French Leave Finesse

D0806508

Richard Binns

Chiltern House

For
all cuckoos, like me, living in Cloud-cuckoo land!

Contents

A special thank you to P&O European Ferries for their help in providing some complimentary ferry crossings on our numerous research trips. The cover watercolour, of Feu Follet at Mougins (see page 235), is by Denis Pannett; for details of his exhibitions write to the artist at Heathers, 1 Woodland Drive, Beaconsfield, Bucks HP9 1JY.

© Richard Binns October 1996 (Text and Maps)
Published by Richard Binns, 4 Waterside, The Moorings, Myton Road, Leamington Spa, Warwickshire CV31 3QA. (T/A Chiltern House Publishers.)

ISBN 0-9516930-8-5 (PB) and 0-9516930-9-3 (HB)

Maps drawn by the author
Typeset in Concorde (text) and Gill (maps) by Art Photoset Limited, 64 London End, Beaconsfield, Bucks HP9 2JD
Printed by Butler & Tanner Limited, The Selwood Printing Works, Caxton Road, Frome, Somerset BA11 1NF

Abbreviations

Each entry has an introductory summary of the main facilities provided (for details of the **FW** – **Franc-Wise** – symbol please read the notes at the bottom of this page and also on page 5); and a concluding section where essential information is shown as follows:

Menus   range of cost of fixed-price menus (*prix-fixe*) or, if not available, the minimum cost of three courses from the *à la carte* menu; see price bands listed below

Rooms   number of bedrooms (in brackets) and price band range (for the bedroom). The word "Disabled" indicates that some bedrooms are accessible to guests in wheelchairs

Cards   accepted: AE American Express; DC Diners Club; MC Mastercard (Access & Eurocard); V Visa. Always check ahead

Closed   annual holidays (if any) and days of the week closed. Always check ahead, as changes are often made. If no details provided then the establishment is open all the year

Post   post code, village or town name, *département*

Region   for details of regional cuisine, specialities and cheeses see the region(s) indicated on the grey-edged pages 397-416

Tel   telephone number: new 10-digit numbers are listed; see box below

Fax   fax number, where available: again, see box below

Mich   page number and grid square on which the entry is located in the spiral-bound *Michelin Motoring Atlas France*

Map   map number (1-6) on which entry is located; grey-edged pages 7-13

From 18 October '96 (22.00 GMT) all phone/fax numbers will have 10 digits. The old 8-digit numbers will be preceded by 2 new digits according to 5 geographical zones (01-05). **Omit the 0 if calling from abroad**. (Use all 10 digits in France – inc' 01 for Paris; do not use the old "16" code.)

Prices

A	under 100 Francs	D	200 to 250 Francs
B	100 to 150 Francs	E	250 to 350 Francs
C	150 to 200 Francs	F	350 to 500 Francs
		G	over 500 Francs

(a) (b) (c) (d): menus not available at weekends or on public holidays. G2, G3, G4: multiply G by figure indicated. Price bands include service and taxes but not wines and breakfasts. Agree pension terms in advance.

To win a **Franc-Wise** – **FW** – accolade cuisine must be of a **Cooking 1-2** or higher rating (see page 5) and establishments must offer one or more menus within two price bands: **A** (under 100 francs); **B** (between 100 and 150 francs) – a range from under £10 to a ceiling of £20 ($15 to $30). The qualifying menu(s) may not be available in the evenings, at weekends, or on public holidays; this represents an important change from the onerous condition set in earlier guides. Towns and villages with a **FW** entry are clearly identified on the maps and in the text.

Introduction

DIY publishing is precarious. In 1980, when I started, 38,000 new books were published in the UK; in 1995 – 90,000! Guides to France? The choice today is ten or more times greater. To make matters worse my recent research costs have been sky-high. So, for this final edition of *French Leave*, commercial realities must prevail: production and paper costs (the latter alarmingly high) must be kept to a minimum; the price must be competitive; the front cover must pack a sales punch; and the finished guide must look and feel "good value" (hence the new format).

French Leave Finesse (*FLF*) will also be the last "Chiltern House" guide sold in bookshops. Future publications, if any, will only be available directly from the author; if you would like details please send me your name and address (to Leamington Spa – see page 2).

FLF is in an A-Z format. The regional introductions in *French Leave Encore* (*FLE*) have been dropped – as have the wine notes and maps; so please keep your copy of *FLE* for future reference. Lists and notes on the cuisine, specialities and cheeses of France's mainland regions are on the grey-edged pages at the back of the guide. No establishment pays to be included and, for the first time, every entry gets equal "democratic" coverage. With my eyesight not as effective as it used to be, the new layout makes for much easier reading – for both of us.

La guillotine has fallen on many previous entries (particularly the more expensive places). Please also note the following:

1) Over 750 entries are **Franc-Wise** (**FW**) recommendations. These offer clients one or more value-for-money, quality cooking menus (see pages 3 and 5). The French have the ideal label to summarise exactly what I mean: *rapport qualité-prix* (*RQP*). The key word in *RQP* is **qualité**.

2) The *Non-FW* entries include scores of "Base" hotels – all *sans restaurant* and, with few exceptions, in either quiet or secluded locations (see pages 22/23); over 50 recommendations with a cooking rating below the minimum required for a **FW** award; and more than 130 others, including hotels where comfort is of a high standard and restaurants where prices exceed the **FW** ceiling – many by just a whisker.

3) A few caveats. *FLF* is for the independent motorist. **I deliberately do not direct you into the centres of cities and the largest towns** – where noise, traffic, thefts from cars, parking and navigation are all nightmares. When I use the word **basic** to describe bedrooms, that's exactly what I mean. Thefts from cars – especially along the Med coast – are rampant; leave nothing in your vehicle and watch where you park (if your car is broken into get a "police report" – essential for insurance claims). Observe speed limits, obey all road signs and markings and don't drink and drive: new on-the-spot fines are draconian. Britons should take a form E111 for medical treatment ("magic" wrote one reader) – available from post offices.

Finally, a big "thank you" to all those readers who "inspected" many of the new **FW** entries – and to the four-figure number of readers who, each year, send me invaluable feedback on all earlier recommendations.

Culinary Comments

Let me remind you how I categorise cooking standards – a system which has taken years to evolve and which I first used in *French Leave Encore*. I use five ratings – but now with five important variations which allow me to solve the problem where, from day to day, or even from course to course, standards can vary up or down. I know of no better system.

Cooking 1 Simple, straightforward cooking which, more often than not, will consist of *cuisine Bourgeoise* specialities. A **Cooking 0-1** rating is used for hotel dining rooms serving the most basic fare.

Cooking 2 Good, competent cooking. (Most Gault-Millau one *toque* & Michelin *"Repas"* (*"R"*) restaurants win this rating.) When standards vary, up or down, I use **Cooking 2-3** or **Cooking 1-2** as a rating.

Cooking 3 Very good level of cooking. Some faults but close or equal to a Michelin one-star restaurant standard. If standards are sometimes higher I use **Cooking 3-4** as a rating.

Cooking 4 Excellent cooking, often innovative and ambitious and rarely flawed. A few exceptional chefs win a **Cooking 4-5** rating.

Cooking 5 Superb, flawless cooking.

To win a **Franc-Wise** (**FW**) accolade cuisine must be of a **Cooking 1-2** or higher rating. Towns and villages with a **FW** entry are clearly identified on the maps and in the text. The place names of recommendations with a **Cooking 3** or better rating are shown on the maps as follows: Roye*

Finally, some comments on culinary terms. I have included a Glossary of Menu Terms and notes and lists on the cuisine, specialities and cheeses of France's mainland regions (grey-edged pages 379-416). I would also like to provide you with thumbnail-sized descriptions of the different French cooking styles – key terms which I refer to constantly.

La cuisine Bourgeoise. Straightforward home cooking using good produce and invariably done well. The repertoire often seems to revolve around 20 to 30 dishes – wherever you are in France: *terrine, escalope, jambon, côte de veau, côte d'agneau, entrecôte, gigot, poulet* and so on.

La cuisine Régionale. Self-explanatory. Alas, authentic regional cooking continues to wither away at an alarming rate. (*Cuisine du terroir*: cooking of the local area, including both produce and ancient recipes.)

La haute cuisine (classical cooking). A repertoire of hundreds of rich sauces and garnishes combined with carved-in-stone recipes, techniques and preparation, developed over the last 200 years, make this style of cooking France's greatest contribution to the culinary arts. Many chefs bring a lighter, less rich, more modern touch to classical cuisine – described in this guide as neo-classical cooking.

La cuisine moderne. Dishes prepared to preserve natural flavours and with the simplest of sauces. Simplicity, and the quality and purity of produce, are essential keys. Improvisation, too, plays a vital part.

To reserve bedrooms; options on right (in brackets)

1 Would you please reserve a room	(2 rooms, etc.,)
2 with a double bed	(with 2 single beds)
	(one room with) (each room with)
3 and bathroom/WC	(and shower/WC)
4 for one night	(2 nights, etc.,)
5 (*indicate day, date, month*)	
6	(We would like *pension* (half-*pension*) terms for our stay)
7 Please confirm the reservation as soon as possible and please indicate the cost of the rooms	(your *pension* terms for each person)

8 An International Reply Coupon is enclosed

9 Yours faithfully

1 Pouvez-vous, s'il vous plaît, me réserver une chambre	**(2 chambres, etc.,)**
2 avec un grand lit	**(avec les lits jumeaux)**
	(une chambre avec)
	(chaque chambre avec)
3 avec salle de bains/WC	**(et douche/WC)**
4 pour une nuit	**(2 nuits, etc.,)**
5 le (*indicate day, date, month*)	
6	**(Nous voudrions pension complète (demi-pension) pour notre séjour)**
7 Veuillez confirmer la réservation dès que possible, et indiquer le tarif des chambres	**(le tarif de pension par personne)**

8 Ci-joint un coupon-réponse international

9 Je vous prie, Monsieur, d'accepter l'expression de mes salutations distinguées

If appropriate: Can I have a room/table overlooking the water

Puis-je avoir une chambre/une table qui donne sur l'eau

To reserve tables; options (in brackets)

Would you please reserve a table for ___ persons for lunch (dinner) on (*indicate day, date, month*). We will arrive at the restaurant at ___ hours (*use 24-hour clock*). (We would like a table on the terrace.) Please confirm the reservation. An International Reply Coupon is enclosed. Yours faithfully

Pouvez-vous me réserver une table pour ___ personnes pour déjeuner (dîner) le (*indicate day, date, month*). Nous arriverons au restaurant à ___ heures (*use 24-hour clock*). (Nous aimerons une table sur la terrasse.) Veuillez confirmer la réservation. Ci-joint etc., (see 8 above). **Je vous prie, etc.,** (see 9 above)

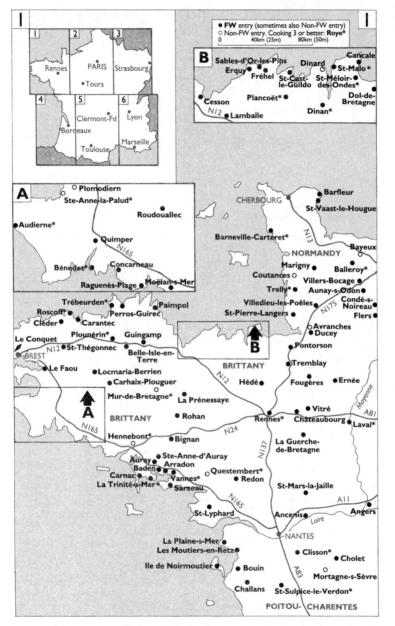

2

● FW entry (sometimes also Non-FW entry)
○ Non-FW entry. Cooking 3 or better: **Roye***
0   40km (25m)   80km (50m)

A

Cresserons

Honfleur
Conteville*
Beuzeville ●
Beaumont-en-Auge ●

● Bénouville
CAEN
N13

● Beuvron-en-Auge*

● Fleury-s-Orne
N175

● Lisieux

Calais
● Dunkerque*
● Bergues*
● Ardres
● Marquise
A16
Wimereux* ● St-Omer
Lumbres ● ● Aire-s-la-Lys
Boulogne-s-Mer ●
Le Touquet ●
Montreuil* ●
St-Josse-s-Mer ●
Quend ●
● Hesdin
● Favières

NORTH
A25
LILLE
A26

● Arras*
● Bapaume
● Cambrai

● Abbeville

AMIENS
● Dury
N28
● Caulières

● St-Quentin
● Ham
● Roye*
A26

Veules-les-Roses* ●
● Le Bourg-Dun*
● Cany-Barville
NORMANDY
Croix-Mare ●
Caudebec-en-Caux* ●
LE HAVRE
Routot ●
Duclair ●
ROUEN
La Bouille ●
● Forges-les-Eaux

Oise
Laon ●
● Compiègne*

Pont-Audemer ●
A13
CAEN
A
N138
Vernon ●
St-Pierre-du-Vauvray ●
Bernay ●

● Bazincourt
● Les Andelys*
Seine
● Fleurines*
Chantilly ●
Ermenonville ○
Germigny-l'Evèque ●

● Etouy

ILE DE FRANCE
● Fontaine-Chaalis
A4
Marne
● La Ferté-s/s-Jouarre*
Couilly-Pont-aux-Dames*

● Thury-Harcourt
● Clécy
Falaise
NORMANDY
Orbec ●
Beaumesnil ●
Evreux ●
A13

● Orgeval ○

PARIS

● Versailles
Houdan* ●
Voisins-le-Bretonneux ○
● Châteaufort*
Senlisse ●

Fontenay-Tresigny* ● N4
● Melun
● Les Ecrennes*
Seine

● Putanges-Pont-Ecrepin
● La Ferrière-aux-Etangs
● Bagnoles-de-l'Orne
● Juvigny-s/s-Andaine
L'Aigle ●

● St-Vrain

● Barbizon

● Thomery*

A5
○ Flagy

● Alençon
● Nocé*
Javron* ● St-Pierre-des-Nids
St-Léonard-des-Bois
Nogent-le-Rotrou
A11

ILE DE FRANCE

● Buthiers

● Evron
A81

LE MANS
● Saulges
Arnage* ●
N138

● Oucques
○ Orléans
St-Benoit-s-Loire ○
● Lorris
● Les Bézards*
● Villeneuve-s-Yonne
Courtenay* ● ● Joigny
● Migennes
● Auxerre*

La Flèche
Luché-Pringé ●

Souvigny-en-Sologne ●
N7
● Vaux
● Gien*
Mailly-le-Château

Molineuf ● Blois*
Onzain ●
Cour-Cheverny ●
Chitenay ●
● Brinon-s-Sauldre*
Nouan-le-Fuzelier ●
BURGUNDY

LOIRE
Semblançay ●
Neuillé-le-Lierre ●
Amboise ●
Candé-s-Beuvron ●
Les Rosiers-s-Loire ●
Tours* ●
LOIRE
● Léré
Vailly-s-Sauldre ● ● Cosne-s-Loire*
Doué-la-Fontaine ●
Bourgueil ●
Bléré ● Pontlevoy ●
Azay-le-Rideau ●
Romorantin-Lanthenay* ●
Vignoux-s-Barangeon ●
● Pouilly-s-Loire

Fontevraud-l'Abbaye ●
Chinon ●
Genillé ●
Montreuil-Bellay ●
Loches ●
Vienne
A10
Berry-Bouy ●
Sancerre ●
La Charité-s-Loire

● Thouars*
BOURGES
BERRY-
BOURBONNAIS

Le Grand-Pressigny ●
Le Petit-Pressigny* ●
○ Issoudun*
Bannegon ●
Magny-Cours*
○
○ Sancoins

● Leigné-les-Bois
Ardentes ●
St-Amand-Montrond ●
N20
● Tronçais

2

8

3

A
Velars-s-Ouche ●
Gevrey-
Chambertin* ●
DIJON
Flagey-Echezeaux ● ● Echigey
Bouilland* ●
Aloxe-Corton ○
Bouze-lès-
Beaune
Beaune* ● ○Levernois*
● Meursault

B
Mittelbergheim ●
Sélestat* ●
Thannenkirch ● Baldenheim* ○
Riquewihr ● ○Illhaeusern
Lapoutroie ○ Kaysersberg ●
Orbey ○ Ammerschwihr* ●
Les Trois-Epis ● Artzenheim ●
COLMAR
Le Valtin ● Eguisheim* ○
Gérardmer* ● ● Herrlisheim
Muhlbach* ● Rouffach* ●
La Bresse ●
Westhalten* ●
Murbach ●

● **FW** entry (sometimes also Non-FW entry)
○ Non-FW entry. Cooking 3 or better: **Roye***
0   40km (25m)   80km (50m)

Dourlers ●
● Sars-Poteries*
Avesnes ●
● Givet
Fourmies ●

Oise

○ Vervins

CHAMPAGNE-ARDENNE

Ste-Preuve ● ● Bièvres
Longuyon* ●
● Neufchâtel-s-Aisne
○ Rugy
Reims* ● METZ St-Avold ●
Sept-Saulx ● ● Niedersteinbach
Ste-Menehould
Ambonnay ● La Petite-Pierre ●
Marne
Pont-à-Mousson ● Brumath ●
Vertus ● L'Epine* ● Wangenbourg ●
Revigny-s-Ornain* ● ● Bar-le-Duc Aingeray ● Marlenheim* ○
Toul* ● NANCY STRASBOURG
Stainville ●
Ottrott-le-Haut ●
🚂 St-Dizier
CHAMPAGNE- ARDENNE **ALSACE**
B
Troyes* ● ○ La Rothière Chaumousey ●
● Arsonval
Colombey-les-2-Eglises ●
○ Montigny-le-Roi
St-Florentin* ● Plombières-les-Bains ●
Beine ● Langres ● Fougerolles* ○
○ Chablis* Froideterre ●
Vincelottes ● Combeaufontaine ●
L'Isle-s-Serein ● Vaux-s/s- Port-s-Saône* ○ Belfort* ● BALE
Avallon ● ○Semur-en-Auxois Aubigny
St-Père-s/s-Vézelay* ● **BURGUNDY**
Val-Suzon ●
Goumois ●
Quarré-les-Tombes* ● DIJON Valdahon ● **JURA** ○Le Noirmont*
Alligny-en-Morvan ○ Ornans ● Cirque de Consolation ●
A Mouchard ●
Autun ● Mouthier-Haute-Pierre ●
Chaussin ● ○ Arbois*
Etang-s-Arroux ● Mercury ● ● Oye-et-Pallet
Torcy ● Poligny ● Malbuisson*
St-Martin-en-Bresse ● Champagnole ●
Loire Courlans* ● ● Lons-le-Saunier

3

9

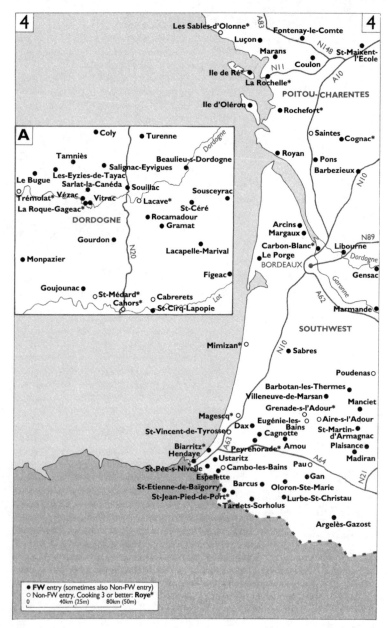

4

Les Sables-d'Olonne*
Fontenay-le-Comte
Luçon
Marans
St-Maixent-l'Ecole
Coulon
Ile de Ré*
La Rochelle*
POITOU-CHARENTES
Ile d'Oléron
Rochefort*
Saintes
Cognac*
Royan
Pons
Barbezieux

A

Coly
Turenne
Tamniès
Beaulieu-s-Dordogne
Salignac-Eyvigues
Le Bugue
Les-Eyzies-de-Tayac
Sarlat-la-Canéda
Souillac
Trémolat*
Vézac
Vitrac
Lacave*
Sousceyrac
La Roque-Gageac*
St-Céré
DORDOGNE
Rocamadour
Gramat
Gourdon
Lacapelle-Marival
Monpazier
Figeac
Goujounac
St-Médard*
Cabrerets
Cahors*
St-Cirq-Lapopie

Arcins
Margaux
Carbon-Blanc*
Libourne
Le Porge
BORDEAUX
Gensac
Mimizan*
Sabres
SOUTHWEST
Marmande
Poudenas
Barbotan-les-Thermes
Villeneuve-de-Marsan
Manciet
Grenade-s-l'Adour*
Magescq*
Aire-s-l'Adour
Eugénie-les-Bains
St-Martin-d'Armagnac
Dax
St-Vincent-de-Tyrosse
Cagnotte
Biarritz*
Peyrehorade*
Amou
Plaisance
Hendaye
Ustaritz
Madiran
St-Pée-s-Nivelle
Cambo-les-Bains
Pau
Espelette
Gan
St-Etienne-de-Baïgorry*
Barcus
Oloron-Ste-Marie
St-Jean-Pied-de-Port*
Lurbe-St-Christau
Tardets-Sorholus
Argelès-Gazost

● FW entry (sometimes also Non-FW entry)
○ Non-FW entry. Cooking 3 or better: **Roye***
0   40km (25m)   80km (50m)

10

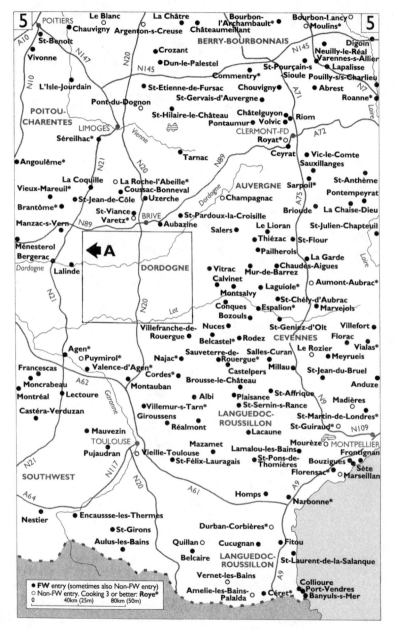

5

POITIERS
Le Blanc
La Châtre
Bourbon-l'Archambault*
Bourbon-Lancy
Chauvigny Argenton-s-Creuse Châteaumeillant
Moulins*

St-Benoît
BERRY-BOURBONNAIS
Digoin

Vivonne
Crozant
Neuilly-le-Réal
Varennes-s-Allier
St-Pourçain-s-
Lapalisse

Dun-le-Palestel
Sioule Pouilly-s/s-Charlieu

Commentry*
Chouvigny

L'Isle-Jourdain
St-Etienne-de-Fursac
Abrest

Pont-du-Dognon
St-Gervais-d'Auvergne
Roanne*

POITOU-
CHARENTES
St-Hilaire-le-Château
Châtelguyon
Riom

LIMOGES
Pontaumur Volvic
CLERMONT-FD

Séreilhac*
Royat*

Angoulême*
Tarnac
Ceyrat
Vic-le-Comte
Sauxillanges

La Coquille La Roche-l'Abeille*
AUVERGNE
Sarpoil*
St-Anthème

Vieux-Mareuil*
Coussac-Bonneval
Pontempeyrat

St-Jean-de-Côle Uzerche
Champagnac

Brantôme*
St-Viance
Brioude La Chaise-Dieu

Manzac-s-Vern
Varetz*
BRIVE St-Pardoux-la-Croisille

Aubazine
Salers
Le Lioran St-Julien-Chapteuil

Ménesterol
Thiézac St-Flour

Bergerac
Pailherols
La Garde

Lalinde
DORDOGNE
Vitrac
Chaudes-Aigues

Calvinet
Mur-de-Barrez
Aumont-Aubrac*

Montsalvy
Laguiole*

Conques Espalion* St-Chély-d'Aubrac
Marvejols

Bozouls

Villefranche-de-
Rouergue
Nuces
St-Geniez-d'Olt
Villefort

Belcastel* Rodez
CEVENNES
Florac

Agen*
Sauveterre-de-
Rouergue*
Salles-Curan
Le Rozier
Vialas*

Puymirol*
Najac*
Millau
Meyrueis

Francescas
Valence-d'Agen*
Castelpers
St-Jean-du-Bruel

Moncrabeau
Cordes*
Brousse-le-Château
Anduze

Montréal Lectoure
Montauban
St-Affrique

Castéra-Verduzan
Albi
Plaisance
Madières

Villemur-s-Tarn*
St-Sernin-s-Rance

Giroussens
LANGUEDOC-
ROUSSILLON
St-Martin-de-Londres*

Mauvezin
Réalmont
St-Guiraud*

TOULOUSE
Lacaune

Pujaudran
Mazamet
Mourèze
MONTPELLIER

Vieille-Toulouse
Lamalou-les-Bains
Frontignan

SOUTHWEST
St-Félix-Lauragais
St-Pons-de-
Thomières
Bouzigues

Florensac
Sète
Marseillan

Homps

Narbonne*

Nestier
Encausse-les-Thermes
Durban-Corbières*

St-Girons
Quillan
Cucugnan
Fitou

Aulus-les-Bains
Belcaire
LANGUEDOC-
ROUSSILLON
St-Laurent-de-la-Salanque

Vernet-les-Bains

• FW entry (sometimes also Non-FW entry)
○ Non-FW entry. Cooking 3 or better: **Roye***
Collioure
Port-Vendres

0   40km (25m)   80km (50m)
Amélie-les-Bains-
Palalda
Céret*
Banyuls-s-Mer

A

5

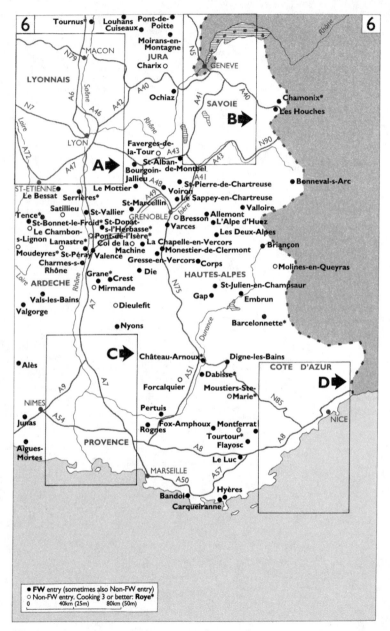

Legend:

- **FW** entry (sometimes also Non-FW entry)
- ○ Non-FW entry. Cooking 3 or better: **Roye***

0   40km (25m)   80km (50m)

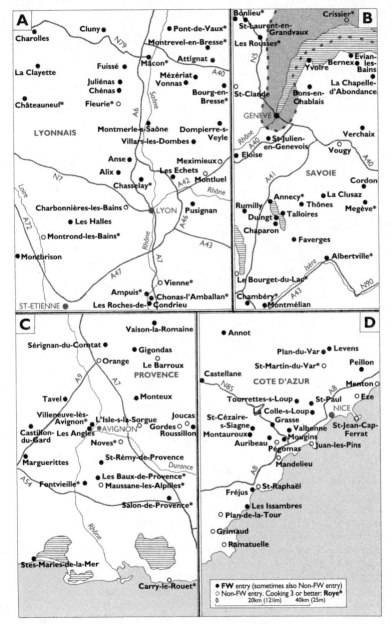

Scornful stirrings
France and the French

I have known and loved France for more than 40 years. Today, alas, I find her a deeply unhappy, soul-searching lady. The current general air of depression in *la belle France* is overwhelming.

What on earth has caused Europe's "First Lady" to become so depressed? A two-word answer: her politicians. (Is that not true for Britain too?)

At 60 I am a case-hardened cynic, scornful of soul-selling, ego-driven politicians, editors, writers, businessmen and sundry bullshitters. I have a passion for history and geography; a deep interest in finance and economics; and an innate understanding of what is required to succeed in the shark-infested world of competitive business. I have a great love for France and a longing for peace in Europe. However, none of the above has stopped me, over 20 years, from becoming the most sceptical of Euro-sceptic "cuckoos". I say "yes" to co-operation and a single market; but an emphatic "no" to control by a federal European Union (EU). No-one has ever given me one good valid reason for Britain to "stay in" the EU.

Britain's politicians have sold our nation's soul for "Europe" – the French even more so. Our hard-earned sovereignty is fast disappearing down a bureaucratic black hole called the EU; our laws are diluted daily by "European Law"; our fishermen have been treated shamefully (the Conman Fisheries Policy is as outrageous as the Conman Agricultural Policy) and the thought that this nation's economic policies (both fiscal and monetary) should be controlled by a single European "state", linked to the "Euro" (a single European currency), fills me with the bleakest gloom. How can we end a glorious millennium so shamefully?

France is hell-bent on being at the heart of the new European order; for historical reasons alone, I understand why. But she has been stopped in her tracks by a *franc-fort* policy and by politicians unwilling to take-on the public service unions and loath to prune public spending. They are unwilling to make the painful decisions needed for a change of course. I pray the "markets" soon bring an end to the *franc-fort* policy: only then will economic sense prevail, as it did here four years ago.

France's hotel and restaurant "industry"

This is her biggest, both in terms of income and employees and, in addition, is the largest foreign currency earner. I know this "industry" better than probably any other Briton; since 1980 I have talked and listened to hundreds of chefs and hotel owners throughout France.

Bluntly, most of them are on their knees – for all sorts of reasons. One trio: excessive VAT charges (20.6%); high minimum wages (over £600 per month); and Mont-Blanc-sized employers' social security taxes. One other stands out however – that *franc-fort* policy again. Against all currencies, other than those in the mark bloc, the franc is overvalued (no wonder unemployment in France is so high). The strong currency and both higher direct and indirect taxes (e.g. petrol) mean less francs in the pockets of foreign tourists and French consumers respectively.

(France's social security budget (taxes!) is set to rise inexorably. No doubt employers will have to pick up the tab (the UK in the future?) – primarily to subsidise the state's huge unfunded, pay-as-you-go pension scheme. France's private pension fund assets are only a fraction of the UK's.)

As a consequence owners now close less often, employ fewer staff (with less being paid into the state's coffers; the welfare deficit is vast and growing), and take more and more short cuts. Not surprisingly, standards of service, skill and facilities – in dining rooms, kitchens and bedrooms respectively – are lower than ever before.

The problems besetting France's hotel and restaurant "industry" should be a salutary reminder to us all of why we should "stay out" of the EU.

Michelin's shameful flaws

On p18/19 I give the guidebook pot a good stir. Here I want to expose Michelin's most serious flaws – ones which leave readers playing blind man's buff. At 7½ to 8frs per £ (5frs a $) choosing the wrong restaurant or hotel, because of a lack of information, can be an expensive mistake.

Michelin's obsessive secretiveness is their Achilles' heel: silence is the easiest way to mislead and arguably they are guilty of exactly that. They give readers no clues to their inspection policies; nor will they say how many inspectors they employ in France. What seems certain though is that inspectors' efforts appear to be primarily devoted to "policing" (testing by eating meals and paying bills) the standards of both existing and potential star chefs. It is rumoured that 10-20, or more, inspections are made before star promotions are confirmed or withheld.

Amazingly, the France red guide provides a culinary "opinion" or "rating" (one, two and three stars and the *"Repas"* award) for only 886 of 10,012 recommendations (6,154 hotels and 3,858 restaurants) – less than 9% of the total. For the remaining 9,126 entries (some are *sans restaurant*) readers are given no advice whatsoever on cooking standards.

"Facilities" will have been checked at all 6,154 hotels – but how many dining rooms were inspected? Michelin should find some way of indicating which hotel dining rooms have been visited and are worth eating in (perhaps a separate restaurant entry, as they do in many cities).

The flaws combine to leave readers sticking pins in pages. From hundreds of examples I'll identify just two. The Ti al-Lannec at Trébeurden and the Beatus in Cambrai get the same rating for hotel facilities: three *pavillons* – a category of *très confortable*. Readers are given no help with cooking standards. Read the entries in this guide to discover the vast culinary gulf that divides the two hotels. Multiply the same problem, at all price and comfort levels, by many thousands, and you get some idea of Michelin's sloth. Sloth? Yes: read on.

Study Megève in the red guide as a further example of how readers are left groping in the dark: 19 hotels (with dining rooms) are listed plus two restaurants. No ratings are given for the latter duo (one is star quality – see p216); and the better hotel chefs are not identified.

Michelin have the resources and profits (600,000 France red guides are sold annually) to correct these serious shortcomings: so why don't they?

Stirring the French culinary pot!

"We maintain that eating out in provincial Britain is in many ways more enjoyable than the French equivalent: eclectic repertoires and a far greater variety of choice are the big pluses here."

Those words first appeared in *Allez France!* two years ago. Two years on and nothing has changed. Most French chefs are stuck in ramrod-straight classical cooking tramlines. Culinary styles from other parts of Europe and the globe have made almost zero impact on French cuisine and the words "eclectic", "cosmopolitan" and "liberation" mean little. Kit Chapman, of the Castle Hotel at Taunton, put it succinctly in his invigorating book *Great British Chefs 2* (1995: Mitchell Beazley): "France has become constipated in her own orthodoxy."

Kit again – writing about the thrill of eating with the best British chefs: "We are unfettered by any orthodoxy. It has made us braver, more curious, more experimental." I agree. We are constantly put down by Europeans for our insularity – in all things. Yet I maintain we are the most open-minded race on this planet – study our history and the deep depth of knowledge and love Britons have for all parts of the earth. No wonder then we have drawn from all culinary styles, adding them, happily and willingly, to our own cooking traditions – the latter a touch tarnished but steadily reviving. Our wholehearted acceptance of any new ideas – cooking or otherwise – is a non-starter concept for the French.

The pace of improvement in Britain is dramatic: not just London but in the regions too. South-west England is a shining example. Ring the West Country TB (01392 425426) and ask for *The Trencherman's West Country* restaurant guide: 32 examples of what I meant in the first paragraph above. Other examples, favourites all, include Simpsons (Kenilworth), Poppies (Brimfield), Old Beams (Waterhouses) & Merchant House (Ludlow).

Some words of qualification: the French culinary pyramid is many times larger than the British equivalent and there are many more consistently good cafés, bistros, brasseries, *rôtisseries* and restaurants in France. Also, there seems no point, as many older francophiles tend to do, in harking back to nostalgic days, decades ago, when every French village had its own time-warp, regional cooking restaurant. Times have changed. All businesses have had to adjust to consumers' changing needs: that's true for chefs too. Nor do I have any truck with self-indulgent readers who keep mum about enterprising chefs they encounter on their travels. Tell the world about them: they need support, not selfish silence.

In Britain a reliable guide is essential: the *British Michelin* (over a third of its 1,000 GB restaurant entries lead you to ethnic cooking), *The Good Food Guide* and *The Good Pub Guide* all do the job well.

The real cause of France's culinary "constipation" is the attitude of the French themselves. Their blinkered arrogance and insularity – in many things – is staggering. Talk to chefs, talk to restaurateurs, talk to *sommeliers* – those that have travelled abroad: they'll tell you what an impossible task they face in "persuading" their French clients to try "foreign" food or "foreign" wines. A teaspoon of curry powder here, or a touch of lemon grass or soy sauce there, do not equate to eclectic culinary liberation. (Another aside: the same professionals – at all price levels – unanimously vote the "French", especially Parisians, as their worst customers. They reckon the French are grasping, mean, miserable, complaining, never satisfied, unbearable snobs and selfish!)

In *"franc-fort"* France hotels and restaurants continue to have a tough time: increased VAT charges (20.6% for restaurants); higher-than-ever minimum wages (over £600 per month); fearsome competition; Mont Blanc-high employers' social security taxes (about 50% of employees' gross wages); and high interest rates are all excruciating burdens.

At the very top of the culinary pyramid matters are even worse: large numbers of staff; fewer French clients (higher taxes); far less British, American, Spanish and Italian customers (care of the overvalued franc); and fabulous cellars full of thousands of bottles of expensive wines – most of which will never be ordered – all add to the tales of woe.

Readers will already know how, since the mid 80s, I have increasingly become disenchanted with all but a few of the "5P" superstar restaurants (pretentious, pompous, precious, poncy and pricey – some very pricey!). Many others agree. Paris-based Suzanne Lowry of *The Daily Telegraph*: "I have come to dread grand restaurants: the hushed atmosphere and the mixture of obsequiousness and arrogance in the staff."

The multi-starred dinosaurs will have to change. The most important word missing at many shrines is "enjoyable" – the essential pleasure in any eating-out visit (read those first three lines again). Many of the culinary Gods have opened *rapport qualité-prix* (*RQP*) bistros, brasseries, *rôtisseries* and simpler restaurants (a few have bistro "chains" – of up to six establishments). French chefs should follow the example of two of the Battaglia brothers who, after the 20 years we've known them (we were the first to write about the duo), now regularly serve well over 1,000 and 1,500 clients each week at their respective Valbonne and Mougins restaurants. Why? They offer clients *RQP* meals.

RQP ought to be the everyday norm in Britain. The resounding success of the annual *Financial Times* two-course "Lunch for £5, £7.50 & £10" promotion (in January) should be a lesson for all chefs: clients roll-up in their thousands, filling 330 restaurants during a two-week bonanza. Chefs: make that an all-year event – and at 3,300 British restaurants!

Finally, some of the gripes readers have about standards in French hotels and restaurants – in random order: lumpy mattresses, stale bread, broken fittings, lack of mirrors and shelves, threadbare linen, poor lighting, incorrect billing (one reader was overcharged on three consecutive nights), lack of vegetables and fruit, poorly-cooked rice, baths and basins which "leak", no no-smoking areas, awful and/or expensive breakfasts, fixed snorkel taps, lack of cleaning, lack of facilities for the disabled, charging for the use of tennis courts, the frequent absence of "service", a frosty welcome, ever-rising bedroom prices, expensive wines, and on and on – the list of grumbles is long.

Stirring the guidebook pot!

A fact of life: the older you get the more cynical you become. I suppose I have reached an age, 60, when I have encountered, at first hand, too many "fiddles" – in a career spanning accountancy (a word synonymous with "fiddling"), computing (when I was involved with the insider *modus operandi* of hundreds of companies) and guidebook publishing (read on).

Guidebooks have numerous shortcomings: readers – and, sadly, all journalists – remain woefully ignorant of what they are.

I have used guides voraciously for over 40 years. In addition, since 1980, I have researched, written and published more than a dozen of my own French and British guides. All the major guides, on France and Britain, in French and English, have serious shortcomings. If my books have their faults critics must say what they are – but I feel I am now qualified enough to comment on the shortcomings of other publications.

The most serious fault of the leading French guides is their passion to include as many thousands of entries as possible. The editors do not guillotine ruthlessly enough. For varying reasons I have cut hundreds of entries over the years; all but a few remain in the main guides.

Perversely, in 1995/96, Michelin cleared out numerous *sans restaurant* hotels, many of which have been great favourites of my readers. Just two examples follow. After 30 years in the red guide, the entry for du Bosquet in Pégomas (a 1996 *France Travelauréat* winner) was guillotined without a word of explanation to the owners. Why? This simple hotel has long been my readers' number one favourite. Did Simone Bernardi, who calls a spade a spade, offend some Parisienne? The Mazets, both lovable angels, at the Europe in Vals-les-Bains, also had the chop. Why?

Michelin's *"Repas"* (R) "good value" rating needs an overhaul: cooking standards vary **wildly** at the 352 French R establishments; and, far too often, an award made one year is cut 12 months later. Bizarrely, only 352 entries win a R award. I maintain Michelin should be able to at least treble that number; the proof is in *FLF*. Michelin France should introduce the British *"Meals"* (M) award (where "good value" is not a criterion) which has always been of a higher standard than the R. Then many of the better French R ratings could be upgraded – and the less reliable French one-stars could be given the more appropriate M award. The French R rating should be introduced in Britain – alongside the M. Rumour has it that 1997 will see the R replacing the M in Britain. What a thoroughly retrograde step. Both countries need both ratings.

(The French roly-poly tyre men are deflated, slow-puncture slouches. Several dozen of their recent R discoveries were places I had previously recommended to readers in earlier books. Why do they roll so slowly?)

One final Bibendum moan. Every village/town/city in the red France guide has a map and grid reference, indicating the Michelin "detailed" yellow *carte* on which the place is located. You need to spend over £80 to cover all France with these maps – yet few readers have the lot as the spiral-bound *Motoring Atlas* is a much better buy, saving you £70 in the process. If I can provide the atlas page number and grid reference for each place name in *FLF*, then Michelin could easily do the same.

Gault Millau, too, are now including more and more entries (among a total of almost 8,000) where no effort is made to give culinary ratings. Where the latter are given, their inconsistency varies outrageously from region to region. For hundreds of GM restaurant entries there's no mention of bedrooms when, in fact, they are available for clients.

Bottin Gourmand offer no cooking ratings for the vast majority of its thousands of entries – and both BG and GM fail lamentably with one aspect of their large town and city recommendations: BG provide no town or city maps at all; and GM have a few – but these are utterly useless. The irony is that you must have the Michelin red guide – with its superb 521 town and city maps – if you are to locate, easily, any of the BG/GM big town recommendations! (I, too, plead guilty though I have always turned my back on the centres of cities and the bigger towns.)

Equally heavy criticism is reserved for other guides – for both France and Britain, in French and English versions. The *Logis de France* guide is no more than a listing of its thousands of paid-up members; in some cases cooking standards are so bad that the "recommendations" should be scuttled. Other general guides, published by motoring organisations and reputable publishers/editors, are also no more than "lists" of hotels and restaurants (some with written comments). How do they collect the information provided? Not surprisingly culinary ratings are not given.

My stirring doesn't stop there. My blood boils when I think of the unspoken "tricks" many publishers/editors use (a few have become very wealthy as a result). As a condition of entry some guides request payments from their "recommendations" (or a commission on the income earned) – from as low as three figures to £2,000 and more. Some guides charge establishments for "inspection" and "administrative" costs. Not one of them tell its readers all this – of course not. Others require the owners of their recommendations to buy a minimum number of guides (say 20) as a condition of entry. Not bad for a guide with say 500 entries; that's a minimum sale of 10,000 copies. Not bad at all!

The mushrooming crop of guides which rely on pictures and sycophantic prose to describe their recommendations have one obvious failure: read them and you will soon grasp that the publishers and editors hardly ever put culinary standards to the test at most of the establishments they praise to the skies. Of course not: that would cost money!

Money? All my criticism boils down to "money" when I stop stirring the pot. Dining rooms for every entry are not "inspected" (bills paid for by the publishers) because that would ensure financial disaster. To check out all the new entries alone in this guide cost well into five figures – my own costs plus those paid to readers who "inspected" scores of dining rooms for me. I wonder if even the most prestigious "independent" guides published in Britain (relying on readers' feedback and, I quote, "unpaid inspectors") spend five-figure sums on "inspection" costs.

All is most certainly not what it seems in the world of guidebooks!

Top-rated Restaurants

Listed in regional order under the cooking rating categories of **5**, **4-5**, **4** and **3-4**. Within each region the establishments are in town/village name alphabetical order. The restaurant or hotel name, chef's name (if also the owner), page number of the entry and map page location (1-6) are also provided (within brackets). **FW: Franc-Wise** menus (see p3).

Cooking 5

JURA **Crissier** (Girardet, p128, Map 6)

Cooking 4-5

BURGUNDY **St-Père-sous-Vézelay** (L'Espérance, Meneau, p317, Map 3)
LOIRE **Tours** (Bardet, p350, Map 2)
MASSIF CENTRAL (AUVERGNE) **Laguiole** (Michel Bras, p193, Map 5)
SOUTHWEST **Puymirol** (L'Aubergade, Trama, p268, Map 5)

Cooking 4

ALSACE **Marlenheim** (Le Cerf, MM. Husser, p212, Map 3)
BRITTANY **Questembert** (Bretagne, Paineau, p269, Map 1)
BURGUNDY **Bouilland** (Host. du Vieux Moulin, Silva, p73, Map 3)
Gevrey-Chambertin (Les Millésimes, MM. Sangoy, p169, Map 3)
COTE D'AZUR. **St-Martin-du-Var** (Jean-François Issautier, p312, Map 6)
Tourtour (Les Chênes Verts, Bajade, p351, Map 6)
JURA **Arbois** (Jean-Paul Jeunet, p38, Map 3)
Le Noirmont (Gare, Wenger, p243, Map 3)
Romorantin-Lanthenay (Gd Hôtel Lion d'Or, Clément, p283, Map 2)
LYONNAIS **Fleurie** (Auberge du Cep, p153, Map 6)
Montrond-les-Bains (Host. La Poularde, Etéocle, p232, Map 6)
MASSIF CENTRAL (ARDECHE) **Pont-de-l'I**. (Michel Chabran, p262, Map 6)
St-Bonnet-le-Froid (Auberge des Cimes, Marcon, p294, Map 6)   **FW**
Vienne (La Pyramide, Henriroux, p368, Map 6)
SAVOIE **Le Bourget-du-Lac** (Ombremont, Jacob, p79, Map 6)
Chamonix (Albert 1er, Carrier, p98, Map 6)

Cooking 3-4

ALSACE **Ammerschwihr** (Aux Armes de F., MM. Gaertner, p32, Map 3)
Fougerolles (Au Père Rota, Kuentz, p160, Map 3)
Gérardmer (Host. des Bas-Rupts, Philippe, p167, Map 3)
Port-sur-Saône (Château de Vauchoux, Turin, p265, Map 3)   **FW**
Toul (Le Dauphin, Vohmann, p346, Map 3)
BERRY-BOURBONNAIS **Commentry** (Michel Rubod, p119, Map 5)   **FW**
Brittany Bénodet (Ferme du Letty, Guilbault, p65, Map 1)   **FW**
Mur-de-Bretagne (Aub. Gd'Maison, Guillo, p239, Map 1)

Base Hotels *(sans restaurant: see page 4 – note 2)*
The regional lists below identify the hotels. In each region the town/village names are in alphabetical order. Within brackets are the hotel name, entry page no. & map page no. (1-6). <u>Hotel</u> names underlined are personal favourites – with an extra special plus. (MC: Massif Central.)

ALSACE (Map 3) **Gérardmer** (Bains, p166) (Echo de Ramberchamp, p166) **Herrlisheim** (Au Moulin, p179) **Illhaeusern** (La Clairière, p185) **Kaysersberg** (<u>Remparts</u>, p191) **Riquewihr** (Couronne, p275) (Hôtel Le Schoenenbourg, p275) (Le Riquewihr, p275) **Rouffach** (Bollenberg, p286) **Le Valtin** (Le Vétiné, p361)

BERRY-BOURBONNAIS **Bourbon-Lancy** (La Roseraie, p76, Map 5) **Sancoins** (Parc, p329 Map 2)

BRITTANY (Map 1) **Bénodet** (Menez-Frost, p65) **Dinard** (<u>Manoir de la Rance</u>, p134) (Reine Hortense, p134) **Moëlan-sur-Mer** (<u>Manoir de Rertalg</u>, p223) **Plomodiern** (Relais Porz-Morvan, p259) **Quimper** (Sapinière, p270) (La Coudraie, p270) **Raguenès-Plage** (Men Du, p271) **St-Malo** (Alba, p309) (Brocéliande, p309) (Terminus, p310) (La Korrigane, p310) (Le Valmarin, p310) **Ste-Anne-d'Auray** (Le Myriam, p325) **Vannes** (Moulin de Lesnuhé, p361)

BURGUNDY (Maps 2 & 3) **Aloxe-Corton** (<u>Clarion</u>, p30) **Auxerre** (Le Maxime, p48) **Avallon** (Avallon-Vauban, p49) (<u>Moulin des Templiers</u>, p49) **Beaune** (Le Cep, p62) (La Closerie, p62) (Ch. de Challanges, p63) **Gevrey-Chamb**. (Les Grands Crus, p168) (Arts et Terroirs, p170) **Levernois** (Parc, p200)

CHAMPAGNE-ARDENNE (Map 3) **Fourmies** (Ibis, p160) **Givet** (Val St-Hilaire, p171) **Sars-Poteries** (Hôtel Fleuri, p332) **Troyes** (Chantereigne, p354)

COTE D'AZUR (Map 6) **La Colle-sur-Loup** (Marc Hély, p116) **Fréjus** (L'Oasis, p162) **Grimaud** (Athénopolis, p176) **Juan-les-Pins** (Mimosas, p189) (Welcome p189) **Mandelieu** (Acadia, p210) **Menton** (Princess et Richmond, p218) **Pégomas** (<u>du Bosquet</u>, p253) **Plan-de-la-Tour** (Mas des Brugassières, p257) (Parosolis, p258) **Ramatuelle** (Ferme d'Hermès, p272) **St-Jean-Cap-Ferrat** (Brise Marine, p301) (Clair Logis, p301) **St-Paul** (<u>Le Hameau</u>, p315)

DORDOGNE (Map 5) **Les Eyzies-de-Tayac** (Les Rochers, p147) **Monpazier** (Edward 1er, p226) **Sarlat-la-Canéda** (Mas de Castel, p331) **Souillac** (Le Quercy, p338)

HAUTES-ALPES (Map 6) **Château-Arnoux** (Villiard, p105) **Moustiers-Ste-Marie** (Le Colombier, p236)

ILE DE FRANCE (Map 2) **Chantilly** (Parc, p101) **Ermenonville** (<u>Le Prieuré</u>, p142) **Versailles** (Home St-Louis, p365) (Aérotel, p365) **Voisins-le-Bretonneux** (Port Royal, p375)

LANGUEDOC-ROUSSILLON (Map 5) **Albi** (Cantepau, p27) **Céret** (Les Arcades, p94) **Collioure** (Casa Païral, p117) (Madeloc, p117) **Marseillan** (Château du Port, p214) **Mourèze** (Hauts de Mourèze, p236) **Narbonne** (La Residence, p240) **Vernet-les-Bains** (Le Mas Fleuri, p364) **Vieille-Toulouse** (La Flânerie, p368)

LOIRE (Map 2) **Bourgueil** (Le Thouarsais, p80) **Chinon** (Diderot, p110) **Nouan-le-Fuzelier** (Charmilles, p243) **Onzain** (Château des Tertres, p247) **Orléans** (Orléans Parc Hôtel, p249) **St-Benoit-sur-Loire** (Labrador, p293) **Tours** (Chantepie, p349) (Cèdres, p350)

LYONNAIS (Map 6) **Bourg-en-Bresse** (Le Logis de Brou, p78) (Prieuré, p79) **Charbonnières-les-Bains** (Beaulieu, p102) **Cluny** (Saint-Odilon, p114) **Fleurie** (Grands Vins, p154) **Mâcon** (Nord, p206) **Montluel** (Le Petit Casset p229) **Tournus** (Hôtel de Greuze, p347)

MC (ARDECHE) (Map 6) **Vals-les-Bains** (Europe, p359) **Vienne** (Midi, p368)

MC (AUVERGNE) (Map 5) **Ceyrat** (La Châtaigneraie, p96) **Laguiole** (Lou Mazuc, p193)

MC (CEVENNES) (Map 5) **Millau** (La Capelle, p221)

NORMANDY **Avranches** (Le Pratel, p50, Map 1) **Bagnoles-de-l'Orne** (Ermitage p52, Map 2) **Bayeux** (Argouges, p59, Map 1) **Ducey** (Moulin de Ducey, p137, Map 1)

NORTH (Map 2) **Arras** (Les 3 Luppars, p43) **Boulogne** (Métropole, p75)

POITOU-CHARENTES **Argenton-sur-Creuse** (Manoir de Boisvillers, p41, Map 5) **Bouin** (Martinet, p74, Map 1) **Challans** (Antiquité, p97, Map 1) **Coulon** (Au Marais, p125, Map 4) **Ile d'Oleron** (Motel Ile de Lumière, p184, Map 4) **L'Isle-Jourdain** (Val de Vienne pl86, Map 5) **La Rochelle** (Les Brises, p279, Map 4) (Le Rochelois, p280, Map 4)

PROVENCE (Map 6) **Bandol** (Golf-Hôtel, p53) **Fontvieille** (Host. St-Victor, p157) **Gordes** (Le Gordos, p171) **Maussane** (Castillon des Baux, p215) (Pré des Baux, p215) **Orange** (Mas des Aigras, p248) **Roussillon** (Rés. des Ocres, p287) **St-Rémy-de-Provence** (Canto Cigalo, p320) (Soleil, p321)

SAVOIE (Map 6) **Annecy** (Motel le Flamboyant, p36) **St-Alban** (St-Alban-Plage, p292) **St-Julien** (Le Soli, p305) **Talloires** (Les Pres du Lac, p340)

SOUTHWEST (Map 4) **Agen** (Host. des Jacobins, p24) **Aire-s-l'Adour** (Adour Hôtel, p26) **Cambo-les-Bains** (Errobia, p87) **Pau** (Bilaa, p253) **St-Jean-Pied-de-P.** (Plaza Berri, p302) **St-Vincent-de-T.** (Côte d'Argent, p323)

ABBEVILLE
Auberge de la Corne

Comfortable restaurant/Cooking 2 | FW |

Two dining rooms: one described as *anglo-normande*; the other a warm, panelled *salle*. There's an equally warm welcome from *patronne*, Maryse Lematelot (she speaks some English). Her husband, Yves, walks a classical path and is competently adept with alternative specialities ranging from *morue fraîche, fondue et poireaux* to a hearty *faux filet de sauce échalote*. One regional must is a filling *ficelle picarde*.
Menus ABDE. Cards All. (Rooms: nearby Relais Vauban; 100m walk E.)
Closed Sun evg. Mon. (Rest. W of station, parking and N1.)
Post 32 chaussée du Bois, 80100 Abbeville, Somme. Region North.
Tel 03 22 24 06 34. Fax 03 22 24 03 65. Mich 6/C3. Map 2.

ABREST
La Colombière

Comfortable restaurant with rooms/Cooking 2 | FW |
Gardens/Parking/Air-conditioning (restaurant)

The terraced gardens, panoramic views over the Allier Valley, pepperpot tower and dovecote (*colombière*) are the first eye-catching pluses. Enjoy the same views from the dining room as you tuck into Michel Sabot's ultra rich classical specialities. Even menu B has opulent classics like *foie gras en terrine* and *chartreuse de volaille farci au foie gras*.
Menus aBCDE. Rooms (4) CDE. Cards All. (2km SE of Abrest; use D906.)
Closed Mid Jan to mid Feb. 14-22 Oct. Sun evg. Mon.
Post 03200 Abrest, Allier. Region Berry-Bourbonnais.
Tel 04 70 98 69 15. Fax 04 70 31 50 89. Mich 100/B4. Map 5.

AGEN
Hostellerie des Jacobins

Comfortable hotel (no restaurant)
Quiet/Closed parking/Air-conditioning

"Superb" & "special" are two words I'll happily use for this captivating 19thC residence. Both the house & old furniture appeal. But, beating them all, is an angel of a lady, Gisèle Bujan – a flying whirlwind. She, too, like Françoise Verrier at Ramatuelle, has a Welsh terrier called Hermes. Visiting Michel Trama at Puymirol? Save francs and stay here.
(From A62 use N21 on Garonne's R bank; R just past Ch. of Comm.)
Rooms (15) FG. Cards All. (In northern shadow of Les Jacobins church.)
Post 1 ter pl. Jacobins, 47000 Agen, Lot-et-Garonne. Region Southwest.
Tel 05 53 47 03 31. Fax 05 53 47 02 80. Mich 137/D3. Map 5.

AGEN (Bon-Encontre)   Parc/Rest. Mariottat

Comfortable restaurant with rooms/Cooking 3
Terrace/Parking/Air-conditioning (restaurant)

A *logis* in the village of Bon-Encontre, 5km SE of Agen (entrance from
N113 easily missed – E side Hôtel du Midi). A string of credits: tree-
shaded terrace; lovely hostess, Christiane Mariottat; and modern *plats*
(many fish dishes) from husband Eric. Relish, in their brick and stone
salle, typical delights like *ballotine de poissons au poivre vert*.
Menus aC(inc' fish menu)DE. Rooms (10) CDE. Cards All.
Closed Sun evg (not rooms in summer). Mon.
Post r. République, 47240 Bon-Encontre, Lot-et-Garonne. Reg. Southwest.
Tel 05 53 96 17 75. Fax 05 53 96 29 05. Mich 137/D3. Map 5.

L'AIGLE   Dauphin

Very comfortable hotel/Cooking 2-3   FW
Closed parking

A 17thC *relais de poste*, owned by the Bernard family since 1925; present
patron, Michel, is an extrovert, involved host. His father, Eléonor, won a
Michelin star in 1931; it's been held ever since – a record. Out-&-out
classical cuisine with top-notch succulent desserts: *soufflé glacé à la
Mandarine Impériale* is a not-too-sweet, not-too-sour masterpiece. Over
50 half-bottles (& wine by the glass). (Tues a.m.: town's famed market.)
Menus A(brasserie: Cooking 1)BCDEF. Rooms (30) F. Cards All.
Post pl. Halle, 61300 L'Aigle, Orne. Region Normandy. (Park in *place*.)
Tel 02 33 84 18 00. Fax 02 33 34 09 28. Mich 33/E4. Map 2.

AIGUES-MORTES   Arcades

Comfortable restaurant with rooms/Cooking 1-2   FW
Terrace/Air-conditioning

A 16thC house with a stone, beamed & flower-filled dining room; an
arcade; super *escalier*; tiny patio garden; and stylish bedrooms. Modest
classical fare: home-made *soupe de poissons*; flavoursome *rable de lapin
farci sauce à la sauge*; and simple *fraises au sucre* or *tarte aux pommes*.
Enter the fortified town halfway along the N wall (bd Gambetta).
Menus BCDE. Rooms (6) FG. Cards All. (Cheaper rooms: Croisades.)
Closed 11-27 Feb. 12-18 Nov. Mon (not July/Aug). Tues midday.
Post 23 bd Gambetta, 30220 Aigues-Mortes, Gard. Regions Lang-Rouss/Prov.
Tel 04 66 53 81 13. Fax 04 66 53 75 46. Mich 157/D3. Map 6.

A100frs & under. B100–150. C150–200. D200–250. E250–350. F350–500. G500+

AINGERAY

La Poêle d'Or

Comfortable restaurant/Cooking 1-2

A modest, tiny hamlet in an attractive section of the Moselle Valley, just SW of Liverdun. A flower-bedecked exterior and a beamed dining room complement, to a tee, the classical/neo-classical cooking of *cuisinière* Maryvonne Metzelard; she's also loyal to her *terroir*. Alas, no choice on any menu. Signature creations inc' *foie gras de canard* (from Landes in this case) *et son gelée au champagne* – a silken-smooth seducer.
Menus BCEF. Cards MC, V. (Rooms: L'Europe, Toul; simple drive SW.)
Closed Feb sch.hols. Sun evg. Mon. Tues. (Or Novotel Ouest, Nancy.)
Post 54460 Aingeray, Meurthe-et-Moselle. Region Alsace.
Tel 03 83 23 22 31. Fax 03 83 23 32 80. Mich 41/D4. Map 3.

AIRE-SUR-L'ADOUR

Adour Hôtel

Comfortable hotel (no restaurant)
Quiet/Swimming pool/Garage/Parking

A new security-conscious building (gates & TV cameras) on the right bank of the River Adour; good views of the latter. Across the river is the town's *arènes*; this is bull-fighting terrain. I've used the hotel to visit Guérard's bistro at Eugénie (see the entry) and also the Pain Adour at Grenade (see the entry) – saving many francs in the process.
Rooms (31) D. Disabled. Cards MC, V.
Closed Nov. Region Southwest.
Post 28 av. 4 Septembre, 40800 Aire-sur-l'Adour, Landes.
Tel 05 58 71 66 17. Fax 05 58 71 87 66. Mich 150/B2. Map 4.

AIRE-SUR-LA-LYS

Hostellerie Trois Mousquetaires

Very comfortable hotel/Cooking 1-2
Secluded/Gardens/Parking

"Ornate" was the word in *FLE*; Paddy Burt (of *The DT*) did better with "Hansel-&-Gretel-land". Friendly welcome from Mme Venet, 7-acre park, lake, ducks, great *cave* & super service. Debits? Over-the-top interior; UHT milk with bkft; dear extras & inconsistent classical/neo-classical fare from Phillipe Venet. Should I guillotine? The hotel – not the chef!
Menus bCDE. Rooms (33) FG. Cards All.
Closed Mid Dec to mid Jan. Region North.
Post Château de la Redoute, 62120 Aire-sur-la-Lys, Pas-de-Calais.
Tel 03 21 39 01 11. Fax 03 21 39 50 10. Mich 3/D3. Map 2.

A 100frs & under. B 100–150. C 150–200. D 200–250. E 250–350. F 350–500. G 500+

ALBERTVILLE

Bouchon des Adoubes (Chez Uginet)

Comfortable restaurant/Cooking 2
Terrace

FW

Times are hard in France: as they are for young Eric & Josie Guillot. All change from *FLE*: a new name and a new *RQP* formula. The couple hope this will get more clients on seats; they need to survive. Eric's menu A has some super neo-classical *plats*: examples are colourful *terrine de ratatouille froid* and encore-please *filet de volaille sauce vin rouge*.
Menus AB. Cards All. (Rooms: Le Berjann; 5-10 minute walk to SE.)
Closed 25 June-5 July. Nov sch. hols. Tues evg. Wed.
Post Pont des Adoubes, 73200 Albertville, Savoie. Region Savoie.
Tel 04 79 32 27 43. Fax 04 79 31 21 41. Mich 118/C2. Map 6.

ALBERTVILLE

Million

Very comfortable hotel/Cooking 3
Terrace/Gardens/Lift/Garage/Parking/Air-cond. (rest.)

Fluent English-speaking Philippe Million, and his wife Renée, are the 7th-generation at the refurbished town-centre hotel. A self-effacing chef, his lack of ego matched by the least wordy menus I've ever seen. Neo-classical & regional dishes: among the latter a *fritot* (crisp, thin pastry) *de grenouilles* and *blanc de Féra au blé grué*. Many half bottles.
Menus CDEG. Rooms (26) FG. Cards All. (Near N212 N exit of town.)
Closed Hotel: Sun evg (Sept-mid July). Rest: Sun evg. Mon.
Post 8 pl. Liberté, 73200 Albertville, Savoie. Region Savoie.
Tel 04 79 32 25 15. Fax 04 79 32 25 36. Mich 118/C2. Map 6.

ALBI (also see next page)

Cantepau

Simple hotel (no restaurant)
Lift/Parking

As simple as they come. North of the River Tarn and east of the busy N88. Parking a major benefit; so is the lift. A two-minute walk to the Jardin des Quatre Saisons; about one km to the ideally-sited Moulin de La Mothe (on the Tarn's right bank); and a much cheaper alternative to La Reserve (3km NW) where you can enjoy menus b (lunch) or low-end C.
Rooms (33) D. Cards All.
Closed 21 Dec to 6 Jan.
Post 9 r. Cantepau, 81000 Albi, Tarn. Region Languedoc-Rousillon.
Tel 05 63 60 75 80. Fax 05 63 47 57 91. Mich 154/A1. Map 5.

A100frs & under. B100–150. C150–200. D200–250. E250–350. F350–500. G500+

ALBI (also see previous page) **Jardin des Quatre Saisons**

Comfortable restaurant/Cooking 2-3 FW
Air-conditioning

Georges Bermond, after an absence of 20 years, has returned to his *pays*.
The inventive, modern *cuisinier*, together with his blond wife Martine,
weave a *RQP* cloth of gold. Numerous starters, a dozen main courses
(divided equally between fish and meat offerings) and many scrumptious
desserts. Excellent cellar. *Quatre saisons* is an apt restaurant name.
Menus BC. Cards AE, MC, V. (Rooms: Cantepau – 150m to E; parking.)
Closed Mon. (Rest. on Tarn's R bank, near river & main town bridge.)
Post 19 bd Strasbourg, 81000 Albi, Tarn. Region Languedoc-Roussillon.
Tel 05 63 60 77 76. Fax 05 63 60 77 76. Mich 154/A1. Map 5.

ALBI Moulin de La Mothe

Very comfortable restaurant/Cooking 2 FW
Terrace/Gardens/Parking/Air-conditioning

An invigorating site: on the Tarn's R bank, down river from the railway
bridge and red-brick cathedral. Marie-Claude Pellaprat is proud as punch of
her gorgeous rest. Husband Michel is an able neo-classicist, making the
most of regional produce. Much to our liking (on menu B) was a
croustillant de boudin noir aux pommes & a refreshing plate of sorbets.
Menus BC. Cards All. (Rooms Mercure & Cantepau; NE near main bridge.)
Closed Feb sch. hols. Nov sch. hols. Sun evg & Wed (not July/Aug).
Post r. de la Mothe, 81000 Albi, Tarn. Region Languedoc-Roussillon.
Tel 05 63 60 38 15. Fax 05 63 60 38 15. Mich 154/A1. Map 5.

ALBI La Réserve

Very comfortable hotel/Cooking 2-3
Secluded/Terr/Gardens/Swim pool/Tennis/Parking/Air-cond.

A blissful setting: a handsome villa in five acres of grounds on the Tarn's
right bank – with the pool between the river & hotel. Hélène & Jean-
François Rieux are the 5th-generation owners. Dip into chef Sylvain
Martin's classical pool: *persillé de jarret au foie gras, filets de truite
poêlés & vacherin glacé à la mascarpone et aux café* are typical.
Menus b(lunch)C(low-end)E. Rooms (20)F(top-end)G,G2. Cards All.
Closed Nov to Apl. (3km NW of Albi; D600 towards Cordes.)
Post rte de Cordes, 81000 Albi, Tarn. Region Languedoc-Roussillon.
Tel 05 63 60 80 80. Fax 05 63 47 63 60. Mich 154/A1. Map 5.

A100frs & under. B100–150. C150–200. D200–250. E250–350. F350–500. G500+

ALENCON
Au Petit Vatel

Very comfortable restaurant/Cooking 2-3 | FW |

The town's most famous restaurant – rightly so, as the window-boxed exterior provides an attractive *entrée* to the culinary patterns so delicately woven by classicist, Michel Lerat. (The restaurant is almost next door to the Musée des Beaux-Arts with its fine lace collection.) Precision *plats* like *délice de cèpes, duo de sole et saumon sauce cardinal, coq au vin à la Solognotte* and super sorbets et *glaces*.
Menus B(lunch)CD. Cards All. (Rooms: Ibis, 300 metre-walk away to E.)
Closed Feb sch. hols. 28 July-17 Aug. Sun evg. Wed. (Parking nearby.)
Post 72 pl. Cdt Desmeulles, 61000 Alençon, Orne. Region Normandy.
Tel 02 33 26 23 78. Fax 02 33 82 64 57. Mich 51/D2. Map 2.

ALES (Méjannes-lès-Alès)
Auberge des Voutins

Comfortable restaurant/Cooking 2-3 | FW |
Terrace/Gardens/Parking

SE of Alès: D981, 8km. Mireille Turonnet welcomes you to her stone-built villa with shady terrace and neat gardens – as eye-pleasing as the modern, inventive cooking of husband René: *filet de rascasse demi-sel* with tomato, garlic and olive oil is just one typical taste explosion. Debit? Poor cellar – but clever use of regional wines in many dishes.
Menus B(top-end)CE. Cards All. (Rooms: Ibis, at St-Christol to SW.)
Closed Feb sch. hols. Sun evg & Mon (not pub. hols).
Post Méjanne-lès-Alès, 30340 Salindres, Gard. Region Provence.
Tel 04 66 61 38 03. Mich 143/D4. Map 6.

ALIX
Le Vieux Moulin

Simple restaurant/Cooking 1-2 | FW |
Terrace/Parking

Annie and Gerard Umhauer's mill shines with pride – literally, as the *moulin* is constructed from the local golden stone (*pierres dorées*). Gérard's cooking is Lyonnais fare at its most Pavlovian: temptations tagged *terrine maison, grenouilles, poulet à la crème, andouillette de "Chez Besson" sauce moutarde, fromage blanc* and *sorbet vigneron*.
Menus BCD. Cards MC, V. (Rooms: many A6 autoroute hotels at Limonest.)
Closed 11 Aug- 9 Sept. Mon & Tues (not pub. hols). (Above SE of Alix.)
Post 69380 Alix, Rhône. Region Lyonnais.
Tel 04 78 43 91 66. Fax 04 78 47 98 46. Mich 115/F1. Map 6.

A100frs & under. B100–150. C150–200. D200–250. E250–350. F350–500. G500+

ALLEMONT

Giniès

Simple hotel/Cooking 1-2
Quiet/Terrace/Gardens/Parking

A colourful, shady garden is one big bonus; a second is the enterprising Giniès family – Robert and Gilberte, their chef son, Philippe, and his wife, Isabelle. Run-of-the-mill *Bourgeoise* and classical cuisine – of the *terrine maison, truite meunière, escalope de veau* variety. Order *raclette* and *fondue* (regional winners) at least two hours in advance.
Menus aBC. Rooms (27) DE. Disabled. Cards MC, V.
Closed Rest: mid Sept to Apl (except evgs during Feb sch. hols).
Post 38114 Allemont, Isère. Regions Hautes-Alpes/Savoie.
Tel 04 76 80 70 03. Fax 04 76 80 73 13. Mich 132/B2. Map 6.

ALLIGNY-EN-MORVAN

Auberge du Morvan

Very simple restaurant with basic rooms/Cooking 1

Auberges don't come simpler or more unpretentious than Jean Branlard's quintessential Morvan home. Humble is perhaps the word; but a smile is guaranteed when you settle the bill. Stick with Morvan and Burgundian dishes – *jambon cru du Morvan, jambon persillé, jambon en saupiquet* and *crêpe Morvandiau* (a dessert); or the basics – *truite meunière, gigot d'agneau* and similar. Note when closed.
Menus a(lunch)BCD. Rooms (5) C. Cards MC, V.
Closed 26 Nov to end Feb. Every evg (not Sat) & Thurs (out of season).
Post 58230 Alligny-en-Morvan, Nièvre. Region Burgundy.
Tel 03 86 76 13 90. Mich 87/D1. Map 3.

ALOXE-CORTON

Clarion

Comfortable hotel (no restaurant)
Secluded/Gardens/Parking

"Delightful" is the word for the 320-year-old manor house: for English-speaking Edmée & Christian Voarick; the quality breakfasts; the tranquil setting, tucked away on the village's northern edges; the shady gardens and lime trees overlooking the famed Corton vineyards; the neighbour's climbing rose; and the patterned roof of Château Corton-André. Two more pluses: the owners' cellar (wines for sale) – and a babysitting service.
Rooms (10) G. Cards MC, V.
Post 21420 Aloxe-Corton, Côte-d'Or. Region Burgundy.
Tel 03 80 26 46 70. Fax 03 80 26 47 16. Mich 88/A2. Map 3.

A100frs & under. B100–150. C150–200. D200–250. E250–350. F350–500. G500+

L'ALPE D'HUEZ

Gérard Astic (Le Lyonnais)

Comfortable restaurant/Cooking 2-3

FW

As you drive the 3000-ft climb with two dozen *lacets* think of the Tour de France cyclists using only pedal power to reach the top. Your car-aided efforts are well rewarded by Gérard Astic's classical & Lyonnais *plats*: *carpaccio de thon frais à la coriandre, quenelle de brochet soufflé au coulis crustacés* (what memories) and *cervelle de Canut* (*fromage frais aux herbes*) are typical. Closed lunch in winter.
Menus BCD. Cards MC, V. (Rooms: Alp'Azur, 500m-walk to NE.)
Closed Lunch (winter). May. June. Sept-Nov. Regs H-Alpes/Savoie/Lyon.
Post r. du Coulet, 38750 L'Alpe d'Huez, Isère.
Tel 04 76 80 68 92. Mich 132/B2. Map 6.

AMBOISE

Novotel

Very comfortable hotel/Cooking 1-2
Secluded/Terrace/Swim pool/Tennis/Lift/Parking/Air-cond. (rooms)

This Novotel is one of the most striking & most pleasantly situated of the breed – in an elevated position, S of the town & off the D31 southern bypass. Fine views of the château, Amboise forest & the Loire Valley. Cooking, a mix of styles, is of a slightly higher standard than other Novotels. Avoid pool-side rooms: noisy Germans (both late & early)!
Menus C(*à la carte*). Rooms (121) G(low-end). Disabled. Cards All.
Post r. Sablonnières, 37400 Amboise, Indre-et-Loire. Region Loire.
Tel 02 47 57 42 07. Fax 02 47 30 40 76. Mich 68/A4. Map 2.
(Bookings: UK 0171 724 1000; US toll free 800 221 4542.)

AMBONNAY

Auberge Saint Vincent

Comfortable hotel/Cooking 2

FW

An ivy-covered, window-boxed and refurbished *logis* at the heart of the Champagne village (with plenty of chances to buy direct). Classical and regional cooking from Jean-Claude Pelletier. His wife Anne-Marie will offer you menus with no less than 17 *Recettes du Terroir* listed with others too among the 9 top-notch desserts. Menu A could typically include *ballotin de volaille en gelée* and *jambon d'os à l'ancienne*.
Menus ACE. Rooms (10) EF. Cards All.
Closed Sun evg & Mon.
Post 51150 Ambonnay, Marne. Region Champagne-Ardenne.
Tel 03 26 57 01 98. Fax 03 26 57 81 48. Mich 38/B2. Map 3.

A100frs & under. B100–150. C150–200. D200–250. E250–350. F350–500. G500+

AMELIE-LES-BAINS-PALALDA

Castel Emeraude

Comfortable hotel/Cooking 1
Secluded/Terrace/Gardens/Lift/Parking

Twin turrets from the last century give this otherwise largish and modern *Relais du Silence* an odd-ball look. Jean-Pierre Lignon's hotel is much liked: in Feb *"printemps en hiver* – sun, blue sky & mimosa"; and a "haven of peace and charm". On the Tech's left bank. Modest classical and neo-classical cuisine: "copious cooking" is the most apt tag.
Menus aBCE. Rooms (59) DEF. Disabled. Cards AE, MC, V.
Closed Dec. Jan. (W of spa, N bank Tech.) Region Languedoc-Roussillon.
Post rte Corniche, 66110 Amelie-les-Bains-Palalda, Pyrénées-Orientales.
Tel 04 68 39 02 83. Fax 04 68 39 03 09. Mich 177/D4. Map 5.

AMMERSCHWIHR

A l'Arbre Vert

Simple hotel/Cooking 1-2

FW

Across the road and just W of the famous Aux Armes de France – well away from the busy N415. All members of the Gebel-Tournier family speak English. They are as proud as punch of one dining room (for non-smokers) which has superb carved panels and beams. Chef Joël Tournier carves his own regional/classical *plats*: best seen on *RQP* menu a – with, among others, *presskopf, poulet au Riesling* & *mousse glacée au Kirsch*.
Menus aBD. Rooms (17) DEF. Cards All.
Closed 10 Feb to 25 Mar. 18-28 Nov. Tues.
Post 68770 Ammerschwihr, Haut-Rhin. Region Alsace.
Tel 03 89 47 12 23. Fax 03 89 78 27 21. Mich 61/D3. Map 3.

AMMERSCHWIHR

Aux Armes de France

Very comfortable restaurant with rooms/Cooking 3-4
Parking

Philippe & François (the *pâtissier*) Gaertner, aided by their wives, Simone & Sylvie, maintain the high standards established by their father Pierre in the 60s-80s. A mix of styles. The *foie gras* is perhaps the best in Alsace; & desserts & *petits fours* are brilliant creations. *RQP* half-bottles. Unhurried, precise service in magnificent dining rooms.
Menus F. Rooms (10) F. Cards All.
Closed Wed. Thurs (not rest. in evgs from Mar to Dec).
Post 68770 Ammerschwihr, Haut-Rhin. Region Alsace.
Tel 03 89 47 10 12. Fax 03 89 47 38 12. Mich 61/D3. Map 3.

A100frs & under. B100–150. C150–200. D200–250. E250–350. F350–500. G500+

AMMERSCHWIHR

Aux Trois Merles

Comfortable restaurant with rooms/Cooking 1-2
Parking

A *logis* alongside the main N415 – and without the interior character of the Arbre Vert. Anne-Marie & Didier Louveau more than compensate for the unattractive exterior. Chef Didier offers 7 no-choice menus with both regional and neo-classical alternatives: of the *gâteau de lapereau, escalope de saumon frais sur tagliatelles sauce basilic* variety.
Menus ABCDE. Rooms (16) CDE. Cards AE, MC, V.
Closed 1-15 Feb. Sun evg. Mon.
Post 68770 Ammerschwihr, Haut-Rhin. Region Alsace.
Tel 03 89 78 24 35. Fax 03 89 78 13 06. Mich 61/D3. Map 3.

AMOU

Commerce

Simple hotel/Cooking 2
Terrace/Garage/Parking

As colourful an exterior as you'll find in France: window boxes, blinds, awnings and creeping vines. The Darracq family enterprise is geared up for entertaining individuals and large gatherings. Classical, *Bourgeois* and regional repasts: *terrine maison, quenelles d'oie, confit de porc* and *gâteau Basque* (from wide-choice menu B) will quench any appetite.
Menus aBCD. Rooms (20) DE. Cards All.
Closed 10-30 Nov.
Post 40330 Amou, Landes. Region Southwest.
Tel 05 58 89 02 28. Fax 05 58 89 24 45. Mich 149/E3. Map 4.

AMPUIS

La Côte Rôtie

Comfortable restaurant/Cooking 3 FW
Terrace

Young chef Manuel Viron and his efficient wife, Marie, are a modern duo – in every way. Blue & white façade (& blue shutters) and creative contemporary cooking from Manuel. Also excessively wordy menus (25+ for some *plats*!). One cracker of a dish – with a précis: *rôti de lapereau entièrment désossé* with herbs, almonds & aubergine *ratatouille*.
Menus b(lun)CDE. Cards MC, V. (Rooms: Bellevue, Les Roches-de-Condrieu.)
Closed 1 wk Jan. 20 Aug-10 Sept. Sun evg. Mon. (Above easy drive S.)
Post pl.Eglise, 69420 Ampuis, Rhône. Regions Lyonnais/MC (Ardèche).
Tel 04 74 56 12 05. Fax 05 74 56 00 20. Mich 116/A3. Map 6.

A100frs & under. B100–150. C150–200. D200–250. E250–350. F350–500. G500+

ANCENIS

Les Terrasses de Bel Air

Comfortable restaurant/Cooking 2-3 `FW`
Terrace/Gardens

E of the town and N side of N23 – high above the Loire (and TGV line). Tradition is the label here: for the correct welcome from Geneviève Gasnier, *la patronne*; for the décor; and the classical/regional cuisine from her husband Jean-Paul. *Blanc de sandre beurre Nantais* is a stylish interpretation; as is a lighter, delicate *saumon mariné à la mélisse*.
Menus aCDE. Cards MC, V. (Rooms: Akwaba – in town.)
Closed 1-15 Aug. Sun evg. Mon.
Post rte Angers, 44150 Ancenis, Loire-Atlantique. Region Loire.
Tel 02 40 83 02 87. Fax 02 40 83 33 46. Mich 65/D4. Map 1.

Les ANDELYS

Chaîne d'Or

Very comfortable restaurant with rooms/Cooking 3 `FW`
Quiet/Closed parking

A well-organised Seine-side *relais*, built in 1751 as a toll house (hence the name, a chain strung across the river as a barrier). Impeccably run by Monique & Jean-Claude Foucault. Readers have praised the classical & neo-classical cooking of chef Francis Chevalliez to the skies: he, too, deserves a *chaîne d'or* for his skilled, masterful work. Fine cellar.
Menus BDE. Rooms (10) FG. Cards AE, MC, V.
Closed Jan. Sun evg. Mon.
Post 27 r. Grande, 27700 Les Andelys, Eure. Region Normandy.
Tel 02 32 54 00 31. Fax 02 32 54 05 68. Mich 34/C1. Map 2.

ANDUZE (Tornac)

Demeures du Ranquet

Very comfortable hotel/Cooking 2-3 `FW`
Secluded/Terrace/Gardens/Swimming pool/Parking

A heavenly, wooded site S of Anduze and Tornac. Anne Majourel is a self-taught *cuisinière*; her *Menu du Jardin Aromatique* is Provence at the table. Fine use of *terroir* produce. Two mouthwatering memories – *filet de merlan au jus de persil plat, quenelle de ratatouille* and *charlotte aux aubergines, trait de sauge.* (Cheaper rooms? Porte des Cévennes.)
Menus B(top-end)DF. Rooms (10) G. Cards MC, V. (Above NW Anduze.)
Closed 12 Nov-end Feb. Tues evg & Wed (not mid June to mid Sept).
Post Tornac, 30140 Anduze, Gard. Regions Languedoc-Roussillon/Provence.
Tel 04 66 77 51 63. Fax 04 66 77 55 62. Mich 142/C4 & 143/D4. Map 5.

A100frs & under. B100–150. C150–200. D200–250. E250–350. F350–500. G500+

ANGERS (St-Sylvain-d'Anjou)   Le Clafoutis

Comfortable restaurant/Cooking 2   ┌────┐
Parking/Air-conditioning   │ FW │
                                               └────┘

Well clear of Angers (to the NE): beside N23, S of A11 exit 14. Modest
dining room perhaps but there's nothing modest about chef Serge Lebert's
classical offerings on menu B: *poissons fumés (saumon, anguille, thon,
flétan), medaillon de filet de lotte pochée, fromage* & a terrific *soufflé
glace au Cointreau* (Angers is the home of the renowned liqueur).
Menus aBCDE. Cards AE, MC, V. (Rooms: Acropole – across the road.)
Closed Feb sch. hols. 21 July to 17 Aug. Sat midday. Sun. Mon evg.
Post rte Paris, 49480 St-Sylvain-d'Anjou, Maine-et-Loire. Region Loire.
Tel 02 41 43 84 71. Fax 02 41 34 74 80. Mich 66/A3. Map 1.

Les ANGLES   Côté Bouchon

Simple restaurant/Cooking 1-2   ┌────┐
Gardens/Parking   │ FW │
                                               └────┘

W of the Rhone, alongside D900 & part of the Ermitage-Meissonnier
rest.; a side room in the main building with separate parking. Excellent
selection of Provençals and classical *plats*: the likes of *darne de saumon
pâtes basilic* & *terrine de foie de lotte aïoli* as starters; a main course of
gâteau d'agneau aux aubergines; & *tarte fine aux pommes*.
Menus B(bottom-end). Cards All. (Rooms: next entry; cheaper ones below.)
Closed Sun evg (Nov-Mar). Mon (not evgs July/Aug). (Le Petit Manoir.)
Post 34 av. de Verdun, 30133 Les Angles, Gard. Region Provence.
Tel 04 90 25 41 68. Fax 04 90 25 11 68. Mich 158/B1. Map 6.

Les ANGLES   Host. Ermitage/Rest. Ermitage-Meissonnier

Comfortable hotel & restaurant/Cooking 2-3
Terrace/Gardens/Swimming pool/Closed parking

W of the Rhône, alongside D900, in adjacent buildings. Dropped from *FLE*;
now restored. Michel Meissonnier will never achieve his father Paul's
supreme standards but his neo-classical/Provençale cuisine is adequate
enough. A low-end menu C (no choice) could be *saumon fumé, jambonnette
de volaille sauce crème et morilles*, cheese and *tatin aux pommes*.
Menus CEF. Rooms (16) DEFG(bottom-end). Cards All.
Closed Hotel: Jan-Feb. Rest: Sun evg (Nov-Mar). Mon (not evgs July/Aug).
Post 34 av. de Verdun, 30133 Les Angles, Gard. Region Provence.
Tel 04 90 25 41 68. Fax 04 90 25 11 68. Mich 158/B1. Map 6.

A100frs & under. B100–150. C150–200. D200–250. E250–350. F350–500. G500+

ANGOULEME (La Vigerie)   Host. du Moulin du Maine Brun

Very comfortable hotel/Cooking 3   `FW`
Secluded/Terrace/Gardens/Swimming pool/Parking

Logis de France don't come better than this! A renovated old *moulin*, astride a mill-race, and richly furnished. As much as Nature & man-made benefits appeal pay a visit for chef Bruno Nicollet's neo-classical and classical creations. Two vivid memories: *carpaccio de foie gras séché à la fleur de sel* and *tarte aux pommes caramélisées au miel d'acacia*.
Menus aBC. Rooms (18) FG. Cards All. (8km to W; N of N141.)
Closed Nov-Apl. Sun evg & Mon (in May, Sept & Oct).
Post La Vigerie, 16290 Hiersac, Charente. Region Poitou-Charentes.
Tel 05 45 90 83 00. Fax 05 45 96 91 14. Mich 108/B2. Map 5.

ANNECY (Annecy-le-Vieux)   Clos des Sens

Very comfortable restaurant/Cooking 3   `FW`
Terrace

One km N of Motel le Flamboyant (see entry for directions). Laurent & Martine Petit do a resoundingly "big" job at their new home (distant lake views from a shaded terrace); they used to be at the Péché Gourmand, Briançon. Bravura lunch menu b: *soupe légère de lentilles & pétoncles*; *pot-au-feu de canard*; *fromage blanc*; *pyramide chocolat*.
Menus b(lunch)CE. Cards All. (Rooms: Motel le Flamboyant.)
Closed Feb sch. hols. Sun evg & Mon (not mid July to end Aug).
Post 13 r. J.Mermoz, 74940 Annecy-le-Vieux, Haute-Savoie. Region Savoie.
Tel 04 50 23 07 90. Fax 04 50 66 56 54. Mich 118/B1. Map 6.

ANNECY (Annecy-le-Vieux)   Motel le Flamboyant

Comfortable hotel (no restaurant)
Parking

Don't be put off by the word "motel". This is an excellent "base" and has justifiably proved popular with readers for many years. English-speaking owners. 20 bedrooms have small kitchens. Approach from the NE corner of Lac d'Annecy: use D129 (rue de Verdun); hotel is on the left. Flamboyant? The bar/lounge wood panelling is certainly that. (Clos des Sens restaurant: continue NW on D129, cross D5, ascend hill, on left.)
Rooms (32) F(low-end). Cards All. Region Savoie.
Post 52 r. Mouettes, 74940 Annecy-le-Vieux, Haute-Savoie.
Tel 04 50 23 61 69. Fax 04 50 27 97 23. Mich 118/B1. Map 6.

A100frs & under. B100–150. C150–200. D200–250. E250–350. F350–500. G500+

ANNECY (Sévrier)   Le Bistrot du Port

Simple restaurant/Cooking 1-2
Terrace

Great position but pity about the building in which the glass-fronted
bistro is housed. Still, the lakeside site, 5km S of Annecy and looking E
across the *lac* is a big plus. Even bigger pluses are the *RQP* grills and
classical *plats* from the Fenestraz family's chef, Patrick Couvert:
brochettes d'agneau, féra & *friture* from the lake and similar.
Menus aBC. Cards AE, MC, V. (Rooms: Résidel – *sans rest.*)
Closed mid Sept to mid May.
Post au port, 74320 Sévrier, Haute-Savoie. Region Savoie.
Tel 04 50 52 45 00. Fax 04 50 52 68 58. Mich 118/B1. Map 6.

ANNOT   Avenue

Simple hotel/Cooking 2   FW

A warm welcome at the much-liked *FLE* favourite (now "discovered" by
both Michelin & Gault Millau; about time) – ideally sited for mountains to
N. Enterprising *Bourgeoise* and classical cooking with Italian touches from
chef/patron Jean-Louis Genovesi: starters such as *cannellonis de homard
au coulis de crustacés* and *millefeuille de truites rosées*; and welcome
main courses like *daube légère de pigeon en couronne de fettucine.*
Menus AB. Rooms (14) CDE. Cards MC, V.
Closed Nov to Mar. Regions Côte d'Azur/Hautes-Alpes.
Post 04240 Annot, Alpes-de-Haute-Provence.
Tel 04 92 83 22 07. Fax 04 92 83 34 07. Mich 147/E4. Map 6.

ANSE   St-Romain

Comfortable hotel/Cooking 2
Quiet/Terrace/Gardens/Closed parking

Guy & Micheline Levet's old farm has several pluses: quiet site, sunny
terrace, beamed & flower-filled *salle* and a smiling *patronne.* Another
plus is the classical cuisine of Bruno Levet: try perhaps *a melon glacé
aux 4 fruits rouges* or a well-executed *truite de mer en crépinette,
crème ciboulette.* Alas, one minus: only "so-so" sweets from the trolley.
Menus aBCE. Rooms (24) DE. Cards All.
Closed 1-8 Dec. Sun evg (Nov to Apl).
Post rte Graves, 69480 Anse, Rhône. Region Lyonnais.
Tel 04 76 40 24 46. Fax 04 76 67 12 85. Mich 116/A1. Map 6.

A100frs & under. B100–150. C150–200. D200–250. E250–350. F350–500. G500+

37

ARBOIS

Jean-Paul Jeunet

Very comfortable hotel/Cooking 4
Quiet & Gardens (annexe)/Lift/Garage/Parking (annexe)

Jean-Paul's invention is manifest and the complicated execution of some dishes is faultless. Among his modern creations a *lièvre à la royale* is a masterpiece (assembled as a largish roll and served as a thick slice). Both Claude, a delightful manageress, & Nadine Jeunet speak fluent English. The 17thC main building much modernised. Noisy church clock!
Menus CEF. Rooms (17) FG(both bottom-end). Cards All.
Closed Dec. Jan. Tues & Wed midday (not Sept & sch. hols).
Post r. de l'Hôtel de Ville, 39600 Arbois, Jura. Region Jura.
Tel 03 84 66 05 67. Fax 03 84 66 24 20. Mich 89/E3. Map 3.

ARCINS

Lion d'Or

Simple restaurant/Cooking 1-2
FW

As simple as they come but, at lunch, the Lion d'Or is a ferocious beast, fairly growling with hectic activity. The à la carte formula is great: 10 starters; 10 main courses; and a handful of sweets; final prices range from B to D. Classical/regional/*Bourgeoise* from lion-tamer chef Jean-Paul Barbier: gutsy grub of the *boudin de Béarn poêlé, saumon d'Ecosse grillé tout simple, crème brûlée au rhum* variety.
Menus A(menu – but not Sat evg)BCD(*à la carte*). Cards AE, MC, V.
Closed July. 23-31 Dec. Sun. Mon. (Rooms: Pont Bernet, Louens.)
Post 33460 Arcins, Gironde. Region Southwest. (Above 18km drive to S.)
Tel 05 56 58 96 79. Mich 121/D2. Map 4.

ARDENTES

Chêne Vert

Comfortable restaurant with rooms/Cooking 2
FW

All hotels in this neck of the woods claim to be in *"Au pays de George Sand"*; Chopin, too, is often quoted in hotel literature. This is true of the Green Oak *logis*, alongside the main D943. *Patronne* Claudine Mimault speaks good English and her husband, chef François, cooks both classical and Berrichonne specialities: a typical tasty treat could be *filet de truite de l'Anglin* (due E, sheet 82) *à la crème de lentilles du Berry*.
Menus bCD. Rooms (7) EF. Cards All.
Closed 2-21 Jan. 1-11 Aug. Sun evg. Mon.
Post 36120 Ardentes, Indre. Region Berry-Bourbonnais.
Tel 02 54 36 22 40. Fax 02 54 36 64 33. Mich 84/A4. Map 2.

A100frs & under. B100–150. C150–200. D200–250. E250–350. F350–500. G500+

ARDENTES

Comfortable restaurant/Cooking 1-2
Parking

Why do some French guides (Gault Millau & Bottin Gourmand) ignore many scores of Michelin-accoladed restaurants? This is one – SW of the D943 and E of the Indre. Terrific choice on single menu (C wk-ends). Eclectic classical/*Bourgeoise*: *assiette Lyonnaise, feuilleté de moules au curry, tête de veau sauce gribiche* & *piéce de boeuf Dijonnaise* are typical.
Menus bC. Cards MC, V. (Rooms: Aub. Arc en Ciel, *sans rest.*, 8km to NW.)
Closed Feb sch. hols. Aug. Sun evg. Mon. (Above at La Forge de l'Ile.)
Post 36120 Ardentes, Indre. Region Berry-Bourbonnais.
Tel 02 54 36 20 24. Mich 84/A4. Map 2.

ARDRES

Very comfortable hotel/Cooking 1-2
Secluded/Gardens/Parking

Mixed reports: should I chop? An 18thC château with handsome stonework and set in a large park (N of TGV). Other guides talk of "beautifully restored rooms" & "*belles chambres*"; my readers reckon some are in a bad state & need re-decoration. Cooking is modest neo-classical & classical. Big plus: "veritable treasure trove" cellar for stocking-up wine buyers. New owners.
Menus bCDE. Rooms (24) FG. Cards All. (Cocove marked on Michelin maps.)
Closed 24-26 Dec. (8km SE Ardres; N N43, A26 exit 2 & D217; use D226.)
Post 62890 Recques-sur-Herm, Pas-de-Calais. Region North.
Tel 03 21 82 68 29. Fax 03 21 82 72 59. Mich 2/B2 & 2/C2. Map 2.

ARDRES

Comfortable hotel/Cooking 2
Quiet/Gardens/Garage/Parking/Air-conditioning (rest.)

The Coolens have gone; new owners are working hard to restore a tattered reputation. Interior newly & nicely decorated; the façade needs a facelift. Disorganised service; compensated by well-presented dishes from chef Michel Pingeon, using fresh, top-quality produce. Classical menus: cream sauces with almost everything, little choice, no simple dishes.
Menus ABD. Rooms (16) DE. Cards All. (Are bedrooms being improved?)
Closed 7 Jan-4 Feb. Mon. (Remember *FLE*: endless grumbles about rooms.)
Post 91 espl. Mar. Leclerc, 62610 Ardres, Pas-de-Calais. Region North.
Tel 03 21 82 25 25. Fax 03 21 82 98 92. Mich 2/B2. Map 2.

A100frs & under. B100–150. C150–200. D200–250. E250–350. F350–500. G500+

ARGELES-GAZOST

Hostellerie Le Relais

Simple hotel/Cooking 1-2
Terrace/Parking/Air-conditioning (restaurant)

FW

Jeannette Hourtal's flowers on the shady terrace and in the main rooms are colourful eye-catchers. Husband Jean's copious classical, regional and *Bourgeoise* fare is not prissy stuff. Highly satisfying grub of the *flan de cèpes, pâté de lièvre confiture d'oignons, tranche de gigot de mouton poêlée* and *coupe aux myrtilles flambées* variety.

Menus aBCD. Rooms (23) DE. Cards MC, V.
Closed Oct to Jan. Region Southwest.
Post 25 r. Mar. Foch, 65400 Argelès-Gazost, Hautes-Pyrénées.
Tel 05 62 97 01 27. Mich 168/B3. Map 4.

ARGELES-GAZOST

Miramont/Rest. Le Casaou

Comfortable hotel/Cooking 2
Gardens/Lift/Parking/Air-conditioning (restaurant)

FW

The label "gardens" does not do justice to the colourful, smart *jardins* surrounding the contemporary-styled hotel – opposite the spa's circular park. Marcelle Pucheu is as friendly a hostess as any. Her husband Louis now leaves much of the classical/regional cooking to their son, Pierre: *piperade de thon à la Basquaise* is typical. Welcome back to *FL*.

Menus aBCD. Rooms (27) E. Disabled. Cards MC, V.
Closed 4 Nov to 10 Dec. Region Southwest.
Post 44 av. Pyrénées, 65400 Argelès-Gazost, Hautes-Pyrénées.
Tel 05 62 97 01 26. Fax 05 62 97 56 67. Mich 168/B3. Map 4.

ARGELES-GAZOST (Beaucens)

Thermal

Simple hotel/Cooking 1
Secluded/Gardens/Swimming pool/Parking

A fort-like *logis* with its own thermal spring – in a 20-acre park with woods, pastures and fine views. The new pool is an added attraction. Readers speak highly of Gisèle Coiquil, the hotel's *directrice*. There's nowt special about Jean Coiquil's basic *Bourgeoise*/classical fare. (Note also that studio-appartments are available on a rent by week basis.)

Menus aBC. Rooms (28) DE. Cards MC, V.
Closed 30 Sept to 26 May. (Beaucens is 5km SE of Argelès-Gazost.)
Post Beaucens, 65400 Argelès-Gazost, Hautes-Pyrénées. Region Southwest.
Tel 05 62 97 04 21. Fax 05 62 97 16 60. Mich 168/B3. Map 4.

A100frs & under. B100–150. C150–200. D200–250. E250–350. F350–500. G500+

40

ARGELES-GAZOST (St-Savin) Viscos

Comfortable restaurant with rooms/Cooking 2-3   `FW`
Terrace

St-Savin is an elevated site S of Argelès. English-speaking Françoise St-Martin is a friendly hostess & husband Jean-Pierre a talented cook climbing modern culinary mountain tracks. Inventive pretty *plats* make clever use of varying flavouring agents and he's keen on vegetables. Signature dish: a perfect *charlotte d'agneau*. Super breakfasts.
Menus bCDE. Rooms (16) E. Cards AE, MC, V. (Off-road parking is easy.)
Closed 1-27 Dec. Rest: Mon (not sch. hols).
Post 65400 St-Savin, Hautes-Pyrénées. Region Southwest.
Tel 05 62 97 02 28. Fax 05 62 97 04 95. Mich 168/B3. Map 4.

ARGENTON-SUR-CREUSE Manoir de Boisvillers

Simple hotel (no restaurant)
Quiet/Gardens/Swimming pool/Closed parking

An 18thC manor house, winning no prizes for looks, is a hop-step-&-jump away from the River Creuse. The hotel is on the river's right bank, just upstream from the *vieux pont*. Owners Monique & Jean-Pierre Gonich are well-liked by readers. Restaurants? Readers speak well of La Criée (3km SE, use D48); & Moulin des Eaux Vives at Tendu (8km NE).
Rooms (14) EF. Cards AE, MC, V.
Closed 2 Dec to 6 Jan. Region Poitou-Charentes.
Post 11 r. Moulin de Bord, 36200 Argenton-sur-Creuse, Indre.
Tel 02 54 24 13 88. Fax 02 54 24 27 83. Mich 97/E1. Map 5.

ARNAGE Auberge des Matfeux

Very comfortable restaurant/Cooking 3   `FW`
Gardens/Parking

An unmemorable building, in a garden setting, SW of Arnage (near junc. of D147S & N23). The classical/neo-classical dishes from Alain Souffront & son Xavier are anything but unmemorable – including on menu D *ravioles de langoustines*, succulent *poulet fermier* from nearby Loué & a delicious *poire rôtie au miel & aux épices*. Menu B (no choice) is *RQP* budget fare.
Menus BCDE. Cards All. (Rooms: Campanile, N of Arnage & N23.)
Closed Feb sch. hols. 14 July to 13 Aug. Sun evg. Mon. Pub. hols evgs.
Post 289 rte Nationale, 72230 Arnage, Sarthe. Region Loire.
Tel 02 43 21 10 71. Fax 02 43 21 25 23. Mich 67/D1. Map 2.

A100frs & under. B100–150. C150–200. D200–250. E250–350. F350–500. G500+

ARRADON

L'Arlequin

Comfortable restaurant/Cooking 2
Terrace/Gardens/Parking

`FW`

Alongside the D101, at the spot marked Boloré on the map (W of Vannes).
Manuel Caradec is a *RQP* fanatic. Modern, classical and regional touches:
witness *millefeuille de saumon, crème d'agrumes; tournedos de rumsteack;*
and *petit far minute aux pommes et calvados.* Two more pluses: fine *cave*
with many half-bottles; and lunch under umbrellas on the terrace.
Menus BCE. Cards All. (Rooms: Le Logis de Parc er Gréo; off D101 to W.)
Closed Sun evg. (Above is *sans rest.*; secluded site; & swimming pool.)
Post Parc Botquelen, 56610 Arradon, Morbihan. Region Brittany.
Tel 02 97 40 41 41. Fax 02 97 40 52 93. Mich 62/C2. Map 1.

ARRAS

Ambassadeur

Very comfortable restaurant/Cooking 2-3

`FW`

A posh name for a swish show. But, for all railway nuts, this is the
ultimate *buffet gare* – a real "stop" *par excellence. Haute cuisine* TGV
classics share the line with anything but punk regional puffers: among the
latter *tarte aux maroilles, ficelles à la Picarde* and *andouillette d'Arras*
– all boiler-stoking fare; the former may number *escalope de saumon à la
creme aneth* and *rable lapin à la crème de moutarde de Meaux.*
Menus BD. Cards All. (Rooms: Les 3 Luppars – a brisk 5-min walk to N.)
Closed Sun evg. (Parking for restaurant adjacent to station.)
Post gare, pl. Foch, 62000 Arras, Pas-de-Calais. Region North.
Tel 03 21 23 29 80. Fax 03 21 71 17 07. Mich 8/A2. Map 2.

ARRAS

La Faisanderie

Very comfortable restaurant/Cooking 3

In 1986 the Dargents moved lock, stock & barrel from Pommera (*FL3*).
The 17thC brick-arched basement *cave*, in the glorious Grand'Place, was
once a stable: note the *escalier*, trough & tethering hooks. Great wine list;
many halves. Marie-Laurence & her brother, Francis Gaudin, are polished
patrons; her husband, Jean-Pierre, is an inventive neo-classical and
modern master. A big readers' favourite: "worth every penny" says one.
Menus CEF. Cards All. (Rooms: Les 3 Luppars, 25m away.)
Closed 1-12 Jan. 4-25 Aug. Sun evg. Mon. (Park in Grand'Place.)
Post 45 Grand'Place, 62000 Arras, Pas-de-Calais. Region North.
Tel 03 21 48 20 76. Fax 03 21 50 89 18. Mich 8/A2. Map 2.

A100frs & under. B100–150. C150–200. D200–250. E250–350. F350–500. G500+

ARRAS

Simple hotel (no restaurant)
Lift

Robert Troy's new Arras enterprise (he was the *chef/patron* at Chanzy for
a couple of decades) in the superb Grand'Place (use its underground car
park) has been a great success with readers. They heap praise on Viviane
de Troy – "absolutely delightful" & "a lovely lady" are typical readers'
compliments. Ask Robert to show you his formidable wine cellar. Les 3 is
just yards from La Faisanderie & a 5-min brisk walk to Ambassadeur.
Rooms (42) DE. Cards All.
Post 49 Grand'Place, 62000 Arras, Pas-de-Calais. Region North.
Tel 03 21 07 41 41. Fax 03 21 24 24 80. Mich 8/A2. Map 2.

ARSONVAL

La Chaumière

Comfortable restaurant with basic rooms/Cooking 1-2   FW
Terrace/Gardens/Parking

Alongside the N19, 6km NW of Bar-sur-Aube – the rustic dining room of
chef Bernard Guillerand and his wife Susan, a Leamington Spa lass. A
mélange of classical and *Bourgeoise* dishes: on one hand a rich, filling
tournedos Périgourdin; on the other tasty home-made teasers like *saumon
fumé* & *terrine de canard*. Grumbles? Unfriendly & indifferent service.
Menus B(bottom-end)CDE. Rooms (3) CDE. Cards AE, MC, V.
Closed Sun evg and Mon (not July/Aug; not pub. hols).
Post Arsonval, 10200 Bar-sur-Aube, Aube. Region Champagne-Ardenne.
Tel 03 25 27 91 02. Fax 03 25 27 90 26. Mich 57/E3. Map 3.

ARTZENHEIM

Auberge d'Artzenheim

Comfortable restaurant with rooms/Cooking 2-3   FW
Quiet/Terrace/Gardens/Parking

The gardens are a special eye-pleaser; the flower-filled interior is a
colourful mixture of old and new – in pleasing contrasts. Some bedrooms
smallish. Edgar Husser, the *chef/patron*, mixes old, new and regional in
his cracking, no-choice menus: a belt-loosening *médaillons de biche*; a
lighter *ravioles de fruits de mer*; and a heady *mousse au kirsch*.
Menus b(lunch)CDE. Rooms (10) E. Cards MC, V.
Closed 15 Feb to 15 Mar. Rest: Mon evg. Tues evg.
Post 68320 Artzenheim, Haut-Rhin. Region Alsace.
Tel 03 89 71 60 51. Fax 03 89 71 68 21. Mich 61/E3. Map 3.

A100frs & under. B100–150. C150–200. D200–250. E250–350. F350–500. G500+

ATTIGNAT
Dominique Marcepoil

Very comfortable restaurant with rooms/Cooking 2-3 | FW |
Terrace/Gardens/Parking

A perfect lunch: a covered terrace with a retina-piercing tapestry and vast colourful mural; and, better still, eye-catching cooking from *chef/ patron*, the bubbly DM. A well-balanced *repas* of salmon marinaded in olive oil and dill, a *quiche de ris de veau au Côtes de Jura*, a fresh goat's cheese *quenelle* and strawberry tart. Perfection?
Menus BCDF. Rooms (10) DEF. Cards AE, MC, V.
Closed Sun evg & Mon (not July/Aug).
Post 01340 Attignat, Ain. (On E side of D975.) Region Lyonnais.
Tel 04 74 30 92 24. Fax 04 74 25 93 48. Mich 103/D3. Map 6.

AUBAZINE
de la Tour

Simple hotel/Cooking 1-2 | FW |
Quiet

A captivating corner of green Corrèze; the village sits high above the Corrèze Valley; opp. the *logis* is the fine façade of a 12thC Cistercian abbey. The recent record has been mixed: for some the food is great; for others not so good. Jacques Lachaud juggles regional (*confits* galore) & classical balls. Arlette's watchful hand is, alas, sorely missed.
Menus aBCD. Rooms (20) BCDE. Cards MC, V.
Closed 1-15 Jan. Sun evg & Mon midday (Oct to May).
Post 19190 Aubazine, Corrèze. Region Dordogne.
Tel 05 55 25 71 17. Fax 05 55 84 61 83. Mich 124/C2. Map 5.

AUDIERNE
Le Goyen

Very comfortable hotel/Cooking 3
Terrace/Lift

The hotel, with terraces & balconies, & exuberantly decorated, overlooks the busy fishing port. Attentive staff. Some grumbles about smallish bedrooms and *les patrons*, M & Mme Bosser. Chef Adolphe Bosser rows with neo-classical oars and, inevitably, fish and shellfish predominate. A signature flourish is a meaty *tronçon de turbot rôti au jus de viande*.
Menus C(lunch: bottom-end)EF. Rooms (24) EFG. Cards AE, MC, V.
Closed Mid to end Jan. Nov to mid Dec. Rest: Mon (out of season).
Post 29770 Audierne, Finistère. Region Brittany.
Tel 02 98 70 08 88. Fax 02 98 70 18 77. Mich 44/B2. Map 1.

A100frs & under. B100–150. C150–200. D200–250. E250–350. F350–500. G500+

AUDIERNE

Roi Gradlon

Comfortable hotel/Cooking 1-2
Parking

From the road, behind the Roi, the *logis* is modern ugly. But appearances often deceive: bedrooms are on the other side, down the cliff face to the beach. Dining room views are stunning. *Le patron* Gaston Auclert is an English-speaking charmer. Wide choice on classical menu C: oysters, *civet de lotte* & *escalope de saumon au beurre rouge* are typical dishes.
Menus BC(bottom-end)D. Rooms (19) EF. Cards All.
Closed Rest: Sun evg & Mon (Oct to Easter).
Post la plage, 29770 Audierne, Finistère. Region Brittany.
Tel 02 98 70 04 51. Fax 02 98 70 14 73. Mich 44/B2. Map 1.

AUDIERNE

Ty Frapp

Comfortable hotel/Cooking 1-2
Parking

A large modern three-storey *logis*, alongside the D784 at Plouhinec, 4 km SE of Audierne. An immediate neighbour is a vast Intermarché. Jeanne Urvois is *la patronne* and her chef/husband Pierre's neo-classical and classical cooking compensates for the uninspiring site. Some robust meat courses: *côte de boeuf au bleu de Bresse* & *filet de canard aux fruits*.
Menus ABCD. Rooms (16) E. Cards MC, V.
Closed 7-20 Oct. 23 Dec to 21 Jan. Sun evg & Mon (not July/Aug).
Post r. de Rozavot, 29780 Plouhinec, Finistère. Region Brittany.
Tel 02 98 70 89 90. Fax 02 98 70 81 04. Mich 44/B2. Map 1.

AULUS-LES-BAINS

Terrasse

Simple hotel/Cooking 2
Terrace

Step over the bridge and travel back in time 30 years – furnishings, service and cooking as they used to be; so, too, is Madame, Rose Amiel, a headmistress martinet. No modern frills here. Chef Jean-François Maurette is a true-blue classics/regional fan: savour rich dishes like *tourte de foie gras de canard* and *cuisse de canard confite du Gers*.
Menus a(lunch)BCDE. Rooms (17) CDE. Cards MC. V. (Cash preferred!)
Closed Oct to Apl (but not Feb sch. hols). (Essential to book ahead.)
Post 09140 Aulus-les-Bains, Ariège. Region Southwest.
Tel 05 61 96 00 98. Mich 170/C4. Map 5.

A100frs & under. B100–150. C150–200. D200–250. E250–350. F350–500. G500+

AUMONT-AUBRAC

Grand Hôtel Prouhèze

Comfortable hotel/Cooking 3
Parking

The new toll-free A75 brings two benefits: the main road is quieter; and access to English-speaking Guy Prouhèze's hotel is easy as pie. Chef Guy is the 4th generation; his repertoire is modern & regional with the odd classic – Aubrac beef with shallots in a red wine sauce is thumpingly good. Top-notch desserts. His wife Catherine is an extrovert hostess.
Menus cEFG. Rooms (27) EFG. Cards MC, V.
Closed Nov to Apl (not Feb sch. hols). Sun evg & Mon (not July/Aug).
Post 48130 Aumont-Aubrac, Lozère. Region Massif Central (Auvergne).
Tel 04 66 42 80 07. Fax 04 66 42 87 78. Mich 127/E4. Map 5.

AUNAY-SUR-ODON

St-Michel

Comfortable restaurant with basic rooms/Cooking 1-2 | FW |

A modern stone *logis* – in a town destroyed by RAF bombers in 1944; the entire heart of Aunay was rebuilt. A well-appreciated, franc-saving recommendation for 14 years now; I'll be charitable and award a 1-2 rating. Copious classical and regional grub: get stuck into *terroir* produce of the *gâteau d'andouille chaude au beurre de cidre* (a dish which is the very essence of Normandy) & *tarte aux pommes* variety.
Menus aBCD. Rooms (7) CD. Cards MC, V. (Parking is easy.)
Closed 15-31 Jan. Sun evg & Mon (not July/Aug).
Post r. Caen, 14260 Aunay-sur-Odon, Calvados. Region Normandy.
Tel 02 31 77 63 16. Fax 02 31 77 05 83. Mich 31/F2. Map 1.

AURAY

Loch et Rest. La Sterne

Comfortable hotel/Cooking 2 | FW |
Quiet/Gardens/Lift/Parking

An architectural disaster (they get paid for this?) but a cool dining room and tree-shaded gardens (on Loch's R bank) compensate. So do the classical servings from the kitchen: aromatic *saumon d'Ecosse parfumé au basilic*; pungent *faux-filet à la crème de Cognac*; and an intense-tasting *plat, cassolette de coquilles St-Jacques au beurre d'estragon*.
Menus BCDE. Rooms (30) E. Cards MC, V.
Closed Rest: Sun evg (October to Easter but not during sch. hols).
Post La Forêt, 56400 Auray, Morbihan. Region Brittany.
Tel 02 97 56 48 33. Fax 02 97 56 63 55. Mich 46/C4. Map 1.

A 100frs & under. B 100–150. C 150–200. D 200–250. E 250–350. F 350–500. G 500+

AURIBEAU

Auberge Nossi-Bé

Comfortable restaurant with rooms/Cooking 2-3
Terrace

Dark-eyed Anne-Marie Retoré, a Cannes girl, welcomes you; husband Jean-Michel cooks a range of neo-classical/modern/regional *plats*. Good choice menus b & D. An inconsistent record over the last decade. Typical dishes are *raviolis de lapereau dans leur jus aux cèpes sec* & *daube de gigot d'agneau Avignonnaise*. Their classic cars have gone: now they're fliers.
Menus b(lun)CD. Rooms (6) E. Cards AE, MC, V.Closed 15-31 Jan. 15-30 Nov. Mon *midi* (season). Tues evg (out of seas). Wed (not evgs seas).
Post 06810 Auribeau-sur-Siagne, Alpes-Maritimes. Region Côte d'Azur.
Tel 04 93 42 20 20. Fax 04 93 42 33 08. Mich 164/C4. Map 6.

AUTUN

Chalet Bleu

Comfortable restaurant/Cooking 1-2

FW

Papa Bouché, Georges, was once the chef at the French Embassy in London. Here he runs the front of house and his son, Philippe, is *le cuisinier*. Regional, classical and neo-classical alternatives: *saupiquet de jambon vieux Morvan, jambon persillé à la Bourguignonne, pièce de boeuf rôtie au fumet de Bourgogne* and *fondant de crabe océan* are a representative quartet. High-standard old-time desserts. (Near *mairie* – town hall.)
Menus aBCD. Cards All. (Rooms: Commerce et Touring; 5-min walk to NW.)
Closed 29 Jan to 14 Feb. Mon evg. Tues.
Post 3 r. Jeannin, 71400 Autun, Saône-et-Loire, Region Burgundy.
Tel 03 85 86 27 30. Fax 03 85 52 74 56. Mich 87/E3. Map 3.

AUTUN

Vieux Moulin

Comfortable restaurant with rooms/Cooking 2
Quiet/Terrace/Gardens/Garage/Parking

FW

Autun, Roman *Augustodunum* (once called the "sister of Rome" by Julius Caesar), is a delight; so, too, is the setting for the *moulin* (once a forge & sawmill) just outside the N Roman gate, the Porte d'Arroux (D980 to Saulieu). Dominique Tarel forges neo-classical & classical *plats: tournedos Talleyrand* & *St-Jacques au vermouth* are typical offerings.
Menus A(lunch)CE (both bottom-end). Rooms (16) DEF. Cards AE, MC, V.
Closed Dec to Feb. Sun evg & Mon (out of season).
Post porte d'Arroux, 71400 Autun, Saône-et-Loire. Region Burgundy.
Tel 03 85 52 10 90. Fax 03 85 86 32 15. Mich 87/E3. Map 3.

A100frs & under. B100–150. C150–200. D200–250. E250–350. F350–500. G 500+

AUXERRE

Barnabet

Luxury restaurant/Cooking 3
Terrace

Jean-Luc & Marie Barnabet are now well-established at their spacious new home (once a garage). A gleaming kitchen, behind glass, is their pride & joy. He's a *faites simple* modern chef. One vivid memory remains: superb *pot-au-feu de boeuf en gelée* (a 3cm-deep blockbuster burger). Handsome, English-speaking *sommelier* Jean-Claude Mourguiart is still *in situ*.
Menus DE. Cards AE, MC, V. (Rooms: Le Maxime, 200m to N.)
Closed 23 Dec-4 Jan. Sun evg. Mon. (Park opp. rest. on quayside.)
Post 14 quai République, 89000 Auxerre, Yonne. Region Burgundy.
Tel 03 86 51 68 88. Fax 03 86 52 96 85. Mich 72/A2. Map 2.

AUXERRE

Hôtel Le Maxime

Comfortable hotel (no restaurant)
Lift/Garage

Few town-centre hotels have such an exhilarating setting: to the front the tree-lined River Yonne; to the rear the giant walls of the *chevet*, transept and tower of Auxerre cathedral – and, just a touch downstream, the ancient abbey of St-Germain. A fine mix of old & new in a well-run family hotel: quieter rooms at rear; front rooms have a river view.
Rooms (25) EF. Cards All. (Parking easy.)
Closed 20 Dec-10 Jan. Sun (Nov to Mar).
Post 2 quai Marine, 89000 Auxerre, Yonne. Region Burgundy.
Tel 03 86 52 14 19. Fax 03 86 52 21 70. Mich 72/A2. Map 2.

AUXERRE

Jardin Gourmand

Very comfortable restaurant/Cooking 2 | FW |

Some guides rate Pierre Boussereau the equal of his Auxerre neighbour, Jean-Luc Barnabet. Two visits here and several over the years to J-L have left me backing Barnabet as the hands down winner. Innovative and inconsistent modern cooking – a mix of poor and super: poor – *crème de poireaux* soup and leathery pigeon breasts; super – a flavoursome *tarte aux pommes et aux St-Jacques, beurre d'ail doux*. Chic service & décor.
Menus BCE. Cards AE, MC, V. (Rooms: Normandie, *sans rest*, across road.)
Closed 10-25 Mar. 1-16 Sept. Mon (not July/Aug). Tues.
Post 56 bd Vauban, 89000 Auxerre, Yonne. Region Burgundy.
Tel 03 86 51 53 52. Fax 03 86 52 33 82. Mich 72/A2. Map 2.

A100frs & under. B100–150. C150–200. D200–250. E250–350. F350–500. G500+

48

AUXERRE (La Coudre)   Le Moulin

Comfortable restaurant with rooms/Cooking 2 | FW |
Terrace/Parking

Just N of Auxerre-Sud exit (follow signs from N65). Jean-Pierre Vaury is
highly regarded by his regional peers. A mainly classical repertoire confirms
their opinions: a rarely seen *pied de veau, sauce ravigote*; a hearty and
well-conceived *magret de canard fumé aux pommes tièdes*; and a
drooling *tarte aux pommes*. The rooms are new; the site should be quiet.
Menus bCDE. Rooms (5) E. Cards MC, V.
Closed Jan. Sun evg. Mon.
Post La Coudre, 89290 Venoy, Yonne. Region Burgundy.
Tel 03 86 40 23 79. Fax 03 86 40 23 55. Mich 72/A2. Map 2.

AVALLON   Avallon-Vauban

Comfortable hotel (no restaurant)
Fairly quiet/Gardens/Lift/Parking

Whilst my vote for the ideal base in this neck of the woods would go to
the Moulin des Templiers, nevertheless the Vauban has long been my
next best favourite. Though the hotel is beside the N6 it does have some
advantages over the *moulin*: modern bedrooms, some with kitchens; it's
open all year; has large gardens at the rear (bedrooms at the back are
fairly quiet); and is a neighbour of the excellent Relais des Gourmets.
Rooms (30) E(bottom-end)F. Disabled. Cards AE, MC, V.
Post 53 r. Paris, 89200 Avallon, Yonne. Region Burgundy.
Tel 03 86 34 36 99. Fax 03 86 31 66 31. Mich 72/B3. Map 2.

AVALLON (also see next page)   Moulin des Templiers

Simple hotel (no restaurant)
Secluded/Gardens/Parking

Mill wheels have turned at this idyllic spot, beside the tree-lined River
Cousin, since the 12th century. The present-day small hotel was
converted from the last working mill in 1925. Marie-Françoise Hilmoine
is proud of her immaculate *moulin*. Bedrooms are small – a regular moan;
but the terrace, trees, and the metre-high weir more than compensate.
Rooms (14) EF(both bottom-end). Cards not accepted.
Closed Nov to Mar.
Post 89200 Avallon, Yonne. Region Burgundy.
Tel 03 86 34 10 80. Mich 72/B3. Map 3. (4km W of Avallon.)

A100frs & under. B100–150. C150–200. D200–250. E250–350. F350–500. G500+

AVALLON (also see previous page)

Relais Fleuri

Comfortable hotel/Cooking 1-2
Quiet/Gardens/Swimming pool/Tennis/Parking

FW

For me a long-overdue visit to the well-named *logis*. Enter past two snoozing Labradors, to the much modernised, greatly extended Schiever family hotel (part motel). Chef Stéphane Blanchet's wide repertoire is classical/neo-classical with eclectic provincial touches: *rillette de haddock, daube de boeuf à la Provençale, crepinette de pintade sauce bigarade* & *millefeuille tout choc* – all on wide-choice menu B.
Menus BC. Rooms (48) F. Cards All. (Due E 6km; N6 towards Saulieu.)
Post 89200 Avallon, Yonne. Region Burgundy. (3km SW of A6 exit).
Tel 03 86 34 02 85. Fax 03 86 34 09 98. Mich 72/B3-C3. Map 3.

AVESNES

La Crémaillère

Comfortable restaurant/Cooking 2

FW

Francis Lelaurain has worked hard to restore this famous restaurant's good name – after he took over the kitchens, following his father's death. Classical offerings of a high standard with, more likely than not, old established *plats* like *bouribout aux arômates de Provence* (see *bourride*) and a bang-in-the-mouth *rôtie Avesnoise* (or *Maroilles*) cheese course. One welcome plus: a *Menu de la Mer* (4 courses, cheese, sweet.)
Menus BDE. Cards All. (Rooms: base hotels at Fourmies & Sars-Poteries.)
Closed Mon evg & Tues (not pub. hols). Regions Champagne-Ardenne/North.
Post 26 pl. Gén. Leclerc, 59440 Avesnes-sur-Helpe, Nord.
Tel 03 27 61 02 30. Mich 10/A3. Map 3.

AVRANCHES

Le Pratel

Comfortable hotel (no restaurant)
Fairly quiet/Gardens/Parking

Upgraded main roads have made this an entirely viable base hotel for the many *FLF* restaurants within say half-an-hour drive. The N175 Avranches western bypass is a boon; the town is now much quieter. The small, modern house is ringed by trees and, in the spring, provides a stunning show of cyclamen. On the east side of the Mont-St-Michel road.
Rooms (7) E. Cards AE, MC, V.
Closed Nov to Feb.
Post 24 r. Vanniers, 50300 Avranches, Manche. Region Normandy.
Tel 02 33 68 35 41. Fax 02 33 68 33 50. Mich 30/C4. Map 1.

AZAY-LE-RIDEAU

L'Aigle d'Or

Comfortable restaurant/Cooking 2-3
Terrace

FW

A pleasure in every sense: a pastel-shaded dining room with flowers on each table; a garden terrace for eating out; an attractive hostess, Ghislaine Fèvre; and classical cooking from her husband Jean-Luc. *Crème d'oseille et quenelles de brochet, jambonnette de volaille à la crème de morilles* and *craquant aux fraises* remain three lip-smacking memories.
Menus a(lunch)BCE. Cards MC, V. (Rooms: de Biencourt; *sans restaurant*.)
Closed 7 Feb-4 Mar. 15-25 Dec. Sun evg. Tues evg (out of season). Wed.
Post 37190 Azay-le-Rideau, Indre-et-Loire. Region Loire.
Tel 02 47 45 24 58. Fax 02 47 45 90 18. Mich 82/A1. Map 2.

BADEN

Le Gavrinis

Comfortable hotel/Cooking 2-3
Terrace/Gardens/Parking

FW

A sparkling, multi-faceted family affair. Alain Justum and sons, Olivier (*le pâtissier*) and Frédéric, man the stoves; mum, Michèle, looks after the front of house. Modern and neo-classical *plats* executed with flair, harmony and good taste. Star-quality sweets. Modern hotel with flower-bedecked terrace. Admire, too, the fine Staffordshire pottery.
Menus bCDF(bottom-end). Rooms (20)EF. Cards All.
Closed 15 Nov-31 Jan. Mon (Oct-Apl). Rest: Mon midday (15 June-15 Sept).
Post Toulbroch, 56870 Baden, Morbihan. Region Brittany.
Tel 02 97 57 00 82. Fax 02 97 57 09 47. Mich 62/B2-C2. Map 1.

BAGNOLES-DE-L'ORNE (also see next page)

Bois Joli

Comfortable hotel/Cooking 1-2
Quiet/Terrace/Gardens/Lift/Parking

FW

A large, handsome red and white *maison Normande*, surrounded by trees and 50m from the spa lake. Modest classical cooking of the *carré d'agneau en croûte d'aubergine* and *fricassée de volaille à l'estragon* variety. The owners, Serge & Claudine Gatti, have a formidable cellar. Recent additions to the facilities include a gym, sauna and Turkish bath.
Menus BCDE. Rooms (20) EF. Cards All.
Closed Rest: Jan. Wed (Nov to Mar).
Post av. Ph. du Rozier, 61140 Bagnoles-de-l'Orne, Orne. Region Normandy.
Tel 02 33 37 92 77. Fax 02 33 37 07 56. Mich 50/B1. Map 2.

A 100frs & under. B 100–150. C 150–200. D 200–250. E 250–350. F 350–500. G 500+

BAGNOLES-DE-L'ORNE (also see previous page)   Ermitage

Comfortable hotel (no restaurant)
Quiet/Gardens/Lift/Garage/Parking

Bagnoles-de-l'Orne is France at the start of the century: a flower-filled spa, clean streets, casino, fine large houses and encircling woods are pleasing features. So, too, is the stone exterior Ermitage – in a quiet street & with a small sun-trap garden. Marie-Claude Planché is an energetic, smiling *patronne*. High-tech garage keeps cars safe.
Rooms (37) DE. Cards MC, V.
Closed Nov to 6 Apl.
Post 24 bd P. Chaivet, 61140 Bagnoles-de-l'Orne, Orne. Region Normandy.
Tel 02 33 37 96 22. Fax 02 33 38 59 22. Mich 50/B1. Map 2.

BAGNOLES-DE-L'ORNE   Manoir du Lys

Very comfortable hotel/Cooking 2-3   FW
Secluded/Terrace/Gardens/Lift/Tennis/Parking

W of the spa, in an isolated wooded setting – the latter part of the Forêt des Andaines. The attractive manor house, with a stone & half-timbered façade, is a delight; so are the rooms. Five members of the talented Quinton family care for clients. Neo-classical/regional fare. Fair choice on menu B: *merlu poêlé aux algues* was especially appetising.
Menus BCDE. Rooms (23) EFG. Disabled. Cards All. (D235, 3km to W.)
Closed 6 Jan-10 Feb. Sun evg & Mon (Nov-Easter).
Post 61140 Bagnoles-de-l'Orne, Orne. Region Normandy.
Tel 02 33 37 80 69. Fax 02 33 30 05 80. Mich 50/B1. Map 2.

BALDENHEIM   La Couronne

Very comfortable restaurant/Cooking 3

The enjoyment rating is sky-high: a pleasing house with wood-panelled, flower-filled dining rooms; a courteous welcome from Marcel Trébis & his pretty daughter, Chantal; and impeccable neo-classical and regional cooking from her husband, Daniel Rubiné, and her mother, Argèle. Typical treats could include *matelote du Ried (de sandre, de brochet, d'anguille* – Ried is the marshy Rhine plain). (Rooms: see Riquewihr & Illhaeusern.)
Menus C(bottom-end)DEF. Cards AE, MC, V.
Closed 2-9 Jan. 22 July to 5 Aug. Sun evg. Mon.
Post r. Sélestat, 67600 Baldenheim, Bas-Rhin. Region Alsace
Tel 03 88 85 32 22. Fax 03 88 85 36 27. Mich 61/E2. Map 3.

BALLEROY

Manoir de la Drôme

Very comfortable restaurant/Cooking 3   FW
Gardens/Closed parking

Alongside the D13, NW of the village & beside the Drôme. Bespectacled Christine provides a smiling welcome. Husband Denis provides his pleasing pleasures from the kitchen – quality classical/regional *plats*. Two memorable menu B dishes: a richly satisfying *pièce de boeuf à la citronelle* and a quintessential *aumonière de pomme à la cannelle*.
Menus B(top-end)C(top-end). Cards AE, MC, V. (Rooms: Argouges, Bayeux.)
Closed Feb sch. hols. 1-8 Sept. Sun evg. Mon. (Bayeux 18km to NE.)
Post 14490 Balleroy, Calvados, Region Normandy.
Tel 02 31 21 60 94. Fax 02 31 21 88 67. Mich 31/E1. Map 1.

BANDOL

Auberge du Port

Comfortable restaurant/Cooking 2-3   FW
Terrace

A vast operation (numerous menus) with large shaded terrace – part by yellow awnings & part by palm trees. Nevertheless owner, M. Ghiribelli, ensures standards are kept high. Great emphasis on fish/shellfish *bien sûr* on the more expensive menus. Menu B (low-end) offers fine quality classical & Provençals *plats*: a *terrine de poireaux, anchoïde de moruette riz pilaf* and *crème caramel* is one typical permutation.
Menus BCDE. Cards All. (Rooms: Baie or Golf Hôtel; both *sans rest.*)
Post 9 allées J. Moulin, 83150 Bandol, Var. Region Provence.
Tel 04 94 29 42 63. Fax 04 94 29 44 59. Mich 160/B4. Map 6.

BANDOL (also see next page)

Golf Hôtel

Simple hotel (no restaurant)
Fairly quiet/Closed parking/Air-conditioning

You could literally practice bunker shots at the Golf: the hotel is on the plage Rénecros. Just west of Bandol promenade, around a headland and facing west. Don't expect miracles from the simple hotel: the site is everything and two recommended restaurants are just minutes away. Over the years readers have had no problems at the Golf.
Rooms (24) F(Bottom-end)G. Cards MC, V.
Closed Nov to Mar.
Post plage Rénecros, 83150 Bandol, Var. Region Provence.
Tel 04 94 29 45 83. Fax 04 94 32 42 47. Mich 160/B4. Map 6.

A100frs & under. B100–150. C150–200. D200–250. E250–350. F350–500. G500+

BANDOL (also see previous page) **Réserve**

Comfortable restaurant with rooms/Cooking 2 FW
Terrace/Closed parking/Air-conditioning (bedrooms)

A regular favourite for my family 30 years ago – a late 19thC building beside the Med and with its toes in both the sea and the beach. New owners now, Jeanine & Jacques Jacquet. His *"Ma Provence"* menu (B) has sure classical & regional treats: flavoursome *crêpinette de cabillaud au basilic* & an old-time tasty *jarret de veau braisé à la sarriette*.
Menus BDF. Rooms (13) EFG. Cards All.
Closed 10 Nov to 10 Dec. Rest: Sun evg & Mon (Nov to Easter).
Post rte de Sanary, 83150 Bandol, Var. Region Provence.
Tel 04 94 29 30 00. Fax 04 94 29 30 13. Mich 160/B4-C4. Map 6.

BANNEGON **Auberge Moulin de Chaméron**

Very comfortable restaurant with rooms/Cooking 2-3 FW
Secluded/Terrace/Gardens/Swimming pool/Parking

English-speaking Jacques & Annie Candoré are the informed & entertaining *patrons* at the 18thC mill with tiny milling museum (his gt-grandfather worked at the *moulin*). Son-in-law, chef Jean Mérilleau, conjures up both neo-classical & modern tricks: *flan de langoustines au vin blanc de Sancerre* & *feuillantine de framboises* are vivid examples of his skills.
Menus BCD. Rooms (13) F. Cards AE, MC, V.
Closed Mid Nov to end Feb. Rest: Tues (out of season).
Post 18210 Bannegon, Cher. Region Berry-Bourbonnais.
Tel 02 48 61 83 80. Fax 02 48 61 84 92. Mich 85/D4. Map 2.

BANYULS-SUR-MER **Les Elmes/Rest. La Littorine**

Comfortable hotel/Cooking 1-2 FW
Parking/Air-conditioning (bedrooms)

Beside the N114 N entrance to Banyuls; bad news – the *logis* is near a railway line; good news – it overlooks a *plage*. Jean Sannac, the owner, employs competent chefs and, invariably, they tread classical/regional waters: menu B last year included *croustillant d'anchois, demi-homard (vapeur ou grillé)* & a *sorbet aux pêches du Roussillon* – all top-notch.
Menus ABCE. Rooms (31) E. Cards All. Region Languedoc-Roussillon.
Closed Tues evg & Wed (Nov-15 Mar). Rest: 2-20 Jan. 25 Nov-15 Dec.
Post plage des Elmes, 66650 Banyuls-sur-Mer, Pyrénées-Orientales.
Tel 04 68 88 03 12. Fax 04 68 88 53 03. Mich 177/F4. Map 5.

A100frs & under. B100–150. C150–200. D200–250. E250–350. F350–500. G500+

BAPAUME

Paix

Comfortable hotel/Cooking 2
Garage/Parking

FW

Things are looking up in Bapaume. The refurbished, stylishly fitted-out hotel (with white stone exterior) is on the W side of the N17, just S of its junc. with the N30. Complex classical/regional dishes from Remy Hautecoeur – but enjoyable nevertheless: filling *plats* like *gigotin de poularde farci aux navets confits* & *contrefilet grillé vert pré*.
Menus aCD. Rooms (13) DE(bottom-end). Cards MC, V
Closed Sun evg.
Post av. A.-Guidet, 62450 Bapaume, Pas-de-Calais. Region North.
Tel 03 21 07 11 03. Fax 03 21 07 43 66. Mich 8/A3. Map 2.

BARBEZIEUX

La Boule d'Or

Comfortable hotel/Cooking 1-2
Terrace/Gardens/Lift/Garage

FW

Modern, town-centre site, in a tree-lined *bd* 150m W of the N10/D5 junc. (Bypass open end 96.) Soundproofed bedrooms. Lovely, tree-shaded garden & terrace is a calm oasis. Wide choice on Jean Charrier's classical & regional menus: *marinière de saumon à l'aneth & huile d'olive, mouclade, cotelettes d'agneau aux herbes* & *entrecôte grillé sauce au vieux Bordeaux* are typical menu A *plats*. That's real *RQP* fare: agreed?
Menus ABC(top-end). Rooms (20) DE. Disabled. Cards All.
Post 9 bd Gambetta, 16300 Barbezieux-St-Hilaire, Charente. Reg. Poit-Ch.
Tel 05 45 78 64 13. Fax 05 45 78 63 83. Mich 107/F3. Map 4.

BARBIZON

Les Pléiades

Comfortable hotel/Cooking 2
Quiet/Terrace/Gardens/Parking

FW

Once the home of the artist Daubigny. Present owners, Roger & Yolande Karampournis, claim *"le charme d'autrefois allié au confort d'aujourd' hui."* The classical cooking, from chef Jean-Marc Héry, can also be tagged *"autrefois"*. Little choice on menu b (top-end): *mousse blonde de foies de volaille au Sauterne, onglet de boeuf mignonnette, brie de Meaux* & *tarte fine aux mirabelles* are not for the anorexic-minded!
Menus b(top-end)cDE. Rooms (15) EFG. Cards All.
Post 77630 Barbizon, Seine-et-Marne. Region Ile de France.
Tel 01 60 66 40 25. Fax 01 60 66 41 68. Mich 54/B2. Map 2.

A100frs & under. B100–150. C150–200. D200–250. E250–350. F350–500. G500+

BARBOTAN-LES-THERMES

Château Bellevue

Comfortable hotel/Cooking 2
Quiet/Terrace/Gardens/Swimming pool/Lift/Parking

FW

Michèle Consolaro's 19thC château, at Cazaubon – 3km SW of the spa, has many admirers. Readers like the elegant mansion, the large park and its century-old cedars. Chef Bruno Roussel's cooking is largely *Bourgeoise* and neo-classical. Raise your berets to both Bruno and Michèle for introducing, and persevering with a *"Menu Tout Poisson"*. Bravo!
Menus AC(bottom-end). Rooms (25) DEFG. Cards All.
Closed Jan-mid Feb.
Post 32150 Cazaubon, Gers. Region Southwest.
Tel 05 62 09 51 95. Fax 05 62 09 54 57. Mich 150/B1-C1. Map 4.

BARCELONNETTE

La Mangeoire

Comfortable restaurant/Cooking 3
Terrace

FW

Hard to find: NE corner of town, W side Eglise St-Pierre. Once found you'll love the vaulted 17thC *salle* and, even more so, the *Provençale* cuisine – in the high mountains – of Laurent Dodé. From menu B relish treats like *terrine de ratatouille vinaigret au basilic, cabillaud pané au pistou huile d'olive* and *crème brûlée à la lavande* – all made in heaven.
Menus ABCD(top-end). Cards AE, MC, V. (Rooms: Gde Epervière or Azteca.)
Closed May. Oct-Nov. Mon & Tues (not sch. hols). Regions Hte-Alpes/Prov.
Post pl. 4-Vents, 04400 Barcelonnette, Alpes-de-Haute-Provence.
Tel 04 92 81 01 61. Fax 04 92 81 01 61. Mich 147/D2. Map 6.

BARCUS

Chez Chilo

Very comfortable restaurant with rooms/Cooking 2-3
Terrace/Gardens/Swimming pool/Parking

FW

Pierre & Martine Chilo are the 3rd-generation *patrons* (a family renowned locally for their rugby links). Scrum down for his classical/regional culinary balls – among them *piments "piquillos" farcis à la morue*, hearty *civet de marcassin* and yummy *gâteau Basque au coulis de cerises noires*. Front of house operations a let down. 8 super new bedrooms.
Menus aBCE. Rooms (14) CDEF. Disabled. Cards All.
Closed 15 Jan-3 Feb. 24-30 Mar. Sun evg & Mon (not high season).
Post 64130 Barcus, Pyrénées-Atlantiques. Region Southwest.
Tel 05 59 28 90 79. Fax 05 59 28 93 10. Mich 167/E2. Map 4.

A100frs & under. B100–150. C150–200. D200–250. E250–350. F350–500. G500+

BARFLEUR

Moderne

Comfortable restaurant with basic rooms/Cooking 2

A small pepperpot tower is an unusual man-made exterior feature. Mme Le Roulier is a friendly, helpful *patronne*. Her husband, chef Evrard, tacks a classical course and capitalises on the nearby ocean's piscatorial harvests: *soupe de poissons*, oysters and a *choucroute de poisson au beurre blanc* are typical culinary catches. Patterned plates reflect the rather busy cooking style. Home-made breads & pasta. Many half-bottles.
Menus aBC. Rooms (8) BCD. Cards MC, V.
Closed 15 Jan-15 Mar. Tues & Wed (15 Sept-15 Jan).
Post 50760 Barfleur, Manche. Region Normandy.
Tel 02 33 23 12 44. Fax 02 33 23 91 58. Mich 12/C1. Map 1.

BAR-LE-DUC

Meuse Gourmande

Comfortable restaurant/Cooking 2-3
Terrace

In the Ville Haute, adjacent to the Tour de l'Horloge (with a Trumpton clock facing E) – a fine 18thC house, the home of Frédérique & Franck Damien. Franck strikes neo-classical/modern culinary chimes – notably in eclectic menu C (bottom-end) *plats* such as *carpaccio de thon rouge au gingembre & au soja* and a pleasurable *jarret de veau braisée aux herbes*.
Menus a(lunch)CDE. Cards All. (Rooms: Gare, town centre; see next line.)
Closed Feb sch. hols. Sun evg. Wed. (Or La Source, Trémont-s-Saulx; SW.)
Post 1 r. F.de Guise, 55000 Bar-le-duc, Meuse. Region Champagne-Ardenne.
Tel 03 29 79 28 40. Fax 03 29 45 40 71. Mich 39/F3-F4. Map 3.

BARNEVILLE-CARTERET

Marine

Very comfortable hotel/Cooking 3
Quiet/Terrace/Parking

Before a meal relax with an *apéritif* on the terrace overlooking the estuary with distant views of Jersey. Then savour the neo-classical and modern creations of Laurent Cesne, the chef son of owners Bernadette & Emmanuel, who run the show with authority & friendliness. Fish/shellfish dishes are flavoursome masterpieces. (Cheaper rooms: Les Isles.)
Menus bCF. Rooms (31) FG. Cards All. Closed Nov-mid Feb. Rest: Sun evg (Feb/Mar/Oct). Mon (not July/Aug; not evgs Apl/May/June/Sept).
Post Carteret, 50270 Barneville-Carteret, Manche. Region Normandy.
Tel 02 33 53 83 31. Fax 02 33 53 39 60. Mich 12/A3. Map 1.

A100frs & under. B100–150. C150–200. D200–250. E250–350. F350–500. G500+

Le BARROUX   Géraniums

Comfortable hotel/Cooking 1
Quiet/Terrace/Closed parking

The terrain, views, *les terrasses*, the *café de la place* and the medieval village are the main reasons for seeking out Agnes and Jacques Roux's *logis*. Take dark glasses: the colour pink overwhelms. Smallish bedrooms and cavernous dining room with, alas, zero charm. Classical, *Bourgeoise* and Provençale cuisine: of the *lapin à la sarriette* variety.
Menus aBCD. Rooms (22) D. Cards All.
Closed Jan. Feb. Wed (Nov to Mar).
Post 84330 Le Barroux, Vaucluse. Region Provence. (NE of Carpentras.)
Tel 04 90 62 41 08. Fax 04 90 62 56 48. Mich 144/C3. Map 6.

Les BAUX-DE-PROVENCE   Mas d'Aigret

Comfortable hotel/Cooking 3   FW
Quiet/Terrace/Gardens/Swimming pool/Parking

A delightful, sparkling hotel where man and Nature combine seductively. The "man" is Pip (Patrick Ivor) Philipps, who makes the place buzz together with his French wife, Chantal, and her brother Fred Laloy. The 250-year-old farmhouse (*mas*) has several troglodyte rooms, including the dining room. Chef Pascal Johnson is a young modern cooking master.
Menus A(lunch)CEF. Rooms (16) G. Cards All.
Closed 3-22 Feb. Wed midday. (Cheaper rooms: see St-Rémy base hotels.)
Post 13520 Les Baux-de-Provence, Bouches-du-Rhône. Region Provence.
Tel 04 90 54 33 54. Fax 04 90 54 41 37. Mich 158/B2. Map 6.

Les BAUX-DE-PROVENCE   La Riboto de Taven

Very comfortable restaurant with rooms/Cooking 3
Secluded/Terrace/Gardens/Closed parking

Taven – a "fairy"; *la riboto* – a "feast of the table" (Mistral). The garden, a riot-of-colour Eden, sits under a high rock face (the bedrooms are troglodyte). Jean-Pierre Novi & brother-in-law Philippe Thème man the stoves and conjure up a *cuisine libre* of modern & Provençale dishes. Christine Thème is a delectable *patronne*. All three speak English.
Menus c(lunch)EF. Rooms (3) G. Cards All. (Cheaper rooms: see St-Rémy.)
Closed 9 Jan-15 Mar. Tues evg (out of season). Wed.
Post 13520 Les Baux-de-Provence, Bouches-du-Rhône. Region Provence.
Tel 04 90 54 34 23. Fax 04 90 54 38 88. Mich 158/B2. Map 6.

A100frs & under. B100–150. C150–200. D200–250. E250–350. F350–500. G500+

BAYEUX Argouges

Comfortable hotel (no restaurant)
Quiet/Gardens/Parking

Daniel and Marie-Claude Auregan are rightly proud of their 18thC *hôtel particulier*. The bedrooms are in two buildings well back from the road; they are sensibly furnished and have high ceilings and beams. Argouges is within a half-mile walk of both the cathedral and the world-famous Bayeux tapestry. Additional pleasures are the numerous man-made and natural attractions which ring the town.
Rooms (23) EF. Cards All.
Post 21 r. St-Patrice, 14400 Bayeux, Calvados. Region Normandy.
Tel 02 31 92 88 86. Fax 02 31 92 69 16. Mich 13/E3-E4. Map 1.

BAZINCOURT-SUR-EPTE Château de la Rapée

Comfortable hotel/Cooking 2
Secluded/Gardens/Closed parking

Built in 1825, the château style is Anglo-Norman baroque. In an isolated site, on the edge of woods and with extensive views north; both the setting and the approach would suit a Brontë novel. Philippe Bergeron has taken over the kitchens (his parents bought the property in 1973); his repertoire is classical/neo-classical – with few Normandy touches.
Menus cD. Rooms (12) FG (low-end). Cards All. (NW of village.)
Closed Feb. Rest: 15-29 Aug. Wed.
Post 27140 Bazincourt-sur-Epte, Eure. Regions Ile de France/Normandy.
Tel 02 32 55 11 61. Fax 02 32 55 95 65. Mich 17/D4. Map 2.

BEAULIEU-SUR-DORDOGNE Central Hôtel Fournié

Simple hotel/Cooking 2 | FW |
Terrace/Closed parking

No surprise to see Bernard Bessière win a Michelin accolade last year at his brown-shuttered *logis*. An all-fish menu is a welcome surprise. Menu B could include a *pillaw de calmar encre, foie de canard frais en terrine de maison* and a middling-only *navarin d'agneau et ses pâtes fraîches*. Regional/classical styles in an enjoyable rustic environment.
Menus aB. Rooms (27) CDE. Cards MC, V.
Closed Mid Nov to mid Mar. Region Dordogne.
Post 4 pl. Champ-de-Mars, 19120 Beaulieu-sur-Dordogne. Corrèze.
Tel 05 55 91 01 34. Fax 05 55 91 23 57. Mich 125/D3. Map 5.

A100frs & under. B100–150. C150–200. D200–250. E250–350. F350–500. G500+

BEAUMESNIL

L'Etape Louis XIII

Comfortable restaurant/Cooking 2-3
Terrace/Gardens/Parking

FW

New young owners at the ivy-covered 17thC half-timbered cottages: Christian, the chef, and Christine Ravinel. No discordant notes with his neo-classical *plats*. For those with few francs menu a is champion: *marinade de saumon à l'huile d'olive, chou farci de morue fraîche*, super goat's cheese with walnut oil & *pain perdu aux pommes* is typical.
Menus aC(top-end)E. Cards AE, MC, V. (Rooms: Acropole, SW of Bernay.)
Closed 2 Jan-5 Feb. 23 June-l July. Sun evg. Mon.
Post 27410 Beaumesnil, Eure. Region Normandy.
Tel 02 32 44 44 72. Fax 02 32 45 53 84. Mich 33/F2. Map 2.

BEAUMONT-EN-AUGE

La Haie Tondue

Comfortable restaurant/Cooking 1-2
Terrace/Parking

FW

Chef Dominique Tolmais is a regular menu changer; every three weeks a new version appears. Menus B&C provide a choice of five starters, five main courses, followed by many cheeses and even more puds. Appetite-quenching classical and *Bourgeoise* grub: like *terrine campagnarde, terrine de poisson verte* and *faux-filet grillé maître d'hôtel*.
Menus BCD. Cards MC, V. (Rooms: Climat de France, Pont-l'Evêque.)
Closed Feb sch hols. 23 Ju-1 Jul. 30 Sep-7 Oct. Mon evg (not Aug). Tues.
Post 14130 la Haie Tondue, Beaumont-en-Auge, Calvados. Region Normandy.
Tel 02 31 64 85 00. Fax 02 31 64 69 34. Mich 32/C1. Map 2. (2km to S.)

BEAUNE

Auberge Toison d'Or

Comfortable restaurant/Cooking 1-2
Air-conditioning

FW

Annick & Philippe Clergue's *auberge* is on E side of Beaune's inner ring road (park in *place* to SE). Smoked glass walls in the *salle* can make the place gloomy – but not so Philippe's classical, Bourgogne & Périgord repertoire. Evidence? *Cabillaud aux 5 poivres, beurre au crémant de Bourgogne*, a filling *fricassée d'oie aux raisins* – all on menu B.
Menus ABCD. Cards AE, MC, V. (Rooms: see Beaune/Levernois base hotels.)
Closed 24 Dec-7 Jan. Sun evg. Mon.
Post 4 bd Jules Ferry, 21200 Beaune, Côte d'Or. Region Burgundy.
Tel 03 80 22 29 62. Fax 03 80 24 07 11. Mich 88/A2. Map 3.

A100frs & under. B100–150. C150–200. D200–250. E250–350. F350–500. G500+

BEAUNE

Le Bénaton

Comfortable restaurant/Cooking 2-3
Terrace

Isabelle & Bruno Monnoir do a first-rate job in their small dining room (with the bonus of a terrace). Bruno is an inventive modernist with a strong liking for both regional & old-fashioned classics. Menu a is *RQP* pleasing – inc' *jambon persillé* or *gâteau de foies blonds de volaille à la crème de langoustines* & a main course *volaille farci aux champignons*.
Menus aC(low-end)D. Cards MC, V. (Rooms: see Beaune/Levernois hotels.)
Closed 18-24 Nov. Wed. Thurs midday. Region Burgundy.
Post 25 r. Fg Bretonnière, 21200 Beaune, Côte-d'Or. (N74 S exit.)
Tel 03 80 22 00 26. Fax 03 80 22 51 95. Mich 88/A2. Map 3.

BEAUNE

Bernard Morillon

Very comfortable restaurant/Cooking 3
Terrace

One of the supreme outposts of authentic French classical cuisine; also one of the supreme readers' favourites. Martine Morillon, a vivacious, larger-than-life extrovert, is *la patronne*; chef Bernard, trained by Eugénie Brazier, is a technical wizard; sauces are 3-star. A signature classic? What about a *volaille de Bresse mijotée au Gevrey-Chambertin*.
Menus cEF. Cards All. (Rooms: see Le Cep or other Beaune base hotels.)
Closed 2-22 Jan. 9-16 Aug. Mon. Tues midday.
Post 31 r. Maufoux, 21200 Beaune, Côte-d'Or. Region Burgundy.
Tel 03 80 24 12 06. Fax 03 80 22 66 22. Mich 88/A2. Map 3.

BEAUNE (also see next page)

Central

Comfortable hotel/Cooking 2

Aptly named – at the heart of the flower-covered town, a tennis court length from the multi-hued Hôtel-Dieu patterned roof. Bright, pretty patterns grace chef Jean Garcin's creations: menus include *jambon persillé fait maison* & *veritable coq au vin à l'ancienne mode* – regional treats; & more traditional classics – *filet de charolais poêle à l'infusion de vin rouge* & *millefeuille de pied de cochon à l'ail doux*.
Menus aBC. Rooms (20) EF. Cards MC, V.
Closed 25 Nov to 20 Dec.
Post 2 r. V. Millot, 21200 Beaune, Côte-d'Or. Region Burgundy.
Tel 03 80 24 77 24. Fax 03 80 22 30 40. Mich 88/A2. Map 3.

A 100frs & under. B 100–150. C 150–200. D 200–250. E 250–350. F 350–500. G 500+

BEAUNE (also see previous page)   **Le Cep**

Very comfortable hotel (no restaurant)
Fairly quiet/Lift/Garage

What a tremendous restoration job has been done to this 17th-century Renaissance-styled town house. Particularly noteworthy is the rear courtyard with arcades, sculptures and a fine stone staircase; all the stonework is exceedingly handsome. The stylish bedrooms have all mod cons. Prices are steep – but not so when one considers the high-quality furnishings & fittings. Restaurant Bernard Morillon in same building.
Rooms (53) G. Cards All. (Just inside inner ring road; N74 S entrance.)
Post 27 r. Maufoux, 21200 Beaune, Côte-d'Or. Region Burgundy.
Tel 03 80 22 35 48. Fax 03 80 22 76 80. Mich 88/A2. Map 3.

BEAUNE   La Closerie

Comfortable hotel (no restaurant)
Quiet/Gardens/Swimming pool/Closed parking

The hotel is ultra modern (attractive is not a label that comes to mind) & is out of town – on E side of N74, SW of Beaune. There are several good reasons for my recommendation: rooms for the disabled; plenty of parking; reasonable prices; the swimming pool & gardens; and a site which gives easy access to the many restaurants in Beaune & environs.
Rooms (47) EFG. Disabled. Cards All.
Closed 24 Dec to 15 Jan.
Post rte Autun, 21200 Beaune, Côte-d'Or. Region Burgundy.
Tel 03 80 22 15 07. Fax 03 80 24 16 22. Mich 88/A2. Map 3.

BEAUNE   L'Ecusson

Comfortable restaurant/Cooking 3-4   `FW`

A dream of a meal at the vine-covered home of Jean-Pierre Senelet. Polished wooden floors, polished modern cooking – assiduously executed. Even the cheap menu B – with no less than five *plats* – appeals; it's tagged *Les Premiers Plaisirs*. Two signature dishes from that menu: *joues d'agneau braisées aux olives & légumes d'ici* and *gelée de noix de coco et sorbets framboise à la praline rose*. Don't miss L'Ecusson!
Menus BCDE. Cards All. (Rooms: see Beaune/Levernois base hotels.)
Closed 11 Feb-4 Mar. 1-10 Dec. Sun. Wed evg. (D973 Dole road.)
Post pl. Malmédy, 21200 Beaune, Côte-d'Or. Region Burgundy.
Tel 03 80 24 03 82. Fax 03 80 24 74 02. Mich 88/A2. Map 3.

A100frs & under. B100–150. C150–200. D200–250. E250–350. F350–500. G500+

BEAUNE

Jardin des Remparts

Very comfortable restaurant/Cooking 3
Terrace/Parking

A delicious restaurant – in every sense – and with the really useful advantage of a site below and outside the town's ramparts (just S of the Hôtel-Dieu). Chef Roland Chanliaud's modern and neo-classical repertoire has many inspired eclectic touches. Desserts are especially fine: one three-star winner is his signature *millefeuille caramélisé aux tomates*.
Menus BCDE. Cards MC, V. (Rooms: see Beaune/Levernois base hotels.)
Closed Mid Feb to mid Mar. 1-8 Aug. Sun & Mon (not pub. hols).
Post 10 r. Hôtel-Dieu, 21200 Beaune, Côte-d'Or. Region Burgundy.
Tel 03 80 24 79 41. Fax 03 80 24 92 79. Mich 88/A2. Map 3.

BEAUNE (Challanges)

Château de Challanges

Comfortable hotel (no restaurant)
Quiet/Gardens/Closed parking

Another extremely welcome *sans restaurant* base hotel in the Beaune area – 4km E of the wine town (just N of Levernois & E of the A6 autoroute). The Schwarz's 100-year-old Burgundian house is a treat (both ancient & modern); but the 17-acre park is even better (trees, stream & fountain). Ghislaine Francis speaks excellent English. (4km E Beaune; use D111.)
Rooms (9) FG. Cards All.
Closed Dec to Mar.
Post r. Templiers, Challanges, 21200 Beaune, Côte-d'Or. Region Burgundy.
Tel 03 80 26 32 62. Fax 03 80 26 32 52. Mich 88/A2. Map 3.

BEINE

Le Vaulignot

Comfortable restaurant/Cooking 1-2
Parking

Beside the D965, 6km W of Chablis & 6km from the Auxerre-Sud A6 exit. Jean-Claude Dubois believes in choice: a rich mix of classical, regional & *Bourgeoise* grub. Ditch your diet & dig into a nostalgic *saucisson chaud de Beaujolais pommes à l'huile*; *sole meunière*; *fromage blanc*; & *baba au rhum et sa crème anglaise* (a typical four-course permutation).
Menus bCDE. Cards MC, V. (Rooms: Ibis, Chablis; Ibis, A6 exit.)
Closed 5-28 Feb. 14-30 Oct. Sun evg. Mon.
Post Beine, 89800 Chablis, Yonne. Region Burgundy.
Tel 03 86 42 48 48. Mich 72/B2. Map 3.

A100frs & under. B100–150. C150–200. D200–250. E250–350. F350–500. G500+

BELCAIRE

Bayle

Very simple restaurant with rooms/Cooking 1-2   `FW`
Terrace/Gardens/Parking

A very simple *logis* at the heart of glorious wooded Cathar country.
Massive Guy Bayle, once a formidable rugby forward, provides copious
classical, regional & Bourgeois *plats*. Scrum down for belt-stretching
tuck: *assiette de charcuteries du village, filet de flétan Dugléré,
caneton poêlé à l'orange*, cheese & dessert is typical multi-choice menu.
Menus ABCD. Rooms (13) CDE. Cards MC, V.
Closed 2 Nov to 15 Dec. Mon (not June & Sept & sch. hols).
Post 11340 Belcaire, Aude. Region Languedoc-Roussillon.
Tel 04 68 20 31 05. Fax 04 68 20 35 24. Mich 176/A2. Map 5.

BELCASTEL

Vieux Pont

Comfortable restaurant with rooms/Cooking 3-4   `FW`
Quiet/Gardens/Parking/Air-conditioning (restaurant)

A super scenic spot & seductive modern, natural cooking from self-
taught chef, Nicole Fagegaltier-Rouquier (new hubby Bruno is in the
kitchen with her); sister Michèle runs the *salle*. Great use of oil (olive,
walnut & hazelnut) & light cooking reductions: e.g. *essence de morilles
& lait d'amandes*. New bedrooms on opp. river bank. Pricey wines.
Menus BCDE. Rooms (7) F. Cards MC, V.
Closed Jan-Feb. Mo *midi* (Jul/Aug). Su evg & Mo (Sep-Jun; not pub. hols).
Post 12390 Belcastel, Aveyron. Region Massif Central (Cévennes).
Tel 05 65 64 52 29. Fax 05 65 64 44 32. Mich 140/A2-B2. Map 5.

BELFORT

Host. du Château Servin

Very comfortable restaurant with rooms/Cooking 3   `FW`
Quiet/Terrace/Gardens/Lift/Closed parking

Step back in time at Lucie Servin's ugly house in a quiet side street: to
rooms decorated in the styles of Louis XIII to Louis XVI; & classical
masterpieces, created by chef Dominique Mathy, in a modern, lighter
style. Sumptuous *foie gras maison*; a *fricassée d'écrevisses René Servin*;
& sweets fit to put before the "Sun King" himself (Louis XIV).
Menus BDEF. Rooms (9) EF. Cards All.
Closed Aug. Sun evg. Fri.
Post 9 r. Gén. Négrier, 90000 Belfort, Ter.-de-Belfort. Region Alsace.
Tel 03 84 21 41 85. Fax 03 84 57 05 57. Mich 76/C2. Map 3.

A 100frs & under. B 100–150. C 150–200. D 200–250. E 250–350. F 350–500. G 500+

BELLE-ISLE-EN-TERRE

Relais de l'Argoat

Comfortable restaurant with rooms/Cooking 2-3 FW
Parking

Delightful views of the pretty village below you as you descend from the
NE (D116). The *logis* is modest but that label most certainly does not
apply to Pierre Marais' classical dishes. Good choice for each course on
menu C: well-executed *duo de ris de veau et saumon en gelée de cerfeuil*
& a much appreciated lightish *filets de rouget barbet beurre blanc.*
Menus BCE. Rooms (8) CD. Cards MC, V.
Closed Feb. Sun evg. Mon.
Post 22810 Belle-Isle-en-Terre, 22810 Côtes d'Armor. Region Brittany.
Tel 02 96 43 00 34. Fax 02 96 43 00 76. Mich 28/A2. Map 1.

BENODET

Ferme du Letty

Comfortable restaurant/Cooking 3-4 FW
Terrace

Perhaps the best *RQP* cooking in Brittany. An old farm, authentically
rustic, gives the impression that cooking may be *ancien régime*; no way,
Jean-Marie Guilbault is a modern master, using the rich harvests of the
Armor & Argoat in tantalising temptations. Flavours & *aromates* are
used in innovative tongue-teasing ways. Papa, Jean-Paul, is *le patron.*
Menus AB(top-end)CEF. Cards All. (Rooms: Menez-Frost and others.)
Closed Mid Oct to 25 Feb. Wed (not evgs July/Aug). Thurs midday.
Post au Letty, 29950 Bénodet, Finistère. Region Brittany. (To SE.)
Tel 02 98 57 01 27. Fax 02 98 57 25 29. Mich 45/D3. Map 1.

BENODET

Menez-Frost

Very comfortable hotel (no restaurant)
Secluded/Gardens/Swimming pool/Tennis/Garage/Parking

Centrally situated, the Menez-Frost is a mixture of several buildings –
both old and new – in a tranquil site away from traffic. The *jardin fleuri*
is a particular highlight. Some rooms have small *cuisinettes.* During the
dozen or so years I have been recommending the hotel I have received
nothing but praise from readers.
Rooms (46) FG. Cards MC, V.
Closed Oct to 10 May.
Post près poste, 29950 Bénodet, Finistère. Region Brittany.
Tel 02 98 57 03 09. Fax 02 98 57 14 73. Mich 45/D3. Map 1.

A100frs & under. B100–150. C150–200. D200–250. E250–350. F350–500. G500+

BENOUVILLE

Manoir d'Hastings et la Pommeraie

Very comfortable restaurant with rooms/Cooking 2
Quiet/Terrace/Gardens/Closed parking

FW

New owners, Carole & José Aparicio, praised by readers, have injected a new lease of life into the 17thC priory. Classical/regional cooking and a wide choice for each course, Faultless technique with specialities such as *terrine de foie gras au vieux porto, ris de veau aux morilles* and *tarte chaude Normande.* The rooms are dear: cheaper ones at La Glycine.
Menus b(lunch)CDEF. Rooms (15)G. Cards All.
Closed 12 Nov to 2 Dec. Rest: Sun evg & Mon (not July/Aug).
Post 14970 Bénouville, Calvados. Region Normandy.
Tel 02 31 44 62 43. Fax 02 31 44 76 18. Mich 32/B1. Map 2.

BERGERAC

Le Cyrano

Comfortable restaurant/Cooking 2-3
Air-conditioning

FW

Don't be put off by the faded, tired façade. Jean-Paul Turon doubles as chef & head waiter; he's the mastermind behind the clever formula menus B&C. From a wide choice enjoy classics or Périgord fillers: *galantine de volaille au foie gras* (touch fatty); *entrecôte pommes sautées* – in deep, delicious meat sauce; & excellent pink *magret.* Super *kir* & *petits fours.*
Menus ABCDE. Cards All. (Rooms: Europe, *sans rest*, 200m walk N.)
Closed 22-26 Dec. Sat midday & Sun (not pub. hols). (Parking opp. rest.)
Post 2 bd Montaigne, 24100 Bergerac, Dordogne. Region Dordogne.
Tel 05 53 57 02 76. Fax 05 53 57 78 15. Mich 122/C3 & 123/D3. Map 5.

BERGUES

Cornet d'Or

Very comfortable restaurant/Cooking 3

FW

Many readers have written about their enjoyable visits to the old-world style at the handsome house in, for me, the most evocative of the North's fortified *villes.* Chef Jean-Claude Tasserit is a classicist master – his cooking laced with many subtle, lighter touches. Typical flourishes: *soles de sable dorées au beurre* (perfection), *rognon de veau aux 3 moutardes* (tasty) & *tarte fine aux pommes au caramel* (heaven).
Menus b(top-end)DE. Cards AE, MC, V. (Rooms: Commerce or Au Tonnelier.)
Closed Sun evg & Mon (not pub. hols). (Rest. just S of D3, N edge town.)
Post 26 r. Espagnole, 59380 Bergues, Nord. Region North.
Tel 03 28 68 66 27. Fax 03 28 68 66 27. Mich 3/D1. Map 2.

A100frs & under. B100–150. C150–200. D200–250. E250–350. F350–500. G500+

BERNAY

Moulin Fouret

Comfortable restaurant with rooms/Cooking 2-3
Secluded/Terrace/Gardens/Parking

4km SW of Bernay. Approach from NE, via D833 & beech-tunnel lane. Ivy-covered mill beside the Charentonne; gorgeous terrace, 2½-acre gardens & mill-stream. Edwige Deduit is *la patronne*; husband François flows down classical/neo-classical/regional streams. Trickle-slow service. One winner: *poêlée d'andouille au lard & son croustillant de Camembert*.
Menus AC(bottom-end)E. Rooms (8) D. Cards AE, MC, V.
Closed Sun evg & Mon (not May-Aug).
Post 27300 Bernay, Eure. Region Normandy.
Tel 02 32 43 19 95. Fax 02 32 45 55 50. Mich 33/E2. Map 2.

BERNEX

Chez Tante Marie

Comfortable hotel/Cooking 1-2
Quiet/Terrace/Gardens/Lift/Parking

South of the village, in the shadow of the well-named Dent d'Oche. *Les patrons* at the chalet are Marcel (the chef) & Marie Birraux (no relation of the Bois Joli family). Relish, in the quintessential *Savoyarde salle*, classical/regional grub: *charcuterie fumée maison, civet de sanglier, gratin Dauphinois* & *crème caramel* is a typical menu B permutation.
Menus ABCD. Rooms (27) F(low-end). Cards DC, MC, V.
Closed Mid Oct to mid Dec.
Post Bernex, 74500 Evian-les-Bains, Haute-Savoie. Region Savoie.
Tel 04 50 73 60 35. Fax 04 50 73 61 73. Mich 105/E2. Map 6.

BERNEX (St-Paul-en-Chablais)

Bois Joli

Comfortable hotel/Cooking 2
Secluded/Terrace/Gardens/Swimming pool/Tennis/Parking

Since its introduction in *FLE* Bois Joli has emerged as a huge favourite; readers return regularly to the large chalet hotel, with super camera-friendly views S, run so well by Joëlle & François Birraux. Dig into classical & regional fare: tasty *tartiflette* (potato, bacon, onions & *Reblochon*), *filet de féra* & filling *filet de boeuf au vin de Mondeuse*.
Menus BCD. Rooms (24) E. Cards All. (2km NW of Bernex; at La Beunaz.)
Closed 15 Mar to 3 Apl. 20 Oct to 20 Dec. Wed (not July/Aug).
Post La Beunaz, 74500 Evian-les-Bains, Haute-Savoie. Region Savoie.
Tel 04 50 73 60 11. Fax 04 50 73 65 28. Mich 105/E2. Map 6.

A100frs & under. B100–150. C150–200. D200–250. E250–350. F350–500. G 500+

BERRY-BOUY
La Gueulardière

Comfortable restaurant/Cooking 2
Terrace/Gardens

A small house in a tiny village (S of the X-roads) where Jean-Claude & Betty Poquet do a thoroughly competent job. Chef Jean-Claude is a classical fan. Little choice in menu B but enjoyable nevertheless: *terrine du vendangeur, daurade rose aux raisins, salade de chevre chaud & tarte aux mirabelles* were a flavoursome lunchtime foursome.
Menus ABCDE. Cards All. (Rooms: Novotel, easy drive, exit 7 A71, to SE.)
Closed 19 Feb-14 Mar. Sun evg. Mon. Tues. (Novotel; use Bourges bypass.)
Post 18500 Berry-Bouy, Cher. Region Berry-Bourbonnais.
Tel 02 48 26 81 45. Fax 02 48 26 01 72. Mich 84/B2. Map 2.

Le BESSAT
La Fondue "Chez l'Père Charles"

Comfortable restaurant with rooms/Cooking 1-2 **FW**

The over 3800 ft-high village is at the heart of the Pilat Regional Park – a green lung for industrial St-Etienne, 18km to the NW. Before your meal make the short detour to the observation platform atop Mont Pilat. La Fondue comes in a wedge-shaped stone building. Enjoy *Bourgeois* and classical basics like mussels and leeks in a cream sauce, venison *à l'ancienne*, stuffed *lapereau*, goat's cheese & desserts from a trolley.
Menus aBCDE. Rooms (9) CDE. Cards All.
Closed Dec to Feb.
Post 42660 Le Bessat, Loire. Regions Lyonnais/Massif Central (Ardèche).
Tel 04 77 20 40 09. Fax 04 77 20 45 20. Mich 115/E4-F4. Map 6.

BEUVRON-EN-AUGE
Pavé d'Auge

Very comfortable restaurant/Cooking 3

The restaurant, once the oak-beamed covered market, is the centre-point of the unbelievably evocative Normandy village. One new addition: a fine Pays d'Auge *cheminée*. Jérôme Bansard uses *terroir* produce superbly in his sensible neo-classical/modern ways. Susan, his wife, a self-effacing English lass, is a 3-star *patissière*; she does the sweets. (Rooms: use Manoir de Sens (1km E); mini Pays d'Auge estate; Tel 02 31 79 23 05.)
Menus bCDE. Cards MC, V. (Above secluded *sans rest*; use postcode below.)
Closed 2 Dec to mid Jan. Mon. Tues (Sept-Apl).
Post 14430 Beuvron-en-Auge, Calvados. Region Normandy.
Tel 02 31 79 26 71. Fax 02 31 39 04 45. Mich 32/C1. Map 2.

A100frs & under. B100–150. C150–200. D200–250. E250–350. F350–500. G500+

BEUZEVILLE

Petit Castel/Auberge du Cochon d'Or

Comfortable hotel (annexe) & restaurant with rooms/Cooking 2 | FW |
Gardens (hotel)

A much-liked family show: Charles and Monique Folleau, aided by their English-speaking daughter, Catherine, and her husband, Oliver Martin. Classical & regional delights: spiky *safranée de truite aux champignons*, stylish *gâteau de pleurotes au beurre échalotes* and saucy *faux-filet grillé Béarnaise*. The hotel annexe (Petit Castel) is across the road.
Menus abCD. Rooms (20: 16 in annexe) CDE. Cards MC, V
Closed Mid Dec to mid Jan. Rest: Mon. (Parking in huge *place*.)
Post 27210 Beuzville, Eure. Region Normandy. Mich 15/D4. Map 2.
Tel (H) 02 32 57 76 08. (R) 02 32 57 70 46. Fax 02 32 42 25 70.

Les BEZARDS

Auberge des Templiers

Luxury hotel/Cooking 3-4
Quiet/Terrace/Gardens/Swimming pool/Tennis/Garage/Parking

The ultimate *auberge*; the bedrooms & suites are located in cottages dotted around the 15-acre grounds. Magnificent gardens & furnishings. Classical, *ancien régime* cooking. Still in place are Alain, a super MD, & Jean-Paul, a so-knowledgeable *sommelier*; both speak English. Philippe Dépée & his wife, elegant Françoise, are consummate hoteliers.
Menus E(lunch)FG. Rooms (22) G,G2. Disabled. Cards All.
Closed Feb.
Post Les Bézards, 45290 Boismorand, Loiret. Region Loire.
Tel 02 38 31 80 01. Fax 02 38 31 84 51. Mich 70/C2. Map 2.

BIARRITZ (also see next page)

Bistrot Bellevue

Simple restaurant/Cooking 2-3 | FW |

Didier Oudill & Gary Duhr have a winning formula at their *RQP* bistro – which occupies a ground-floor corner of the famed Café de Paris. Choose from a *menu carte*: each of the three courses provides a minimum of 7 alternative choices. Some mouthwatering classics: *carpaccio de tranche au pistou, tagliatelles primavera* is typical of many eclectic treats – especially the Spanish variety. (See next entry for rooms; alas dear.)
Menus B. Cards All. (Many cheaper *sans rest.* hotels in resort.)
Closed 6 Jan to end Mar. Region Southwest.
Post 5 pl. Bellevue, 64200 Biarritz, Pyrénées-Atlantiques.
Tel 05 59 24 19 53. Fax 05 59 24 18 20. Mich 148/B3. Map 4.

A100frs & under. B100–150. C150–200. D200–250. E250–350. F350–500. G500+

BIARRITZ (also see previous page)   **Café de Paris**

Very comfortable restaurant with rooms/Cooking 3-4
Lift

Didier Oudill, who made such a success of Pain Adour & Fantaisie (rating 4) has moved further W, to the world-famed Café de Paris. In partnership with fellow chef Gary Duhr, his style remains involved & complicated modern/neo-classical – full of attention to small details. The site & ocean view are spectacular. Spacious bedrooms. See previous entry.
Menus EF. Rooms (18) FG(low-end). Disabled. Cards All. (Park in *place*.)
Closed 6 Jan-31 Mar. Rest: Tues & Wed midday (mid Sept to mid June).
Post 5 pl. Bellevue, 64200 Biarritz, Pyrénées-Atlantiques. Reg S/West.
Tel 05 59 24 19 53. Fax 05 59 24 18 20. Mich 148/B3. Map 4.

BIEVRES   Relais de St-Walfroy

Comfortable restaurant/Cooking 1-2 | FW |
Parking/Air-conditioning

A hidden hamlet, NW of Montmédy and S of the N43. Michel Vignol is the mayor of Bièvres and the *directeur* of the rustic *relais*. Chef Jean-Noël Vignol treads *Bourgeois*/classical/regional paths: *terrine de campagne, quiche Ardennaise, faux-filet maître d'hôtel, canard à l'orange, coq au vin rouge, tarte maison* & similar. Franc-Wise is the Vignol motto.
Menus AB. Cards MC, V. (Rooms: Le Mâdy, Montmédy to SE.)
Closed Tues.
Post 08370 Bièvres, Ardennes. Region Champagne-Ardenne.
Tel 03 24 22 61 62. Fax 03 24 27 53 04. Mich 22/B3. Map 3.

BIGNAN   Auberge La Chouannière

Very comfortable restaurant/Cooking 2 | FW |

Jean-Luc and Anne-Marie Simon opened their restaurant, with a Louis XVI-style dining room, in 1971. Champion classical fare: on the cheapest menu you could find *pintadeau à l'orange*; on a typical menu C a crunchy and moist *croustillant de saumon à l'oseille* or, loosen the belts, a *pièce de boeuf grillée sauce verte* with a robust *galette de pommes de terre*, *Brie de Meaux* and *nougat maison glacé.*
Menus bCDE. Cards MC, V. (Rooms: France or Château, Josselin to E.)
Closed Feb sch. hols. 7-19 Oct. Sun evg. Mon. (Above easy drive.)
Post 56500 Bignan, Morbihan. Region Brittany.
Tel 02 97 60 00 96. Fax 02 97 44 24 58. Mich 62/C1. Map 1.

A100frs & under. B100–150. C150–200. D200–250. E250–350. F350–500. G500+

Le BLANC   Domaine de l'Etape

Comfortable hotel/Cooking 1
Secluded/Gardens/Parking

"Gardens"? Hardly – in reality a 350-acre park. There's also a 40-acre *étang* for fishing & boating; & horse riding is possible all the year. The 19thC house, not the best-looking in the world, is old-fashioned comfortable. The kitchen uses produce from the property's farm. Dinner only for residents – classical & *Bourgeois* fare. Best of all however is owner Nicole Seiller, much liked by readers for over a decade.
Menus B. Rooms (35) DEF. Cards All. (D10, 6km SE of Le Blanc.)
Post rte de Bélâbre, 36300 Le Blanc, Indre. Region Poitou-Charentes.
Tel 02 54 37 18 02. Fax 02 54 37 75 59. Mich 96/C1. Map 5.

BLERE   Cheval Blanc

Comfortable hotel/Cooking 2-3   `FW`
Terrace/Gardens/Swimming pool/Parking

The façade is all-white, the interior is all beams and fine furnishings; but the super small courtyard/garden beats the lot. Michel & Micheline Blériot do a great job; the cooking is classical/neo-classical. Rating not quite 3 for two just-off-the-mark *plats: gateau de foie de volaille aux raisins* & *civet de cuisse de canette à l'ancienne.*
Menus aCE. Rooms (12) EF. Cards All.
Closed Jan-mid Feb. Rest: Sun evg & Mon (not July/Aug).
Post pl. Eglise, 37150 Bléré, Indre-et-Loir. Region Loire.
Tel 02 47 30 30 14. Fax 02 47 23 52 80. Mich 68/A4. Map 2.

BLOIS (also see next page)   La Péniche

Comfortable restaurant/Cooking 1-2   `FW`
Air-conditioning

Some of you will perhaps recall Gérard & Germain Bosque at their Botte d'Asperges in Contres. For the last 14 years they've been afloat, on a large & handsome, renovated *péniche* (barge) tied-up on the Loire's R bank – just downstream from the D174 bridge. Classical cooking with an emphasis on fish/shellfish (there's a seawater tank in the dining room).
Menus B(top end). Cards All. (Rooms: Ibis/Campanile; N Blois, A10 exit.)
Closed Sun (not pub. hols). (Quayside for parking.) (Above easy drive.)
Post promenade Mail, 41000 Blois, Loir-et-Cher. Region Loire.
Tel 02 54 74 37 23. Mich 68/C3. Map 2.

A100frs & under. B100–150. C150–200. D200–250. E250–350. F350–500. G500+

BLOIS (also see previous page)

Rendez-vous des Pêcheurs

Comfortable restaurant/Cooking 3 | FW
Air-conditioning

Menu B (top-end) at the tiny home of young master chef Eric Reithler does not always appear in written form. Ask the waitress to get Eric to explain the daily-changing menu – in French or English. Typical bursting-with-flavour modern *plat* is *rouelles de cabillaud aux pommes de terre en anchoïade*. (Rooms: Le Savoie & Anne de Bretagne; 400m to NW.)
Menus B(top-end)D&E(*à la carte*). Cards AE, MC, V. (Rest 300m S château.)
Closed Feb sch. hols. 28 July-18 Aug. Sun. Mon midday. Pub. hols.
Post 27 r. Foix, 41000 Blois, Loir-et-Cher. Region Loire.
Tel 02 54 74 67 48. Fax 02 54 74 47 67. Mich 68/B3-C3. Map 2.

BONLIEU

La Poutre

Comfortable restaurant with rooms/Cooking 3 | FW
Parking

The façade is now looking far more cheerful. Inside the well-named "beamed" home of Denis Moureaux lurks an able chef and his delicious regional/classical dishes. How about *tête de veau, crêpes Jurassienes* – or a *gratin d'écrevisses aux morilles* – scrumptious. *Macvin* in sauces and a *baba au mac-vin?* Answers: local grape juice & *marc* (spirit).
Menus BCE. Rooms (10) BCDEF. Cards MC, V.
Closed 12 Nov-10 Feb. Sun evg & Mon (not pub. hols & sch. hols).
Post 39130 Bonlieu, Jura. Region Jura.
Tel 03 84 25 57 77. Fax 03 84 25 51 61. Mich 89/F4. Map 6.

BONNEVAL-SUR-ARC

Auberge Le Pré Catin

Simple restaurant/Cooking 1-2 | FW
Terrace

Alpine from boots to helmet: a stone-built chalet; mountain flowers and decorations; and filling *Bourgeoise*/regional tucker. Daniel Delaplace, a Parisian, and his wife Josiane, from Normandy, serve up gutsy grub: mainly grills (*feu de bois*) – like *entrecôte* and *agneau*; tasty cheeses, j*ambon de Savoie*, locally-dried meats and *ravioles de Royans*.
Menus BC. Cards MC, V. (Rooms: A la Pastourelle, *sans rest*.)
Closed 6 May to 20 June. 22 Sept to 20 Dec. Mon.
Post 73480 Bonneval-sur-Arc, Savoie. Region Savoie.
Tel 04 79 05 95 07. Mich 119/F4. Map 6.

A100frs & under. B100–150. C150–200. D200–250. E250–350. F350–500. G500+

BONS-EN-CHABLAIS

Progrès

Comfortable hotel/Cooking 2
Lift/Parking

The dining room is alongside the main road; the modern bedrooms in an annexe behind the restaurant (note the lift). Brigitte Colly is an obliging *patronne*. Her husband, Charles, is a champion classicist: reference an excellently executed *filet de féra au Crépy* (a local white wine) and an intense *suprême de pintade à la crème d'échalottes*.
Menus aBCE. Rooms (10) E. Disabled. Cards MC, V.
Closed 29 Dec-14 Jan. 29 June-22 Jul. Sun evg & Mon (not 22 Jul-23 Aug).
Post 74890 Bons-en-Chablais, Haute-Savoie. Region Savoie.
Tel 04 50 36 11 09. Fax 04 50 39 44 16. Mich 104/C2. Map 6.

BOUILLAND

Host. du Vieux Moulin

Very comfortable hotel/Cooking 4
Secluded/Terr/Gardens/Swim pool (indoor)/Parking/Air-cond. (rest.)

What vast changes over 15 years. "Ultra modern" is the tag I'd use now: both the costly-to-build annexe (with vast rooms, a gym and pool) & the restyled dining room; & for the modern, creative cooking of Jean-Pierre Silva (including reworked classics). He & Isabelle have shown terrific resilience & fortitude over the years; daughter Laura is still not 100%.
Menus CDEF. Rooms (24) FG. Disabled. Cards MC, V.
Closed 2-24 Jan. Wed (not evgs May-Oct). Thurs midday (not pub. hols).
Post 21420 Bouilland, Côte-d'Or. Region Burgundy.
Tel 03 80 21 51 16. Fax 03 80 21 59 90. Mich 88/A2. Map 3.

La BOUILLE

Les Gastronomes

Comfortable restaurant/Cooking 2
Terrace

FW

A super site a hop-step-&-jump away from the Seine. The colourful small house, with window boxes & awnings, sits two-yards away from the stained-glass windows of the village *église*. In the first-floor dining room relish Jacques Marrière's neo-classical, lots-of-choice menus; one dish, *jambonnette de canard Rouennais au citron vert*, is a virtuoso effort.
Menus bD. Cards All. (Rooms: nearby Bellevue.)
Closed 1-20 Feb. 14-22 Sept. Wed evg. Thurs. (Parking nearby.)
Post 76530 La Bouille, Seine-Marîtime. Region Normandy.
Tel 02 35 18 02 07. Mich 15/F4. Map 2.

A100frs & under. B100–150. C150–200. D200–250. E250–350. F350–500. G500+

BOUIN

Le Courlis

Comfortable restaurant/Cooking 1-2
Gardens/Parking

FW

Don't park by the D758 & use the front door. Drive to the rear where the car park & gardens are an attractive *entrée* to the rustic interior. Jean-Marc Rabiller conjures up neo-classical tricks. Two piscatorial pleasures on menu B (wide choice) are *croustillant de sardines à la crème de chou-fleur sauce curry* & *feuilleté de raie aux salicornes*.
Menus aBC. Cards MC, V. (Rooms: Martinet, see next entry.)
Closed 23 Dec to 2 Jan. 23 June to 1 July. Mon.
Post 85230 Bouin, Vendée. Region Poitou-Charentes.
Tel 02 51 68 64 65. Mich 78/B2. Map 1.

BOUIN

Martinet

Comfortable hotel (ignore restaurant)
Quiet/Gardens/Swimming pool/Closed parking

A *maison vendéenne*, tucked away in a quiet side street/cum *place*, W of D578 & near the church. A seductive base, like stepping back into a French scene from the 30s. Owner Françoise Huchet is a friendly charmer and the rear gardens with a swimming pool are gorgeous. A new venture started in 1996: meals are served from May-Sept; I suggest use as base. Fancy a *dégustation* of oysters? Madame will make arrangements for you.
Menus AB (not recommended). Rooms (21) E. Disabled. Cards All.
Post pl. de la Croix Blanche, 85230 Bouin, Vendée. Region Poitou-Char.
Tel 02 51 49 08 94. Fax 02 51 49 83 08. Mich 78/B2. Map 1.

BOULOGNE-SUR-MER

La Matelote

Very comfortable restaurant/Cooking 3

Nothing but praise for the highly-liked Tony Lestienne at the helm of his light, airy restaurant, N of the port & opposite the entertaining Nausicaa. As I wrote in *FLE* he's less inventive these days and has developed a fine repertoire of personalised classical & neo-classical specialities. Dive into his richly-rewarding sea-water pool of culinary pleasures. Régine Lestienne, *la patronne*, wins many readers' plaudits.
Menus C(low-end)D. Cards AE, MC, V. (Rooms: nearby Ibis-Plage & also)
Closed 24 Dec to 10 Jan. Sun evg (not July/Aug). (see next entry.)
Post 80 bd Ste-Beuve, 62200 Boulogne-s-Mer, Pas-de-Calais. Region North.
Tel 03 21 30 17 97. Fax 03 21 83 29 24. Mich 2/A3. Map 2.

A100frs & under. B100–150. C150–200. D200–250. E250–350. F350–500. G500+

BOULOGNE-SUR-MER   Métropole

Comfortable hotel (no restaurant)
Gardens/Lift/Garage

Writing this entry, more than any other, reminds me how the years are rushing by: we first stayed here, as teenagers, over 40 years ago. Little has changed: still an ideal base & the spacious bedrooms have been modernised. The garden is a big bonus; & make sure you pay a call on Philippe Olivier's famed *fromagerie* (43 r. Thiers; same street).
Rooms (25) EF. Cards All.
Closed 20 Dec-6 Jan.
Post 51 r. Thiers, 62200 Boulogne-sur-Mer, Pas-de-Calais. Region North.
Tel 03 21 31 54 30. Fax 03 21 30 45 72. Mich 2/A3. Map 2.

BOULOGNE-SUR-MER   Rest. de Nausicaa

Comfortable restaurant/Cooking 1-2 | FW |
Air-conditioning

A second reason for visiting Nausicaa, the world's largest sea centre. The huge rest. is supervised by Tony Lestienne (the *chef/patron* of La Matelote just across the road). If you cannot afford his prices then dive into this cheaper classical pool. Not surprisingly fish *plats* dominate: *fruits de mer, choucroute de poissons* & *bulots mayonnaise* are typical. No problems with parking & at the S end of a sandy beach.
Menus aB. Cards MC, V. (Rooms: Ibis-Plage, short walk to N.)
Post bd Ste-Beuve, 62200 Boulogne-s-Mer, Pas-de-Calais. Region North.
Tel 03 21 33 24 24. Fax 03 21 30 15 63. Mich 2/A3. Map 2.

BOULOGNE-SUR-MER (Hesdin-l'Abbé) (also see next page) Cléry

Comfortable hotel (ignore restaurant)
Secluded/Gardens/Tennis/Parking

Hesdin-l'Abbé is 9km S of Boulogne; turn N, just W of the traffic lights on the N1. The 18thC château sits contentedly in a 12-acre park with many fine trees. Most bedrooms are on the first & second floors; others are in what was once a stable block & a small pavilion in the grounds. A new 1996 venture: dinner available for residents. Ignore: use as a base.
Menus B (not recommended). Rooms (19) EFG. Cards All.
Closed 14 Dec to 29 Jan. Rest: Sat. Sun. Pub. hols.
Post 62360 Hesdin-l'Abbé, Pas-de-Calais. Region North.
Tel 03 21 83 19 83. Fax 03 21 87 52 59. Mich 2/A3. Map 2.

A100frs & under. B100–150. C150–200. D200–250. E250–350. F350–500. G500+

BOULOGNE-SUR-MER (also see previous page)   **Host. de la Rivière**
(Pont-de-Briques)
Very comfortable restaurant with rooms/Cooking 3
Gardens

True enough, the unattractive house sits beside the River Lianne, though
the stream is no scenic shakes. Who cares: the interior is elegantly fitted-
out & the owners, Jean & Odette Martin, are lovely people. Chef Jean,
helped by his son Dominique, is an able classicist. Some northern stomach
warmers too: one example – a lip-smacking *flamiche aux poireaux.*
Menus c(low-end)DE. Rooms (8)E. Cards AE, MC, V. (5km S of Boulogne.)
Closed Feb sch. hols. 15 Aug-7 Sept. Sun evg & Mon (not pub. hols).
Post 17 r. Gare, 62360 Pont-de-Briques, Pas-de-Calais. Region North.
Tel 03 21 32 22 81. Fax 03 21 87 45 48. Mich 2/A3. Map 2. (200m W N1.)

BOURBON-LANCY   La Roseraie

Very simple hotel (no restaurant)
Gardens

Modest prices, old-world charm, large bedrooms, a pleasant garden, the
nearby thermal baths, woods and parks are the agreeable pluses at this
small hotel at the heart of a relaxing spa. Francs saved here can be used
to eat at the Manoir de Sornat restaurant, 2km to the W; alas, not
included after a very disappointing inspection visit. Reports please.
Rooms (11) BCD. Cards DC, MC, V.
Closed 20 Dec to 5 Jan. Region Berry-Bourbonnais.
Post r. Martyrs-de-la-Libération, 71140 Bourbon-Lancy, Saône-et-Loire.
Tel 03 85 89 07 96. Mich 100/C1. Map 5.

BOURBON-L'ARCHAMBAULT   Thermes

Comfortable hotel/Cooking 3
Terrace/Gardens/Garage/Air-conditioning (restaurant)

A much-appreciated favourite with many readers. In a Louis XVI-styled
décor savour the out-&-out classical/regional specialities (huge helpings)
of a master chef, Guy Barichard: *foie gras d'oie poêlé aux morilles
farcies, filet mignon d'agneau à la Connétable* & *omelette Brayaude*
are typical. Roger Barichard is both *maître d'* & *sommelier.*
Menus aCDE. Rooms (21) CDEF(low-end). Cards AE, MC, V. (Opp. spa baths.)
Closed Nov to mid Mar. Region Berry-Bourbonnais.
Post av. Ch.-Louis-Philippe, 03160 Bourbon-l'Archambault. Allier.
Tel 04 70 67 00 15. Fax 04 70 67 09 43. Mich 99/F1. Map 5.

A 100frs & under. B 100–150. C 150–200. D 200–250. E 250–350. F 350–500. G 500+

Le BOURG-DUN

Auberge du Dun

Comfortable restaurant/Cooking 3
Parking

What a classy restaurant: Pierre Chrétien is as smart a chef as his dining rooms are stylish. Menu B epitomises *RQP* at its most rewarding franc-saving best: an aptly-named *aumonière de coquillages;* some *paupiettes de saumon aux épinards*; a selection of creamy regional cheeses; & *sable au citron meringué*. A masterly neo-classical feast.
Menus BDE. Cards MC, V. (Rooms: Mercure, St-Valery-en-Caux, to W.)
Closed 17 Aug-4 Sept. 1-15 Dec. Sun evg & Mon (not pub. hols).
Post 76740 Le Bourg-Dun, Seine-Maritime. Region Normandy.
Tel 02 35 83 05 84. Mich 15/F1. Map 2.

BOURG-EN-BRESSE

Auberge Bressane

Very comfortable restaurant/Cooking 2
Terrace/Parking

Jean-Pierre & Dominique Villin's *auberge* is opposite the superb Eglise de Brou. Unlike the church chef J-P's cooking is not what it was back at the start of the 80s. Uninspired these days but two FW menus compensate. Classical & Lyonnaise cooking with due devotion to Brillat-Savarin (a Bugey son) &, rightly so, to the magnificent *poulardes de Bresse*. Among fish dishes a *paupiette de saumon & saumon fumé* was much enjoyed.
Menus aBCEF. Cards All. (Rooms: see following two bases.) Reg Lyonnais.
Post 166 bd Brou, 01000 Bourg-en-Bresse, Ain. (Above only 2-min walk.)
Tel 04 74 22 26 68. Fax 04 74 23 03 15. Mich 103/D3. Map 6.

BOURG-EN-BRESSE (also see next page)

France/Rest. Jacques Guy

Comfortable hotel/Cooking 3
Terrace/Lift/Garage

The hotel & rest. are run as separate businesses. Regional, classical & neo-classical *plats* from Jacques Guy (at Coligny in the early 80s) in two dining rooms – one Louis XVI, one rustic. Two memorable dishes: a mussel soup starter – a palette teaser; *cuisses & poitrine de pigeonneau rôti* – a quality/technique *tour de force*. Menu C just above FW ceiling.
Menus CDEF. Rooms (46) DEF. Cards All. (Parking easy.) Region Lyonnais.
Closed Rest: 4-19 Mar. 11-27 Nov. Sun evg. Mon. Mich 103/D3. Map 6.
Post 19 pl. Bernard, 01000 Bourg-en-Bresse, Ain. Tel (R) 04 74 45 29 11.
(H) 04 74 23 30 24. Fax (R) 04 74 24 73 69. (H) 04 74 23 69 90.

A100frs & under. B100–150. C150–200. D200–250. E250–350. F350–500. G500+

BOURG-EN-BRESSE (also see previous page)　　　La Galerie

Comfortable restaurant/Cooking 2　　　FW

A modest, shop-fronted look about La Galerie but a redoubtable *RQP* outpost, particularly when 3 other rest. entries provide such formidable competition. Here Michel, the chef, and Dominique Chanteloup beguile with regional, neo-classical & classical pleasures – reference *persillé de tête de veau, crépinette de sanglier aux châtaignes, noisettes de lièvre au genièvre* & a star-quality *fromage frais de Bresse à la crème.*
Menus BC. Cards DC, MC, V. (Rooms: see next entry – 800m walk to SE.)
Closed Sat midday. Sun.
Post 4 r. Th. Riboud, 01000 Bourg-en-Bresse, Ain. Region Lyonnais.
Tel 04 74 45 16 43. Fax 04 74 45 16 43. Mich 103/D3. Map 6.

BOURG-EN-BRESSE　　　Le Logis de Brou

Comfortable hotel (no restaurant)
Lift/Garage/Parking

The first of two *sans restaurant* base hotels in Bourg – in a town, and its environs, studded with first-class chefs. Like the other base, the Logis has long been a readers' favourite – for many reasons: the owners Pierre & Monique Marillat; the modern facilities; and for the flowers – virtually everywhere outside. The hotel is on the west side of the N75, north of the Eglise de Brou. Use A40 exit 7; then 8km to north-west.
Rooms (30) DEF. Cards All.
Post 132 bd Brou, 01000 Bourg-en-Bresse, Ain. Region Lyonnais.
Tel 04 74 22 11 55. Fax 04 74 22 37 30. Mich 103/D3. Map 6.

BOURG-EN-BRESSE　　　Mail

Very comfortable restaurant with rooms/Cooking 2-3　　　FW
Garage/Parking/Air-conditioning (restaurant)

Beside the D936, where the road passes under the railway line on the W side of Bourg. However, not a noisy site. Lovely welcome from Bernadette Charolles and excellent service (praised by many, many readers). Chef Roger Charolles' repertoire is classical & Lyonnais – making exceptional use of the rich larder surrounding him. *Cuisine terroir* at its finest.
Menus BCDE. Rooms (9) CDE. Cards All.
Closed 23 Dec-7 Jan. 14 July-5 Aug. Sun evg. Mon.
Post 46 av. Mail, 01000 Bourg-en-Bresse, Ain. Region Lyonnais.
Tel 04 74 21 00 26. Fax 04 74 21 29 55. Mich 103/D3. Map 6.

BOURG-EN-BRESSE

Prieuré

Very comfortable hotel (no restaurant)
Fairly quiet/Gardens/Lift/Parking

More expensive than the other Bourg-en-Bresse base, but the extra cost pays handsome dividends: for *les patronnes*, sisters Yvonne Guerrin and Andrée Alby; for the colourful large gardens; and for the stylish Louis XV & XVI furniture. Soundproofed bedrooms – most of which have a terrace or balcony. The hotel is just north of the glorious Eglise de Brou – on the east side of the N75. Use A40 exit 7; then 8km to the north-west.
Rooms (14) FG. Cards All.
Post 49 bd Brou, 01000 Bourg-en-Bresse, Ain. Region Lyonnais.
Tel 04 74 22 44 60. Fax 04 74 22 71 07. Mich 103/D3. Map 6.

Le BOURGET-DU-LAC

Ombremont et Rest. Le Bateau Ivre

Very comfortable hotel/Cooking 4
Secl'd/Terr/Gardens/Swim pool/Lift/G'ge/Parking/Air-cond. (rooms)

Sensational is the word for the view: of Lac du Bourget far below you; & the wall of Mont Revard across the lake. The terrace is one France's most spectacular. There's now another reason to visit: Jean-Pierre Jacob (ex Bateau Ivre, down the road), *chef/patron*, is a modern master; his fish dishes are 3-star creations – full of mysterious, subtle tastes.
Menus C(top-end)FG. Rooms (14) G,G2,G3. Cards All. (N on N504.)
Closed Nov-Apl. Rest Tues (not July/Aug). (Care: turn off N504 tricky.)
Post 73370 Le Bourget-du-Lac, Savoie. Region Savoie. (Approach from S.)
Tel 04 79 25 00 23. Fax 04 79 25 25 77. Mich 117/F2. Map 6.

BOURGOIN-JALLIEU (also see next page)

Bernard Lantelme

Comfortable restaurant/Cooking 2-3
Terrace/Parking/Air-conditioning

FW

At La Grive. NW of town & S side of N6. Old farm with a beamed & stone dining room. Attractive, smiling Christine Lantelme is an ideal hostess; husband Bernard is a neo-classicist chef. Menu B was the vehicle for 3 wonderful dishes: *terrine de saumon en gelée sauce emulsionnée au paprika, volaille à la fondue de poireaux* & perfect *crème brûlée.*
Menus BCD. Cards MC, V. (Rooms: Ibis, 2km to NW.)
Closed 4-24 Aug. Sat midday. Sun.
Post La Grive, 38080 L'Isle-d'Abeau, Isère. Region Lyonnais.
Tel 04 74 28 19 12. Fax 04 74 93 78 88. Mich 116/C3. Map 6.

A100frs & under. B100–150. C150–200. D200–250. E250–350. F350–500. G500+

BOURGOIN-JALLIEU (also see previous page)   Chavancy

Comfortable restaurant/Cooking 2-3   FW
Air-conditioning

An orange-hued oasis in a bustling town (400m N of N6, near the hospital
& close to parking). Bruno Chavancy drives all carriageways. Menu B (top
end of 2) offers the chance to try a Lyonnais culinary landmark – *petit
pâté chaud*, followed by a light *saumon beurre aux herbes*. Try another
area highlight – a Bresse *suprême de volaille* (with *curry, riz sauvage*).
Menus B(low & top-end)DE. Cards All. (Rooms: Ibis/Climat to W of town.)
Closed 19 July to 19 Aug. Sun evg. Mon.
Post av. Tixier, 38300 Bourgoin-Jallieu, Isère. Region Lyonnais.
Tel 04 74 93 63 88. Fax 04 74 28 42 44. Mich 116/C3. Map 6.

BOURGUEIL   Le Thouarsais

Very simple hotel (no restaurant)
Fairly quiet/Gardens

As simple as they come – but make no mistake, this base is a big-hearted
much loved hotel. For many reasons: for *les patrons*, Bernard & Dominique
Caillault – so friendly, helpful & welcoming; for the site – away from main
roads & railway line; and for the garden – where you are welcome to enjoy a
picnic if you so wish. Easy drive to Chinon's restaurants.
Rooms (23) BCDE. Cards MC, V.
Closed 3-20 Oct. 27 Dec-1 Jan. Sun evg (Oct-Easter).
Post pl. Hublin, 37140 Bourgueil, Indre-et-Loire. Region Loire.
Tel 02 47 97 72 05. Mich 81/E1. Map 2.

BOUZE-LES-BEAUNE   La Bouzerotte

Simple restaurant/Cooking 2   FW
Terrace

Captivating: for smile-making names of village & rest; the tiny chalet with
minuscule dining room & cheerful fire; the young owners, Olivier (the
chef) & Christine Robert, providing gilt-edged *RQP*; and menus studded
with honest-to-goodness classical/regional crackers: from *jambon braisé
au Porto* (A) to succulent *volaille de Bresse à la crème* (C).
Menus ACD. Cards MC, V. (Rooms: see base hotels in Beaune/Levernois.)
Closed 2-18 Jan. 31 July-22 Aug. Mon evg. Tues. Region Burgundy.
Post Bouze-lès-Beaune, 21200 Beaune, Côte-d'Or. (7km NW Beaune; D970.)
Tel 03 80 26 01 37. Fax 03 80 26 01 37. Mich 88/A2. Map 3.

A100frs & under. B100–150. C150–200. D200–250. E250–350. F350–500. G500+

BOUZIGUES

Côte Bleue

Very comfortable hotel/Cooking 2-3
Quiet/Terrace/Gardens/Swimming pool/Parking

The Bassin de Thau is famed for *coquillages*; the hotel overlooks its still lagoon. Chefs come & go but the Archimbeau family ensure that high standards are kept up. Modern/neo-classical creations based, *bien sûr*, on the harvests plucked from the *bassin*, the Med & other seas: *moules, huîtres, St-Pierre, turbot, langoustines, rougets, morue* & many more.
Menus b(top-end)CDEF. Rooms (32) EF (bottom-end). Cards AE, MC, V.
Closed Rest: Jan. Tues evg & Wed (not July/Aug).
Post 34140 Bouzigues, Hérault. Region Languedoc-Roussillon.
Tel 04 67 78 31 42. Fax 04 67 78 35 49. Mich 156/B4. Map 5.

BOZOULS

A la Route d'Argent

Simple hotel/Cooking 1-2 FW
Swimming pool/Garage/Parking

The best testimonial for this simple place comes from the staff at Michel Bras' Laguiole home; they regularly eat here, tucking into a mixed bag of regional/classical/*Bourgeoise* grub. You don't leave with a *trou* in your stomach with fare like *pot-au-feu de tête de veau, joues de lotte poêlées au beurre d'orange*. Bravo, too, for the swimming pool.
Menus aBC. Rooms (18) CD. Cards All.
Closed Feb. Sun evg (out of season). Regions MC (Auvergne/Cévennes).
Post rte d'Argent (D988), 12340 Bozouls, Aveyron.
Tel 05 65 44 92 27. Fax 05 65 48 81 40. Mich 140/C2. Map 5.

BOZOULS

Le Belvédère

Comfortable restaurant with rooms/Cooking 1-2 FW
Quiet/Terrace

Overlooking the Trou de Bozouls (a small, wooded, meandering *cirque* and the plus of a handsome *église*), Marcel Girbelle keeps matters plain & simple in his rustic dining room. The chimney's roaring fire provides grills for the main courses (*boeuf* or *magret de canard*); *Roquefort* cheese features in tasty first & second course dishes.
Menus ABC. Rooms (11) DE. Cards MC, V.
Closed Dec. Sun evg.
Post 12340 Bozouls, Aveyron. Regions Massif Central (Auvergne/Cévennes).
Tel 05 65 44 92 66. Fax 05 65 48 87 33. Mich 140/C2. Map 5.

A100frs & under. B100–150. C150–200. D200–250. E250–350. F350–500. G500+

BRANTOME

Moulin de l'Abbaye

Very comfortable hotel/Cooking 3-4
Terrace/Gardens/Garage/Parking

A 15thC mill (not the prettiest building), beside the Dronne, converted by Régis (*Relais & Châteaux* president) & Cathy Bulot into one of the region's finest hotels. Consistently praised. A new chef swims the modern stream and capitalises on Périgord's bountiful larder to mightily good effect – especially succulent dishes featuring *foie gras* & *truffes*.
Menus DEF. Rooms (17) G. Cards All.
Closed Nov to Apl. Rest: Mon midday.
Post rte de Bourdeilles, 24310 Brantôme, Dordogne. Region Dordogne.
Tel 05 53 05 80 22. Fax 05 53 05 75 27. Mich 109/D4. Map 5.

BRANTOME (Champagnac-de-Belair)

Moulin du Roc

Very comfortable hotel/Cooking 3 | FW |
Secluded/Terr/Gardens/Swim pool (indoor)/Tennis/Parking

Solange Gardillou is one of the most self-effacing *cuisinières* I know, yet her 17thC mill has evolved into one of the most fussy, over-the-top hotels in France. Newcomers will be none the wiser; fans from the early 80s will need Prozac. Son Alain has joined mum in the kitchen; regional & neo-classical cuisine. Husband Lucien masterminds a formidable *cave*.
Menus b(lunch: top-end)DE. Rooms (10) FG. Cards All. (6km NE Brantôme.)
Closed 2 Jan-5 Mar. Rest: Tues. Wed midday.
Post 24530 Champagnac-de-Belair, Dordogne. Region Dordogne.
Tel 05 53 54 80 36. Fax 05 53 54 21 31. Mich 109/D4. Map 5.

La BRESSE

Les Vallées

Very comfortable hotel/Cooking 1
Terrace/Gardens/Swim pool (indoor)/Tennis/Lift/Garage/Parking

I'll repeat the introduction I used in *FLE*: considering the range of facilities prices are not unreasonable at the huge Remy family complex. Apart from the 53 bedrooms there are also 60 studios with kitchens. Cooking ranges from old-timed classical to belt-loosening *Bourgeoise*: from *tournedos sauté au St-Emilion* to *bavette de boeuf poêlée*. Some *Logis de France*: more akin to a mini holiday camp – *par excellence*.
Menus aBCD. Rooms (53) EF. Cards All.
Post 31 r. P. Claudel, 88250 La Bresse, Vosges. Region Alsace.
Tel 03 29 25 41 39. Fax 03 29 25 64 38. Mich 60/B4. Map 3.

A100frs & under. B100–150. C150–200. D200–250. E250–350. F350–500. G500+

BRESSON

Luxury restaurant with rooms/Cooking 2-3
Terrace/Gardens/Swimming pool/Lift/Parking/Air-conditioning

This handsomely furnished luxury rest, with a seductive tree-shaded terrace, appeals for many reasons: the seriously classical cooking from Jean-Pierre Chavant (his father, Emile, started the business in 1933); an attentive, hospitable welcome from sister Danièle; & the huge plus of being just 8km SE from noisy Grenoble. Many functions during the week.
Menus CD. Rooms (9) G. Cards All.
Closed 26-31 Dec. Rest: Mon (Oct to May). Sat midday.
Post 38320 Bresson, Isère. Regions Hautes-Alpes/Savoie.
Tel 04 76 25 15 14. Fax 04 76 62 06 55. Mich 131/E2. Map 6.

BRIANCON

Vauban

Comfortable hotel/Cooking 2   FW
Gardens/Lift/Parking

A striking apricot & cream façade ensures you cannot miss the Semiond family hotel in the lower town. Utterly straightforward classical & *Bourgeois plats*: *quenelles aux fruits de mer, canard à l'orange, tarte Tatin* & *soufflé au Grand Marnier* – all well executed & precisely cooked. André Semiond, a true caring gentleman, speaks fluent English.
Menus BC. Rooms (44) F. Cards MC, V.
Closed 5 Nov to 20 Dec. Region Hautes-Alpes.
Post 13 av. Gén. de Gaulle, 05100 Briançon, Hautes-Alpes.
Tel 04 92 21 12 11. Fax 04 92 20 58 20. Mich 133/D3. Map 6.

BRINON-SUR-SAULDRE

La Solognote

Comfortable hotel/Cooking 3
Quiet/Gardens/Parking/Air-conditioning (restaurant)

Andrée Girard is a warm-hearted, smiling *patronne*: husband Dominique is a classical specialist, capitalising on his *pays* and its rich, bountiful larder. Beamed dining rooms in old red-brick Sologne cottages; bedrooms in a modern extension at rear. Menu C (low-end) *plats* such as *feuilleté de lotte au fenouil* & earthy *joues de porc braisées au Menetou rouge*.
Menus CDE. Rooms (13) EF. Cards MC, V. Closed 6 Feb-13 Mar. 27 May-5 June. 9-18 Sept. Tue *midi* & Wed *midi* (summer). Tue evg & Wed (Oct-June).
Post 18410 Brinon-sur-Sauldre, Cher. Region Loire.
Tel 02 48 58 50 29. Fax 02 48 58 56 00. Mich 69/F3. Map 2.

A100frs & under. B100–150. C150–200. D200–250. E250–350. F350–500. G500+

BRIOUDE

Poste et Champanne

Simple hotel/Cooking 1-2 |FW|
Closed parking

I was hard on the Chazal-Barge family hotel (the annexe, around the corner, is quieter) in *FLE*. No real moans from readers since – so let's give Hélène Chazal's classical & regional cooking a just squeaked-in FW rating of 1-2. Try numerous Auvergne tummy-fillers: *tripoux, potée* & "rediscovered" versions like *tourte au chou* & *palette de veau*.
Menus aBC. Rooms (20) CD. Cards MC, V.
Closed 2 Jan-1 Feb. Sun evg (15 Sept-15 June). Region MC (Auvergne).
Post 1 bd Dr Devins (N102), 43100 Brioude, Haute-Loire.
Tel 04 71 50 14 62. Fax 04 71 50 10 55. Mich 127/F1. Map 5.

BROUSSE-LE-CHATEAU

Relays du Chasteau

Simple hotel/Cooking 1-2 |FW|
Quiet/Parking/Air-conditioning (restaurant)

An endearing riverside village pleases the eye; & the efforts of young English-speaking Sybile & Phillipe Senegas, both lovely people, please the spirits & taste buds. Copious regional & classical offerings : one, *filet de truite à la mer à la crème de Roquefort*, certainly pleased us. Enjoy the "travelling *pichet*", from table to table. Modernised bedrooms.
Menus ABC. Rooms (12) CD (top-end). Cards MC, V.
Closed 20 Dec to 20 Jan. Fri evg & Sat midday (Oct to Apl).
Post 12480 Brousse-le-Château, Aveyron. Region MC (Cévennes).
Tel 05 65 99 40 15. Mich 140/C4. Map 5.

BRUMATH

L'Ecrevisse/Krebs'Stuebel

Very comfortable rest. with rooms/Cooking 2-3 (see text) |FW|
Terrace/Gardens/Garage/Parking/Air-conditioning (restaurant)

Seven generations of the Orth family, over more than 150 years, have built a formidable regional reputation. Today, Jean & son Michel man the stoves. Classical & Alsace grub served in palatial dining rooms (one with columns & exuberant ceiling). Super eclectic French *cave*. Gym, sauna & solarium. FW rating for cheaper Krebs'Stuebel (cooking 1-2).
Menus DEF (L'Ecrevisse); ABC (Krebs'Stuebel). Rooms (21) EF. Cards All.
Closed Mon evg. Tues.
Post 4 av. Strasbourg, 67170 Brumath, Bas-Rhin. Region Alsace.
Tel 03 88 51 11 08. Fax 03 88 51 89 02. Mich 43/E3. Map 3.

A 100frs & under. B 100–150. C 150–200. D 200–250. E 250–350. F 350–500. G 500+

Le BUGUE

Royal Vézère/Rest. L'Albuca

Very comfortable hotel/Cooking 2-3
Terraces/Swimming pool/Air-conditioning

The hotel sits beside the Vézère. The most appealing features are the terraces: one on the roof, where the pool is situated; the other is adjacent to the restaurant & overlooks the river. Christian Rouffignac & chef Thierry Gauteron keep to right royal neo-classical & regional – with many creative eclectic touches. Liked by readers for 16 years.
Menus BC. Rooms (49) DEFG. Cards All.
Closed Oct to Apl. Rest: Mon midday. Tues midday.
Post 24260 Le Bugue, Dordogne. Region Dordogne. Mich 123/E3. Map 5.
Tel (R) 05 53 07 28 73. (H) 05 53 07 20 01. Fax 05 53 03 51 80.

BUTHIERS

Roches Gourmandes

Comfortable restaurant/Cooking 2

FW

As straightforward as they come: in the shape of the stone & beamed dining room; the enclosed terrace & tiny garden underneath the rockface – *roches* – at the rear; the friendly, helpful patrons – chef Emile Bellais & his wife Arlette; and the classical fare with numerous fish dishes in wide-choice menus. Tuck into piscatorial treats like *langoustines* or *tourteau mayonnaise, moules* & *darne de colin meunière.*
Menus aBC. Cards MC, V. (Rooms: Ecu de France, Malesherbes.)
Closed 10-30 Sept. Mon (not *midi* mid Mar-mid Oct). Tues. (Above 2km NW.)
Post 77760 Buthiers, Seine-et-Marne. Region Ile de France.
Tel 01 64 24 14 00. Mich 4/B3. Map 2.

CABRERETS

Auberge de la Sagne

Simple hotel/Cooking 1
Quiet/Terrace/Gardens/Swimming pool/Parking

Recharge the batteries at this much appreciated spot – in captivating terrain. One acid test is passed easily: popular with French families, all of whom return often. Gardens, the shady terrace, pool & *les patrons*, the Labrousse duo. Cooking is down-to-earth regional & *Bourgeoise*: the likes of *magret de canard au miel d'acacia* & *escalope de porc poêlée.*
Menus AB. Rooms (10) E. Cards MC, V.
Closed Oct to mid May. Rest: lunchtime.
Post 46330 Cabrerets, Lot. Region Dordogne.
Tel 05 65 31 26 62. Fax 05 65 30 27 43. Mich 138/C2. Map 5.

A100frs & under. B100–150. C150–200. D200–250. E250–350. F350–500. G500+

CAGNOTTE

Le Fournil

Comfortable restaurant with rooms/Cooking 2
Terrace/Swimming pool/Parking

This delectable spot is at the southern end of the Landes *département* – in gentle hill-walking country. Annie Demen is a capable *cuisinière*; a mix of classical & re-worked regional recipes is her forté. Shellfish & fish play an important part in well-executed *plats*: no wonder – husband Jacques (he speaks some English) is a wholesale fishmonger.
Menus a(lunch)BCD. Rooms (10) CDE. Cards AE, MC, V.
Closed Jan. 21-31 Oct. Sun evg & Mon (mid Sept-mid June).
Post 40300 Cagnotte, Landes. (8km NE of Peyrehorade.) Region Southwest.
Tel 05 58 73 03 78. Fax 05 58 73 13 48. Mich 149/D3. Map 4.

CAHORS

Terminus/Rest. Le Balandre

Very comfortable hotel/Cooking 3
Lift/Parking/Air-conditioning (restaurant)

Gilles Marre is one of the region's best chefs. Almost 40, and with training stints at several 3-star shrines, he has assured, masterful skills – primarily classical & regional but with many modern touches as well. *Pièce de boeuf poêlée sauce au vin* is a rich signature starter; as are several sumptuous chocolat desserts. Wife Jacqueline is *la patronne*.
Menus c(lunch)DE. Rooms (22) EFG. Cards AE, MC, V. (Near station.)
Closed Rest: Sun evg & Mon (not July/Aug).
Post 5 av. Ch. de Freycinet, 46000 Cahors, Lot. Region Dordogne.
Tel 05 65 35 24 50. Fax 05 65 22 06 40. Mich 138/B2. Map 5.

CALAIS

Au Côte d'Argent

Comfortable restaurant/Cooking 2

For many readers Bertrand Lefebvre is the best chef in the busy channel port. His modern restaurant, overlooking both the Channel and the bustling port entrance – plus the bonus of a huge public car park at the door – is a classical haven. The *Menu Douceur* (A) keeps wallets full: a filling *caudière*, a fresh-from-the-sea cod filet in a tangy, perfectly executed *beurre blanc* sauce and a knockout sweet to finish.
Menus ABCE. Cards All. (Rooms: Richelieu & Windsor; both 5 min walk.)
Closed 3-9 Mar. 22 Sept-5 Oct. Sun evg. Mon. (Both above *sans rest.*)
Post 1 digue G. Berthe, 62100 Calais, Pas-de-Calais. Region North.
Tel 03 21 34 68 07. Fax 03 21 96 42 10. Mich 2/B1. Map 2.

A100frs & under. B100–150. C150–200. D200–250. E250–350. F350–500. G500+

CALAIS

Comfortable restaurant/Cooking 2
Air-conditioning

José (Jo) & Monique Crespo (*France Travelauréat* winners) do a great job but don't call with excessive expectations. Monique speaks English & Jo digs a classical tunnel with, not surprisingly, a significant reliance on fish delights: from *langoustines* to *turbotin*. A channel-wide choice for all courses on menu C (low-end). Cellar? 600 wines & 60,000 bottles.
Menus aCDE. Cards All. (Rooms: Richelieu & Windsor; both 3 min walk.)
Closed 25 July-8 Aug. 19 Dec-9 Jan. Sun evg (not pub. hols). Tues.
Post 3 bd Résistance, 62100 Calais, Pas-de-Calais. Region North.
Tel 03 21 34 42 30. Fax 03 21 97 42 43. Mich 2/B1. Map 2.

CALVINET

Beauséjour

Comfortable restaurant with rooms/Cooking 2-3
Terrace/Parking

FW

Louis-Bernard Puech is a desperately shy host; get to know him & he's a cheerful, helpful soul. The interior has been refurbished & whitewashed; L-B's cooking has a brighter face. Real *cuisine terroir* with regional & classical *plats*: a punchy *filet de boeuf sauce Béarnaise* is one example. A welcome plus: several fish dishes. Try a tot of *crème chataigne!*
Menus a(lunch)BCE. Rooms (12) DE. Cards MC, V.
Closed Mid Jan to mid Feb. Sun evg & Mon (not July/Aug; not pub. hols).
Post 15340 Calvinet, Cantal. Region Massif Central (Auvergne).
Tel 04 71 49 91 68. Fax 04 71 49 98 63. Mich 126/A4. Map 5.

CAMBO-LES-BAINS

Errobia

Comfortable hotel (no restaurant)
Secluded/Gardens/Swimming pool/Parking

Let's give the mixed-bag Errobia another chance – dropped from *FLE*. Pluses? Several: the beamed and panelled interior, full of antique furniture; the quintessential Basque house; rhododendrons & camellias, which in May, are a dazzling show; and the 4-acre unkempt grounds above the Nive Valley. Debits? For some "seedy" & "small" bedrooms.
Rooms (13) CDEF. Cards MC, V. (N of NW exit from spa.)
Closed Nov to Apl. Region Southwest.
Post av. Chantecler, 64250 Cambo-les-Bains, Pyrénées-Atlantiques.
Tel 05 59 29 71 26. Fax 05 59 29 96 36. Mich 148/B4. Map 4.

A100frs & under. B100–150. C150–200. D200–250. E250–350. F350–500. G 500+

CAMBRAI

Beatus

Very comfortable hotel/Cooking 1
Quiet/Gardens/Parking

Mme Gorczynski & Philippe, her English-speaking son, are likeable, caring *patrons*. Philippe is an enthusiastic, knowledgeable host: ask to see his own guide to Cambrai, in English, and natter with him about the regional battlefields (especially those involving World War I tank battles). Classical/regional dishes (dinner only for residents).
Menus CD(*à la carte*). Rooms (32) EF. Cards All. (N44 S exit from town.)
Closed Rest: Aug. Fri. Sat. Sun. Every midday.
Post 718 av. Paris, 59400 Cambrai, Nord. Region North.
Tel 03 27 81 45 70. Fax 03 27 78 00 83. Mich 8/C3. Map 2.

CAMBRAI

Château de la Motte Fenelon/Rest. Les Douves

Very comfortable hotel/Cooking 1-2
Quiet/Gardens/Tennis/Closed parking

FW

The mystery continues: as I wrote in *FLE* – a mouthfilling string of words name yet I get no feedback whatsoever about the 19thC château. A series of buildings in a 20-acre wooded park; the dining room is in a brick vaulted cave. Cooking? Classical with little invention. (NE corner of town: use N30, then NE on Allée St-Roch, 300m SE of Peugeot garage.)
Menus BCD. Rooms (40) EFG,G2. Cards All.
Closed Rest: Sun evg. Pub. hols (evgs). (Cheaper rooms: Ibis/Campanile.)
Post sq Château, 59400 Cambrai, Nord. Region North. (Above at A2 exit.)
Tel 03 27 83 61 38. Fax 03 27 83 71 61. Mich 8/C3. Map 2.

CANCALE

Le Bistrot de Cancale

Simple restaurant/Cooking 2
Terrace

FW

A busy site, tiny dining room, bare floors, simple terrace – overlooking the Port de la Houle. But chef Jacques Granville's classical fare is big-hearted in every way. Menu B is real *RQP* largesse: *pot au feu de la mer* (or, inevitably, Cancale oysters), *filet de saumon doré, fricassée de poulet aux amandes et courgettes* & *crème brûlée* are typical *plats*.
Menus a(lunch)BCD. Cards MC, V. (Rooms: Nuit et Jour & Le Chatellier.)
Closed 27 Jan-19 Feb. Mon. Tues (Nov-Mar).
Post quai Gambetta, 35260 Cancale, Ille-et-Vilaine. Region Brittany.
Tel 02 99 89 92 42. Mich 30/A4. Map 1.

A100frs & under. B100–150. C150–200. D200–250. E250–350. F350–500. G500+

CANCALE

Le Cancalais

Comfortable restaurant with rooms/Cooking 1-2 | FW |

The talented English-speaking Jean-Claude Pierpaoli – one-time director of the legendary Mère Poulard hotel on Le Mont-St-Michel – has moved from his Moidrey restaurant, S of the honeypot shrine, to a new home overlooking the busy quai Gambetta & Port de la Houle. He's an effervescent, most likeable professional. With wife Joëlle the duo provide a sea-water pool of classical *RQP* pleasures.

Menus aBC. Rooms (10) EF. Cards MC, V.
Closed Mid Dec to mid Feb. Sun evg & Mon (not July/Aug).
Post 12 quai Gambetta, 35260 Cancale, Ille-et-Vilaine. Region Brittany.
Tel 02 99 89 61 93. Fax 02 99 89 89 24. Mich 30/A4. Map 1.

CANCALE

Le St-Cast

Comfortable restaurant/Cooking 2 | FW |
Terrace

Overlooking the bay, port & with distant views of Le Mont-St-Michel. Fish & shellfish are the star performers in Michel St-Cast's classical repertoire. Fair choice on menu C: first course starters like *salade de haddock aux pommes de terre tièdes* (tasty); *assiette de fruits de mer*; and a star-winning *gâteau de poissons beurre blanc au fines herbes*.

Menus bCD(all bottom-end). Cards AE, MC, V. (Rooms: see entry p88.)
Closed 17-31 Mar. 15 Nov-20 Dec. Tues (not July/Aug). Wed.
Post rte Corniche, 35260 Cancale, Ille-et-Vilaine. Region Brittany.
Tel 02 99 89 66 08. Fax 02 99 89 89 20. Mich 30/A4. Map 1.

CANDE-SUR-BEUVRON

Hostellerie de la Caillère

Comfortable restaurant with rooms/Cooking 2-3 | FW |
Terrace/Gardens/Parking

Once a great favourite with readers; now the *hostellerie* just squeaks in! The setting appeals to all (vine-covered 18thC cottages) but Jacky & Françoise Guindon – he paddles modern/neo-classical streams – have become a touch stingy: little choice & often no veg with the main course on menus a&C. The 9 new bedrooms are not liked; "too small & too dark."

Menus aCDE. Rooms (14) EF. Disabled. Cards AE, MC, V.
Closed 2 Jan-28 Feb. Rest: Sun evg (Nov-Mar). Wed.
Post rte Monteils, 41120 Candé-sur-Beuvron, Loir-et-Cher. Region Loire.
Tel 02 54 44 03 08. Fax 02 54 44 00 95. Mich 68/B3. Map 2.

A100frs & under. B100–150. C150–200. D200–250. E250–350. F350–500. G500+

CANY-BARVILLE

Manoir de Barville

Very comfortable restaurant with rooms/Cooking 2
Secluded/Gardens/Parking
FW

A gorgeous setting, S of the town at the marked *gué* (ford); to avoid the latter approach from the D131. Magnificent trees, the River Durdent, colourful gardens and a handsome house – plus Lionel Morin's classical cooking: menu B (top-end) of *brouillade d'oeuf aux champignons des bois & avocat, filet de truite de la Durdent* (the delectable river which forms the ford), cheese & strawberry tart was thoroughly enjoyable.
Menus B(top-end)CD. Rooms (4) EF. Cards AE, MC, V.
Post 76450 Cany-Barville, Seine-Maritime. Region Normandy.
Tel 02 35 97 79 30. Fax 02 35 57 03 55. Mich 15/E1-E2. Map 2.

CARANTEC

Le Cabestan

Comfortable restaurant/Cooking 1-2
FW

The bustling enterprise is on the Carentec peninsula – as you start the *"route submersible"* to Ille Callot. 3 alternatives: La Cambuse is a brasserie; Le Balcon & Le Cabestan are upstairs – head for the latter. A fish/shellfish extravaganza inc' oysters, *chaudrée de pétoncles, marinière de coquillages, dorade de ligne mi-fumée* &, best of all, an à la carte *assiette de fruits de mer* worth every franc (low-end C).
Menus BCD. Cards MC, V. (Rooms: Falaise, *sans rest.*)
Closed 3 Nov to 15 Dec. Mon evg (not July/Aug). Tues.
Post 29660 Carantec, Finistère. Region Brittany.
Tel 02 98 67 01 87. Mich 27/E2. Map 1.

CARBON-BLANC

Marc Demund

Very comfortable restaurant/Cooking 3
Terrace/Gardens/Parking
FW

Welcome back to *FL* Marc Demund – a Swiss chef (trained by Girardet) I first met in 1980 at Chaumont-s-Loire. A lovely shaded park & terrace add big pluses to Marc's happy home & his modern/neo-classical skills. A summer lunch (menu b) was perfect – especially *pauchouse de coquillages et poissons* & a crackling good *craquant de coquelet aux herbes*.
Menus bEF(low-end). Cards All. (Rooms Ibis/Novotel; W, across river.)
Closed Sun evg. Mon. (Rest. just N A10/A630; exit 34 from NE; 2 from W.)
Post av. Gardette, 33560 Carbon-Blanc, Gironde. Region Southwest.
Tel 05 56 74 72 28. Fax 05 56 06 55 40. Mich 121/E3. Map 4.

A100frs & under. B100–150. C150–200. D200–250. E250–350. F350–500. G500+

CARHAIX-PLOUGUER

Auberge du Poher

Comfortable restaurant/Cooking 1-2
Gardens/Parking

Robert Le Roux tows both classical & *Bourgeoise* cooking barges at his modern *auberge* – at Port-de-Carhaix, S of the Nantes-Brest canal. An austere dining room, attractive gardens, streams & views. Wide choice on all menus. Anorexics beware: for a real tuck-in the likes of *terrine de chef, faux filet grillée, boeuf en daube, truite au Roquefort* & similar.
Menus aBCD. Cards MC, V. (Rooms: D'Ahès, Carhaix-Plouguer.)
Closed 2-16 Feb. 21 July-3 Aug. Sun evg. Mon.
Post 29270 Carhaix-Plouguer, Finistère. Region Brittany.
Tel 02 98 99 51 18. Fax 02 98 99 55 98. Mich 46/A1. Map 1.

CARNAC

Alignements

Comfortable hotel/Cooking 2
Lift

An all-modern, 4-storey hotel with every bedroom having its own tiny terrace. Geoffroy Bernardi's menu C offers choice, quantity & quality classical fare: *assiette de fruits de mer*, an entire *cannette de Challans aux épices* (for two) & a calorie-boosting *gâteau aux deux chocolats* will test readers with the most whopping of appetites.
Menus AC(low-end)D. Cards (27) EF. Cards AE, MC, V. (D781 Lorient road.)
Closed Oct-Mar.
Post 45 r. St-Cornély, 56340 Carnac, Morbihan. Region Brittany.
Tel 02 97 52 06 30. Fax 02 97 52 76 56. Mich 62/B2. Map 1.

CARQUEIRANNE

Les Pins Penchés

Very comfortable restaurant/Cooking 2-3
Terrace/Air-conditioning

At Port des Salettes, S of D559, 100m from front. Young chef, Stéphane Lelièvre & his pretty wife, Sandrine, mean business at their serious & stylish home. Innovative neo-classical/Provençale cuisine. Two laser-sharp memories remain (menu B): *bouillabaisse de morue* with safran & tomatoes; & *andouillette de dinde en croûte farcie aux morilles*.
Menus BC. Cards All. (Rooms: Plein Sud; in same avenue.)
Closed 2-10 Jan. Su evg & Mo (Sept-June). Mo *midi* & Wed *midi* (July/Aug).
Post av. Gen. de Gaulle, 83320 Carqueiranne, Var. Region Côte d'Azur.
Tel 04 94 58 60 25. Fax 04 94 58 69 04. Mich 161/D4. Map 6.

A100frs & under. B100–150. C150–200. D200–250. E250–350. F350–500. G500+

CARRY-LE-ROUET

L'Escale

Very comfortable restaurant/Cooking 3
Terrace/Gardens

Dany & Gérard Clor's 30s-style rest. has terraces with views over the port & far beyond, to Cap Croisette. All the major guides award multi-stars & *toques*; not so my readers. Some say "superb"; some say "bizarre combinations". Gérard's neo-classical cooking (emphasis on fish *bien sûr*) has had a mixed record; so has service; & Dany's welcome. Oh dear!
Menus E. Cards AE, MC, V. (Rooms: Paradoy-Méditer'ée; Sausset-les-Pins.)
Closed Nov-Jan. Sun evg. Mon (not evgs July/Aug). (Above to W.)
Post 13620 Carry-le-Rouet, Bouches-du-Rhône. Region Provence.
Tel 04 42 45 00 47. Fax 04 42 44 72 69. Mich 159/D4. Map 6.

CASTELLANE

Nouvel H. Commerce

Comfortable hotel/Cooking 2-3
Terrace/Gardens/Lift/Parking

The rear entrance is more exciting: looming above you is the 184m-high Notre-Dame du Roc and below it the River Verdon. The newish hotel offers all creature comforts but the highlight is the neo-classical cooking: *raviolis de daube et blettes à la provençale, blanc de pintade piqué à la sauge* & *pastilla d'abricots et glace Gd-Marnier* – a memorable menu B.
Menus BCE. Rooms (43) EF. Cards All.
Closed Nov to early Apl. Regions Hautes-Alpes/Provence.
Post 04120 Castellane, Alpes-de-Haute-Provence.
Tel 04 92 83 61 00. Fax 04 92 83 72 82. Mich 163/D1. Map 6.

CASTELPERS

Château de Castelpers

Comfortable restaurant with rooms/Cooking 1-2
Secluded/Gardens/Parking

The large park (with old lofty trees) is a welcoming tonic – contrasting the out-of-character red paintwork on the 17thC stone château with its equally odd-ball Gothic add-on. The adjoining River Céor is also a plus. The little-choice classical menu B has welcome fish dishes: *feuilleté aux fruits de mer* & a tangy *truite de mer à la creme de citron*.
Menus (residents only) B. Rooms (8) EF. Cards All.
Closed Oct to Mar. (Note: meals only served to residents.)
Post Castelpers, 12170 Ledergues, Aveyron. Region MC (Cévennes).
Tel 05 65 69 22 61. Fax 05 65 69 25 31. Mich 140/B4. Map 5.

A100frs & under. B100–150. C150–200. D200–250. E250–350. F350–500. G500+

CASTERA-VERDUZAN

Hôtel Ténarèze/Rest. Florida

Simple hotel & comfortable restaurant/Cooking 2-3
Terrace

FW

Castéra is a tiny thermal spa. Bernard Ramounéda, the English-speaking 3rd-generation chef, mixes classical/regional/*Bourgeoise*: menu B could be *potage, poule farci Henri IV, épaule d'agneau rôtie aux herbes* & *3 chocolates (marquise, mousse, glace)*. Hotel run as separate business.
Menus a(lunch)BCD. Rooms (24) CD. Cards (R) All. (H) MC, V.
Closed (R) Feb sch. hols. Sun evg & Mon (Oct-Mar). Wed (Apl-Sept).
Closed (H) Nov-Mar. Sun evg & Mon (Apl & Oct). Region Southwest.
Post 32410 Castéra-Verduzan, Gers. Tel (R) 05 62 68 13 22. (H) 05 62 88 10 22. Fax (R) 05 62 68 10 44. (H) 05 62 68 14 69. Mich 151/E2. Map 5.

CASTILLON-DU-GARD

L'Amphitryon

Comfortable restaurant/Cooking 2-3

FW

A medieval "manger" restored by Serge Lanoix, the previous owner (*FLE* p324). New *patrons*, Philippe Trichard (in his late 20s and trained by Serge) and his wife Fati, do a remarkable job in retaining high modern and neo-classical standards. The tastes of the south – both *terre et mer*: *tournedos de lapin aux olives* & *jus d'herbes fraîches* and *rascasse rôti à l'huile d'olive fenouil braisé* & *coulis de poivrons doux* are typical.
Menus aBCE. Cards MC, V. (Rooms: Moderne; Remoulins.)
Closed Annual – not known. Wed. (Above hotel easy 4km drive to SE.)
Post 30210 Castillon-du-Gard, Gard. Region Provence.
Tel 04 66 37 05 04. Mich 157/F1. Map 6.

CAUDEBEC-EN-CAUX (also see next page)

Manoir de Rétival

Very comfortable restaurant/Cooking 3-4
Terrace/Parking

FW

An 18thC neo-Gothic *relais de chasse*, with turret and high above the Seine and, to the immediate E, is the vast harp-like Brotonne bridge. Jean-Luc Tartarin is an assertive young *cuisine moderne* chef who's going places; helped by brother Jean-Paul, *le pâtissier* – who plays delicate tunes with his light-touch fingers. Sister Nathalie runs the front of house.
Menus b(lunch: top end)CEF. Cards All. (Rooms: Normotel-La Marine.)
Closed Jan. Mon. Tues midday. (For above see next entry.)
Post 76490 Caudebec-en-Caux, Seine-Maritime. Region Normandy. (To E.)
Tel 02 35 96 11 22. Fax 02 35 96 29 22. Mich 15/E3. Map 2.

A 100frs & under. B 100–150. C 150–200. D 200–250. E 250–350. F 350–500. G 500+

CAUDEBEC-EN-CAUX (also see previous page) Normotel-La Marine

Simple hotel/Cooking 1
Lift/Closed parking

The Lefebvres have done much to improve the Seine-side hotel: they've restored the old name (Marine); and given the rooms a facelift (double-glazing is a bonus). From the dining room you can watch the barges chugging by (not such a curse now at night); they are as entertaining as the cheap and cheerful classical/regional and *Bourgeoise* cooking.
Menus ABCD. Rooms (31) EF. Cards AE, MC, V. Region Normandy.
Closed 2-31 Jan. Fri, Sat midday & Sun evg (Mid Oct to mid Mar).
Post quai Guilbaud, 76490 Caudebec-en-Caux, Seine-et-Marine.
Tel 02 35 96 20 11. Fax 02 35 56 54 40. Mich 15/E3. Map 2.

CAULIERES Auberge de la Forge

Very comfortable restaurant /Cooking 2-3 `FW`

Once the village *café/tabac/épicerie* & facing the forge which, in times past, must have been kept busy shoeing horses whilst their riders fed *en face*. Alan, the *cuisinier*, & Michele Mauconduit make you welcome at their half-timbered inn & rustic dining room. Regional & classical fare: from *cuisse de lapin au cidre* (a Normandy tempter) & *ficelle Picarde* (a northern teaser) to *saumon à l'oseille*. (Bedroom annexe planned.)
Menus aBCE. Cards DC, MC, V. (Rooms: Le Cardinal, Poix-de-Picardie.)
Closed Feb. Tues evg. Wed. (Rest. is 7km W of Poix-de-Picardie.)
Post 80590 Caulières, Somme. Regions Normandy/North.
Tel 03 22 38 00 91. Fax 03 22 38 08 48. Mich 17/E2. Map 2.

CERET Les Arcades

Simple hotel (no restaurant)
Lift/Garage

A modern, multi-storey hotel – in a shady *place* & just a few paces from the excellent Les Feuillants rest. (next entry). Owners, the Astrou brothers, are a helpful, friendly duo. Five of the bedrooms are studios with *cuisinettes* (let on a weekly basis). At the end of April/early May the Tech Valley is famed for cherry blossom and Céret claims to be the *capitale de la cerise*. Don't miss the town's Musée d'Art Moderne.
Rooms (26) E(bottom-end)F. Cards MC, V. Region Languedoc-Roussillon.
Post 1 pl. Picasso, 66400 Céret, Pyrénées-Orientales.
Tel 04 68 87 12 30. Fax 04 68 87 49 44. Mich 177/D4. Map 5.

A100frs & under. B100–150. C150–200. D200–250. E250–350. F350–500. G500+

CERET   Les Feuillants

Very comfortable restaurant with rooms/Cooking 3-4 (see text) FW
Terrace/Lift/Garage/Air-conditioning

English-speaking *patronne*, Marie-Louise Banyols, is a *sommelière* with
nous; a huge *cave* with terrific *vins de pays*; & light, flavoursome modern
& Catalane cuisine from chef Didier Banyols – a small details addict. One
new addition: a brasserie with *RQP* fare (rating 2, hence FW award).
Ochre-shaded house in plane tree-shaded *place*. Super bedrooms.
Menus Brass B. Rest EF. Rooms (3) G. Cards AE, MC, V. (See Les Arcades;)
Closed Mon *midi* (July/Aug). Sun evg & Mon (Sept-June). (cheaper rooms.)
Post 1 bd La Fayette, 66400 Céret, Pyrénées-Orientales. Reg Lang-Rouss.
Tel 04 68 87 37 88. Fax 04 68 87 44 68. Mich 177/D4. Map 5.

CESSON   Croix Blanche

Very comfortable restaurant/Cooking 2-3 FW
Gardens/Parking/Air-conditioning

Just E of the N12 St-Brieuc *voie express* – between Ginglin & Cesson. An
all modern restaurant with a charming welcome from *la patronne*, Martine
Mahé. Chef/husband Michel is a neo-classicist. On menu B two first-rate
refreshing fish dishes: *salade de carrelet en vinaigrette de piment doux au
chevre frais*; & *millefeuille de truite de mer* – a masterpiece.
Menus ABCD. Cards All. (Rooms: Campanile, Langueux – 3km S.)
Closed 4-21 Aug. Sun evg. Mon. Region Brittany.
Post 61 r. Genève, Cesson, 22000 St-Brieuc, Côtes d'Armor.
Tel 02 96 33 16 97. Fax 02 96 62 03 50. Mich 28/C3 & 29/D3. Map 1.

CESSON   Le Quatre Saisons

Comfortable restaurant/Cooking 2-3 FW
Terrace/Gardens

A stone-built building with pastel-shaded interior, attractive gardens &
quiet site – 1km E of earlier entry & nearer the sea. Patrick Faucon is a
modern cooking fan (a well-named restaurant): a *brochette de noix de St-
Jacques aux lardons, légumes sauce échalote* was outstanding. So, too, a
yummy *gâteau Breton, pommes tièdes à la cannelle, crème anglais*.
Menus ABCDE. Cards MC, V. (Rooms: Campanile, see above.) Reg Brittany.
Closed Feb sch. hols. 23 Sept-6 Oct. Sun evg. Mon evg. Sat midday.
Post 61 ch. Courses, Cesson, 22000 St-Brieuc, Côtes d'Armor.
Tel 02 96 33 20 38. Fax 02 96 33 77 38. Mich 28/C3 & 29/D3. Map 1.

A100frs & under. B100–150. C150–200. D200–250. E250–350. F350–500. G500+

CEYRAT

La Châtaigneraie

Comfortable hotel (no restaurant)
Quiet/Parking

An ideal Auvergne "base" hotel: high above the village with extensive views to the E. Use the D133 from Ceyrat. Perfectly situated for Le Montrognon rest. (see next entry: 2km S); the Radio at Royat (see entry: 4km N) – where bedrooms are expensive; & La Renaissance rest. in Ceyrat (not inspected). Superb terrain to the N, S & W.
Rooms (17) DEF. Cards MC, V.
Closed Sun (Nov to Apl). Region Massif Central (Auvergne).
Post av. Châtaigneraie, 63122 Ceyrat, Puy-de-Dôme.
Tel 04 73 61 34 66. Mich 113/D2. Map 5.

CEYRAT (Saulzet-le-Chaud)

Le Montrognon

Comfortable restaurant/Cooking 2   FW
Terrace/Parking/Air-conditioning

Gilles & Florence Bettiol have moved into their spanking new restaurant (Saulzet is 2km S of Ceyrat). Spanking good neo-classical menus too – changed every 3 days. Dig into Gilles' varied kaleidoscope of treats: among them *meunière de saumon au coulis de crustacés, vinaigrette de volaille aux myrtilles* & *rable de lapereau aux champignons des bois*.
Menus BCDE. Cards MC, V. (Rooms: La Châtaigneraie; see entry above.)
Closed 24 Aug to 4 Sept. Sun evg. Mon. Region Massif Central (Auvergne).
Post Saulzet-le-Chaud, 63540 Romagnat, Puy-de-Dôme.
Tel 04 73 61 30 51. Fax 04 73 61 53 11. Mich 113/D2. Map 5.

CHABLIS

Hostellerie des Clos

Very comfortable restaurant with rooms/Cooking 3
 Quiet/Gardens/Lift/Parking/Air-conditioning (restaurant)

Michel & Marié Vignaud have not changed their habits since I first met them at the Aub. de l'Artre (Quarré-les-Tombes): she uses simple yet stylish furnishings in their old town hospice; he's a contemporary cuisine convert – influenced by Marc Meneau, his original teacher. Typical dish: *dos de sandre rôti au jus de volaille*. Stunning *cave*.
Menus CEF. Rooms (26) EFG. Cards AE, MC, V. (Cheaper rooms: Ibis.)
Closed 23 Dec-10 Jan. Wed & Thurs midday (Oct to Apl).
Post 89800 Chablis, Yonne. Region Burgundy.
Tel 03 86 42 10 63. Fax 03 86 42 17 11. Mich 72/B2. Map 3.

A100frs & under. B100–150. C150–200. D200–250. E250–350. F350–500. G500+

La CHAISE-DIEU

Au Tremblant

Simple hotel/Cooking 1-2   FW
Gardens/Garage/Parking

Check before visiting: Jean (he's not well) & Josette Boyer (the third generation) are selling their family hotel (opened in 1902). Josette has a beaming smile. Jean's menus are beaming classical/*Bourgeois* with a sofa-wide range of choice: *soufflé de foies de volailles forestières, truite belle meunière, pâté de brochet* & *coquelet au vin* are typical.
Menus ABCD. Rooms (27) DE. Cards MC, V. (Beside D906.)
Closed Nov to Apl.
Post 43160 La Chaise-Dieu, Haute-Loire. Region Massif Cent. (Auvergne).
Tel 04 71 00 01 85. Fax 04 71 00 08 59. Mich 128/B1. Map 5.

CHALLANS

Antiquité

Comfortable hotel (no restaurant)
Fairly quiet/Gardens/Swimming pool/Closed parking

Renovated rooms overlook the garden. The family Flaire, all speak English, also specialise in selling old fireplaces & *carrelages*. One caveat & black mark for the family: ensure any deposit cheque sent (even if drawn on a French bank) is cashed by owners – & not handed back to you on departure (a nasty problem for a reader with little cash on him).
Rooms (16) EF. Disabled. Cards All (worth having in view of above).
Closed 24 Dec to 3 Jan. (Just W of Palais des Expositions.)
Post 14 r. Gallieni, 85300 Challans, Vendée. Region Poitou-Charentes.
Tel 02 51 68 02 84. Fax 02 51 35 55 74. Mich 78/C3. Map 1.

CHALLANS

Le Pavillon Gourmand

Comfortable restaurant/Cooking 2-3   FW

The unprepossessing façade means the tiny restaurant is easily missed (beside the D753 & between the town centre & Renault & Citroën garages). A happy welcome from *chef/patron* Serge Pierron. Happy mixture, too, of neo-classical/classical specialities: *lotte sauce légère au poivre, jambonette de canard de Challans à la rhubarbe* (a town famed for its ducks) & *mousse glacé parfumée au whisky* are a flavoursome trio.
Menus b(lunch)CDE. Cards MC, V. (Rooms: see above entry.)
Closed 1-10 July. 20 Dec-2 Jan. Sun evg. Mon. Region Poitou-Charentes.
Post 4 r. St-Jean-de-Monts, 85300 Challans, Vendée.
Tel 02 51 49 04 52. Mich 78/C3. Map 1.

A100frs & under. B100–150. C150–200. D200–250. E250–350. F350–500. G500+

CHAMBERY

Very comfortable restaurant/Cooking 3
Terrace/Air-conditioning

FW

As good as any *RQP* cooking in the French Alps. Young Jean-Michel Bouvier, trained by Guérard & Senderens, is a modern cooking addict: a *filet de rouget poêlé à la tapenade dans son jus acidulé aux herbes fraîches* is the Med on a plate; & a *moëlleux au chocolat chaud, glace pistache aux zestes d'orange confits* is an intense, mouthwatering sweet.
Menus b(lunch)C(bottom-end)E. Cards AE, MC, V. (Rooms: Mercure; lift;)
Closed 1-15 Aug. Sat midday. Sun (July/Aug). (has garage; above rest.)
Post 183 pl. Gare, 73000 Chambéry, Savoie. Region Savoie.
Tel 04 79 96 97 27. Fax 04 79 96 17 78. Mich 117/F3. Map 6.

Le CHAMBON-SUR-LIGNON

Clair Matin

Comfortable hotel/Cooking 1
Secluded/Terr/Gardens/Swimming pool/Tennis/Garage/Parking

Alain Bard's modern chalet-styled *logis* is over 3000ft above sea-level and in an isolated forest setting, E of the village (D185). In addition to the list of facilities listed above add a gym, sauna and solarium. Cooking? No FW rating alas: just run-of-the-mill *Bourgeoises*/classical basics – *rôti de veau, entrecôte rôti, cotelette d'agneau* and similar.
Menus ACD. Rooms (30) EF. Disabled. Cards All.
Closed Mid Nov to mid Dec. Region Massif Central (Ardèche).
Post 43400 Le Chambon-sur-Lignon, Haute-Loire.
Tel 04 71 59 73 03. Fax 04 71 65 87 66. Mich 129/E2. Map 6.

CHAMONIX

Albert 1er

Very comfortable hotel/Cooking 4
Gardens/Swimming pool/Lift/Garage/Parking

Continual improvement to the hotel's fabric (see the new *sapin* panelling & glass in the front *salle*). Self-effacing *chef/patron* Pierre Carrier & his wife, Martine, both English speakers, are great favourites. Modern French with many Piemont, Nice & Savoie touches/produce – as befits the old state of Savoie. Ask Dominique, the *sommelier*, to show you the *cave*.
Menus cEF. Rooms (19) G. Cards All. (Near station – to N.)
Closed 4-13 May. 20 Oct-4 Dec. Rest: Wed.
Post 74400 Chamonix-Mont-Blanc, Haute-Savoie. Region Savoie.
Tel 04 50 53 05 09. Fax 04 50 55 95 48. Mich 105/F4. Map 6.

A100frs & under. B100–150. C150–200. D200–250. E250–350. F350–500. G500+

CHAMONIX

Comfortable restaurant/Cooking 2   FW
Air-conditioning

A central site, beside La Poste & with the fast-flowing Arve roaring past the rear windows. Dutch owners Paul & Wim Robberse (*in situ* for 10 yrs) and a top-notch *MD*, Didier Guillemot. Well-named rest. – for the cosy panelled dining room. Grub? Three winners on menu B (low-end): *jambonnette de volaille farci au thym, filet de féra au fumet d'Apremont & pain perdu*. One regional alternative: satisfying *fondue Savoyarde*.
Menus B. Cards All. (Rooms: Au Bon Coin; 400m SW.)
Post 123 pl. Balmat, 74400 Chamonix, Haute-Savoie. Region Savoie.
Tel 04 50 55 97 97. Fax 04 50 53 38 96. Mich 105/F4. Map 6.

CHAMONIX

Auberge du Bois Prin

Very comfortable hotel/Cooking 2-3   FW
Secluded/Terrace/Gardens/Lift/Garage/Parking

Plus upon plus at the flower-bedecked chalet: the most spectacular view in Europe (shared by all bedrooms); the terrace (on a budget? call for a cuppa); caring English-speaking hosts, Denis & Monique Carrier; and his neo-classical/regional cooking skills. Signature *plat*: *filets de féra à la crème d'estragon* – a taste explosion. Great sweets. Note *RQP* menu b.
Menus b(lunch)CDEF. Rooms (11)G, G2. Cards All. Region Savoie.
Closed 14 Apl-1 May. 28 Oct-5 Dec. Rest: Wed midday.
Post aux Moussoux, 74400 Chamonix-Mont-Blanc, Haute-Savoie.
Tel 04 50 53 33 51. Fax 04 50 53 48 75. Mich 105/F4. Map 6.

CHAMONIX (also see next page)

La Savoyarde

Comfortable hotel/Cooking 1-2   FW
Quiet/Gardens/Garage/Parking

Recently purchased by Denis & Monique Carrier; the small chalet & its modern extension are 300m N of their Bois Prin hotel (see above). Great views & a chance to try tasty, authentic Savoyarde cooking. Menus are in price bands AB, but choose *à la carte* for the best *RQP* (B&C): inc' *tartiflette* (see regional specialities), *fondue, raclette* & *farçon*.
Menus AB(*à la carte* BC). Rooms (14) FG(low-end). Cards MC, V.
Closed 8-22 May. 2-19 Dec. Region Savoie.
Post 28 rte Moussoux, 74400 Chamonix-Mont-Blanc, Haute-Savoie.
Tel 04 50 53 00 77. Fax 04 50 55 86 82. Mich 105/F4. Map 6.

A100frs & under. B100–150. C150–200. D200–250. E250–350. F350–500. G500+

CHAMONIX (Les Praz) (also see previous page)   L'Eden

Comfortable restaurant with rooms/Cooking 2   FW
Terrace/Parking

A new yellow-ochre exterior & stylish, light interior. Odette Lesage is an elegant *patronne*; bearded husband Gérard skis classical *pistes*. Relish the majestic views & also the restrained mastery of accomplished specialities like *terrine de poisson à la croûte d'algues* (in the Alps) & a tasty c*ontre filet de boeuf marchand de vin* – the sauce a stunner.
Menus BCDF. Rooms (10) EF. Cards All. (Les Praz is NE of Chamonix.)
Closed 1-15 June. Nov. Tues (not high season).
Post Les Praz, 74400 Chamonix-Mont-Blanc, Haute-Savoie. Region Savoie.
Tel 04 50 53 18 43. Fax 04 50 53 51 50. Mich 105/F4. Map 6.

CHAMPAGNAC   Château de Lavandès

Comfortable hotel/Cooking 2
Secluded/Terrace/Gardens/Swimming pool/Parking

The hotel, a handsome old manor house, is gorgeously situated – between the high Auvergne & green Périgord. Louisette Gimmig is the hostess; husband Gérard, a prize-winning desserts champ, paddles classical & regional courses: a *chartreuse de canard confit vinaigrette de pied de porc* & *fondant et sa glace au miel de pays* confirm his pedigree.
Menus CDE. Rooms (8) FG. Cards MC, V.
Closed Mid Dec to mid Feb. Sun evg & Mon (mid Sept to mid May).
Post 15350 Champagnac, Cantal. Regions Dordogne/MC (Auvergne).
Tel 04 71 69 62 79. Fax 04 71 69 65 33. Mich 112/A4. Map 5.

CHAMPAGNOLE   La Vouivre

Comfortable hotel/Cooking 1-2   FW
Quiet/Terrace/Gardens/Swimming pool/Tennis/Parking

A reappearance for La Vouivre, previously *sans rest* in *FL3*. "Beautiful" is not a word I would use for the hotel – but the 7-acre park is an eye-pleasing plus. Véronique & Philippe Pernot are helpful hosts. Nothing special about the classical/regional fare which includes *poulet au Comté* & *saucisse de Morteau à la cancoillotte* (see Jura cheeses/specialities).
Menus BC. Rooms (20) F. Cards MC, V. (N5 to NW; L at railway line.)
Closed Early Oct to Apl. Rest: Wed midday.
Post r. Gédéon David, 39300 Champagnole, Jura. Region Jura.
Tel 03 84 52 10 44. Fax 03 84 52 04 07. Mich 89/F4. Map 3.

A100frs & under. B100–150. C150–200. D200–250. E250–350. F350–500. G500+

CHANTILLY

Parc

Very comfortable hotel (no restaurant)
Gardens/Lift/Parking

Parc is well-named. Though only one of a few base hotels in *FLF* with no "quiet" tag the site compensates in many other ways. The Parc is across the road from the Bois Bourillon & the renowned racecourse with the Grands Ecuries & the Musée du Cheval on the northern edge of the track; and, a little further E, the handsome château with its water-dotted park & Jardin Anglais. Other pluses; rooms for the disabled; and a lift.
Rooms (58) F. Disabled. Cards All.
Post 36 av. Mar. Joffre, 60500 Chantilly, Oise. Region Ile de France.
Tel 03 44 58 20 00. Fax 03 44 57 31 10. Mich 36/A1. Map 2.

CHANTILLY (Lys-Chantilly)

Hostellerie du Lys

Comfortable hotel/Cooking 2   FW
Secluded/Terrace/Gardens/Parking

New owners – and an eager-to-please, English-speaking *directrice*, Lydie Simon – have brought a welcome gust of fresh air to the modern buildings in wooded grounds, SW of Chantilly (Ascot look-alike terrain). Classical cuisine is vastly improved – with an enterprising choice on menu C. How about *gelée de poireaux* (1 of 6 starters); *jambonette de volaille aux pleurottes* (1 of 6 main courses); finishing with 1 of 8 sweets?
Menus aBCD. Rooms (35) EF. Cards All. (9km SW of Chantilly.)
Post Lys-Chantilly, 60260 Lamorlaye, Oise. Region Ile de France.
Tel 03 44 21 26 19. Fax 03 44 21 28 19. Mich 36/A1. Map 2.

CHAPARON

La Châtaigneraie

Comfortable hotel/Cooking 1-2   FW
Secluded/Terrace/Gardens/Tennis/Parking

An alluring setting for a family hotel (½km W of Lac d'Annecy), led by English-speaking Martine Millet & her husband Robert – a friendly, helpful duo. Competent classical/*Bourgeoise*, ranging from *terrine maison* & *filet de haddock fumé sur lit de salade* to an ambitious *jambonette de volaille farcie sauce poivre vert*. Some rooms have *cuisinettes*.
Menus BCDE. Rooms (19) F. Cards All. (SW of Brédannaz.)
Closed Nov to Jan. Sun evg & Mon (Oct to Apl).
Post Chaparon, 74210 Faverges, Haute-Savoie. Region Savoie.
Tel 04 50 44 30 67. Fax 04 50 44 83 71. Mich 118/B1. Map 6.

A 100frs & under. B 100–150. C 150–200. D 200–250. E 250–350. F 350–500. G 500+

La CHAPELLE-D'ABONDANCE

L'Ensoleillé

Comfortable hotel/Cooking 1-2
Gardens/Lift/Parking

FW

A large chalet-style *logis* at the heart of the now over-developed village –
in the valley famed for its cheese. The best *RQP* comes in André Trincaz'
Menu du Montagnard (B) – classical/regional crackers. Two main
courses were tastebud pleasures: *triolet de saumon, sandre & féra crème
légère safranée*; & a hearty ideal *escalope de veau Savoyarde*.
Menus aBCDE. Rooms (34) E. Cards MC, V.
Closed Easter to end May. 21 Sept to Christmas.
Post 74360 La Chapelle-d'Abondance, Haute-Savoie. Region Savoie.
Tel 04 50 73 50 42. Fax 04 50 73 52 96. Mich 105/E2. Map 6.

La CHAPELLE-EN-VERCORS

Bellier

Comfortable hotel/Cooking 1-2
Quiet/Terrace/Gardens/Swimming pool/Parking

FW

Important changes at this much-loved hotel, at the heart of the wondrous
Vercors. Cooking at the small mountain-style chalet is now done by two
younger members of M. & Mme Bellier's family: Fabienne, their daughter,
in winter; & their nephew Stéphane, in summer. Cooking? Regional,
classical & *Bourgeoise*. Elyane, an employee, speaks good English.
Menus ABCD. Rooms (13) F. Cards All.
Closed Tues evg & Wed (Nov to Apl but not sch. hols).
Post 26420 La Chapelle-en-Vercors, Drôme. Regions Hautes-Alpes/Savoie.
Tel 04 75 48 20 03. Fax 04 75 48 25 31. Mich 131/D3. Map 6.

CHARBONNIERES-LES-BAINS

Beaulieu

Comfortable hotel (no restaurant)
Lift/Parking

Lyon is, of course, one of the large, ultra-busy French cities that I have
avoided over the years for *French Leave* editions. However, for some
readers, visits to its famed restaurants are a culinary must; the old town
too is another must. If so, then head for Charbonnières, a small, green
spa in the hills W of Lyon; only 8km away but it could be 1,000. There's
nothing special about the hotel; the site is everything.
Rooms (40) DE. Cards All. Region Lyonnais.
Post 19 av. Gén. de Gaulle, 69260 Charbonnières-les-Bains, Rhône.
Tel 04 78 87 12 04. Fax 04 78 87 00 62. Mich 116/A2. Map 6.

A100frs & under. B100–150. C150–200. D200–250. E250–350. F350–500. G500+

La CHARITE-SUR-LOIRE   Grande Monarque

Comfortable restaurant with rooms/Cooking 1-2   FW
Gardens/Garage

James & Monique (a smasher) Grennerat's riverside restaurant overlooks the Loire & the town's 16thC bridge. Classical cooking from *chef/patron* James: *rumsteack poêlé, sauce Bordelaise* exemplifies the alternatives on the FW menus; *tournedos de filet de boeuf "Lili"* & *écrevisses au Champagne* are among the typical dishes on menus DE. Lovely views.
Menus BDE. Rooms (9) DEF. Cards All. Region Berry-Bourbonnais.
Closed Feb sch hols. Fri evg & Sun evg (10 Nov-31 Mar – not pub. hols).
Post 33 quai Clemenceau, 58400 La Charité-sur-Loire, Nièvre.
Tel 03 86 70 21 73. Fax 03 86 69 62 32. Mich 85/E1. Map 2.

CHARIX   Auberge du Lac Genin

Very simple restaurant with basic rooms/Cooking 1
Secluded/Parking

If you have my earlier guides you'll know how much I love Lac Genin, a 20-acre unspoilt emerald, protected by a circular couch of beech, spruce & pine wooded cushions. Jean Godet's *auberge* beside the lake, originally a farm, was built by his father, Gustave. Basic *Bourgeoise* & grills *au feu de bois: côte de veau moutardée* is typical. "Excellent *fondue.*"
Menus AB. Rooms (5) BCD. Cards MC, V.
Closed 15 Oct to end Nov. Sun evg. Mon..
Post Lac Genin, 01130 Charix, Ain. Region Jura.
Tel 04 74 75 52 50. Fax 04 74 75 51 15. Mich 103/F3. Map 6.

CHARMES-SUR-RHONE   Autour d'une Fontaine (Vieille Auberge)

Comfortable restaurant with rooms/Cooking 2-3   FW
Air-conditioning

Christiane & Jean-Maurice Gaudry's *auberge* is 100m W of the busy N86. Jean-Maurice is a *Maître Cuisinier de France* &, like most members of the group, is a classicist/neo-classicist. Enjoy the vaulted dining room &, even in menu B (the dearer of 2) pleasures like a refreshing *filets de lieu noir, poché fondue de tomates, epinards, ratatouille confite*.
Menus BCDE. Rooms (7) DE. Cards All.
Closed Sun evg. Mon.
Post 07800 Charmes-sur-Rhône, Ardèche. Region Massif Central (Ardèche).
Tel 04 75 60 80 10. Fax 04 75 60 87 47. Mich 130/A3. Map 6.

A 100frs & under. B 100–150. C 150–200. D 200–250. E 250–350. F 350–500. G 500+

CHAROLLES

Poste

Very comfortable restaurant with rooms/Cooking 2 **FW**
Terrace/Garage

An attractive, colourful *maison Bourgeoise* with an intriguing collection of antique clocks. Classical cuisine from chef Daniel Doucet. This is Charollais *pays* so what better than a gutsy hard-to-beat *entrecôte Charollaise à la plaque* (the beef served sizzling on a cast-iron dish). First-rate sweets (5 served on a plate). Garage some distance away.
Menus bCEF. Rooms (6) DE(low-end) Cards AE, MC, V. (Near *église*.)
Closed 24 Nov to 17 Dec. Sun evg. Mon midday. (Parking nearby.)
Post av. Libération, 71120 Charolles, Saône-et-Loire. Region Lyonnais.
Tel 03 85 24 11 32. Fax 03 85 24 05 74. Mich 101/E2. Map 6.

CHASSELAY

Guy Lassausaie

Very comfortable restaurant/Cooking 3-4 **FW**
Closed parking/Air-conditioning

Brilliant is the word to sum up the efforts of young Guy Lassausaie – an imaginative, modern master chef. Menu B (ceiling) is culinary largesse: 4 exuberant courses with 2 *petites surprises* at start & finish (melon balls in a cream sauce; and a small crème brûlée). Of the 4 courses a *cuisse de lapin braisée à la coriandre et basilic* was scented heaven.
Menus B(top-end)DEF. Cards All. (Rooms: see Charbonnières-les-Bains.)
Closed 15-25 Feb. 31 July-23 Aug. Tues evg. Wed. (Above easy 14km S.)
Post r. Belcize, 69380 Chasselay, Rhône. Region Lyonnais.
Tel 04 78 47 62 59. Fax 04 78 47 06 19. Mich 116/A1. Map 6.

CHATEAU-ARNOUX

La Bonne Etape

Very comfortable hotel/Cooking 3
Quiet/Gardens/Swimming pool/Parking/Air-conditioning

Fewer grumbles during the last 4 years about Pierre & Arlette Gleize's 18thC posthouse, handsomely furnished (in true *R&C* livery) & tucked away from the busy N85. Anglophile Jany, the couple's son, has control of the kitchen these days: bravura modern with imaginatively (sometimes a touch bizarre) personalised creations. Super regional produce/wines/cheeses.
Menus DEFG. Rooms (18) G,G2. Cards All. (Cheaper rooms: Villiard.)
Closed 3 Jan to 12 Feb. Sun evg & Mon (Nov-Mar). (Above: see next page.)
Post 04160 Château-Arnoux-St-Auban, Alpes-de-Hte-Prov. Regs Htes-A/Prov.
Tel 04 92 64 00 09. Fax 04 92 64 37 36. Mich 146/B4. Map 6.

A100frs & under. B100–150. C150–200. D200–250. E250–350. F350–500. G500+

CHATEAU-ARNOUX

L'Oustaou de la Foun

Very comfortable restaurant/Cooking 2-3
Terrace/Parking/Air-conditioning

FW

Young Natalie & Gérald Jourdan (the chef) have moved from Digne to a gorgeous old farm with cool, stylish, spacious rooms & a pleasing central courtyard. Great emphasis on regional produce & specialities. Gérald's claims that the tastes & perfumes of Haute-Provence dominate his cooking are vividly demonstrated. (2km N; use N85; near A51 exit.)
Menus BCDE. Cards All. (Rooms: Ibis, Sisteron; Villiard – next entry.)
Closed Mon (not July/Aug). Pub. hols. (Ibis at N end of A51.)
Post 04160 Château-Arnoux-St-Auban, Alpes-de-Hte-Prov. Regs Htes-A/Prov.
Tel 04 92 62 65 30. Fax 04 92 62 65 32. Mich 146/B3-B4. Map 6.

CHATEAU-ARNOUX (St-Auban)

Villiard

Comfortable hotel (no restaurant)
Gardens/Parking

Initial expectations are not high: a tatty exterior & on W side of N96, 4km S of Ch.-Arnoux. But don't be put off as the hotel is more than adequate. There are various reasons for using the Villiard: first, save francs on bedrooms if you eat at La Bonne Etape; and, second, ideally situated for other recommended restaurants: see above; see Dabisse.
Rooms (20) EF. Cards AE, MC, V. (St-Auban 4km S of Château-Arnoux.)
Closed 20 Dec to 5 Jan. Sat & Sun midday (Oct-Mar).
Post 04600 St-Auban, Alpes-de-Haute Provence. Region Hautes-Alpes.
Tel 04 92 64 17 42. Fax 04 92 64 23 29. Mich 146/B4. Map 6.

CHATEAUBOURG

Pen'Roc

Comfortable hotel/Cooking 2-3
Terrace/Gardens/Swimming pool/Lift/Parking

FW

A real corker, on all counts, for this modern hotel, next door to the Eglise Notre Dame at La Peinière, 6km E of the town. Wonderful welcome from Mireille Froc. Colour, brightness & freshness dominate her rooms & husband Joseph's neo-classical cooking. Clever choice formula. One vivid memory: *filet de sandre, velouté de potimaron et poireaux frits* – magic.
Menus bCDE. Rooms (33) F. Cards All. Regions Brittany/Normandy.
Closed Sch. hols Feb & Nov. Rest: Sun evg (Sept-Apl).
Post La Peinière, 35220 Châteaubourg, Ille-et-Vilaine.
Tel 02 99 00 33 02. Fax 02 99 62 30 89. Mich 49/D3. Map 1.

A100frs & under. B100–150. C150–200. D200–250. E250–350. F350–500. G500+

CHATEAUFORT

La Belle Epoque

Comfortable restaurant/Cooking 3-4
Terrace

Alain Rayé, a huge readers' favourite at Albertville in the 80s, has deserted Paris; with his delightful English-speaking wife, Brigitte, the couple have bought the old Peignaud house with the most seductive Ile de France terrace. Savour, too, Alain's seductive cooking – a mix of modern & neo-classical. Deserts, pre-meal starters & *petits fours* are champion.
Menus DEF. Cards All. (Rooms: see entry at Voisins-le-Bretonneux.)
Closed 14-28 Aug. Sun evg. Mon. (Above base hotel easy 5-min. drive W.)
Post 78117 Châteaufort, Yvelines. Region Ile de France.
Tel 01 39 56 21 66. Fax 01 39 56 87 96. Mich 35/E4. Map 2.

CHATEAUMEILLANT

La Piet à Terre

Comfortable restaurant with rooms/Cooking 2 | FW |

What a captivating place. An all blue exterior (apt as the *gendarmerie nationale* is next door) greets you but better still is the welcome from Sylvie Piet & and her elegantly furnished dining rooms (one beamed). She has an eagle eye; & chef Thierry Finet is great on the small details in his neo-classical repertoire. No choice on very wordy 5-course menu B. Typical of attention to small details is the chef's super *petits fours*.
Menus AB(top-end)E. Rooms (7) E. Cards MC, V. (S of D943.)
Closed 2 Jan to 20 Mar. Sun evg & Mon (not high season).
Post 18370 Châteaumeillant, Cher. Region Berry-Bourbonnais.
Tel 02 48 61 41 74. Mich 98/B1. Map 5.

CHATEAUNEUF

La Fontaine

Simple restaurant/Cooking 3 | FW |
Parking

Yves & Anne Jury's tiny home is a touch odd-ball. But there's nowt oddball about his modern & neo-classical repertoire. Menu C (bottom-end) is a superlative *RQP* bargain: perhaps a *salade de saumon fumé au vinaigre balsamique*; some *noix d'agneau au coulis d'olive*; a *fromage du charolais chaud en salade*; and brilliant sweets tagged *délices de la Fontaine*.
Menus bCE. Cards MC, V. (Rooms: Relais de l'Abbaye, Charlieu.)
Closed 13 Jan-13 Feb. 1-9 Oct. Tues evg. Wed. (Above 10km to S.)
Post 71740 Châteauneuf, Saône-et-Loire. Region Lyonnais.
Tel 03 85 26 26 87. Mich 101/E3. Map 6.

A100frs & under. B100–150. C150–200. D200–250. E250–350. F350–500. G500+

CHATELGUYON

Comfortable hotel/Cooking 2
Gardens/Lift/Air-conditioning (restaurant)

FW

French spas are having a tough time; I hope the Kapustics survive their nation's present difficulties. Old-fashioned service & classical cooking in a 5-storey turn-of-the-century house. Menu B can include tastes from the past too: *terrine de canard aux noisettes & pistaches*, gutsy *pièce Charolais façon Paris* & a *chariot de desserts* – loaded with temptations.
Menus ABC. Rooms (62) DE. Cards MC, V. (Public parking nearby.)
Closed 17-27 Mar. 3 Oct-7 Nov. Rest: Sun evg. Region MC (Auvergne).
Post r. Dr Levadoux, 63140 Châtelguyon, Puy-de-Dôme.
Tel 04 73 86 00 12. Fax 04 73 86 21 85. Mich 113/D1. Map 5.

La CHATRE (St-Chartier)

Château Vallée Bleue

Comfortable hotel/Cooking 2
Secluded/Terrace/Gardens/Swimming pool/Parking

FW

Once the home of Dr Pestel (George Sand's doctor), the *"logis"* stands in a 10-acre park, studded with fine trees (especially ancient oaks). Lots of English touches in the lounge & bedrooms. *Patron* Gérard Gasquet is a caring hotelier. Chef Emmanuel Maganto plays a classical/regional piano, inspired by Chopin. Good no-choice, 4-course *Menu Berrichon* (B).
Menus BCE. Rooms (13) EFG. Cards MC, V. (St-Chartier: 9km N La Châtre.)
Closed Feb. Sun evg & Mon (Oct-Mar). (Use D69 to E of St-Chartier.)
Post St-Chartier, 36400 La Châtre, Indre. Region Berry-Bourbonnais.
Tel 02 54 31 01 91. Fax 02 54 31 04 48. Mich 98/A1-B1. Map 5.

CHAUDES-AIGUES (Pont de Lanau)

Auberge Pont de Lanau

Comfortable restaurant with rooms/Cooking 2
Terrace/Parking

FW

Most hoteliers who have featured in my guides instantly recognise the titles *French Leave/Hidden France*. Here, despite 14 years of entries, Josette Cornut has no idea the books exist. *C'est la vie!* Readers rate her as charming & her chef/husband, Jean-Michel, as talented. *Plats* span the classical/neo-classical/Auvergne styles. Soundproofed bedrooms.
Menus aCE. Rooms (8) EF. Cards MC, V. (5km N of Chaudes-Aigues.)
Closed Jan. Feb. Tues evg & Wed (Sept-May).
Post Pont de Lanau, 15260 Neuvéglise, Cantal. Region MC (Auvergne).
Tel 04 71 23 57 76. Fax 04 71 23 53 84. Mich 127/D3. Map 5.

A100frs & under. B100–150. C150–200. D200–250. E250–350. F350–500. G500+

CHAUMOUSEY

Le Calmosien

Comfortable restaurant/Cooking 2
Terrace

Drive 10km SW of Epinal, on the D460, to a whitewashed, window-boxed exterior & a pleasing *belle époque* interior. Chef Jean-Marc Béati paddles all culinary streams: an encore-shouting *saucisson de canard au foie gras, chutney de pommes vertes;* a hearty *civet de cochon fermier;* & a *hérisson* (hedgehog) *de chocolat noir à l'orange* will please all.
Menus BCDE. Cards MC, V. (Rooms: Epinal; Ariane, Ibis, Azur & Mercure.)
Closed Sun evg. (All above hotels an easy drive. Garage at Ibis/Ariane.)
Post 37 r. d'Epinal, 88390 Chaumousey, Vosges. Region Alsace.
Tel 03 29 66 80 77. Fax 03 29 66 89 41. Mich 59/F3. Map 3.

CHAUSSIN

Chez Bach

Comfortable hotel/Cooking 2-3
Quiet/Parking

FW

Near *la gare*: don't take ear plugs – there's no line. Modern *logis* with forests of greenery in the cool *salle*. A cascade of menus from young Christophe Vernay who plays both Bach's Jura & classic tunes adroitly: a robust *assiette Jurassienne* (mountain ham, *brési, terrine,* etc.); & *feuilleté de quenelles de volaille au vin jaune* – a polished melody.
Menus aBCDE. Rooms (23) DE. Cards AE, MC, V.
Closed 2-15 Jan. Fri evg & Sun evg (not July/Aug).
Post pl. Ancienne Gare, 39120 Chaussin, Jura. Region Jura.
Tel 03 84 81 80 38. Fax 03 84 81 83 80. Mich 89/D2. Map 3.

CHAUVIGNY

Lion d'Or

Simple hotel/Cooking 1-2
Parking

FW

Parking? If you own a Volvo (or similar) then endless point-to-point turns to get out. A friendly welcome from helpful hosts, Simone & Yves Chartier. Regional, classical & *Bourgeoise* grub: readers have insisted I raise the old rating. *Farci poitevin* & *cuisses de grenouille poitevin* are typical; "veal kidneys" delicious. 16 rooms in annexe at rear.
Menus aBD. Rooms (26) E. Disabled. Cards MC, V.
Closed 15 Dec-10 Jan. Sat (Nov-Mar).
Post 8 r. Marché, 86300 Chauvigny, Vienne. Region Poitou-Charentes.
Tel 05 49 46 30 28. Fax 05 49 47 74 28. Mich 95/F1. Map 5.

CHENAS

Daniel Robin

Comfortable restaurant/Cooking 2
Terrace/Gardens

FW

Restored *Beaujolaise* farm with views over the vines to the Saône Valley beyond. Chef Robin hops from classical to regional perches; I chirped on about high prices in *FLE* – not only has he dropped them, he's won a gong from Michelin. You'll love fillers like *poulet de Bresse rôti au four* (or as a contrast *à la crème*) & *pièce de Charollais sauce Bourguignonne*.
Menus BCD. Cards All. (Rooms: see Grands Vins entry at Fleurie.)
Closed Feb. Tues evg. Wed. (Above hotel *sans restaurant*.)
Post Les Deschamps, 69840 Chénas, Rhône. Region Lyonnais.
Tel 03 85 36 72 67. Fax 03 85 33 83 57. Mich 102/B3. Map 6.

CHINON

Au Plaisir Gourmand

Very comfortable restaurant/Cooking 3-4
Air-conditioning

Superlative standards & saucing at the 17thC tufa stone house. Jean-Claude Rigollet is an unassuming classical master. His wife, elegant Danielle, is proud of her two new staff members – her sons, English-speaking Laurent, a knowledgeable *sommelier* (L'Echo Chinon wines from the family vineyard) & Jérôme, in the kitchen. Menu C is a *RQP* cracker.
Menus CDE. Cards AE, MC, V. (Rooms: see Diderot, *sans rest*. entry.)
Closed 7-28 Feb. 17 Nov-2 Dec. Sun evg. Mon. (Park on quayside.)
Post quai Charles VII, 37500 Chinon, Indre-et-Loire. Region Loire.
Tel 02 47 93 20 48. Fax 02 47 93 05 66. Mich 81/F1-F2. Map 2.

CHINON (also see next page)

Château de Marçay

Very comfortable hotel/Cooking 2-3
Secluded/Terrace/Gardens/Swimming pool/Tennis/Lift/Parking

FW

Here advertising blurbs match reality: 20thC luxury in a 15thC fortress. The public rooms, bedrooms & bathrooms are archetypal *Relais & Châteaux*, with the addition of handsome, medieval beams. Classical/neo-classical cooking continues to get mixed reports from readers: often praised, often thumped. 3 cheers for the FW-rated weekday lunch (b ceiling).
Menus b(lunch: top-end)EF. Rooms (32)G,G2,G3. Cards All.
Closed Feb-mid Mar. Rest: Sun evg & Mon (Nov-Apl but not pub. hols).
Post Marçay, 37500 Chinon, Indre-et-Loire. Region Loire. (D116, 7km S.)
Tel 02 47 93 03 47. Fax 02 47 93 45 33. Mich 81/F2. Map 2.

A100frs & under. B100–150. C150–200. D200–250. E250–350. F350–500. G500+

CHINON

Diderot

Simple hotel (no restaurant)
Quiet/Terrace/Closed parking

What a charmer – in several respects: the vine-covered 18thC town house; the sun-trap terrace when, in May/June, lilies & roses are sensual pleasures; the quiet site – at the E end of Chinon, 250m from the Loire; and English-speaking Théodore Kazamias, the Cypriot owner for whom nothing is too much trouble. Home-made breakfast jams. Cycles for hire.
Rooms (28) EF. Disabled. Cards All.
Closed 20 Dec to 5 Jan.
Post 4 r. Buffon, 37500 Chinon, Indre-et-Loire. Region Loire.
Tel 02 47 93 18 87. Fax 02 47 93 37 10. Mich 81/F1-F2. Map 2.

CHINON

La Giraudière

Simple hotel/Cooking 2   FW
Secluded/Terrace/Gardens/Parking

Fluent English-speaking Jean-Jacques Daviet – an attentive, friendly owner, who is universally liked, is making big efforts to win a culinary reputation for the 17thC manor. Young chef Marc de Passorio is a neo-classicist: *blanquette de veau légèrement parfumé au gingembre* adds zing to an old timer. Alas, some rooms (& towels) are old timers too.
Menus BCD. Rooms (25) DEF. Cards All. (*Cuisinettes* available.)
Closed Rest: Dec-mid Feb.Tue (not evgs July/Aug). Wed *midi*. Reg. Loire.
Post 37420 Beaumont-en-Véron, Indre-et-Loire. (5km NW: 1km off D749.)
Tel 02 47 58 40 36. Fax 02 47 58 46 06. Mich 81/E1. Map 2.

CHINON

L'Orangerie

Comfortable restaurant/Cooking 2-3   FW

Bruno Marcel Guiot is a newcomer to Chinon; his restaurant is in the same building as Rigollet's famed shrine – and immediately above the latter's dining room. Service is reckoned to be slow & amateurish: but who cares when you can tuck into neo-classical & modern *RQP* sparklers like *langoustines en ravioli sur risotto parfumé au safran, civet de lotte au Bonnezeau* & *millefeuilles à la mousse de chocolat*.
Menus AB. Cards AE, MC, V. (Rooms: see Diderot & Giraudière entries.)
Closed 15-31 Jan. 15-30 Nov. Sun evg & Wed *midi* (Oct-Mar). (Park quay.)
Post 79 bis r. Hte-St-Maurice, 37500 Chinon, Indre-et-Loire. Reg. Loire.
Tel 02 47 98 42 00. Fax 02 47 93 92 50. Mich 81/F1-F2. Map 2.

A100frs & under. B100–150. C150–200. D200–250. E250–350. F350–500. G500+

CHITENAY

Auberge du Centre

Comfortable hotel/Cooking 2
Terrace/Gardens/Closed parking

FW

A great success with readers. Colourful freshness permeates the *auberge*, inside & out. English-speaking chef, Gilles Martinet, was born in the house in the year his grandmother started the business (1951). With his attractive blond wife, Brigitte, the duo have transformed the *logis* in the 6 years since they took over the reins. Ambitious classical cooking.
Menus B(bottom-end)CE. Rooms (23) EF. Disabled. Cards All.
Closed 12-26 Feb. Sun evg & Mon (out of season).
Post 41120 Chitenay, Loir-et-Cher. Region Loire.
Tel 02 54 70 42 11. Fax 02 54 70 35 03. Mich 68/C3. Map 2.

CHOLET

Le Belvédère

Very comfortable restaurant with rooms/Cooking 2-3
Secluded/Terrace/Parking

FW

SE of the town, above the Lac de Ribou (all types of watersports: rowing windsurfing, pedalos, sailing, etc.). Nice views & modernised bedrooms. Chef, Japanese Daisuke Inagaki, tacks an innovative modern course: a subtle tasty seducer – *pigeonneau rôti au citron vert* & *au gingembre;* & *gâteau de noisettes d'agneau à l'aubergine* are typical signature dishes.
Menus bDE. Rooms (8) EF. Cards All. Regions Loire/Poitou-Charentes.
Closed 24 Feb-2 Mar. 28 July-20 Aug. Sun evg. Mon midday.
Post Lac de Ribou, 49300 Cholet, Maine-et-Loire. (5km to SE of Cholet.)
Tel 02 41 62 14 02. Fax 02 41 62 16 54. Mich 80/A2. Map 1.

CHONAS-L'AMBALLAN

Domaine de Clairefontaine

Comfortable hotel/Cooking 3
Quiet/Terrace/Gardens/Tennis/Garage/Parking/Air-cond (rest.)

FW

Mme Girardon & her chef sons, Philippe (ex-Michel Roux student) & Hervé, have injected new life into this ideally-situated hotel. Menu B(ceiling) is a good excuse for a visit: *velouté de moules aux fins légumes, cuissot de volaille farci Grande-mère, fromage blanc* & caramelised *gratin de poires William* is impressive neo-classical 4-course *RQP* fare.
Menus B(top-end)DEF. Rooms (16) CDEF. Cards All. (9km S of Vienne.)
Closed Dec. Jan. Rest: Sat *midi* (Jul/Aug). Su evg. Mo (not evg Jul/Aug).
Post 38121 Chonas-l'Amballan, Isère. Regions Lyonnais/MC (Ardèche).
Tel 04 74 58 81 52. Fax 04 74 58 80 93. Mich 116/A3-A4. Map 6.

A100frs & under. B100–150. C150–200. D200–250. E250–350. F350–500. G500+

CHOUVIGNY

Gorges de Chouvigny

Simple restaurant with basic rooms/Cooking 1-2
Quiet/Terrace/Parking

W of Ebreuil & the A71 exit 12 – in a riverside setting on the Sioule's north (right) bank. Spartan bedrooms are in an ivy-covered house across the road. Eric & Sylvie Fleury, with a young family, work hard. Service not slick. *Cuisine Bourgeoise*: *terrine de saumon, truite meunière, coq au vin* (too dry) & *petite friture*. Don't accept *pension* terms.
Menus ABC. Rooms (8) DE (both bottom-end). Cards MC, V.
Closed Mid Dec-Feb. Tues evg & Wed (not high season).
Post 03450 Chouvigny, Allier. Regions Berry-Bourbonnais/MC (Ardèche).
Tel 04 70 90 42 11. Mich 99/F4. Map 5.

CIRQUE DE CONSOLATION

Hôtel de la Source

Simple restaurant with basic rooms/Cooking 1
Secluded/Parking

Nature reigns supreme: the Dessoubre Valley & park at the 17thC Abbey of Notre Dame are tonics. The hotel is hidden among woods above the abbey – the dining room perched on stilts above a stream feeding the Dessoubre. *Bourgeois* & regional *plats* from Marie-Jo Joliot (a caring, helpful hostess). Enjoy, too, her Great Dane Gypsy. Central heating installed.
Menus ABCD. Rooms (10) CD. Cards MC, V.
Closed Mon & Tues (Oct-June). Region Jura.
Post Cirque de Consolation, 25390 Orchamps-Vennes, Doubs.
Tel 03 81 43 55 38. Mich 90/C1. (Rest. marked on Michelin maps.) Map 3.

La CLAYETTE

Gare

Comfortable restaurant with rooms/Cooking 2
Terrace/Gardens/Swimming pool/Garage/Parking

FW

The well-kitted out *logis* is in the capable hands of Simone Thoral & her classicist *cuisinier* husband Michel. Even menu A is a humdinger: perhaps a *dodine de colvert aux noisettes, confiture d'oignons* to start; then *cuisse de pain farcie à l'ail et aux olives noires, sauce au romorain*; finishing with the ubiquitous *fromage blanc à la crème*. Terrific *RQP*.
Menus ABCDE. Rooms (8) EF. Cards MC, V. (S entrance to town.)
Closed 25 Dec-15 Jan. Sun evg. Mon.
Post av. Gare, 71800 La Clayette, Saône-et-Loire. Region Lyonnais.
Tel 03 85 28 01 65. Fax 03 85 28 03 13. Mich 101/E3. Map 6.

A100frs & under. B100–150. C150–200. D200–250. E250–350. F350–500. G500+

CLECY
Moulin du Vey

Very comfortable hotel/Cooking 1-2 FW
Secluded/Terrace/Gardens/Parking

I've described the beguiling river setting at Clécy in books & articles;
pestered by readers I've at last visited the old corn mill with garden &
superb terrace beside the weir on the Orne's right bank. Gorgeous is the
word for the hotel. The classical/regional cooking is more pedestrian: of
the *terrine, blinis d'andouille* & *nage de raie en ravigote* variety.
Menus BDEF. Rooms (25) FG. Cards All.
Closed Dec. Jan. (Some bedrooms in two annexes – 400m & 3km.)
Post 14570 Clécy, Calvados. Region Normandy.
Tel 02 31 69 71 08. Fax 02 31 69 14 14. Mich 32/A3. Map 2.

CLEDER
Le Baladin

Comfortable restaurant/Cooking 2 FW

In a quiet side street, E of the church. Pierre Queffelec's dining room
may be spartan but his cooking is most certainly not. Modern & classical
specialities: the latter includes a *faux-filet Béarnaise*, the former a
colourful *mosaïque de St-Jacques aux légumes*. Sweets? *Feuilleté
caramélisé aux fraises* & *crème brûlée à l'orange* are typical delights.
Wines by the glass are a welcome innovation: just ask.
Menus ABCD. Cards MC, V. (Rooms: several hotels at Roscoff to NE.)
Closed Mon & Tues evg (not July/Aug). (Or Caravelle, Plouescat, 5km W.)
Post 9 r. Armorique, 29233 Cléder, Finistère. Region Brittany.
Tel 02 98 69 42 48. Mich 27/D1. Map 1.

CLISSON
Bonne Auberge

Very comfortable restaurant/Cooking 3 FW
Gardens

A delightful series of *salles* – the main one, a glass conservatory,
overlooks the garden. Chantale Poiron is a delectable hostess; & husband
Serge an innovative modern magician (with a few classic tricks up his
sleeve). Some snags: when full service can be stretched – little details sink
without trace; & a pigeon dish was awfully tough. Super sweets.
Menus a(lunch)CF. Cards AE, MC, V. (Rooms: Gare – 100m walk; basic.)
Closed 1-15 Jan. 10-31 Aug. Sun evg. Mon. Regions Loire/Poitou-Char.
Post 1 r. O. de Clisson, 44190 Clisson, Loire-Atlantique.
Tel 02 40 54 01 90. Fax 02 40 54 08 48. Mich 79/E2. Map 1.

A100frs & under. B100–150. C150–200. D200–250. E250–350. F350–500. G500+

CLUNY

Bourgogne

Comfortable hotel/Cooking 2
Garage

Opposite the abbey. Michelle & Jean-Claude Gosse are justifiably proud of the stonework, timbers & period furnishings in their 180-year-old hotel. Bruno Dupasquier is a classical chef. Specialities range from *entrecôte du Charollais (bien sûr)* to r*avioles de langoustines aux herbes*. Formidable dessert trolley. Some readers say cooking is "tired".
Menus B(lunch)DEF. Rooms (12) F. Cards All. (Parking 200m.)
Closed 21 Nov-4 Mar. Tues. Wed midday.
Post pl. Abbaye, 71250 Cluny, Saône-et-Loire. Region Lyonnais.
Tel 03 85 59 00 58. Fax 03 85 59 03 73. Mich 102/B2. Map 6.

CLUNY

Saint-Odilon

Simple hotel (no restaurant)
Gardens/Closed parking

Robert Berry's new, unusually-styled hotel (with handsome Romanesque tower at its centre) is just across the River Grosne, about 400m from the once proud but now sad remains of the ancient abbey. Apart from its proximity to so many man-made treasures in all directions, the hotel is also close to Cluny's *piscine*. (Hotel alongside D15, to E of Cluny.)
Rooms (36) E(bottom-end). Cards AW, MC, V.
Closed 20 Dec-10 Jan.
Post rte Azé, 71250 Cluny, Saône-et-Loire. Region Lyonnais.
Tel 03 85 59 25 00. Fax 03 85 59 06 18. Mich 102/B2. Map 6.

La CLUSAZ

L'Ourson

Simple restaurant/Cooking 2-3

FW

Next door to *Maison du Tourisme* – both S of church. Last winter saw the restaurant being fitted out with a new interior (and panelling). English-speaking chef Vincent Lugrin once worked for 3-star wonder boy Veyrat &, more realistically, for Pierre Carrier at Chamonix. That shows to good effect in his formidable value, modern cooking, multi-course menus. One star dish: *aiguillettes de canard aigre-doux aux pêches*.
Menus ABCD. Cards AE, MC, V. (Rooms: several hotels in resort.)
Closed May-mid June. Nov-10 Dec.
Post 74220 La Clusaz, Haute-Savoie. Region Savoie.
Tel 04 50 02 49 80. Mich 118/C1. Map 6.

A100frs & under. B100-150. C150-200. D200-250. E250-350. F350-500. G500+

COGNAC

Very comfortable restaurant with rooms/Cooking 1-2
Terrace/Gardens/Parking

Jacques Tachet is the classical cuisine chef; brother Jean-Michel is *le sommelier*; and English-speaking sister, Catherine, is *la patronne*. The 17thC *relais de poste* has a quietish site, well-clear of the town centre. Bedrooms are dear for the facilities. Choose the cheaper of the two menus C; at least it has limited choice. Poor quality desserts.
Menus BCD. Rooms (7) EF. Cards All. (Beside D731 Poitiers road.)
Closed Rest: Sun evg. (Alternative rooms: Mercure, SE edge of town.)
Post 110 r. J.-Brisson, 16100 Cognac, Charente. Region Poitou-Charentes.
Tel 05 45 82 16 36. Fax 05 45 82 29 29. Mich 107/E2. Map 4.

COGNAC (Bourg-Charente)

Very comfortable restaurant/Cooking 3
Terrace/Gardens/Parking

A delectable spot – on the left bank of the Charente with terrace & gardens overlooking the river. Geranium-filled window boxes are a colourful plus but the best pleasures come after Patricia welcomes you: then Thierry Verrat's modern light creations seduce – witness *salade de primeurs, moules & encornets au basilic* and a *feuillantine aux pommes*.
Menus BCDE. Cards All. (Rooms: Mercure, E side Cognac; 6km to W.)
Closed 15 Jan-15 Feb. Sun evg (out of season). Mon. (Above easy drive.)
Post 16200 Bourg-Charente, Charente. Region Poitou-Char. (E of Cognac.)
Tel 05 45 81 30 54. Fax 05 45 81 28 05. Mich 107/F2. Map 4.

COGNAC (L'Echassier)

Very comfortable hotel/Cooking 3
Quiet/Terrace/Gardens/Swimming pool/Parking

Two separate buildings, stylishly furnished – just N of the N141/D15 junction SE of Cognac. The line of benefits above appeal (away from the town centre) but the classical/neo-classical *plats* from Jean Loccussol seduce far more: menu B could include s*aumon fumé crème ciboulette* (home-smoked), *fricassée de volaille au pineau* & n*ougat glacé sauce au thé*.
Menus BCDE. Rooms (22) F(low-end)G. Disabled. Cards All.
Closed Feb & Nov sch. hols. Sat midday & Sun (not mid June-mid Sept).
Post 16100 Châteaubernard, Charente. Region Poitou-Charentes.
Tel 05 45 35 01 09. Fax 05 45 32 22 43. Mich 107/E2. Map 4.

A 100frs & under. B 100–150. C 150–200. D 200–250. E 250–350. F 350–500. G 500+

COL DE LA MACHINE

du Col de la Machine

Simple hotel/Cooking 1
Secluded/Swimming pool/Garage/Parking

A remarkable family, site & view at this modest *logis*. Jacques & Eliane Faravellon are the 5th generation of the family (the business was started by their ancestors in 1848). Their son, Eric (trained by Albert Lecomte at St-Vallier; see entry), will be the 6th. Basic *Bourgeoise* with *gratin Dauphinois à la crème* & *pommes Dauphines* on all menus.
Menus ABC. Rooms (14) CDE. Cards MC, V. Region Hautes-Alpes/Savoie.
Closed 17-24 Mar. 12 Nov-5 Dec. Sun evg & Mon (Oct-May).
Post Col de la Machine, 26190 St-Jean-en-Royans, Drôme. (11km to SE.)
Tel 04 75 48 26 36. Fax 04 75 48 29 12. Mich 130/C3 & 131/D3. Map 6.

La COLLE-SUR-LOUP

Marc Hély

Comfortable hotel (no restaurant)
Quiet/Gardens/Swiming pool/Parking

A mixture of styles: Provençale farmhouse & modern bedrooms with welcome refrigerated mini-bars & terraces which give fine views of perched St-Paul, further up the valley. Gardens are the highlight. A typical reader's comment sums up Marc Hély: "nothing special but M. & Mme Seigle are very helpful owners." The hotel is alongside the D6, SE of village – close to restaurants, perched villages to the N and the coast.
Rooms (13) F. Cards AE, MC, V. Region Côte d'Azur.
Post 535 rte de Cagnes, 06480 La Colle-sur-Loup, Alpes-Maritimes.
Tel 04 93 22 64 10. Fax 04 93 22 93 84. Mich 165/D3-D4. Map 6.

La COLLE-SUR-LOUP

La Stréga

Comfortable restaurant/Cooking 2   FW
Terrace/Parking

An unprepossessing exterior (easily missed) but a pretty Provençal interior. A light, neo-classical & modern approach from Chef Gilbert Stella. *Fleurs de courgette farcies à la mousseline de rascasse* can be so fresh you may even see the flowers being delivered. *Brie-de-Meaux* for cheese, followed by a sweet like *crème brûlée à la vanille et cassonade*.
Menus B(ceiling). Cards MC, V. (Rooms: nearby Marc Hély; see above.)
Closed Jan. Feb. Sun evg (Sept-June). Mon. Tues midday (July/Aug).
Post 06480 La Colle-sur-Loup, Alpes-Maritimes. Region Côte d'Azur.
Tel 04 93 22 62 37. Mich 165/D3-D4. Map 6. (D36 SE of village.)

COLLIOURE

Casa Païral

Very comfortable hotel (no restaurant)
Quiet/Gardens/Swimming pool/Parking

A 19thC Moorish-style house at the very heart of the town's old port. The highlight is the truly tiny delectable walled garden/patio – full of firs, palm trees & camellias. Tucked away in a corner is a minuscule swimming pool – the surrounding walls covered in roses & wisteria. No grumbles for some years now about the stingy owners: three cheers!
Rooms (28) FG(top-end). Disabled. Cards AE, MC, V.
Closed Nov-Mar. Region Languedoc-Roussillon.
Post impasse Palmiers, 66190 Collioure, Pyrénées-Orientales.
Tel 04 68 82 05 81. Fax 04 68 82 52 10. Mich 177/F3. Map 5.

COLLIOURE

La Frégate

Comfortable hotel/Cooking 2   FW
Terrace/Lift/Air-conditioning

Both the English-speaking *chef/patron*, Yves Costa, & La Frégate have had a new lease of life. New style dining rooms with handsome Portuguese-made tiles (costa lot). Air-conditioned, double-glazed bedrooms (perfect on hot summer nights). As always a wide choice of *Catalane*, classical & modern: the *anchois* & *poissons* alternatives are cracking *plats*. Locked private parking (500m away) is both patience & vehicle testing.
Menus BC. Rooms (24) EFG. Cards MC, V. Region Languedoc-Roussillon.
Post 24 quai de l'Amirauté, 66190 Collioure, Pyrénées-Orientales.
Tel 04 68 82 06 05. Fax 04 68 82 55 00. Mich 177/F3. Map 5.

COLLIOURE (also see next page)

Madeloc

Comfortable hotel (no restaurant)
Quiet/Gardens/Parking

Five hundred metres to the west of the port and the various beaches. That's no handicap as there are several rewarding compensations: a quiet site; modern facilities; rooms with loggias & many with private terraces (some quite sizeable) – all facing the Pyrénées; and, best of all, the very friendly and much-praised owners, the Pouchairet-Ramona family.
Rooms (22) EF. Cards All.
Closed Jan. Region Languedoc-Roussillon.
Post r. R.-Rolland, 66190 Collioure, Pyrénées-Orientales.
Tel 04 68 82 07 56. Fax 04 68 82 55 09. Mich 177/F3. Map 5.

A100frs & under. B100–150. C150–200. D200–250. E250–350. F350–500. G500+

COLLIOURE (also see previous page)

Nouvelle Vague

Comfortable restaurant/Cooking 2
Terrace

Claude Nourtier, the young owner, is a passionate champion of both *Catalane* cuisine & Roussillon wines. The *Menu Catalan* (low-end C) could include *les rillettes de pain à la fleur de thym, les figues au vinaigre* (two flavours not quite jelling); *"paupilles" d'agneau aux pignons et à la Soubressade*; and a luscious *crème Catalane*. Bravo chef Pierre Jiquet.
Menus ACE. Cards MC, V. (Rooms: see entries for Casa Païral & Madeloc.)
Closed Feb. Sun evg & Mon (mid Oct to Easter). Region Languedoc-Rouss.
Post 7 r. Voltaire, 66190 Collioure, Pyrénées-Orientales.
Tel 04 68 82 23 88. Mich 177/F3. Map 5. (S of château.)

COLOMBEY-LES-DEUX-EGLISES Auberge de la Montagne

Comfortable restaurant with rooms/Cooking 2 **FW**
Quiet/Gardens/Parking

A Gén.-de-Gaulle hatful of pluses: away from the N19; Arlette Natali is an attractive, smiling *patronne*; & her extrovert husband, Gérard, is an able chef. Appetite-quenching *plats*: a duo of *hures – sanglier et lapereau*, one slice of each in jelly; & several rounds of tasty *noix de veau aux pleurottes*. Debits? Small bedrooms; moody waitress.
Menus bCDE. Rooms (7) DE(bottom-end). Cards AE, MC, V.
Closed Mid Jan-mid Feb. Mon evg. Tues. Region Champagne-Ardenne.
Post 52330 Colombey-les-deux-Eglises, Haute-Marne.
Tel 03 25 01 51 69. Fax 03 25 01 53 20. Mich 57/F3. Map 3.

COLY

Manoir d'Hautegente

Very comfortable hotel/Cooking 2 **FW**
Secluded/Terrace/Gardens/Swimming pool/Parking

An adorable, creeper-covered *manoir* in a delectable woodland & garden setting. In centuries past the site was both a forge & mill, power courtesy of the pool & river. "Great air of peace & very good for the soul," says a reader. Owned by Hamelin family for 300 + years. Classical & regional fare from Edith Hamelin. Impeccable bedrooms & taste.
Menus B(lunch: ceiling)CE. Rooms (12) G. Cards AE, MC, V.
Closed Nov-Mar. Rest: midday on Mon, Tues, Wed.
Post 24120 Coly, Dordogne. Region Dordogne. (E of Montignac.)
Tel 05 53 51 68 03. Fax 05 53 50 38 52. Mich 124/B2. Map 5.

A100frs & under. B100–150. C150–200. D200–250. E250–350. F350–500. G500+

COMBEAUFONTAINE

Balcon

Comfortable hotel/Cooking 2-3   FW
Garage

Yvette & Christian Parnet (see Oye-et-Pallet) gave me the nod about
their *copains* – Claudine, *la patronne*, & her husband, chef Gérard
Gauthier. He's a classical/neo-classical rider but also finds room for Jura
plats: a *poulet au vin jaune et morilles* was a gem. Save francs by trying
a bargain local *vin de pays* – from nearby Champlitte (to SW).
Menus BDEF. Rooms (17) DEF. Cards All.
Closed 23 Jun-2 Jul. Sun evg. Mon.
Post 70120 Combeaufontaine, Haute-Saône. Regs Champ-Ard/Jura.
Tel 03 84 92 11 13. Fax 03 84 92 15 89. Mich 75/E2. Map 3.

COMMENTRY

Michel Rubod

Comfortable restaurant/Cooking 3-4   FW

If you are heading S for the toll-free A75, leave the A71 (exit 10) and make
the easy 15km detour to the home of a *cuisine moderne* chef. Michel
Rubod is a creative master & he uses superb produce. Among his *plats*:
nothing mod about *andouillette Dromart* (*en noir et blanc*) – the best in
France; drooling *saumon fumé à la maison* – *chaud au beurre de pomme
de terre*; & a luscious *pain perdu d'autrefois*. (D69: E of town centre.)
Menus BCEF. Cards MC, V. (Rooms: St-Christophe, *sans rest*, to W.)
Closed 23 Dec-6 Jan. 28 Jul-19 Aug. Sun evg. Mon. (Rest. parking easy.)
Post 47 r. J.-J. Rousseau, 03600 Commentry, Allier. Region Berry-Bourb.
Tel 04 70 64 45 31. Fax 04 70 64 33 17. Mich 99/E3. Map 5.

COMPIEGNE (also see next page)

Hostellerie Royal-Lieu

Very comfortable restaurant with rooms/Cooking 2-3
Terrace/Gardens/Closed parking

Much liked by readers. Angelo Bonechi is not a shy classicist. Old style,
old traditions & cooking from the past shows in the service, furnishings,
decorations & his repertoire (increasingly with some lighter creations):
cuisse de lapin braisé à la sauge sauce au cidre & a richer *poulet
braisé à la crème de morilles* are typical signature *plats*. (To SW, beside
the D932A, r. de Senlis, well clear of Compiègne centre.)
Menus C(low-end)DF. Rooms (17) FG. Cards All. Region Ile de France.
Post 9 r. Senlis, Royal-Lieu, 60200 Compiègne, Oise.
Tel 03 44 20 10 24. Fax 03 44 86 82 27. Mich 18/B4. Map 2.

A 100frs & under. B 100–150. C 150–200. D 200–250. E 250–350. F 350–500. G 500+

COMPIEGNE (also see previous paqe)   La Part des Anges

Comfortable restaurant/Cooking 3   FW
Terrace/Parking

A great find. Modern, spacious dining room (park at rear). Just E of Univ. (from bypass, continue NE from D200 & A1). Modern cooking from Francis Carpentier. Two-way choice each course menu B. On a hot summer day perfection came in the form of *rillettes de truite de mer au cerfeuil* & d*os de cabillaud poêlé purée de cocos à l'huile d'olive*.
Menus BE. Cards AE, MC, V. (Rooms: Université, *sans rest*, 200m walk.)
Closed 1st 3 weeks Aug. Sun evg. Mon midday.
Post 18 r. Bouvines, 60200 Compiègne, Oise. Regions Ile de France/North.
Tel 03 44 86 00 00. Fax 03 44 86 09 00. Mich 18/B4. Map 2.

COMPIEGNE   Rive Gauche

Very comfortable restaurant/Cooking 2-3   FW

Upstream from the town centre bridge, on the left bank of the Oise. The puce-hued dining room may be a bit off-putting – but not the modern & neo-classical cuisine, full of delicate subtleties, from chef Franck Carpentier-Dervin. Menu B offers good choice: enjoyable fare such as *salade tiède de saucisson de canard à l'avocat* (yummy); *jambonnette de volaille*; & a touch bizarre *crème brûlée à la banane et au curry*.
Menus BC. Cards MC, V. (Rooms: de Harlay, by bridge, 400m walk.)
Closed Sat midday. Mon. (Park by quayside, opposite rest.)
Post 13 cours Guynemer, 60200 Compiègne, Oise. Regions Ile de F/North.
Tel 03 44 40 29 99. Fax 03 44 40 38 00. Mich 18/B4. Map 2.

CONCARNEAU   Chez Armande

Comfortable restaurant/Cooking 2   FW

Facing the Port de Plaisance (Avant-Port): neat & tidy & blue & white. Chef Jean-Luc Dupuis has evolved a rewarding formula for clients – *plats* which can be deceptively simple or cooked in traditional classic ways. Menu B is unusual in providing 12 starters, 3 main courses, cheese & 12 sweets: alternatives like *moules marinières, mouclade au safran, tarte de lotte aux asperges, barbue grillée beurre citronée* & *forêt noir*.
Menus aBC. Cards All. (Rooms: Les Halles, *sans rest*, 2 min walk away.)
Closed 20 Dec-20 Jan. Tues evg (not July/Aug). Wed. Region Brittany.
Post 15 bis av. Dr Nicolas, 29900 Concarneau, Finistère.
Tel 02 98 97 00 76. Mich 45/D3. Map 1. (Parking in front of rest.)

A100frs & under. B100–150. C150–200. D200–250. E250–350. F350–500. G500+

120

CONCARNEAU

Les Sables Blancs

Comfortable hotel/Cooking 1-2
Terrace

FW

The aptly-named Chabrier family *logis*, NW of the port, has its toes in both the beach & sea. Classical/*Bourgeoise* cooking from Pierre-Bernard. Aromatic *soupe de poissons maison, moules à la crème* (60 no less), melt-in-the-mouth *magret de canard, faux-filet au poivre vert, poire Belle-Hélène* & *galette Concarnoise flambée*. Plenty of half-bottles.
Menus ABC. Rooms (48) CDEF. Cards All.
Closed Mid Oct-Mar. Region Brittany. Mich 45/D3.
Post Plage des Sables-Blancs, 29182 Concarneau, Finistère. Map 1.
Tel 02 98 97 01 39. (02 98 97 86 93 out of season.) Fax 02 98 50 65 88.

CONDE-SUR-NOIREAU

Cerf

Simple restaurant with rooms/Cooking 2
Closed parking

FW

A vine-covered *logis*, alongside D36 Aunay road (take care turning in). Catherine Malgrey is a helpful soul; her chef/husband, Patrice, pedals classical & regional wheels – & is a dedicated follower of *produits du terroir*. Good choice on menu B: typical meal could be *saumon fumé, filet de flétan, piéce de boeuf Béarnaise*, cheese & *crème caramel*. Tummy full?
Menus aBC. Rooms (9) D. Cards All.
Closed Sun evg.
Post 18 r. Chêne, 14110 Condé-sur-Noireau, Calvados. Region Normandy.
Tel 02 31 69 40 55. Fax 02 31 69 78 29. Mich 31/F3. Map 1.

CONQUES

Ste-Foy

Comfortable hotel/Cooking 1-2
Quiet/Terrace/Lift

FW

In 1982 I described Ste-Foy as an utter gem, creeper-covered, medieval & in the shadow of one of France's most precious sites – Eglise Ste-Foy. Chefs come & go alas – but owners, the Garcenots, keep standards high. A new chef in place this year with a regional/neo-classical repertoire. Snags? Some rooms slant; the place is busy; parking is 250m away.
Menus b(lunch)CE. Rooms (17) G. Cards AE, MC, V.
Closed Nov to Easter.
Post 12320 Conques, Aveyron. Regions Massif Central (Auvergne/Cévennes).
Tel 05 65 69 84 03. Fax 05 65 72 81 04. Mich 140/B1. Map 5.

A100frs & under. B100–150. C150–200. D200–250. E250–350. F350–500. G500+

Le CONQUET

Comfortable hotel/Cooking 1-2
Lift/Parking

FW

An ugly, ultra-modern concrete & glass structure with a spectacular site on rocks above the sea – 24km W of Brest. Exhilarating views; near sandy beach. Menu B(top-end) has huge choice with fish dishes predominating. Classical sauces – *Béarnaise, hollandaise, beurre blanc* & mayonnaise – with salmon, white fish & crab as examples. Several meat dishes also.
Menus aB(top-end)DF. Rooms (49) CDEFG. Disabled. Cards All.
Closed 12 Nov-17 Dec. Rest: Mon (not July-mid Sept).
Post 29217 Le Conquet, Finistère. Region Brittany.
Tel 02 98 89 00 26. Fax 02 98 89 14 81. Mich 26/A3. Map 1.

CONTEVILLE

Auberge du Vieux Logis

Very comfortable restaurant/Cooking 3

FW

The delectable brown & white half-timbered cottages catch the eye as you meander along the D312. Behind the beams waits Maryse Louet to give you a warm welcome; behind the stoves stand hubby Yves & son Guillaume, a well-matched tandem turning classical/regional pedals. Uplifting glories of the *sole soufflé au Noilly ancien régime* type; & appetite smashers – of the *andouille de Vire chaud aux pommes* & *au cidre* variety.
Menus B(lunch)cDE. Cards All. (Rooms: see Beuzeville, Petit Castel.)
Closed 20 Jan-1 Mar. Tues evg. Wed.
Post 27120 Conteville, Eure. Region Normandy.
Tel 02 32 57 60 16. Fax 02 32 57 45 84. Mich 15/D4. Map 2.

La COQUILLE

Voyageurs

Simple hotel/Cooking 1-2
Gardens/Garage/Parking

FW

A *Logis de France*, alongside the N21. Surprisingly service can be very swish (*maître D* dressed in formal style). *Chef/patron* Gilbert Saussot sticks with tradition, in both furnishings & cuisine. Menus C offers a good choice with a couple of punchy dishes laced with hard stuff: *melon de Cavaillon au Pineau* & *feuilleté de lotte au whisky*.
Menus B(bottom-end)CDE. Rooms (10) DE. Cards DC, MC, V.
Closed Oct-Apl. Sun evg (May & Jun). Rest: Mon.
Post 24450 La Coquille, Dordogne. Region Dordogne.
Tel 05 53 52 80 13. Fax 05 53 62 18 29. Mich 109/F3. Map 5.

A 100frs & under. B 100–150. C 150–200. D 200–250. E 250–350. F 350–500. G 500+

P. lombières

Theatrical? Extravagant? Extrovert? Yes all 3. (Atop a hill-top stunner called Cordes-sur-Ciel.) A Gothic wonder with stone, timbers & lavish furnishings. Yves Thuriès plays his part: good chef & supreme *pâtissier-chocolatier*. He weaves neo-classical tapestries; his desserts are out of this world. He is also a foodie entrepreneur *par excellence* to boot.
Menus CEF. Rooms (12) G. Cards All. (Parking can be tricky.)
Closed Nov to Easter. Mon & Tues midday (not July/Aug & pub. hols).
Post 81170 Cordes-sur-Ciel, Tarn. Region Massif Central (Cévennes).
Tel 05 63 56 01 03. Fax 05 63 56 18 83. Mich 139/E4. Map 5.

CORDES   Hostellerie du Vieux Cordes

Comfortable hotel/Cooking 1-2   FW
Secluded (annexe quiet)/Terrace

A second Yves Thuriès enterprise, one which is easily affordable. This, too, is a medieval house with an unusual, inviting terrace plus distant views. Less extrovert fare from chef Bernard Lafon: classical/regional & neo-classical specialities such as *hure de saumon au poivre vert, magret pommes sautées* & *gratin de pommes*. Once again parking can be tricky.
Menus ABC. Rooms (21) EF; annexe (8) DE. Cards All. Mich 139/E4.
Closed Jan. Rest: Sun evg & Mon (Oct-Apl). Annexe: mid Oct-mid Apl.
Post 81170 Cordes-sur-Ciel, Tarn. Region Massif Central (Cévennes).
Tel 05 63 56 00 12. Annexe 63 56 03 53. Fax 05 63 56 02 47. Map 5.

CORDON (also see next page)   Le Cordonant

Comfortable hotel/Cooking 1-2   *very good*   FW
Quiet/Terrace/Parking

A flower-bedecked chalet with the most friendly of owners in the shape of Gisèle Pugnat. Stand on the flower-filled terrace, turn your eyes SE & revel in the superb view of the Mont Blanc *massif*. Alain Pugnat keeps his classical fare simple: *fera au beurre blanc, gigot d'agneau rôti, osso bucco* (a nice change) & similar temptations. New addition: a gym.
Menus bC. Rooms (16) EF(low-end). Cards MC, V. (SW of Sallanches.)
Closed 16 Apl-7 May. 25 Sept-20 Dec.
Post 74700 Cordon, Haute-Savoie. Region Savoie.
Tel 04 50 58 34 56. Fax 04 50 47 95 57. Mich 105/E4. Map 6.

A100frs & under. B100–150. C150–200. D200–250. E250–350. F350–500. G500+

123

CORDON (also see previous page)　　　　　　　**Roches Fleuries**

Very comfortable hotel/Cooking 2　　　　　　　　　| FW |
Secluded/Terrace/Gardens/Swimming pool/Garage/Parking

100m W of Le Cordonant; same majestic Mt-Blanc views. Superb panelling in the public rooms/bedrooms of the chalets. Jocelyne & Gérard Picot are proud *patrons*. Chef Dominique Weber skis neo-classical slopes: one spicy sizzler – *canard rôti au poivre de Sechuan*. Separate *rest*. – La Boîte à Fromages – *fondues, raclettes*, etc. (C, low-end; dinner only).
Menus BCE. Rooms (28) Demi-pension only FG. Cards All.
Closed 15 Apl-7 May. 28 Sept-20 Dec. (Cheaper rooms: Solneige.)
Post 74700 Cordon, Haute-Savoie. Region Savoie. (SW Sallanches.)
Tel 04 50 58 06 71. Fax 04 50 47 82 30. Mich 105/E4. Map 6.

CORPS　　　　　　　　　　　　　　　　**Boustigue Hôtel**

Simple hotel/Cooking 1
Secluded/Gardens/Swimming pool/Tennis/Parking

Several roadside signs encourage you to keep going as you wind your way up the long wooded climb to the hotel's panoramic site (4000-ft) high above Corps (views of mountain needles to W). Facilities & setting are everything; as are the owners, the Dumas family. Cooking? Modest classical from Dumas *fils*: *filet de boeuf sauce poivre vert* variety.
Menus aC(low-end). Rooms (30) DE. Cards MC, V. (To NE; use D212.)
Closed 21 Oct-20 Apl. (Hotel site marked on Michelin maps.)
Post 38970 Corps, Isère. Regions Hautes-Alpes/Savoie.
Tel 04 76 30 01 03. Fax 04 76 30 04 04. Mich 132/A3. Map 6.

CORPS　　　　　　　　　　　　　　　　　　　**Poste**

Comfortable restaurant with rooms/Cooking 2　　　| FW |
Terrace/Garage

Young Gilbert & Christiane Delas are steaming ahead. Their extrovert N85 (busy) outpost is a huge sucess. Now they've also opened the swish Ch. des Herbeys at Chauffayer (SE of Corps: pool/tennis/calm). A classical passage from Gilbert, once chef on the liner *France*. Even the cheapest menu offers wide-choice, four-course, appetite-scuttling grub.
Menus abCE. Rooms (20) DEF. Cards AE, MC, V.
Closed Dec-mid Jan.
Post 38970 Corps, Isère. Regions Hautes-Alpes/Savoie.
Tel 04 76 30 00 03. Fax 04 76 30 02 73. Mich 132/A3. Map 6.

A100frs & under. B100–150. C150–200. D200–250. E250–350. F350–500. G500+

COSNE-SUR-LOIRE

Le Sévigné

Comfortable restaurant/Cooking 3 `FW`

A tiny restaurant in a maze of one-way streets; leave the *village fleuri* town centre to the NW, towards *la gare*. One caveat: book ahead. There's no choice on menu B other than the 7 sweets on offer. That's no hardship when you can savour modern/neo-classical seducers like a *tarte chaude au crottin de Chavignol tomates au thym l'huile d'olives* (a Provençale & local cheese marriage). Bravo Stéphane Derbord! Well worth the detour.
Menus aBCD. Cards All. (Rooms: St-Christophe, opposite *la gare*.)
Closed 2-8 Jan. 8-16 June. Sun evg. Mon. (Above 2-3 minute-walk away.)
Post 16 r. 14 Juillet, 58200 Cosne-sur-Loire, Nièvre.
Tel 03 86 28 27 50. Mich 71/D4. Map 2. Regions Berry-Bourbonnais/Loire.

COUILLY-PONT-AUX-DAMES

Auberge de la Brie

Comfortable restaurant/Cooking 3 `FW`
Terrace/Gardens/Parking/Air-conditioning

Just N of the village, on D436 Quincy road. A simple house with light green shutters (once an old Brie farmhouse); but Alain Pavard's modern cooking (trained by Meneau) is anything but simple or old-fashioned. Two wizard treats (menu B; ceiling); *cuisse de canard aux pêches rôties, feuillantine de Brie*; & *soupe glacée de rhubarbe aux abricots*.
Menus BD. Cards AE, MC, V. (Rooms: Campanile; A140 S of Meaux.)
Closed Feb sch. hols. 2-27 Aug. Sun evg. Mon. Wed evg. (Above 4-mins N.)
Post 77860 Couilly-Pont-aux-Dames, Seine-et-Marne. Region Ile de France.
Tel 01 64 63 51 80. Fax 01 64 63 51 80. Mich 36/C3. Map 2.

COULON (also see next page)

Au Marais

Comfortable hotel (no restaurant)
Parking

A welcome return to *French Leave* with energetic new owners – Martine & Alain Nervière – & a new breath-of-fresh-air *sans restaurant* formula. Two old houses, in smart blue livery, overlooking the right bank of the Sèvre Niortaise. Martine is a smashing, helpful hostess. One other plus: "mosquito-free" bedrooms. A marvellous base for the Marais Poitevin.
Rooms (18) F. Cards AE, MC, V.
Closed 5-24 Jan.
Post 79510 Coulon, Deux-Sèvres. Region Poitou-Charentes.
Tel 05 49 35 90 43. Fax 05 49 35 81 98. Mich 93/F2. Map 4.

A100frs & under. B100–150. C150–200. D200–250. E250–350. F350–500. G500+

125

COULON (also see previous page)   **Central**

Comfortable restaurant/Cooking 1-2   `FW`
Terrace

The name is spot on; central it is. Anny Monnet is the *cuisinière* at the smart *logis*; husband Jean is the attentive front-of-house boss. Be sure to book ahead if you want to punt with a host of classical/*Bourgeois plats* such as as *daube de joue de boeuf à l'ancienne* & *oeufs à la neige*. Lots of local produce: *mogettes* (small pulse beans) for example.
Menus aC. Cards AE, MC, V. (Rooms: see base hotel above.)
Closed 15 Jan-8 Feb. 22 Sept-8 Oct. Sun evg. Mon.
Post 79510 Coulon, Deux-Sèvres. Region Poitou-Charentes.
Tel 05 49 35 90 20. Fax 05 49 35 81 07. Mich 93/F2. Map 4.

COUR-CHEVERNY   **Trois Marchands**

Comfortable hotel/Cooking 1-2   `FW`
Parking

The Bricault family, from papa to son, have owned the hotel since 1865. Classical cooking from the past, too, with some Sologne flavours: among chef Laurent Lemarchand's *plats* are *fricassée de girolles, cuisse de grenouilles fraîches*, asparagus & chicken breast in a cream sauce, & *rognon de veau entier grillé Béarnaise*. Readers dislike annexe rooms.
Menus bCDE. Rooms (36) CDE. Cards All.
Closed 5 Feb-14 Mar. Mon midday (Easter-June). Mon (Oct-Easter).
Post 41700 Cour-Cheverny, Loir-et-Cher. Region Loire.
Tel 02 54 79 96 44. Fax 02 54 79 25 60. Mich 68/C3. Map 2.

COURLANS   **Auberge de Chavannes**

Very comfortable restaurant/Cooking 3-4
Terrace/Gardens/Parking/Air-conditioning

Taste is all to chef Pierre Carpentier. Modern/classical/neo-classical dishes: luscious *goujonnettes de sole en vinaigrette tiède aux truffes d'été*; & *suprême de poularde de Bresse en rouelles, galette de riz au gras et morille farcie* – a complex construction of contrasting flavours. Monique Carpentier is an elegant, knowledgeable *patronne/sommelière*.
Menus CDE. Cards MC, V. (Rooms: Parenthèse at Chille; 9km NE of town.)
Closed Feb. 24 June-1 July. Sun evg. Mon. (Above easy drive.)
Post 39570 Courlans, Jura. Region Jura. (N78, 6km W of Lons-le-Saunier.)
Tel 03 84 47 05 52. Fax 03 84 43 26 53. Mich 89/D4. Map 3.

A100frs & under. B100–150. C150–200. D200–250. E250–350. F350–500. G500+

COURTENAY

Auberge Clé des Champs

Very comfortable restaurant with rooms/Cooking 3 | FW |
Secluded/Gardens/Parking

A 17thC farm, much modernised & with many rustic touches. Owned by same family for over 200 years. Regional & classical specialities from Marc Delion. On no-choice (first 2 courses) menu C dig into hearty Burgundian fare: *Bourguignon de joue en vinaigrette* & *andouillette à la moutarde ancienne*; delectable desserts (from 7).
Menus ACE. Rooms (7) FG. Disabled. Cards AE, MC, V.
Closed 6-29 Jan. 13-29 Oct. Tues evg. Wed.
Post 45320 Courtenay, Loiret. Region Burgundy. (2km SE; use D32.)
Tel 02 38 97 42 68. Fax 02 38 97 38 10. Mich 55/D4. Map 2.

COUSSAC-BONNEVAL

Voyageurs

Comfortable restaurant with rooms/Cooking 2 | FW |
Gardens/Air-conditioning (restaurant)

The vine-covered *logis* of Henri Robert, an English-speaking chef & great promoter of his beloved *pays*, Limousin, snoozes in the shadow of a 15thC castle – deep in the heart of Richard Coeur de Lion terrain. Henri is a classical/regional crusader: *tournedos Rossini* is typical of the former; Périgord (*confits* & *foies*) & Limousin (*cèpes* & *clafoutis*) do their bit.
Menus aBCD. Rooms (9) D(top-end). Cards MC, V.
Closed Jan. Sun evg & Mon (Oct to Easter).
Post 87500 Coussac-Bonneval, Hte-Vienne. Regions Dord/Poitou-Char.
Tel 05 55 75 20 24. Fax 05 55 75 28 90. Mich 10/B3. Map 5.

COUTANCES

Cositel

Comfortable hotel/Cooking 1
Quiet/Parking

Alongside the D44, 1km W of the cathedral town. Please do not be put off by the name of this *Logis de France*. Claude Holley runs a tight, large ship (54 rooms); modern facilities & panoramic views of the town & cathedral from the restaurant. Not far from town's *piscine*. *Bourgeois* & classical grub & pleasing number of fish specialities. Poste at Marigny (to the W) provides better *RQP* meals: use the Cositel as a base.
Menus ABCD. Rooms (54) EF. Disabled. Cards All.
Post 50200 Coutances, Manche. Region Normandy.
Tel 02 33 07 51 64. Fax 02 33 07 06 23. Mich 30/C2. Map 1.

A100frs & under. B100–150. C150–200. D200–250. E250–350. F350–500. G500+

CRESSERONS
La Valise Gourmande

Very comfortable restaurant/Cooking 2
Terrace/Gardens/Parking

FW

A wisteria-clad, 18thC *maison Bourgeoise*. New *chef/patronne* Linda de Souza continues the good work of her predecessor, Jean-Jacques Hélie. Modern & neo-classical specialities: choose from *clafoutis de moules au jus safrané, tourte d'andouille au beurre de cidre* (regional produce combining to perfection), *pavé de morue* & similar tasty treats.
Menus bCE. Cards MC, V. (Rooms: Novotel & Ibis, by N bypass of Caen.)
Closed Sun evg & Mon (not pub. hols).
Post rte Lion-sur-Mer, 14440 Cresserons, Calvados. Region Normandy.
Tel 02 31 37 39 10. Fax 02 31 37 59 13. Mich 32/B1. Map 2.

CREST
Grand Hôtel

Simple hotel/Cooking 2
Garage

FW

Danielle & René Lattiers' *logis* is 300m or so from the Tour de Crest, a formidable medieval dungeon reckoned to have the highest walls in France. Chef René's cooking is no less formidable with classical & *Bourgeois plats* in each of the multi-choice menus. Step back in time to *terrine de foies, faux filet marchand de vin* & *pêche Melba*.
Menus aBD, Rooms (20) BCDE. Cards MC, V. Closed 22 Dec-22 Jan.
23 Feb-3 Mar. Sun evg (5 Sept-13 June). Mon (not evgs Apl-Oct).
Post 60 r. Hôtel de Ville, 26400 Crest, Drôme. Regions Htes-Alpes/Sav.
Tel 04 75 25 08 17. Fax 04 75 25 46 42. Mich 130/B4. Map 6.

CRISSIER
Girardet

Very comfortable restaurant/Cooking 5
Air-conditioning

If there's a "4-star" restaurant this is it – home of the supreme chef, Frédy Girardet. Innovative modern technique & exemplary good taste. All the culinary arts are on show (inc' the dying skills of carving at table – a feature of both menus). Plus no finer *maître d'hôtel* anywhere, English-speaking Louis Villeneuve. Dear? Yes, thanks to the Swiss fr. *plus fort*.
Menus SF180-195. *àlc* SF100-155. Cards not taken. (Rooms: Novotel/Ibis.)
Closed 1st 3 wks Aug. Xmas-mid Jan. Sun. Mon. (Above mins away to W.)
Post CH 1023 Crissier, Vaud, Switzerland. (Rest. NW Lausanne; E of N1.)
Tel 021 634 05 05. Fax 021 634 24 64. Mich 105/D1. Map 6.

A100frs & under. B100–150. C150–200. D200–250. E250–350. F350–500. G500+

CROIX-MARE

Auberge de la Forge

Comfortable restaurant/Cooking 2
Parking

FW

Don't be put off by the run-down, decrepit exterior. Three immaculate rustic dining rooms (once separate cottages) will cheer you up no end. A mix of styles from Christian Truttmann: *oeufs cocotte crème de haddock, escalope de saumon frais crème de courgettes au curry* & *pièce de boeuf sauce marinade* are a typical filling, flavoursome trio. (Park at rear.)
Menus ABCD. Cards All. (Rooms: Havre at nearby Yvetot to NW.)
Closed Tues evg & Wed (not pub. hols).
Post N15, Croix-Mare, 76190 Yvetot, Saine-Maritime. Region Normandy.
Tel 02 35 91 25 94. Mich 15/F3. Map 2.

CROZANT

Auberge de la Vallée

Comfortable restaurant/Cooking 1-2

FW

I've had mixed reports on the *auberge* (hence the down-rating) – with waitresses dressed in Marchois folk costumes. Françoise Guilleminot & daughter Béatrice are *les patronnes*; & husband Jean turns classical, regional & *Bourgeoises* pages in the kitchen. *Jambon demi sel au porto; aloyau* (sirloin) *Limousin rôti* (famed *terroir* beef); & *magret de canard aux cèpes* (acclaimed Limousin mushrooms) are three examples.
Menus aBD. Cards MC, V. (Rooms: Joly; Dun-le-Palestel; 9km S.)
Closed 2 Jan-2 Feb. Mon evg & Tues (mid Sept-end June).
Post 23160 Crozant, Creuse. Region Poitou-Charentes.
Tel 05 55 89 80 03. Fax 05 55 89 83 22. Mich 97/E2. Map 5.

CUCUGNAN

Auberge de Cucugnan

Simple restaurant/Cooking 1-2
Parking

Climb the stepped lanes to reach the *auberge*, once a barn. The village is within sight of two of the famous Cathar castles. Menu A is not for the diet squeamish: start with a plate of *crudités* or a *charcuterie* assortment; then *coq au vin, lapin au saupiquet* (a Burgundian touch) or *pintadeau en salmis*; vegetables; cheese; dessert. Are you still peckish?
Menus ACD. Cards MC, V. (Rooms: Alta Riba at Rivesaltes to ESE.)
Closed Feb sch. hols. Wed (Jan-Mar). (Above has lift, garage, parking.)
Post 11350 Cucugnan, Aude. Region Languedoc-Roussillon.
Tel 04 68 45 40 84. Fax 04 68 45 01 52. Mich 175/F2. Map 5.

A100frs & under. B100–150. C150–200. D200–250. E250–350. F350–500. G500+

CUISEAUX

Comfortable restaurant with rooms/Cooking 2   `FW`
Swimming pool/Garage/Parking

A stone-built *logis* in an evocative village, bypassed by the very busy N83. Jean & Viviane Vuillot are regional addicts, *naturellement*, but we chose the oh-so-welcome, light *Menu Pêcheur*: a *rosace de langoustines au beurre de safran* (choice of 3 courses); *filet de sandre à l'oseille* (choice of 2); *fromage blanc à la crème*; and strawberry ice-cream.
Menus aBCDE. Rooms (16) CDE. Cards MC, V.
Closed Jan. Sun evg (Oct-May; not pub.hols). Rest: Mon.
Post 71480 Cuiseaux, Saône-et-Loire. Regions Jura/Lyonnais.
Tel 03 85 72 71 79. Fax 03 85 72 54 22. Mich 103/E1. Map 6.

DABISSE

Very comfortable restaurant/Cooking 3   `FW`
Terrace/Parking

Sylvain & Marie Nowak's farm was once a *relais de poste*. A rustic dining room & handsome terrace, shaded by two proud trees. Sylvain is an inventive modern cook, doing a remarkable job in an out-of-the-way spot. Worth a detour for tomatoes stuffed with *ratatouille & chèvre, sauce basilic*; & *pintadeau poêlée aux gousses d'ail en chemise*.
Menus BCDE. Cards All. (Rooms: Villiard, Château-Arnoux – N; see entry.)
Closed 1-8 Jan. Sun evg (not July/Aug). Wed. Regions Htes-Alpes/Prov.
Post Dabisse, 04190 Les Mées, Alpes-de-Haute-Provence. (S of village.)
Tel 04 92 34 32 32. Fax 04 92 34 34 26. Mich 146/A4. Map 6.

DAX (St-Paul-lès-Dax)

Very comfortable restaurant/Cooking 2   `FW`
Terrace/Parking

Old, converted mill beside a lily-ringed *étang*; all-in-all an attractive spot & a swish conversion. Thierry Berthelier's no-choice menu B was regional hearty (other dishes neo-classical): *salade Landaise, confit de canard pommes sautées* & *nougat glacé au miel*. The *àlc* list had a smiler: *hamburger de foie gras mi-cuit façon Mac Dolandes* (sic)! Landes: got it?
Menus BCE. Cards All. (Rooms: Climat de France, 500m S.)
Closed Sun evg. Mon. (Above in fine site overlooking lake.)
Post 40990 St-Paul-lès-Dax, Landes. (NW of Dax.) Region Southwest.
Tel 05 58 91 31 03. Fax 05 58 91 37 97. Mich 149/D2. Map 4.

A100frs & under. B100–150. C150–200. D200–250. E250–350. F350–500. G500+

DAX (St-Paul-lès-Dax)   La Renardière

Comfortable restaurant/Cooking 2   FW
Terrace/Gardens/Parking

Head W from St-Paul-lès-Dax, past all the commercial enterprises & you
will nose out the "fox's earth", on the right near the D16 junc. The
dining rooms have a touch of the country about them. Serge Panzolato,
a neo-classicist/regional chef, provides good choice; one dish, *escalope
de loup grillé au Jurançon moelleux*, was "worth the trip" – heaven.
Menus aBC. Cards All. (Rooms: Campanile; to E; same route Bayonne.)
Closed Sun evg. Wed.
Post 168 av. de la Résistance, 40990 St-Paul-lès-Dax, Landes.
Tel 05 58 91 57 30. Mich 149/D2. Map 4. Region Southwest.

Les DEUX-ALPES   Chalet Mounier

Comfortable hotel/Cooking 2   FW
Terrace/Gardens/Swim pools (indoor & out)/Tennis/Lift/Parking

Add a gym & a heart-stopping view from the "cliff" (some cliff) at the back,
over Venosc/Véneon Valley, to the list. Georgia & Robert Mounier's
chalet is smart & busy; some culinary details need polishing up. Menu C
could include a starter, then spicy *meurson en brioche* (tasty pork
sausage), *filet de flétan à la crème de ciboulette* & a top-notch sweet.
Menus bC. Rooms (48) FG. Cards MC, V.
Closed May. June. Sept-21 Dec.
Post 38860 Les Deux-Alpes, Isère. Regions Hautes-Alpes/Savoie.
Tel 04 76 80 56 90. Fax 04 76 79 56 51. Mich 132/B2. Map 6.

DIE   La Petite Auberge

Comfortable restaurant with rooms/Cooking 1-2   FW
Terrace/Gardens/Parking

Simple, traditional pleasures please: the classical cooking of chef Patrick
Montero (now 47) – *jambonnette de volaille aux cèpes et bolets* &
aiguillette de veau aux morilles à la crème are typical; the warm,
welcoming Maryse, his wife; & proud Dad, Gaston Montero, who still
helps the hardworking duo. Particularly tasty desserts. Well-lit dining room.
Menus aBCD. Rooms (11) E. Cards MC, V. Closed 15 Dec-20 Jan. 22-28 Sept.
Sun evg & Wed (Sept-June). Rest Mon (July/Aug).
Post av. Sadi-Carnot, 26150 Die, Drôme. Regions Hautes-Alpes/Savoie.
Tel 04 75 22 05 91. Fax 04 75 22 24 60. Mich 131/D4. Map 6. (Opp. *gare*.)

A100frs & under. B100–150. C150–200. D200–250. E250–350. F350–500. G500+

DIEULEFIT
Les Hospitaliers

Very comfortable hotel/Cooking 2-3
Secluded/Terrace/Swimming pool/Parking

Part of the restored medieval Vieux Village, high above Poët-Laval, 5km W of Dieulefit. The terrace is an ingenious creation. Yves Morin is the *patron/sommelier*; son Bernard is *le cuisinier*. He paints from a palette of both modern & neo-classical colours: *omble chevalier aux vermicelles craquants baies roses & saveur d'asperge* is one culinary work of art.
Menus C(low-end)DEF. Rooms (24) G,G2(low-end). Cards All.
Closed Feb. Sun evg, Mon, Tues, Wed, Thurs, Sat *midi* (mid Nov-mid Mar).
Post Vieux Village, 26160 Poët-Laval, Drôme. Regions Htes-A/MC(Ardèche).
Tel 04 75 46 22 32. Fax 04 75 46 49 99. Mich 144/C1. Map 6.

DIGNE-LES-BAINS
Mistre

Comfortable hotel/Cooking 2   FW
Garage

In the plane tree-lined bd Gassendi (town centre). Rolland Comte (the 3rd generation owner) demonstrates his devotion to classical ways, to Provence & his terroir. Good choice on menu B offers several appetising dishes: *champignons de pins à la provençale, potage tous sanglier, darne de saumon en bourride & gigot d'agneau rôti au thym* – a tasty quartet.
Menus BCDE. Rooms (19) F. Cards AE, MC, V.
Closed 10-30 Nov. Rest: Sun evg. Mon (not high season).
Post 65 bd Gassendi, 04000 Digne-les-Bains, Alpes-de-Haute-Provence.
Tel 04 92 31 00 16. Mich 146/C4. Map 6. Regions Htes-Alpes/Provence.

DIGNE-LES-BAINS
L'Origan

Comfortable restaurant with basic rooms/Cooking 2   FW
Terrace

Up a small, pedestrian-only side street – 100m NE of the Grand Paris hotel & public car park. The beamed dining room is tiny but is a stylish affair. Classical concoctions from Philippe Cochet with many an alluring Provençal aspect: *mousse de loup à la crème d'ail, fricassée de lapin au basilic & caillette de pays au marc de Provence* all feature on menu A.
Menus ABC. Rooms (9) AB. Cards AE, MC, V.
Closed 18-27 Dec. Sun. Regions Hautes-Alpes/Provence.
Post 6 r. Pied-de-Ville, 04000 Digne-les-Bains, Alpes-de-Haute-Provence.
Tel 04 92 31 62 13. Mich 146/C4. Map 6.

DIGOIN

Diligences et Commerce

Comfortable restaurant with rooms/Cooking 1-2 | FW |
Terrace/Parking

Many readers pressed me to include this long-established *relais*, now rejuvenated by the hands of *chef/patron*, Gilles Soujaeff. Near the Loire's right bank, the D&C has a quieter site than its competitor, the Gare. Classical grub using top-notch produce: witness *filet de Charolais grillé, ravioles aux langoustines* & *nougat glacé au coulis de framboise*. Menus ABDE. Rooms (6) E. Cards All. Region Berry-Bourbonnais. Closed 17-21 June. Mid Nov-mid Dec. Mon evg & Tues (not July/Aug). Post 14 r. Nationale, 71160 Digoin, Saône-et-Loire Tel 03 85 53 06 31. Fax 03 85 88 92 43. Mich 101/D2. Map 5.

DIGOIN

Gare (Jean-Pierre Mathieu)

Comfortable restaurant with rooms/Cooking 2-3 | FW |
Gardens/Parking

Jean-Pierre & Jacqueline Mathieu have won plenty of praise from readers since they took over the controls from the TGV high-flier Billoux, now in Dijon. J-P steams a classical track – with many a bright interlude: *panaché de poissons de mer aux baies roses* & *filet de canard et foie gras poêlé aux myrtilles* are typical specialities. (Some rooms noisy.) Menus BCDE. Rooms (13) E. Cards MC, V. Closed Mid Jan-mid Feb. Wed (not July/Aug). Region Berry-Bourbonnais. Post 79 av. Gén. de Gaulle, 71160 Digoin, Saône-et-Loire. Tel 03 85 53 03 04. Fax 03 85 53 14 70. Mich 101/D2. Map 5.

DINAN (also see next page)

Caravelle

Comfortable restaurant/Cooking 3 | FW |

Bravo Jean-Claude (the chef) & Christiane Marmion; you continue to make many friends with your stunning *RQP* menu B. Consider the evidence: to start perhaps a *lapereau en gelée, crépinette aux herbes, marmalade d'oignons et de primeurs* – a wordy mouthful but intense & colourful; then a *tranche de lieu doré au paprika* – pretty & punchy; cheese; & a sweety finish – *crêpes soufflé aux cerises à la verveine de jardin*. Menus BCDEF. Cards All. (Rooms: easy walk to Le d'Avaugour or Arvor.) Closed 13-20 Mar. 12 Nov-6 Dec. Sun evg & Wed (6 Dec-7 July). Post 14 pl. Duclos, 22100 Dinan, Côtes d'Armor. Region Brittany. Tel 02 96 39 00 11. Mich 29/F3. Map 1.

A100frs & under. B100–150. C150–200. D200–250. E250–350. F350–500. G500+

DINAN (also see previous page)   **Les Grands Fossés**

Very comfortable restaurant/Cooking 2   FW
Parking

The bespectacled duo, Alain Colas & Jacqueline, his charming wife,
opened their *maison Bourgeoise*, opposite the ramparts (NW corner), in
1990. Relish Alain's neo-classical offerings in two handsome dining
rooms: an ace *terrine de ris de veau à l'hydromel*; wholesome *sole
entière poêlee à l'échalote confite*; and a pretty *palette des sorbets*.
Menus aCDE. Cards MC, V. (Rooms: Le d'Avaugour & Arvor in Dinan.)
Closed 27 Jan-3 Feb. Thurs. (Parking is easy for both above hotels.)
Post 2 pl. Gén. Leclerc, 22100 Dinan, Côtes d'Armor. Region Brittany.
Tel 02 96 39 21 50. Mich 29/F3. Map 1.

DINARD   Manoir de la Rance

Comfortable hotel (no restaurant)
Secluded/Gardens/Parking

One of the great *French Leave* base hotels: superlative is an adjective
which can be applied to many of the hotel's charms. An invigorating site
above the left bank of the Rance estuary; delightful gardens – colourful in
spring; handsome bedrooms in a 10thC manor house; & English-speaking
Mme Jasselin, a highly-appreciated *patronne*. All-in-all – a winner.
Rooms (9) FG. Cards MC, V. (4km S of the D168 – the southern bypass.)
Closed Jan. Feb.
Post La Jouvente, 35730 Pleurtuit, Ille-et-Vilaine. Region Brittany.
Tel 02 99 88 53 76. Fax 02 99 88 63 03. Mich 29/F2. Map 1.

DINARD   Reine Hortense

Very comfortable hotel (no restaurant)
Quiet/Parking

Idiosyncratic & luxurious, the *belle époque* hotel was built as a private
villa for the mother of Napoléon III, Queen Hortense. The bedrooms,
with over-the-top decorations, are spacious & airy. The views, across the
Plage de l'Ecluse to the Pointe du Moulinet headland & beyond, are
superb; & don't forget the sea-water pool on the far side of the beach.
Rooms (10) G. Cards All.
Closed 16 Nov-24 Mar.
Post 19 r. Malouine, 35800 Dinard, Ille-et-Vilaine. Region Brittany.
Tel 99 46 54 31. Fax 99 88 15 88. Mich 29/F2. Map 1.

A100frs & under. B100–150. C150–200. D200–250. E250–350. F350–500. G500+

DOL-DE-BRETAGNE

La Bresche Arthur

Comfortable restaurant with rooms/Cooking 2   FW
Gardens/Parking

Philippe Martel's refurbished *logis* (fire damaged shortly after he bought
the "breach") is much liked by readers. Revitalised, pick-me-up, modern
fare leaves Cognac-clear memories (he's well named): *carpaccio de
saumon à la vinaigrette de concombre, escalopes de barbue en vapeur
d'algues et petits oignons nouveaux* & *crème brûlée à la vanille.*
Menus ABC. Rooms (24) CDE. Cards MC, V.
Closed Feb. Sun evg & Mon (Oct-June). Region Brittany.
Post 36 bd Deminiac, 35120 Dol-de-Bretagne, Ille-et-Vilaine.
Tel 02 99 48 01 44. Fax 02 99 48 16 32. Mich 48/B1. Map 1.

DOL-DE-BRETAGNE

v. good

Bretagne

Comfortable hotel/Cooking 1
Terrace

Catherine & Patrick Haelling-Morel's whitewashed *logis*, recently and
expensively renovated, is a dependable provider: a family atmosphere
where kiddies are welcome; *Bourgeoise*/classical/*Bretons plats*, cooked
by Catherine; & modest prices. Dour for some but not for us over the 30
years we've known it. Sundays: *gigot d'agneau de prés salés.*
Menus ABC. Rooms (27) BCDE. Cards DC, MC, V. (Park in *place* opp.)
Closed Feb sch. hols. Oct. Sat (Nov-Easter). Region Brittany.
Post pl. Châteaubriand, 35120 Dol-de-Bretagne, Ille-et-Vilaine.
Tel 02 99 48 02 03. Fax 02 99 48 25 75. Mich 48/B1. Map 1.

DOMPIERRE-SUR-VEYLE

Aubert

Very simple restaurant with very basic rooms/Cooking 1-2   FW
Gardens

Down-to-earth in every sense. Joëlle Subtil keeps her repertoire basic
with few subtle frills. *Bourgeoise*, classical & *Bressane* grub – *cuisine
terroir* at its most evocative: *grenouilles fines herbes, terrine de carpe,
soufflé de brochet, poulet à la crème, vacherin praliné, fromage blanc
(à la crème)* & *omelette Norvégienne.* A weight-watcher's nightmare.
Menus bCD. Rooms (2) B(low-end). Cards MC, V. (Other rooms: Montluel)
Closed 7 Feb-8 Mar. 17-27 July. Sun evg. Wed evg. Thurs. (& Bourg-en-B.)
Post 01240 Dompierre-sur-Veyle, Ain. Region Lyonnais. (See entries.)
Tel 04 74 30 31 19. Fax 04 74 30 36 98. Mich 103/D4. Map 6.

A 100frs & under. B 100–150. C 150–200. D 200–250. E 250–350. F 350–500. G 500+

DOUE-LA-FONTAINE

Auberge Bienvenue

Comfortable restaurant/Cooking 2
Terrace/Parking

The spanking new building, with colourful terrace & intimate dining room, is easily found: opp. the zoo, near the W end of the D960 bypass. Marie-Line & Michel Roche have a winning formula – plenty of choice & a classical/*Bourgeois* repertoire: *terrine de pigeonneau, aile de raie rôti, noisettes d'agneau rôti & quenelles au chocolat noir et blanc.*
Menus ABCDE. Cards MC, V. (Rooms: Splendid, Montreuil-Bellay.)
Closed Feb sch. hols. Sun evg (not July/Aug). Mon. (Above easy drive.)
Post rte Cholet, 49700 Doué-la-Fontaine, Maine-et-Loire. Region Loire.
Tel 02 41 59 22 44. Fax 02 41 59 93 49. Mich 81/D1. Map 2.

DOURLERS

Auberge du Châtelet

Very comfortable restaurant/Cooking 2
Gardens/Parking

Pierre Carlier, a genial, English-speaking host, welcomes you to his neo-rustic *auberge* – beside the N2, N of Avesnes. His son, François, prepares the specialities for the classical/neo-classical menus. One appetite buster: *La Marmite Yolande* (with fish & vegetables) – in memory of Pierre's *cuisinière* wife who died in 1990. Good-choice *cave*.
Menus b(ceiling)DEF. Cards All. (Rooms: see Fourmies & Sars-Poteries.)
Closed 2-8 Jan. 15 Aug-6 Sept. Sun evg. Pub. hols evgs.
Post Dourlers, 59440 Avesnes-sur-Helpe, Nord. Regions Champ-Ard/North.
Tel 03 27 61 06 70. Fax 03 27 61 20 02. Mich 10/A2. Map 3.

DUCEY

Auberge de la Sélune

Comfortable hotel/Cooking 1-2
Gardens

The small, weed-choked gardens have a view of the Sélune, a famed salmon river. Chef Jean-Pierre Girres & his wife Josette offer classical catches such as *terrine d'aubergines, paupiettes de saumon, pie au crabe* (soup with a pastry topper), *truite soufflée à la ducéene* and, alas, a comatose *tarte aux pommes*. Extensive refurbishments/improvements 1995.
Menus aBC. Rooms (20) E. Cards All.
Closed Mid Jan-mid Feb. Mon (Oct-Feb).
Post 50220 Ducey, Manche. Regions Brittany/Normandy.
Tel 02 33 48 53 62. Fax 02 33 48 90 30. Mich 30/C4. Map 1.

A100frs & under. B100–150. C150–200. D200–250. E250–350. F350–500. G500+

DUCEY

Comfortable hotel (no restaurant)
Quiet/Lift/Parking

Henri-Jacques Dewitte's transformation of the large 16thC mill, beside the River Sélune, has been remarkably well done. His father was once the miller at the *moulin*, before fire destroyed the watermill in 1985. *"Les pieds dans l'eau"* is literally true; try to ensure you do not have rooms by the noisy mill race. Bedrooms have all mod-cons & some bedrooms are fitted out for the disabled (note the lift). Ideally placed for touring.
Rooms (28) EF. Disabled. Cards All.
Post 50220 Ducey, Manche. Regions Brittany/Normandy.
Tel 02 33 60 25 25. Fax 02 33 60 26 76. Mich 30/C4. Map 1.

DUCLAIR

Poste

Simple hotel/Cooking 2
Lift

FW

A busy site beside the Seine. The restaurant is on the first floor & the bustling river traffic & ferry ensure there's never a dull visual moment. Eric Montier does the same with his classical dishes: *terrine de canard au porto, filet de lotte sauce Nantua, fromage blanc* & a *tarte Normande* makes a great lunch. A long-established family hotel.
Menus aBCD. (Grill: aBC.) Rooms (16) DE. Cards All.
Closed Sch. hols Feb & Nov. 1-14 July. Sun eg (not pub. hols). Rest: Mo.
Post 76480 Duclair, Seine-Maritime. Region Normandy.
Tel 02 35 37 50 04. Fax 02 35 37 39 19. Mich 15/F3. Map 2.

DUINGT

Lac

Comfortable hotel/Cooking 2
Terrace/Gardens/Lake swimming/Lift/Parking

FW

A seductive setting, W of the château: gorgeous views & the restaurant's toes literally in Lac d'Annecy. Thierry & Anne Borsoi are rightly proud of their tonic hotel. Chef Marc Catellani treads water in the modern cooking pool: delight in exuberant catches like *bisquit de truite rose au curry* & *carpaccio de volaille en marinière de sauce vierge.*
Menus BCD. Rooms (23) F. Cards MC, V.
Closed Hôtel: Nov-Easter. Sun evg & Mon (out of season). Rest: Oct-Apl.
Post 74410 Duingt, Haute-Savoie. Region Savoie.
Tel 04 50 68 90 90. Fax 04 50 68 50 18. Mich 118/B1. Map 6.

A 100frs & under. B 100–150. C 150–200. D 200–250. E 250–350. F 350–500. G 500+

DUNKERQUE

Le Soubise

Very comfortable restaurant/Cooking 2-3
Gardens/Parking

Well clear of Dunkerque, at Couderkerque-Branche, S of A16 (exit 31) & on W side of D916. Don't be put off by the scruffy frontage. Michel Hazebroucq is a creative classicist. His *saumon et canard* menu C has six starters & seven main courses. How about *carpaccio de canard, cotelletes de saumon grillées Béarnaise* & a *chocolat/nougat* dessert?
Menus ABC. Cards All. (Rooms: Campanile/Mercure; Lac d'Armbouts-Cappel.)
Closed Sat midday. Sun evg. (Both above hotels 4km to W – near N225.)
Post 49 rte Bergues, 59210 Coudekerque-Branche, Nord. Region North.
Tel 03 28 64 66 00. Fax 03 28 25 12 19. Mich 3/D1. Map 2.

DUNKERQUE (Téteghem)

La Meunerie

Very comfortable restaurant with rooms/Cooking 3-4
Quiet/Gardens/Garage/Parking/Air-conditioning (restaurant)

Marie-France Delbé, helped by her pretty, English-speaking daughter Laurence, battles on in tough times. No shortcuts: in the flowers, always a delight; in the impeccable furnishings; & in the immaculate neo-classical *plats* from Alain Gellé (trained by the late Jean-Pierre). 3-star sweets (14 on trolley) & Philippe Olivier cheeses. Super bedrooms.
Menus EF. Rooms (10) G. Cards AE, MC, V.
Closed 20 Dec-17 Jan. Sun evg & Mon. Region North.
Post 59229 Téteghem, Nord. (D4, two miles S of A16 exit 34.)
Tel 03 28 26 14 30. Fax 03 28 26 17 32. Mich 3/D1. Map 2.

DUN-LE-PALESTEL

Joly

Simple hotel/Cooking 1-2

FW

The Creuse is ideal walking/cycling *pays*. No wonder then that Claude Monceaux is happy to welcome walkers & cyclists to his *logis*; he's well equipped to give you sound advice. Step back in time: to Jacqueline's (a touch too formal) dining room; & to her husband's classical fare (little details need watching Claude). *A faux-filet de Limousin mousseline de cèpes* is a local *terroir* joy. Also a welcome *Special Poissons Menu*.
Menus ABCD. Rooms (27) DE. Disabled. Cards MC, V.
Closed 1-20 Mar. 4-24 Oct. Sun evg. Mon midday.
Post 23800 Dun-le-Palestel, Creuse. Region Poitou-Charentes.
Tel 05 55 89 00 23. Fax 05 55 89 15 89. Mich 97/E3. Map 5.

A100frs & under. B100–150. C150–200. D200–250. E250–350. F350–500. G500+

DURBAN-CORBIERES   Le Moulin

Very comfortable restaurant/Cooking 3-4
Parking/Air-conditioning

What a stunning show. All the staff, led by Corinne Moreno, speak English. A "Foreign Legion" fort! Semi-circular *salle* with panoramic windows. Chef David Moreno, a Spaniard, lives & breathes good taste. Menu C could be *tarte fine de tomate et anchois*, clearcut simpicity; a fish creation; a choice of 40 cheeses; & a sumptuous *crème brûlée*.
Menus CDE. Cards MC, V. (Rooms: hotels A9/A61 junc. S Narbonne.)
Closed 15 Jan-end Feb. Sun evg & Mon (out of season). Mon *midi* (season).
Post 11360 Durban-Corbières, Aude. Region Languedoc-Roussillon.
Tel 04 68 45 81 03. Fax 04 68 45 83 31. Mich 172/C3. Map 5.

DURY   La Bonne Auberge

Comfortable restaurant/Cooking 2   `FW`
Parking

A retina-searing, flower-covered exterior with a touch forced rustic interior. Nowt forced or prissy about Raoul Beaussire's regional & classical juggling. Menu B has a good range of choice: a typical meal could start with *ficelles Picardes*, move on to a *pintade crème de champignon* & finish with a copious *fruits de jour Melba*.
Menus aBCE. Cards AE, MC, V. (Rooms: Novotel to E; N of Boves.)
Closed Sun evg & Mon (not pub. hols). (Above near junc. N29/D934.)
Post 63 rte Nationale, 80480 Dury, Somme. Region Normandy.
Tel 03 22 95 03 33. Fax 03 22 45 37 38. Mich 17/F1. Map 2.

Les ECHETS   Marguin

Very comfortable restaurant with rooms/Cooking 2-3   `FW`
Terrace/Gardens/Garage/Parking

Busy N83 roadside site, close to A46 Les Echets exit. Years ago I knew *les patrons*, Jacques & Adrienne Marguin. Now their young son Christophe (the first non-Parisian to win *Prix Prosper Montagne*) & his likeable wife, Niçole, run the show. Regional/neo-classical grub. Typical menu a *plats*: *gâteau de ratatouille de légumes d'été* & *quenelles de brochet*.
Menus aBCE. Rooms (8) DE. Cards All.
Closed 24 Dec-3 Jan. 1st 3 wks Aug.
Post 01700 Les Echets, Ain. Region Lyonnais.
Tel 04 78 91 80 04. Fax 04 78 91 06 83. Mich 116/B1. Map 6.

A100frs & under. B100–150. C150–200. D200–250. E250–350. F350–500. G500+

ECHIGEY

Comfortable restaurant with basic rooms/Cooking 1-2
Gardens/Closed parking

 FW

A quiet village, SE of Dijon. The *logis* is well-appointed and has basic but entirely adequate bedrooms. Chef Dany Rey provides a good choice for each menu course. Nothing flashy with specialities such as shrimp & avocado cocktail; gutsy *pièce de boeuf*, touch spoiled by veg overpowered with nutmeg; top-notch cheese chariot; & dessert trolley. All on menu a.
Menus aBCD. Rooms (13) BCD(low-end). Cards All.
Closed Jan. 3-11 Aug. Sun evg & Mon (not pub. hols).
Post Echigey, 21110 Genlis, Côte-d'Or. Region Burgundy.
Tel 03 80 29 74 00. Fax 03 80 29 79 55. Mich 88/C1. Map 3.

Les ECRENNES

Auberge Briarde

Comfortable restaurant/Cooking 3
Terrace

FW

Jean & Monique Guichard left their Velay *pays* (the area around Le Puy) & set up their new rustic home in Brie terrain at the start of the 90s. Nothing 90s about his cooking – consummate classical with Velay touches: Le Puy lentils & Verveine du Velay (see Auvergne notes) are just two. Saliva-stirring *plats: filet de boeuf grillé Béarnaise* & *turbot au Champagne.*
Menus bcEF. Cards All. (Rooms: Ibis; beside N105, N of Melun.)
Closed 1-20 Aug. Sun evg & Mon (not pub. hols). Region Ile de France.
Post 77820 Les Ecrennes, Seine-et-Marne. (D213, E Le Châtelet-en-Brie.)
Tel 01 60 69 47 32. Fax 01 60 66 60 11. Mich 54/C1. Map 2.

EGUISHEIM

Caveau d'Eguisheim

Comfortable restaurant/Cooking 2-3

FW

Many changes at the historic *caveau* since *FLE*. The flower-bedecked inn, at the very heart of honeypot Eguisheim, remains the same: the new owner is the Societé de Propagande des Vins d'Eguisheim; their chef is Olivier Nasti. Nothing nasty or pretty about his regional/neo-classical dishes: *tarte à l'oignon, choucroute comme au temps du Pape* & *baeckaoffa (sur commande)*; & a so-so-welcome, *melting sandre rôti et cuit à la vapeur.*
Menus BEF. Cards All. (Rooms: see many Alsace base hotels, *sans rest.*)
Closed Jan. Feb. Wed.
Post 3 pl. Château St-Léon, 68420 Eguisheim. Haut-Rhin. Region Alsace.
Tel 03 89 41 08 89. Fax 03 89 23 79 99. Mich 61/D3. Map 3.

A100frs & under. B100–150. C150–200. D200–250. E250–350. F350–500. G500+

EGUISHEIM

La Grangelière

Comfortable restaurant/Cooking 3   `FW`

Eguisheim is a 4-star *village fleuri*; the medieval half-timbered, peach-washed, blue-shuttered, geranium window-boxed restaurant does its best to match the flower rating. In an elegant first-floor *salle* enjoy Karine Finkbeiner's welcome & husband Alain's modern, neo-classical & regional delights: no-choice menu B (with wine) seduced with *gâteau de lapereau aux lentilles vertes de Puy* & *jambonnette de volaille à la moutarde*.
Menus BCF. Cards MC, V. (Rooms: see Alsace base hotels, *sans rest*.)
Closed Feb. Thurs (not high season). (Restaurant on W edge of village.)
Post 59 r. Rempart Sud, 68420 Eguisheim, Haut-Rhin. Region Alsace.
Tel 03 89 23 00 30. Fax 03 89 23 61 62. Mich 61/D3. Map 3.

ELOISE

Le Fartoret

Comfortable hotel/Cooking 1-2   `FW`
Secluded/Terrace/Gardens/Swimming pool/Tennis/Lift/Parking

The family Gassiloud's Fartoret (*logis*) is quite a business complex. 40 bedrooms mean the place gets too busy at times; when full service & cooking suffer. However, the dead-end village road ensures peace; there's plenty of walking; extensive views; A40 (exit 11) is close; & classical cuisine, just squeaking a FW rating, is of the *filet de canard sauce Madère* & *escalope de truite de mer crème d'épinard* variety.
Menus bCDE. Rooms (40) EF. Cards All. Region Savoie.
Post Eloise, 01200 Bellegarde-sur-Valserine, Ain. (5km SE of town.)
Tel 04 50 48 07 18. Fax 04 50 48 23 85. Mich 104/A4. Map 6.

EMBRUN

Mairie

Simple hotel/Cooking 1-2   `FW`
Terrace/Air-conditioning (restaurant)

Chantal & Jean-Pierre François' *logis* is at the heart of Embrun, opp. the Fontaine St-Pierre (follow signs for Centre Ville/Hôtel de Ville). Chef J-P is from the Southwest, hence his fondness for *foie gras de canard* & *magret de canard fumé*. Menus provide great *RQP* with a good choice (extra for *foie gras naturellement*). Classical/*Bourgeoise* grub.
Menus aB. Rooms (22) DE(low-end). Cards All.
Closed 1st 3 wks May. Oct. Nov. Sun evg & Mon (not sch. hols).
Post pl. Mairie, 05200 Embrun, Hautes-Alpes. Regions Htes-Alpes/Savoie.
Tel 04 92 43 20 65. Fax 04 92 43 47 02. Mich 147/D1. Map 6.

A 100frs & under. B 100–150. C 150–200. D 200–250. E 250–350. F 350–500. G 500+

ENCAUSSE-LES-THERMES

Marronniers

Comfortable restaurant with basic rooms/Cooking 1-2
Quiet/Terrace/Gardens/Parking

The well-named Marronniers sits snugly beside the Job with a chestnut-shaded terrace between the building & river. Equally unspoilt as the setting are *les patrons* – Michel, the chef, & his English-speaking wife Christiane. Warm, friendly welcome assured. Classical/regional fare: *cassoulet Commingeois* (local *pays*) & *gâteau des Prélats* are typical.
Menus aBC. Rooms (10) BC. Cards MC, V. (S of St-Gaudens.)
Closed Sun evg & Mon (out of season). Rooms: mid Nov-Mar. Rest: Jan.
Post 31160 Encausse-les-Thermes, Haute-Garonne. Region Southwest.
Tel 05 61 89 17 12. Mich 169/F2. Map 5.

L'EPINE

Aux Armes de Champagne

Very comfortable hotel/Cooking 3-4 **FW**
Gardens/Tennis/Parking

Jean-Paul & Denise Pérardel continue to refurbish the much-loved family hotel, across the road from the flamboyant Gothic basilica. J-P doesn't miss a thing. Patrick Michelon is a 90s chef: witness his irresistible *ambroisie chaude de turbot sur un velouté de crustaces*. Exceptional service (as one reader so dramatically witnessed). Wine cellar & shop.
Menus b(lunch)D(low-end)EF. Rooms (37) FG. Cards AE, MC, V.
Closed 5 Jan-11 Feb. Sun evg & Mon (Nov-Mar).
Post 51460 L'Epine, Marne. Region Champagne-Ardenne.
Tel 03 26 69 30 30. Fax 03 26 66 92 31. Mich 38/C2. Map 3.

ERMENONVILLE

Le Prieuré

Comfortable hotel (no restaurant)
Gardens/Closed parking

"Quiet" is not listed above but don't be put off. This is a jewel of a base hotel, slumbering contentedly in the shadow of the church. The furnishings may be old-style but the bedrooms have all mod-cons, inc' mini-bar. The most pleasing aspects are Jean-Pierre & Marie-José Treillou's 18thC vine-covered *maison Bourgeoise* & *jardin anglais*.
Rooms (11) FG. Cards All.
Closed Feb.
Post 60950 Ermenonville, Oise. Region Ile de France.
Tel 03 44 54 00 44. Fax 03 44 54 02 21. Mich 36/B2. Map 2.

A 100frs & under. B 100–150. C 150–200. D 200–250. E 250–350. F 350–500. G 500+

ERNEE

Grand Cerf

Comfortable restaurant with rooms/Cooking 1-2 | FW |

The *Logis de France* sits beside the N12. Ask for a rear *chambre au calme* (relatively). Public parking is also at the back – plus the town's tennis courts & swimming pool. On Ascension Day (lunch) the place was packed to the rafters. Noëlle Sémerie, *la patronne*, kept her cool. So did her chef/husband Yves (an expert *chocolatier*). Menu C ("*tradition*") was adequate classical: highlight a *tête de veau sauce ravigote*.
Menus BC. Rooms (8) CD. Cards AE, MC, V.
Closed 15-31 Jan. Sun evg & Mon (out of season).
Post 19 r. A.-Briand, 53500 Ernée, Maynne. Region Normandy.
Tel 02 43 05 13 09. Fax 02 43 05 02 90. Mich 49/E2-F2. Map 1.

ERQUY

L'Escurial

Very comfortable restaurant/Cooking 2-3 | FW |

Views of the bay from the elevated dining room; enjoy the hang gliders too. More excitement comes in the shape of Véronique Bernard's mix of modern & neo-classical melodies. Limited choice but that's no hardship on menu B: *aumonière de pétoncles et fruits de mer; magret de canard aigre doux; profiterolles de fromage chaud*; &, from 8 sweets, a flamboyant *omelette Norvégienne au Grand Marnier*. Beats hang-gliding!
Menus ABC. Cards MC, V. (Rooms: Beauséjour, Erquy.)
Closed Feb sch. hols. 9-15 June. 6-20 Oct. Sun evg & Mon (not July/Aug).
Post bd Mer, 22430 Erquy, Côtes d'Armor. Region Brittany.
Tel 02 96 72 31 56. Fax 02 96 63 57 92. Mich 19/E2. Map 1.

ESPALION (also see next page)

Le Méjane

Comfortable restaurant/Cooking 3-4 | FW |
Air-conditioning

The cooking rating gives the clue to how impressed we were at this most beguiling of FW entries. A young couple going places: Régine Caralp, a vibrant, vivacious hostess; and husband Philippe, a confident, modern master with an eye for technique, presentation & good taste. One superb showpiece: a *jambonnette de pintade rôtie, jus reduit au vin rouge*.
Menus BCDE. Cards All. (Rooms: Moderne; or simpler Central, 20m away.)
Closed Feb sch. hols. 23-25 June. Sun evg & Wed (not Aug).
Post r. Méjane, 12500 Espalion, Aveyron. Region MC (Auvergne/Cévennes).
Tel 05 65 48 22 37. Mich 140/C1. Map 5. (Rest. S of River Lot, E D920.)

A100frs & under. B100–150. C150–200. D200–250. E250–350. F350–500. G500+

ESPALION (also see previous page) Moderne/Rest. L'Eau Vive

Comfortable hotel/Cooking 1-2 FW
Lift/Air-conditioning (restaurant)

An oldish building (some rooms modernised) at the junc. of D921/D920,
N of the Lot. The family Raulhac pride themselves on their freshwater fish
dishes (hence the rest. name): *truite de meunière aux lardons & citrons
verts* was the sole (!) offering on menu B. Otherwise good choice with
mainly classical *plats*: like *pièce de boeuf grillée sauce au Roquefort*.
Menus aBCDE. Rooms (28) E. Disabled. Cards MC, V.
Closed 1-15 Jan. 15 Nov-5 Dec. Sun evg. Rest: Mon.
Post bd Guizard, 12500 Espalion, Aveyron. Regs MC (Auvergne/Cévennes).
Tel 05 65 44 05 11. Fax 05 65 48 06 94. Mich 140/C1. Map 5.

ESPELETTE Euzkadi

Simple hotel/Cooking 2-3 FW
Gardens/Swimming pool/Tennis/Parking

The Basque village is famed for red peppers (*FLE* p402). The vine-covered
Basque house hides many a colourful, tasty treat: in the shape of the
amenities above; in the form of owners Michèle & André Darraïdou; & the
latter's exciting Basque/classical cooking – *ttora* (*soupe de poissons*) &
axoa d'Espelette (*viande de veau & peppers*) are 2 of numerous delights.
Menus ABC. Rooms (32) DE. Disabled. Cards MC, V.
Closed 5 Nov-15 Dec. Mon. Tues (not high season).
Post 64250 Espelette, Pyrénées-Atlantiques. Region Southwest.
Tel 05 59 93 91 88. Fax 05 59 93 90 19. Mich 148/B4. Map 4.

ETANG-SUR-ARROUX Hostellerie du Gourmet

Comfortable restaurant with basic rooms/Cooking 1-2 FW

The geranium-edged frontage is a bright & welcome sight at the Caboche
hostellerie on the southern main road entrance to the village (D994).
Copious & anything but dull could describe a lunch (menu B) of *salade
de noix de pétoncles au vinaigre de framboise*; followed by, first, a *filet
de julienne sauce crustacé* &, next, a *contrefilet vigneronne*; then
fromage; & to finish, a large slice of so-so only *tarte aux pommes*.
Menus aBCD. Rooms (12) C(bottom-end)D. Cards MC, V.
Closed Jan. Sun evg & Mon (not July/Aug).
Post 71190 Etang-sur-Arroux, Saône-et-Loire. Region Burgundy.
Tel 03 85 82 20 88. Mich 87/D3-E3. Map 3.

A100frs & under. B100–150. C150–200. D200–250. E250–350. F350–500. G500+

ETOUY

L'Orée de la Forêt

Very comfortable restaurant with rooms/Cooking 2-3   `FW`
Secluded/Gardens/Closed parking

On S side of village: follow old sign for Gare d'Etouy. An unattractive house, redeemed by a tranquil site & a large park. Some of the classical & neo-classical offerings from chef Nicolas Leclercq disappointed; witness the toughish *pigeon fermier rôti*. For those of you with an ultra sweet tooth, several voluptuous "choc" desserts. Bedrooms a touch basic.
Menus aCDEF. Rooms (4) BCD(low-end). Cards MC, V.
Closed Mid Aug-mid Sept. Fri. Sun evg. Evgs pub. hols.
Post 60600 Etouy, Oise. Regions Ile de France/North. (7km NW Clermont.)
Tel 03 44 51 65 18. Fax 03 44 78 92 11. Mich 18/A4. Map 2.

EUGÉNIE-LES-BAINS

La Ferme aux Grives

Simple restaurant/Cooking 2-3
Gardens/Parking

Enterprise 4 in the growing *"Village Minceur"* Eugénie empire of 3-star chef Michel Guérard. Striking rustic conversion & *la cuisine rustique* – local produce & old recipes. Vast choice: a suckling pig turning on the spit in the fireplace, superb soups, Landes *terrines*, black puddings, *cochon de lait*, roast duck, *méringues* & *tartes*. First-class service.
Menus C. Cards, MC, V. (Rooms: Maison Rose; & see Aire-s-l'Adour entry.)
Closed 3 Jan-8 Feb. Mon evg & Tues (10 Sept-10 July; not pub. hols).
Post 40320 Eugénie-les-Bains, Landes. Region Southwest.
Tel 05 58 51 19 08. Fax 05 58 51 10 10. Mich 150/A2. Map 4.

EVIAN-LES-BAINS

Bourgogne

Comfortable hotel/Cooking 2   `FW`
Lift

Welcome reappearance for the family hotel, in new maroon & cream livery, at the spa's heart & 200m from Lac Léman. Natalie Riga is a pleasant, English-speaking hostess; her chef husband, Christophe, is an out-&-out classicist. Old-time favourites abound: *filet de boeuf Rossini, ris de veau braisé au porto* & glorious *omble chevalier beurre citronné*. Gym.
Menus bCDE. (Also brasserie A; rating 1-2). Rooms (31) FG. Cards All.
Closed Nov-mid Dec. Rest: Sun evg. Mon. (Parking 100m N & W.)
Post pl. Charles Cottet, 74500 Evian-les-Bains, Hte-Savoie. Reg. Savoie.
Tel 04 50 75 01 05. Fax 04 50 75 04 05. Mich 105/D2. Map 6.

A100frs & under. B100–150. C150–200. D200–250. E250–350. F350–500. G500+

EVREUX

Very comfortable restaurant with rooms/Cooking 2-3   FW
Gardens/Parking

Almost not included as Evreux is busy. A refurbished *logis* with a tiny arm of the River Iton at the rear; *patron* Bernard Meyruey has nous; & a great menu price formula (dishes chosen from *àlc* list) persuaded me to include the France. Modern/classical/neo-classical *plats*: *compote de lapin au cidre* & *soufflé de poire à la Williamine* are typical treats.
Menus BC. Rooms (15) E. Cards All. (500m N cathedral; quietish street.)
Closed Rest: Sun evg. Mon.
Post 29 r. St-Thomas, 27000 Evreux, Eure. Region Normandy.
Tel 02 32 39 09 25. Fax 02 32 38 38 56. Mich 34/B2. Map 2.

EVRON (Mézangers)   Relais du Gué de Selle

Comfortable hotel/Cooking 2   FW
Quiet/Terrace/Gardens/Swimming pool/Parking

A restored stone farm with modern amenities & the most seductive of terraces/gardens at the rear – backing on to the tranquil Gué de Selle (pool). Neo-classical sums up the cooking – with many personal touches. Normandy specialities too on *Menu Terroir* (B). Didier Paris & Didier Peschard, the chef, have a real winner on their hands. Gym.
Menus BCDE. Rooms (25) EF. Disabled. Cards All. (7km NW of Evron.)
Closed 15 Feb-3 Mar. 23 Dec-8 Mar. Sun evg & Mon (Oct-Apl).
Post Mézangers, 53600 Evron, Mayenne. Region Normandy.
Tel 02 43 90 64 05. Fax 02 43 90 60 82. Mich 50/B3. Map 2.

Les EYZIES-DE-TAYAC

Comfortable hotel/Cooking 2   FW
Terrace

Still the odd grumble about Gérard & Claudine Brun's well-named hotel. A cool, shady terrace – both at lunchtime or, better still, on balmy summer evenings when trees, fountain, river & floodlights seduce. Always busy; service can be so slow & the mechanics of ordering/serving wine are almost non-existent. Food is liked – regional/classical/*Bourgeoise*.
Menus BCDE. Rooms (20) E. Cards MC, V.
Closed Mid Nov-Mar.
Post 24620 Les Eyzies-de-Tayac, Dordogne. Region Dordogne.
Tel 05 53 06 97 13. Fax 05 53 06 91 63. Mich 123/F3. Map 5.

A 100frs & under. B 100–150. C 150–200. D 200–250. E 250–350. F 350–500. G 500+

Les EYZIES-DE-TAYAC

Cro-Magnon

Very comfortable hotel/Cooking 2-3
Terrace/Gardens/Swimming pool/Parking

FW

Anne & I have loved the vine-covered hotel & the genuine, caring owners, Jacques & Christiane Leyssales for almost 40 years. They want to retire & are trying to sell. When they go do still visit. The same chef entices with this typical menu B: subtle *morue fraîche à l'anchoïade; fricassée de pintadeau aux Xèrés*; strawberries & cream. Cool vine-covered terrace.
Menus BCEF. Rooms (18) F(bottom-end)G. Cards All.
Closed 8 Oct-end Apl. Rest: Wed midday.
Post 24620 Les Eyzies-de-Tayac, Dordogne. Region Dordogne.
Tel 05 53 06 97 06. Fax 05 53 06 95 45. Mich 123/F3. Map 5.

Les EYZIES-DE-TAYAC

Moulin de la Beune

Comfortable hotel/Cooking 2-3
Quiet/Terrace/Gardens/Parking

FW

What a happy marriage – of two mills, one built in 1880 & converted into a beguiling hotel 15 years ago (airy modern bedrooms), the other, once a walnut-oil *moulin*, the adjoining rest. of Georges & Annick Soulé. His cooking covers all styles; presentation is especially commendable. The River Beune's "streamlets" give the *moulin* an extra seductive appeal.
Menus BCDE. Rooms (20) E. Cards AE, MC, V.
Closed Hotel: Nov-Mar. Rest: 3 Jan-15 Feb. Tues midday.
Post 24620 Les Eyzies-de-Tayac, Dordogne. Region Dordogne.
Tel 05 53 06 94 33. Fax 05 53 06 98 06. Mich 123/F3. Map 5.

Les EYZIES-DE-TAYAC

Les Roches

Comfortable hotel (no restaurant)
Gardens/Swimming pool/Parking

Jean-Luc Bousquet's new *logis* has been a welcome *sans restaurant* addition to Les Eyzies' many hotels. Alongside the D47 road to Sarlat the largish hotel (41 bedrooms) has particularly attractive gardens – with the added benefits of a shady terrace & a small stream. A fairly quiet site, not too close to the not-too-busy D47 (at night).
Rooms (41) EF(bottom-end). Disabled. Cards MC, V.
Closed Mid Oct-Easter.
Post rte Sarlat, 24620 Les Eyzies-de-Tayac, Dordogne. Region Dordogne.
Tel 05 53 06 96 59. Fax 05 53 06 95 54. Mich 123/F3. Map 5.

A100frs & under. B100–150. C150–200. D200–250. E250–350. F350–500. G500+

EZE

Simple hotel/Cooking 1
Swimming pool/Parking

A small *logis*, high above Eze & off the Grande Corniche (D2564). (Use the D46 from Eze to the Col d'Eze.) Exhilarating views. Chef Gaspard Berardi plays it safe with down to earth basics. Classical (he's an Escoffier disciple)/*Bourgeoise*/regional cooking (& grills) in a rustic, check table-cloth *salle: carré d'agneau à la Provencale* is typical.
Menus aBC. Rooms (14) CDE. Cards AE, MC, V.
Closed Hotel: mid Dec-mid Jan. Rest: mid Oct-mid Feb. Mon. Thurs midday.
Post 06360 Eze (Gde Corniche), Alpes-Maritimes. Region Côte d'Azur.
Tel 04 93 41 00 68. Fax 04 93 41 00 68. Mich 165/E3. Map 6.

FALAISE

Poste

Comfortable hotel/Cooking 1-2
Parking

FW

The only debit is the main road (though now there is a western bypass). The rest are credits: an informative *patronne*, Simone Collias, is a pleaser; as is her judo-loving husband Michel's classical repertoire. (He's also a pilot; take an aerial tour.) Limited choice: *tête de veau ravigote* & *entrecôte grillée sauce moelle* are 2 representative dishes.
Menus aBCD(top-end). Rooms (21) DEF. Cards AE, MC, V.
Closed 15-22 Oct. 20 Dec-15 Jan. Sun evg. Rest: Mon.
Post 38 r. G. Clemenceau, 14700 Falaise, Calvados. Region Normandy.
Tel 02 31 90 13 14. Fax 02 31 90 01 81. Mich 32/B3. Map 2.

Le FAOU

Relais de la Place

Comfortable hotel/Cooking 1-2

FW

No problem with parking in the vast *place* opposite the Relais – a facility shared with its arch rival, the Vieille Renommeé. A handful of menus with a *mélange* of *Bourgeois* & classical courses: at the simple end *lieu sauce Dieppoise* & *noix de veau à la crème*; at the more expensive end, relatively, *homard grillé, sauce aurore, riz pilaff*. Both *les patrons*, M. & Mme Le Floch, speak English; he's *le cuisinier*.
Menus aBCD. Rooms (34) DE. Cards MC, V.
Closed 2-15 Jan. Mid Sept-mid Oct. Sat (Oct-Easter).
Post pl. Mairie, 29580 Le Faou, Finistère. Region Brittany.
Tel 02 98 81 91 19. Fax 02 98 81 92 58. Mich 26/C4. Map 1.

A100frs & under. B100–150. C150–200. D200–250. E250–350. F350–500. G500+

Le FAOU

Vieille Renommée

Comfortable hotel/Cooking 1-2
Lift

FW

Like the Relais de la Place, the hotel is a large, unappealing, modern building (with similar number of rooms). Joëlle Philippe's chef, Daniel Bourhis, sticks to classical/*Bretonne*/*Bourgeoise* fare with highlights of the *truite saumonée au coulis de crustacés* & hearty *pot-au-feu de la mer* type. Parking? No problem; football pitch-sized *place* right opposite.
Menus aBCD(low-end). Rooms (32) EF. Cards MC, V.
Closed Sun evg (Oct-mid June).
Post pl. Mairie, 29580 Le Faou, Finistère. Region Brittany.
Tel 02 98 81 90 31. Fax 02 98 81 92 93. Mich 26/C4. Map 1.

FAVERGES

Florimont

Simple hotel/Cooking 2
Terrace/Gardens/Lift/Parking

FW

Jacques & Marie-Josèphe Goubot (now thawing a bit) let their son, Jean-Christophe, run the kitchen show in their new home, NE of Faverges. Classical & *Bourgeoise* fare: *cuisse de canard aux olives, omble chevalier rôti, magret de canard poêlé et sa sauce aux mûres* & similar. Marie-Claire, J-C's wife, much liked by readers, is a "real charmer".
Menus bCDE. Rooms (27) EF. Disabled. Cards All. (3km NE; N side N508.)
Closed Rest: Sun evg (Oct-June).
Post 74210 Faverges, Haute-Savoie. Region Savoie.
Tel 04 50 44 50 05. Fax 04 50 44 43 20. Mich 118/C2. Map 6.

FAVERGES (Tertenoz)

Gay Séjour

Simple hotel/Cooking 2-3
Secluded/Terrace/Parking

Much liked by readers for many years now: a 17thC *Savoyarde* farmhouse; a captivating site – near mountains, Lac d'Annecy & Tamié Abbey; & the caring family Gay – led by Bernard, a likeable dynamo of a chef. Menus CDE allow you to choose from numerous *à la carte* neo-classical & regional treats. Wide choice of top-notch fish *plats* & home-made sweets.
Menus bCDEF. Rooms (12) E(bottom-end)F. Cards All. (Use D12 S of town.)
Closed 5-26 Jan. Sun evg & Mon (not sch. hols).
Post Tertenoz, 74210 Faverges, Haute-Savoie. Region Savoie.
Tel 04 50 44 52 52. Fax 04 50 44 49 52. Mich 118/C2. Map 6.

A100frs & under. B100–150. C150–200. D200–250. E250–350. F350–500. G500+

FAVERGES-DE-LA-TOUR

Domaine de Faverges

Luxury hotel/Cooking 2-3
Secluded/Terr/Gardens/Golf(9)/Swim pool/Tennis/Lift/Parking

In the early 80s a ruin; today one of *Relais & Châteaux's* finest hotels. English-speaking owner Catherine Tournier, with husband Jo, have worked wonders; ask to see the photos of the restoration. The furniture, public rooms & hall/gallery are all superb. Chefs come & go but cooking pitches between both classical & neo-classical greens. There's a gym too.
Menus C(lunch)EF. Rooms (38) G,G2,G3. Cards All. (N junc. of N75/N516.)
Closed 12 Nov-12 Apl.
Post 38110 Faverges-de-la-Tour, Isère. Regions Lyonnais/Savoie.
Tel 04 74 97 42 52. Fax 04 74 88 86 40. Mich 117/D3. Map 6.

FAVIERES

La Clé des Champs

Comfortable restaurant/Cooking 2   `FW`
Parking

"The key" leads you to blue & white cottages & a rustic interior with many flowers, at the heart of a hamlet in the Somme estuary. Isabelle & Bruno Flasque charm clients in many ways: a warm welcome, competent service, sensible wines & appetising, if a touch fancy, neo-classical dishes: *terrine de poissons aux 3 couleurs* is a typical signature *plat*.
Menus aBC. Cards All. (Rooms : Lion d'Or at Rue, 3km to N.)
Closed Jan. 25 Aug-11 Sept.
Post 80120 Favières, Somme. Region North.
Tel 03 22 27 88 00. Mich 6/C2. Map 2.

La FERRIERE-AUX-ETANGS

Auberge de la Mine

Comfortable restaurant/Cooking 2-3   `FW`

What an off-putting name; but please don't bypass this colourful oasis. A talented young couple, Catherine & Hubert Nobis, have an eye for detail. A bright-as-a-button dining room is the first eye-catcher; followed by Hubert's inventive, modern repertoire: full-of-verve dishes such as *pavé de brochet rôti au gingembre frais*; *filet de rascasse en nage de coriandre*; & *pudding chocolat, crème de réglisse.* Easy parking.
Menus aBC. Cards All. (Rooms: see Ermitage, Bagnoles-de-l'O, 18km SE.)
Closed 2-20 Jan. 3-19 Sept. Tues evg & Wed. (Rest. 2km S, via D21/D825.)
Post Le Gué-Plat, 61450 La Ferrière-aux-Etangs, Orne. Region Normandy.
Tel 02 33 66 91 10. Fax 02 33 96 73 90. Mich 32/A4. Map 2.

A100frs & under. B100–150. C150–200. D200–250. E250–350. F350–500. G500+

La FERTE-SOUS-JOUARRE   Auberge de Condé

Very comfortable restaurant/Cooking 3
Terrace/Closed parking/Air-conditioning

The heroic Emile Tingaud opened the *auberge* in 1947 & manned the stoves until his death, at 81, in 1989. (His son, Jean-Claude, had originally succeeded him but he died, aged 38, in 1973.) Now Pascal, the grandson, continues the Tingaud classical cooking dynasty – with many a lighter touch. Try *poularde de Bresse à la Briarde* with a vibrant *Brie* streak.
Menus d(bottom-end)EF. Cards All. (Rooms: Chât. des Bondons, 2km E.)
Closed Mon evg. Tues. (Or cheaper Climat de France; N3 towards Meaux.)
Post 1 av. Montmirail, 77260 La Ferté-s/s-Jou., Seine-et-Marne. Map 2.
Tel 01 60 22 00 07. Fax 01 60 22 30 60. Mich 37/D3. Reg. Ile de France.

FIGEAC   La Puce à l'Oreille

Comfortable restaurant/Cooking 1-2
Terrace

At the heart of medieval Figeac, N of the post office & W of Notre Dame du Puy. 15thC house: stone, beams & huge *cheminée* are among the man-made eye-pleasers. Chef Jean-Marie Filhol does his classical/regional bit on the plates: a touch heavy-duty fare of the *cuisse de poule confite, salade de magret au miel & au thym, mousse de pruneaux* ilk.
Menus aBCD. Cards All. (Rooms: Pont du Pin, *sans rest*: N140 to E.)
Closed Mon (out of season). (Parking: several car parks – 200m N, E, S.)
Post 5 r. St-Thomas, 46100 Figeac, Lot. Region Dordogne.
Tel 05 65 34 33 08. Mich 139/E1. Map 5.

FITOU   Cave d'Agnès

Simple restaurant/Cooking 1-2   FW
Parking

The last house in the village as you head W on the D50. Originally an old wine *cave* & a touch too dark for a dining room. No problems here with quantities. For both menus the first course is a buffet-style *hors d'oeuvre*; followed by classical *plats* like *sauté de veau à l'estragon*, a toothsome *jambonnette de canard* or a filling *pot au feu de la mer*.
Menus B(two menus). Cards MC, V. (Rooms: Deux Golfs, Port-Leucate.)
Closed Oct-Mar. Wed. (Above *sans restaurant* & easy 18km drive to E.)
Post 11510 Fitou, Aude. Region Languedoc-Roussillon.
Tel 04 68 45 75 91. Mich 177/E1. Map 5.

A100frs & under. B100–150. C150–200. D200–250. E250–350. F350–500. G500+

FLAGEY-ECHEZEAUX Robert Losset

Simple restaurant/Cooking 2 FW
Air-conditioning

No signs: just "*Bar*" & "*Tabac*" in the small place, N of the church. Emphatic, exemplary classics: an intense *terrine de caille*; a light, restrained *mousseline de saumon*; or a punch-in-the-mouth *rognon veau à la moutarde*. Debits? Alas, yes: a frosty, patronising *patronne*. Dear wines and cold shoulder the Domaine Rapet vintages (zero points). Menus BCD. Cards MC, V. (Rooms: see entries at Gevrey-Chambertin.) Closed 1-15 Aug. Sun evg. Tues midday. Wed.
Post Flagey-Echezeaux, 21640 Vougeot, Côte-d'Or. Region Burgundy.
Tel 03 80 62 88 10. Mich 88/B1. Map 3.

FLAGY Hostellerie du Moulin

Very comfortable restaurant with rooms/Cooking 1
Secluded/Terrace/Gardens/Parking

Claude Scheidecker, an attentive English-speaking host, hails from Alsace. His 13thC mill, alongside the Orvanne, is a charmer – helped no end by a nightingale's song from across the stream. Cooking is run-of-the-mill classical: the ubiquitous *sauce Béarnaise* pops up regularly; so does curry powder. The rating goes down a gear – after many grumbles. Menus CD. Rooms (10) E(bottom-end)FG. Cards All. (S of Montereau-F-Y.) Closed 22 Dec-24 Jan. 14-26 Sept. Sun evg & Mon (not pub. hols).
Post 77940 Flagy, Seine-et-Marne. Region Ile de France.
Tel 01 60 96 67 89. Fax 01 60 96 69 51. Mich 55/D3. Map 2.

FLAYOSC L'Oustaou

Comfortable restaurant/Cooking 1-2 FW
Terrace

Pleasant village square setting: lovely out-of-doors on terrace; a touch confined inside. *Provençale* cuisine with several hunky dory *Bourgeois* tummy fillers: *pâté, boeuf en daube, coq au vin, pieds et paquets, magrets grillés*, goat's milk cheeses & above average sweets. One nice touch: help yourself from copper pans brought to the table.
Menus BCE. Cards AE, MC, V. (Rooms: Les Oliviers, 3km to E.)
Closed 11 Nov-9 Dec. Sun evg & Mon.
Post 83780 Flayosc, Var. Region Côte d'Azur. (7km W of Draguignan.)
Tel 04 94 70 42 69. Mich 162/C3. Map 6.

A100frs & under. B100–150. C150–200. D200–250. E250–350. F350–500. G500+

La FLECHE   **Vert Galant**

Comfortable restaurant with rooms/Cooking 1-2   FW
Gardens/Parking

The ivy-covered *logis* is away from the main roads cutting through the
town (itself bypassed). The Bergers are traditionalists: you see that in the
furnishings (public rooms & bedrooms) & in the classical/regional
cooking. Wide choice on menu B: old-timers such as *rillettes, poule au
pot Henry IV, brochet beurre blanc, île flottante & poire Belle Hélène.*
Menus aBC. Rooms (9) DE. Cards MC, V.
Closed 15 Dec-16 Jan. Thurs (not July/Aug).
Post 70 Gde Rue, 72200 La Flèche, Sarthe. Region Loire.
Tel 02 43 94 00 51. Fax 02 43 45 11 24. Mich 66/C2. Map 2.

FLERS   **Au Bout de la Rue**

Comfortable restaurant/Cooking 2   FW
Air-conditioning

The smile-forcing name is a happy start; the cascade of flowers over the
shop-front façade is even better. Marie-Noël Lebouleux is a warm-hearted
hostess & husband Jacky a classical/neo-classical chef. Huge choice on
menu B (top-end) including *salade terre-mer en vapeur de poissons tiède,
rognons de veau à la moutarde* & 10 cracking desserts. Also bistro (A).
Menus B(bottom & top). Cards MC, V. (Rooms: Galion; *sans rest*; parking.)
Closed Sun. Pub. hols. (Above hotel 2 minute-walk to NE.)
Post 60 r. Gare, 61100 Flers, Orne. Region Normandy.
Tel 02 33 65 31 53. Fax 02 33 65 46 81. Mich 32/A4. Map 1.

FLEURIE (also see next page)   **Auberge du Cep**

Very comfortable restaurant/Cooking 4
Air-conditioning

A great favourite. Chef Gérard Cortembert died 6 years ago, in his 40s. His
widow, Chantal, aided by her delectable daughter Hélène (both speak
English fluently) & young chef Michel Guérin, trained by Gérard, do a
magnificent job. His repertoire is Pavlovian mix of terrific classical/
regional cuisine (Bresse/Burgundy/Beaujolais). Ask Hélène: which border?
Menus CDEF. Cards AE, MC, V. (Rooms: Grands Vins; see next entry.)
Closed Mid Dec-mid Jan. 29 July-6 Aug. Sun evg. Mon.
Post pl. Eglise, 69820 Fleurie, Rhône. Region Lyonnais.
Tel 04 74 04 10 77. Fax 04 74 04 10 28. Mich 102/B3. Map 6.

A100frs & under. B100–150. C150–200. D200–250. E250–350. F350–500. G500+

FLEURIE (also see previous page)   Grands Vins

Simple hotel (no restaurant)
Secluded/Gardens/Swimming pool/Closed parking

Jean-Paul Ringuet's hotel is adequate enough – furnished in a mix of
styles, primarily *à l'ancienne*; some rooms are smallish. The secluded
location & the swimming pool are two of its main benefits. A third is the
number of excellent restaurants which are an easy drive away. S of the
famed village, between the D68 & D119E.
Rooms (20) F. Cards MC, V.
Closed Dec-mid Jan. 30 July-6 Aug.
Post 69820 Fleurie, Rhône. Region Lyonnais.
Tel 04 74 69 81 43. Fax 04 74 69 86 10. Mich 102/B3. Map 6.

FLEURINES   Vieux Logis

Very comfortable restaurant/Cooking 3
Terrace/Gardens/Parking

North of Senlis (& A1 exit 8) & at the heart of the Forêt d'Halatte. Yann &
Valerie Nivet hiked their prices upwards after *Franc-wise France* was
published in 1995: no FW rating now! Classical/regional fare, which
pleases both the eyes & taste buds: examples include *cul de lapin à la
bière Picarde* & a Normandy marvel, *douillon aux poires sauce caramel*.
Menus C(top-end)E(low-end). Cards All. (Rooms: Ibis, just W A1 exit 8.)
Closed Feb sch. hols. 1-15 Aug. Sat midday. Sun evg. Mon. (Above 8km S.)
Post 60700 Fleurines, Oise. Regions Normandy/North.
Tel 03 44 54 10 13. Fax 03 44 54 12 47. Mich 36/B1. Map 2.

FLEURY-SUR-ORNE   Ile Enchantée

Comfortable restaurant/Cooking 2-3   FW

Well-named: a pretty, wooded setting, across the road from the River
Orne & adjacent to an easily accessible riverside "green". Luscious
classical food with a varied choice of tastes: light *gourmandise de
saumon à la crème d'herbettes* & *minute de saumon aux huîtres,
sauce lie de vin*; or loosen-your-belts *médaillon de veau à l'anglaise,
crème Vallée d'Auge* & fine *tarte aux pommes chaudes, sauce caramel*.
Menus aBCD. Cards MC, V. (Rooms: Novotel/Ibis; N of Caen; near bypass.)
Closed Feb sch. hols. 1-8 Aug. Sun evg. Mon. (Use bypass for above.)
Post 14123 Fleury-sur-Orne, Orne. (Rest. 4km S Caen.) Region Normandy.
Tel 02 31 52 15 52. Fax 02 31 72 67 17. Mich 32/A1-B1. Map 2.

A100frs & under. B100–150. C150–200. D200–250. E250–350. F350–500. G500+

FLORAC

Grand Hôtel Parc

Comfortable hotel/Cooking 1-2
Terrace/Gardens/Swimming pool/Lift/Parking

FW

The large hotel is a mixture of modern & old, overlooking a large, shady garden with an almost hidden, cool swimming pool. Claude Gleize, the *chef/patron*, rows regional & classical boats: put your oars into gutsy, filling grub – including *charcuteries Cévenoles, salade Cévenole, tripoux Lozèriens, civet de caneton & côtes d'agneau grillées*.
Menus aBC. Rooms (60) CDE. Cards All.
Closed Dec-mid Mar. Mon (not high season). Rest: Sun evg.
Post 48400 Florac, Lozère. Region Massif Central (Cévennes).
Tel 04 66 45 03 05. Fax 04 66 45 11 81. Mich 142/B2. Map 5.

FLORENSAC

Léonce

Comfortable restaurant with rooms/Cooking 3-4
Air-conditioning (restaurant)

FW

Our last visit, at the end of a scorching day, demonstrated the panache of chef Jean-Claude Fabre: *carpaccio de saumon et petits agrumes à l'huile d'olive* was refreshing nectar: & a two-inch thick *mignon de boeuf cuit au lard, le sauce brune relevée au genièvre* was sumptious. One caveat: noise from the *place* below the bedrooms can be awful.
Menus bDE. Rooms (11) DE. Cards All. (Other rooms: see Marseillan.)
Closed Mid Feb-mid Mar. 22 Sept-6 Oct. Sun evg (not July/Aug). Mon.
Post pl. République, 34510 Florensac, Hérault. Region Languedoc-Rouss.
Tel 04 67 77 03 05. Fax 04 67 77 88 89. Mich 156/A4. Map 5.

FONTAINE-CHAALIS

Auberge de Fontaine

Comfortable restaurant with rooms/Cooking 2
Terrace/Gardens/Parking

FW

Michelin have always given a "quiet" rating to the stone-built, family-run *logis*; I dropped the tag years back after readers said traffic could be noisy. Is it still? No arguing about Jacques Campion's safe-as-houses classical & *Bourgeoise* grub: an appetite-quenching *andouillette sauce grain de moutarde* (mustard-town Meaux is down the road) is champion.
Menus BCE. Rooms (7) DE. Cards MC, V.
Closed Feb. Tues (Nov-Mar; not pub. hols).
Post 60300 Fontaine-Chaalis, Oise. Region Ile de France.
Tel 03 44 54 20 22. Fax 03 44 60 25 38. Mich 36/B1. Map 2.

A100frs & under. B100–150. C150–200. D200–250. E250–350. F350–500. G500+

FONTENAY-LE-COMTE

Chouans Gourmets

Comfortable restaurant/Cooking 2 | FW |

Alongside the Vendée's right bank & at the heart of handsome Fontenay.
Stone features overpoweringly in the main dining room; a smaller *salle*
overlooks the dull river view. Madame is an eagle-eyed *patronne. Chef/
patron* Robert Vrignon weaves a mix of culinary patterns: witness *emincé
de porc Cantonnaise*, succulent *canette rôtie au miel et coriandre* &
tender, pink *brochette de gigot d'agneau grillée aux herbes.*
Menus aBCD. Cards All. (Rooms: Rabelais or St-Nicolas at Maillezais.)
Closed 3-15 Jan. Sun evg & Mon (not pub. hols). (Maillezais 12km SE.)
Post 6 r. Halles, 85200 Fontenay-le-Comte, Vendée. Region Poitou-Char.
Tel 02 51 69 55 92. Mich 93/E2. Map 4.

FONTENAY-LE-COMTE (Velluire)

Auberge de la Rivière

Very comfortable restaurant with rooms/Cooking 1-2 | FW |
Quiet

The site, 11km SW of Fontenay, is everything: alongside the River Vendée
& at the northern *portes* of the Marais Poitevin. The modernised, vine-
covered *auberge* is stylishly furnished (antiques in the main building) &
decorated. Robert Pajot is *le patron*; wife Luce is an able exponent of
classical/regional/*Bourgeoise* cuisine. Her fish dishes are exemplary.
Menus b(bottom-end)CD. Rooms (11) F. Cards MC, V.
Closed 3 Jan-25 Feb. Mon (not evgs July/Aug). Rest: Sun evg (Sept-June).
Post 85770 Velluire, Vendée. Region Poitou-Charentes.
Tel 02 51 52 32 15. Fax 02 51 52 37 42. Mich 93/D2. Map 4.

FONTENAY-TRESIGNY

Le Manoir

Very comfortable hotel/Cooking 3
Secluded/Gardens/Swimming pool/Tennis/Parking

The Sourisseau family manor, a creeper-covered, half-timbered,
Normandy-style hunting lodge in 40 acres of woodland, has won praise
from several readers during the last 4 years. Old trees & pools captivate,
as do the stylish splendours of the rich interior. The latter adjectives also
apply to the classical fare; one highlight – magnificent *chateaubriand*.
Menus dF(bottom-end). Rooms (15) G. Cards All. (To the E; N of N4/D402.)
Closed Tues (not pub. hols).
Post 77610 Fontenay-Trésigny, Seine-et-Marne. Region Ile-de-France.
Tel 01 64 25 91 17. Fax 01 64 25 95 49. Mich 36/C4. Map 2.

A100frs & under. B100–150. C150–200. D200–250. E250–350. F350–500. G500+

FONTEVRAUD-L'ABBAYE   Abbaye

Very simple restaurant/Cooking 1-2   `FW`

There's nowt simpler in this edition of *French Leave* – but what pleasure
André Côme has provided for readers over the years. Step back to an
autrefois & relish a series of classical, regional & *Bourgeois plats*: *hors
d'oeuvre, steack grillé Béarnaise, saumon grillé beurre blanc* (a
regional treasure), *filet de turbot forestière, poire belle-Hélène* & other
similar old-time satisfiers. Restaurant on N exit from village.
Menus ABC. Cards MC, V. (Rooms: see *sans rest.* hotels Chinon/Bourgueil.)
Closed 2-26 Feb. 1-25 Oct. Tues evg. Wed. Region Loire.
Post rte Montsoreau, 49590 Fontevraud-l'Abbaye, Maine-et-Loire.
Tel 02 41 51 71 04. Fax 02 41 51 43 10. Mich 81/E1. Map 2.

FONTEVRAUD-L'ABBAYE   La Licorne

Very comfortable restaurant/Cooking 3   `FW`
Terrace/Gardens

A seductive charmer: an 18thC house with an alluring garden (approach
from the SW; car park 50 yds away; use garden entrance); *patron* Jean
Criton; & classical cooking from chef Michel Lecomte. A summer lunch
was a perfectly-balanced triumph: *gâteau de sole aux petits légumes, dos
de saumon poêlé, soufflé au chocolat* – all three "encore please" dishes.
Menus bCDE. Cards All. (Rooms: nearby Hôt. Prieuré St-Lazare.)
Closed Dec-mid Jan. Sun evg & Mon (Oct-Apl). Region Loire.
Post allée Ste-Catherine, 49590 Fontevraud-l'Abbaye, Maine-et-Loire.
Tel 02 41 51 72 49. Fax 02 41 51 70 40. Mich 81/E1. Map 2.

FONTVIEILLE (also see next page)   Hostellerie St-Victor

Very comfortable hotel (no restaurant)
Secluded/Gardens/Swimming pool/Parking/Air-conditioning

A newish, villa-style stone hotel (11 rooms) – first recommended in *FLE*
& a success with readers. St-Victor has an elevated site to the S of the
D17, on the road to Arles. Daudet's *moulin* & museum lie to the E. A
touch expensive though the facilities & seclusion justify the higher
prices. Close to several recommended restaurants – in Fontvieille itself,
at Les Baux & both Maussane & St-Rémy-de-Provence.
Rooms (11) FG. Cards All. Region Provence.
Post chemin des Fourques, 13990 Fontvieille, Bouches-du-Rhône.
Tel 04 90 54 66 00. Fax 04 90 54 67 88. Mich 158/B2. Map 6.

A100frs & under. B100–150. C150–200. D200–250. E250–350. F350–500. G500+

FONTVIEILLE (also see previous page)   **La Regalido**

Very comfortable hotel/Cooking 3
Quiet/Terrace/Gardens/Parking/Air-conditioning

Can so many beguiling pluses be packed into such a tiny area? The old converted oil mill is hemmed in on all sides; yet the bucket-of-colour garden & stylish interior of Regalido (re-awakened flame of the fire – how apt)concentrate the senses wonderfully well. Classical cooking from Jean-Pierre Michel plus both *Sud-Ouest* & *Provençales* specialities.
Menus c(lunch)EF. Rooms (15)G,G2,G3. Cards All.
Closed 2-31 Jan. Rest: Mon (Oct-June). Mon *midi* & Tues *midi* (Jul-Sept).
Post 13990 Fontvieille, Bouches-du-Rhône. Region Provence.
Tel 04 90 54 60 22. Fax 04 90 54 64 29. Mich 158/B2. Map 6.

FONTVIEILLE   **La Table du Meunier**

Simple restaurant/Cooking 1-2   FW
Parking/Air-conditioning

A tiny dining room, sitting 2 dozen or so, E side of church towards Les Baux. Thierry Fel is *le patron*; wife Marie-France *la cuisinière*. Wide choice on her classical/*Provençals* menus: *terrine de rougets, côtes d'agneau au pistou*, an especially appetising *gigotin de volaille à la tapenade, petite chevre à l'huile d'olive* are menu B *terroir* tempters.
Menus BC(both bottom-end). Cards MC, V. (Rooms: see Maussane-les-Alp.)
Closed Sch. hols Feb & Nov. 17-27 Dec. Tues evg. Wed (not evg July/Aug).
Post 42 cours H. Bellon, 13990 Fontvieille, Bouches-du-Rhône.
Tel 04 90 54 61 05. Fax 04 90 54 77 24. Mich 158/B2. Map 6. Region Prov.

FORCALQUIER   **Hostellerie des Deux Lions**

Comfortable hotel/Cooking 2-3
Garage

Old France in a time warp: gentle, caring hosts, Robert & Claude Audier & Michel Montdor-Florent, a classical/regional chef. No-choice menu C (bottom-end) confirms his old-fashioned skills: like *oeuf brouillé au crabe & aux crevettes en aumonière croustillante; potrine d'agneau mitonnée puis grillée aux herbes*; & *mousse au chocolat noir*.
Menus CDE. Rooms (16) EF. Cards AE, MC, V. Region Provence.
Closed 3 Ja-28 Fe. 1-20 De. Sun evg (not Jul/Aug). Mon (not evg season).
Post 11 pl. Bourguet, 04300 Forcalquier, Alpes-de-Haute-Provence.
Tel 04 92 75 25 30. Fax 04 92 75 06 41. Mich 145/F4. Map 6.

A100frs & under. B100–150. C150–200. D200–250. E250–350. F350–500. G500+

FORGES-LES-EAUX   Auberge du Beau Lieu

Comfortable restaurant with rooms/Cooking 2-3
Terrace/Parking

Marie-France Ramelet is a *petite*, attentive *patronne/sommelière* – proud of
her *cave* (40 halves) & beamed dining room (with many paintings by local
artist, William Gantier). Patrick Ramelet is an inventive modern master:
gâteau d'andouille aux pommes confites & *millefeuille de haddock
mariné et salade* are two treats. Bedrooms: touch dampish & cold floors.
Menus C(low-end)DE. Rooms (3) E. Cards All. (2km SE, beside D915.)
Closed Tues (not July/Aug). Region Normandy.
Post Le Fossé, 76440 Forges-les-Eaux, Seine-Maritime.
Tel 02 35 90 50 36. Fax 02 35 90 35 98. Mich 16/C2-C3. Map 2.

FORGES-LES-EAUX   Paix

Comfortable restaurant with rooms/Cooking 1-2   FW
Gardens/Lift/Closed parking

Régine (much-loved) & Rémy Michel claim their culinary philosophy is to
uphold *tradition et terroir*. They do – at their *logis* with its spanking new
bedrooms (& lift). Examples of regional *plats* using *terroir* produce:
*andouillette à la Normande, terrine de canard à la Rouennaise, filets de
sole Dieppoise*, Bray cheeses & hot apple tart. Normandy on a plate x 5!
Menus ABC. Rooms (18) DE. Disabled. Cards All. Region Normandy.
Closed 16 Dec-8 Jan. Sun evg (out of season). Mon (not evg high season).
Post 15 r. Neufchâtel, 76440 Forges-les-Eaux, Seine-Maritime.
Tel 02 35 90 51 22. Fax 02 35 09 83 62. Mich 16/C2-C3. Map 2.

FOUGERES (also see next page)   Le Haut Sève

Comfortable restaurant/Cooking 2   FW

A town centre restaurant (plenty of street parking) with an understated
exterior but a comfortable spacious interior. Thierry Robert's neo-
classical repertoire shows up well on menu C: a humdinger *galettes de
saumon jus de pommes*; a home-made *foie gras de canard breton*; a
filling *magret de canard rôti*; or an easily-digested *limande sole*; &, best
of all, a large selection of desserts (*pain perdu aux poires* – perfection).
Menus BCDE. Cards AE, MC, V. (Rooms: Campanile; easy 2km drive to SE.)
Closed 1-15 Jan. 15 Jul-15 Aug. Sun evg. Mon.
Post 37 bd J. Jaurès, 35300 Fougères, Ille-et-Vilaine.
Tel 02 99 94 23 39. Mich 49/D2-E2. Map 1.

A100frs & under. B100–150. C150–200. D200–250. E250–350. F350–500. G500+

FOUGERES (also see previous page)   **Rest. & Hôtel Voyageurs**

Comfortable restaurant & simple hotel/Cooking 1-2   FW
Lift/Air-conditioning (restaurant)

Run as two separate businesses but within the same building; impressive façade & the flags of 7 nations flying proudly. One plus aspect on all 4 menus is the good choice for each course. Classical offerings. Menu C included welcome fish *plats* for the first 2 courses: a lip-smacking *chaussin de brochet & saumon*; & a light, so-tasty *blanc de sandre poché*.
Menus aBCD. Rooms (37) CDE. Cards AE, MC, V. Regs Brittany/Normandy.
Closed Rest: 21 Aug-3 Sept. Sat & Sun evg (not July/Aug). Mich 49/D2-E2.
Post 10 pl. Gambetta, 35300 Fougeres, I.-&-V. Tel (R) 02 99 99 14 17.
(H) 02 99 99 08 20. Fax (R) 02 99 99 28 89. (H) 02 99 99 99 04. Map 1.

FOUGEROLLES   Au Père Rota

Very comfortable restaurant/Cooking 3-4
Parking

Jean-Pierre & Chantal Kuentz work wonders at this longtime favourite of mine. The town is famed for its *eaux-de-vie* distilleries & surrounding orchards. The local cherries (*griottes et griottines*) feature strongly in *terrine de lapereau* &, *bien sûr*, in desserts. Neo-classical repasts from J-P, in a *salle* which is an oasis of light & modern pastel hues.
Menus cDE. Cards All. (Rooms: Résidence, Le Val-d'Ajol; 6km to NE.)
Closed 2-24 Jan. 23-26 June. Sun evg & Mon (not pub. hols).
Post 8 Gde-Rue, 70220 Fougerolles, Haute-Saône. Region Alsace.
Tel 03 84 49 12 11. Fax 03 84 49 14 51. Mich 76/A1. Map 3.

FOURMIES   Ibis

Simple hotel (no restaurant)
Secluded/Parking (public)

Too many folk – especially the French – are hotel snobs. This "group" Ibis meets all the criteria for my "base" hotels: in quiet (wooded) terrain, beside the Etangs des Moines (pools), SE of Fourmies & N of the D964. The hotel is well placed for restaurants to the N & for exploring the little-known Lac du Val Joly, in wooded hills E of Avesnes.
Rooms (31) E. Cards All. Region Champagne-Ardenne.
Post Etangs des Moines, 59610 Fourmies, Nord.
Tel 03 27 60 21 54. Fax 03 27 57 40 44. Mich 10/A3. Map 3.
(Bookings UK 0171 724 1000; US toll free 800 221 4542.)

A100frs & under. B100–150. C150–200. D200–250. E250–350. F350–500. G500+

FOX-AMPHOUX   Auberge du Vieux Fox

Comfortable restaurant with rooms/Cooking 1-2   FW
Secluded/Terrace/Parking

A narcotic hamlet; the *auberge* was once the presbytery of the adjoining
16thC church (part 900 years old). Jean-Charles Martha has retired; new
English-speaking owners Rudolph (Austrian) & Niçole (French) Staudinger
have brought a new lease of life to the delectable VF. Classical *plats* from
Gilles Unino: *faux-filet de charolais Béarnaise* is typical example.
Menus BD. Rooms (8). Cards All. (11km NW of Cotignac.)
Closed Rest: Tues. Wed midday.
Post Fox-Amphoux, 83670 Barjols, Var. Region Côte d'Azur.
Tel 04 94 80 71 69. Fax 04 98 80 78 38. Mich 162/B3. Map 6.

FRANCESCAS   Relais de la Hire

Very comfortable restaurant/Cooking 2-3   FW
Terrace/Gardens/Parking

High-ceilinged *salles* in an 18thC house with a *parc ombragé* – all at the
door of heart-stirring Gascony. Jean-Noël Prabonne adds his own brand of
musketeer bravura. Tuck into two menus – *l'Ecuyer* & *Chevalier* – &
savour smashing classical largesse like *cromesquis de Ste-Maure, petit de
saumon à la crème de lentilles* & head-clearing *charlotte à l'Armagnac*.
Menus bCE. Cards All. (Rooms: Trois Lys & Logis des Cordeliers; Condom.)
Closed Sun evg & Mon (not pub. hols). (Both above *sans rest.*; 15km SW.)
Post 47600 Francescas, Lot-et-Garonne. Region Southwest.
Tel 05 53 65 41 59. Fax 05 53 65 86 42. Mich 136/C4. Map 5.

FREHEL   Le Victorine

Comfortable restaurant/Cooking 2   FW
Terrace

A tiny jewel where Laurence & Thierry Blandin sparkle. Thierry mixes
modern & neo-classical in innovative ways: a flavoursome *farandole de
poissons fumés* seemed an appropriate match for the smoked-glass ceiling;
filet de saumon à la crème de porto was an encore-shouting hit; &, from a
choice of seven, *croustillant aux fraises* was an ideal summer sweet.
Menus aBC. Cards MC, V. (Rooms: hotels at Sables-d'Or; 5 km NW.)
Closed Tues evg & Wed (not high season).
Post pl. Mairie, 22240 Fréhel, Côtes d'Armor. Region Brittany.
Tel 02 96 41 55 55. Mich 29/E2. Map 1.

A 100frs & under. B 100–150. C 150–200. D 200–250. E 250–350. F 350–500. G 500+

FREJUS

Hôtel Oasis

Simple hotel (no restaurant)
Quiet/Terrace/Parking

The hotel is well-named, a surprising oasis tucked away in a narrow side lane, midway between the busy N98 to St-Raphaël & Fréjus-Plage. The latter is a simple 200m walk & the beach is one of the better sandy versions on the coast. Other pluses: pines provide a shady terrace; parking, too, is *ombragé*; a quiet site (bliss); & fairly modest prices.
Rooms (27) F(bottom-end). Cards MC, V.
Closed Mid Oct-mid Feb. Region Côte d'Azur.
Post impasse Charcot (off av. H. Fabre), 83600 Fréjus, Var.
Tel 04 94 51 50 44. Mich 163/E3. Map 6.

FREJUS

La Toque Blanche

Very comfortable restaurant/Cooking 2
Terrace/Air-conditioning

At the E end of Fréjus-Plage, as you enter St-Raphaël. Stylish, service *sous cloches* & goldfish-bowl glasses. Jacky Collin is a classicist with a light hand: *gratin de moules et huîtres, tournedos sauté forestière, noisettes d'agneau aux gousses d'ail* & *crème brûlée à la vanille* are all menu C possibilities. Prices also shown in *écus*; heaven forbid!
Menus BCE. Cards All. (Rooms: see entry above – 500/600m walk away.)
Closed 24 June-11 July. Mon.
Post 394 av. V. Hugo, 83600 Fréjus-Plage, Var. Region Côte d'Azur.
Tel 04 94 52 06 14. Mich 163/E3. Map 6.

FROIDETERRE

Hostellerie des Sources

Comfortable restaurant/Cooking 2
Terrace/Parking

Several pools & springs justify the restaurant's name. Visit from June-October & you can order *écrevisses* which are bred in the *étangs*. Marcel Brocard is a savvy wine buff; his young son, Valéry, a talented chef. In the beamed dining room dip into eclectic French dishes: *soupe de poisson à la provençale* & *gras double à la lyonnaise* are a typical starter duo.
Menus ACDE. Cards MC, V. (Rooms: Eric Hôtel, Lure – 3km to SW.)
Closed 16 Fe-2 Mar. 3-10 Au. Sa *midi* & Su ev (Oc-Ap). Mo (not pub.hols).
Post 4 r. Grand Bois, 70200 Froideterre, Haute-Saône. Region Alsace.
Tel 03 84 30 13 91. Fax 03 84 30 29 87. Mich 76/B2. Map 3.

A100frs & under. B100–150. C150–200. D200–250. E250–350. F350–500. G500+

FRONTIGNAN

Jas d'Or

Comfortable restaurant/Cooking 2-3
Air-conditioning

FW

Tricky to find: from N112 use D60 from S; rest. on N side of canal, near *la gare*. Your efforts will be repaid handsomely: modern, spacious, cool *salle*, home of elegant Christine Vallon & chef/husband Jean-Jacques. He plays a modern piano with sea tunes: *soupe de homard* & *papillote de poisson sur son lit de choucroute de la mer* are two evocative melodies.
Menus a(lunch)C. Cards MC, V. (Rooms: Campanile, Balaruc-le-Vieux.)
Closed Mon *midi* & Sat *midi* (season). Tues evg & Wed (out of season).
Post 2 bd V. Hugo, 34110 Frontignan, Hérault. Region Languedoc-Rouss.
Tel 04 67 43 07 57. Mich 156/B4. Map 5. (Campanile near A9 exit 33.)

FUISSE

Pouilly Fuissé

Comfortable restaurant/Cooking 1-2
Terrace

FW

Eric & Dominique Point (she's the fourth generation owner) entice with lick-your-lips *RQP* classical, *Bressane* & *Lyonnaise* cuisine. From an avalanche of five menus tuck into the likes of *saladier Lyonnais, filet de perche sauce Duglérée* (sic), *grenouilles poêlées à la persillade* & the much-more-please *crêpes Parmentier sucrées* (potato pancakes).
Menus ABCD. Cards MC, V. (Rooms: Ibis: S of A6 Mâcon-Sud exit.)
Closed 2-24 Jan. 30 July-6 Aug. Wed. (Above where A6 crosses N6.)
Post 71960 Fuissé, Saône-et-Loire. Region Lyonnais.
Tel 03 85 35 60 68. Fax 03 85 35 60 68. Mich 102/B3. Map 6.

GAN

Le Tucq

Simple restaurant/Cooking 1-2
Terrace/Parking

FW

If pennies count & if you would like to lose yourself in the exquisite foothills of the Pyrénées – & if you relish down-to-earth *Béarnaise* & *Bourgeoise* grub – then nose out Michel & Simone Rances. Take an appetite: *garbue Béarnaise, assiette de charcuterie, truite meunière, confit de canard* & six desserts all appear on low-end menu B.
Menus aB. Cards MC, V. (Rooms: see Pau (Lescar) entry; easy 8km to N.)
Closed Oct. Tues. Wed. Region Southwest.
Post rte de Laruns, 64290 Gan, Pyrénées-Atlantiques. (4km S; use D934.)
Tel 05 59 21 61 26. Mich 168/A1. Map 4.

A100frs & under. B100–150. C150–200. D200–250. E250–350. F350–500. G500+

GAP
La Grangette

Simple restaurant/Cooking 2

A small rustic dining room with a touch of swish & a truly big heart. No chance of a *Glamorous Night* here but Ivor's namesake, Raphaël, plays both classical & neo-classical melodies on his culinary piano: excellent tunes such as *carpaccio de saumon à l'huile d'olive, petit pot-au-feu de poisson et crustacés, entrecôte au vin* & renowned local lamb cooked in varying ways, from day to day, all sure to keep the home fires burning.
Menus BC. Cards MC, V. (Rooms: Ibis; 300m to S.)
Closed 12-22 Feb. 11-25 June. Sun evg. Mon.
Post 1 av. Foch, 05000 Gap, Hautes-Alpes. Regions Hautes-Alpes/Savoie.
Tel 04 92 52 39 82. Mich 146/B1. Map 6. (Restaurant is near *la gare*.)

GAP
Le Patalain

Very comfortable restaurant/Cooking 2-3
Air-conditioning

Readers will be sad to read that Bernard Fiore-Rappelin, *chef/patron* of Carré Long, died last year. This stylish rest., opp. the station, is now Gap's best. Warm welcome from Monique Périnet & immaculate neo-classical delights from husband Gérard: *ballotine de volaille à l'estragon* (menu B) & delicious *crépinette de noisette d'agneau au jus de thym*.
Menus BCE. Cards All. (Rooms: Ibis; 300m to S.)
Closed July. Sat midday. Sun.
Post 7 av. Alpes, 05000 Gap, Hautes-Alpes. Regions Hautes-Alpes/Savoie.
Tel 04 92 52 30 83. Mich 146/B1. Map 6.

GAP
Porte Colombe

Comfortable hotel/Cooking 1-2
Lift/Garage/Air-conditioning (restaurant)

A multi-storied, modern building in the town centre (rooms are double-glazed). A pleasing welcome from Christine Reynaud, the English-speaking *patronne*. (Unusual feature: panoramic terrace at the top of the hotel.) Run-of-the-mill classical/*Bourgeoise*/grill tucker: likes of *saumon de Norvège grillé sauce Béarnaise* & *côtes d'agneau de Sisteron grillés*.
Menus BC. Rooms (26) DEF. Cards All.
Closed Rest: 6-28 Jan. Fri evg & Sat (Oct-mid July).
Post 4 pl. F. Euzières, 05000 Gap, Htes-Alpes. Regs Htes-Alpes/Savoie.
Tel 04 92 51 04 13. Fax 04 92 52 42 50. Mich 146/B1. Map 6.

A100frs & under. B100–150. C150–200. D200–250. E250–350. F350–500. G500+

La GARDE

Rocher Blanc

Comfortable hotel/Cooking 1-2 | FW
Terrace/Gardens/Swimming pool/Parking/Air-cond. (rest.)

Logis 2km N from A75 exit 32, beside N9 at altitude of over 3,000 ft.
Fine views E above village of Margeride mountains. Claudine & Pierre
Brunel provide wide-choice classical/*Bourgeoise RQP* grub. Menu B
could include *jambon de pays & saucisson, poulet de ferme au curry &
filet boeuf au poivre vert*. Wed evg in July/Aug: *aligot avec folklore!*
Menus ABC. Rooms (20) DEF(bottom-end). Cards MC, V.
Closed Mid Nov-Easter. Sun evg & Mon (not July/Aug).
Post La Garde, 48200 Albaret-Ste-Marie, Lozère. Region MC (Auvergne).
Tel 04 66 31 90 09. Fax 04 66 31 93 67. Mich 127/E3. Map 5.

GENILLE

Agnès Sorel

Comfortable restaurant with rooms/Cooking 2 | FW
Terrace

A tiny *logis* with a cool dining room & minuscule terrace shaded by a
green & white awning. Green is the word for the delectable Indrois
Valley; delectable is the word for Patrick Le Hay's neo-classical *plats*.
Mouthwatering trio of *terrine de Roquefort au saumon en gelée, queue
de lotte à l'oseille & rable de lapin rôti et betteraves rouges* (menu B).
Menus BCD. Rooms (3) D. Cards MC, V.
Closed Jan. Sun evg & Mon (not pub. hols).
Post 37460 Genillé, Indre-et-Loir. Region Loire.
Tel 02 47 59 50 17. Mich 82/C1. Map 2.

GENSAC

Remparts

Comfortable restaurant with rooms/Cooking 2-3 | FW
Quiet/Terrace/Gardens/Parking

Tucked away in perched village; newly-created bedrooms are in adjacent
restored building. Catherine Poveromo, 30ish, is a brisk, neat *patronne*;
chef/husband Eric is a classicist. Typical dishes: deep-tasting *sandre rôti,
crème de noilly & pleurotes; pigeonneau* in rich *jus* with *galette* of
échalotes confites & excellent *tarte fine aux pommes chaudes*.
Menus aBCD. Rooms (7) E. Cards MC, V. (Order desserts at start of meal.)
Closed Jan. Feb. Mon (not July/Aug). Rest: Sun evg.
Post 33890 Gensac, Gironde. Region Dordogne.
Tel 05 57 47 43 46. Fax 05 57 47 76. Mich 122/B3. Map 4.

A100frs & under. B100–150. C150–200. D200–250. E250–350. F350–500. G500+

GERARDMER

Bains

Simple hotel (no restaurant)
Gardens/Parking

In a side street, 300m due E from the lake, casino & lakeside gardens. Scores of window boxes give the part chalet-style hotel a colourful, bright outlook. The owners, the Leonard family, speak excellent English; the son spent three years in the US. Good value, alternative bedrooms for the restaurants at the Gd Hôtel Bragard & up the hill at Bas-Rupts.
Rooms (55) CDEF. Cards MC, V.
Closed Nov-mid Dec.
Post 16 bd Garnier, 88400 Gérardmer, Vosges. Region Alsace.
Tel 03 29 63 08 19. Fax 03 29 63 23 31. Mich 60/B3. Map 3.

GERARDMER

Chalet du Lac

Simple hotel/Cooking 0-1
Gardens/Parking

Invigorating views across the lake to the densely-wooded hills beyond the southern shore are the big bonuses at the *familles* Bernier (Alain is both friendly & efficient) & Wallcaneras' chalet-style hotel – itself surrounded by pine trees (& red squirrels) 1km W of the resort. Basic cooking: honest-to-goodness *Bourgeoise* grub (*côte de porc* variety).
Menus aB. Rooms (11) E. Cards MC, V.
Closed Oct. Rest: Fri (not sch. hols).
Post rte Epinal (D417), 88400 Gérardmer, Vosges. Region Alsace.
Tel 03 29 63 38 76. Fax 03 29 60 91 63. Mich 60/B3. Map 3.

GERARDMER

Echo de Ramberchamp

Very simple hotel with basic rooms (no restaurant)
Quiet/Gardens/Parking

Base hotels don't come simpler than the chalet-style Echo, W of the resort, off the D69 & on S side of the lake. Guy & Nelly Fleurance-Parisot are *les patrons* (alas, mother died last year). One other plus: there's a bar. Walks abound: along the S shore (on the N side you use the road, which is dangerous) & in wooded hills behind the Echo.
Rooms (16) CDE. Cards AE, MC, V.
Closed 15-31 Jan. 15 Nov- 20 Dec. Mon. Region Alsace.
Post 4 ch. de Sapins, Ramberchamp, 88400 Gérardmer, Vosges.
Tel 03 29 63 02 27. Mich 60/B3. Map 3.

GERARDMER   Grand Hôtel Bragard/Rest. Grand Cerf

Luxury hotel/Cooking 2-3   `FW`
Terrace/Gardens/Swimming pool/Lift/Parking

Don't let "luxury" put you off. Talented Fabienne & Claude Remy continue
to breathe rejuvenating life into this long-established hotel. Chef
Dominique Mervelay tempts with a wide range of classical menus. Soak up
the deluxe environment & tuck into the varied menu fare: *nage de tous nos
poissons* & a *terrine de lapereau* at the bargain end: *emincé de canard
aux morilles* at the more expensive extreme. Gym/sauna/solarium.
Menus bCDEF. Rooms (56) FG. Cards All. (Cheaper rooms? Previous page.)
Post pl. Tilleul, 88400 Gérardmer, Vosges. Region Alsace.
Tel 03 29 63 06 31. Fax 03 29 63 46 81. Mich 60/B3. Map 3.

GERARDMER (Bas Rupts)   A La Belle Marée

Comfortable restaurant/Cooking 2   `FW`
Parking

800m nearer Gérardmer than its famed neighbour, the Philippes home.
"*La Mer à la Montagne*" is the proud boast here – with a vengeance.
Reason? Owner Christian David runs a fish/shellfish delivery service in
Alsace. *Patronne* Laurence Galli is first-rate – as is the formidable choice
of classical fish dishes: based on *coquillages, sole, raie, saumon et al.*
Menus ABCDE. Cards All. (Rooms: two *sans rest.* hotels on previous page.)
Closed 23 June-5 July. Sun evg. Mon.
Post Bas Rupts, 88400 Gérardmer, Vosges. Region Alsace.
Tel 03 29 63 06 83. Mich 60/B4. Map 3.

GERARDMER (Bas Rupts)   Host. des Bas-Rupts/Chalet Fleuri

Very comfortable hotel/Cooking 3-4
Terrace/Gardens/Swimming pool/Tennis/Parking/Air cond. (rest.)

Michel Philippe & his hostess daughter, English-speaking Sylvie, have
found a new lease of life at their flower-bedecked *hostellerie* & aptly-
named chalet annexe in the wooded hills S of Gérardmer. Both modern &
regional specialities from Michel's kitchen, where chef François Lachaud
has brought with him an oversized dose of rare culinary talent. Bikes
provided f.o.c. in the summer. Note: open all year; enjoy winter skiing.
Menus c(low-end)DEF. Rooms (31) FG. Cards AE, MC, V.
Post Bas Rupts, 88400 Gérardmer, Vosges. Region Alsace.
Tel 03 29 63 09 25. Fax 03 29 63 00 40. Mich 60/B4. Map 3.

A100frs & under. B100–150. C150–200. D200–250. E250–350. F350–500. G500+

GERMIGNY-L'EVEQUE

Le Gonfalon

Very comfortable restaurant with rooms/Cooking 2
Quiet/Terrace

Some moans about this delectably-sited restaurant on the Marne's left bank: grumbles over unfriendly service & severe wine mark-ups. Indeed all prices are up: blame Disneyland Paris for that. Pity! Line Colubi, a classicist, loves working with fish & shellfish (there's a 1600-litre seawater tank in the *salle*). Some bedrooms have riverside terraces.
Menus c(top-end)E. Rooms (8) EF. Cards All. (NE of Meaux.)
Closed Jan. Sun evg. Mon.
Post 77910 Germigny-l'Evèque, Seine-et-Marne. Region Ile de France.
Tel 01 64 33 16 05. Fax 01 64 33 25 59. Mich 36/C2. Map 2.

GEVREY-CHAMBERTIN

Le Bonbistrot

Simple restaurant/Cooking 1-2   FW
Terrace/Parking

Pierre Menneveau's *bistrot* is at ground level, above his rightly famed Rôtisserie & is served by the same kitchen. Admire the 19thC pewter bar & chuckle at the toilet's washbasin. Emphatic regional tunes on the Bonbistrot accordion: among them *jambon persillé, fricassée de coq au vin à l'ancienne & ami du Chambertin* cheese. FW wines by the glass.
Menus BC (à la carte). Cards MC, V. (Rooms: see next entry; short walk.)
Closed 15-28 Feb. 1-15 Aug. Sun evg & Mon (not pub. hols).
Post 21220 Gevrey-Chambertin, Côte-d'Or. Region Burgundy.
Tel 03 80 34 35 14. Fax 03 80 34 12 30. Mich 88/B1. Map 3.

GEVREY-CHAMBERTIN

Les Grands Crus

Comfortable hotel (no restaurant)
Quiet/Gardens/Parking

Within sight of the 12thC château, overlooking vineyards & alongside the Route des Grands Crus, the hotel has long been a personal favourite. Built 20 years ago, the modest but smart, flower-bedecked hotel has new owners these days, the Farniers. Despite the modern façade the large hall/breakfast room has the air of an authentic old Burgundian house.
Rooms (24) F. Cards MC, V. (Easy walk to all 4 recommended restaurants.)
Closed Dec-Feb.
Post 21220 Gevrey-Chambertin, Côte-d'Or. Region Burgundy.
Tel 03 80 34 34 15. Fax 03 80 51 89 07. Mich 88/B1. Mich 3.

GEVREY-CHAMBERTIN   Les Millésimes

Very comfortable restaurant/Cooking 4
Terrace/Parking/Air-conditioning

A supreme family enterprise: elegant Monique Sangoy, her daughter Sophie & son Didier (*MD/sommelier*) supervise the opulent cellar *salle*; Laurent & Denis, her younger sons, mastermind the brilliant neo-classical *plats*. One wonderful creation: *escargots en os à moelle*. More? Yes, more than likely the world's greatest collection of Burgundian wines: what a list!
Menus EG. Cards All. (Rooms: see two Gevrey-Chambertin base hotels.)
Closed 22 Dec-25 Jan. Tues. Wed midday.
Post 25 r. Eglise, 21220 Gevrey-Chambertin, Côte-d'Or. Region Burgundy.
Tel 03 80 51 84 24. Fax 03 80 34 12 73. Mich 88/B1. Map 3.

GEVREY-CHAMBERTIN   La Rôtisserie du Chambertin

Very comfortable restaurant/Cooking 3
Parking/Air-conditioning

There are many good reasons for seeking out La Rôtisserie: the owner, Anglophile Pierre Menneveau; the cellar dining room (with stone, wood panelling & discreet lighting); the treasure-chest *cave*; & chef Jean-Pierre Nicholas' multi-styled repertoire. Among highlights a gutsy *tranche saumon frais rôti* with GC sauce; & artful *sandre au vin jaune*.
Menus CDE. Cards MC, V. (Rooms: see two Gevrey-C base hotels.)
Closed 15-28 Feb. 1-15 Aug. Sun evg & Mon (not pub. hols).
Post 21220 Gevrey-Chambertin, Côte-d'Or. Region Burgundy.
Tel 03 80 34 33 20. Fax 03 80 34 12 30. Mich 88/B1. Map 3.

GEVREY-CHAMBERTIN (also see next page)   Sangoy Côté Cour

Simple restaurant/Cooking 2-3   FW
Terrace

"*Millésimes Bistro*", run by Melissa Sangoy (Didier's wife) with vitality & charm (she's an Oregon lass). An old garage converted with flair. Exceptional *RQP* menus & à la carte choice: typical classical, regional & *Bourgeoise* fare inc' *jarret de veau à la croque en sel, langue de boeuf grillé* & *jambon persillé*. Super wines (inc' two dozen half-bottles.)
(Rooms: Arts & Terroirs (next page) 1 min walk; Grands Crus 5 min walk.)
Menus AB. Cards MC, V. (Grands Crus: previous page.) Reg. Burgundy.
Post rte de Beaune (N74), 21220 Gevrey-Chambertin, Côte-d'Or.
Tel 03 80 58 53 58. Fax 03 80 58 52 73. Mich 88/B1. Map 3.

A 100frs & under. B 100–150. C 150–200. D 200–250. E 250–350. F 350–500. G 500+

GEVREY-CHAMBERTIN

Comfortable hotel (no restaurant)
Gardens/Closed parking

First recommended to me by Pierre Menneveau who spoke highly of the owners, the Leclercs, & the attractively furnished interior; many readers have since confirmed the hotel's high reputation. On the E bank of the busy, fast-flowing N74; but don't be put off as 17 of the stylish bedrooms at the rear are surprisingly quiet. Two welcome bonuses: the gardens at the rear; &, unlike Les Grands Crus, the hotel is open all year.
Rooms (20) E(bottom-end)F. Cards All. (Short walk to Sangoy Côté Cour.)
Post rte Dijon (N74), 21220 Gevrey-Chambertin, Côte-d'Or. Reg. Burgundy.
Tel 03 80 34 30 76. Fax 03 80 34 11 79. Mich 88/B1. Map 3.

GIEN

Very comfortable hotel/Cooking 3   FW
Closed parking/Air-conditioning (restaurant)

English-speaking Christian Gaillard & his smiling wife, Ingrid, continue to raise standards at the Loire-side *relais* opened by his parents in 1954. The glass-lined dining room is especially pleasant & has talking-point pictures. Chef Thierry Renou paints modern/neo-classical pictures of his own: typical of which is a *darne de colin rôti au paprika*.
Menus BCDEF. Rooms (16) EFG. Cards All. (Right bank of Loire.)
Closed Rest: 13 Feb-8 Mar. Sun evg (9 Nov-11 Mar).
Post 1 quai Nice, 45500 Gien, Loiret. Region Loire.
Tel 02 38 37 79 00. Fax 02 38 38 10 21. Mich 70/B2. Map 2.

GIGONDAS

Comfortable restaurant with rooms/Cooking 2   FW
Secluded/Terrace/Gardens/Parking

A large tree-shaded terrace is a plus: cool at midday & with lights in the evening. Menu C has a choice of classical/regional/*Bourgeois plats*: *tourte de lapereau au romarin et morilles* & *roulade de pintadeau aux ravioles* have been praised. All-in-all much improved. The Bernard family (Pierre's a charmer) also own a Gigondas vineyard ("sensational wines").
Menus BCD. Rooms (13) F. Cards All. (E of village; shown on Mich. maps.)
Closed Jan. Feb. Tues evg (out of season). Wed.
Post 84190 Gigondas, Vaucluse. Region Provence.
Tel 04 90 65 85 01. Fax 04 90 65 83 80. Mich 144/C3. Map 6.

A100frs & under. B100–150. C150–200. D200–250. E250–350. F350–500. G500+

GIROUSSENS

L'Echauguette

Comfortable restaurant with rooms/Cooking 2
Terrace

La cuisinière, Pierrette Canonica, puts her fingers in varying French regional cooking pots: take your pick from varied delights like *salade Aveyronnaise, gras-double à la Lyonnaise, andouillettes* (Normandy) & an earthy *daube de boeuf au Madiran* (a Gascony wine). Sumptuous home-made *pâtisseries*. Claude, Pierrette's husband, is *le patron*.
Menus aBCDE. Rooms (5) BCDE. Cards All.
Closed 1-21 Feb. 14-29 Sept. Sun evg & Mon (Oct-June).
Post pl. de la Mairie, 81500 Giroussens, Tarn. Region Languedoc-Rouss.
Tel 05 63 41 63 65. Fax 05 63 41 63 13. Mich 153/E2. Map 5.

GIVET

Val St-Hilaire

Comfortable hotel (no restaurant)
Closed parking

The modern, newly-built hotel has a pleasant site, below a high cliff with Vauban's (his work is everywhere) 17thC fortress, the Citadelle de Charlemont, dominating the summit. More importantly the hotel overlooks the Meuse; boat trips downriver to Dinant (in Belgium) are a special plus. Mme Dardenne, *la patronne*, speaks English.
Rooms (20) E. Disabled. Cards MC, V.
Closed 20 Dec-5 Jan. Sun evg (5 Jan-15 Mar).
Post 7 quai des Fours, 08600 Givet, Ardennes. Region Champ-Ard.
Tel 03 24 42 38 50. Fax 03 24 42 07 36. Mich 11/D3. Map 3.

GORDES

Le Gordos

Comfortable hotel (no restaurant)
Quiet/Gardens/Swimming pool/Parking

Lynda Mazet's hotel is SW of Gordes, on the road to Cavaillon – at the heart of *bories* land (ancient dry stone-built, beehive-like structures; visit the nearby Village des Bories). Le Gordos is a modern stone-built structure (with essential mortar); each of the large bedrooms has a private terrace. Useful, if a touch dear, base for nearby restaurants.
Rooms (19) G. Cards AE, MC, V.
Closed 5 Nov-14 Mar.
Post rte Cavaillon, 84220 Gordes, Vaucluse. Region Provence.
Tel 04 90 72 00 75. Fax 04 90 72 07 00. Mich 159/D1. Map 6.

A100frs & under. B100–150. C150–200. D200–250. E250–350. F350–500. G500+

GOUJOUNAC

Hostellerie de Goujounac

Simple restaurant with rooms/Cooking 1-2
Terrace

FW

As I said in *FLE*: who would have thought this modest *FL3* (1983) entry would one day make the Michelin guide. Rustic & endearing apply to the dining room & the Costes family respectively. Jean-Pierre is a *cuisine terroir* chef: *poularde aux cèpes, mique* (see Dordogne specs), *confit de canard, cous farci* – some of many tempters. For one reader "pure magic".
Menus B(bottom-end)CD. Rooms (5) DE. Cards MC, V.
Closed 15-28 Feb. Oct. Sun evg & Mon (Oct-June).
Post 46250 Goujounac, Lot. Region Dordogne.
Tel 05 65 36 68 67. Fax 05 65 36 60 54. Mich 138/A1. Map 5.

GOUMOIS

Moulin du Plain

Simple hotel/Cooking 1-2
Secluded/Parking

FW

One of the most perfect dead-end road hotel settings I've ever seen (only Gidleigh Park is perhaps better). N of Goumois on the left bank of the gorgeous River Doubs, a valley akin to heaven for fishermen & walkers. Thomas Coulet's copious regional/classical fare takes second place: *truite, croûte aux morilles, brési, jambon fumé* & similar.
Menus aBC. Rooms (22) DE. Cards MC, V. (Hotel on Michelin maps.)
Closed Nov-Feb.
Post 25470 Goumois, Doubs. Region Jura.
Tel 03 81 44 41 99. Fax 03 81 44 45 70. Mich 77/D4. Map 3.

GOUMOIS

Taillard

Comfortable hotel/Cooking 2-3
Secluded/Terrace/Gardens/Swimming pool/Parking

FW

A blissful spot, 2000 ft above sea-level, with rejuvenating views across the deep wooded Doubs Valley. A long-established, now modernised, family hotel, founded in 1875. Regional & modern creations from 4th-generation Jean-François Taillard & new young chef in *la cuisine*. One reader wrote: "If you want to be spoilt, I would recommend the Taillard to anyone."
Menus BCEF. Rooms (14) EF. Cards All.
Closed Mid Nov-mid Mar. Wed (not Apl-Sept).
Post 25470 Goumois, Doubs. Region Jura.
Tel 03 81 44 20 75. Fax 03 81 44 26 15. Mich 77/D4. Map 3.

A100frs & under. B100–150. C150–200. D200–250. E250–350. F350–500. G500+

GOURDON
Hostellerie de la Bouriane

Comfortable hotel/Cooking 2
Quiet/Gardens/Lift/Parking/Air-conditioning (rest.)

`FW`

Modern *logis* S of Gourdon's medieval centre. A host of little details make
their mark: tasty appetisers & *petits fours*; & a huge log fire in winter.
Pretty *salle* & caring *patrons* (the Lacams). A spiky *escalope de saumon
grillée au beurre d'épices* & a luscious *coq au vin de Cahors* with a dark
pool of sauce were the high points of a classical cooking *repas*.
Menus ABCDE. Rooms (20) EF(low-end). Cards AE, MC, V.
Closed 15 Jan-5 Mar. Sun evg (Nov-Easter). Mon (not evgs Easter-Oct).
Post pl. Foirail, 46300 Gourdon, Lot. Region Dordogne.
Tel 05 65 41 16 37. Fax 05 65 41 04 92. Mich 124/B4. Map 5.

GRAMAT
Lion d'Or

Very comfortable hotel/Cooking 2-3
Terrace/Lift/Air-conditioning (restaurant)

`FW`

A handsome stone façade with a vine-covered terrace & a warm welcome
from Suzanne & René Mommèjac. René seduces with treats like *carpaccio
de jambon d'Aoste au melon des côteaux du Quercy* (a tasty French &
Italian marriage) & a mouthwatering *saumon rôti au lard, poireaux et
tatin de champignons aux pommes*. Neo-classical & *Quercynoise* cooking.
Menus BCDE. Rooms (15) EF. Cards All. (Park in huge *place* opp. hotel.)
Closed Mid Dec-mid Jan.
Post pl. Republique, 46500 Gramat, Lot. Region Dordogne.
Tel 05 65 38 73 18. Fax 05 65 38 84 50. Mich 125/D4. Map 5.

GRAMAT
Le Relais des Gourmands

Comfortable hotel/Cooking 2-3
Terrace/Gardens/Swimming pool/Parking

`FW`

An enticing mix of ingredients beguile clients: colourful, bright
decorations & furnishings in a modern building, a Scots' welcome from
multi-lingual Susy Curtet & a confident *palette* of regional & classical
specialities from husband Gérard. Memorable *assiette de deux terrines* &
blockbuster *cassoulet Périgourdin au confit d'oie*. A readers' favourite.
Menus aBCD. Rooms (16) EF. Cards MC, V.
Closed Sun evg. Mon midday.
Post av. Gare, 46500 Gramat, Lot. Region Dordogne.
Tel 05 65 38 83 92. Fax 05 65 38 70 99. Mich 125/D4. Map 5.

A100frs & under. B100–150. C150–200. D200–250. E250–350. F350–500. G500+

Le GRAND-PRESSIGNY

Espérance

Comfortable restaurant with basic rooms/Cooking 2-3 | FW |

No complaints about Bernard Torset's modern/neo-classical cooking. For some "marvellous food, atmosphere & staff." For others "fussy & slow, abysmal service." One serious gripe: the numerous cats *demi-sauvages* (Paulette Torset's words) often attracted to the rear patio. One reader counted 17. Mme's dog has unsavoury habits too. I've put both problems to her; I hope by now she has successfully got them sorted out.
Menus BCD. Rooms (10) C (bottom-end). Cards All. (Parking is easy.)
Closed Mon. (Alternative rooms: Moderne, Decartes; 12km to NW.)
Post 37350 Le Grand-Pressigny, Indre-et-Loire. Regions Loire/Poitou-Ch.
Tel 02 47 94 90 12. Mich 82/B3. Map 2.

GRANE

Patrick Giffon

Comfortable hotel/Cooking 3 | FW |
Quiet/Terrace/Swimming pool/Closed parking/Air-cond. (rest.)

Welcome wind of change continues to blow through this old favourite. The small *logis* is still dominated by the *église*; the plane-shaded terrace is as cool as ever; now there's a pool; & the family atmosphere remains. Patrick Giffon's modern/neo-classical skills improve steadily & he makes super use of a bountiful *terroir* – the Rhône Valley & Provence to the S.
Menus b(lunch)CDEF. Rooms (14) DEFG. Cards All.
Closed Sun evg (Oct-Apl). Mon.
Post 26400 Grane, Drôme. Regions Hautes-Alpes/Massif Central (Ardèche).
Tel 04 75 62 60 64. Fax 04 75 62 70 11. Mich 130/B4. Map 5.

GRASSE

Maître Boscq

Very simple restaurant/Cooking 1

No dining room comes smaller or simpler than the tiny home of Patrick & Odile Boscq, both big-hearted, friendly *patrons*. Patrick is the Stormin' Norman of French cuisine; he speaks good English & has a fierce, fighting loyalty for *Grassoise* recipes: *lou fassum*, *fricot de cacho-fuou* & similar treats. Herbs, vegetables, game; everything is authentically Provençal. Park in the nearby car parks at the bus station.
Menus B. Cards MC, V. (Rooms: see du Bosquet, Pégomas entry.)
Closed Evenings (out of season). Sun.
Post 13 r. Fontette, 06130 Grasse, Alpes-Maritimes. Region Côte d'Azur.
Tel 04 93 36 45 76. Mich 163/F2. Map 6.

A100frs & under. B100–150. C150–200. D200–250. E250–350. F350–500. G500+

GRASSE

Pierre Baltus

Very simple restaurant/Cooking 1-2

Next door to longtime old favourites, Patrick & Odile Boscq: will they ever forgive me for introducing you to competition? This *salle* is no bigger than Maître Boscq – but the cooking drives different routes from Patrick's: here expect classical fare laced with many Périgord touches (ideal for Dordogne lovers). Hearty tucker of the *steack de canard comme à Sarlat* & *filet de boeuf à la Périgourdine variety.* (E Pl. aux Aires.)
Menus ABC. Cards not accepted. (Rooms: see du Bosquet, Pégomas entry.)
Closed Mid Feb-mid Mar. 1-15 July. Mon. (Parking: see earlier entry.)
Post 15 r. Fontette, 06130 Grasse, Alpes-Maritimes. Region Côte d'Azur.
Tel 04 93 36 32 90. Mich 163/F2. Map 6.

GRASSE (Opio)

Mas de Géraniums

Comfortable restaurant/Cooking 2
Terrace/Gardens/Parking
FW

A jewel of a *mas*, hidden among the olive groves (now with a new vista of a golf course 300m away). English-speaking owners, Colette & Michel Creusot (he worked for both Surmain at Mougins & Ducloux at Tournus). His classical & Provençale cooking appeals: typical of both are tasty *suprême de volaille farci aux morilles* & *rouget grillé à l'Opidoise.*
Menus BCD. Cards MC, V. (Rooms: Arc Hôtel, beside D3 to Mougins, to S.)
Closed 19/12-1/1. 24/10-27/11. Wed. Th *midi* (Jul/Au). Tu evg (Sep-Jun).
Post 06650 Opio, Alpes-Maritimes. Region Côte d'Azur. (E of Grasse.)
Tel 04 93 77 23 23. Fax 04 93 77 76 05. Mich 163/F2. Map 6. (S D2085.)

GRASSE (Spéracèdes)

La Soleillade

Simple restaurant with basic rooms/Cooking 1
Terrace

Many readers have written to report on their highly satisfactory visits since the new English owners, Jenny Monckton & Shirley Jones, took over from Michel Forest. *Les patronnes* offer a mix of classical & Provençale cooking: the likes of *charcuterie & crudités; bouchées aux fruits de mer & côtes d'agneau aux herbes*; & some of Michel's fine desserts. Bravo!
Menus B. Rooms (9) C. Cards MC, V. (8km W of Grasse.)
Closed Last wk Oct to first wk Dec. Rest: Sun evg. Tues.
Post 06530 Spéracèdes, Alpes-Maritimes. Region Côte d'Azur.
Tel 04 93 60 58 46. Mich 163/E2. Map 6.

A100frs & under. B100–150. C150–200. D200–250. E250–350. F350–500. G500+

GRENADE-SUR-L'ADOUR

Pain Adour et Fantaisie

Very comfortable hotel/Cooking 3-4
Terrace/Air-conditioning (bedrooms)

Didier Oudill has gone W (see Biarritz). New owners have made a terrific start. Véronique Garret & her sister-in-law, Josiane, welcome you; chef/husband Philippe (35; worked for DO at Eugénie & Grenade) seduces with a dazzling array of inventive, modern creations with eclectic facets. The 17thC house, stonework, panelling, Adour-side terrace – all are superb.
Menus CEF. Rooms (12) FG. Cards All.
Closed Sun evg (Sept-June). Mon (not evgs July/Aug). Region Southwest.
Post 14 pl. Tilleuls, 40270 Grenade-sur-l'Adour, Landes.
Tel 05 58 45 18 80. Fax 05 58 45 16 57. Mich 150/A2. Map 4.

GRESSE-EN-VERCORS

Le Chalet

Comfortable hotel/Cooking 2   FW
Quiet/Terrace/Swimming pool/Tennis/Garage/Parking

A *logis* & no chalet. That matters not. The site is tremendous, under the shadow of Gd Veymont & the Vercors' high E wall. Super owners: smiling, helpful Nicole Prayer out front, with husband Paul & son Christophe singing neo-classical/regional duets in the kitchen: such as *panaché de la mer aux petits légumes* & *civet de sanglier, gratin Daupinois*.
Menus aBCE. Rooms (25) EF. Cards MC, V.
Closed 20 Oct-19 Dec. 29 Mar-10 May.
Post 38650 Gresse-en-Vercors, Isère. Regions Hautes-Alpes/Savoie.
Tel 04 76 34 32 08. Fax 04 76 34 31 06. Mich 131/D3-E3. Map 6.

GRIMAUD

Athénopolis

Comfortable hotel (no restaurant)
Secluded/Gardens/Swimming pool/Parking

The prime benefit here is the secluded setting – 3 km NW of Grimaud, in grounds of five acres alongside the D558 & only 10km from the Golfe de St-Tropez & the overcrowded coast. All the bedrooms face N & have either balconies or terraces; they all overlook the pool & face the heavily wooded Massif des Maures. Mini-bars in the bedrooms are another plus.
Rooms (11) G(low-end). Disabled. Cards All.
Closed Nov-Mar.
Post 83310 Grimaud, Var. Region Côte d'Azur.
Tel 04 94 43 24 24. Fax 04 94 43 37 05. Mich 163/D4. Map 6.

A 100frs & under. B 100–150. C 150–200. D 200–250. E 250–350. F 350–500. G 500+

La GUERCHE-DE-BRETAGNE   La Calèche

Comfortable restaurant with rooms/Cooking 1-2   FW
Quiet/Terrace/Garage/Closed parking

Built six years ago, the modern Calèche has large bathrooms – unusual in
so many newly-built French establishments. Service is truly exemplary –
witness the late-night cold dinner laid out for clients who phoned ahead
to say that they had been delayed. Classical/*Bourgeoise* cooking: of the
pavé de saumon, râble de lapereau, peaches poached in wine variety.
Menus aBC. Rooms (10) DE. Cards MC, V.
Closed 1-21 August. Sun evg. Mon. Regions Brittany/Normandy.
Post 16 av. Gén. Leclerc, 35130 La Guerche-de-Bretagne, Ille-et-Vilaine.
Tel 02 99 96 21 63. Fax 02 99 96 49 52. Mich 49/D4. Map 1.

GUINGAMP   Relais du Roy

Very comfortable restaurant with rooms/Cooking 2-3   FW
Quiet

Victoria & Jacques Mallégol's 16thC *hôtel particulier* (town house) has
elegant bedrooms. Jacques' elegant classical cooking has many a Breton
touch. Four fish creations – *petite marmite des Pêcheurs, moules de la
Côte au cidre, filet de mérou bisquine* & *filet de truite de l'Argoat*
evoke to a tee his well-crafted regional *plats* using *terroir* produce.
Menus BCDE. Rooms (7) FG. Cards All. (Cheaper rooms: D'Armor.)
Closed Christmas. Rest: Sun (mid Nov-mid Mar). (Parking in *place* opp.)
Post pl. Centre, 22200 Guingamp, Côtes d'Armor. Region Brittany.
Tel 02 96 43 76 62. Fax 02 96 44 08 01. Mich 28/B2. Map 1.

Les HALLES   Charreton

Comfortable restaurant with rooms/Cooking 2   FW
Parking

The *auberge,* beside the D489 & at the heart of the Monts du Lyonnais,
has views from the rear of both hills & woods. Pierre Charreton is both a
master baker & *cuisinier.* Regional & neo-classical specialities: an
enterprising *Pithiviers au Roquefort*; a sweet toothsome *cuisse de canard
au Banyuls et orange*; and, no surprise, a *fromage blanc* with cream.
Menus BCD. Rooms (5) E. Cards MC, V.
Closed Sun evg. Wed.
Post 69610 Les Halles, Rhône. Region Lyonnais.
Tel 04 74 26 63 05. Mich 115/E2. Map 6.

A100frs & under. B100–150. C150–200. D200–250. E250–350. F350–500. G500+

HAM

France

Comfortable restaurant with rooms/Cooking 1-2

No changes from *FLE*. It's impossible to make merry in this consecrated land. Come with no great expectations & take quiet pleasure from the vine-covered France in the shadow of the town hall's high belfry. Jean-Pierre Malliez rings classical bells, diverting here & there with some regional chimes: *anguille fumé*, filling *ficelle Picarde* & *tarte aux pommes flambées au Calvados* (from Normandy) are typical alternatives.
Menus BC. Rooms (6) D. Cards MC, V.
Closed Sun evg.
Post 5 pl. Hôtel de Ville, 80400 Ham, Somme. Region North.
Tel 03 23 81 00 22. Mich 18/C2. Map 2.

HEDE

Hostellerie Vieux Moulin

Comfortable restaurant with rooms/Cooking 1-2 FW
Terrace/Gardens/Parking

The pretty virgina creeper-covered mill is below the village's W edge, beside the old N137 (now an express-way to the W). The wooded valley is a green pleasure; so is the classical, traditional fare. Good choice on menu B: to start oysters, *terrine de canard* or *feuilleté de fruits de mer*; salmon or lamb; cheese; & *île flottante* or apple tart to finish.
Menus aBCD. Rooms (14) E. Cards All.
Closed 20 Dec-1 Feb. Sun evg & Mon (not mid July-mid Aug).
Post 35630 Hédé, Ille-et-Vilaine. Region Brittany.
Tel 02 99 45 45 70. Fax 02 99 45 44 86. Mich 48/B2. Map 1.

HENDAYE

Chez Antoinette

Simple hotel & annexe/Cooking 1-2 FW
Gardens (annexe)/Closed parking (hotel)

A mile or so from Hendaye Plage & with "a geranium show good enough for Chelsea." A green-shuttered family *logis*, led by Bernard Haramboure, the *chef de cuisine*. Enjoy both Basque & classical fare: *merlu salsa verde, lotte au coulis de crabe, confit de cannette maison* & *noisette d'agneau à la Navarraise* are typical copious choices. Annexe at Hendaye Plage.
Menus B. Rooms (23: of which 7 at annexe) DEF. Cards MC, V.
Closed Nov-Easter. Rest: Mon (not July/Aug). Region Southwest.
Post pl. Pellot, 64700 Hendaye Ville, Pyrénées-Atlantiques.
Tel 05 59 20 08 47. Fax 05 59 48 11 64. Mich 166/A1. Map 4.

A100frs & under. B100–150. C150–200. D200–250. E250–350. F350–500. G500+

HENNEBONT
Château de Locguénolé

Very comfortable hotel/Cooking 3
Secluded/Gardens/Swimming pool/Tennis/Parking

The site is pure enchantment, surrounded by woods & grounds & beside the River Blavet; the richly-decorated interior is typical *R&C* sumptuous; the owners, *châtelaine* Alyette de la Sablière & her son, Bruno, are consummate hoteliers; & cooking, by new chef Marc Angelle, is modern & neo-classical. Flaws? An ugly-duckling exterior & overpriced wines.
Menus cDEF. Rooms (18) G,G2. Also annexe (7) FG. Cards All.
Closed 2 Jan-8 Feb. Rest: Mon (Oct-Apl; not pub. hols). (Use D781 to S.)
Post 56700 Hennebont, Morbihan. Region Brittany.
Tel 02 97 76 29 04. Fax 02 97 76 82 35. Mich 46/B4. Map 1.

HERRLISHEIM
Au Moulin

Comfortable hotel (no restaurant)
Secluded/Gardens/Lift/Parking

A 17thC mill which, as recently as 25 years ago, was still in operation. Converted into an hotel by M. & Mme Raymond Woelffle; she is the daughter of the last miller. The *moulin* is alongside the River Thur (a dozen mills were once active; two still work). Beside the D1, E of Herrlisheim – or W from exit 27 on the A35.
Rooms (17) DEF. Disabled. Cards MC, V.
Closed 4 Nov-end Mar. Region Alsace.
Post rte d'Herrlisheim, 68127 Ste-Croix-en-Plaine, Haut-Rhin.
Tel 03 89 49 31 20. Fax 03 89 49 23 11. Mich 61/D4. Map 3.

HESDIN (also see next page)
Les Flandres

Simple hotel/Cooking 1-2
Closed parking

Simple the *logis* may be but readers love the hotel (& the film-set town). They particularly like *les enfants terribles* – the brothers Marc & Georges Persyn. "Enjoyed immensely" & "adore this hotel" are typical comments. Cooking? Classical, *Bourgeoise* & regional – from grills to *coq au bière flambé au genièvre* (a *terroir* dish *par excellence*).
Menus aBC. Rooms (14) E. Cards MC, V.
Closed 20 Dec-10 Jan. 28 June-7 July.
Post r. Arras, 62140 Hesdin, Pas-de-Calais. Region North.
Tel 03 21 86 80 21. Fax 03 21 86 28 01. Mich 7/D1. Map 2.

A100frs & under. B100–150. C150–200. D200–250. E250–350. F350–500. G500+

HESDIN (also see previous page)   Les Trois Fontaines

Simple hotel/Cooking 1
Quiet/Gardens/Parking

A newish, whitewashed *logis* where Martine & Patrick Herbin, helped by her jovial father, satisfy in unassuming, quiet ways. *La salle* is quintessential French; the site is quiet; the gardens are neat; the bar adds colour & atmosphere. Classical, regional, *Bourgeoise* cooking from Patrick. A one-word summary? "Satisfying" – again. Alas no FW rating.
Menus ABC. Rooms (10) E. Cards All. (At Marconne; 500m S of Hesdin.)
Closed 24 Dec-1 Jan. 31 Aug-9 Sept. Region North.
Post 16 rte Abbeville, Marconne, 62140 Hesdin, Pas-de-Calais.
Tel 03 21 86 81 65. Fax 03 21 86 33 34. Mich 7/D1-D2. Map 2.

HOMPS   Auberge de l'Arbousier

Simple hotel/Cooking 2   FW
Quiet/Terrace/Parking

Don't be put off by first appearances of the "strawberry tree". Ignore the tatty roadside façade; enjoy, instead, the Rosado *logis*, W of the village & on the S side of the Canal du Midi. Classical & regional fare with little choice; no problem with delights like *rillettes de poisson, lapin au sauce citron et miel* & *escalope de veau aux Lucques* (olives).
Menus aBC. Rooms (7) DE. Cards MC. V.
Closed 15 Feb-15 Mar. 1-23 Nov. Su evg & We (Sept-June). Mon (July/Aug).
Post av. Carcassonne, 11200 Homps, Aude. Region Languedoc-Roussillon.
Tel 04 68 91 11 24. Fax 04 68 91 12 61. Mich 172/C1. Map 5.

HONFLEUR   Au P'tit Mareyeur

Simple restaurant/Cooking 2   FW

Christian Chaillou is an assured *cuisinier*. Behind the blue-fronted, ship-shape façade lies a small 18thC dining room. There's a single-price neo-classical menu which confirm's Christian's culinary *nous*: a punchy *velouté de petits crabes son crouton à la crème d'ail*, an artful *escalope de saumon mi-cuit à la réglisse douce* & a saliva-stirring *tarte paysanne au miel et pommeau* are all absolutely cracking creations.
Menus B. Cards MC, V. (Rooms: many *sans restaurant* hotels nearby.)
Closed 7-24 Jan. 13-29 Nov. Mon evg. Tues. (Parking nearby.)
Post 4 r. Haute, 14600 Honfleur, Calvados. Region Normandy. Mich 14/C3.
Tel 02 31 98 84 23. Fax 02 31 98 84 23. Map 2. (NW of La Lieutenance.)

A100frs & under. B100–150. C150–200. D200–250. E250–350. F350–500. G500+

HONFLEUR   Le Butin de la Mer

Very comfortable restaurant with rooms/Cooking 2   FW
Quiet/Terrace/Gardens/Parking

The half-timbered Anglo-Normand *manoir* is an "annexe" for the famed
Ferme St-Siméon (400m to the E). A wooded parkland site overlooking the
Seine Estuary (pity about the distant refineries). *RQP* menu specialising in
classic fish/shellfish delights: *huîtres, morue fraîche, St-Pierre,
langoustines*, etc. (Cheaper rooms: many *sans rest.* hotels in Honfleur.)
Menus B(top-end). Rooms (9) G,G2,G3,G4(!). Cards AE, MC, V.
Closed Rest: 12 Nov-30 Mar. Wed & Thur *midi* (not July-Sept).
Post r. A. Marais, 14600 Honfleur, Calvados. Region Normandy. (D513 SW.)
Tel 02 31 81 63 00. Fax 02 31 89 48 48. Mich 14/C3. Map 2.

HONFLEUR   La Lieutenance

Comfortable restaurant/Cooking 1-2   FW
Terrace

In this case "terrace" means part of the largish *place* on the N side of the
Eglise Ste-Catherine. Plenty of choice on 3 menus – all of which are
laced with Eric Delaunay's classical & Normandy specialities. Fish
dishes dominate of course: menu a includes *soupe de poissons, moules
marinière, saumon grillée* & the ubiquitous *tarte chaude aux pommes*.
Menus aC(low-end)D. Cards MC, V. (Rooms: several *sans rest.* hotels.)
Closed 11 Nov-18 Dec. Sun evg (not high season).
Post 12 pl. Ste-Catherine, 14600 Honfleur, Calvados. Region Normandy.
Tel 02 31 89 07 52. Mich 14/C3. Map 2.

Les HOUCHES   Auberge Beau Site/Rest. Le Pèle

Comfortable hotel/Cooking 1-2   FW
Terrace/Gardens/Lift/Parking

Mont Blanc towers over the hotel but it is the extrovert, colourful
gardens which almost steal the show. Nicole Perrin is an obliging hostess
& hubby Christian is an able chef. Primarily classical *plats* such as *féra
du lac au beurre blanc, travers de porc à la Dijonnaise* & *tarte au
citron*. (Cheaper rooms: Au Bois Coin, Chamonix.)
Menus bC(bottom-end). Rooms (18) F. Cards All. Closed 21 Apl-mid May.
11 Oct-23 Dec. Rest: *midi* (May/June/Oct). Wed (15 May-15 June).
Post 74310 Les Houches, Haute-Savoie. Region Savoie.
Tel 04 50 55 51 16. Fax 04 50 54 53 11. Mich 119/E1. Map 6.

A100frs & under. B100–150. C150–200. D200–250. E250–350. F350–500. G500+

HOUDAN

La Poularde

Very comfortable restaurant/Cooking 3
Terrace/Gardens/Parking

Two *Jeunes Restaurateurs de France* members – Rayé to the E, Bansard to the W – gave me unqualified recommendations for their colleague, Sylvain Vandenameele. The gardens are pleasing, the décor is neo-classical & the chef's cooking is both those plus *classique* as well. One masterpiece is 3-star: *aumônière de poulette de Houdan sauce truffée, sauce suprême.*
Menus bEF. Cards MC, V. (Rooms: Le Beffroi, Dreux; 20km to W.)
Closed 1-15 Mar. Tues evg. Wed. Regions Ile de France/Normandy.
Post 24 av. de la République, 78550 Houdan, Yvelines.
Tel 01 30 59 60 50. Fax 01 30 59 79 71. Mich 34/C4. Map 2.

HYERES

Jardin de Bacchus

Comfortable restaurant/Cooking 2-3
Terrace/Air-conditioning

An elegant spot with the Bacchus theme used at every turn. A top-notch wine list, *bien sûr* – presented by *la patronne/sommelière*, charming Claire Santioni. Her husband, Jean-Claude, paddles in modern Provençales pools: a right champion *marinade de canard en tapenade et huile d'olive* & a tingling-with-flavour *tian de filets de rouges et ratatouille.*
Menus BCE. Cards AE, MC, V. (Rooms: lbis & Centrotel nearby – to S.)
Closed 6-12 Jan. Sat midday (July/ Aug). Sun evg (winter). Mon.
Post 32 av. Gambetta, 83400 Hyères, Var. Regions Côte d'Azur/Provence.
Tel 04 94 65 77 63. Mich 161/D4. Map 6.

ILE DE NOIRMOUTIER (Noirmoutier-en-l'Ile)

Fleur de Sel

Comfortable hotel/Cooking 1-2
Secluded/Terrace/Gardens/Swimming pool/Tennis/Parking

FW

Follow signs to the E of the island where you'll find Pierre & Annick Wattecamps' whitewashed hotel has a Camargue look. Facilities are excellent, inc' bedrooms furnished in the "English" style! Chefs come & go, but neo-classical standards prevail: *plats* like *terrine de raie aux pommes* & *côtes d'agneau et caviar d'aubergines jus à l'olive noire.*
Menus BC. Rooms (35) FG. Disabled. Cards AE, MC, V.
Closed 3 Nov-16 Feb. Rest: Mon midday.
Post 85330 Noirmoutier-en-l'Ile, Vendée. Region Poitou-Charentes.
Tel 02 51 39 21 59. Fax 02 51 39 75 66. Mich 78/A2. Map 1.

A100frs & under. B100–150. C150–200. D200–250. E250–350. F350–500. G500+

ILE DE RE (Ars-en-Ré)   Bistrot de Bernard

Comfortable restaurant/Cooking 2-3   FW
Terrace

An attractive *maison rhétaise* with blue & white façade & small terrace.
Catherine Frigière is the welcoming hostess; her chef/husband pleases by
keeping things simple & sticking to traditional ways with, mainly, fish/
shellfish *plats*. Menus B is great *RQP*. Consider *àlc* as well: *chaudrée
Charentaise* (A) or *assiette de fruits de mer* (A) with 7 different types.
Menus BC. Cards MC, V. (Rooms: Hippocampe, La Flotte.)
Closed 4 Jan-15 Feb. Mon evg & Tues (mid Sept-31 Mar). Region Poit-Char.
Post 1 quai Criée (au port), 17590 Ars-en-Ré, Charente-Maritime.
Tel 05 46 29 40 26. Fax 05 46 29 28 99. Mich 92/B3. Map 4.

ILE DE RE (La Flotte)   Le Lavardin

Comfortable restaurant/Cooking 2-3   FW
Air-conditioning

Owners Georges & Patricia Barbet look after the front of house while
young chef William Donny uses his donnies to mix neo-classical, Danish
& *Charentaises* culinary cocktails. Refreshing, salty & sweet cocktails of
flavours they are too: try a shaker mix of *harengs marinés Baltique,
saumon grillé à la fleur de sel de Ré* and what else but *Ile Flottaise!*
Menus a(lunch)C(low-end)DE. Cards MC, V. (Rooms: Hippocampe.)
Closed 8 Jan-2 Feb. 12 Nov-7 Dec. Tues evg (Oct-Mar). Wed (out of seas.)
Post r. H. Lainé, 17630 La Flotte, Charente-Maritime. Region Poit-Char.
Tel 05 48 09 68 32. Fax 05 46 09 54 03. Mich 92/C3. Map 4.

ILE DE RE (La Flotte) (also see next page)   Richelieu

Very comfortable hotel/Cooking 3
Secluded/Terr/Gardens/Swim pool/Tenn/Parking/Air cond. (rest.)

Luxury in an elegant ensemble of villas & bungalows with views N
towards the mainland. Léon & Jacqueline Gendre are savvy hoteliers;
they look after all the small details. Despite his name, chef Dominique
Bourgeois' cooking is *haute cuisine* with modern & local touches. Menus
could list *mouclade* & certainly a superb *plateaux de fruits de mer*.
Menus EF. Rooms (42) G,G2,G3,G4(!). Cards MC, V.
Closed Rest: 5 Jan-10 Feb. (Plus gym & Thalassotherapy centre.)
Post 17630 La Flotte, Ile de Ré, Charente-Maritime. Region Poit-Char.
Tel 05 46 09 60 70. Fax 05 46 09 50 59. Mich 92/C3. Map 4.

A100frs & under. B100–150. C150–200. D200–250. E250–350. F350–500. G500+

ILE DE RE (also see previous page)　　　　**Auberge de la Marée**
(Rivedoux-Plage)
Comfortable hotel/Cooking 1-2　　　　　　　FW
Terrace/Gardens/Swimming pool/Parking/Air-cond. (bedrooms)

Debits? A roadside site. Credits? Overlooking the sea (views NE) & small
port; air-cond. bedrooms; & prize-winning pool with patio & garden. The
classical cooking is best described as "contra": debits equal credits. No
serious grumbles with basics such as *melon au pineau, saumon fumé,
sole meunière, côte de veau forestière* & *fraises au pineau* (again).
Menus B(lunch)CDE. Rooms (30) FG. Cards MC, V.
Closed 12 Nov-31 Mar. Rest: Oct-mid May. Mon midday. Tues midday.
Post 17490 Rivedoux-Plage, Charente-Maritime. Region Poitou-Charentes.
Tel 05 46 09 80 02. Fax 05 46 09 88 25. Mich 92/C3. Map 4.

ILE D'OLERON (La Cotinière)　　　　**Motel Ile de Lumière**

Comfortable hotel (no restaurant)
Secluded/Gardens/Swimming pool/Tennis/Parking

Motel? No – otherwise well-named. An hotel with a series of pleasant
white bungalows around a swimming pool. Other pluses: a sandy beach;
a gym; the nearby port – famed for its shrimps; friendly owners; sea views
to the SW; & comfortable, spacious bedrooms. A well-liked readers'
favourite for over a decade. Snags? Just one – getting expensive.
Rooms (45) G(bottom-end). Cards MC, V.
Closed Oct-Easter. Region Poitou-Charentes.
Post La Cotinière, 17310 St-Pierre-d'Oléron, Charente-Maritime.
Tel 05 46 47 10 80. Fax 05 46 47 30 87. Mich 106/A1. Map 4.

ILE D'OLERON (St-Pierre-d'Oléron)　　　　**La Campagne**

Very comfortable restaurant/Cooking 2-3　　　FW
Terrace/Gardens/Parking

The stone & beamed restaurant, once the family farm, is 200m N of the
D734. Attractive, perfumed gardens, plus fountain, tease the senses;
followed by more of the same from Bernard Nicolas who uses excellent
produce in regional/neo-classical ways. Two dishes on menu B, *Le Petit
Charentais*, captivated: *soupe de moules* & *estouffade de joue de boeuf*.
Menus B(top-end)CE. Cards AE, MC, V. (Rooms: Les Cleunes, *sans rest.*)
Closed Nov-7 Apl. Sun evg. Mon. (Above hotel at St-Trojan-les-Bains.)
Post 17310 St-Pierre-d'Oléron, Charente-Maritime. Region Poitou-Char.
Tel 05 46 47 25 42. Fax 05 46 75 16 04. Mich 106/A1. Map 4.

A100frs & under. B100–150. C150–200. D200–250. E250–350. F350–500. G500+

ILE D'OLERON (St-Pierre-d'Oléron)　　　Moulin du Coivre

Comfortable restaurant/Cooking 2-3　　　FW
Parking

The *moulin* (once a windmill & still wearing a spiked black-hat roof) is a
visual tonic; the adjacent restaurant was the miller's house. Chef Patrice
Gasses's neo-classical formula keeps the satisfaction wheels turning
happily: *carpaccio de saumon au poivre vert, charlotte d'agneau aux
poivrons doux & clafoutis tiède aux griottes* are colourful evidence.
Menus BCD. Cards MC, V. (Rooms: Les Cleunes, St-Trojan-les-Bains.)
Closed Sun evg & Mon (not sch. hols; not pub. hols). (Above *sans rest*.)
Post 17310 St-Pierre-d'Oléron (D734), Charente-Maritime. Region Poit-Ch.
Tel 05 46 47 44 23. Mich 106/A1. Map 4.

ILLHAEUSERN　　　La Clairière

Very comfortable hotel (no restaurant)
Secluded/Swimming pool/Tennis/Lift/Parking

Marie-France & Roger Loux are justly proud of their stylish hotel – a
modern building constructed in the traditional style. Externally there's
much evidence of timber & there's a high tiled roof; the elegant interior
has all the mod cons you could ever want. *Chambres doubles normales*
(band F) provide the best value. W of village, beside D106.
Rooms (26) FG(top-end). Cards MC, V.
Closed Jan. Feb.
Post rte Guémar, 68970 Illhaeusern, Haut-Rhin. Region Alsace.
Tel 03 89 71 80 80. Fax 03 89 71 86 22. Mich 61/D3. Map 3.

L'ISLE-JOURDAIN (also see next page)　　　La Grimolée

Comfortable restaurant/Cooking (see text)　　　FW
Terrace/Gardens/Parking

Like the stunning Val de Vienne hotel, the *salle*, terrace & gardens are
alongside the Vienne's W bank. Susan Brooker-Carey (see next entry)
has bought the rest. She takes over in Sept 96 &, by then, after *FLF* has
been printed, a new chef should be at work. I've introduced her to many
regional cooks (in *FLF*); they'll ensure she employs a top-notch FW chef.
Menus a(lunch)BCD (projected prices). Cards MC, V. (Rooms: next entry.)
Closed Annual & weekly not known (check with Susan B-C at next entry.)
Post Port de Salles, 86150 Le Vigeant, Vienne. Region Poitou-Charentes.
Tel 05 49 48 75 22. Mich 96/A3. Map 5.

A100frs & under. B100–150. C150–200. D200–250. E250–350. F350–500. G500+

L'ISLE-JOURDAIN (also see previous page)   **Val de Vienne**

Comfortable hotel (no restaurant)
Secluded/Gardens/Swimming pool/Garage/Parking

A fabulous *sans restaurant* base hotel – 7km SW of the town, at Port de
Salles, on the left (W) bank of the Vienne. A single story new building, in
lovely gardens & with a stunning heated pool. The bedrooms have an
English feel – with attractive furnishings & tea-making facilities. No
wonder, as the owner, Susan Brooker-Carey, is English (from Staffs).
Perfect for exploring *Mapaholics' France* Michelin map sheet 96.
Rooms (20) G (bottom-end). Disabled. Cards MC, V.
Post Port de Salles, 86150 Le Vigeant, Vienne. Region Poitou-Charentes.
Tel 05 49 48 27 27. Fax 05 49 48 47 47. Mich 96/A3. Map 5.

L'ISLE-SUR-LA-SORGUE   **Mas de Cure Bourse**

Very comfortable restaurant with rooms/Cooking 2
Secluded/Terrace/Gardens/Swimming pool/Parking

The *mas* (farmhouse), with 5-acre park, is in the maze of market-garden
fields to the SW of the water-wheel town. Once a *relais de poste*; now
the "relaxed" home of *cuisinière* Françoise Donzé. Watch her at work
behind a glass wall between kitchen & reception. Neo-classical/regional
specialities with a welcome number of light fish alternatives.
Menus CDE. Rooms (13) FG. Cards MC, V. (W of D31 bypass; S of D25.)
Closed Rest: 1-15 Jan. 15-31 Oct. Mon. Tues midday.
Post 84800 L'Isle-sur-la-Sorgue, Vaucluse. Region Provence.
Tel 04 90 38 16 58. Fax 04 90 38 52 31. Mich 158/C1. Map 6.

L'ISLE-SUR-SEREIN   **Auberge Pot d'Etain**

Comfortable restaurant with rooms/Cooking 2   ⬛ FW
Terrace/Air-conditioning (restaurant)

An eye-pleasing charmer: a pink & grey façade & a cosy dining room with
large frilly "floppy-hat" lampshades. The old village house is the home of
Catherine & Alain Péchery. A 3-way choice on Alain's classical & neo-
classical menus. Two delights on menu B (top-end): *rumsteack aux 2
poivres* & *rascasse en tapenade fondue de tomates à l'huile d'olives*.
Menus aBCDE. Rooms (8) DEF. Cards MC, V.
Closed Feb. 15-22 Oct. Sun evg & Mon (not July/Aug).
Post 89440 L'Isle-sur-Serein, Yonne. Region Burgundy.
Tel 03 86 33 88 10. Fax 03 86 33 90 93. Mich 72/C3. Map 3.

A100frs & under. B100–150. C150–200. D200–250. E250–350. F350–500. G500+

Les ISSAMBRES

Chante-Mer

Simple restaurant/Cooking 2
Terrace/Air-conditioning

FW

A tiny spot where 20 or so clients eat out on the covered terrace & an equal number share the air-conditioned interior. Chef Mario Battaglia is a classical fan; wife Nanette is a delightful, smiling hostess. Tuck into tempting *soupe de poissons*, drooling *petit pâté chaud*, *contrefilet sauce marchand de vin* & a freshly-made tart or *parfait glacé*.
Menus BCD. Cards MC, V. (Rooms: Plage, *sans rest*; La Nartelle; 6km SW.)
Closed Mid Dec-end Jan. Sun evg & Mon (not July/Aug).
Post 83380 Les Issambres, Var. Region Côte d'Azur.
Tel 04 94 96 93 23. Mich 163/E4. Map 6. (N N98 – at Hôt. Les Calanques.)

ISSOUDUN

La Cognette

Very comfortable restaurant & hotel (annexe)/Cooking 3
Quiet/Garage/Air-conditioning (restaurant)

No welcome is warmer: from Alain Nonnet (with "Roger Royle" laugh), an extrovert English-speaking chef who now spends much time in *la salle*; from his eagle-eyed wife, delightful Nicole; & from daughter Isabelle. Her chef husband, Jean-Jacques Daumy, walks regional, neo-classical & classical paths. An extrovert, cosy dining room. Annexe a touch shabby.
Menus D(low-end)EF. Rooms (11) FG. Disabled. Cards All. (50m to annexe.)
Closed Rest: 6-29 Jan. Sun evg & Mon (not high season; not pub. hols).
Post bd Stalingrad, 36100 Issoudun, Indre. Region Berry-Bourbonnais.
Tel 02 54 21 21 83. Fax 02 54 03 13 03. Mich 84/A3. Map 2.

JAVRON

La Terrasse

Very comfortable restaurant/Cooking 3

One word: GO! Stylish, modern *RQP* cooking of an impeccable standard from a gifted English duo: Alison is the vivacious hostess (& young mum of 2 boys); husband Michel is a champion chef – his desserts are especially sumptuous (better than Laval's famed Bistro de Paris). A stunning cheese course: *terrine de Roquefort aux noix* comes with its own butter (you'll see). Like the BdeP the *àlc* list is fantastic value. Many half-bottles.
Menus ABC. Cards MC, V. (Rooms: see Ermitage, Bagnoles-de-l'Orne.)
Closed Jan. Su evg/Mo (not pub. hols). (Ask Alison re *chambres d'hôtes*.)
Post 53250 Javron-les-Chapelles, Mayenne. Region Normandy.
Tel 02 43 03 41 91. Mich 50/B2. Map 2. (Bagnoles is easy 19km drive NW.)

A100frs & under. B100–150. C150–200. D200–250. E250–350. F350–500. G500+

JOIGNY   Modern'Hôtel Godard

Comfortable hotel/Cooking 2-3   FW
Terrace/Swimming pool/Garage/Parking

The new N6 bypass is a welcome relief; the hotel is on a busy corner of the
old route (opp. *la gare*). Renovated, repainted & refurbished; the Modern
is now just that. Classical/neo-classical fare from Jean-Claude Godard &
his son Christophe. Menu B includes main courses of the *dos de truite de
mer aux moules* & *sauté d'agneau aux petits légumes* variety. Also a
Rôtisserie (lunch only Mon-Sat; bottom-end menu b; rating 1-2.)
Menus BDEF. Rooms (21) CDEFG. Cards All.
Post 17 av. Robert Petit, 89300 Joigny, Yonne. Region Burgundy.
Tel 03 86 62 16 28. Fax 03 86 62 44 33. Mich 71/E1. Map 2.

JOIGNY   Le Rive Gauche

Comfortable hotel/Cooking 1-2   FW
Quiet/Terrace/Gardens/Lift/Tennis/Parking/Air cond. (rest.)

The "pad" is the sure sign that this has to be a 3-star chef's bistro: the
LRG owner is Michel Lorain. The riverside green-roofed hotel (zero
marks for looks) is across the Yonne from the hideous Lorain palace.
Vast choice in the busy *salle*. The big attraction is the buffet-styled
grande table de hors d'oeuvre – followed by classical main courses &
desserts such as *entrecôte marchand de vin* & *profiteroles au chocolat*.
Menus aBCDE. Rooms (42) EFG. Disabled. Cards AE, MC, V.
Post Port au Bois, 89300 Joigny, Yonne. Region Burgundy.
Tel 03 86 91 46 66. Fax 03 86 91 46 93. Mich 71/E1. Map 2.

JOUCAS   Hostellerie Le Phébus

Very comfortable hotel/Cooking 2-3
Secluded/Terr/Gardens/Swim pool/Tenn/Parking/Air-cond. (rooms)

A super dry-stone complex in 10 acres of *garrigue*. "Out of this world"
wrote a reader. Bedrooms are dear (see below for alternative). Enjoy the
setting & chef Xavier Mathieu's classical/Provençale cooking in menu C:
fleurs de courgette farcies de morue fraîche & *charlotte d'agneau de
Sisteron au romarin* are two evocative memories of this seductive hotel.
Menus C(low-end)E. Rooms (17) G,G2. Disabled. Cards AE, MC, V.
Closed Nov-mid Mar. (Cheaper rooms: see Roussillon entry.)
Post rte Murs, 84220 Joucas, Vaucluse. Region Provence.
Tel 04 90 05 78 83. Fax 04 90 05 73 61. Mich 159/D1. Map 6.

A100frs & under. B100–150. C150–200. D200–250. E250–350. F350–500. G 500+

JUAN-LES-PINS

Mimosas

Very comfortable hotel (no restaurant)
Quiet/Gardens/Swimming pool/Parking

Of the two *sans restaurant* base hotels in Juan-les-Pins my preference would be for the Welcome (next entry). But many readers, I suspect, would opt for the Mimosas: for the attractive park ("gardens" don't do it justice); for the swimming pool; & the site – midway between the old N7 (& railway line) through Juan & the new northern relief bypass.
Rooms (34) FG. Cards AE, MC, V.
Closed Oct-Mar. Region Côte d'Azur.
Post r. Pauline, 06160 Juan-les-Pins, Alpes-Maritimes.
Tel 04 93 61 04 16. Fax 04 92 93 06 46. Mich 165/D4. Map 6.

JUAN-LES-PINS

Welcome

Comfortable hotel (no restaurant)
Quiet/Gardens/Lift/Parking

If a lift is essential then the Welcome makes an ideal base, built at the turn-of-the-century. Not that a lift is the only benefit at the hotel, considerably refurbished over the last few years by Annick & Dominique Pollet. Delightful gardens; & the tree-lined, side-street site (150m SE of *la gare*) is well-placed for the beach & town-centre.
Rooms (29) FG. Cards All.
Closed Nov-Feb. Region Côte d'Azur.
Post 7 av. Dr Hochet, 06160 Juan-les-Pins, Alpes-Maritimes.
Tel 04 93 61 26 12. Fax 04 93 61 38 04. Mich 165/D4. Map 6.

JULIENAS (also see next page)

Chez la Rose

Simple restaurant with rooms/Cooking 1-2 | FW |
Terrace

A young, eager-to-please duo, Sylvette & Bertrand Alizer, are the hosts at this lovable *logis*. Bertrand selects his repertoire from regional & neo-classical vines. Typical of his pungent offerings are *gâteau de tomates à la tapenade* (a welcome Med touch), *morue fraîche aux aromates* (a fragrant *plat*) & *andouillette de Fleurie à la moutarde à l'ancienne*.
Menus aCDE. Rooms (11) BCDE. Cards All. Closed 8 Jan-19 Feb.
25 Dec-20 Dec. Tues *midi* (not pub. hols). Rest: Mon (July/Aug).
Post pl. Marché, 69840 Juliénas, Rhône. Region Lyonnais.
Tel 04 74 04 41 20. Fax 04 74 04 49 29. Mich 102/B3. Map 6.

A100frs & under. B100–150. C150–200. D200–250. E250–350. F350–500. G500+

JULIENAS (also see previous page) Le Coq au Vin

Comfortable restaurant/Cooking 2 `FW`
Terrace

Multi-shaded *coqs* reign supreme at Mme Claude Clévenot's blue-shuttered bistro – quintessential *Clochemerle*; the cocks appear ready to scrap with neighbouring "la Rose" anytime. The fare is a mix of neo-classical/modern/regional – with Georges Duboeuf wines almost on tap. We voted one cock of the walk: *coq au vin de Juliénas* – a perfect Beaujolais mating.
Menus aB(top-end)D. Cards All. (Rooms: nearby des Vignes, *sans rest.*)
Closed Mid Dec-mid Jan. Wed (mid Nov-Easter).
Post pl. Marché, 69840 Juliénas, Rhône. Region Lyonnais.
Tel 04 74 04 41 98. Fax 04 74 04 41 44. Mich 102/B3. Map 6.

JUNAS Can Peio

Very simple restaurant/Cooking 1-2 `FW`
Terrace/Parking

The *ancienne gare* is a captivating delight: the waiting room is now *la salle* (picture-filled; some tell a story!); the platform is the terrace; the old line is a fish pool. *La vrai cuisine Catalane* from Peio (*can* is *chez*) Rahola & an engaging welcome from Charlotte. *Esqueixada (salade de morue), jambon Serrano, crème Catalane,* Spanish wines & much more.
Menus B(lunch)BCD(evgs *àlc*). Cards MC, V. (Rooms: Orange, Sommières.)
Closed 20 Dec-7 Jan. 1-15 Sept. Sun evg. Wed. (Above easy drive to W.)
Post rte Aujargues, 30250 Junas, Gard. Region Languedoc-Roussillon.
Tel 04 66 77 71 83. Mich 157/D2. Map 6. (Beside D105 N of Junas.)

JUVIGNY-SOUS-ANDAINE Au Bon Accueil

Comfortable restaurant with rooms/Cooking 2 `FW`
Garage

André Cousin dips his fingers into many a French regional culinary pool at his *logis*: *jambon de Bayonne, terrine de canard à la Rouennaise, foie gras d'oie des Landes, escargots de Bourgogne* & *sorbet Granny Smith* are an eclectic jumble. *Bourgeoise* & classical – *ancien régime* cooking which guarantees contentment. One word from a reader says it all: "splendid!"
Menus BCE. Rooms (8) E. Cards MC, V.
Closed 1 Feb-5 Mar. Sun evg. Mon.
Post 61140 Juvigny-sous-Andaine, Orne. Region Normandy.
Tel 02 33 38 10 04. Fax 02 33 37 44 92. Mich 50/B1. Map 2.

A100frs & under. B100–150. C150–200. D200–250. E250–350. F350–500. G500+

KAYSERSBERG Remparts

Comfortable hotel (no restaurant)
Quiet/Lift (annexe)/Garage/Parking

The hotel has been extensively refurbished & extended during the last few years. But none of the "facilities" can outdo the boss, Christiane Keller, one of the most talented hoteliers. She's effervescent, speaks excellent English & is the driving force behind the town's famed Xmas market. She is also the winner of a 1995 *France Travelauréat*. Some rooms have *cuisinettes* (small kitchens). For the disabled note lift (annexe).
Rooms (41) EF. Disabled (annexe rooms). Cards AE, MC, V.
Post 68240 Kaysersberg, Haut-Rhin. Region Alsace.
Tel 03 89 47 12 12. Fax 03 89 47 37 24. Mich 61/D3. Map 3.

LACAPELLE-MARIVAL Terrasse

Simple hotel/Cooking 2-3 FW
Terrace/Gardens

A smart, whitewashed *logis* near the château & church. Young chef Eric Boussac & his English-speaking wife, Clarisse, are highly thought of by their Quercy peers & nothing is too much trouble for the couple. Proof of Eric's talent shines forth in a herby *terrine de lapereau à la sauge* & a drooling *filet de truite, beurre d'échalotes et Bergerac blanc*.
Menus ABCD. Rooms (9) CDE. Cards MC, V.
Closed 10 Jan-10 Mar. Sun evg & Mon (out of season).
Post 46120 Lacapelle-Marival, Lot. Region Dordogne.
Tel 05 65 40 80 07. Fax 05 65 40 99 45. Mich 125/D4-E4. Map 5.

LACAUNE (also see next page) Calas

Simple hotel/Cooking 2 FW
Gardens/Swimming pool

The *logis* is tucked away, above a small *place*, in a quiet backwater. Annie Calas is *la patronne*; hubby Claude prepares neo-classical/regional dishes, making exceptional use of the renowned Lacaune *charcuterie*. Fair choice on menu B: like Lacaune *jambon et boudin noir, soupe de poissons* & *filet de loup a l'infusion d'échalottes* (two so-welcome fish treats).
Menus ABCD. Rooms (16)CDE. Cards All.
Closed 22 Dec-15 Jan. Fri evg & Sat (mid Oct-Apl).
Post pl. Vierge, 81230 Lacaune, Tarn. Region Languedoc-Roussillon.
Tel 05 63 37 03 28. Fax 05 63 37 09 19. Mich 154/C2. Map 5.

A100frs & under. B100–150. C150–200. D200–250. E250–350. F350–500. G500+

LACAUNE (also see previous page)   Hôtel Fusiès

Comfortable hotel/Cooking 1-2   FW
Terrace/Gardens/Lift/(Swimming pool/Tennis: see text)

What a record: Pierre Fusiès' ancestors first set up shop in Lacaune in 1690! He also owns the casino (500m away; guests can use its swimming pool & tennis court). Huge choice on the classical/regional menus. The *Menu Terroir* is perhaps the best bet: for a start all the famed Lacaune *charcuterie*; soups too are listed (almost extinct in France these days).
Menus ABE. Rooms (56) E. Cards All.
Closed Sun evg (mid Nov-mid Mar).
Post r. République, 81230 Lacaune, Tarn. Region Languedoc-Roussillon.
Tel 05 63 37 02 03. Fax 05 63 37 10 98. Mich 154/C2. Map 5.

LACAVE   Pont de l'Ouysse

Very comfortable restaurant with rooms/Cooking 3-4
Secluded/Terrace/Gardens/Swimming pool/Parking

A roll-call of man-made & natural pleasures: a site beside the Ouysse (clever use made of this seducer), downstream from Rocamadour, just before it joins the Dordogne; Belcastel château; cosseting comforts; & modern/regional masterpieces from Daniel Chambon. Among made-in-heaven treats are *foie de canard "Bonne Maman"* & poultry/lamb specialities.
Menus C(low-end)EFG. Rooms (12) FG. Cards All.
Closed Jan. Feb. Mid Nov-mid Dec. Mon (not evgs high season).
Post 46200 Lacave, Lot. Region Dordogne.
Tel 05 65 37 87 04. Fax 05 65 32 77 41. Mich 124/C3. Map 5.

LAGUIOLE   Grand Hôtel Auguy

Comfortable hotel/Cooking 2   FW
Gardens/Lift/Garage

Isabelle Muylaert-Auguy & her English-speaking husband, Jean-Marc, have capitalised on the cattle town's fame (see Bras). Chef Isabelle makes the most of her bountiful *terroir*. Super neo-classical/regional fare: even menu b has top-notch alternatives like *saucisse grillée avec aligot* or a lighter *pavé de saumon au thym et mosaique de légumes*.
Menus bCD(bottom-end). Rooms (28) DE. Cards MC, V.
Closed 9-16 June. 24 Nov-12 Jan. Sun evg & Mon (not sch. hols).
Post 12210 Laguiole, Aveyron. Region Massif Central (Auvergne).
Tel 05 65 44 31 11. Fax 05 65 51 50 81. Mich 126/C4. Map 5.

LAGUIOLE

Lou Mazuc

Comfortable hotel (no restaurant)
Lift/Parking

This was the old Bras family hotel where Michel first worked his magic (in terrain more akin to Llanidloes in mid-Wales) before flying off to the E. New owners are Alain & Françoise Guillemin. The entry is included purely for those readers who would like to eat at Bras' new home but just cannot contemplate the stratospheric bedroom prices. Stay here; the drive is simple as pie. (Evening meals available in July/Aug.)
Rooms (15) DEF. Cards MC, V.
Post 12210 Laguiole, Aveyron. Region Massif Central (Auvergne).
Tel 05 65 48 48 58. Fax 05 65 48 48 01. Mich 141/D1. Map 5.

LAGUIOLE

Michel Bras

Very comfortable hotel/Cooking 4-5
Secluded/Lift/Parking/Air-conditioning (restaurant)

Michel Bras is a unique creative genius & the most generous & helpful of men (ask Catherine; Oustal del Barry, Najac); wife Ginette wears the most happy smile; & elder son, Sebastien, now works in the huge kitchen. A space station atop an Aubrac mountain; vast views S, W & N. For the couple their communion with Nature & their beloved *pays* is total. Go!
Menus d(low-end)FG. Rooms (15) G2,G3. Disabled. Cards AE, MC, V.
Closed Nov-Mar. Mon & Tues *midi* (not July/Aug). (Also see above entry.)
Post rte d'Aubrac, 12210 Laguiole, Aveyron. Region MC (Auvergne).
Tel 05 65 44 32 24. Fax 05 65 48 47 02. Mich 141/D1. Map 5. (D15 to E.)

LALINDE

Château

Comfortable hotel/Cooking 2-3
Terrace/Swimming pool

FW

A down-at-heel façade for the *logis* (once a prison!) alongside the right bank of the river Dordogne. Guy Gensou's classical/regional treats match the fine site & views: an *omelette aux queues de langoustines* made a pleasant change; & both a *blanquette d'agneau aux trompettes de mortes* & a *tarte aux pommes chaudes* were "well-executed", accomplished dishes.
Menus b(lunch: bottom-end)CD. Rooms (7) FG. Cards AE, MC, V.
Closed 2-31 Jan. 17-22 Sep. Su evg (No-Mar). Rest: Mo (not evgs Jul/Au).
Post 1 r. Verdun, 24150 Lalinde, Dordogne. Region Dordogne.
Tel 05 53 61 01 82. Fax 05 53 24 74 60. Mich 123/D3-E3. Map 5.

A100frs & under. B100–150. C150–200. D200–250. E250–350. F350–500. G500+

193

LAMALOU-LES-BAINS

Comfortable hotel/Cooking 1-2
Terrace/Lift/Parking

A small, shady, cool spa. The *belle époque* hotel is opposite the spa's casino. Ask English-speaking Ernest Bitsch, a friendly host, to show you the fine frescoes in the vast salon. Neo-classical/classical dishes: *tournedos Bordelaise à la moelle* & *omelette Norvégienne* are typical of the latter style. The large terrace is a shady oasis on hot days. (For nicer bedrooms ask to stay at their associated hotel, L'Arbousier.)
Menus ABCD. Rooms (40) BCDE. Cards All.
Post 34240 Lamalou-les-Bains, Hérault. Region Languedoc-Roussillon.
Tel 04 67 95 62 22. Fax 04 67 95 67 78. Mich 155/E3. Map 5.

LAMASTRE

Midi

Comfortable hotel/Cooking 3
Gardens/Garage

In the 30s Joseph Barattéro won 3 stars here. After the war his widow, aided by chef Elie Perrier, maintained JB's high standards. Today Elie's son Bernard & his wife, Marie-George, a happy, involved duo, continue the good work. Classical cuisine with many *plats* paying homage to JB: an exquisite *pain d'écrevisses sauce Cardinal* is one. Few veg; good coffee.
Menus CDEF. Rooms (12) EF. Cards All.
Closed Dec-Feb. Sun evg. Mon (not evgs July/Aug).
Post pl. Seignobos, 07270 Lamastre, Ardèche. Region MC (Ardèche).
Tel 04 75 06 41 50. Fax 04 75 06 49 75. Mich 129/F2. Map 6.

LAMBALLE

Les Alizés

Comfortable hotel/Cooking 1-2
Gardens/Parking

FW

An anonymous modern motel exterior, compensated by nice gardens, on the edge of an industrial estate (N of the furthest W of 4 N12 exits for Lamballe). Classical/*Bourgeoise* cuisine – of the *saumon beurre blanc, entrecôte grillée Béarnaise* type. One welcome plus: a fish menu (B) with alternatives like *langoustines grillées au basilic* & *sole meunière*.
Menus ABC. Rooms (32) E. Disabled. Cards AE, MC, V. (2km W of town.)
Closed 23 Dec-6 Jan. Rest: Sun evg.
Post ZI La Ville-Es-Lan, 22400 Lamballe, Côtes d'Armor. Region Brittany.
Tel 02 96 31 16 37. Fax 02 96 31 23 89. Mich 29/D3. Map 1.

A100frs & under. B100–150. C150–200. D200–250. E250–350. F350–500. G500+

LANGRES

Auberge des Trois Jumeaux

Comfortable restaurant with rooms/Cooking 2   FW
Terrace

Jean-Claude Thomassin continues to please all those who seek out his ever-improving modest establishment – 4km S of Langres (thankfully, not alongside the N74 & a few minutes from the A31 exit 6). Classical menus: *terrine de brochet, jambonnette de canard au choux, mousseline de truite au Champagne, coq au vin & entrecôte Béarnaise* are a typical quintet.
Menus a(lunch)BCDE. Rooms (10) DE. Cards AE, MC, V.
Closed 15-30 Nov. Sun evg (Nov-May). Mon. Regs Burgundy/Champ-Ard.
Post Saints-Geosmes, 52200 Langres, Hte-Marne.
Tel 03 25 87 03 36. Fax 03 25 87 58 68. Mich 74/C1. Map 3.

LANGRES

Grand Hôtel Europe

Comfortable hotel/Cooking 1-2   FW
Parking

Step back several decades to a 17thC town house at the heart of the walled town (S of cathedral; enter by the *porte* at N19/N74 junction). Nostalgia in the rooms, furnishings & cooking; the latter is neither flashy nor cheap & cheerful. Happy memories of times past: *poulet rôti à la broche, pintadeau rôti aux morilles & bavarois de saumon fumé.*
Menus aBD. Rooms (28) DE. Cards All.
Closed 5-19 May. 1-21 Oct. Sun evg. Mon (not evgs 22 May-22 Oct).
Post 23 r. Diderot, 52200 Langres. Hte-Marne. Regions Burg/Champ-Ard.
Tel 03 25 87 10 88. Fax 03 25 87 60 65. Mich 74/C1. Map 3.

LANGRES

Lion d'Or

Comfortable restaurant with rooms/Cooking 1-2   FW
Terrace/Gardens/Parking

If the two entries above are full/closed then use the somewhat listless, faded Lion d'Or. One plus: panoramic views E, shared by the covered terrace & one dining room (for smokers). Classical grub from Pierre-Yves Ouary. Run-of-the-mill competent *plats:* c*assolette de moules aux poireaux* & *pot-au-feu de canard sauce ravigote* are a menu B twosome.
Menus ABC. Rooms (14) CDE. Cards AE, MC, V.
Closed Jan. Fri evg. Sat. Regions Burgundy/Champagne-Ardenne.
Post rte Vesoul (N19), 52200 Langres, Haute-Marne.
Tel 03 25 87 03 30. Fax 03 25 87 60 67. Mich 74/C1. Map 3.

A100frs & under. B100–150. C150–200. D200–250. E250–350. F350–500. G500+

LAON

Bannière de France

Comfortable restaurant with rooms/Cooking 1-2
Garage

A 17thC *relais de poste* at the heart of the majestic hill-top town. Mme
Paul Lefèvre lost her husband four years ago; she continues his work,
helped by chef Dominique Havot. Classical, regional and a few dishes with
an Italian influence. Menu B could include the likes of *terrine de lapin aux
olives, osso bucco Milanaise* & *brochette d'onglet Ardennaise.*
Menus aBCE. Rooms (18) DEF. Cards All. (Parking in nearby *place.*)
Closed 20 Dec-19 Jan. Regions Champagne-Ardenne/North.
Post 11 r. F. Roosevelt, 02000 Laon, Aisne.
Tel 03 23 23 21 44. Fax 03 23 23 31 56. Mich 19/E3-F3. Map 2.

LAON

La Petite Auberge

Very comfortable restaurant/Cooking 2-3
Terrace

Close to *la gare* and underneath the N side of the hill with Laon cathedral
atop its summit. Willy-Marc Zorn mixes modern and neo-classical, often in
odd-ball ways. However, both *onglet de veau poêlé au curry riz basmati à
la crème* and *emincé de boeuf et sa compote d'oignons, jus au soja*
pleased well enough. Also Bistrot St-Amour wine bar: menus A; rating 1.
Menus B(ceiling)BCE. Cards AE, MC, V. (Rooms: Host. St-Vincent; to E.)
Closed Sat midday & Sun (not public holidays).
Post 45 bd Brossolette, 02000 Laon, Aisne. Regions Champ-Ardenne/North.
Tel 03 23 23 02 38. Fax 03 23 23 31 01. Mich 19/E3-F3. Map 2.

LAPALISSE

Galland

Comfortable restaurant with rooms/Cooking 1-2 FW
Closed parking

The first plus is the site: in the town but well S of the N7 (use D7). The
ultimate geranium welcome (boxes and big pots) at this *Logis de France.*
Jean-Marie Duparc's classical cuisine is more down-to-earth than the
bright red welcome outside: typical appetite-scuttling *plats* include *rognon
de veau aux senteurs balsamiques* and *duo de joue et filet de boeuf.*
Menus BCE. Rooms (8) E. Cards MC, V.
Closed 1-15 Mar. 22-29 Nov. Wed.
Post pl. République, 03120 Lapalisse, Allier. Region Berry-Bourbonnais.
Tel 04 70 99 07 21. Fax 04 70 99 34 64. Mich 100/C3. Map 5.

LAPOUTROIE

Les Alisiers

Comfortable restaurant with rooms/Cooking 1-2 `FW`
Secluded/Terrace/Gardens/Parking

Jacques & Ella Degouy's *logis* (2300 ft high)has a sensational site with a panoramic northern vista, a Chartreuse-shaded distillation of Vosges scenery. Raining? Soak in the view from *la salle* with its glass walls. Alsace/*Bourgeoise*/classical fare: of the *choucroute grandmère, truites aux amandes, faux-filet au pinot noir* & *tarte à l'oignon* variety.
Menus ABC. Rooms (13) EF. Cards MC, V. Closed 2-31 Jan. 26 June-2 July. 22-25 Dec. Mon evg & Tues (not rooms 15 Mar-15 Nov).
Post 68650 Lapoutroie, Haut-Rhin. Region Alsace. (3km SW of village.)
Tel 03 89 47 52 82. Fax 03 89 47 22 38. Mich 60/C3. Map 3.

LAPOUTROIE

du Faudé

Comfortable hotel/Cooking 2-3 `FW`
Gardens/Swimming pool (indoor: summer)/Closed parking

No heart-stopping views here but the heart-stirring Baldinger family makes the *logis* buzz. Thierry is the chef; wife Chantal the extrovert, English-speaking *patronne*. Numerous menus: stomach-fillers like *coq au Riesling* & *choucroute garnie* to a silky *terrine de foie de volaille au poivre* served with 12 *hors d'oeuvre et crudités* left at the table.
Menus aBCDEF. Rooms (25) EF. Cards All.
Closed 3-21 Mar. 3 Nov-5 Dec. (In village, which is bypassed to N.)
Post 68650 Lapoutroie, Haut-Rhin. Region Alsace.
Tel 03 89 47 50 35. Fax 03 89 47 24 82. Mich 60/C3. Map 3.

LAPOUTROIE

Hostellerie A La Bonne Truite

Comfortable restaurant with rooms/Cooking 2 `FW`
Parking

To the SE, at Hachimette, beside the N415. Danièle Zavialoff is a proud hostess; husband Michel conjures up regional/classical/modern creations. Choose from either end of the culinary spectrum listed above: perhaps a belt-loosening *choucroute royale au Riesling* or, a welcome change, a *filet de loup de mer et de rascasse à la crème d'ail et au basilic.*
Menus BCDE. Rooms (10) DE. Cards AE, MC, V.
Closed Jan. 17-27 June. 12-28 Nov. Tues & Wed (Oct-June).
Post Hachimette, 68650 Lapoutroie, Haut-Rhin. Region Alsace.
Tel 03 89 47 50 07. Fax 03 89 47 25 35. Mich 60/C3. Map 3.

A100frs & under. B100–150. C150–200. D200–250. E250–350. F350–500. G500+

LAVAL

A la Bonne Auberge

Comfortable restaurant with rooms/Cooking 1-2
Garage/Parking

A vine-covered façade gives no clue to the light, contemporary interior. The site, beside the Rennes N157 road, just E of the western bypass, is busy; but Martine & Marc Mariel more than compensate. Classicist Marc provides a 3-way choice for each course on menu B: *gratinée de fruits de mer, saumon grillée Béarnaise*, cheese & *glacé à la noisette* are typical.
Menus ABCDE. Rooms (11) DE. Cards MC, V.
Closed Feb sch. hols. 1-25 Aug. Sat. Sun. Rest: Fri evg (mid Nov-Feb).
Post 170 r. Bretagne, 53000 Laval, Mayenne. Region Normandy.
Tel 02 43 69 07 81. Fax 02 43 91 15 02. Mich 49/F4. Map 1.

LAVAL

Bistro de Paris

Very comfortable restaurant/Cooking 3

Stunning *RQP* at Guy Lemercier's elegant "bistro" with mirrored walls. The *Image Bistro* menu – 6 choices for each course – is top-end B; a *menu dégustation* is top-end D; & on the *àlc* all 13 starters cost the same – the same pattern for 15 main courses, 4 cheeses & 12 sweets (3 courses in band D). "Cor!" describes *compotée de boeuf aux poireaux* & *brandade de hareng et de lieu jaune estragon* – typical of Guy's modern skills.
Menus BCD. Cards MC, V. (Rooms: 10-min walk to Impérial & Marin'H.)
Closed 12-26 Aug. Sat *midi*. Sun. (Impérial has lift/garage; opp. bank.)
Post 67 r. Val de Mayenne, 53000 Laval, Mayenne. Region Normandy.
Tel 02 43 56 98 29. Fax 02 43 56 52 85. Mich 49/F4. Map 1.

LECTOURE

De Bastard

Comfortable hotel/Cooking 2-3
Quiet/Terrace/Swimming pool/Garage

A handsome 18thC building with stylish rooms & exhilarating views. Anne Arnaud is an informed, English-speaking hostess & her chef husband, Jean-Luc, thankfully offers more than just the usual Gers tummy-filling goose & duck permutations. Savour lighter, modern dishes such as *terrine de poissons aux champignons* & *soupe de moules aux courgettes et safran*.
Menus aBE. Rooms (29) CDEF. Cards All.
Closed 2-20 Jan. Sch. hols Feb & Nov.
Post r. Lagrange, 32700 Lectoure, Gers. Region Southwest.
Tel 05 62 68 82 44. Fax 05 62 68 76 81. Mich 151/E1-F1. Map 5.

A100frs & under. B100–150. C150–200. D200–250. E250–350. F350–500. G500+

LEIGNE-LES-BOIS

Bernard Gautier

Comfortable restaurant/Cooking 2 | FW |

An unpretentious little country restaurant – in a hamlet & across the road from the *église* – with smartly-kitted-out, beamed dining rooms & trying hard to get small details right. Classical pleasures arrive on chef Bernard Gautier's plates: a taste of the local fields with *gâteau de lapereau en gelée*; a fresh, unfussy *cabillaud au beurre d'échalotes*; & an out-for-the-count *tournedos Bernard Gautier* (loosen the belts).
Menus B(bottom-end)CE. Cards MC, V. (Rooms: Europe at La Roche-Posay.)
Closed Feb. 11-30 Nov. Sun evg. Mon. (La Roche-Posay, a spa, 10km to E.)
Post 86450 Leigné-les-Bois, Vienne. Regions Loire/Poitou-Charentes.
Tel 05 49 86 53 82. Fax 05 49 86 58 05. Mich 82/B4. Map 2.

LERE

Lion d'Or

Comfortable restaurant with rooms/Cooking 2 | FW |
Terrace/Air-conditioning (restaurant)

Frédéric Ortéga has taken over the stoves in a kitchen where he was second-in-command to the previous chef, Jean-Paul Ridon. Frédéric's ways are less elaborate & less ingenious. Classical/neo-classical creations predominate: *canard rôti au Banyuls* – perfection; *civet de joue de cochon*; magnificent *fromages du Berry*; & *parfait glacé aux agrumes*.
Menus BCE. Rooms (7) D. Cards MC, V. (Rest. just W of D751.)
Closed Rest: Sun evg & Mon (mid Sept-mid May).
Post 18240 Léré, Cher. Regions Berry Bourbonnais/Loire.
Tel 02 48 72 60 12. Fax 02 48 72 56 18. Mich 70/C4. Map 2.

LEVENS

Les Santons

Simple restaurant/Cooking 1-2 | FW |
Terrace

Tucked away in Levens, high above the Var & Vésubie valleys. The owners, the Pellerins, ask you to take your time & enjoy their hospitality. Mme is a charmer. Provençale fare & numerous fish specialities. Three-star *amuses-gueules*; gutsy *timbale de moules, noisette en beurre*; a *chèvre* quintet; & dessert trolley. Lunch on the terrace is especially pleasant.
Menus BCD. Cards MC, V. (Rooms: nearby La Vigneraie – to SE.)
Closed 6 Jan-12 Feb. 23 June-2 July. 29 Sept-8 Oct. Wed.
Post 06670 Levens, Alpes-Maritimes. Region Côte d'Azur.
Tel 04 93 79 72 47. Mich 165/D2. (Near Levens church.)

A100frs & under. B100–150. C150–200. D200–250. E250–350. F350–500. G500+

LEVERNOIS

Luxury restaurant with rooms/Cooking 3-4
Secluded/Terrace/Gardens/Tennis/Parking/Air cond. (rest.)

Heavenly setting: bungalow-style rooms, with terraces, in single-storey annexe surrounded by a huge park; there's even a stream. Neo-classical & modern cooking from Jean & Christophe Crotet, father & son. Superb *foie gras*; succulent & simple *poulet de Bresse rôti*. Christiane & daughter-in-law Gabrielle, an English lass, are *les patronnes*. 800 wines listed.
Menus d(lunch: bottom-end)FG. Rooms (16) G,G2, G3. Cards All.
Closed 1-15 Feb. Tues (not evgs Apl-Oct). Wed *midi* (Nov-Mar).
Post Levernois, 21200 Beaune, Côte-d'Or. Region Burg. (5km SE Beaune.)
Tel 03 80 24 73 58. Fax 03 80 22 78 00. Mich 88/A2. Map 3.

LEVERNOIS

Parc

Simple hotel (no restaurant)
Secluded/Gardens/Parking

Readers of the first *French Leave* will know of my family's affection for this restfully-sited, well-named hotel – E of the A6 Beaune exit. Christiane Oudot bought the property in 1991 & has made many subtle improvements. Two ancient farm buildings straddle a sun-trap garden patio & centuries-old trees add a pleasing verdant backdrop. Two pluses: eating at the Crotets? – then save francs here; golf course in village.
Rooms (25) DEF. Cards MC, V. (5km SE of Beaune; off D970.)
Post Levernois, 21200 Beaune, Côte d'Or. Region Burgundy.
Tel 03 80 24 63 00. Fax 03 80 24 21 19. Mich 88/A2. Map 3.

LIBOURNE (Les Artigues-de-Lussac)

Chez Servais

Comfortable restaurant/Cooking 2   FW
Terrace/Parking

12km to the NE of Libourne, on the E side of the N89 & part of Libourne Aero Club. No prizes for looks; but plenty of accolades to young Nicole Servais for her welcome & to chef/husband Pierre for lots of choice (5 per course) on his eclectic neo-classical menu B: *terrine de poireaux aux fruits de mer* & *filets de truite de mer sauce au cidre* – a bonny duo.
Menus BE. Cards MC, V. (Rooms: Henri IV, Coutras; *sans rest.*)
Closed Feb sch. hols. 15-31 Aug. Sun evg. Mon. (Above easy 7km drive N.)
Post à l'aérodrome, 33570 Les Artigues-de-Lussac, Gironde.
Tel 05 57 24 31 95. Mich 121/F2-F3. Map 4. Regions Dordogne/Southwest.

Le LIORAN (Super-Lioran)　　　　Grand Hôtel Anglard et du Cerf

Very comfortable hotel/Cooking 2　　　　FW
Quiet/Lift/Parking

High above Super-Lioran (over 3500 ft); surrounded by pines; super
Monts du Cantal views; & super value for the facilities. Jean-Pierre
Anglard is a classicist: *ballotine de dinde au foie gras* is one example. A
lighter dish: *saumon aux lentilles à l'Auvergnate*; & a regional *volcan –
ris de veau vallagnonne (champignons, morilles*, potatoes, pastry). Full?
Menus aBCD. Rooms (38) C(bottom-end)DEF. Cards AE, MC, V.
Closed 1-14 May. 27 May-29 June. Oct-19 Dec.
Post Super-Lioran, 15300 Laveissière, Cantal. Region MC (Auvergne).
Tel 04 71 49 50 26. Fax 04 71 49 53 53. Mich 126/C2. Map 5.

LISIEUX　　　　Ferme du Roy

Very comfortable restaurant/Cooking 2　　　　FW
Terrace/Gardens/Parking

An old farm (combination of timber & Bucks-like brick & flint) 2km to N
(junction with the new NE bypass). Jean-Louis Gallet believes in choice
& he's arguably a passionate regional/classical addict: *andouille de Vire
flambée calvados* is one hearty example of his *métier*. Another heady,
highly-satisfying surprise: a yummy *gâteau Irlandais au whisky*.
Menus aBC. Cards AE, MC, V. (Rooms: Azur & St-Louis, Lisieux.)
Closed Sun evg. Mon.
Post rte Deauville, 14100 Lisieux, Calvados. Region Normandy.
Tel 02 31 31 33 98. Mich 33/D1. Map 2.

LOCHES　　　　George Sand

Comfortable hotel/Cooking 1-2　　　　FW
Terrace

The 15thC *logis* (once a post-house) sits beneath the high walls of the
Cité Médiévale. The "terrace" is the highlight – beside the Indre (& small
weir). A beamed dining room & spiral staircase please the eye; as does a
Menu des Bords de l'Indre from Frédéric Loiseau – a strange mix of
classical & odd-ball: *salade folle de moules au curry, pavé de boeuf au
vin de Touraine* & *crème brûlée* is one trio of dishes. FW rating just.
Menus aBCD. Rooms (20) EFG. Cards MC, V. (Parking nearby.)
Post 39 r. Quintefol, 37600 Loches, Indre-et-Loire. Region Loire.
Tel 02 47 59 39 74. Fax 02 47 91 55 75. Mich 82/C2. Map 2.

A100frs & under. B100–150. C150–200. D200–250. E250–350. F350–500. G500+

LOCMARIA-BERRIEN

Auberge de la Truite

Simple restaurant with basic rooms/Cooking 1-2
Gardens/Garage/Parking

Travel back a few decades, to a captivating corner stuck in a time warp.
Mme Le Guillou's *auberge* is a *Bretonne*-furnished *maison*, surrounded
by trees. Gilbert Quemener's cooking is *Bourgeoise*/classical/*Bretonne*:
truite from the Aulne; *terrine maison*; *coquelet rôti*; *foie gras de
canard*; & a top of the old-time pops, an unctuous *gâteau Breton*.
Menus BCE. Rooms (6) BC. Cards MC, V.
Closed Nov-Easter. Sun evg. Mon.
Post Locmaria-Berrien-Gare, 29690 Huelgoat, Finistère. Region Brittany.
Tel 02 98 99 73 05. Mich 27/E3. Map 1. (7km SE of Huelgoat.)

LONGUYON

Le Mas et Hôtel Lorraine

Comfortable restaurant with rooms/Cooking 3
Terrace/Garage

Few clients leave Gérard & Viviane Tisserant's newly-renovated home
disappointed – though it's best to ask for one of the bedrooms at the rear.
English-speaking Gérard, a self-taught chef with an Everest-sized sense of
humour, has an all-styles repertoire: fish dishes are especially good (ex
Boulogne to *gare* opp.). Bedrooms re-decorated, new terrace & garage.
Menus bDF. Rooms (14) DE. Cards All.
Closed 6 Jan-3 Feb. Rest: Mon (19 Sept-30 June).
Post face gare, 54260 Longuyon, Meurthe-et-Moselle. Region Champ-Ard.
Tel 03 82 26 50 07. Fax 03 82 39 26 09. Mich 22/C3. Map 3.

LONS-LE-SAUNIER

Comédie

Comfortable restaurant/Cooking 2
Air-conditioning

A tiny dining room in a pretty-as-a-picture *place* where every terraced
house seems to be washed in a different pastel shade. Menu A is modern
cooking largesse. Main courses have a special panache: both *joues de
loup grillée au riz noir* & *cuisse de canard de Challans aux mousserons
et navets* are exotic, virtuoso gems. Bravo chef Bernard Hémery.
Menus AC(bottom-end). Cards MC, V. (Rooms: Nouvel; closed parking.)
Closed Easter sch. hols. 4-24 Aug. Sun. Mon evg. (Above 5 min-walk W.)
Post 65 r. Agriculture, 39000 Lons-le-saunier, Jura. Region Jura.
Tel 03 84 24 20 66. Mich 89/D4. Map 3. (Park in place Comédie opp.)

A100frs & under. B100–150. C150–200. D200–250. E250–350. F350–500. G500+

202

LORRIS
Guillaume de Lorris

Comfortable restaurant/Cooking 2-3 `FW`

Lorris is a super little village: plenty of flowers, an old covered market &
the Forêt d'Orléans to the S (seek out the *Résistance* site at its heart).
Jean-Pierre de Boissière gives you even more reasons for a detour: his
old house with bricks & beams – the dining room looked after with care
by his wife Edith; & a mix of neo-classical/classical *plats* – a *pavé de
boeuf au vin de Bourgueil* was an especially hearty delight.
Menus bC, Cards MC, V. (Rooms: Sauvage in the village.)
Closed 20 Feb-10 Mar. 24 July-9 Aug. Sun evg. Tues evg. Wed.
Post 45260 Lorris, Loiret. Regions Ile de France/Loire.
Tel 02 38 94 83 55. Mich 70/B1. Map 2.

LOUHANS
La Cotriade

Comfortable restaurant/Cooking 1-2 `FW`
Air-conditioning

The clue for Philippe Coulon's home *pays* is in the name: Brittany *bien
sûr*. He's no introvert; study the couple of dozen framed diplomas in the
hall for proof of his culinary abilities. Being a *Breton* he's fond of fish: a
Menu du Pêcheur has an *assiette de fruits de mer* & a *dos de sandre au
beurre blanc*. Otherwise regional & classical numbers.
Menus ABC. Cards All. (Rooms: Host. Cheval Rouge; same *rue*; number 5.)
Closed 1-7 July. 15-30 Nov. Tues evg & Thurs evg (not July/Aug).
Post 4 r. Alsace, 71500 Louhans, Saône-et-Loire. Region Lyonnais.
Tel 03 85 75 19 91. Fax 03 85 75 19 91. Mich 103/D1. Map 6.

LOUHANS
Moulin de Bourgchâteau

Comfortable hotel/Cooking 2 `FW`
Gardens/Parking

Patrick & Marie-Christine Gonzalès' 218-year-old Seille-side *moulin* has
some of its machinery still in place (non-operational). Patrick turns neo-
classical/regional gears: get teeth stuck into cogs like *salade Bressane;
poulet de Bresse, sauce fleurette et sa jardinière de légumes; fromage
blanc aux fines herbes*; & *nougat glacé au coulis de pistaches*.
Menus B(bottom-end)C. Rooms (18) DE. Cards AE, MC, V. (E of rte Chalon.)
Closed 20 Dec-20 Jan. Sun (Oct-Easter). Mon *midi*. Tue *midi* (Easter-Oct).
Post r. Guidon, 71500 Louhans, Saône-et-Loire. Region Lyonnais.
Tel 03 85 75 37 12. Fax 03 85 75 45 11. Mich 102/D1. Map 6.

A100frs & under. B100–150. C150–200. D200–250. E250–350. F350–500. G500+

Le LUC

Le Gourmandin

Comfortable restaurant/Cooking 2-3
Air-conditioning

FW

Le Luc has an artistic feel about it. One debit though: the A8 which, literally, towers over the N side of the village. Le Gourmandin is a quaint, engagingly old-fashioned, family restaurant. Patrick Schwartz fashions both a *cuisine terroir*, using fresh, local produce, & classical *plats*. Menu B is terrific *RQP*. Highlight? *Fleurs de courgettes farcies*.
Menus BCD. Cards AE, MC, V. (Rooms: La Grillade au Feu de Bois.)
Closed 1-10 Mar. 24 Aug-9 Sept. Sun evg. Mon. (Above 4km to W.)
Post pl. L. Brunet, 83340 Le Luc, Var. Region Côte d'Azur.
Tel 04 94 60 85 92. Fax 04 94 47 91 10. Mich 161/E2. Map 6.

LUCHE-PRINGE

Auberge du Port des Roches

Simple hotel/Cooking 1-2
Quiet/Gardens/Parking

FW

An isolated *logis* (2km E of village) in a delectable setting: across the lane is a shady garden/terrace, with fountain, beside the Loir. Simple applies to everything – & wholesome is the label for both the welcome from Valérie & Thierry Lesiourd & his classical cooking. Wide choice for *plats* of the *pâté en croute, entrecôte au beurre d'échalotes* variety.
Menus BC. Rooms (12) DE. Cards MC, V.
Closed 20 Jan-10 Feb. Sun evg & Mon (not evgs high season).
Post Port des Roches, 72800 Luché-Pringé, Sarthe. Region Loire.
Tel 02 43 45 44 48. Fax 02 43 45 39 61. Mich 66/C2. Map 2.

LUCON

La Mirabelle

Comfortable restaurant/Cooking 2-3

FW

Chris Oakes, a Michelin-star chef, "inspected" La Mirabelle twice in 1993 for me; the tyre men "discovered" it in 1995. Benoît & Véronique Hermouet are talented. He punts classical/*Vendée* streams: a *préfou* appetiser (garlic bread *galette*); a simple, tender *filet de canard aux aromates et son garniture* was a well-sauced classic; & *terrine froid de jarret de porc purée légère mojettes et préfou* a mouthwatering winner.
Menus aBCDE. Cards MC, V. (Rooms: Central; St-Michel-en-l'Herm.)
Closed Feb & Nov sch. hols. Tues. Sat midday. (Above basic; 15km to SW.)
Post 89 bis r. de Gaulle, 85400 Luçon, Vendée. Region Poitou-Charentes.
Tel 02 51 56 93 02. Fax 02 51 56 35 92. Mich 92/C2. Map 4.

A100frs & under. B100–150. C150–200. D200–250. E250–350. F350–500. G500+

LUMBRES

Aa-St-Omer Golf Club

Simple restaurant/Cooking 1-2
Parking

N of Lumbres & the new N42 bypass (first exit after leaving A26 exit 3). Whether you play or not (two courses: 9-hole, 2,003m; & 18-hole, 6,400m) the new club house facilities, in an elevated site (super views S), are worth the detour. Chef Philippe Courlin plays classical fairways: *coq au vin, caneton sauce au porto* & *tarte maison* are typical menu A chips; *gambas au whisky* & *tournedos Rossini* are representative menu B putts. Menus AB. Cards MC, V. (Rooms: Ibis, St-Omer – 15km E.)
Post Chemin des Bois, Acquin Westbécourt, 62380 Lumbres, Pas-de-Calais.
Tel 03 21 38 59 90. Fax 03 21 38 59 90. Mich 2/C3. Map 2. Region North.

LUMBRES

Moulin de Mombreux

Comfortable hotel/Cooking 2-3
Quiet/Gardens/Parking

Winner of the "love it or hate it" prize. Some readers drool; others give a Harvey Smith sign! The new annexe straddling the Bléquin is an eyesore; the 18thC mill, gardens & stream more than compensate. Staff can be pompous; Danièle Gaudry can be warm & friendly; hubby Jean-Marc's classical/neo-classical fare can range from a rating of 1-2 to 3-4.
Menus DEG. Rooms (24) G. Disabled. Cards All.
Closed 20-29 Dec. (S & W of Lumbres; alongside (& over!) Bléquin.)
Post 62380 Lumbres, Pas-de-Calais. Region North.
Tel 03 21 39 62 44. Fax 03 21 93 61 34. Mich 2/C3. Map 2.

LURBE-ST-CHRISTAU

Au Bon Coin

Comfortable hotel/Cooking 2
Terrace/Gardens/Swimming pool/Parking

His regional chef peers rate Thierry Lassala & his English-speaking wife highly. A well-named hotel – a modern blue & cream, chalet-styled building E of the village. A thumpingly good *garbure*, melting *saumon braisée au Jurançon* & an assiduously executed *charlotte d'agneau au beurre de tomate* confirmed his regional & classical cooking skills.
Menus ABD. Rooms (18) EF. Disabled. Cards MC, V.
Closed Sun evg & Mon (10 Oct-end Feb). Region Southwest.
Post rte des Thermes, 64660 Lurbe-St-Christau, Pyrénées-Atlantiques.
Tel 05 59 34 40 12. Fax 05 59 34 46 40. Mich 167/E3. Map 4.

A100frs & under. B100–150. C150–200. D200–250. E250–350. F350–500. G500+

MACON

Simple hotel (no restaurant)
Lift

As basic as they come – beside the River Saône (on its R bank) & also alongside the N6. Modest prices & the lift is a plus. Parking (closed) about 500 metres away – which *le patron* will willingly take you to. Not the most attractive base, but no readers' grumbles. Ideal for the next entry – the Rocher de Cancale is just a 150m walk away; & the two St-Laurent restaurants (opp. page) on the Saône's L bank – 400m walk.
Rooms (21) BCD. Cards AE, MC, V. (200m N of N79 bridge.)
Post 313 quai J. Jaurès, 71000 Mâcon, Saône-et-Loire. Region Lyonnais.
Tel 03 85 38 08 68. Fax 03 85 39 01 92. Mich 102/B2. Map 6.

MACON

Rocher de Cancale

Comfortable restaurant/Cooking 2   `FW`
Air-conditioning

The first-floor dining room overlooks the Saône. Christian Bourlot is an attentive host & chef Gérard Duc paddles primarily classical streams. Oddly enough, on the inspection visit, despite the name, few fish dishes. Menu B more than compensated with sparklers like a *marinade de lapin à l'huile d'olive, pôelée de rougets sauce pistou* & *clafoutis*.
Menus ABCD. Cards AE, MC, V. (Rooms: Nord; 150m to N; see above.)
Closed Sun evg & Mon (not pub. hols).
Post 393 quai J. Jaurès, 71000 Mâcon, Saône-et-Loire. Region Lyonnais.
Tel 03 85 38 07 50. Fax 03 85 38 70 47. Mich 102/B2. Map 6.

MACON (Charnay-lès-Macon)

Moulin du Gastronome

Comfortable restaurant/Cooking 2-3   `FW`
Terrace/Gardens/Parking/Air-conditioning

N side N79, W side A6 bridge. Once located relish many delights. First the young couple who once worked in Welwyn GC & speak English – the efficient Sylvie Goineau & her twinkly-eyed husband Philippe. Next his neo-classical repertoire: an encore please trio – *jambon braisé, salade de quenelles de poissons et thon fumé* & *demi-coquelet façon Gde-mère*.
Menus BCE. Cards AE, MC, V. (Rooms: Ibis; S of A6 Mâcon Sud exit.)
Closed Easter sch. hols. 26 July-8 Aug. Sun evg. Wed evg.
Post 71850 Charnay-lès-Mâcon, Saône-et-Loire. Region Lyonnais.
Tel 03 85 34 16 68. Fax 03 85 34 37 25. Mich 102/B2. Map 6.

A100frs & under. B100–150. C150–200. D200–250. E250–350. F350–500. G500+

MACON (La Croix-Blanche)   Relais du Mâconnais

Comfortable restaurant with rooms/Cooking 3   FW
Terrace/Parking

A handsome stone *logis*, in a village now bypassed by the new N79. The interior, too, is eye-pleasing, as is the modern/neo-classical cooking of Christian Lannvel. Menu B offers a 3-way choice for each course: colourful *mousseline de cabillaud aux courgettes et tomates au basilic* & *dos de lapin farci aux champignons et aux herbes* – an artful duo.
Menus BDE. Rooms (10) EF. Cards All. (13km NW of Mâcon.)
Closed 15-31 Jan. Sun evg & Mon (not high season). Region Lyonnais.
Post La Croix-Blanche, 71960 Berzé-la-Ville, Saône-et-Loire.
Tel 03 85 36 60 72. Fax 03 85 36 65 47. Mich 102/B2. Map 6.

MACON (St-Laurent-sur-Saône)   Les Capucines

Very comfortable restaurant/Cooking 2   FW
Air-conditioning

A cascade of menus at the beamed, old-fashioned dining room on the Saône's left bank (alas no terrace & no river views here). Chef Pierre Harmelle, based previously on the Côte d'Azur (oh for some Med touches), keeps to old-time culinary traditions, using his *terroir* to advantage. *Menu Terroir* (B) has unabashed, robust fare like *cassolette d'escargots aux orties sauvages* & a succulent *volaille de Bresse au Pouilly Fuissé.*
Menus ABCDE. Cards All. (Rooms: Beaujolais; 100m walk; *sans rest.*)
Post 47 r. J. Jaurès, 01620 St-Laurent-sur-Saône, Ain. Region Lyonnais.
Tel 03 85 39 11 05. Fax 03 85 38 29 60. Mich 102/B2-C3. Map 6.

MACON (St-Laurent-sur-Saône)   Le Saint-Laurent

Simple restaurant/Cooking 2   FW
Terrace

Part of the Georges Blanc empire (Vonnas 3-star chef). A busy, evocative bistro – in the 30s café style, on the Saône's L bank, across the bridge from Mâcon. Great river views. Chef Marc Drillien digs up all-styles bounty (inc' both Burgundy & Lyonnais): menu A could include *oeufs en meurette, lapin sauté chausseur, jambonneau braisé* & *fromage blanc.*
Menus ACD. Cards AE, MC, V. (Rooms: Beaujolais; l00m walk; *sans rest.*)
Closed Mid Nov-mid Dec. Region Lyonnais.
Post 1 quai Bouchacourt, 01620 St-Laurent-sur-Saône, Ain.
Tel 03 85 39 29 19. Fax 03 85 38 29 77. Mich 102/B2-C3. Map 6.

A100frs & under. B100–150. C150–200. D200–250. E250–350. F350–500. G500+

MADIERES

Château de Madières

Very comfortable hotel/Cooking 1-2
Secluded/Terrace/Gardens/Swimming pool/Parking

Credits? Superb views, terrain & setting – above the wooded Gorges de la Vis; 14km from the stunning Cirque de Navacelles; all mod-cons & swish furnishings in a 14thC fortified house; & a warm welcome from English-speaking Bernard Brucy & his *cuisinière* wife, Françoise. Debits? Dear; & classical cooking which desperately needs far more attention to detail.
Menus C(top-end)EF. Rooms (10) G,G2. Cards All. (Gym also available.)
Closed 5 Nov-28 Mar. Regions Languedoc-Roussillon/MC (Cévennes).
Post Madières, 34190 Ganges, Hérault.
Tel 04 67 73 84 03. Fax 04 67 73 55 71. Mich 156/A1-B1. Map 5.

MADIRAN

Le Prieuré

Simple hotel/Cooking 2
Quiet/Terrace/Gardens/Parking

FW

Michel (the chef) & Danielle Cuénot's handsome stone hotel was once the abbey at the famous wine village. Cleverly modernised public rooms; but a touch spartan bedrooms (once monks' cells!). Neo-classical/regional fare – like light *filets de rougets aux oignons frits* & tender *agneau de lait des Pyrénées à l'ail confit.* Top-notch sweets. Noisy church clock!
Menus aCD. Rooms (10) DE. Cards AE, MC, V.
Closed Sun evg & Mon (Oct-May).
Post 65700 Madiran, Hautes-Pyrénées. Region Southwest.
Tel 05 62 31 92 50. Fax 05 62 31 90 66. Mich 150/B3. Map 4.

MAGESCQ

Relais de la Poste

Very comfortable hotel/Cooking 3-4
Quiet/Terr/Gards/Swim pool/Tenn/Garage/Parking/Air-cond. (rest.)

The Basque-style Relais is a formidable family enterprise – led by Bernard Coussau & his son Jean, both of whom cook impeccable classical & regional creations, all of which profit from their rich Landes larder (*foie gras, confits, magret, palombes, canards, lamproie* & much else). A second son, Jacques, is both a polished *MD* & knowledgeable *sommelier.*
Menus EF. Rooms (12) G(low-end). Cards All.
Closed 11 Nov-20 Dec. Mon midday (July/Aug). Mon evg & Tues (Sept-June).
Post 40140 Magegcq, Landes. Region Southwest.
Tel 05 58 47 70 25. Fax 05 58 47 76 17. Mich 148/C2. Map 4.

A100frs & under. B100–150. C150–200. D200–250. E250–350. F350–500. G500+

MAGNY-COURS

La Renaissance

Very comfortable hotel/Cooking 3
Quiet/Parking

Jean-Claude Dray, born in 1941, has worked in the kitchen here for 33 years: restrained good taste is his Renaissance culinary hallmark. Authentic classical/neo-classical twists & turns: *filet de charolais à la crème et aux morilles* & *foie gras de canard poêlé, compote de rhubarbe* are just two varying examples of his succulent style spectrum.
Menus CDEF. Rooms (9) F(bottom-end)G. Cards AE, MC, V.
Closed 9 Feb-18 Mar. 25 July-8 Aug. Sun evg. Mon.
Post 58470 Magny-Cours, Nièvre. Region Berry-Bourbonnais.
Tel 03 86 58 10 40. Fax 03-86 21 22 60. Mich 85/F3. Map 2.

MAILLY-LE-CHATEAU

Le Castel

Comfortable restaurant with rooms/Cooking 1-2   FW
Quiet/Gardens

An old-world corner of France. Readers adore the village, the perched site, the views over the Yonne, the church, the 400-year-old lime tree, the old-fashioned charm of Le Castel &, above all, the friendliest of owners – English-speaking Michel Breerette & his wife Janet. *Bourgeois*, regional & classical menus: excellent local trout, cheeses & sweets.
Menus ABC. Rooms (12) DEF. Cards MC, V. (Opposite church.)
Closed Mid Nov-mid Mar. Tues evg & Wed (Oct-Mar).
Post 89660 Mailly-le-Château (Le Haut), Yonne. Region Burgundy.
Tel 03 86 81 43 06. Fax 03 86 81 49 26. Mich 72/A3. Map 2.

MALBUISSON (also see next page)

Le Bon Accueil

Comfortable hotel/Cooking 2-3   FW
Gardens/Garage/Parking

Aptly-named chalet; a cheerful welcome from English-speaking Catherine Faivre. Husband Marc, happy in his Franche-Comté *terroir*, mixes modern, neo-classical & regional – in enterprising, sometimes off-key tunes: *truite au bleu* for the latter but brilliantly redeemed with a *croûte aux champignons* (including heavenly *morilles*) & a rich *civet de lièvre*.
Menus BCDE. Rooms (12) E(Bottom-end)F. Cards MC, V.
Closed 9 Dec-15 Jan. 8-15 Apl. Sun evg (Oct-mid Apl). Mon. Tues midday.
Post 25160 Malbuisson, Doubs. Region Jura.
Tel 03 81 69 30 58. Fax 03 81 69 37 60. Mich 90/B3. Map 3.

A100frs & under. B100–150. C150–200. D200–250. E250–350. F350–500. G500+

MALBUISSON (also see previous page)　　　**Jean-Michel Tannières**

Very comfortable restaurant with rooms/Cooking 3　　
Terrace/Gardens/Garage/Parking

Jean-Michel & Fabienne continue to make welcome improvements at their family *auberge*, a smart, green-shuttered, whitewashed roadside *logis*. Refurbished bedrooms; an elegant *salle*; & spanking new modern kitchen. Classical/regional *plats*: supreme *suprême de sandre au vin jaune* (crisp skin & velvety sauce) & *petite brioche farcie à la crème de morilles*.
Menus BCEF. Rooms (6) DE. Cards All.
Closed 3-25 Jan. 8-18 Apl. Sun evg (Oct-May). Mon (not evgs July/Aug).
Post 25160 Malbuisson, Doubs. Region Jura.
Tel 03 81 69 30 89.Fax 03 81 69 39 16. Mich 90/B3. Map 3.

MANCIET　　　**La Bonne Auberge**

Comfortable restaurant with rooms/Cooking 1-2　　FW

Perfectly sited for motor racing fans: 8km NE of the Nogaro circuit. The Sampietro family run a tight restaurant track: the parents are front-of-house & Eric, their son, drives both regional & classical cooking cars. One serious misfire: no-choice menus. Crash into gutsy grub: a typical menu A could be *filet de truite poêlé*, *bavette de boeuf avec légumes* & *tarte citron*. Menu C is far more interesting. Very popular with locals.
Menus ACE. Rooms (13) EF(both bottom-end). Cards All.
Closed Sun evg.
Post 32370 Manciet, Gers. Region Southwest.
Tel 05 62 08 50 04. Fax 05 62 08 58 84. Mich 150/C2. Map 4.

MANDELIEU　　　Acadia

Simple hotel (no restaurant)
Quiet/Gardens/Swimming pool/Tennis/Lift/Parking

An old favourite of readers – both recently & in the days when the hotel was called Sant-Angelo. The site, just minutes away from the beach, port, golf course & A8 autoroute exit, is unusual in that the River Saigne almost encircles the Acadia (the hotel has its own boat landing jetty). The lift is another welcome benefit for many readers.
Rooms (27) F. Cards AE, MC, V.
Closed 15 Nov-27 Dec. Region Côte d'Azur.
Post 681 av. Mer, 06210 Mandelieu-La-Napoule, Alpes-Maritimes.
Tel 04 93 49 28 23. Fax 04 92 97 55 54. Mich 163/F3. Map 6.

MANZAC-SUR-VERN

Lion d'Or

Comfortable restaurant with rooms/Cooking 2 FW
Terrace/Gardens

Jean-Paul & Nelly Beauvais created their oasis of *RQP* charm in 1980.
Bright & airy applies to both *la salle* & neo-classical cooking. Menu B
may offer a first-rate *terrine de foie gras* or *salade de St-Jacques et
saumon*; *méli-mélo* (an assortment) *de poissons au beurre de safran* or
magret de canard poêlée sauce au vin de noix; & one of six desserts.
Menus a(lunch)BD(bottom-end). Rooms (7) CD(low-end). Cards All.
Closed Feb sch. hols. 25 Oct-10 Nov. Sun evg (not July/Aug). Mon.
Post 24110 Manzac-sur-Vern, Dordogne. Region Dordogne.
Tel 05 53 54 28 09. Fax 05 53 54 25 50. Mich 123/D2. Map 5.

MARANS

Porte Verte

Simple restaurant/Cooking 1-2 FW
Terrace

Colourful flowers, greenery & gourds. Once a fisherman's quayside home
with a small, cool, handsome interior. Even smaller terrace. Didier
Montéran keeps things classically simple: *assiette de fruits de mer* or
terrine de lapin; *bavette sauce porto* or various fish alternatives (so
fresh, still wriggling); cheese & dessert (like iced *nougat terrine*).
Menus ABC. Cards MC, V. (Rooms: St-Nicolas, Maillezais – to NE.)
Closed Feb sch. hols. Sun evg (not high season). Wed.
Post 20 quai Foch, 17230 Marans, Charente-Maritime. Region Poitou-Char.
Tel 05 46 01 09 45. Mich 93/D2. Map 4.

MARGAUX

Le Savoie

Comfortable restaurant/Cooking 2 FW
Terrace

Yves Fougeras' two *RQP* menus boldly state his culinary philosophy: *la
cuisine est un art; tout art est patience*. True enough: even low-cost
classical & neo-classical menus need time & sure, skilled hands; Yves
certainly has those. Two memorable menu B pleasures: *terrine d'aileron
de raie aux câpres* & *crème de pommes au cidre doux*.
Menus AB. Cards not accepted. (Rooms: Pont Bernet; Louens – 12km to S.)
Closed Feb sch. hols. Sun. Mon evg (winter). Pub. hols.
Post 33460 Margaux, Gironde. Region Southwest.
Tel 05 57 88 31 76. Fax 05 57 88 31 76. Mich 121/D2. Map 4.

A 100frs & under. B 100–150. C 150–200. D 200–250. E 250–350. F 350–500. G 500+

MARGUERITTES

L'Hacienda

Comfortable hotel/Cooking 2-3
Secluded/Terrace/Gardens/Swimming pool/Parking

Well-named: an old restored farm in a green oasis of calm, 2km SE of the village; follow the dozen or so signposts. The pool is unusual: dining rooms & kitchen make up the 4 sides! The Chauvins ensure chefs keep high neo-classical standards, evidenced by two ideal summer lunch *plats*: *soupe glacée à la tomate et basilic* & *saumon frais gros sel Camarguais*. Menus a(lunch)D(low-end)E. Rooms (12)FG(low-end). Cards MC, V. Closed Jan. Feb. (Cheaper rooms: Ibis, nr A9/A5 junc to SW; easy drive.) Post 30320 Marguerittes, Gard. Regions Languedoc-Roussillon/Provence. Tel 04 66 75 02 25. Fax 04 66 75 45 58. Mich 157/E1. Map 6.

MARIGNY

Poste

Comfortable restaurant/Cooking 2

FW

The odd-ball blue-and-white façade – with three large panels depicting the varied harvests garnered from land, sea & air (& vines to boot) – leaves you in no doubt about the Manche-wide repertoire of award-winning chef, Joël Meslin. Examples include *filet de carrelet au Camembert* – a happy marriage; & an artful *noisettes de jeune cerf sur petite vinaigrette aux ciboulettes*. Sadly, banal sweets. Stylish dining room. Menus bCDE. Cards All. (Rooms: Ibis, St-Lô to E. Easy 12km drive.) Closed 22 Sept-9 Oct. Sun evg. Mon. Post pl. Westport, 50570 Marigny, Manche. Region Normandy. Tel 02 33 55 11 08. Fax 02 33 55 25 67. Mich 31/D2. Map 1.

MARLENHEIM

Le Cerf

Very comfortable restaurant with rooms/Cooking 4
Terrace/Gardens/Closed parking & parking

A richly-rewarding Cerf: modern/neo-classical/re-jigged regional *plats*; an intimate *salle* with Spindler marquetry gems; unfussy service; a super *MD*, English-speaking Daniel Krier; Marcelle Husser & daughter-in-law Cathy are caring *patronnes*; grandma Irmgard, 82, still lends a hand; &, best of all, Robert, 60, & son Michel are innovative master chefs. Menus E(2 menus: one lunch bottom-end)FG. Rooms (15) EFG. Cards All. Closed Tues. Wed. Post 30 r. du Gén.-de-Gaulle, 67520 Marlenheim, Bas-Rhin. Region Alsace. Tel 03 88 87 73 73. Fax 03 88 87 68 08. Mich 43/D4. Map 3.

A100frs & under. B100–150. C150–200. D200–250. E250–350. F350–500. G500+

MARMANDE

Capricorne/Rest. Le Trianon

Comfortable hotel/Cooking 2-3 | FW |
Gardens/Swimming pool/Closed parking/Air-conditioning (rest.)

Modern building beside the N113 (SE town exit – by an Intermarché).
What makes this *logis* tick is the restaurant, run as a separate business
by Patricia & Thierry (the chef) Arbeau. They do a great job. A clever mix
of neo-classical/regional, though little choice on menu B. Highlights:
cailles grillées à la crème d'herbes & *tarte chaude aux pommes*.
Menus aBCD(bottom-end). Rooms (34) E. Cards All.
Closed 20 Dec-5 Jan. Rest: 2-7 Jan. Sat midday. Sun. Region Southwest.
Post rte Agen, 47200 Marmande, Lot-et-Garonne. Mich 136/B1. Map 4.
Tel (H) 05 53 64 16 14. (R) 05 53 20 80 94. Fax (H) 05 53 20 80 18.

MARMANDE (Virazeil)

Auberge Moulin d'Ané

Comfortable restaurant/Cooking 2-3 | FW |
Parking/Air-conditioning

An attractive spot with umbrella-shaded terrace & dining room above a
pool, cascade & River Trec. (Virazeil E of Marmande; S of D933; beside
D267.) Good choice Menu C. Classical/neo-classical *plats* from Jacques
Amiel: welcome light *filets de rougets au coulis de poivron doux; baron
de mouton grillé* was, alas, not so light. Fish menu B (Fri/Sat).
Menus ABCD. Cards All. (Rooms: Europ'H, Marmande; *sans rest.*)
Closed Feb sch. hols. Sun evg & Mon (not pub. hols).
Post 47200 Virazeil, Lot-et-Garonne. Region Southwest.
Tel 05 53 20 18 25. Fax 05 53 89 67 99. Mich 136/B1. Map 4.

MARQUISE

Le Grand Cerf

Comfortable restaurant/Cooking 2-3 | FW |

The Cerf has had a long-overdue face-lift: but has the cosmetic surgery
spoilt things too much? English-speaking Stéphane Pruvot is a skilled
chef. Our lunch menu B – *croustillant de crabe à la fondue de poireaux*
was worthy of a 3-star God; followed by a pan-fried *rascasse* with a purée
of courgettes & potato *crêpe*; finishing with an *omelette aux pommes
sauce pistache* – was the essence of modern simplicity & subtlety.
Menus BCDE. Cards AE, MC, V. (Rooms: several hotels in Boulogne/Calais.)
Closed 15 Aug-5 Sept. Sun evg. Mon.
Post 62250 Marquise, Pas-de-Calais. Region North.
Tel 03 21 87 55 05. Fax 03 21 33 61 09. Mich 2/A2. Map 2.

A100frs & under. B100–150. C150–200. D200–250. E250–350. F350–500. G500+

MARSEILLAN

Château du Port

Comfortable hotel (no restaurant)
Garage/Parking

Noilly Prat & *coquillaqe pays*. The 100-year-old quayside château (built originally for a wine *négociant*) has views of the Basin de Thau. The interior décor is in the style of the Second Empire. The hotel is a great favourite with readers. Golf, tennis, horse riding, water-skiing – all can be organised for you. Also bikes for hire at the hotel.
Rooms (15) EFG(low-end). Cards All.
Closed Mid Oct-Mar. Region Languedoc-Roussillon.
Post 9 quai Résistance, 34340 Marseillan, Hérault.
Tel 04 67 77 65 65. Fax 04 67 77 67 98. Mich 156/A4. Map 5.

MARVEJOLS

Viz Club

Comfortable restaurant/Cooking 1-2   FW
Parking

A most unlikely looking chalet-restaurant – & the name is, initially, odd-ball. Don't be put off (at island, N entrance to town). Christian Vizier (viz) describes himself as an *artisan cuisinier*. A comfortable interior & copious regional/classical food. Little choice on menu A: *pâté de volaille aux morilles* & *glace aux marrons* are typical *plats*.
Menus ACD. Cards All. (Rooms: Gare et Rochers; S of town.)
Closed 2-31 Jan. Sun evg.
Post rte du Nord, 48100 Marvejols, Lozère. Region MC (Auvergne).
Tel 04 66 32 17 69. Mich 141/F1. Map 5.

MAUSSANE-LES-ALPILLES

La Petite France

Comfortable restaurant/Cooking 3
Parking/Air-conditioning

Regional tunes from young neo-classicist chef Thierry Maffre-Bogé; wife Isabelle is a gentle *patronne*. Order anything which features the famed olive oil from nearby Mouriès & tuck into evocative delights like *tomates tièdes farcies de brandade de morue au pistou* (Provence on a plate) & *terrine de gigot d'agneau à l'ail confit*. Scrumptious desserts.
Menus C(low-end)DE. Cards MC, V. (Rooms: base hotels on opp. page.)
Closed 3-31 Jan. 13-20 Nov. Wed. Thurs midday. Region Provence.
Post av. Vallée des Baux, 13520 Maussane-les-Alpilles, Bouches-du-Rhône.
Tel 04 90 54 41 91. Fax 04 90 54 52 50. Mich 158/B2. Map 6.

A100frs & under. B100–150. C150–200. D200–250. E250–350. F350–500. G500+

MAUSSANE-LES-ALPILLES Castillon des Baux

Comfortable hotel (no restaurant)
Quiet/Swimming pool/Parking/Air-conditioning

New name (previously the Touret) and new management; three cheers for the latter. W of the village, alongside & S of the D17. Credits? Well, the list of facilities above for a start; so is the slightly elevated site with views S over the Plaine de la Crau; the pines & olive trees are welcome; but, best of all, the prices are modest. In addition, well placed for the La-Petite France restaurant – a short walk away to the E.
Rooms (16) E. Cards All. Region Provence.
Post rte Paradou, 13520 Maussane-les-Alpilles, Bouches-du-Rhône.
Tel 04 90 54 31 93. Fax 04 90 54 51 31. Mich 158/B2. Map 6.

MAUSSANE-LES-ALPILLES Pré des Baux

Comfortable hotel (no restaurant)
Secluded/Gardens/Swimming pool/Closed parking

Another successful recommendation which first appeared in *FLE* – just after the small seductive haven was opened. Cécile Salério's single-storey hotel has all 10 bedrooms overlooking the swimming pool & enclosed garden – described, accurately, by *la patronne* as *jardin exotique*. S of the D17 through the village. Cool, quiet, modern rooms.
Rooms (10) G(low end). Cards AE, MC, V.
Closed 6 Jan-14 Mar. 26 Nov-19 Dec. Region Provence.
Post r. Vieux Moulin, 13520 Maussane-les-Alpilles, Bouches-du-Rhône.
Tel 04 90 54 40 40. Fax 04 90 54 53 07. Mich 158/B2. Map 6.

MAUVEZIN La Rapière

Comfortable restaurant/Cooking 2 FW
Terrace/Air-conditioning

Michel Fourreau, just turned 50, started cooking at the age of 14 in the Loire's Sologne. Marie-Thérèse, his wife, welcomes you & Michel then challenges you to classical & regional duels with menus notable for their exceedingly generous choice. Signature *plats*: *terrine de faisan, saumon sauce hollandaise* & luscious *glace aux pruneaux à l'Armagnac.*
Menus a(lunch)BCDE. Cards All. (Rooms: Coin de Feu, Gimont.)
Closed 15-30 June. 1-15 Oct. Tues evg. Wed. (Above 14km to S.)
Post 32120 Mauvezin, Gers. Region Southwest.
Tel 05 62 06 80 08. Fax 05 62 06 80 08. Mich 152/A2. Map 5.

A100frs & under. B100–150. C150–200. D200–250. E250–350. F350–500. G500+

MAZAMET

Hôtel Jourdon

Simple hotel/Cooking 2
Air-conditioning

FW

An unprepossessing exterior, completely forgotten when you relish the
bonus of air-conditioning & the talents of Brigitte & Henri Jourdon. His
classical & regional menus offer good choice. A variety of dishes delight:
*jambon de pays, brandade de morue aux croutons frits, couscous à
l'épaule d'agneau* & *cassoulet de canard confit* to name just four.
Menus ABCE. Rooms (11) CDE. Cards AE, MC, V.
Closed Sun (not public holidays). (Parking nearby.)
Post 7 av. A. Rouvière, 81200 Mazamet, Tarn. Region Languedoc-Rouss.
Tel 05 63 61 56 93. Fax 05 63 61 83 38. Mich 154/B3-B4. Map 5.

MAZAMET (Pont-de-Larn)

Host. du Château de Montlédier

Very comfortable hotel/Cooking 1-2
Secluded/Terrace/Gardens/Swimming pool/Parking

FW

Step back in time to the 12thC castle high above the Gorges du Banquet
& the River Arn – & with extensive views S beyond Mazamet to the
Montagne Noire. Vaulted dining room & bedrooms from an *autre temps*.
Cooking, too, is from the classical past: *boeuf Stroganoff, gigot de poulet
farci en crépinette* &, a much lighter *trois poissons sauce à l'oseille*.
Menus BC. Rooms (9) FG. Cards MC, V. (Cheaper rooms: see next line.)
Closed Jan. Rest: Sun evg & Mon (not July/Aug). (Les Comtes d'Hautpoul.)
Post 81660 Pont-de-Larn, Tarn. Region Languedoc-Roussillon. (Use D54.)
Tel 05 63 61 20 54. Fax 05 63 98 22 51. Mich 154/B3-B4. Map 5.

MEGEVE

Michel Gaudin

Comfortable restaurant/Cooking 3-4

FW

Alongside the N212. I would drive a long way to relish the delights at
Michel & Monique Gaudin's small, homely *salle* with its beamed &
panelled ceiling. Both speak English; they once worked in London & met &
married there. One of the finest examples of modern/neo-classical/regional
RQP: wake up Michelin. From the winter appetiser, *pormonaise* (brioche
pastry with minced meat, cabbage, etc.) to the desserts: all first-rate fare.
Menus BCDF. Cards MC, V. (Rooms: L'Auguille; 3 min walk to N.)
Closed Mon & Tues (not high season). (Above quiet/*sans rest.*/parking.)
Post carrefour d'Arly, 74120 Megève, Haute-Savoie. Region Savoie.
Tel 04 50 21 02 18. Mich 119/D1. Map 6.

MELUN

La Melunoise

Comfortable restaurant/Cooking 2   `FW`

In an unpretentious side street on the left bank of the River Seine,
between the railway bridge & the main N-S Melun bypass road. Twins
Michel & Claude Hainaut are proud to boast that everything is home-
made: bread, ice-cream, chocolates and so on. They should be equally
proud of their good-choice neo-classical menu B: an especially well-
judged *terroir* creation is an *entrecôte poêlée sauce au brie de Melun*.
Menus BCE(bottom-end). Cards DC, MC, V. (Rooms: Ibis; N105 N bypass.)
Closed Feb sch. hols. Aug. Sat. Sun evg. Mon evg. (Above easy drive.)
Post 5 r. Gâtinais, 77000 Melun, Seine-et-Marne. Region Ile de France.
Tel 01 64 39 68 27. Fax 01 64 39 81 81. Mich 54/C1. Map 2.

MELUN (Plessis-Picard)

La Mare au Diable

Comfortable restaurant/Cooking 2-3
Terrace/Parking

Just off the N6, NW of Melun (before the A5a). Quite a complex in large
park; ivy-covered façade & beamed interior. Michèle & Franz Eberwein
employ top-notch chefs; the current *cuisinier* is a modern/neo-classical
fan. A typical signature speciality is *caille rôtie aux pommes cidre et
miel* – a toothsome marriage of mouthwatering tastes.
Menus C(bottom-end)D. Cards All. (Rooms: Ibis; N105 N Melun bypass.)
Closed Sun evg. Mon. (Above hotel is easy drive to SE.)
Post 77550 Plessis-Picard, Melun, Seine-et-Marne. Region Ile de France.
Tel 01 64 10 20 90. Fax 01 64 10 20 91. Mich 54/B1. Map 2.

MENESTEROL

Auberge de l'Eclade

Comfortable restaurant/Cooking 2   `FW`
Terrace/Air-conditioning

A colourful façade & a rustic interior at the Auberge – in Ménesterol, N of
the River Isle & Montpon-Ménesterol. Chef Christian Moutin includes
Spanish touches in his neo-classical repertoire – in a sunny & tempting trio
of *piccata de saumon fumé maison à l'oeuf poché tiède; cabillaud
poché au piment et poivron doux*; & *crème Catalane et sa glace au miel.*
Menus a(lun)BCD. Cards MC, V. (Rooms: Puits d'Or, Montpon-Ménesterol.)
Closed 1-20 Mar. 24 Sept-19 Oct. Tues evg. Wed.
Post Ménesterol, 24700 Montpon-Ménesterol, Dordogne. Region Dordogne.
Tel 05 53 80 28 64. Mich 122/B2. Map 5.

A100frs & under. B100–150. C150–200. D200–250. E250–350. F350–500. G500+

MENTON Princess et Richmond

Very comfortable hotel (no restaurant)
Lift/Air-conditioning

Of the numerous Côte d'Azur base hotels in *FLF* this is the only one which has neither a "quiet" nor a "secluded" label. Don't let that put you off: the modern hotel overlooks the *plage* & Promenade du Soleil & all the bedrooms on the front, overlooking the Med, have balconies. There's also a roof terrace, a nice sunbathing alternative to the beach.
Rooms (45) FG(low-end). Cards All. (Close to public parking.)
Closed 5 Nov-17 Dec. Region Côte d'Azur.
Post 617 prom. Soleil, 06500 Menton, Alpes-Maritimes.
Tel 04 93 35 80 20. Fax 04 93 57 40 20. Mich 165/F3. Map 6.

MERCUREY Hôtellerie du Val d'Or

Comfortable hotel/Cooking 2-3 `FW`
Gardens/Garage/Parking

The epitome of a traditional family-run hotel: in this case the Cogny family is, in every way, typical of the very best of the breed. Monique is an unassuming, gentle *patronne* & husband Jean-Claude a self-effacing chef with a smile & bags of skill. Burgundian treasures, classical old-timers & some modern gems. Don't miss the Michel Juillot village wines.
Menus b(lunch)CDEF. Rooms (13) F. Cards MC, V.
Closed 15 Dec-17 Jan. Mon (not midday pub. hols). Tues midday.
Post 71640 Mercurey, Saône-et-Loire. Region Burgundy.
Tel 03 85 45 13 70. Fax 03 85 45 18 45. Mich 88/A3. Map 3.

MEURSAULT Relais de la Diligence

Comfortable restaurant/Cooking 2 `FW`
Parking

Beside the D23, SE of the N74 (near *la gare*). A modern building with four dining rooms & fine views W of *la côte*. Several menus, efficient service & pleasing ambience. Typical appetising *plats* include a tasty *mousse d'avocat* with fresh shrimps; a well-chosen *panaché de poisson aux deux sauces*; & an excellent multi-choice *plateau de fromages*.
Menus aBC. Cards All. (Rooms: Les Magnolias or Les Charmes in village.)
Closed 5 Dec-18 Jan. Tues evg. Wed. (Both above quiet & *sans rest*.)
Post rue de la gare, 21190 Meursault, Côte-d'Or. Region Burgundy.
Tel 03 80 21 21 32. Fax 03 80 21 64 69. Mich 88/A2-A3. Map 3.

A100frs & under. B100–150. C150–200. D200–250. E250–350. F350–500. G500+

MEXIMIEUX Claude Lutz

Very comfortable restaurant with rooms/Cooking 2-3
Parking/Air-conditioning (restaurant)

Once again no changes to report at this reliable *Bressan* restaurant. A warm welcome from Evelyne Lutz & an in-the-tramlines consistency from chef Claude. Fine classical & regional cuisine: a mite-too-rich *poulet de Bresse & ris de veau à la crème et morilles* is one typical example. Drink Bugey (to the E) wines – both Gamay & Chardonnay varieties.
Menus C(bottom-end)DE. Rooms (14) CDE. Cards AE, MC, V.
Closed 14-21 July. 28 Oct-15 Nov. Sun evg. Mon.
Post 17 r. Lyon, 01800 Meximieux, Ain. Region Lyonnais.
Tel 04 74 61 06 78. Fax 04 74 34 75 23. Mich 116/C1. Map 6.

MEYRUEIS Château d'Ayres

Very comfortable hotel/Cooking 2 `FW`
Secluded/Terrace/Gardens/Swimming pool/Tennis/Parking

A 12thC Benedictine monastery in wooded grounds – with giant redwoods & oaks – E of Meyrueis (use D57). The hotel's façade is one of the most evocative, & photogenic, in France. The Montjou family's haven of peace also seduces with classical/*Cévenols* menus: nothing sizzling – just enjoyable fare like *tarte aux cèpes, pintadeau aux choux* & *crème brûlée*.
Menus B(lunch)C(bottom-end)E. Rooms (26) G. Cards All.
Closed Mid Nov-Mar. (Cheaper rooms: Grand Hôtel de France, in village.)
Post 48150 Meyrueis, Lozère. Region Massif Central (Cévennes).
Tel 04 66 45 60 10. Fax 04 66 45 62 26. Mich 141/F3. Map 5.

MEYRUEIS (also see next page) Europe

Comfortable hotel/Cooking 1-2 `FW`
Lift/Closed parking/(also see text)

The first of two Robert family-owned hotels. Here Frédéric Robert is *le patron*; his sister, Stella, is the hostess at the Mont Aigoual, 200m to the S (you can use garden & pool). Their dad, Jean-Paul, mans the Europe kitchen. Copious, basic classical/regional grub, just scraping 1-2: the *terrine de veau, saumon grillée à l'oseille, croquette de poulet* type.
Menus AB. Rooms (29)DE. Cards MC, V.
Closed Nov-Easter.
Post 48150 Meyrueis, Lozère. Region Massif Central (Cévennes).
Tel 04 66 45 60 05. Fax 04 66 45 65 31. Mich 141/F3. Map 5.

A100frs & under. B100–150. C150–200. D200–250. E250–350. F350–500. G500+

MEYRUEIS (also see previous page) Mont Aigoual

Comfortable hotel/Cooking 2
Gardens/Swimming pool/Lift/Closed parking

The second of the two Robert family enterprises. Here Stella Robert, an energetic *patronne*, runs the *logis*. Chef Daniel Lagrange concocts a mix of tummy-filling regional, classical & neo-classical *plats*: on menu B they range from *ragout de ris d'agneau aux écrevisses* & *magret de canard aux épices* to *gigot de mouton sa galette de pommes au roquefort*.
Menus AB(ceiling). Rooms (30) E. Cards AE, MC, V.
Closed Nov-Mar. (Alongside D986 to S.)
Post 48150 Meyrueis, Lozère. Region Massif Central (Cévennes).
Tel 04 66 45 65 61. Fax 04 66 45 64 25. Mich 141/F3. Map 5.

MEZERIAT Les Bessières

Simple restaurant with rooms/Cooking 1-2 FW
Terrace/Garage

To the W of the *village fleuri*, near *la gare*. Joël & Raymonde Foraison are friendly, gentle folk – complementing perfectly the unassuming restaurant, shady terrace & classical/regional fare. Enjoy local *plats*: *mousse de brochet sauce Nantua, filet de carpe des Dombes aux cerfeuil* & *fromage blanc à la crème*. One more pleasing plus: very attentive staff.
Menus aBC. Rooms (6) CD(top-end). Cards MC, V.
Closed 15 Nov-Jan. Mon & Tues (not July/Aug).
Post 01660 Mézériat, Ain. Region Lyonnais.
Tel 04 74 30 24 24. Mich 102/C3. Map 6.

MIGENNES Paris

Comfortable restaurant with rooms/Cooking 2 FW
Air-conditioning (restaurant)

A vine-covered building beside a busy main road (D943). Ghastly décor, in the style only the French know how to do so brilliantly. Attentive service, with a touch of humour, & plenty of flowers compensate – as does the classical cooking of Patrice Chauvin, the *chef/patron*. Notable dishes include a lip-smackingly good *île flottante crème anglaise*.
Menus aBC. Rooms (9) CDEF. Cards MC, V.
Closed 2-7 Jan. 1-28 Aug. Fri evg. Sat midday. Sun evg.
Post 57 av. J.Jaurès, 89400 Migennes, Yonne. Region Burgundy.
Tel 03 86 80 23 22. Fax 03 86 80 31 04. Mich 72/A1. Map 2.

A100frs & under. B100–150. C150–200. D200–250. E250–350. F350–500. G500+

MILLAU   La Capelle

Simple hotel (no restaurant)
Quiet

Jane Rouquet is a friendly, helpful owner; with her mother's help they run their hotel with tender loving care. Despite its central location – park in the large *place* opposite the hotel – the site is quiet. More than anything else the prime benefit here is that you are just a few minutes walk away from 3 recommended restaurants. Much liked favourite.
Rooms (46) B(top-end)CDE. Cards MC, V.
Closed Oct-Easter. (At other times use Campanile, on Rodez road to NW.)
Post 7 pl. Fraternité, 12100 Millau, Aveyron. Region MC (Cévennes).
Tel 05 65 60 14 72. Mich 141/E4. Map 5.

MILLAU   Capion

Simple restaurant/Cooking 1-2   `FW`

Patrick (from the Vosges) & Corinne (she's from the Aveyron) Mougeot maintain the high standards set by Blaise Trespaillé-Barrau. No prizes for the décor but the classical (*sole sauce Cardinal* & *gibiers Grand Veneur*), regional (*tripous Aveyronnais*) & neo-classical (*tarte aux sardines fraîches oignons confits* & *encornet farci en fine ratatouille coulis de tomates*) specialities should please all – at *RQP* prices.
Menus ABC. Cards All. (Rooms: see entry above.)
Closed Wed (not July/Aug). (Above 250m walk to E.)
Post 3 r. J.-F. Alméras, 12100 Millau, Aveyron. Region MC (Cévennes).
Tel 05 65 60 00 91. Fax 05 65 60 42 13. Mich 141/E4. Map 5.

MILLAU (also see next page)   Château de Creissels

Comfortable hotel/Cooking 1-2   `FW`
Quiet/Terrace/Gardens/Parking

Retained by a whisker – only because a new chef has been employed. I've supported the Austruy family hotel (2km SW) for 15 years & Michelin (with a "*Repas*" award) for 5/6 years; but recently cooking standards did slip badly. Classical/regional tucker. Well-appointed bedrooms, a counterpoint to the old-world gentility of the main public rooms.
Menus BCD. Rooms (33) DEF. Cards All. (Use D992.) Closed 29 Dec-12 Feb.
Sun evg (mid Nov-mid Mar). Rest: Sun evg & Mon midday (not high season).
Post rte St-Affrique, 12100 Millau, Aveyron. Region MC (Cévennes).
Tel 05 65 60 16 59. Fax 05 65 61 24 63. Mich 141/E4. Map 5.

A100frs & under. B100–150. C150–200. D200–250. E250–350. F350–500. G500+

221

MILLAU (also see previous page) International

Very comfortable hotel/Cooking 2
Lift/Closed parking/Air-conditioning (restaurant)

A mini Park Lane Hilton. The multi-storey hotel is in the town centre; the 3rd-generation *patrons* are Jean-François & Caroline Pomarède. On a boiling summer's day the air-cond. was the ideal cooler for the huge-choice classical *Menu Touristique* (B): *paupiette de truites au lard, fondue de poireaux* & *tarte à la banane* made ideal hot weather dishes.
Menus BCDE. Rooms (110) EF. Cards All.
Closed Rest: Sun evg & Mon (not high season).
Post 1 pl. Tine, 12100 Millau, Aveyron. Region MC (Cévennes).
Tel 05 65 59 29 00. Fax 05 65 59 29 01. Mich 141/E4. Map 5.

MILLAU La Marmite du Pêcheur

Simple restaurant/Cooking 2 FW
Terrace

Albert Négron is no longer with us. He died in 1993, aged 79 & after working 65 years in various kitchens. His widow, the smiling Janine, continues Albert's classical & regional traditions – aided by 33-year-old chef Christian Aveline. Best treats are *petite marmite du pêcheur* &, from 16 sweets, *bolet du chef Albert* – a 3-star winner. Bravo Janine!
Menus ABCD(top-end). Cards AE, MC, V. (Rooms: La Capelle, 200m N.)
Closed Wed (Dec-Apl). (See previous page for details of above hotel.)
Post 14 bd Capelle, 12100 Millau, Aveyron. Region MC (Cévennes).
Tel 05 65 61 20 44. Mich 141/E4. Map 5. (Park in large *place* 100m N.)

MIMIZAN Au Bon Coin du Lac

Very comfortable restaurant with rooms/Cooking 3-4
Quiet/Terrace/Gardens/Garage/Parking/Air cond. (rest.)

Before your meal walk the 250m-long *promenade fleuri* which runs from the Bon Coin beside the Etang d'Aureilhan. Then relish the idyllic home of Jean-Pierre & Jacqueline Caule. She's a vivacious, larger-than-life soul & he's a beguiling neo-classicist who capitalises cleverly on both his *pays* & the nearby ocean's harvests. Breakfast is one of France's finest.
Menus c(low-end)EDF. Rooms (4) G(low-end). Cards AE, MC, V.
Closed Feb. Sun evg & Mon (mid Sept-June). Region Southwest.
Post 40200 Mimizan, Landes. (N of Mimizan-Bourg; use D87.)
Tel 05 58 09 01 55. Fax 05 58 09 40 84. Mich 134/A3. Map 4.

MIRMANDE

La Capitelle

Simple hotel/Cooking 1
Quiet/Terrace

Previous owners, the Bouchers, were extremely well-liked; I've had no input yet on the new *patrons*, Bernard Melki & his wife. What doesn't change however is the super 16thC Renaissance stone-built hotel with its colourful façade, terrace & extensive views. Cooking? Unadventurous classical continues; of the *pigeon farci au foie gras de canard* type.
Menus aB. Rooms (11) EF. Cards All. (3km SE Saulce-sur-Rhône.)
Closed 15 Jan-20 Feb. Tues & Wed midday (not July/Aug).
Post 26270 Mirmande, Drôme. Regions Hautes-Alpes/MC (Ardèche).
Tel 04 75 63 02 72. Fax 04 75 63 02 50. Mich 130/A4. Map 6.

MITTELBERGHEIM

Winstub Gilg

Comfortable restaurant with rooms/Cooking 1-2   FW
Parking

Quintessential Alsace: an evocative *vin* village, where wine merchants & geraniums rule; & a half-timbered, window-boxed 17thC *winstub* with beamed interior. George Gilg prepares neo-classical/regional creations. On no-choice menu b *tarte à l'oignon* & *vacherin glacé*; on bottom-end menu C a welcome *saumon frais poêlé au Noilly et crème d'oseille*.
Menus bCDE. Rooms (15) DEF. Cards All.
Closed 6-29 Jan. 23 June-9 July. Tues evg. Wed.
Post 67140 Mittelbergheim, Bas-Rhin. Region Alsace.
Tel 03 88 08 91 37. Fax 03 88 08 45 17. Mich 61/D1. Map 3.

MOELAN-SUR-MER (also see next page)   Manoir de Kertalg

Very comfortable hotel (no restaurant)
Secluded/Gardens/Parking

What a gorgeous hotel, originally the stables of the adjacent manor & in 217 acres of a wooded park, overlooking the Bélon estuary (8km inland!). The long access drive is a carbon copy of the road on the L bank of Wales' Llyfnant Valley (S Machynlleth). Splendid interior. The owners's English-speaking son, "Brann", is a talented modern artist.
Rooms (9) G. Cards AE,MC, V. (Off D24, 3km to W.)
Closed Nov-Easter.
Post 29350 Moëlan-sur-Mer, Finistère. Region Brittany.
Tel 02 98 39 77 77. Fax 02 98 39 72 07. Mich 45/E3. Map 1.

A100frs & under. B100–150. C150–200. D200–250. E250–350. F350–500. G500+

MOELAN-SUR-MER (also see previous page) Les Moulins du Duc

Very comfortable hotel/Cooking 1-2　　　　　　　　　**FW**
Secluded/Gardens/Swimming pool (indoor)/Parking

Dropped from *FLE* but reinstated for the Quistreberts' efforts in introducing FW menus at their delectable 16thC water mills' complex beside the Bélun, a famed salmon river, & with the pluses of 6 *étangs*, cascades & 150 acres of wooded grounds. Rooms dear (in granite cottages) but perfect for a FW classical cuisine meal in a most alluring setting.
Menus a(lunch)BC. Rooms (22) G. Cards All. (2km N of village.)
Closed Jan-Feb. (Moëlan-sur-Mer is 8km from the coast.)
Post 29350 Moëlan-sur-Mer, Finistère. Region Brittany.
Tel 02 98 39 60 73. Fax 02 98 39 75 56. Mich 45/E3. Map 1.

MOIRANS-EN-MONTAGNE　　　　　　Auberge Jurassienne

Simple restaurant/Cooking 1-2　　　　　　　　　**FW**
Terrace/Parking

A large, unattractive *Jurassienne* farm, now the restaurant home of a young, enterprising couple, Laurent & Laurence Fieret. N of the village at the D470/D301 junc. Appetite & wallet satisfying classical & regional offerings from Laurent: *filet de truite rose en timbale d'écrevisses* & *aiguillette de volaille au Comté au jambon cru* are a representative duo.
Menus a(lunch)BD(both low-end). Cards MC, V. (Rooms: Host. Lacuzon.)
Closed Sun evg & Mon (not July/Aug). (Above hotel in village.)
Post 39260 Moirans-en-Montagne, Jura. Region Jura.
Tel 03 84 42 01 32. Fax 03 84 42 33 62. Mich 103/F2. Map 6.

MOLINES-EN-QUEYRAS　　　　　　　　　L'Equipe

Simple hotel/Cooking 0-1
Quiet/Terrace/Parking

Reasons for inclusion? Simple: the clue is in the word Queyras; for details read pages 139-143 in *Mapaholics' France*. The Catalins' *logis* is a modest chalet-styled hotel with simple *Bourgeoise* nosh & some rock-solid regional dishes (*fondues, raclette* & *tarte aux myrtilles* are bright sparklers). Adolphe Catalin will put you wise on the best walks.
Menus ABC. Rooms (22) E. Cards All.
Closed 8 Apl-22 May. 3 Nov-15 Dec. Rest: Sun evg & Mon (Oct).
Post 05350 Molines-en-Queyras, Hautes-Alpes. Region Hautes-Alpes.
Tel 04 92 45 83 20. Fax 04 92 45 81 85. Mich 133/E4. Map 6.

A100frs & under. B100–150. C150–200. D200–250. E250–350. F350–500. G500+

MOLINEUF

Poste

Comfortable restaurant/Cooking 2
Parking/Air-conditioning

FW

An attractive village in wooded terrain (W Blois). Modern, light dining room with striking wall frescoes. An up-and-coming young chef, Thierry Poidras, certainly means business. Classical & neo-classcal dishes: a hunky dory duo of *dos de flétan au coulis et ravioli de homard* & *magret de canard aux langoustines et jus de truffes* were perfection.
Menus aCD. Cards All. (Rooms: Ibis & Campanile: N Blois, near A10 exit.)
Closed Feb. Sun evg. Wed. (Above easily reached; 13km drive.)
Post 41190 Molineuf, Loir-et-Cher. Region Loire.
Tel 02 54 70 03 25. Fax 02 54 70 12 46. Mich 68/B3. Map 2.

MONCRABEAU

Le Phare

Comfortable restaurant with rooms/Cooking 2
Terrace/Gardens

FW

A *logis* in a delightful perched village. The shady terrace with views of the village's swimming pool & unusual bell tower is a cool oasis on a burning hot day. Michel Lestrade, with the help of his daughter, rings both regional/neo-classical cooking bells: *magret de canard grillé* & *filets de rougets à la fondue de tomate* are typical. Super bedrooms.
Menus ABC. Rooms (8) DEF. Cards All.
Closed Feb. Oct. Mon evg & Tues (not July/Aug).
Post 47600 Moncrabeau, Lot-et-Garonne. Region Southwest.
Tel 05 53 65 42 08. Fax 05 53 97 04 87. Mich 136/C4. Map 5.

MONESTIER-DE-CLERMONT

Au Sans Souci

Simple hotel/Cooking 2
Quiet/Terrace/Gardens/Swimming pool/Tennis/Garage/Parking

FW

The Maurice family celebrated 60 years of ownership in 1994. The fourth generation, Frédéric, the chef, & Michelle, *la patronne*, do a sterling job at their mountain *logis*. Extensive choice on the classical & *Bourgeois* menus: *ravioles du Royans* (W of Vercors), *omble chevalier aux amandes, filet d'agneau aux cèpes* & *fromage blanc* – winners all.
Menus ABCD. Rooms (11) CDE. Cards MC, V. (N of village; W of N75.)
Closed 15 Dec-Jan. Sun evg & Mon (not July/Aug). Regions Htes-Alpes/Sav.
Post St-Paul-lès-Monestier, 38650 Monestier-de-Clermont, Isère.
Tel 04 76 34 03 60. Fax 04 76 34 17 38. Mich 131/E3. Map 6.

A100frs & under. B100–150. C150–200. D200–250. E250–350. F350–500. G500+

MONPAZIER

La Bastide

Comfortable restaurant/Cooking 1-2

FW

Monpazier is the best of the *bastides* between the Dordogne & Lot; the fortified village's arcaded square is a joy – with perfectly proportioned stone buildings. Gérard Prigent's largish medieval rest. (120 *couverts*) is hardly evocative of his *Breton pays*; it's relentless *cuisine Périgourdine*. Tuck into *foie gras de canard au torchon, rognon de veau fourré au foie gras* & similar – served on Limoges crockery.

Menus ABCD. Cards AE, MC, V. (Rooms: see base hotel below.)
Closed 19 Feb-end Mar. Mon.
Post 52 r. St-Jacques, 24540 Monpazier, Dordogne. Region Dordogne.
Tel 05 53 22 60 59. Fax 05 53 22 09 20. Mich 123/E4. Map 5.

MONPAZIER

Edward 1er

Comfortable hotel (no restaurant)
Quiet/Gardens/Swimming pool/Parking

Monpazier is my favourite *bastide* – built in 1284 by Edward I, King of England & Duke of Aquitaine (read first 2 lines of entry above); hence the name of this evocative mini 19thC château (hotel opened in 1990). Stylish is an apt adjective for the interior; some rooms have a jacuzzi & steam bath & all the rooms have a mini-bar & satellite TV channels.

Rooms (13) FG,G2. Disabled. Cards All.
Closed Nov-Apl.
Post 24540 Monpazier, Dordogne. Region Dordogne.
Tel 05 53 22 44 00. Fax 05 53 22 57 99. Mich 123/E4. Map 5.

MONPAZIER (Lolme)

Les Peyrouliers

Simple restaurant/Cooking 2
Terrace/Parking

FW

On the D660 E side, 6km NW of Monpazier. Delightful in many ways: the terrace; the warm welcome from Marie Buisson (charmer with a marvellous memory); & the classical/*Périgord* cooking from her husband Jean-Claude. The two hail from Normandy: bits of the latter in the cooking; & super Calvados *bien sûr*. Enterprising veg. Simple & seductive; don't miss it.

Menus ABCD. Cards MC, V. (Rooms: Edward 1er (above); Lac at Villéreal.)
Closed Mid Nov-mid Dec. Mon (not high season).
Post 24540 Lolme, Dordogne. Region Dordogne.
Tel 05 53 22 66 10. Fax 05 53 23 33 13. Mich 123/E4. Map 5.

A100frs & under. B100–150. C150–200. D200–250. E250–350. F350–500. G500+

MONTAUBAN Ambroisie

Comfortable restaurant/Cooking 2
Air-conditioning

Sybette Fournales is the hostess at the contemporary-styled restaurant;
husband Jean-Pierre mans the *fours* in the kitchen. Copious, multi-
choice menus with classical, *Bourgeois* & regional specialities of the
*parfait de foie de volaille, filet de truite poêlée aux champignons,
faux-filet sauce au poivre vert, îles flottantes* variety.
Menus B(bottom-end)C. Cards MC, V. (Rooms: Climat de France; 4km NE.)
Closed 23 Dec-5 Jan. 13 July-4 Aug. Sun (not midday Sept-June). Mon.
Post 41 r. Comédie, 82000 Montauban, Tarn-et-Garonne. Region Southwest.
Tel 05 63 66 27 40. Mich 138/B4. Map 5.

MONTAUBAN La Cuisine d'Alain et Hôtel Orsay

Very comfortable restaurant with rooms/Cooking 2-3 FW
Terrace/Lift/Closed parking/Air-conditioning (bedrooms)

Opposite the station but soundproofed rooms take the sting out of
moving trains. Alain Blanc regales clients with a neo-classical display,
notable for a mix of fish dishes – *gratin de poissons aux poireaux* is one
example – & filling creations such as a *galinette de veau pâtes fraîches*.
High-quality trolley of light sweets. Nicole is *la patronne*.
Menus BCDE. Rooms (20) E. Cards All.
Closed 23 Dec-2 Jan. 11-24 Aug. Sun. Mon midday.
Post face gare, 82000 Montauban, Tarn-et-Garonne. Region Southwest.
Tel 05 63 66 06 66. Fax 05 63 66 19 39. Mich 138/B4. Map 5.

MONTAUROUX Auberge du Puits Jaubert

Comfortable restaurant with rooms/Cooking 1-2
Secluded/Terrace/Gardens/Parking

Brothers Henri & Fabien Fillatreau have given the 15thC *bergerie* a
welcome fillip since they bought the *auberge* 10 years ago. Some grumbles
about the food (rating has been downgraded) & slip-slap attention to detail
in the bedrooms. Classical cooking with the odd Provençale touch. Site is
the prime plus: near to but not overlooking Lac de St-Cassien.
Menus B(ceiling)E. Rooms (8) DE(low-end). Cards MC, V.
Closed 15 Nov-15 Dec. Tues. Region Côte d'Azur.
Post Montauroux, 83440 Fayence, Var. (Due S of Montauroux & D562.)
Tel 04 94 76 44 48. Mich 164/C4. Map 6. (Site marked on Michelin maps.)

A100frs & under. B100–150. C150–200. D200–250. E250–350. F350–500. G500+

MONTBRISON

Rest. Yves Thollot/Hôtel Marytel

Comfortable restaurant & simple hotel/Cooking 2 FW
Terrace (restaurant)/Parking

At Savigneux, beside D946 to E. Two colourful, ultra-modern buildings side-by-side. Odd-ball bright umbrellas in dining room. Nothing odd-ball about Yves' neo-classical repertoire: a spirited *panaché de lotte et saumon* & an accomplished, full-of-flavour marriage of *magret de canard aux chanterelles* are sunny memories under the indoor umbrellas.
Menus bCDE. Rooms (33) DE. Cards (R) AE, MC, V. (H) All. Mich 115/D3.
Closed Rest: Feb sch. hols. 21 July-11 Aug. Sun evg. Mon. Map 6.
Post 93/95 rte Lyon, 42600 Montbrison, Loire. Region MC (Auvergne).
Tel (R) 04 77 96 10 40. (H) 04 77 58 72 00. Fax (H) 04 77 58 42 81.

MONTEUX

Blason de Provence

Comfortable hotel/Cooking 1-2 FW
Terrace/Gardens/Swimming pool/Tennis

Two English-speaking owners Joan & Roger Duvillet are keen as mustard & are determined. Yet I continue to get the odd complaint about the food (classical & Provençale cuisine) & that both wines & the buffet-style breakfast (50F or so) are expensive. The Blason just squeaks a cooking 1-2 rating (FW): tell me if I'm wrong – either way.
Menus b(bottom-end)CE. Rooms (20) EF. Cards All.
Closed 15 Dec-15 Jan. Rest: Sat midday.
Post 84170 Monteux, Vaucluse. Region Provence. (To E of village.)
Tel 04 90 66 31 34. Fax 04 90 66 83 05. Mich 144/C4. Map 6.

MONTFERRAT

Ferme du Baudron

Simple restaurant/Cooking 1-2 FW
Terrace/Gardens/Swimming pool/Tennis/Parking

Note: lunch only (except July/Aug) at the Faivre family farm. Rustic is the tag at this Alpine-like ski-lodge, complete with vast chimney & log fire where Daniel Faivre does most of his cooking. Readers adore the sauces & a mushroom sextet *façon de grand-mère*. *Pâtés*, grilled *faux-filet* & *côte de porc* & similar (& instant-whip chocolat mousse?).
Menus A (not Sun when *à la carte* C). Cards not accepted.
Closed 15 Jan-Feb. All evenings (not July/Aug). Wed. (Studios for rent.)
Post 83131 Montferrat, Var. Region Côte d'Azur. (1km S of Montferrat.)
Tel 04 94 70 91 03. Mich 163/D2. Map 6. (Rooms: Parc, Draguignan.)

A100frs & under. B100–150. C150–200. D200–250. E250–350. F350–500. G500+

MONTIGNY-LE-ROI

**Comfortable hotel/Cooking 1
Garage/Parking**

An hotel I first came across when researching *En Route*, my autoroute guide. Head W from exit 8 on the A31; up the D417 hill & the hotel is N of the village at the junction with the D74. Henri Maillot is the owner of the unprepossessing establishment; Eric Buiatti is *le cuisinier*. He drives utterly safe, straightforward classical roads – *filets de sole à la tomate* & *rognonnade de veau à la Dijonnaise* are signature km posts.
Menus ABCD. Rooms (26) DE. Disabled. Cards All.
Post 52140 Montigny-le-Roi, Haute-Marne. Region Champagne-Ardenne.
Tel 03 25 90 30 18. Fax 03 25 90 71 80. Mich 58/B4. Map 3.

MONTLUEL

Le Petit Casset

**Simple hotel (no restaurant)
Fairly quiet/Gardens/Parking**

For long a great readers' favourite – especially in the days of Jeannine Perronier & her parrot. New owners, Mireille & Bernard Kiehl, don't have a talking bird but the rest of the appeal formula remains the same. Ideally sited for Pérouges (be sure not to miss it) & Lyon-Satolas airport. (At La Boisse; N (about 100m) of the N84; 2km SW of Montluel; Lyon is 24km to the SW; & the A42 exit 5 is 6km to the SW.)
Rooms (15) E. Cards MC, V.
Post La Boisse, 01120 Montluel, Ain. Region Lyonnais.
Tel 04 78 06 21 33. Fax 04 78 06 55 20. Mich 116/B1. Map 6.

MONTMELIAN

Viboud

**Simple restaurant with basic rooms/Cooking 1-2
Garage/Parking/Air-conditioning (restaurant)**

FW

On the hill in the old town, well away from the N6. Jacques Viboud is a great rugger enthusiast – witness the intriguing memorabilia & the town team's many cups displayed in the bar. Old-fashioned cooking (little choice) with classics such as *terrine de canard au pistaches et noisettes* & a mundane but appetising *faux-filet poêlé*. Average sweets.
Menus ABC. Rooms (8) C. Cards All.
Closed 1-15 Jan. Oct. Sun evg. Mon.
Post Vieux Montmélian, 73800 Montmélian, Savoie. Region Savoie.
Tel 04 79 84 07 24. Fax 04 79 84 44 07. Mich 118/B3. Map 6.

A100frs & under. B100–150. C150–200. D200–250. E250–350. F350–500. G500+

MONTMERLE-SUR-SAONE

Rivage

Comfortable hotel/Cooking 1-2
Terrace/Parking

FW

Readers like the shady, paved terrace (which, at night, is lamplit) overlooking the river & suspension bridge. Josette Job, *la patronne*, provides an engaging welcome; husband Emile takes care of the kitchen from which flows a cascade of classical/regional dishes. Simpler treats please too: like *petite friture* from the Saône & *terrine anguille*.
Menus aCDE. Rooms (21) EF. Cards AE, MC, V.
Closed 1-7 Mar. Nov. Sun evg (Oct-May). Mon (not evgs June-Sept).
Post 01090 Montmerle-sur-Saône, Ain. Region Lyonnais.
Tel 04 74 69 33 92. Fax 04 74 69 49 21. Mich 102/B4. Map 6.

MONTREAL

Chez Simone

Simple restaurant/Cooking 1-2
Terrace

FW

Chez Simone, tucked away near the fortified *église* in the perched *bastide* of Montréal, is a cool oasis of culinary Gers charm. Three plane trees provide a shady terrace; a beamed *salle* is the indoor option. Landes & Gers *terroir* tummy fillers from Bernard Daubin: *salmis de palombe* & *confit de canard* are typical. Toothsome *hors d'oeuvre*.
Menus aBCD. Cards All. (Rooms: 3 Lys & Logis des Cordeliers, Condom.)
Closed Sat. (Both above hotels are *sans rest.* & easy 15km drive to E.)
Post pl. Eglise, 32250 Montréal, Gers. Region Southwest.
Tel 05 62 29 44 40. Fax 05 62 29 49 94. Mich 151/D1. Map 5.

MONTREUIL

Château de Montreuil

Very comfortable hotel/Cooking 3-4
Secluded/Terrace/Gardens/Garage/Closed parking

Our last visit confirmed conclusively that Christian Germain is cooking better than ever. Menus D&E were studded with neo-classical & modern gems – drawing cleverly on the chef's *terroir*, other parts of France & Europe & the tropics. More long-loved pluses: the relaxing garden; the retina-reeling *potager* (ask to see it); & Lindsay G – an English rose.
Menus D(low-end lunch)EF. Rooms (13) G. Cards All.
Closed 15 Dec-8 Feb. Mon (Sept-May). Thurs midday (not pub. hols).
Post chaussée Capucins, 62170 Montreuil, Pas-de-Calais. Region North.
Tel 03 21 81 53 04. Fax 03 21 81 36 43. Mich 2/A4. Map 2.

A100frs & under. B100–150. C150–200. D200–250. E250–350. F350–500. G500+

230

MONTREUIL   Auberge la Grenouillère

Very comfortable restaurant with rooms/Cooking 3-4   `FW`
Quiet/Terrace/Parking

Arguably one of readers' most-loved favourites in the North. Frogs are
the theme in the converted whitewashed farm cottages, beside the tree-
lined River Canche. Chuckle at the dining room frescoes, enjoy the
crackling fire, then relish the pleasures of Jura-born Roland Gauthier's
neo-classical & modern repertoire – polished *plats* all.
Menus b(ceiling)DEF. Rooms (4) F. Cards All.
Closed 2 Jan-15 Feb. Tues & Wed (not July/Aug). Region North.
Post 62170 La Madelaine-sous-Montreuil, Pas-de-Calais. (NW; off D139.)
Tel 03 21 06 07 22. Fax 03 21 86 36 36. Mich 2/A4. Map 2.

MONTREUIL   Les Hauts de Montreuil

Comfortable restaurant with rooms/Cooking 1-2   `FW`
Terrace/Parking

Run as a "business" by the energetic, black-bearded Jacques Gantiez.
The "show" can be overwhelming. The half-timbered house at the front
is 16thC (a *monument historique*); the rest is modern. *Cave* with 400
choices; cheese cellar; & boutique (you can buy goodies from all three).
Cooking? Wide choice classical/regional. Magnificent breakfasts.
Menus b(top-end)CD. Rooms (27) EF. Cards MC, V. (In town centre.)
Closed Rest: 3 Jan-mid Feb.
Post 21-23 r. P. Ledent, 62170 Montreuil, Pas-de-Calais. Region North.
Tel 03 21 81 95 92. Fax 03 21 86 28 83. Mich 2/A4. Map 2.

MONTREUIL-BELLAY   Splendid et Annexe Relais du Bellay

Simple hotel & comfortable annexe/Cooking 1
Gardens, Swimming pool (indoor) & Lift at annexe/Parking

I continue to receive mixed reports. Some readers speak highly of a warm
& comfortable, old-fashioned French rest. & the well-appointed bedrooms.
The *relais* (41 rooms) is a modern annexe. Cooking is straightforward
classical, regional & *Bourgeoise*: of the *hors d'oeuvre, filet de boeuf au
poivre, sandre beurre blanc* & *ris de veau Véronique* variety.
Menus ABCD. Rooms (63) CDEF. Disabled. Cards MC, V.
Closed Rest: Sun evg (Oct-Feb). Region Loire. Mich 81/D2. Map 2.
Post r. Dr Gaudrez, 49260 Montreuil-Bellay, Maine-et-Loire.
Tel 02 41 53 10 00. 02 41 53 10 10 (annexe). Fax 02 41 52 45 17.

A100frs & under. B100–150. C150–200. D200–250. E250–350. F350–500. G500+

MONTREVEL-EN-BRESSE

Le Comptoir

Very simple restaurant/Cooking 1-2
Air-conditioning

Louis Monnier, *chef/patron* of the Léa rest. which he opened in 1980 (see next entry) describes his "annexe" as a *"Bistrot Lyonnais"*. Run by his son Cédric. Tuck into *Bourgeoise*/Lyonnais grub – of the *assiette de rosette* (superb pork sausage), *saucisson chaud pommes à l'huile, poulet à la crème, fromage blanc à la crème* variety. No second mortgages here.
Menus AB. Cards MC, V. (Rooms: see next entry.)
Closed 23 Dec-10 Jan. 25 June-11 July. Tues evg & Wed.
Post 01340 Montrevel-en-Bresse, Ain. Region Lyonnais.
Tel 04 75 25 45 53. Mich 103/D2. Map 6.

MONTREVEL-EN-BRESSE

Léa

Comfortable restaurant/Cooking 3

Montrevel is famed for Bresse poultry. Not surprisingly *poulet/poularde de Bresse* feature on Louis Monnier's classical & regional menus. An elegant flower-filled *salle* & a warm welcome from Marie-Claude provide an enticing setting for her husband's skilled cooking: Lyonnais legends like *gâteau de foies, cuisses de grenouilles* & *poulet à la crème*; & many classics of which m*arquise au chocolat amer* is a heavenly concoction.
Menus B(ceiling)E. Cards MC, V. (Rooms: Le Pillebois, 2km S – D975.)
Closed 23 Dec-10 Jan. 25 June-11 July. Sun evg. Wed.
Post 01340 Montrevel-en-Bresse, Ain. Region Lyonnais.
Tel 04 74 30 80 84. Fax 04 74 30 85 66. Mich 103/D2. Map 6.

MONTROND-LES-BAINS

Hostellerie La Poularde

Very comfortable hotel/Cooking 4
Garage/Air-conditioning

Some reports suggested "not what it was". Back we went, yet again, & we left satisfied that the rating needed raising to 4. Modern master, Gilles Etéocle, is back to form; wife Monique is as captivating as ever. English-speaking, prize-winning *sommelier*, Eric Beaumard, has a lovely personality; what a joy to watch his wine & customer-handling skills.
Menus dEFG. Rooms (11) EFG. Cards All.
Closed 2-15 Jan. Mon (not pub. hols). Tues midday.
Post 42210 Montrond-les-Bains, Loire. Region Lyonnais.
Tel 04 77 54 40 06. Fax 04 77 54 53 14. Mich 115/D3. Map 6.

A100frs & under. B100–150. C150–200. D200–250. E250–350. F350–500. G500+

MONTSALVY

Comfortable hotel/Cooking 2
Gardens/Parking

Jean Crayon, a cheerful, energetic *patron*, runs the front of house; his wife, Mauricette, is *la cuisinière* at the much modernised hotel. Readers speak warmly of her artistic skills with regional/classical/*Bourgeoises* offerings such as *terrine de légumes en jardinière, quiche crèmeuse aux girolles & filet de St-Pierre, doré, au Noilly*. One debit: awful bread.
Menus ABCDE. Rooms (23) CDE. Cards All.
Closed Jan-Mar.
Post 15120 Montsalvy, Cantal. Region Massif Central (Auvergne).
Tel 04 71 49 20 03. Fax 04 71 49 29 00. Mich 126/B4. Map 5.

MORTAGNE-SUR-SEVRE

France/Rest. La Taverne

Comfortable hotel/Cooking 2
Gardens/Swimming pool (indoor)/Lift/Air-cond. (rest.)

The *relais'* ivy-covered exterior, a coaching inn for 400 years, hides many facets of olden-days France: service; furnishings; courtesy; from the 4th-generation owners, Guy & Marie-Claude Jagueneau (soon to retire; they're looking for a buyer); & classical cuisine. Fine sauces: witness *omble chevalier au beurre de romoran*. The indoor pool is magnificent.
Menus CDE (brasserie A; rating 1). Rooms (24) EF. Cards All.
Closed 20 Dec-16 Jan. Sat (Sept-May). Region Poitou-Charentes.
Post pl. Dr Pichat, 85290 Mortagne-sur-Sèvre, Vendée.
Tel 02 51 65 03 37. Fax 02 51 65 27 83. Mich 80/A2. Map 1.

Le MOTTIER

Les Donnières

Comfortable restaurant/Cooking 2-3

FW

You dine not so much in a rest. as the home of Jean-Luc & Line Boland. The ancient barn is 70m N of the *mairie*, on the R (sign is hidden). A pretty garden & an old-world interior with table settings to match. Classical fare with old-fashioned finesse; impeccable saucing; & daily-changing *plats*. Signature flourishes: *saucisson chaud d'agneau au madère & filet de boeuf poêlé au St-Joseph*. Book ahead; & arrive on time!
Menus B(*à la carte*). Cards AE. (Rooms: H. de France, La Côte-St-André.)
Closed Jan. Mid July-mid Aug. Sun evg. Wed. Thurs.
Post 38260 Le Mottier, Isère. Region Lyonnais/Savoie.
Tel 04 74 54 42 06. Mich 116/C4. Map 6.

A100frs & under. B100–150. C150–200. D200–250. E250–350. F350–500. G500+

MOUCHARD

Chalet Bel'Air/Rôtisserie

Comfortable rest. with rooms/Cooking 2-3 (Rest.); 1-2 (Rôt.) | FW |
Terrace (Rôtisserie)/Gardens/Parking/Air-cond. (rest.)

Chalet-style *logis* just W of N83. Bruno & Monique Gatto do an excellent job. Try stylish regional/neo-classical dishes in the restaurant; in the Rôtisserie (with FW rating), from the large chimney's open fire, relish tasty grills with vegetables cooked in olden-day ways: *jambon grillée, faux-filet grillé maître d'hôtel & caille dorée en brioche* are typical.
Menus ABC(Rôt:*àlc*)CDEF(Rest.). Rooms (9)DEF. Cards All.
Closed 18-25 June. 20 Nov-11 Dec. Wed (not sch. hols).
Post 39330 Mouchard, Jura. Region Jura.
Tel 03 84 37 80 34. Fax 03 84 73 81 18. Mich 89/E2. Map 3.

MOUDEYRES

Auberge Pré Bossu

Comfortable hotel/Cooking 3
Secluded/Parking

A stone & thatched cottage built 25 years ago (designer "rusticity"). A Belgian duo, Carlos & Marlène Grootaert, work wonders at the isolated site in the 20 years they've been *in situ*. English-speaking Carlos walks modern/neo-classical paths & uses his *terroir* imaginatively (e.g. green Velay lentils in a *gnocchi* creation). Mme can be austere & reserved.
Menus CEF. Rooms (10) F. Cards AE, MC, V.
Closed Dec-Mar. Midday (out of season; but not Sun lunch).
Post 43150 Moudeyres, Haute-Loire. Region Massif Central (Ardèche).
Tel 04 71 05 10 70. Fax 04 71 05 10 21. Mich 129/D3. Map 6.

MOUGINS

L'Amandier de Mougins

Simple restaurant/Cooking 2 | FW |
Terrace

This is the café-restaurant of the famed Roger Vergé (I guillotined his then 3-star Moulin de Mougins years ago). Lots of appeal here though: the village; the terrace with a panorama of Grasse & its backdrop of mountains; & for the wide-choice menus of Provençals/neo-classical *plats* – most simple creations. Tempters like *gaspachio de tomate avec son emincé de saumon fumé* & succulent *gigot d'agneau rôti à la broche*.
Menus BC. Cards All. (Rooms: see entry for du Bosquet, Pégomas – to W.)
Post au village, 06250 Mougins, Alpes-Maritimes. Region Côte d'Azur.
Tel 04 93 90 00 91. Fax 04 93 90 18 55. Mich 163/F2. Map 6.

A100frs & under. B100–150. C150–200. D200–250. E250–350. F350–500. G500+

MOUGINS (front cover watercolour)   **Feu Follet**

Comfortable restaurant/Cooking 2-3   FW
Terrace

At the heart of film-set Mougins, the most expensive real estate on the
coast. English-speaking Jean-Paul & Micheline Battaglia have worked
wonders to create their success; the place is always busy (it has to be to
survive). Quality classical fare; no stinting; wide choice; opulent desserts.
Take a peek at the high-tech kitchen (cost 1 million francs).
Menus BC(low-end). Cards AE, MC, V. (Rooms: see Pégomas entry.)
Closed Mar. Mon. Tues *midi* (out of seas). (Also Arc H.; D3 to Valbonne.)
Post pl. Mairie, 06250 Mougins, Alpes-Maritimes. Region Côte d'Azur.
Tel 04 93 90 15 78. Fax 04 92 92 92 62. Mich 163/F2. Map 6.

MOUGINS   **Manoir de l'Etang**

Comfortable hotel/Cooking 2   FW
Secluded/Terrace/Gardens/Swimming pool/Parking

The Gridaine-Labro family hotel is seductive: in elevated position E of
Mougins (S of D35); 17 acres with *étangs* & mountain views; light, airy
salle; & covered terrace overlooking the pool & gardens. Provençals &
neo-classical *plats* from Lionel Goyard: no choice menu B could include
the likes of *agneau à la crème d'ail doux* & *tarte tatin au caramel*.
Menus BC(both top-end). Rooms (14) G. Cards AE, MC, V.
Closed Nov-Jan (not Xmas-New Year). Rest: Tues (out of season).
Post allée du Manoir, 06250 Mougins, Alpes-Mar. Region Côte d'Azur.
Tel 04 93 90 01 07. Fax 04 92 92 20 70. Mich 163/F2. Map 6.

MOUGINS   **Relais à Mougins**

Comfortable restaurant/Cooking 2   FW
Terrace

English-speaking André Surmain is a redoubtable chef, a real survivor –
a trick he acquired in the Big Apple. Wily pricing on classical/regional
menus (especially lunch menu B). Employees may come & go but typical
treats are the likes of *carpaccio de thon, dos de saumon fumé par nos
soins, grillée, crème ciboulette* & *blanquette de veau à l'ancienne*.
Menus B(lunch)C(bottom-end)DF. Cards MC, V. (Rooms: see Pégomas.)
Closed Sun evg & Mon (not July/Aug). (du Bosquet, Pégomas to W.)
Post pl. Mairie, 06250 Mougins, Alpes-Maritimes. Region Côte d'Azur.
Tel 04 93 90 03 47. Fax 04 93 75 72 83. Mich 163/F2. Map 6.

A100frs & under. B100–150. C150–200. D200–250. E250–350. F350–500. G500+

MOULINS

Very comfortable hotel/Cooking 3
Terrace/Swimming pool/Lift/Closed parking/Air-cond. (rest.)

What a refreshing breeze has blown through the famous hotel. New owners Louis & Anne-Françoise de Roberty (they ran the nearby Jacquemart rest.) have brought a modern freshness to the previously dead-on-its-feet Paris cooking. Breathe-in the likes of *lanières de turbot cloutées aux anchois grillées au safran* & tuck into a top-notch sweet trolley.
Menus CEF. Rooms (28) FG. Cards All. (Cheaper rooms: Ibis, S of town.)
Closed Feb sch. hols. Rest: 4-24 Aug. Sun evg. Mon.
Post 21 r. Paris, 03000 Moulins, Allier. Region Berry-Bourbonnais.
Tel 04 70 44 00 58. Fax 04 70 34 05 39. Mich 100/A1. Map 5.

MOUREZE

Simple hotel (no restaurant)
Secluded/Terrace/Gardens/Swimming pool/Parking

Both the delightful hotel & the village are surrounded by the weird Cirque de Mourèze, a battlefield of gigantic, dolomitic-shaped rocks. The hotel has a wonderful secluded location – with views of the *cirque*, a 2½-acre park & a sun-trap kidney-shaped pool. *Patronne* Mme Navas is a friendly soul. Use this as a base for Mimosa at St-Guiraud, 15km NE.
Rooms (16) EF(both bottom-end). Cards MC, V. (Above easy drive.)
Closed Mid Oct-Mar.
Post 34800 Mourèze, Hérault. Region Languedoc-Roussillon.
Tel 04 67 96 04 84. Fax 04 67 96 25 85. Mich 156/A3. Map 5.

MOUSTIERS-STE-MARIE

Simple hotel (no restaurant)
Quiet/Gardens/Tennis/Parking

Built 10 years ago the modest hotel is an ideal base – to the W of & below the D952, S of Moustiers. Ideally placed for Les Santons (next entry) & the new La Bastide de Moustiers. The latter (rooms are G,G2) is Alain Ducasse's own business (he's the 3-star God from Monaco) – an evocative 17thC *bastide*. Reports please on the grub from chef Sonja Lee.
Rooms (22) DE. Disabled. Cards MC, V. Region Côte d'Azur/Hautes-Alpes.
Closed Dec. Jan.
Post rte Castellane, 04360 Moustiers-Ste-Marie, Alpes-de-Hte-Provence.
Tel 04 92 74 66 02. Fax 04 92 74 66 70. Mich 162/C1. Map 6.

A100frs & under. B100–150. C150–200. D200–250. E250–350. F350–500. G500+

MOUSTIERS-STE-MARIE

Les Santons

Comfortable restaurant/Cooking 3-4
Terrace

English-speaking André Abert & his partner, Claude Fichot, both culinary
magicians, weave seductive webs at their tiny cottagey dining rooms.
Classical/regional specs sparkle with sunny tastes of Provence: witness a
masterly *poulet fermier au miel de lavande aux aromates et épices*
doux; & a 3-star *nougat glacé aux noisettes et amandes de Valensole*.
Menus c(lunch: top-end)EF. Cards All. (Rooms: see previous entry.)
Closed Dec. Jan. Mon evg (not July/Aug). Tues. Regions Htes-Alpes/Prov.
Post pl. Eglise, 04360 Moustiers-Ste-Marie, Alpes-de-Haute-Provence.
Tel 04 92 74 66 48. Fax 04 92 74 63 67. Mich 162/C1. Map 6.

MOUTHIER-HAUTE-PIERRE

La Cascade

Comfortable hotel/Cooking 1-2   **FW**
Quiet/Parking

The *logis* has scintillating views of the wooded Loue Valley far below.
Chef/patron René Savonet juggles regional & *Bourgeoises* balls on
menu b (classical, too, on CDE): *croûte forestière, pâté aux foies de*
volaille ou crudités; truite belle meunière, épaule de veau sauce
paprika ou côtes d'agneau grillée; cheeses; dessert. One blot: awful tea.
Menus bCDE. Rooms (23) E. Disabled. Cards MC, V.
Closed Mid Nov-mid Feb.
Post 25920 Mouthier-Haute-Pierre, Doubs. Region Jura.
Tel 03 81 60 95 30. Fax 03 81 60 94 55. Mich 90/A2-B2. Map 3.

Les MOUTIERS-EN-RETZ

Bonne Auberge

Comfortable restaurant/Cooking 2   **FW**

Patrice & Catherine Raimbault have bags of nous: neo-classical/classical
plats; a smart dining rooms with flowers; & a profusion of professional
touches. A clever *nouvelle formule* menu allows you to permutate five
different prices (good choice too). Chef Patrice's talents shine in
numerous fish/shellfish dishes like *palourdes farcies au beurre d'ail,*
marinade d'anguilles & *coquillage à la crème de curry.*
Menus BCDE. Cards MC, V. (Rooms: Alizés, *sans rest;* Pornic, 8km NW.)
Closed Feb & Nov sch. hols. Sun evg & Mon (not July/Aug).
Post av. Mer, 44580 Les Moutiers-en-Retz, Loire-Atlantique.
Tel 02 40 82 72 03. Fax 02 40 64 68 37. Mich 78/B2. Map 1. Reg Poit-Ch.

A100frs & under. B100–150. C150–200. D200–250. E250–350. F350–500. G500+

MUHLBACH

Perle des Vosges

Comfortable hotel (very comfortable annexe)/Cooking 1
Quiet/Lift/Parking

A largish, whitewashed *Logis de France* (with a modern extension), high
above the village & the cheese-renowned Munster Valley, & with
extensive views S to the high wooded Ballon peaks. No grumbles about
the owners, the Benz & Ertlé families. (M. Ertlé speaks excellent English.)
Cooking is much less inspired – run-of-the-mill classical & *Bourgeoise*.
Menus ABCD. Rooms (44) DEF. Cards DC, MC, V.
Closed 1 Jan-2 Feb. 15 Nov-1 Dec.
Post 68380 Muhlbach-sur-Munster, Haut-Rhin. Region Alsace.
Tel 03 89 77 61 34. Fax 03 89 77 74 40. Mich 60/C4. Map 3.

MURBACH

Hostellerie St-Barnabé

Comfortable hotel/Cooking 2-3   FW
Quiet/Terrace/Gardens/Tennis/Closed parking

A re-appearance for a pleasingly situated hotel, just below the superb
Romanesque "half-church". Nature dominates: a dead-end wooded valley
under the Gd Ballon peak to the S; & both flowers & a stream tease the
senses. Chef Eric Orban treads classical/neo-classical tracks; a nice
surprise in Alsace – many Med touches. Wife Clémence is *la patronne*.
Menus BCDE. Rooms (27) FG. Cards All. (5km NW of Guebwiller.)
Closed Feb sch. hols. Sun evg (Nov-Mar).
Post 68530 Murbach, Haut-Rhin. Region Alsace.
Tel 03 89 76 92 15. Fax 03 89 76 67 80. Mich 60/C4. Map 3.

MUR-DE-BARREZ

Auberge du Barrez

Comfortable hotel/Cooking 1-2   FW
Quiet/Gardens/Parking

A contemporary-styled, ultra-modern *auberge*, to the SE of high-on-a-
hill Mur-de-Barrez. *Chef/patron* Christian Gaudel's culinary brush is a
lot more traditional & unfussy: few regional colours but this is more than
compensated for by well-judged flavoursome dishes such as *terrine de
lapin en gelée, canette braisée au vin rouge* & *terrine de fraises*.
Menus aBC. Rooms (18) D(bottom-end)EF. Cards AE, MC, V.
Closed Jan. Rest: Sun evg (Nov-Easter). Mon (not pub.hols).
Post 12600 Mur-de-Barrez, Aveyron. Region Massif Central (Auvergne).
Tel 05 65 66 00 76. Fax 05 65 66 07 98. Mich 126/C3. Map 5.

A100frs & under. B100–150. C150–200. D200–250. E250–350. F350–500. G500+

MUR-DE-BRETAGNE Auberge Grand'Maison

Very comfortable restaurant with rooms/Cooking 3-4

No praise is high enough for Jacques & Brigitte Guillo – two angels & among the most loved of readers' favourites. Chef Jacques, a treasure, is much fitter now. Top-notch modern cooking: melt-in-the-mouth pigeon & lamb; fish cooked in light, lip-smacking ways; supreme sweets (*fenouil confit, mousse au chocolat pralinée, glace vanille et sauce caramel aux épices* is a winner). First-class breakfasts. Effective insulation.
Menus cDEF. Rooms (12) EFG. Cards All. (Parking is easy.)
Closed Feb sch. hols. Oct. Sun evg. Mon.
Post 22530 Mur-de-Bretagne, Côtes d'Armor. Region Brittany.
Tel 02 96 28 51 10. Fax 02 96 28 52 30. Mich 28/B4. Map 1.

NAJAC Belle Rive

Simple hotel/Cooking 1-2   `FW`
Secluded/Terrace/Gardens/Swimming pool/Tennis/Parking

Some site: the *logis* beside the Aveyron; & across the river, high above the wooded valley, is Najac's ruined castle. Add to Nature's appeal the list of man-made benefits above. English-speaking Jacques Mazières is 5th-generation *patron*. Classical *plats*: of the *entrecôte à l'échalotte*, *crème brûlée* variety. Inexpensve grill lunches beside pool (July/Aug).
Menus ABCD. Rooms (37) E. Cards DC, MC, V.
Closed Nov-Easter. Sun evg (Oct).
Post 12270 Najac, Aveyron. Regions Dordogne/Massif Central (Cévennes).
Tel 05 65 29 73 90. Mich 139/E3. Map 5. (N of Najac, west bank Aveyron.)

NAJAC (also see next page) Longcol

Very comfortable hotel/Cooking 2-3   `FW`
Secluded/Terrace/Gardens/Swimming pool/Tennis/Parking

A lavish restoration of a 17thC farm, high above the winding & wooded Aveyron Valley (N of Najac: 4km S of Monteils, beside D638). Furnishings are stylish; *la directrice*, fluent English-speaking Fabienne Luyckx, is elegance personified; a S-facing suntrap pool/terrace; & neo-classical & modern fare from young chef Arnaud Dare. Exceptional in every way.
Menus B(lunch)CE. Rooms (17)G. Cards AE, MC, V.
Closed Mid Nov-Easter. Rest: Tues midday (not mid June-mid Sept).
Post 12270 Najac, Aveyron. Regions Dordogne/Massif Central (Cévennes).
Tel 05 65 29 63 36. Fax 05 65 29 64 28. Mich 139/E3. Map 5.

A100frs & under. B100–150. C150–200. D200–250. E250–350. F350–500. G500+

NAJAC (also see previous page)   **Oustal del Barry**

Very comfortable restaurant with rooms/Cooking 3   FW
Terrace/Gardens/Lift/Garage

Jean-Marie Miquel died in a tragic 1994 tractor accident. His gentle, graceful widow, Catherine (she speaks excellent English), has achieved wonders since the chef's death – supported by José Garcia & Alexandre Lasfargeas (youngsters trained by J-M). Our last meal was modern cooking at its very best. Don't miss the "surprise" 2½-acre hillside garden.
Menus a(lunch: ceiling)BCDE. Rooms (21) EF. Cards AE, MC, V.
Closed Nov-Mar. Mon (not July-Sept). (Parking is easy.)
Post 12270 Najac, Aveyron. Regions Dordogne/Massif Central (Cévennes).
Tel 05 65 29 74 32. Fax 05 65 29 75 32. Mich 139/E3. Map 5.

NARBONNE   La Résidence

Comfortable hotel (no restaurant)
Fairly quiet/Lift/Garage

A 19thC town house *par excellence* – a family home converted by Georges & Marie-Rose Aiguille 37 years ago into a richly-furnished hotel. The town is a bustling, busy place; La Résidence is a cool oasis of charm – the ideal counterpoint. Just W of the cathedral & an easy drive S to Claude Giraud's new home (yet another; see next entry). (Ask to see the owners *Livre d'Or* with its vast number of famed visitors' signatures.)
Rooms (26) EF. Cards AE, MC, V.
Post 6 r. 1er Mai, 11100 Narbonne, Aude. Region Languedoc-Roussillon.
Tel 04 68 32 19 41. Fax 04 68 65 51 82. Mich 173/D2. Map 5.

NARBONNE   La Table St-Créscent

Comfortable restaurant/Cooking 3-4   FW
Terrace/Gardens/Parking

Another move for Claude Giraud & his delectable wife Sabine. The *RQP* goldmine moves S from the town-centre L'Olibo to a new home opp. the *piscine municipale/complexe sportif* (N9; N of A9 exit 38). (Prior to L'Olobo CG won 2 Michelin stars at his Réverbère rest. – which, alas, went bust.) Modern culinary nuggets; great *cave* (400 regional wines).
Menus aB(top-end)CE. Cards AE, MC, V. (Rooms: Novotel/Ibis.)
Closed Check ahead: open all year 1996. (Above nearby to S.)
Post Domaine St-Créscent le viel, rte Perpignan, 11000 Narbonne. Reg LR.
Tel 04 68 41 37 37. Fax 04 68 41 01 22. Mich 173/D2. Map 5.

NESTIER

Relais du Castéra

Comfortable restaurant with rooms/Cooking 2-3
Terrace/Parking

FW

At the northern door of spectacular terrain (Col d'Aspin to the SW; St-Bertrand-de-Comminges to the SE). Man & Nature tease the eyes; here Serge Latour tempts the taste buds with regional & neo-classical creations: put my claims to the test with the likes of *croustillant de truite, cassoulet* & *feuilleté tiède aux pruneaux*. Rooms not very comfy.
Menus BCD. Rooms (8) DE(both bottom-end). Cards AE, MC, V.
Closed 4-20 Jan. 14-19 June. Sun evg. Mon.
Post 65150 Nestier, Hautes-Pyrénées. Region Southwest.
Tel 05 62 39 77 37. Fax 05 62 39 77 29. Mich 169/E2. Map 5.

NEUFCHATEL-SUR-AISNE

Le Jardin

Comfortable restaurant/Cooking 2
Terrace/Gardens

FW

The A26 (exit 14) is 10km to the W – so ideal for a first/last lunch. Well-named; the glassed-in terrace overlooking the garden is a delight. Jean-Claude Chevallier is *le patron* & master pastry cook; son Thierry is the chef; both look the part. Knockout classical/regional *plats*: *soufflé d'anguille* & *filet de carpe*; & *croustillant de Picardie* (sweet) are two.
Menus aCDE. Cards All. (Rooms: Novotel & Ibis – W of Reims.)
Closed 15-30 Jan. Sun evg. Mon. Tues evg. (Above at A4/A26 junction.)
Post 02190 Neufchâtel-sur-Aisne, Aisne. Regions Champ-Ard/North.
Tel 03 23 23 82 00. Fax 03 23 23 84 05. Mich 20/C3. Map 3.

NEUILLE-LE-LIERRE

Auberge de la Brenne

Comfortable restaurant/Cooking 2
Parking

FW

François Sallé is the helpful host (ask him to fix up a nearby *chambre d'hôte*) & his wife, Ghislaine, conjures up unfussy classical/regional culinary tricks – among them *salade tourangelle, rillettes* of pork, duck & goose cooked slowly & perfectly over a log fire & *joue de boeuf mijotée* with an unctuous black sauce (*vin de Bourgueil*).
Menus aBC. Cards AE, MC, V. (Rooms: Lurton, *sans rest*, Château-Renault.)
Closed 15 Jan-5 Mar. Tues evg. Wed. (Above easy 10km drive to N.)
Post 37380 Neuillé-le-Lierre, Indre-et-Loire. Region Loire.
Tel 02 47 52 95 05. Fax 02 47 52 29 43. Mich 68/A3. Map 2.

A100frs & under. B100–150. C150–200. D200–250. E250–350. F350–500. G500+

NEUILLY-LE-REAL

Logis Henri IV

Comfortable restaurant/Cooking 2
Terrace

FW

Valdi & Patricia Persello are justly proud of their half-timbered 16thC hunting lodge. They should be just as chuffed by their *RQP* menu B. Consider the evidence: a well-judged *cassolette de moules au safran, compotée d'endives*; tender *noisettes d'agneau de pays à la sarriette; fromage*; & a mouthwatering *nougat glacé au miel des Cévennes*.
Menus a(lunch)BCD. Cards MC, V. (Rooms: Ibis (N7); S of Moulins.)
Closed Feb sch. hols. 1-7 Sept. Sun evg. Mon. (Above hotel 12km to NW.)
Post 03340 Neuilly-le-Réal, Allier. Region Berry-Bourbonnais.
Tel 04 70 43 87 64. Mich 100/B2. Map 5.

NIEDERSTEINBACH

Cheval Blanc

Comfortable hotel/Cooking 2-3
Quiet/Terrace/Gardens/Swimming pool/Tennis/Parking

FW

Interconnected buildings, both old & new, at the White Horse *logis* in the densely wooded northern Vosges. Charles & Michel Zinck, father & son, run a successful set-up. Regional/classical specialities: delicious *presskopf de lapereau* (rabbit terrine), *filet de sandre aux nouilles* (for weightwatchers) & *cailles farcies au chou*; all safe-as-houses fare.
Menus aBCDE. Rooms (26) E. Cards MC, V. Closed Feb-10 Mar. 12-26 June. 1-10 Dec. Rest: Thurs. Fri midday (not high season).
Post 67510 Niedersteinbach, Bas-Rhin. Region Alsace.
Tel 03 88 09 55 31. Fax 03 88 09 50 24. Mich 43/D2. Map 3.

NOCE

Auberge des Trois J

Very comfortable restaurant/Cooking 3

FW

I love the terrain of Le Perche (wooded hills & *manoirs*) to the N of the village. How Stéphane Joly survives here is a mystery. Survive he does, capitalising on the produce from his bountiful *terroir*. He's a modern fanatic – and he adds numerous eclectic touches to his *cuisine*. A couple of dishes illustrate what I mean: *morue fraîche et chorizo en écrin de pommes de terre*; & *curry de saumon rizotto de tomate & coriandre*.
Menus BCE. Cards AE, MC, V. (Rooms: Du Golf, Bellême; 8km to W.)
Closed 2-16 Feb. 14-29 Sept. Sun evg (not Jul/Aug); Mon (not pub. hols.)
Post 61340 Nocé, Orne. Region Normandy.
Tel 02 33 73 41 03. Fax 02 33 83 33 66. Mich 51/F2. Map 2.

A100frs & under. B100–150. C150–200. D200–250. E250–350. F350–500. G500+

NOGENT-LE-ROTROU

Host. de la Papotière

Comfortable restaurant/Cooking 1-2
Parking

| FW |

A stunning 16thC half-timbered & stone *maison* with a beamed interior. Chefs come & go (you may rate the cooking higher) but *la patronne*, Mme Beule, has nous. Menu A is a simple *rôtisserie* meal; Menu B is champion classical with a wide choice. Filling, rich fare epitomised by *tournedos d'agneau aux pignons de pin* & *clafoutis de pommes caramélisées*.
Menus AB(top end). Cards AE, MC, V. (Rest. is 50m E of Rue du Paty.)
Closed Sun evg. Mon. (Rooms: Lion d'Or, easy walk N.) Region Normandy.
Post 3 r. Bourg-le-Comte, 28400 Nogent-le-Rotrou, Eure-et-Loir.
Tel 02 37 52 18 41. Fax 02 37 52 94 71. Mich 52/A2. Map 2.

Le NOIRMONT

Gare

Very comfortable restaurant with rooms/Cooking 4
Parking/Air-conditioning (restaurant)

Tour de force show by a supreme master: precision kitchen organisation; varying tastes, textures & colours; & differing presentation from dish to dish. Georges Wenger, a gentle, English-speaking Swiss, influenced by stints with Senderens & Stucki, is a consummate modern chef. Andrea, his wife, is a sparkling English-speaking hostess. Superb *cave* & bedrooms.
Menus SwissF28-52(1unch)60-140(dinner). Rooms (3) SF130-260(inc' bkft).
Cards AE, MC, V. Closed Feb. Rest: Sun evg. Mon.
Post CH2725 Le Noirmont, Jura, Switzerland. (Cheaper rooms: Soleil.)
Tel 039 53 11 10. Fax 039 53 10 59. Mich 91/D1. Map 3. Region Jura.

NOUAN-LE-FUZELIER (also see next page)

Charmilles

Simple hotel (no restaurant)
Quiet/Gardens/Parking

A favourite with readers for over a decade – but far less so now, since Dominique Sené handed over the hotel to his daughter from his first marriage. Charmilles, a *maison Bourgeoise* built at the turn of the century and converted into an hotel in 1972, backs onto six acres of woods (ideal for quiet walks); there are also two small ponds.
Rooms (13) DEF. Cards MC, V. (Use D122 to SE.)
Closed Mid Dec-mid Mar. Region Loire.
Post rte Pierrefitte-sur-Sauldre, 41600 Nouan-le-Fuzelier, Loir-et-Cher.
Tel 02 54 88 73 55. Mich 69/E3. Map 2.

A100frs & under. B100–150. C150–200. D200–250. E250–350. F350–500. G500+

NOUAN-LE-FUZELIER (also see previous page)   Le Dahu

Comfortable restaurant/Cooking 2   FW
Terrace/Gardens/Parking

A beamed & cleverly glassed-in dining room in an old *Solognote* farm with
English-style gardens. English-speaking chef, Jean-Luc Germain. Cooking?
Neo-classical. Marie-Thérèse, J-L's wife, is an attentive, friendly hostess.
(Ask the couple to arrange accommodation at a super *chambre d'hôte*, La
Renardie, at Le Ferté-Imbault, 20km to the SW.) Le Dahu? Ask!
Menus bCD. Cards AE, MC, V. (Alternative rooms: see previous entry.)
Closed 10 Feb-20 Mar. Tues evg & Wed (not July/Aug).
Post 14 r. H. Chapron, 41600 Nouan-le-Fuzelier, Loir-et-Cher.
Tel 02 54 88 72 88. Mich 69/E3. Map 2. Region Loire.

NOUAN-LE-FUZELIER   Moulin de Villiers

Simple hotel/Cooking 0-1
Secluded/Gardens/Parking

Go for just one reason: 17 acres of private woodlands, an *étang*, streams &
marshes; a mini Sologne. Cooking is basic *Bourgeoise*. Atrocious décor.
Gérard & Gladys Andrieux (her grandfather bought the estate in 1929) are
no longer good-humoured "angels"; Mme now has a short-fuse temper.
They are weary; I hope they soon find a buyer who'll do justice to the mill.
Menus aBC. Rooms (19) DEF(low-end). Cards MC, V. (D44, 3km to NE.)
Closed 8 Jan-15 Mar. 1-15 Sept. Tues evg & Wed (Nov/Dec).
Post rte Chaon, 41600 Nouan-le-Fuzelier, Loir-et-Cher. Region Loire.
Tel 02 54 88 72 27. Fax 02 54 88 78 87. Mich 69/E3. Map 2.

NOUAN-LE-FUZELIER   Le Raboliot

Comfortable restaurant/Cooking 2   FW

Consistently good reports arrived during 1994-96, so we sought out
Philippe Henry & his *"raboliot"* (?Ask!). None of the captivating man-
made benefits of the *"dahu"* but excellent classical/neo-classical
specialities: *persillé de volaille au gingembre à l'huile de noisette* –
clever contrasts; *faux-filet marchand de vin* – to make Escoffier proud;
Brie; & top-class *crème brûlée*; all on menu B (wine included).
Menus ABCD. Cards AE, MC, V. (Rooms: see entry on previous page.)
Closed 14 Jan-21 Feb. Tues evg (Dec-Mar). Wed. (Rest. E side N20.)
Post av. Mairie, 41600 Nouan-le-Fuzelier, Loir-et-Cher. Region Loire.
Tel 02 54 88 70 67. Fax 02 54 88 77 86. Mich 69/E3. Map 2.

A100frs & under. B100–150. C150–200. D200–250. E250–350. F350–500. G500+

NOUAN-LE-FUZELIER (St-Viâtre)   Auberge de la Chichone

Comfortable restaurant with rooms/Cooking 1-2   `FW`
Terrace

A smashing village: visit the *Maison des Etangs* (down the road) & nearby *étangs*. The old hunting inn, now a *logis*, has plenty of beams, character & fine hosts in the Cléments. Alas, chefs come & go – too frequently. André Clément keeps standards high. Classical cooking: of the *filet de boeuf poêlé sauce aux baies roses* & *tarte Tatin* (what else?) variety.
Menus ABC. Rooms (7) E. Cards AE, MC, V. (8km W of Nouan.)
Closed Mar. Tues evg. Wed.
Post pl. Eglise, 41210 St-Viâtre, Loir-et-Cher. Region Loire.
Tel 02 54 88 91 33. Fax 02 54 96 18 06. Mich 69/E3. Map 2.

NOVES   Auberge de Noves

Luxury hotel/Cooking 3-4
Secluded/Terr/Gards/Swim pool/Tenn/Lift/Closed parking/Air-cond.

For many readers a Garden of Eden. *La famille* Lalleman is talented & proud: André runs a tight ship; Robert, his son, nearing 40, puts his chef's philosophy simply – a subtle marriage of *tradition, continuité, changement et renouvellement*. Both speak perfect English, both are true gentlemen. Exquisite terrace where a lunch (D) is *RQP* seduction.
Menus DEF. Rooms (19) G2,G3. Cards All. (NW of village; D28.)
Closed Rest: Sun evg & Mon (not high season).
Post 13550 Noves, Bouches-du-Rhône. Region Provence.
Tel 04 90 94 19 21. Fax 04 90 94 47 76. Mich 158/B1. Map 6.

NUCES   La Diligence

Very comfortable restaurant with rooms/Cooking 2-3   `FW`
Terrace/Gardens/Garage/Parking

Alongside the busy N140. Don't be put off. What a surprise the stylish, cool dining room is, matched by the terrace, shaded by four large trees. Jean-Claude Lausset is the dining room gaffer; Joël Delmas is the chef. Neo-classical, inventive *plats* with desserts stealing the show, witness a *biscuit au chocolate noisette, glace à l'amande amère*.
Menus a(lunch)BCE. Rooms (7) D. Cards MC, V. Closed 1st wk Sept. Sun evg & Mon (Apl-June & Sept). Tues evg & Wed (Oct-Mar).
Post Nuces, 12330 Valady, Aveyron. Region Massif Central (Cévennes).
Tel 05 65 72 60 20. Mich 140/B2. Map 5.

A100frs & under. B100–150. C150–200. D200–250. E250–350. F350–500. G500+

NYONS

La Charrette Bleue

Comfortable restaurant/Cooking 2
Terrace/Parking

Four menus – *tradition, découverte, regal & saveur* – at this single-storey, stone-built "cart". Rein in regional & classical *plats*: Mme Medard takes the orders; Denis Jadon prepares them. Great olives (no surprise that) & two special highlights: *terrine de lapin aux senteurs de Provence & bavette poêlée à la tapenade*. Very popular with locals.
Menus aBC. Cards MC, V. (Rooms: Caravelle, Nyons; *sans rest.*)
Closed 6 Jan-6 Feb. 12-18 Dec. Tues evg (not July/Aug). Wed.
Post rte de Gap, 26110 Nyons, Drôme. Region Provence. (D94, 7km to NE.)
Tel 04 75 27 72 33. Fax 04 75 26 05 72. Mich 144/C2. Map 6.

NYONS

Le Petit Caveau

Comfortable restaurant/Cooking 2-3
Air-conditioning

An aptly-named medieval site at the heart of Nyon. Christian Cormont's seven-year-stint with Joël Robuchon in Paris gave him a modern cooking itch. This, married to a Provençale style, results in many flavoursome humdingers: *bouillabaisse minute de rouget et rascasse aux pistils de safran* is just one. Muriel Cormont is an expert *patronne/sommelière*.
Menus BC. Cards AE, MC, V. (Rooms: Caravelle, *sans rest.*)
Closed Dec. Sun evg. Mon. (Parking: use huge *place* 100m to W.)
Post 9, r. V. Hugo, 26110 Nyons, Drôme. Region Provence.
Tel 04 75 26 20 21. Mich 144/C2. Map 6.

OCHIAZ

Auberge de la Fontaine

Comfortable restaurant with rooms/Cooking 2-3
Terrace/Gardens/Parking

A flower-bedecked *logis* with Bugey's Plateau de Retord forming a high wooded backdrop. Colette Ripert is a friendly, involved hostess; husband Claude is a loyal classicist. Clues to that label lie in evidence such as *quenelle de brochet à la Nantua, feuilleté chaud de canard, filet de loup au vermouth* & a luscious *filet de turbot champagne Fernand Point*.
Menus bCDE. Rooms (7) CD. Cards All.
Closed 7 Jan-1 Feb. 3-19 June. Sun evg. Mon.
Post Ochiaz, 01200 Châtillon-en-Michaille, Ain. Regions Lyonnais/Savoie.
Tel 04 50 56 57 23. Mich 104/A3. Map 6. (SW of A40 exit 10.)

A100frs & under. B100–150. C150–200. D200–250. E250–350. F350–500. G 500+

OLORON-STE-MARIE

Alysson

Very comfortable hotel/Cooking 2
Terrace/Gardens/Swim pool/Lift/Parking/Air-cond. (rest.)

FW

Spanking-new hotel, surrounded by grass "gardens", W of the town. Mod-cons everywhere plus stirring views of the Pyrénées' wall to the S. Plenty of choice between chef Philippe Maré's stop-the-tummy-rumbling regional grub & lighter fish alternatives: pick from the likes of *emincé de magret de canard au fumet de cèpes* & *tranche de thon poêlé Basquaise*.
Menus a(lunch)BCD. Rooms (34) EF. Disabled. Cards AE, MC, V
Closed Rest: 25 Nov-15 Dec. Sat & Sun evg (out of season). Region SW.
Post bd Pyrénées, 64400 Oloron-Ste-Marie, Pyrénées-Atlantiques.
Tel 05 59 39 70 70. Fax 05 59 39 24 47. Mich 167/F2. Map 4.

ONZAIN

Château des Tertres

Comfortable hotel (no restaurant)
Quiet/Gardens/Parking

I receive many letters of praise for Paul Valois & his delectable 19thC château, an elegant looking charmer in an attractive park. Readers speak highly of *les patrons* & the stylishly furnished, comfortable bedrooms. In an elevated position, W of village (D58). (Do call on Owen Watson, potter *extraordinaire*; Les Fraisiers; D65 ½km S of Mesland; W side.)
Rooms (14) F. Cards AE, MC, V.
Closed 12 Nov-31 Mar.
Post rte de Monteaux, 41150 Onzain, Loir-et-Cher. Region Loire.
Tel 02 54 20 83 88. Fax 02 54 20 89 21. Mich 68/B3. Map 2.

ONZAIN

Domaine des Hauts de Loire

Luxury hotel/Cooking 3-4
Secluded/Terrace/Gardens/Swimming pool/Tennis/Parking

I've been a fan of the Bonnigal family for two decades. Fluent English-speaking Pierre-Alain, Gaston & Janine's son, is a consummate hotelier; & the 18thC creeper-covered hunting lodge, surrounded by woods, is in as romantic a setting you could wish to find. Luxury is the label: timbers, stonework, furniture *et al*. Chef Rémy Giraud beats a neo-classical drum.
Menus EF. Rooms (25) G(top-end)G2. Disabled. Cards All. (D1 to NW.)
Closed Dec-5 Feb. Rest: Mon (Feb/Mar). Tues midday.
Post rte de Herbault, 41150 Onzain, Loir-et-Cher. Region Loire.
Tel 02 54 20 72 57. Fax 02 54 20 77 32. Mich 68/B3. Map 2.

A100frs & under. B100–150. C150–200. D200–250. E250–350. F350–500. G500+

ORANGE

Mas des Aigras

Comfortable hotel (no restaurant)
Secluded/Gardens/Swimming pool/Tennis/Parking

Readers speak well of the gardens; & the bedrooms – just 11 of them. The gardens & small Provençal *mas* certainly do appeal, as does the site, to the W of the N7 and 4km N of Orange. *Table d'hôtes* meals are available but are most definitely not recommended. Not much praise for the owners, the Pernelles. Good base for exploring both Roman Provence to the S & the attractive, largely deserted mountain terrain to the E.
Rooms (11) F. Cards MC, V.
Post ch. des Aigras, 84100 Orange, Vaucluse. Region Provence.
Tel 04 90 34 81 01. Fax 04 90 34 05 66. Mich 144/B3. Map 6.

ORBEC

Au Caneton

Comfortable restaurant/Cooking 2 | FW |

A 17thC half-timbered house with a *feu à l'âtre* keeping you warm in the rustic dining room during the winter; the exterior is a mix of colourful peach wash, ivy & geranium-filled window boxes. Hearty classical & regional cooking with plenty of choice on *Menu Normande* (B): oysters, if you're hooked on them (I'm not); *pâté de canard maison et sa mousse de foie gras*; *rognons de veau en crème de cidre*; & similar rich fare.
Menus aBDE. Cards AE, MC, V. (Rooms: France, also in rue Grande.)
Closed 2-16 Jan. Sun evg & Mon (not pub. hols.)
Post 32 r. Grande, 14290 Orbec, Calvados. Region Normandy.
Tel 02 31 32 73 32. Fax 02 31 62 48 91. Mich 33/D2. Map 2.

ORBEC

L'Orbecquoise

Simple restaurant/Cooking 2 | FW |

An unattractive shop-window frontage with a small beamed dining room. Prices are pitched the same as those at Au Caneton. Karine welcomes you; & Hervé Doual puts eclectic neo-classical, modern & neo-classical balls. *Menu Découverte* (B) could include *beignets de poisson crème de laitue* & *nougatine fine mousse caramel au lait d'amandes*. One guide reckons *chorizo et brandade* a dangerous liaison! Surely not?
Menus ABCD. Cards MC, V. (Rooms: France, also in same rue Grande.)
Closed Sun evg. Mon.
Post 60 r. Grande, 14290 Orbec, Calvados. Region Normandy.
Tel 02 31 62 44 99. Mich 33/D2. Map 2.

A100frs & under. B100–150. C150–200. D200–250. E250–350. F350–500. G500+

ORBEY

Croix d'Or

Simple hotel/Cooking 1
Terrace/Air-conditioning (restaurant)

The *logis* has been owned by the Thomann family for 104 years; chef Jean Bertin Thomann is the third-generation *chef/patron*. Jocelyne, his wife, gives you a warm welcome; JB's contribution is gutsy regional/classical grub (though one menu is *minceur*): *coq au Riesling* & *entrecôte au pinot noir* are typical. *Baeckaoffa* served on Thurs evgs (in high season).
Menus aBCDE. Rooms (19) E. Cards All.
Closed 16 Nov-19 Dec. Mon *midi* (high season). Wed (not evgs high seas).
Post r. Eglise, 68370 Orbey, Haut-Rhin. Region Alsace.
Tel 03 89 71 20 51. Fax 03 89 71 35 60. Mich 60/C3. Map 3.

ORGEVAL

Moulin d'Orgeval

Comfortable hotel/Cooking 1-2
Secluded/Terrace/Gardens/Swimming pool/Parking

Orgeval stream is the star at the Douvier's evocative mill (a *moulin* was *in situ* here as long ago as the 13thC); the waters flow alongside the covered terrace & bridges allow you to cross to island gardens. The woods & gardens share second billing. Classical cooking (*pavé Charolais* is typical) takes third place. Heated pool. Also *sauna/bronzarium*!
Menus CDEFG. Rooms (14) FG. Cards All.
Closed 20-31 Dec.
Post r. l'Abbaye, 78630 Orgeval, Yvelines. Region Ile de France.
Tel 01 39 75 85 74. Fax 01 39 75 48 52. Mich 35/E3. Map 2.

ORLEANS

Orléans Parc Hôtel

Comfortable hotel (no restaurant)
Quiet/Gardens/Closed parking

The ideal base if you want to explore Orléans & La Sologne to the S. (Off the N152, just W of A71 exit 1 – Orléans-Ouest.) The 19thC house, much modernised, sits in 7 acres of parkland alongside the Loire's right bank; there are some magnificent old trees in the grounds. Christian Pisivin & Françoise Julien are justly proud of their hotel. (Separate restaurant, Ciel de Loire, in the same grounds; reports please.)
Rooms (34) EFG. Disabled. Cards All.
Post 55 rte Orléans, 45380 La Chapelle-St-Mesmin, Loiret. Region Loire.
Tel 02 38 43 26 26. Fax 02 38 72 00 99. Mich 69/E1. Map 2.

A100frs & under. B100–150. C150–200. D200–250. E250–350. F350–500. G500+

ORNANS

good food
poor service

France

Comfortable hotel/Cooking 2
Gardens/Parking

FW

Town centre *logis* combining charming traditional furniture & fittings & all mod-cons. Charming is the word for *les patronnes*, Nicole Gresset & Marie-Claude Vincent; hubbies Marcel & Serge are *les chefs*. Fair choice on menu B: a welcome *salade de raie aux câpres*, an evocative *truite au bleu beurre citronné* & tasty *Edel de Cléron (vache frais)* cheese.
Menus bCE. Rooms (31) CDEF. Cards DC, MC, V.
Closed 15 Dec-15 Feb. Sun evg (not sch. hols). Rest: Mon.
Post r. P. Vernier, 25290 Ornans, Doubs. Region Jura.
Tel 03 81 62 24 44. Fax 03 81 62 12 03. Mich 90/A2. Map 3.

ORNANS (Bonnevaux-le-Prieuré)

Moulin du Prieuré

Very comfortable restaurant with rooms/Cooking 2-3
Secluded/Terrace/Gardens/Parking

FW

The mill, which dates back to the 13thC, was converted into a restaurant 20 years ago. Some machinery is still in place. Classical cooking from *chef/patron* Marc Gatez, a fan of Aberdeen Angus beef (what now?). Ask Renée G to send details of their remote Lodge de la Piquette where the "beat" is on the idyllic Loue, some of the finest fly fishing in France.
Menus b(lunch & Sun evg)DEF. Rooms (8) EF(low-end). Disabled. Cards All.
Closed Mid Nov-4 Mar. Tues & Wed midday (not July/Aug).
Post 25620 Bonnevaux-le-Prieuré, Doubs. Region Jura. (8km N of Ornans.)
Tel 03 81 59 21 47. Fax 03 81 59 28 79. Mich 90/Al-A2. Map 3.

OTTROTT-LE-HAUT

A l'Ami Fritz

Comfortable restaurant & simple hotel (annexe)/Cooking 2
Secluded (hotel)/Terrace/Gardens & Closed parking (hotel)

FW

The restaurant is in a house built in 1790; the bedrooms are in a new annexe about 300m away. Sophie & Patrick Fritz are a highly capable duo. Classical dishes & bravo to Patrick for re-creating ancient *recettes Alsaciennes*. Knockout *strudel boudin noir*; *gilerle* (cockerel) *au Riesling*; & *boeuf au rouge d'Ottrott* (from Fritz vineyards). Parking OK.
Menus BCE. Rooms (17) EF. Cards All.
Closed 4-24 Jan. Rest: Wed.
Post 67530 Ottrott-le-Haut, Bas-Rhin. Region Alsace. Mich 61/D1. Map 3.
Tel (R) 03 88 95 80 81. (B) 03 88 95 87 39. Fax 03 88 95 84 85.

A100frs & under. B100–150. C150–200. D200–250. E250–350. F350–500. G500+

OTTROTT-LE-HAUT

Very comfortable hotel/Cooking 1-2
Terrace/Garage/Parking

All change at this much-liked readers' favourite. Martin & Brigitte
Schreiber have gone; new *patrons* are at the helm. The chef too has
gone; the current incumbent treads classical/regional paths. One
glorious feature remains in place: the beamed "Spindler" dining room
with its stunning marquetry. Rating (non FW) is low; reports please.
Menus D (*àlc* DE). Rooms (15) EFG. Cards MC, V.
Closed 31 Jan-l Mar. 27 July-6 Aug. Rest: Mon & Tues (not high season).
Post pl. de l'Eglise, 67530 Ottrott-le-Haut, Bas-Rhin. Region Alsace.
Tel 03 88 95 80 61. Fax 03 88 95 86 41. Mich 61/D1. Map 3.

OUCQUES

Commerce

Comfortable restaurant with rooms/Cooking 1-2   `FW`
Garage/Air-conditioning

The dark-shuttered *logis* is beside the D917, to the E of the D924. The
very much contemporary-styled, colourfully-upholstered dining room &
bedrooms come as quite a surprise (take dark glasses). *La patronne*, Jo
Lanchais, is a delight; husband Jean-Pierre drives classical/*Bourgeoises*
routes – like *crépinette de poularde aux champignons des bois*.
Menus aBCE. Rooms (12) DE. Cards AE, MC, V.
Closed 20 Dec-20 Jan. Sun evg & Mon (not July/Aug; not pub. hols).
Post 41290 Oucques, Loir-et-Cher. Region Loire.
Tel 02 54 23 20 41. Fax 02 54 23 02 88. Mich 68/B2. Map 2.

OYE-ET-PALLET

Parnet

v good

Comfortable hotel/Cooking 1-2   `FW`
Gardens/Swimming pool/Tennis/Garage/Parking

A fourth generation family *logis*, in a time warp, where Christian &
Yvette Parnet are friendly hosts. The small pool is heated. A charge is
made for tennis & the use of sauna & Turkish bath (*hamman*). Christian
rows classical/regional courses; for one reader "cream & flour cuisine".
Typical signature dish: *truite saumonée aux Jura blanc à la créme*.
Menus bCDE. Rooms (16) EF. Cards MC, V.
Closed 20 Dec-6 Feb. Sun evg & Mon (not sch. hols).
Post 25160 Oye-et-Pallet, Doubs. Region Jura.
Tel 03 81 89 42 03. Fax 03 81 89 41 47. Mich 90/B3. Map 3.

A100frs & under. B100–150. C150–200. D200–250. E250–350. F350–500. G500+

PAILHEROLS

Auberge des Montagnes

Simple hotel/Cooking 2   FW
Quiet/Terrace/Gardens/Swim pools (indoor & outdoor)/Parking

A warm-hearted family, led by André & Denise Combourieu, fusses over you at the high-altitude *auberge*. *Bourgeois*/classical/*Auvergnats* appetite-quenching meals: *pounti, truffade, tripoux* & *cornet de Murat* on one of the menus a; *terrine d'aiglefin, pavé de Salers* (*terroir* beef) & a light, tempting plate of three hiqh-quality *pâtisseries* on menu B.
Menus aB. Rooms (23) E (bottom-end). Cards MC, V.
Closed 10-24 Oct. 5 Nov-20 Dec.
Post 15800 Pailherols, Cantal. Region Massif Central (Auvergne).
Tel 04 71 47 57 01. Fax 04 71 49 63 83. Mich 126/C3. Map 5.

PAIMPOL

Marne

Comfortable restaurant with rooms/Cooking 2-3   FW
Parking

The *logis* has a modest stone exterior & rue Marne is busy. Don't be put off: Michelle & chef Stéphane Kokoszka do a wonderful job. Especially noteworthy is the *menu carte* (BCD): choose *à la carte*; prices depend on the courses chosen – great neo-classical/modern *RQP* cooking. *Jambonette de lapin poêlée en daube* & *Brie rôti au caramel de Xérès* were super.
Menus ABCDF. Rooms (12) E. Cards AE, MC, V.
Closed Feb sch. hols. Xmas. Thurs evg & Fri (not July/Aug & pub. hols).
Post 30 r. Marne, 22500 Paimpol, Côtes d'Armor. Region Brittany.
Tel 02 96 20 82 16. Fax 02 96 20 92 07. Mich 28/B1. Map 1.

PAIMPOL

Le Repaire de Kerroc'h

Comfortable restaurant with rooms/Cooking 2   FW
Lift

An 18thC *"malounière"* (a château like St-Malo's Valmarin) overlooking the port. Soundproofed rooms – they need to be (a quayside fun fair on our visit). Modern/neo-classical cuisine from chef Jean-Claude Broc. Menu B has modern marine flavour: *pressé de raie en terrine* & *pavé de cabillaud rôti à la peau, choux vert et gingembre* – both champion.
Menus a(lunch)BCF. Rooms (12) F. Cards MC, V. (Parking nearby.)
Closed Rest: 5 Jan-15 Feb. Tues & Wed midday (not July-15 Sept).
Post 29 quai Morand, 22500 Paimpol, Côtes d'Armor. Region Brittany.
Tel 02 96 20 50 13. Fax 02 96 22 07 46. Mich 28/B1. Map 1.

A100frs & under. B100–150. C150–200. D200–250. E250–350. F350–500. G500+

PAU

Bilaa

Comfortable hotel (no restaurant)
Quiet/Lift/Parking

You will never find the Bilaa in any guide with the word "charming" as a recommendation objective. Why? This is a modern, ugly-looking concrete box; but I've been recommending the place since 1980 and I've had no grumbles. Low prices; a friendly *patron*; & a quiet site between Lescar & Lons (both NW of Pau; hotel shown on Michelin's large-scale maps).
Rooms (80) BCD(bottom-end). Cards AE, MC, V.
Closed 24 Dec-5 Jan. Region Southwest.
Post chemin de Lons, 64230 Lescar, Pyrénées-Atlantiques.
Tel 05 59 81 03 00. Fax 05 59 81 15 24. Mich 150/A4. Map 4.

PEGOMAS

du Bosquet

Simple hotel (no restaurant)
Secluded/Gardens/Swimming pool/Tennis/Closed parking

Together with the Albert 1er in Chamonix, this is our most loved French favourite. For 30 years we have been enchanted by the adorable Bernardi family: irrepressible Simone; her daughter Chantal, a mum look-alike who now runs the show; & Jean-Pierre, Simone's husband, who takes things a bit more easily these days. *France Travelauréat* 1996 winners. Bravo!
Rooms (17) DE. Studios (7) EF. Cards not accepted.
Closed 10 Jan-10 Feb. Region Côte d'Azur. (Off D209 Mouans-Sartoux rd.)
Post 74 ch. des Périssols, 06580 Pégomas, Alpes-Maritimes.
Tel 04 92 60 21 20. Fax 04 92 60 21 49. Mich 163/F2. Map 6.

PEILLON

Auberge de la Madone

Comfortable hotel/Cooking 2-3 | FW |
Secluded/Terrace/Gardens/Tennis/Parking

A heavenly perched oasis lovingly tended by the Millo family: Aimée, *la mère*; Christian, her chef son, the flavours of Provence flowing through his veins; & his sister, Marie-Josée, a charismatic smasher (her English an infectious tonic). Roger, too, the perpetual-motion waiter. 1996 was La Madone's 50th birthday; Christian's too. *La vrai cuisine Provençale.*
Menus b(lunch) DE. Rooms (20) FG. Cards MC, V.
Closed 7-24 Jan. 20 Oct-20 Dec. Wed.
Post 06440 Peillon, Alpes-Maritimes. Region Côte d'Azur.
Tel 04 93 79 91 17. Fax 04 93 79 99 36. Mich 165/E3. Map 6.

A100frs & under. B100–150. C150–200. D200–250. E250–350. F350–500. G500+

PERROS-GUIREC

Les Feux des Iles

Comfortable hotel/Cooking 2
Quiet/Tennis/Gardens/Parking

FW

Gardens, sea views & a modern stone building impress as much as
patron/chef Antoine La Roux's cooking. Limited choice menu B could
include a rainbow-hued *terrine de poissons et saumon tiède au velouté
vert* – or oysters; tasty & tarty *fricassée de volaille au cidre et pommes
acidulées* – or a vivid *pièce de cabillaud rôtie à la bisque d'étrilles*.
Menus BCE. Rooms (15) FG. Cards All. (Much cheaper rooms: Les Sternes.)
Closed 1-10 Mar. 1-6 Oct. Sun evg (Oct-Apl). Rest: Mon. Region Brittany.
Post 53 bd Clemenceau, 22700 Perros-Guirec, Côtes d'Armor.
Tel 02 96 23 22 94. Fax 02 96 91 07 30. Mich 28/A1. Map 1.

PERROS-GUIREC

Le Sphinx

Comfortable hotel/Cooking 1-2
Quiet/Gardens/Lift/Parking

FW

Well-named. Site & sea views don't come better than this: multi-storied
building (part turn-of-the-century/part modern) with one end of *la salle*
literally out in space. Chef Le Vergé's classical cooking doesn't match the
superb setting, but it's adequate enough. Stick with fish: colourful *aspic
de raie aux piments d'azur* & tasty *daurade au romarin* are typical.
Menus BCDE. Rooms (20) G. Cards AE, MC, V. (Cheaper rooms: Les Sternes.)
Closed 6 Jan-20 Feb. Rest: Mon midday (not pub. hols). Fri (Oct-Apl).
Post 67 chemin de la Messe, 22700 Perros-Guirec, Côtes d'Armor.
Tel 02 96 23 25 42. Fax 02 96 91 26 13. Mich 28/A1. Map 1.

PERROS-GUIREC (Ploumanac'h)

Rochers

Very comfortable restaurant with rooms/Cooking 2-3

FW

Bracing views of a landlocked bay from Renée Justin's acclaimed Rochers
will leave you with laser-etched memories. New chef Christian Bellet &
his *équipe* don't impress quite as much. Neo-classical/classical/modern
plats with, *bien sûr*, great emphasis on fish: *filet de carrelet au coulis de
langoustines* on menu C; *raie bouclée aux baies roses et épices douces*
or *nage de langoustines, seiches et palourdes* on menu D.
Menus B(lunch)CDF. Rooms (14) EFG. Cards MC, V. (Cheaper rms: Europe.)
Closed Oct-3 Apl. Rest: Wed (4 Apl-11 June).
Post Ploumanac'h, 22700 Perros-Guirec, Côtes d'Armor. Region Brittany.
Tel 02 96 91 44 49. Fax 02 96 91 43 64. Mich 28/A1. Map 1.

A100frs & under. B100–150. C150–200. D200–250. E250–350. F350–500. G500+

PERTUIS

Le Boulevard

Comfortable restaurant/Cooking 2
Air-conditioning

FW

A small, first-floor dining room perhaps – but big *rapport qualité-prix*
from chef Pierre Bontoux. His *Menu Gastronomique* (B) provides a
good choice of classical culinary crackers. A summer lunch of *fleurs de
courgettes farcies, pavé de cabillaud graines de moutarde, fromages*
(inc' a delicious fresh goat's cheese) & *nougat glacé* was perfection.
Menus a(lun)BC. Cards AE, MC, V. (Rooms: Fenouillets, La Tour d'Aigues.)
Closed 5-19 Jan. 30 July-13 Aug. Sun evg. Wed. (Above 5km NE Pertuis.)
Post 50 bd Pecout, 84120 Pertuis, Vaucluse. Region Provence.
Tel 04 90 09 69 31. Fax 04 90 09 09 48. Mich 159/E2. Map 6.

La PETITE-PIERRE

Auberge d'Imsthal

Comfortable hotel/Cooking 1-2
Secluded/Terrace/Gardens/Lift/Parking

FW

Silence, wooded hills, tiny *étang* (with island), chestnut-cool terrace,
walks galore & two differently-styled chalets make up this dead-end,
seductively-sited spot. Nowt special about Hans Michaely's regional &
classical repertoire, at its best in the autumn. Hunter Hans may well
have bagged the game in a filling *pâté de gibier au poivre* or a *civet de
gibier*; tasty *cèpes* dishes (& *crème de bolets*). Exercise? Use the gym!
Menus aBCD. Rooms (23) DEFG. Cards All. Region Alsace.
Post 67290 La Petite-Pierre, Bas-Rhin. (4km SE of La Petite-Pierre.)
Tel 03 88 01 49 00. Fax 03 88 70 40 26. Mich 42/C3. Map 3.

Le PETIT-PRESSIGNY

La Promenade

Very comfortable restaurant/Cooking 3-4
Air-conditioning

FW

"Petit" village astride the Aigronne, 10km E of Gd-Pressigny. *"Grande"*
for the superlative modern cooking of Jacky Dallais. *Menu du Marché* (b)
is *RQP* largesse: my mouth waters (& wallet smiles) at the memory of
*oeufs coque à la crème de champignons, géline rôtie à la creme de
morilles et oignons nouveaux*, cheese & *clafoutis aux cérises & pralines*.
Menus bCDEF. Cards MC, V. (Rms: St-Roch or Europe; La Roche-Posay SW.)
Closed 6-28 Jan. 22 Sept-7 Oct. Sun evg & Mon (not pub. hols).
Post 37350 Le Petit-Pressigny, Indre-et-Loire. Regions Loire/Poit-Char.
Tel 02 47 94 93 52. Fax 02 47 91 06 03. Mich 82/C3. Map 2.

A100frs & under. B100–150. C150–200. D200–250. E250–350. F350–500. G500+

PEYREHORADE

Central

Comfortable hotel/Cooking 3
Lift

FW

A *RQP* sizzler. What a transformation I've seen over 20 years (pity about the Muzak though). Sylvie de Lalagade has worked wonders; the building is now a contemporary-styled sparkler; & her brother, Eric Galby, is a young *cuisine moderne* dazzler. Past tastebud pleasures have included *sandre soufflé aux pleurottes* & *sable aux fraises, crème vanillée*.
Menus bCD. Rooms (16) E. Cards All.
Closed 4-12 Mar. 16-30 Dec. Sun evg & Mon (not July/Aug).
Post pl. A. Briand, 40300 Peyrehorade, Landes. Region Southwest.
Tel 05 58 73 03 22. Fax 05 58 73 17 15. Mich 149/D3. Map 4.

La PLAINE-SUR-MER (Port de Gravette)

Anne de Bretagne

Comfortable hotel/Cooking 2-3
Quiet/Terrace/Gardens/Swimming pool/Tennis/Parking

FW

A modern hotel at Port de Gravette (NW) with fine views across the Loire Estuary. Michèle Vételé is *la patronne/sommelière*; chef/husband Philippe concentrates on the harvests from the oceans. Among neo-classical *plats*, all light and well-executed, enjoy *terrine de poissons de la côte* & a flavoursome *lotte rôtie au four au beurre d'Anjou rouge*.
Menus ACDE. Rooms (25) FG. Cards AE, MC, V. Closed 2 Jan-23 Feb.
Rest: Mon midday (20 May-9 Sep). Sun evg & Mon (out of season).
Post 44770 La Plaine-sur-Mer, Loire-Atlantique. Regions Loire/Poit-Char.
Tel 02 40 21 54 72. Fax 02 40 21 02 33. Mich 78/A1-B1. Map 1.

PLAISANCE (Aveyron)

Les Magnolias

Comfortable restaurant with rooms/Cooking 2-3
Quiet/Terrace/Gardens

FW

A bewitching spot: a 14th-17thC vine-covered *logis* with stones & beams & an emerald of a garden. Marie-France & Francis Roussel are charmers too. She's the English-speaking *patronne*; he's a highly competent *cuisinier* with a light, neo-classical touch. Hereabouts dishes like *dos de truite et son court bouillon à l'ail rose de Lautrec* are a welcome surprise.
Menus ABCE. Rooms (6) E. Cards AE, MC, V.
Closed Jan-Mar. Mon (mid Oct-Dec).
Post 12550 Plaisance, Aveyron. Region Languedoc-Roussillon.
Tel 05 65 99 77 34. Fax 05 65 99 70 57. Mich 154/C1. Map 5.

A100frs & under. B100–150. C150–200. D200–250. E250–350. F350–500. G500+

PLAISANCE (Gers)   Ripa Alta

Comfortable restaurant with rooms/Cooking 2-3   `FW`

Big-hearted, English-speaking Maurice Coscuella, cooking for 37 years
(& shortly to retire), has had his fair share of problems over the decades
I've known him & his gentle wife, Irène. He's one of a rare breed – a
truly innovative chef capable of pulling modern/neo-classical/regional
tricks from his culinary *valise. Quod sapit nutrit* he claims: spot-on
with delights like a *soupe de châtaigne aux grattons de foie gras.*
Menus ABCD. Rooms (13) CDE. Cards All.
Closed Rest: Mon midday (mid Sept-mid Mar).
Post 32160 Plaisance, Gers. Region Southwest.
Tel 05 62 69 30 43. Fax 05 62 69 36 99. Mich 150/C3. Map 4.

PLANCOET   Jean-Pierre Crouzil

Very comfortable restaurant with rooms/Cooking 3-4   `FW`
Terrace/Gardens/Parking/Air-conditioning (restaurant)

In Plancoët's "lower" town, overlooking a basin on the River Arguenon.
Extrovert furnishings. An attentive welcome from smart Colette, followed by
an astonishingly good, modern show from chef J-PC. Two dishes summed
up his style to a tee: an *aumônière de saumon aux filaments de légumes*;
& a drooling *filet de canard grillé, poivre et sel, la sauce au miel.*
Menus b(lunch)CDEF. Rooms (7) G. Cards AE, MC, V. Closed 6-20 Jan.
Rooms: Sun evg & Mon (Oct-Apl). Rest: Sun evg (not July/Aug). Mon.
Post 22130 Plancoët, Côtes d'Armor. Region Brittany.
Tel 02 96 84 10 24. Fax 02 96 84 01 93. Mich 29/E3. Map 1.

PLAN-DE-LA-TOUR (also see next page)   Mas des Brugassières

Comfortable hotel (no restaurant)
Secluded/Gardens/Swimming pool/Tennis/Parking

Sometimes you have to choose descriptive adjectives with great care: this
is most certainly a spot where "heavenly" is entirely appropriate.
Alongside the D44, just S of the village, the wooded grounds are a cool,
delectable haven: to the N the tree-covered Massif des Maures; & to the
S, beyond the St-Pierre peak, the St-Tropez bee-hive is just 10km away.
Rooms (14) FG. Cards MC, V.
Closed Mid Oct-mid Mar.
Post rte Grimaud, 83120 Plan-de-la-Tour, Var. Region Côte d'Azur.
Tel 04 94 43 72 42. Fax 04 94 43 00 20. Mich 163/D4. Map 6.

A100frs & under. B100–150. C150–200. D200–250. E250–350. F350–500. G500+

PLAN-DE-LA-TOUR (also see previous page)   **Parasolis**

Simple hotel (no restaurant)
Secluded/Gardens/Swimming pool/Closed parking

At Courruero, 2km further S from the Mas des Brugassières (the previous entry) & Plan-de-la-Tour. The slightly higher elevation provides better views of the wooded mountains. The swimming pool is newly built. The *patron* is a friendly soul; all bedrooms are on one level; & the 5-acre estate is well-named – dominated by several umbrella pines.
Rooms (15) F(bottom-end)G. Cards not accepted.
Closed Mid Oct-mid Mar. Region Côte d'Azur.
Post rte Grimaud, Courruero, 83120 Plan-de-la-Tour, Var.
Tel 04 94 43 76 05. Fax 04 94 43 77 09. Mich 163/D4. Map 6.

PLAN-DU-VAR   **Cassini**

Comfortable restaurant with basic rooms/Cooking 2 | FW |
Terrace

Beside the N202. A rural-style dining room & a warm welcome from the Cassini-Martin foursome, all talented restaurateurs. Philippe Martin is a clever classicist with many light-fingered touches. Two main courses epitomise those skills: a super *truite saumonée à la creme de persil* & a gutsy *pavé de boeuf aux morilles*. Delicious desserts – like *tiramisu*.
Menus ABCD. Rooms (20) BCD. Cards AE, MC, V. Region Côte d'Azur.
Closed 1-15 Feb. 4-19 June. Sun evg & Mon (not July/Aug).
Post rte National, Plan-du-Var, 06670 Levens, Alpes-Maritimes.
Tel 04 93 08 91 03. Fax 04 93 08 45 48. Mich 165/D2-D3. Map 6.

PLOMBIERES-LES-BAINS   **Fontaine Stanislas**

Simple hotel/Cooking 1
Secluded/Gardens/Garage/Parking

Seclusion (a dead-end), beech woods, birds, fine views & a nearby spring (Fontaine Stanislas) are the natural pleasures at the Lemercier hotel. 4th-generation, English-speaking Marie-Line Bilger & her chef/husband Michel, work hard to please. Simple *Bourgeoise*/classical fare – of the *andouille, truite meunière (ou amandes), mignon de porc à la creme* type.
Menus ABCE. Rooms (19) C(bottom-end)DE. Cards AE, MC, V.
Closed Oct-Mar. (Hotel is 4km SW of spa; follow signs from D63.)
Post 88370 Plombières-les-Bains, Vosges. Region Alsace.
Tel 03 29 66 01 53. Fax 03 29 30 04 31. Mich 59/F4. Map 3.

A 100frs & under. B 100–150. C 150–200. D 200–250. E 250–350. F 350–500. G 500+

PLOMODIERN

Relais Porz-Morvan

Simple hotel (no restaurant)
Secluded/Gardens/Tennis/Parking

A restored 160-year-old farm (*ferme* was originally part of the name) with a dozen modern, some smallish, bedrooms. (There's one largish family room, called *"Penty"*.) Small garden, facing S, is ideal for sunbathing; the coast & beaches are just minutes away; tennis for the active; a *crêperie* is *in situ*; & old Breton furniture in *le salon*.
Rooms (12) E (family room bottom-end G). Cards MC, V.
Closed Oct-Mar.
Post 29550 Plomodiern, Finistère. Region Brittany.
Tel 02 98 81 53 23. Mich 44/C1. Map 1.

PLOUNERIN

Patrick Jeffroy

Very comfortable restaurant with rooms/Cooking 3-4 FW
Parking

No question about it: one of the best young chefs in Brittany. (Patrick Fer worked wonders too in this hamlet a decade ago: see *FL3*.) PJ keeps his modern repertoire simple & lets Nature work for him. Proof of that is at every turn: *truite de mer sesames sauce vièrge*; & *gigot d'agneau rôti aux shitakées, légumes printaniers* were two blue-chip marvels.
Menus b(lunch)C(ceiling)EF. Rooms (3) F(low-end). Cards MC, V.
Closed 29 Jan-12 Feb. 25 Nov-9 Dec. Sun evg & Mon (out of season).
Post 22780 Plounérin, Côtes d'Armor. Region Brittany.
Tel 02 96 38 61 80. Fax 02 96 38 66 29. Mich 27/F2. Map 1.

POLIGNY (also see next page)

Cellier St-Vernier

Simple restaurant/Cooking 2-3 FW

The modest dining room can be tricky to locate: take the N5 through the village & park in the main place Nationale; on the W side, between *Axa Assurances* & *Banque Populaire* you'll find the stairs that lead down to Dominique & Caroline Fieux's *cellier*. Memorable modern, neo-classical & regional sparklers from Dominique: *caille des Dombes farci de marmelade de raisins réduction de Banyuls* was three-star brilliance.
Menus b(lunch)CEF. Cards AE, MC, V. (Rooms: Nouvel Hôtel, to NW.)
Closed Sun evg. Mon.
Post 21 pl. Nationale, 39800 Poligny, Jura. Region Jura.
Tel 03 84 37 21 65. Mich 89/E3. Map 3.

A100frs & under. B100–150. C150–200. D200–250. E250–350. F350–500. G500+

259

POLIGNY (also see previous page)   **Host. Monts de Vaux**

Very comfortable hotel/Cooking 2
Quiet/Terrace/Gardens/Tennis/Garage/Closed parking

Run by two generations of the English-speaking Carrion family. "You are made to feel like a weekend guest of the family in a warm, old-fashioned atmosphere," says one reader. Another writes "kids not welcome." Views of the Culée de Vaux (valley) are sensational. Regional/classical/neo-classical cooking: *poulet de Bresse au vin jaune* is one of the best.
Menus C(lunch)F. Rooms (7)FG(top-end). Cards All. (N5: 4km SE Poligny.)
Closed Nov. Dec. Tues *midi* (July/Aug). Tues evg & Wed *midi* (Sept-June).
Post Monts de Vaux, 39800 Poligny, Jura. Region Jura.
Tel 03 84 37 12 50. Fax 03 84 37 09 07. Mich 89/E3. Map 3.

POLIGNY   Paris

Simple hotel/Cooking 1-2
Swimming pool (indoor)/Garage

André Biétry's ugly *logis* is in the centre of Poligny. A choice for each course is a big plus – as is the indoor pool. Choose from alternatives such as *terrine* or *soupe de poissons*; *truite meunière*, *civet de lièvre* – the latter both rich & filling – or *lapereau aux herbes garni*; Jura cheeses & a vast selection of tummy-stretching sweets.
Menus ABC. Rooms (23) DE. Cards MC, V.
Closed 3 Nov-1 Feb. Rest: Mon. Tues midday.
Post 7 r. Travot, 39800 Poligny, Jura. Region Jura.
Tel 03 84 37 13 87. Fax 03 84 37 23 39. Mich 89/E3. Map 3.

POLIGNY (Passenans)   Le Revermont

Comfortable hotel/Cooking 1-2   FW
Secluded/Terr/Gardens/Swim pool/Tennis/Lift/Garage/Parking

Michel & Marie-Claude Schmit own an odd-looking, modern *logis*, run as a business" in a lovely setting N of Passenans. Ideal for families with something always going on. Principally classical offerings: *mitonnée de magret de canard à la crème de lentilles* (an in-vogue dish) is a stomach filler; *petite assiette de pâtisseries* is a sumptuous sweet.
Menus BCDE. Rooms (28) EF. Cards AE, MC, V.
Closed 25 Dec-1 Mar. Sun evg & Mon (Oct-Mar).
Post 39230 Passenans, Jura. Region Jura. (11km SW of Poligny.)
Tel 03 84 44 61 02. Fax 03 84 44 64 83. Mich 89/E3. Map 3.

A100frs & under. B100–150. C150–200. D200–250. E250–350. F350–500. G500+

PONS

Auberge Pontoise

Comfortable hotel/Cooking 2-3
Terrace/Garage/Air-conditioning (restaurant)

Not a trouble-free performance since the *auberge* appeared in *FLE*. Poor welcome, incorrect bills & cooking have all been criticised. Modern stylish interior (scruffy exterior) & a colourful patio/terrace (pity about the artificial flowers). Jeaninne Chat is *la patronne*; hubby Philippe & chef Alain Gargarit play classical/neo-classical tabby games.

Menus CF(both bottom-end). Rooms (22) EF. Cards MC, V. (In town centre.)
Closed 20 Dec-Jan. Sun evg (mid Sept-June). Mon (not evg July-mid Sept.)
Post 23 av. Gambetta, 17800 Pons, Charente-Maritime. Region Poitou-Char.
Tel 05 46 94 00 99. Fax 05 46 91 33 40. Mich 107/D3. Map 4.

PONS

Bordeaux

Comfortable hotel/Cooking 2　　　　　　　　FW
Terrace/Garage

The Chats, to the N, will have to look to their laurels: owner Cornélia Muller & young chef, Pierre Jaubert, offer first-rate *RQP* at their town-centre *logis*. Pierre's repertoire is a mix of modern, some regional & neo-classical: typical *plats* are *blanc de sandre en gribiche d'huîtres* & an artful *roulade de sole purée de cresson* – a touch out of sync.

Menus ABCD. Rooms (16) DE. Cards AE, MC, V. (Parking nearby.)
Closed Sun & Mon midday (Oct-Apl).
Post 1 r. Gambetta, 17800 Pons, Charente-Maritime. Region Poitou-Char.
Tel 05 46 91 31 12. Fax 05 46 91 22 25. Mich 107/D3. Map 4.

PONT-A-MOUSSON

Auberge des Thomas

Simple restaurant/Cooking 2　　　　　　　FW
Terrace

Flowers please the eyes both inside & on the terrace at Michel & Solange Thomas' *auberge* – at Blénod, 2km 5 of the town, in an unattractive part of the Moselle Valley. Neo-classical specialities from the chef: good use is made of local wine in a masterly *sandre à la lie de pinot noir de Toul* & his desserts are formidable – witness *charlotte à la poire*.

Menus ABCE. Cards All. (Rooms: Bagatelle, Pont-à-Mousson; *sans rest.*)
Closed 19-26 Feb. 1st 3 wks Aug. Sun evg. Mon. Wed evg. Regs Als/Ch-Ard.
Post 100 av. V. Claude, 54700 Blénod-lès-Pont-à-Mousson, Meurthe-et-M.
Tel 03 83 81 07 72. Fax 03 83 82 34 94. Mich 41/D3. Map 3.

A100frs & under. B100–150. C150–200. D200–250. E250–350. F350–500. G500+

PONT-AUDEMER
Auberge du Vieux Puits

Comfortable restaurant with rooms/Cooking 2
Gardens/Parking

The superb 17thC *maison Normande*, originally a tannery, has become almost a national tourist monument. The fabulous interior is praised by everyone; as are the English-speaking owners, Jacques & Hélène Foltz (a touch "over solicitous"?); but high prices are not appreciated. Cooking remains classical & authentic *Normande*: what else? Limited-choice menus.
Menus d(lunch: ceiling)E. Rooms (12) EF. Disabled. Cards MC, V.
Closed 17 Dec-26 Jan. Mon evg & Tues (out of season).
Post 6 r. N.-D.-du-Pré, 27500 Pont-Audemer, Eure. Region Normandy.
Tel 02 32 41 01 48. Fax 02 32 42 37 28. Mich 15/D4. Map 2.

PONTAUMUR
Poste

Simple hotel/Cooking 1-2
Garage

FW

Pierette Quinty is a welcoming hostess; & her husband, Jean-Paul, is both an enthusiastic rugger fan & lover of *Auvergnats*, classical & *Bourgeois* specialities: *tête de veau gribiche, jambon d'Auvergne* & *rable de lièvre aux figues* are among the many Quintyssential pleasures. *Nougat glacé au miel et aux noix* is a lip-licking sweet. Great cellar.
Menus aBCDE. Rooms (15) DE. Cards MC, V.
Closed Mid Dec-Jan. Sun evg & Mon (not July/Aug).
Post 63380 Pontaumur, Puy-de-Dôme. Region Massif Central (Auvergne).
Tel 04 73 79 90 15. Fax 04 73 79 73 17. Mich 112/C1. Map 5.

PONT-DE-L'ISERE
Michel Chabran

Luxury restaurant with rooms/Cooking 4
Terrace/Closed parking/Air-conditioning

Michel, just turned 50, is fast restoring his past reputation – but now with a classical/neo-classical style – in a much refurbished restaurant, once a garage. Low-end lunch menu d is superb value (with wine & *café*): *soupe au pistou, tranche de gigot poêlée à la minute* & *tarte fine aux poires Williams, sorbet caramel* is one choice permutation. Gentle, self-effacing Rose-Marie Chabran, *la patronne*, is as much loved as ever.
Menus d(lunch)EFG. Rooms (12) FG. Cards All. (Also see Valence entry.)
Post RN7, 26600 Pont-de-l'Isère, Drôme. Region Massif Central (Ardèche).
Tel 04 75 84 60 09. Fax 04 75 84 59 65. Mich 130/B2. Map 6.

A100frs & under. B100–150. C150–200. D200–250. E250–350. F350–500. G500+

PONT-DE-POITTE

Ain

Comfortable restaurant with rooms/Cooking 1-2
Air-conditioning (restaurant)

FW

Pretty as a picture: first, the view of the Ain from the bridge; & next the *logis* with its stone façade, explosion of geraniums & the plane tree shaded small *place* in front of the rest. Michel & Yvonne Bailly are helpful, friendly hosts. Cooking? *Bourgeois*/classical/regional dishes (plus a *poisson* menu). Typical *plat truite meunière*. Wide-choice menus.
Menus BCE. Rooms (10) DE. Cards MC, V.
Closed 23 Dec-Jan. Sun (out of season). Mon. Tues midday (July/Aug).
Post 39130 Pont-de-Poitte, Jura. Region Jura.
Tel 03 84 48 30 16. Fax 03 84 48 36 95. Mich 103/F1. Map 6.

PONT-DE-VAUX

Le Raisin

Comfortable restaurant with rooms/Cooking 3
Closed parking/Air-conditioning (restaurant)

FW

A coffee-shaded façade in a street of houses with many-hued exteriors. Menus, too, have many taste & choice shades. Consider Gilles Chazot's regional/classical cheapest: from 4 starters *terrine et assiette de crudités*; from a main-course trio, a robust *paillard de boeuf grillée; crêpes Parmentier*; & from 4 sweets, *fromage blanc à la crème*.
Menus BCDE. Rooms (18) E. Cards All.
Closed 8-31 Jan. Sun evg & Mon (out of season; not pub. hols).
Post 01190 Pont-de-Vaux, Ain. Region Lyonnais.
Tel 03 85 30 30 97. Fax 03 85 67 89. Mich 102/C2. Map 6.

PONT-DU-DOGNON

Rallye

Simple hotel/Cooking 1
Secluded/Parking

Overlooking the River Taurion (here a narrow, winding, man-made lake) the not-so-pretty-as-a-picture *logis* is well-liked: for the peace & quiet; views; above average standards; & for the good-value provided by René & Nicole Périéras, *les patrons*. Classical/*Bourgeoise*/regional (*terroir*) cooking – but alas, no FW: *cèpes, jambon, truites*, etc.
Menus aBC. Rooms (18) CDE. Cards MC, V. Region Poitou-Charentes.
Closed Oct-mid Apl. Mon (not evg season). Tues (not evg out of season).
Post Pont-du-Dognon, 87340 St-Laurent-les-Eglises, Haute-Vienne.
Tel 05 55 56 56 11. Fax 05 55 56 50 67. Mich 110/C1. Map 5.

A100frs & under. B100–150. C150–200. D200–250. E250–350. F350–500. G500+

263

PONTEMPEYRAT

Mistou

Comfortable hotel/Cooking 2-3   FW
Secluded/Gardens/Parking

An 18thC watermill (once used to preserve eggs) in a 2-acre park beside the River Ance. Jacqueline Roux is a "particularly agreeable" hostess; husband Bernard, an English-speaking chef, has a liking for fish in his neo-classical repertoire: witness a *millefeuille de sandre langoustines roses jus au cidre*. Flies, from the next-door farm, can be a pest.
Menus bCDE. Rooms (28) EF. Cards AE, MC, V. Region MC (Auvergne).
Closed Nov-Easter. Rest: midday (not July/Aug; week-ends; pub. hols).
Post Pontempeyrat, 43500 Craponne-sur-Arzon, Haute-Loire. (S of D498.)
Tel 04 77 50 62 46. Fax 04 77 50 66 70. Mich 114/C4. Map 5.

PONTLEVOY

de l'Ecole

Comfortable restaurant with rooms/Cooking 1-2   FW
Terrace/Gardens/Closed parking

The enchanting terrace/gardens & refreshing fountain are the highlights of this charminq *demeure* – run with panache by chef Guy Preteseille. Old-time character is the label for both the décor & the classical fare: good-choice menus – mouthwatering treats of the *feuilleté d'asperges sauce mousseline, escalope de veau sauce crème* & *crème brûlée* variety.
Menus ABCD. Rooms (11) EF. Cards MC, V.
Closed Feb. Tues (not July/Aug).
Post 41400 Pontlevoy, Loir-et-Cher. Region Loire.
Tel 02 54 32 50 30. Fax 02 54 32 33 58. Mich 68/B4. Map 2.

PONTORSON

Bretagne

Comfortable hotel/Cooking 2   FW

A puce-shaded façade is an off-putting starter at the town-centre *logis*. Things improve significantly when you enter: Yvette Carnet is an elegant *patronne* – proud as punch of her young son, chef Jérôme. A cascade of menus – all with plenty of choice. Classical/*Bourgeoise* fare. Highlights were *pièce de boeuf sauce au poivre*; &, for this *pays*, a "different" cheese course, *feuilleté de Fourme d'Ambert* (Auvergne) *chaud à la poire*.
Menus ABCE. Rooms (12) DEF. Cards AE, MC, V.
Closed 5 Jan-10 Feb. Mon (out of season).
Post r. Couesnon, 50170 Pontorson, Manche. Regions Brittany/Normandy.
Tel 02 33 60 10 55. Fax 02 33 58 20 54. Mich 48/C1. Map 1.

A100frs & under. B100–150. C150–200. D200–250. E250–350. F350–500. G500+

Le PORGE

Vieille Auberge

Comfortable restaurant/Cooking 1-2   `FW`
Terrace/Gardens/Parking

A series of pluses: a handsome building with a welcome terrace; a cool dining room; & regional/classical dishes which would make Escoffier happy – of the *terrine de ris de veau aux cèpes et son coulis de tomates & cuisse de confite de canard confite* (menu B). One debit: lunches are fine but where can one stay overnight other than the suggestion below?
Menus B (*àlc* Sun: CD). Cards MC, V. Region Southwest.
Closed 20 Jan-20 Feb. Tues evg (mid Nov-Easter). Wed.
Post 33680 Le Porge, Gironde. (Rooms: Etoile d'Argent, Lacanau-Océan.)
Tel 05 56 26 50 40. Mich 120/B2. Map 4. (Above 24km to NW.)

PORT-SUR-SAONE (Vauchoux)

Château de Vauchoux

Very comfortable restaurant/Cooking 3-4   `FW`
Terrace/Gardens/Swimming pool/Tennis/Parking

Jean-Michel Turin & his adorable wife, Franceline, find life tough at their handsome restaurant home, once a Louis XV hunting lodge. Seductive neo-classical *plats*: sole filets in a scallops *fumée* – the taste of the sea on a plate; succulent *pigeonneau* on a bed of *chou vert, lardons, pied à veau* & oxtail; & 3-star sweets. Have lunch: use the facilities.
Menus BEF. Cards MC, V. (Rooms: Ibis & Gd Hôtel, Vesoul; 16km to E.)
Closed Feb. Mon. (Gd Hôtel owned by Turins: Tel 03 84 75 02 56.)
Post Vauchoux, 70170 Port-s-Saône, Hte-Saône. Region Alsace. (3km to S.)
Tel 03 84 91 53 55. Fax 03 84 91 65 38 (also Gd H.). Mich 75/F2. Map 3.

PORT-VENDRES

Côte Vermeille

Comfortable restaurant/Cooking 2   `FW`
Air-conditioning

The brothers Bessière – Philippe, younger by two years, is the chef; Guilhem runs the front of house – are fish addicts. The trawler alternatives are a knockout: like *soupe de poissons, anchois de Collioure marinés, fantasie de poissons et crustacés marinés, merlan de palangre et pétoncles* & *filets de rougets de roche en salmis*.
Menus a(lunch)BCD. Cards AE, MC, V. (Rooms: St-Elme, *sans rest.*)
Closed Tues (not July/Aug).
Post quai Fanal, 66660 Port-Vendres, Pyrénées-Orientales.
Tel 04 68 82 05 71. Mich 177/F3. Map 5. Region Languedoc-Roussillon.

A100frs & under. B100–150. C150–200. D200–250. E250–350. F350–500. G500+

POUDENAS   Le Moulin de la Belle Gasconne

Comfortable restaurant with rooms/Cooking 2-3
Quiet/Gardens/Swimming pool/Parking

Marie-Claude Gracia is a remarkable chef by any measure. A mother of 5, she's an indefatigable lady; M-C & her husband Richard have an intuitive sympathy for their *pays*. Tuck into authentic classical/regional fare: prize-winning *foies gras*; strongly-flavoured *civet de canard*; home-made *fromageon*; & much else. Bedrooms in mill beside Gélise. Not what it was.
Menus CE. Rooms (7) FG. Cards All.
Closed Jan-Mar. Sun evg.
Post 47170 Poudenas, Lot-et-Garonne. Region Southwest.
Tel 05 53 65 71 58. Fax 05 53 65 87 39. Mich 136/B4. Map 4.

POUILLY-SOUS-CHARLIEU   de la Loire

Very comfortable restaurant/Cooking 2-3 | FW |
Terrace/Gardens/Parking

Brigitte & Alain Rousseau (he trained at Troisgros in Roanne) have a handsome dining room & lime tree-shaded terrace – 100m from the Loire. Alain rings all the culinary-style bells: *rillette aux deux saumons*; a blockbuster pan-fried *pièce Charolaise au beurre vigneron* or a lighter *filet de cabillaud à la Basquaise*; & a dessert duo – all on menu C.
Menus aCDE. Cards AE, MC, V. (Rooms: Relais de l'Abbaye, Charlieu.)
Closed Feb sch. hols. 25-30 Aug. Sun evg. Mon. (Above 5 min-drive E.)
Post 42720 Pouilly-sous-Charlieu, Loire. Region Lyonnais.
Tel 04 77 60 81 36. Fax 04 77 60 76 06. Mich 101/E3. Map 5.

POUILLY-SUR-LOIRE   Hôtel de Pouilly/Rest. Relais Grillade

Comfortable hotel/Cooking 1
Terrace/Gardens/Parking

English-speaking Robert Fischer is a professional, helpful hotelier. The Relais Grillade has been *in situ* for 25 years; the hotel, opened in 1992, is nicely furnished & has all mod-cons. The restaurant terrace & two rustic dining rooms have views of *la Loire sauvage*. Cooking? Basic *Bourgeoise*, grills & some French regional additions: *raie aux câpres*, *gigot d'agneau à la Provençale* & the ubiquitous *choucroute* (Oct-May).
Menus ABC. Rooms (23) DEF. Disabled. Cards All. (2km to S of Pouilly.)
Post 58150 Pouilly-sur-Loire, Nièvre. Region Berry-Bourbonnais.
Tel 03 86 39 03 00. Fax 03 86 39 07 47. Mich 85/E1. Map 2.

La PRENESSAYE   Motel d'Armor/Rest. Le Boléro

Comfortable hotel/Cooking 2   FW
Terrace/Gardens/Parking

On the N side of the N164, 8km E of Loudéac. Wooded grounds, a warm
welcome from Madeleine Fraboulet & both modern & neo-classical
cooking from her husband Daniel. Menus BCD are cleverly contrived &
provide a wide choice: typical treats could include *dos de saumon à la
sauce des prés, filet de lieu côtier à l'estragon* & *faux-filet grillée*.
Menus aBCD. Rooms (10) DE. Cards MC, V.
Closed Feb sch. hols. Rest: Sun evg.
Post La Prénessaye, 22210 Plémet, Côtes d'Armor. Region Brittany.
Tel 02 96 25 90 87. Fax 02 96 25 76 72. Mich 47/D1. Map 1.

PUJAUDRAN   Puits St-Jacques

Very comfortable restaurant/Cooking 2   FW

N of N124. A handsome façade: window boxes, red brick window surrounds,
sand-shaded walls. Elegant, spacious interior. Fabienne & Jean-Pierre
Retureau are *les patrons*. His repertoire is modern/neo-classical. Two fine
memories from menu b: *croustillant d'anchois frais et sa quenelle de
tapenade* & *méli-mélo de fruits au Madiran*. Main courses not so good. Pre-
cooked & warmed up? A problem everywhere in France: cutting corners!
Menus b(lunch)CE(all bottom-end). Cards All. (Rooms: Host du Lac 8km W.)
Closed Feb sch. hols. 1-15 Aug. Sat *midi*. Mon. (Above L'Isle-Jourdain.)
Post 32600 Pujaudran, Gers. Regions Languedoc-Roussillon/Southwest.
Tel 05 62 07 41 11. Fax 05 62 07 44 09. Mich 152/B3. Map 5.

PUSIGNAN   La Closerie

Very comfortable restaurant/Cooking 2-3   FW
Terrace/Gardens

Gilles Troump's Louis XV-styled restaurant is more easily found if
Pusignan is approached from the A432 Satolas airport road. Classical is
the best tag for cooking, service & fittings. An original *carpaccio de
canard* – which didn't quite work – & impressive *blanquette de veau* (no
relation to the basic mundane version) were enjoyable. Pretty gardens.
Menus BCE. Cards All. (Rooms: Sofitel & Climat de France; 7km to S.)
Closed 4-18 Aug. Sun evg. Mon. (Both above at Lyon-Satolas airport.)
Post 4 pl. Gaîté, 69330 Pusignan, Rhône. (Also see Montluel entry.)
Tel 04 78 04 40 50. Fax 04 78 04 44 05. Mich 116/B2. Map 6. Reg Lyon.

A100frs & under. B100–150. C150–200. D200–250. E250–350. F350–500. G500+

PUTANGES-PONT-ECREPIN

Lion Verd

Simple hotel/Cooking 1-2
Gardens/Closed parking

FW

Modern, stone-built, Orne-side *logis* in a visual tonic setting (photo *Hidden France* p128). *Chef/patron* Jean-Pierre Guillais steers a middle of the river course: a mix of classical, *Normande & Bourgeoise*. Debits? Small bedrooms; some beds are uncomfortable; & Ginette Guillais, a prolific tapestry weaver, is not the most welcoming of *patronnes*.
Menus ABCDE. Rooms (19) BCDE. Cards MC, V.
Closed 23 Dec-31 Jan. Rest: Fri evg (out of season).
Post 61210 Putanges-Pont-Ecrepin, Orne. Region Normandy.
Tel 02 33 35 01 86. Fax 02 33 39 53 32. Mich 32/B4. Map 2.

PUYMIROL

Les Loges de l'Aubergade

Very comfortable hotel/Cooking 4-5
Quiet/Terrace/Garage/Air-conditioning

Michel Trama is a neuro-surgeon modern chef, the ultimate technician; he's also a culinary magician & has the rare ability to make you scratch your head & smile on seeing his myriad creations (latest is a "Corona" dessert). He's also a dedicated family man, putting Maryse, his wife, children & grandchildren before all else. We adore him, as man & chef.
Menus c(lunch)EG. Rooms (10) G2. Cards All. (Cheaper rooms: see Agen.)
Closed Feb sch. hols. Mon (out of season; not pub. hols).
Post 52 r. Royale, 47270 Puymirol, Lot-et-Garonne. Region Southwest.
Tel 05 53 95 31 46. Fax 05 53 95 33 80. Mich 137/E3. Map 5.

QUARRE-LES-TOMBES

Auberge de l'Atre

Very comfortable restaurant with rooms/Cooking 3
Gardens/Parking

FW

An 18thC granite farmhouse, 5km S of Quarré. The terrain is delectable; so is the garden. Owners, Odile & English-speaking Francis Salamolard, are accomplished hosts. Francis is an exuberant chef, mixing all styles: top marks for the many Morvan-grown herbs; the 30 desserts he offers clients; a *cave* of over 350 *RQP* wines; & tasty regional cheeses.
Menus b(lunch: top-end)DE. Rooms (6: ready Oct 96) F. Cards All.
Closed 20 Jan-10 Mar. 25 Nov-10 Dec. Tues evg & Wed (14 Sept-19 June).
Post Les Lavaults, 89630 Quarré-les-Tombes, Yonne. Region Burgundy.
Tel 03 86 32 20 79. Fax 03 86 32 28 25. Mich 72/C4. Map 3.

A100frs & under. B100–150. C150–200. D200–250. E250–350. F350–500. G500+

QUARRE-LES-TOMBES

Auberge des Brizards

Comfortable hotel/Cooking 1-2
Secluded/Terrace/Gardens/Tennis/Parking

FW

Take your Tardis & travel back in time: to a remote, heavily-wooded *coin* in the Morvan; to an idiosyncratic family *auberge*. Glamorous Françine Besancenot is *la patronne*; son Jérôme is the chef, helped by grandma Odette. Hearty, anything but frivolous Burgundian fare: home-cured hams, *charcuterie, crapinaud* & *le vrai boudin*. Breakfast a treat. Farm & *étang* (fishing) *in situ*. "Could have stayed longer" wrote a reader.
Menus BCE. Rooms (23) EFG. Cards All. (D55/D355/V7; 8km SE.)
Post Les Brizards, 89630 Quarré-les-Tombes, Yonne. Region Burgundy.
Tel 03 86 32 20 12. Fax 03 86 32 27 40. Mich 72/C4. Map 3.

QUEND

Auberge Le Fiacre

Comfortable restaurant with rooms/Cooking 1-2
Secluded/Gardens/Parking

FW

At Routhiauville, midway between Quend & Fort-Mahon-Plage, 150m S of D32. An old, half-timbered farm houses *les salles*; modernised bedrooms are at the rear. A warm welcome from Martine Masmonteil & above average classical *plats* from her chef/husband Jean-Pierre. *Aumonière de bar florentine beurre blanc* remains a vivid memory. Fish at best in June & Oct.
Menus aB(ceiling)CD. Rooms (11) F(bottom-end). Cards MC, V.
Closed Mid Jan-mid Feb.
Post 80120 Quend, Somme. Region North.
Tel 03 22 23 47 30. Fax 03 22 27 19 80. Mich 6/B2-C2. Map 2.

QUESTEMBERT

Bretagne

Luxury restaurant with rooms/Cooking 4
Terrace/Gardens/Parking

Guides shower stars/*toques* on *chefs/patrons* Georges Paineau & son-in-law Claude Corlouër. My readers are not 100% convinced. Arguably highly inventive, contemporary cooking (one 3-star creation: cheek of beef in luscious dark Chinon sauce). Ultra-modern, glitzy furnishings (3-cheers for panelled *salle*). Wholesome *patronnes* Michèle P & daughter Natalie.
Menus c(lunch)EFG. Rooms (13)G,G2. Disabled. Cards AE, MC, V.
Closed 2-10 Dec. Mon & Tues midday (Sept-June; not pub. hols).
Post r. St-Michel, 56230 Questembert, Morbihan. Region Brittany.
Tel 02 97 26 11 12. Fax 02 97 26 12 37. Mich 63/D2. Map 1.

A100frs & under. B100–150. C150–200. D200–250. E250–350. F350–500. G500+

QUILLAN

Cartier

Comfortable hotel/Cooking 1
Lift

Henri Cartier's town-centre *logis* is hidden behind a curtain of trees. Grills/classical/*Bourgeois*/regional fare: especially tasty are *rouzolle* (eggs & *jambon* in a local vegetable soup) & *cèpes sautés Provençale*. Order the local "sparklers": Blanquette de Limoux (*méthode champenoise*) & Blanquette Méthode Ancestrale (made in traditional local way).
Menus AB. Rooms (30) CDEF. Cards AE, MC, V.
Closed 15 Dec-31 Mar. Rest: mid Dec-Feb. Sat (Oct-Apl).
Post bd Ch. de Gaulle, 11500 Quillan, Aude. Region Languedoc-Roussillon.
Tel 04 68 20 05 14. Fax 04 68 20 22 57. Mich 171/F3. Map 5.

QUIMPER

Sapinière

Simple hotel (no restaurant)
Tennis/Parking

Certainly not the world's most attractively-sited hotel; but, to its credit, I've received no really serious grumbles over the 13 years I've included the Sapinière in *FL*. Another important plus: your hard-earned French francs will go further here. Rooms at the rear justify a "fairly quiet" label. 4km S of Quimper, alongside the D34 Bénodet road.
Rooms (39) BCDE. Cards All.
Closed Mid Sept-mid Oct.
Post rte Bénodet, 29000 Quimper, Finistère. Region Brittany.
Tel 02 98 90 39 63. Fax 02 98 64 76 00. Mich 45/D2. Map 1.

QUIMPER (Pluguffan)

La Coudraie

Simple hotel (no restaurant)
Quiet/Gardens/Parking

For once, a building without the essential *Breton* whitewashed exterior coat. The hotel is in a quiet side road, S of the church, at Pluguffan – 7km W of Quimper. A pleasant garden with the interesting bonus of a handsome walnut tree. Both Quimper base hotels are ideal for the budget conscious reader; both are out-of-town with easy parking.
Rooms (11) DE. Cards MC, V.
Closed Feb & Nov sch. hols. Sat & Sun (winter).
Post impasse du Stade, 29700 Pluguffan, Finistère. Region Brittany.
Tel 02 98 94 03 69. Fax 02 98 94 08 42. Mich 44/C2. Map 1.

A100frs & under. B100–150. C150–200. D200–250. E250–350. F350–500. G500+

QUIMPER (Ty Sanquer)

Auberge Ty Coz

Comfortable restaurant/Cooking 1-2
Parking

Beside the D770 – 7km N of Quimper & E of the N165 *voie express* –
the sombre, dark granite exterior is brightened-up no end by a splash of
flowers. Jean-Pierre Marrec's classical & *Bourgeois* wide-choice menus
brighten-up spirits no end & fill empty stomachs: oysters, mussels,
smoked salmon, *gigot, faux-filet, St-Pierre, confit de canard* & similar.
Menus aBCD. Cards MC, V. (Rooms: Ibis, NE corner of Quimper.)
Closed 18 Apl-8 May. 5-23 Sept. Sun evg. Mon. (Above easy 5km drive.)
Post Ty Sanquer, 29000 Quimper, Finistère. Region Brittany.
Tel 02 98 94 50 02. Mich 45/D2. Map 1.

RAGUENES-PLAGE

Chez Pierre

Comfortable hotel/Cooking 1-2
Quiet/Gardens/Parking

FW

Chez Pierre has had many a face-lift over the decades I've known it –
including a new modern annexe. Gentle, self-effacing, English-speaking
patronne, Dany Guillou, & her chef/husband Xavier, are charming, helpful
hosts. Copious classical/*Bourgeois* cooking with the odd fizzing firework
(*filet de turbot au champagne* for one). Desserts are greatly improved.
Menus BCE. Rooms (35) DEF. Disabled. Cards MC, V.
Closed 26 Sept-6 Apl. Rest: Wed (11 June-10 Sept).
Post Raguenès-Plage, 29139 Névez, Finistère. Region Brittany.
Tel 02 98 06 81 06. Fax 02 98 06 62 09. Mich 45/E3. Map 1.

RAGUENES-PLAGE

Men Du

Comfortable hotel (no restaurant)
Secluded/Gardens/Parking

What a great success the Men Du has proved to be with readers. *Les
patrons*, the Oliviers, have been greatly appreciated – but not for their
machine-gun rattle French. Typical *Bretonne* seaside house – with an
extensive sea view from all the bedrooms. An isolated site with easy
access to the beach. Sun-trap, out-of-the-wind verandah.
Rooms (14) E. Cards MC, V.
Closed Oct-Mar.
Post Raguenès-Plage, 29139 Névez, Finistère. Region Brittany.
Tel 02 98 06 84 22. Fax 02 98 06 76 69. Mich 45/E3. Map 1.

A100frs & under. B100–150. C150–200. D200–250. E250–350. F350–500. G500+

RAMATUELLE

Ferme d'Hermès

Comfortable hotel (no restaurant)
Secluded/Gardens/Swimming pool/Parking

A small Provençale house, in a lovely setting, surrounded by vines (caveat: sprayed every 2 weeks) & bedrooms (alas, no air-cond.) with space-saving kitchens. Great welcome from Hermès (17) & Hermès Jnr, two Welsh terriers; & the English-speaking owner, Françoise Verrier. (Winter bookings: Tel Paris 01 48 28 75 75; or write 15 r. Peclet, 75015 Paris.)
Rooms (8) G. Cards MC, V. (S of D93.)
Closed Nov-Mar.
Post rte l'Escalet, 83350 Ramatuelle, Var. Region Côte d'Azur.
Tel 04 94 79 27 80. Fax 04 94 79 26 86. Mich 161/F3. Map 6.

REALMONT

Noël

Very comfortable restaurant with rooms/Cooking 2
Terrace

Young chef Jean-Paul Granier hangs classical & regional *plats* on the Noël tree; his wife Michèle takes your requests. The green-shuttered house & shady terrace remain the same from times past -- as does the cooking. Menus B could be a *salade de foie de dinde au vinaigre de Xérès; noix de boeuf au poivre*; cheeses; & *croustillant aux pommes*.
Menus BCE(bottom-end). Rooms (8) CDE. Cards All.
Closed Feb sch. hols. Sun evg & Mon (Sept-July).
Post r. H. de Ville, 81120 Réalmont, Tarn. Region Languedoc-Roussillon.
Tel 05 63 55 52 80. Mich 154/A2. Map 5.

REDON

Jean-Marc Chandouineau

Very comfortable restaurant with rooms/Cooking 2-3
Parking

Redon is an astonishing inland "port". An astonishing mouthful of a name for the restaurant: no prizes for the surroundings but the interior has old-time style; so does J-M's classical cuisine (with modern touches). A menu cascade. Good choice on menu B: a typical meal could be *magret de canard fumé, lotte sur coulis d'étrilles* & a pyramid of sorbets.
Menus BCDE. Rooms (7) EF. Cards All.
Closed 22 Apl-1 May. 9-27 Aug. Sat & Sun evg (not July/Aug).
Post 10 av. Gare, 35600 Redon, Ille-et-Vilaine. Region Brittany.
Tel 02 99 71 02 04. Fax 02 99 71 08 81. Mich 63/F2. Map 1.

A100frs & under. B100–150. C150–200. D200–250. E250–350. F350–500. G500+

REIMS (Champigny-sur-Vesle)   La Garenne

Very comfortable restaurant/Cooking 3
Parking/Air-conditioning

Beside N31, W of Reims & A4/A26 junction (exit 26). On the apex of the once infamous Thillois hairpin, part of the old Reims racing circuit. Laurent Laplaige (wife Corinne is *la patronne*) has made speedy progress from the grid. Neo-classical with a *forté* for fish: *pavé de turbot rôti aux germes de blé* & *lotte rôtie en crepine* – both hard to resist.
Menus b(ceiling)DF. Cards All. (Rooms: Ibis/Novotel; to E, A4/A26 exit.)
Closed 28 July-18 Aug. Sun evg. Mon.
Post 51370 Champigny-sur-Vesle, Marne. Region Champagne-Ardenne.
Tel 03 26 08 26 62. Fax 03 26 84 24 13. Mich 38/A1. Map 3.

RENNES (Cesson-Sévigné)   Germinal

Comfortable hotel/Cooking 1
Quiet/Terrace/Lift/Parking

A converted 113-year-old mill on an island site in the River Vilaine, 6km E of Rennes. The *moulin* has been owned by Louis & Danielle Goualin's family for three generations; Louis' father was the miller as recently as 1970. The terrace & glass-walled dining room are attractive pluses. A vast choice of classical/*Bourgeoise* specialities – on menus & *àlc*.
Menus aCD. Rooms (19) EF. Cards AE, MC, V.
Closed 23 Dec-2 Jan. Rest: Sun evg. Regions Brittany-Normandy.
Post 9 cours de la Vilaine, 35510 Cesson-Sévigné, Ille-et-Vilaine.
Tel 02 99 83 11 01. Fax 02 99 83 45 16. Mich 48/C3. Map 1.

RENNES (Chevaigné) (also see next page)   La Marinière

Comfortable restaurant/Cooking 3   FW
Terrace/Gardens/Parking

An isolated stone building on the W side of the D175 (take care from S), 12km N of Rennes. A rustic dining room & well-executed, authentic classical specialities from Yves Lejeune. Two main courses illustrated his skills to a tee: succulent *saumon frais à l'oseille;* & luscious *aile de canette au Chinon. Agneau de pré-salé*: on menus DE (Easter-mid Aug).
Menus a(lunch)BCDE. Cards All. (Rooms: La Reposée, Liffré; to E.)
Closed Sun evg. Mon evg. Pub. hols (evgs). Regions Brittany/Normandy.
Post rte Mont-St-Michel, 35250 Chevaigné, Ille-et-Vilaine.
Tel 02 99 55 74 64. Fax 02 99 55 89 65. Mich 48/C3. Map 1.

A100frs & under. B100–150. C150–200. D200–250. E250–350. F350–500. G500+

RENNES (Noyal-sur-Vilaine) (also see previous page) **Host. les Forges**

Comfortable restaurant with rooms/Cooking 2-3 `FW`
Parking

André Pilard, an ex-student of the Strasbourg hotel school, is the chef; wife Laurette is *la patronne*. André plays a classical cooking fiddle, his bow well-tuned to the sauces strings. Among a rich repertoire of nostalgic old-time tunes the likes of *filet de boeuf sauté Périgourdine, magret de canard au cassis* & *gratin d'oranges au Gd-Marnier* are typical.
Menus ABCE. Rooms (11) DE. Cards All. (12km E of Rennes.)
Closed 11-24 Aug. Sun evg. Pub. hols (evgs). Regions Brittany/Normandy.
Post 35530 Noyal-sur-Vilaine, Ille-et-Vilaine.
Tel 02 99 00 51 08. Fax 02 99 00 62 02. Mich 48/C3. Map 1.

REVIGNY-SUR-ORNAIN   Les Agapes

Comfortable restaurant/Cooking 3 `FW`

A modest window-boxed stone frontage gives no clue to the pleasures awaiting within the modernish interior. Chef Jean-Marc Joblot mixes traditional with new – a fine example of the best neo-classical cuisine. There's a no-choice *RQP* menu a (lunch) – but go, instead, for low-end menu C (three-way choice each course). Two sharp memories: *croustillant de saumon* (so succulent) & mouthwatering *île flottante au miel d'acacia*.
Menus a(lun)CD. Cards All. (Rooms: Aub. de la Source, Trémont-s-Saulx.)
Closed 26 Dec-2 Jan. 4-11 Mar. 28 July-19 Aug. Sun evg. Mon. (Above SE.)
Post 7 r. A. Maginot, 55800 Revigny-s-Ornain, Meuse. Region Champ-Ard.
Tel 03 29 70 56 00. Fax 03 29 70 59 30. Mich 39/E3. Map 3. (D994 road.)

RIOM   Moulin de Villeroze

Comfortable restaurant/Cooking 2 `FW`
Terrace/Parking

A colourful, inviting dining room creates a welcoming first impression. Neo-classical *plats* from chef Dominique Juvigny with a 3-way choice for each course on menu B (top-end). Two fish dishes were aromatic winners: *mesclun de rouget et jus au vin de Graves* & *escalopes de sandre et compote d'oignons*. Hard to find: use D83 to SW; just N of D446 bypass.
Menus BCE. Cards All. (Rooms: Mikégé, in Riom; 3kn NE; garage.)
Closed 1-15 Aug. Sun evg. Mon.
Post rte de Marsat, 63200 Riom, Puy-de-Dôme. Region MC (Auvergne).
Tel 04 73 38 58 23. Fax 04 73 38 92 26. Mich 113/D1. Map 5.

A100frs & under. B100–150. C150–200. D200–250. E250–350. F350–500. G500+

RIQUEWIHR   Couronne

Comfortable hotel (no restaurant)
Quiet/Parking

A lemon-hued exterior at the character 16thC Couronne; the interior is chock-a-block full of sturdy beams. There's no shortage, however, of modern amenities. Danielle Claudel is a delightful, English-speaking *patronne*. The hotel is within the walls of the picture-book pretty medieval village, S of the Riquewihr main *rue* (Gén.-de-Gaulle). (Seek out the Beauvillé textile factory; D416 W exit from Ribeauvillé.)
Rooms (37) EFG. Cards All. (Some rooms have small kitchens.)
Post 5 r. de la Couronne, 68340 Riquewihr, Haut-Rhin. Region Alsace.
Tel 03 89 49 03 03. Fax 03 89 49 01 01. Mich 61/D3. Map 3.

RIQUEWIHR   Hôtel Le Schoenenbourg

Comfortable hotel (no restaurant)
Quiet/Gardens/Lift/Garage/Parking

The hotel's only debit is that the building is a touch too ultra modern. An elevated site at the foot of the famous Schoenenbourg vineyards & just outside the village. Note the name of the street (another nearby plus). More pluses? A gymnasium, sauna & solarium. The owner, Jacques Kiener, is the brother of François, the chef at the renowned Auberge du Schoenenbourg restaurant next door to the hotel.
Rooms (45) F(low-end)G. Disabled. Cards AE, MC, V.
Post r. Piscine, 68340 Riquewihr, Haut-Rhin. Region Alsace.
Tel 03 89 49 01 11. Fax 03 89 47 95 88. Mich 61/D3. Map 3.

RIQUEWIHR   Le Riquewihr

Comfortable hotel (no restaurant)
Lift/Parking

Perhaps the best of the village's base hotels: though the site is only fairly quiet the main benefit is that access is easy & parking is simple as pie. Newly-built & E of Riquewihr, facing the famous Schoenenbourg vineyards on the hillside to the N. Philippe Dubich's hotel has won a "thumbs-up" appreciation from readers over the years.
Rooms (49) E. Cards All.
Closed Feb.
Post rte Ribeauvillé, 68340 Riquewihr, Haut-Rhin. Reqion Alsace.
Tel 03 89 47 83 13. Fax 03 89 47 99 76. Mich 61/D3. Map 3.

A100frs & under. B100–150. C150–200. D200–250. E250–350. F350–500. G500+

ROANNE

Central

Simple restaurant/Cooking 2 FW

Face à la gare – like its owners' nearby home, the famed Troisgros rest.
Michel Troisgros (Pierre's son) & his wife Marie-Pierre opened their
stylish *"café-épicerie"* (you can buy all sorts of produce) in June 1995.
Ex-Troisgros staff run both *la cuisine et la salle*, supervised by M-P. An
open-plan kitchen is a novel touch. Regional/neo-classical/modern
styles – plus grills (*Charolais* beef *bien sûr*) from *la cheminée*.
Menus B(lunch)BC(dinner *à la carte*). Cards MC, V.
Closed 1-15 Aug. Sun. Mon *midi*. (Rooms: Terminus & Gd Hôtel; 50-100m.)
Post 20 cours République, 42300 Roanne, Loire. Region Lyonnais.
Tel 04 77 67 72 72. Fax 04 77 72 57 67. Mich 101/E4. Map 5.

ROANNE (Le Coteau)

Artaud

Comfortable hotel/Cooking 2-3 FW
Garage/Air-conditioning (restaurant)

Nicole & Alain (he's the 3rd-generation) Artaud's colourful small *logis* is
at Le Coteau (Loire's R bank; less busy than Roanne), 100m E of the
station. Authentic classical/*Lyonnaise* cooking: the *Menu du Terroir* (A)
is notable for an appetite-quenching *fricassée de volaille au vinaigre de
vin petites crêpes Parmentier* (small, addictive, potato pancakes).
Menus ACE(top-end). Rooms (25) EF. Cards AE, MC, V.
Closed Rest: 24 July-14 Aug. Sun (not *fêtes* days).
Post 133 av. Libération, 42120 Le Coteau, Loire. Region Lyonnais.
Tel 04 77 68 46 44. Fax 04 77 72 23 50. Mich 101/E4. Map 5.

ROANNE (Le Coteau)

Auberge Costelloise

Very comfortable restaurant/Cooking 3-4 FW
Air-conditioning

On the Loire's R bank, overlooking the bridge to Roanne. Terrific *RQP*.
Solange Alex runs the front of house; her chef husband Daniel conjures
up delicious modern & neo-classical delights. Evidence? From menu b
(4-way choice each course) saliva-stirring *gâteau de foies blonds au
coulis de langoustines* & *lapin rôti au Romarin* (a dream of a dish).
Menus bCEF. Cards AE, MC, V. (Rooms: Ibis; to SE, towards N7 bypass.)
Closed 2-10 Jan. 15 Aug-4 Sept. Sun. Mon.
Post 2 av. Libération, 42120 Le Coteau, Loire. Region Lyonnais.
Tel 04 77 68 12 71. Fax 04 77 72 26 78. Mich 101/E4. Map 5.

A 100frs & under. B 100–150. C 150–200. D 200–250. E 250–350. F 350–500. G 500+

ROANNE (Renaison)   Jacques-Coeur

Comfortable restaurant with rooms/Cooking 2   FW

The *logis* is at the central x-roads (NE corner) of the small town of
Renaison, 12km W of Roanne. Pascaline Giraudon provides a warm
welcome; husband Jean-Yves steers a classical course – but with many,
breath-of-fresh-air, eclectic touches in his repertoire. Menu B pleased with
two flavoursome *plats* – *blanc de cabillaud rôti à l'oriental* & a hunky dory
saltimbocca de veau au craquelin de gruyère; a real mix of cooking pots.
Menus aBC. Rooms (8) DE. Cards MC, V. (Park in large *place*.)
Closed Mid Feb-mid Mar. Sun evg. Mon.
Post 42370 Renaison, Loire. Region Lyonnais.
Tel 04 77 64 25 34. Fax 04 77 64 43 88. Mich 101/D4. Map 5.

ROANNE (Villerest)   Château de Champlong

Comfortable restaurant/Cooking 3   FW
Terrace/Gardens/Parking

Villerest is 6km SW of Roanne; the 16thC château (impressive façade but
not on closer inspection) is on maps. Ignore the cosmetics; concentrate
instead on Véronique Boizet's welcome & her chef husband Olivier's
masterful modern/neo-classical creations. An authentic & brilliant
carpaccio de boeuf, vinaigrette tapenade et son toast à l'ail (menu B).
Menus BCDE. Cards AE, MC, V. (Rooms: Ibis; Le Coteau, Loire's R bank.)
Closed 1-21 Jan. Sun evg. Mon. (To reach above, use D56.)
Post rte Golf, 42300 Villerest, Loire. Region Lyonnais.
Tel 04 77 69 69 69. Fax 04 77 69 71 08. Mich 101/D4. Map 5.

ROCAMADOUR   Beau Site/Rest. Jehan de Valon

Very comfortable hotel/Cooking 2-3   FW
Terrace/Lift/Parking (limited)

A well-named site, halfway up the cliff-hanger medieval *cité*. Modern &
old apply to the two buildings (straddling the pedestrian-crowded road)
& to Christophe Besse's cooking. On one hand a melting *millefeuille de
truite rose à la crème de ciboulette*; on the other a belt-stretching
cuisse de canard confite à l'ancienne. Wide choice on menus.
Menus ABCDF. Rooms (44) EF. Cards All. (Cheaper rooms: Comp'Hostel.)
Closed 13 Nov-4 Feb. (Above *sans rest.* at L'Hospitalet, above village.)
Post 46500 Rocamadour, Lot. Region Dordogne.
Tel 05 65 33 63 08. Fax 05 65 33 65 23. Mich 124/C4. Map 5.

A 100frs & under. B 100–150. C 150–200. D 200–250. E 250–350. F 350–500. G 500+

ROCHEFORT

La Corderie Royale

Very comfortable hotel/Cooking 1-2 `FW`
Quiet/Terrace/Gardens/Swim pool/Lift/Parking/Air-cond. (rest.)

N of the renowned Corderie Royale & beside the R bank of the Charente. Bedrooms dear but menus b(lunch; bottom-end) & B provide *RQP* in swish surroundings. Wide choice on B. How about these classical/regional dishes: *mouclade au citron vert, dos de saumon sauce à l'américaine, jonchée du marais* (see cheeses) & *granité de pineau et fruits rouges.*
Menus b(see text)BC. Rooms (50) FG. Disabled. Cards All.
Closed 2-18 Feb. Sun evg (Oct-Easter). Rest: Mon. (Cheaper rooms: Ibis.)
Post r. Audebert, 17300 Rochefort, Char.-Mar. Reg. Poitou-Charentes.
Tel 05 46 99 35 35. Fax 05 46 99 78 72. Mich 106/B1-C1. Map 4.

ROCHEFORT

Escale de Bougainville

Very comfortable restaurant/Cooking 3 `FW`
Terrace/Air-conditioning

The spacious, airy dining room is on the ground floor of the modern Résidence Atlantica, overlooking a marina. Patrick Labouly welcomes you & chef Daniel Barret seduces with innovative modern & regional *plats*. Even menu B, simplicity itself, pleases: *minute de sardines demies-sel; morue fraîche à nôtre façon*; & *trilogie de desserts.*
Menus BCD. Cards MC, V. (Rooms: nearby Ibis; 250m walk.)
Closed Feb sch. hols. Sun evg. Mon. Region Poitou-Charentes.
Post quai Louisiane, 17300 Rochefort, Charente-Maritime.
Tel 05 46 99 54 99. Fax 05 46 99 54 99. Mich 106/B1-C1. Map 4.

ROCHEFORT

Tourne-Broche

Comfortable restaurant/Cooking 1-2 `FW`

Dina Klein & her husband, chef Jean, contrive to pull off a series of culinary rope tricks with no less than four menus. The two C menus (one ceiling) are largesse: *nos propositions du marché* offers you a wide choice for each course; a *dégustation* has 8 courses. Fish, shellfish, *grillades au feu de bois*, classical & regional alternatives provide the most varied options. Simpler grills on menus B (both bottom/top ends). Menus BC(both with bottom & top-ends). Cards AE. MC, V. (Rooms: Ibis.)
Closed 5-19 Jan. Sun evg. Mon. Region Poitou-Charentes.
Post 56 av. Ch. de Gaulle, 17300 Rochefort, Charente-Maritime.
Tel 05 46 99 20 19. Fax 05 46 99 72 06. Mich 106/B1-C1. Map 4.

A100frs & under. B100–150. C150–200. D200–250. E250–350. F350–500. G500+

ROCHEFORT (Soubise)   Le Soubise

Comfortable restaurant with rooms/Cooking 1-2   FW
Gardens/Parking

Lilyane Benoit retired in 1994, after working as a *cuisinière* for 40 years. New owner, Dennis Caudrelier, & his chef David Duban, have chosen to introduce a more modern/neo-classical repertoire – but still make clever use of *Charentais* produce. Typical signature dishes include *ris de veau aux gingembre et citron vert*. Try *jonchée*, a fresh cream cheese.
Menus ABC. Rooms (24) CDEF. Cards All. (Soubise 7km SW Rochefort.)
Closed 15 Jan-3 Feb. 14-28 Oct. Sun evg & Mon (not Jul/Aug & pub. hols.)
Post 17780 Soubise, Charente-Maritime. Region Poitou-Charentes.
Tel 05 46 84 92 16. Fax 05 46 84 91 35. Mich 106/B1. Map 4.

La ROCHE-L'ABEILLE   Moulin de la Gorce

Very comfortable hotel/Cooking 3-4
Secluded/Gardens/Parking

A preposterously pretty 16thC *moulin* with an *étang*, cascade & opulent bedrooms (tapestries, antiques, the indulgent lot). Of the two dining rooms readers do not like the modern version. Jean Bertranet's 90s repertoire is a mix of rich classical & neo-classical – putting his *terroir* produce to good use. One gripe: his wife Annie has little charm.
Menus CEF. Rooms (10) FG(top-end). Cards All. (E of D704.)
Closed 2 Jan-6 Feb. Sun evg & Mon (Oct-Mar).
Post 87800 La Roche-l'Abeille, Haute-Vienne. Regs Dordogne/Poit-Char.
Tel 05 55 00 70 66. Fax 05 55 00 76 57. Mich 110/B3. Map 5.

La ROCHELLE (also see next page)   Les Brises

Very comfortable hotel (no restaurant)
Secluded/Terrace/Lift/Garage/Parking

No road runs between the six-storey high hotel (ground floor plus five with 50 bedrooms) one km W of the famed port. Highlights are the south facing, sun-trap terrace & exhilarating sea views. Bedrooms overlooking the sea have balconies & superb bathrooms. From the terrace edge admire the view to the left of the port & its towers; better still go to the roof & soak in an even more terrific panorama – especially so at night.
Rooms (50) FG. Cards AE, MC, V. Region Poitou-Charentes.
Post ch. digue Richelieu (av.P.-Vincent), 17000 La Rochelle. Char.-Mar.
Tel 05 46 43 89 37. Fax 05 46 43 27 97. Mich 92/C3. Map 4.

A100frs & under. B100–150. C150–200. D200–250. E250–350. F350–500. G500+

279

La ROCHELLE (also see previous page)   Bistro de l'Entracte

Comfortable restaurant/Cooking 2-3   `FW`
Air-conditioning

L'Entracte is Michelin 2-star chef Richard Coutanceau's bistro (about
300m E from his rest.) A "theatre-programme" menu: four acts (starters,
fish, *viandes*, desserts) & you choose from three. Wide choice of modern,
classical & regional specialities like *mouclade, morue fraîche, faux-filet
grillée sauce Bordelaise* & *jonchée* (see Poitou-Charentes cheeses).
Menus B(top-end). Cards MC, V. (Rooms: see base hotels; also Majestic.)
Closed Sun. (Rest. easy to reach from W; park near Tour de la Lanterne.)
Post 22 r. St-Jean-du-Pérot, 17000 La Rochelle, Charente-Maritime.
Tel 05 46 50 62 60. Fax 05 46 41 99 45. Mich 92/C3. Map 4. Reg Poit-Ch.

La ROCHELLE   Richard Coutanceau

Luxury restaurant/Cooking 3-4
Air-conditioning

"Magnificent" sums up the site, beside a beach just W of the handsome
Tour de la Lanterne; the gorgeous sea views; & the *RQP* menu D (bottom-
end). Chef Richard, a small, friendly man, is a modern/neo-classical &
regional master; his sauces are superb. His wife Maryse, attractive &
elegant, is as down-to-earth as her husband. They do their *pays* proud.
Menus D(bottom-end)F. Cards All. (Parking easy. Rooms: see base hotels.)
Closed Sun. Region Poitou-Charentes. (See Les Brises; 2-min drive.)
Post plage de la Concurrence, 17000 La Rochelle, Charente-Maritime.
Tel 05 46 41 48 19. Fax 05 46 41 99 45. Mich 92/C3. Map 4.

La ROCHELLE   Le Rochelois

Simple hotel (no restaurant)
Swimming pool/Tennis/Lift/Garage/Parking

An unattractive, modern building, 500m W of Les Brises (see entry) &
with views of the sea. (Like Les Brises approach from the N237 bypass;
due S of airport.) The most useful appeal is that bedrooms don't cost the
earth & the hotel is well W of the busy town centre. Apart from the
facilities above the place is a veritable health club: gym, sauna, jacussi,
Turkish baths *et al*. Some family rooms with small kitchens.
Rooms (44) DEFG(low-end). Disabled. Cards MC, V. Region Poitou-Char.
Post 66 bd Winston Churchill, 17000 La Rochelle, Charente-Maritime.
Tel 05 46 43 34 34. Fax 05 46 42 10 37. Mich 92/C3. Map 4.

Les ROCHES-DE-CONDRIEU

Bellevue

Comfortable hotel/Cooking 1-2
Garage

FW

The highlights of the Bouron family hotel are the riverside views & the site on the Rhône's left bank. There's also a busy marina below the well-named Bellevue. On cool evenings a log fire crackles in *la salle*; less crackling is Jean Bouron's cast-in-stone classical fare – like *turbot braisée au champagne* & *entrecôte grillée au beurre d'échalotes*.
Menus a(lunch)BE. Rooms (16)DE. Cards All.
Closed 10 Feb-12 Mar. 22-28 Oct. Sun evg (Oct-Jan). Rest: Mon.
Post 38370 Les Roches-de-Condrieu, Isère. Region MC (Ardèche).
Tel 04 74 56 41 42. Fax 04 74 56 47 56. Mich 116/A4. Map 6.

RODEZ

Goûts et Couleurs

Simple restaurant/Cooking 2-3
Terrace

FW

Michel Bras (Laguiole) & the Fagegaltier sisters (Belcastel) urged me to try this fine rest. A tiny patio was the ideal lunch setting for a wide-choice menu B – modern, colourful cooking from Jean-Luc Fau (admire his paintings): a triumphant trio of *anchois frais marinés jus de poivron rouges, thon mi-cuit pané à la poudre d'ail* & *mousse choco b&n*.
Menus a(lunch)BCE. Cards AE, MC, V. (Rooms: Biney, short walk away.)
Closed 15 Jan-8 Feb. 10-21 Sept. Sun. Mon. (Rest. is NE of cathedral.)
Post 38 r. Bonald, 12000 Rodez, Aveyron. Region MC (Cévennes).
Tel 05 65 42 75 10. Fax 05 65 78 11 20. Mich 140/B2-C2. Map 5.

RODEZ (also see next page)

St-Amans

Comfortable restaurant/Cooking 2
Air-conditioning

FW

Jack Amat is fast approaching his 50th birthday. 30 years ago he won the coveted best apprentice chef in France award (& he had a 7-year stint at Taillevent). His polished skill shows in a classical & neo-classical repertoire: menu B could be *oeuf poché aux asperges; saumon poêlé aux algues; granité; filet de porc au citron vert; fromage*; and a dessert.
Menus BE. Cards MC, V. (Rooms: Tour Maje, adjacent to parking.)
Closed 10 Feb-10 Mar. Sun evg. Mon. (Above 220m walk to NW.)
Post 12 r. Madeleine, 12000 Rodez, Aveyron. Region MC (Cévennes).
Tel 05 65 68 03 18. Mich 140/B2-C2. Map 5. (Rest. 300-400m S cathedral.)

A100frs & under. B100–150. C150–200. D200–250. E250–350. F350–500. G500+

RODEZ (Olemps) (also see previous page)   **Les Peyrières**

Comfortable hotel/Cooking 2   FW
Quiet/Terrace/Swimming pool/Parking

A largish new hotel in a modern housing estate at Olemps, to the W of
both the N88 & Rodez. The word that comes to mind is "functional" – for
the anonymous building, public rooms & bedrooms. Philippe Panis offers
wide-choice classical menus. Menu B had 5 courses: highlights were *blanc
de plie à l'olivade* & *pavé de veau au fumet de morilles* (what an aroma).
Menus aBCE. Rooms (50) EF (bottom-end). Disabled. Cards AE, MC, V.
Closed Rest: Sun evg & Mon midday (not July/Aug).
Post 12510 Olemps, Aveyron. Region Massif Central (Cévennes).
Tel 05 65 68 20 52. Fax 05 65 68 20 52. Mich 140/B2-C2. Map 5.

ROGNES   **Les Olivarelles**

Comfortable restaurant/Cooking 2-3   FW
Terrace/Gardens/Parking

Hard to find: 6km NW (use D66, D66D; just R of words Caire-Val on
maps). Small, modern villa lost in attractive terrain. How do Paul & Eliane
Dietrich survive? Well – with Paul's classical/neo-classical/Provençale
cuisine providing the answers: *poitrine de pintade, terrine de homard* &
mouthwatering *jambon chaud à l'estragon* – just 3 of his canny clues.
Menus aCDEF. Cards MC, V. (Rooms: Mas de Livany; La Roque d'Anthéron.)
Closed Sun evg & Mon (not pub. hols). (Above short, easy drive N.)
Post 13840 Rognes, Bouches-du-Rhône. Region Provence.
Tel 04 42 50 24 27. Fax 04 42 50 17 99. Mich 159/D2. Map 6.

ROHAN   **L'Eau d'Oust**

Comfortable restaurant/Cooking 2
Terrace

The simple stone building, once an old barn, overlooks a small lake,
wooded park & the Brest-Nantes canal. Delicious classical offerings. Menu
B (top-end) includes two choices for each of three courses: *terrine de foie
gras de canard maison; escalope de saumon moutarde à l'ancienne;* &
nougat glacé et son coulis de fruits was a well-balanced meal.
Menus aBCD. Cards AE, MC, V. (Rooms: France, Loudéac.)
Closed Feb sch. hols. Sun evg. Mon. (Above 13km to N.)
Post rte de Loudéac, 56580 Rohan, Morbihan. Region Brittany.
Tel 02 97 38 91 86. Mich 47/D2. Map 1.

A100frs & under. B100–150. C150–200. D200–250. E250–350. F350–500. G500+

ROMORANTIN-LANTHENAY   Grand Hôtel Lion d'Or

Luxury hotel/Cooking 4
Terrace/Lift/Parking/Air-conditioning (restaurant)

A talented family is the heart & soul of this exquisite hotel: Colette & Alain Barrat; their gifted daughter Marie-Christine & her husband Didier Clément (the happiest of marriages). Didier, now 40, has matured into a confident, full-of-good-taste, creative modern chef. Fish/shellfish creations are 3-star wonders. Superb shaded indoor courtyard. (Most *àlc* dishes can be "shared": use this formula for band E meals per person.)
Menus FG. Rooms (13) G,G2,G3. Dis'd. Cards All. Closed 15 Feb-15 Mar.
Post 69 r. Clemenceau, 41200 Romorantin-L, Loir-et-Cher. Region Loire.
Tel 02 54 94 15 15. Fax 02 54 88 24 87. Mich 69/D4. Map 2.

ROMORANTIN-LANTHENAY   Le Lanthenay

Comfortable restaurant with rooms/Cooking 3   `FW`
Quiet/Gardens

100m W of the D922, by Lanthenay *église*. A family *logis*: Philippe Valin is *le cuisinier*, a classical master; brother-in-law Michel Talmon is *le sommelier*; his sister, Evelyne (PV's wife), & his wife, Martine, run *la salle* with him. High-class *RQP* even on menu a: how about *assiette de poisson crus* & *fumés, fricassée de poulet* & *tarte fine aux pommes*?
Menus aCDE. Rooms (10)E. Cards All. (Parking easy across road.)
Closed 21 Dec-14 Jan. 14-29 July. Sun evg. Mon.
Post Lanthenay, 41200 Romorantin-Lanthenay, Loir-et-Cher. Region Loire.
Tel 02 54 76 09 19. Fax 02 54 76 72 91. Mich 69/D4. Map 2.

La ROQUE-GAGEAC (also see next page)   Belle Etoile

Comfortable hotel/Cooking 1-2   `FW`
Terrace/Garage/Air-conditioning (restaurant)

Guy & chef Regis Ongaro's *logis* has a fabulous Dordogne-side site. The first-floor terrace is a cool haven for summer lunches. Plenty of choice but no little extras. A typical menu could be a drooling *ballotine de canard au foie gras et sa salade*, a *magret de canard sauce citron, cabécou de Rocamadour* & a "so-so" *crème brûlée à la cassonade*.
Menus BCDE. Rooms (17) E. Cards AE, MC, V.
Closed Mid Oct-Mar. Rest: Mon (Mar-June).
Post 24250 La Roque-Gageac, Dordogne. Region Dordogne.
Tel 05 53 29 51 44. Fax 05 53 29 45 63. Mich 124/A3. Map 5.

A100frs & under. B100–150. C150–200. D200–250. E250–350. F350–500. G500+

La ROQUE-GAGEAC (also see previous page)   Plume d'Oie

Comfortable restaurant with rooms/Cooking 3-4

What a happy & exhilarating surprise our visit proved to be. *La patronne* is Biddy – an involved, friendly, multi-lingual Dutch lady; husband Marc-Pierre Walker, an Englishman, is a confident, inventive *cuisinier* – a quiet, unassuming chef, brimful of modern & neo-classical creative ideas. The enjoyment factor is sky-high. The use of vegetables, varying flavours & desserts are all brilliantly done. Where's the star Michelin?
Menus CEF. Rooms (4) F(bottom-end). Cards MC, V.
Closed Feb. Rest: Sat *midi* & Mon *midi* (Jul/Au). Sun evg & Mon (Sep-Jun).
Post 24250 La Roque-Gageac, Dordogne. Region Dordogne.
Tel 05 53 29 57 05. Fax 05 53 31 04 81. Mich 124/A3. Map 5.

ROSCOFF   Le Temps de Vivre

Very comfortable restaurant/Cooking 3   FW

Don't miss one of Brittany's most creative chefs: Jean-Yves Crenn had stints in several superstar chefs' kitchens, including Robuchon/Bardet. J-Y is a modern master, capitalising cleverly on Finistère's rich & varied larder. Simple, complex & robust sit cheek by jowl. Evidence? *Langoustines poêlées, asperges, artichaut et jambon maison*; & a *museau de cochon farci* are both star-winning, good-taste stunners.
Menus bCDEF. Cards AE, MC, V. (Rooms: adjacent Ibis.)
Closed Feb & Nov sch. hols. Sun evg (not July/Aug). Mon.
Post pl. Eglise, 29680 Roscoff, Finistère. Region Brittany.
Tel 02 98 61 27 28. Fax 02 98 61 27 28. Mich 27/D1. Map 1.

Les ROSIERS-SUR-LOIRE   La Toque Blanche

Very comfortable restaurant/Cooking 2   FW
Parking/Air-conditioning

What a super show: an airy, elegant dining room overlooking both the Loire & a tiny garden-patio; a pleasant welcome from Françoise Klein; & equally pleasant & elegantly presented neo-classical/regional offerings from her chef/husband Gilles. A lunchtime *mousse de rouget et gâteau de brochet* & *filet de sandre au beurre blanc* got our thumbs-up approval.
Menus BCD. Cards MC, V. (Rooms: Ducs d'Anjou; quiet & *sans rest*.)
Closed Tues evg. Wed. (Above is annexe of Jeanne de Laval rest.)
Post rte Angers, 49350 Les Rosiers-sur-Loire, Maine-et-Loire.
Tel 02 41 51 80 75. Fax 02 41 38 06 38. Mich 66/B4. Map 2. Region Loire.

A100frs & under. B100–150. C150–200. D200–250. E250–350. F350–500. G500+

La ROTHIERE

Auberge de la Plaine

Simple restaurant with rooms/Cooking 1
Terrace/Parking

A modest *Logis de France*, in a lonely site alongside the D396, 6km S of
Brienne-le-Château. The Galton family, led by Jean-Pierre the chef, have
been at La Rothière almost 30 years; the bedrooms & new dining room
were built at the start of the 80s. *Bourgeoise*/classical cooking &
appetite-quenching grills. Bravo, too, for several welcome fish dishes.
Menus aBCDE. Rooms (18) CDE. Cards All.
Closed Fri (Oct-Mar). Rest: 2-20 Jan. Fri evg & Sat midday (Oct-Mar).
Post La Rothière, 10500 Brienne-le-Château, Aube. Region Champ-Ard.
Tel 03 25 92 21 79. Fax 03 25 92 26 16. Mich 57/D2. Map 3.

ROUDOUALLEC

Bienvenue

Simple restaurant/Cooking 2-3   FW
Parking

Don't be fooled by the run-of-the-mill, dour exterior; the airy, cool
dining room is a refreshing pleasure (the turquoise wall covering is
English). Refined neo-classical cuisine from Jean-Claude Spégagne.
Some fizzing specialities: *langoustines géantes grillées flambées au
whisky*: & *filet de boeuf au foie gras et vieux porto* are two firecrackers.
Menus ACDE. Cards MC, V. (Rooms: Relais de Cornouaille – see next line.)
Closed Feb sch hols. Mon. (At Châteauneuf-du-Faou; easy drive NW.)
Post 56110 Roudouallec, Morbihan. Region Brittany.
Tel 02 97 34 50 01. Mich 45/E1. Map 1.

ROUFFACH (also see next page)

A la Ville de Lyon/
Rest. Philippe Bohrer

Simple hotel & very comfortable restaurant/Cooking 3   FW
Terrace & Lift (hotel)/Parking/Air-conditioning (restaurant)

Two adjacent buildings (not the most attractive of hotels). Attentive
service from young waitresses. Neo-classical offerings from chef PB: a
sensuous *sandre rôti au gewürztraminer*; flavoursome *blanc de volaille
aux senteurs des Mascareignes* & a saliva-stirring *terrine de quetsches
et sa glace cannelle*. Cheaper Chez Julien *winstub* (wine bar: rating 1-2)
Menus bCEF. Rooms (43) EF. Cards All. (Nicer, quieter hotel?)
Closed 26 Feb-17 Mar. Rest: Mon. (See next entry & also Herrlisheim.)
Post r. Poincaré, 68250 Rouffach, Haut-Rhin. Region Alsace. Mich 61/D4.
Tel (H) 03 89 49 65 51. (R) 03 89 49 62 49. Fax 03 89 49 76 67. Map 3.

A100frs & under. B100–150. C150–200. D200–250. E250–350. F350–500. G500+

ROUFFACH (Bollenberg) (also see pevious page)   **Bollenberg**

Simple hotel (no restaurant)
Secluded/Gardens/Parking

Start the climb to this dead-end hamlet from the D18B (SW of
Rouffach). Up through vineyards to a collection of houses (hotel; Vieux
Pressoir rest; & the Clos Ste-Apolline *cave*). The *logis* is straightforward
enough – with first-class gym & *bains bouillonnants* (whirlpool); but
whether you eat or not at the Vieux Pressoir restaurant across the road,
under no account must you fail to see the eccentric over-the-top interior.
Rooms (45) EF(bottom-end). Cards All.
Post Bollenberg, 68250 Rouffach, Haut-Rhin. Region Alsace.
Tel 03 89 49 62 47. Fax 03 89 49 77 66. Mich 61/D4. Map 3.

Les ROUSSES   Arbez Franco-Suisse

Comfortable restaurant with rooms/Cooking 1-2
Terrace/Parking

At La Cure, SE of Les Rousses, literally on the Franco-Suisse border.
Indeed, if you want to avoid customs walk from the front entrance to the
back (the rest. has both French & Swiss addresses). Bernard Arbez is no
mean chef: dig into tummy-filling classical/regional grub like *truite
meunière aux amandes, civet de porc au romarin* & *saucisse de Morteau*.
Menus BCD. Rooms (10) E. Cards MC, V.
Closed 15-30 Nov. Mon evg & Tues (May/June/Oct). Region Jura.
Post La Cure, 39220 Les Rousses, Jura. (Also CH1265 La Cure, Suisse.)
Tel 03 84 60 02 20. Fax 03 84 60 08 59. Mich 104/B1. Map 6.

Les ROUSSES   France

Very comfortable hotel/Cooking 3   **FW**
Terrace/Parking

Madame Petit, a welcoming *patronne*, aided by chef Jean-Pierre Ducrot
– for so long at Roger Petit's right hand – continues the neo-classical &
classical traditions of her late husband. The wood panelling of both the
lounge & *la salle* is warm & welcoming (the mountain chalet-hotel in
the centre of the resort is 1100m above sea-level). Plenty of half-bottles.
Menus B(top-end)DEF. Rooms (32) FG. Cards All.
Closed 9-27 June. 18 Nov-13 Dec.
Post 39220 Les Rousses, Jura. Region Jura.
Tel 03 84 60 01 45. Fax 03 84 60 04 63. Mich 104/B1. Map 6.

A100frs & under. B100–150. C150–200. D200–250. E250–350. F350–500. G500+

ROUSSILLON

David

Comfortable restaurant/Cooking 1-2
Terrace

Jean David's restaurant sits atop one of the pupil-piercing red & ochre cliffs which make the village so colourfully renowned. You cannot quite claim the same for chef Georges Mazzolini's cooking, a mix of classical, Provençale & *Bourgeoise*. Tuck into treats of the *paillardise de veau à la sauge* & *cassolette de rascasse au safran* variety.
Menus bCE. Cards DC, MC, V. (Rooms: see next entry.)
Closed 21 Nov-19 Mar. Mon (not pub. hols).
Post pl. Poste, 84220 Roussillon, Vaucluse. Region Provence.
Tel 04 90 05 60 13. Fax 04 90 05 75 80. Mich 159/D1. Map 6.

ROUSSILLON

Résidence des Ocres

Simple hotel (no restaurant)
Quiet/Garage/Parking/Air-conditioning

Outside the village & close to the red & ochre cliffs which make the village such a spectacular technicolour extravaganza. Apart from the facilities there's another which is even more worthwhile: bedroom prices, for this neck of the woods, are reasonable. Rose-Marie & Jean-Louis Torregrossa's base is handy for nearby recommended restaurants.
Rooms (16) EF(low-end). Cards MC, V.
Closed 10 Jan-15 Feb. 15 Nov-23 Dec.
Post rte de Gordes, 84220 Roussillon, Vaucluse. Region Provence.
Tel 04 90 05 60 50. Fax 04 90 05 73 06. Mich 159/D1. Map 6.

ROUTOT

L'Ecurie

Comfortable restaurant/Cooking 2-3

FW

Danièlle & Jacques Thierry are a delightful, ambitious couple. Great dining room (not the *écurie* – stable – which is used for large parties) & equally stylish menus, a roll-call of sumptuous classical dishes. Try these for size: *les rouelles de lapereau tièdes, vinaigrette au jus de truffe; trois terrines maison; canard de Duclair façon Ecurie;* Normandy cheeses (cream/cream/scream!); & *charlotte au chocolate crème au café.*
Menus b(bottom-end)CD. Cards MC, V. (Rooms: see Normotel, Caudebec.)
Closed 1-7 Jan. Feb sch. hols. 28 July-4 Aug. Sun evg. Mon. Wed evg.
Post 27350 Routot, Eure. Region Normandy. (Caudebec is 20km to N.)
Tel 02 32 57 30 30. Mich 15/E4. Map 2. (Park in huge *place* opp. rest.)

A100frs & under. B100–150. C150–200. D200–250. E250–350. F350–500. G500+

ROYAN

Trois Marmites

Very comfortable restaurant/Cooking 2
Terrace

An intimate dining room with English-style furniture – & a small, but colourful garden. Charming welcome from Monique Verzura & polished classical cooking from Guy Boudreault. Excellent choice on Menu B: *bisque de homard, agneau poêlè à l'estragon,* cheese & *crêpes flambées* is one perm. (D141ES; behind *Sapeurs-Pompiers*; 500m N of *Marché Central.*)
Menus BCD. Cards All. (Rooms: Pasteur, SE of *Marché Central.*)
Closed Sun evg & Mon (Oct-June; but not sch. hols).
Post 37 av. Ch. Regazzoni, 17200 Royan, Charente-Maritime.
Tel 05 46 38 66 31. Mich 106/B2. Map 4. Region Poitou-Charentes.

ROYAT (Chamalières)

Radio

Very comfortable hotel/Cooking 3
Quiet/Gardens/Lift/Parking/Air-conditioning (restaurant)

Awkwardly-styled hotel with a high-ceilinged art deco interior. Yvette Mioche is still in place, a delightful hostess. Husband Michel, once a volcanic neo-classical talent, is not now tuned-in to his old waveband; he leaves the cooking to younger lieutenants. Same style with clever use made of *lentilles vertes du Puy* – in both fish & *ris de veau plats*.
Menus cDEF. Rooms (25)EFG. Cards All. (Cheaper rooms: see Ceyrat.)
Closed Jan. Rest: Sun (not midday in winter). Mon (not evgs in summer).
Post 43 av. P.-Curie, 63400 Chamalières, Puy-de-Dôme. Region MC (Auv).
Tel 04 73 30 87 83. Fax 04 73 36 42 44. Mich 113/D2. Map 5. (Near *gare.*)

ROYE

Central et Restaurant Florentin

Comfortable restaurant with rooms/Cooking 2

A smart-looking, modern spot in the centre of the town (near the huge place H. de Ville). The dining room, with garish neo-classical pillars & murals, is much too crowded for comfort. Chef Denis Devaux does a competent classical/regional cuisine job: enjoy, from a wide choice for each course on menu B, *tourteau froid mayonnaise*; gutsy *coq au vin*; cheese; & a filling, intense *gâteau au chocolat* (a typical selection).
Menus aBD. Rooms (8) DE. Cards All.
Closed 23 Dec-5 Jan. 18-31 Aug. Sun evg. Mon.
Post 36 r. Amiens, 80700 Roye, Somme. Region North.
Tel 03 22 87 11 05. Fax 03 22 87 42 74. Mich 18/B2. Map 2.

A100frs & under. B100–150. C150–200. D200–250. E250–350. F350–500. G500+

ROYE
La Flamiche

Very comfortable restaurant/Cooking 3-4 | FW |

An astonishing transformation. Marie-Christine Klopp (her father's name &
the chef who started the business) got fed up with cooks coming & going;
so 3 years ago she decided to have a go herself! She has worked wonders
– with modern, creative specialities which make you drool. Husband
Gérard Borck, with a young team, masterminds the front of house in his
usual smiling manner. Treasure-chest *cave*. (Rooms: Les Lions.)
Menus b(inc' Sat *midi*)CEFG. Cards All. (Above hotel E side A1 exit 12.)
Closed 21 Dec-13 Jan. 8-14 July. Sun evg Mon. (Park in *place* opp. rest.)
Post pl. H. de Ville, 80700 Roye, Somme. Region North.
Tel 03 22 87 00 56. Fax 03 22 78 46 77. Mich 18/B2. Map 2.

Le ROZIER
Grand Hôtel Muse et Rozier

Very comfortable hotel/Cooking 1
Secluded/Terrace/Gardens/Swimming pool/Parking

A striking, ultra-modern structure (rebuilt in 1982, after a 1979 fire),
squeezed between the Tarn & D907. The spectacular wooded, riverside
site catches the eye; at night clever lighting illuminates the rejuvenating
scene. Cooking? No bright lights here alas, just a basic 1 rating: grills &
both classical & neo-classical fare with little choice.
Menus B(lunch)CD. Rooms (35) FG. Cards All.
Closed Mid Nov-mid Mar.
Post à la Muse, 12720 Peyreleau, Aveyron. Region MC (Cévennes).
Tel 05 65 62 60 01. Fax 05 65 62 63 88. Mich 141/E3. Map 5.

RUGY
La Bergerie

Comfortable hotel/Cooking 1
Quiet/Terrace/Gardens/Parking

Convenience & a quiet site are the prime benefits. Leave the A4 at the
Argancy/Ennery exit 37, just E of the River Moselle; Rugy is to the N. La
Bergerie (sheepfold) is, in part, a 16thC farmhouse; most bedrooms are in a
single storey modern annexe. "Traditional" cooking – classical & *Bourgeoise*.
Michel & Michèle Keichinger are highly regarded by readers – though
celebration parties can tarnish the *Relais du Silence* claim.
Menus bCD. Rooms (48) EF. Disabled. Cards MC, V.
Post Rugy, 57640 Argancy, Moselle. Regions Alsace/Champagne-Ardenne.
Tel 03 87 77 82 27. Fax 03 87 77 87 07. Mich 24/B3. Map 3.

A100frs & under. B100–150. C150–200. D200–250. E250–350. F350–500. G 500+

RUMILLY

L'Améthyste

Comfortable restaurant/Cooking 2-3
Air-conditioning

FW

Julien Valéro, a modern chef, was once a student of glamour-puss Marc Veyrat (near Annecy). JV's invention shows – though not in a *noisette de thon au curry*. Better successes are *cuisse de lapereau au jus de thyme* & a cleverly-executed strawberry dessert (*duo chaud-froid*). Irène Valéro is *la patronne*. (Rest. easily found: enter from N; on R before bridge.)
Menus ABCDEF. Cards MC, V. (Rooms: Relais du Clergeon; Moye.)
Closed 26 July-15 Aug. Sun evg. Mon evg. (Above quiet; 4km NW.)
Post 27 r. Pont-Neuf, 74150 Rumilly, Haute-Savoie. Region Savoie.
Tel 04 50 01 02 52. Mich 118/A1. Map 6. (Good cooking at the Relais.)

Les SABLES-D'OLONNE

Beau Rivage

Very comfortable restaurant with rooms (see text)/Cooking 3

Overlooking Le Remblai, the resort's fine sand beach, the Beau Rivage has won many readers' plaudits since I first recommended Jean Drapeau & his classical/neo-classical cooking in the early 80s. He capitalises brilliantly on piscatorial and *terroir* harvests: Limousin beef & veal are especially good. (Bedrooms: I'm not happy about what would happen in the event of a fire. Use the nearby Alizé Hôtel; cheaper rooms too.)
Menus cEF. Rooms (11) F. Cards All. Region Poitou-Charentes.
Closed Jan. 29 Sept-9 Oct. Sun evg & Mon (Oct-May; not pub. hols).
Post 40 prom. G.Clemenceau, 85100 Les Sables-d'Olonne, Vendée.
Tel 02 51 32 03 01. Fax 02 51 32 46 48. Mich 92/A1. Map 4.

SABLES-D'OR-LES-PINS

Voile d'Or/La Lagune

Comfortable hotel/Cooking 1-2
Gardens/Parking

FW

No views of the open sea from the *logis* but overlooking a small inlet & 400m from the famed sands. Théo Orio, wisely, capitalises on the rich bounty trawled from the seas, putting it to good use in a range of classical dishes: *palourdes ou praires farcies à l'orange et aux amandes* & *escalope de lieu jaune sauce agrume* feature on menu B (huge choice).
Menus aBCDEF. Rooms (26) EF. Disabled. Cards MC, V.
Closed Mid Nov-mid Mar. Mon & Tues midday (Oct).
Post Sables-d'Or-les-Pins, 22240 Fréhel, Côtes d'Armor. Region Brittany.
Tel 02 96 41 42 49. Fax 02 96 41 55 45. Mich 29/E2. Map 1.

SABRES

Auberge des Pins

Comfortable hotel/Cooking 2
Quiet/Terrace/Gardens/Parking

A Landaise flower-strewn, chalet-style *maison* surrounded by pines – a mini Landes scene. Rooms in the newer building are a better bet. Michel Lesclauze is an imaginative neo-classical/regional chef – profiting from his *terroir*: enjoy *la salle* with its old furniture & relish delights like *foie gras de canard* & *filets de rouget et langoustines rôties*.
Menus aCDF. Rooms (23)EFG. Disabled. Cards MC, V.
Closed 1-21 Jan. Sun evg Mon. (Near town's *piscine*.)
Post 40630 Sabres, Landes. Region Southwest.
Tel 05 58 07 50 47. Fax 05 58 07 56 74. Mich 134/C3. Map 4.

ST-AFFRIQUE

Moderne

Comfortable hotel & very simple annexe/Cooking 2

FW

A considerable favourite with readers over the years. Built in 1970, the *logis* lives up to its modern-day name as the place has been extensively refurbished & painted up a treat; the interior is a permanent art exhibition. Jean-François Decuq does the brush work front of house; brother Yves mixes the colours in the kitchen. Classical & regional canvases with Roquefort (down the road) popping up all over the show.
Menus ABCE. Rooms (28) DEF. Annexe (18) ABC. Cards AE, MC, V.
Closed 20 Dec-20 Jan. Rest: 7-13 Oct. Region MC (Cévennes).
Post 54 av. A.-Pezet, 12400 St-Affrique, Aveyron. Mich 155/D1.
Tel 05 65 49 20 44. Annexe 05 65 99 07 24. Fax 05 65 49 36 55. Map 5.

ST-ALBAN-DE-MONTBEL (also see next page) Novalaise-Plage

Comfortable hotel/Cooking 1-2
Quiet/Terrace/Gardens/Lake swimming/Parking

FW

At Novalaise-Lac, a few km N of St-Alban, close to A43 exit 11. Plage is just that: with its own beach & between the road & Lac d'Aiguebelette. The terrace provides super lake & mountain views. Christiane Bergier is a helpful *patronne*. Classical & *Bourgeoise* fare: the best catches are *friture de lac, truite rosée* & *filet de lavaret au beurre blanc*.
Menus aBC. Rooms (10) E. Cards MC, V. (On W bank of lake.)
Closed Oct-Mar. Tues (not mid June-Aug).
Post 73470 Novalaise-Lac, Savoie. Region Savoie.
Tel 04 79 36 02 19. Fax 04 79 36 04 22. Mich 117/E3. Map 6.

A100frs & under. B100–150. C150–200. D200–250. E250–350. F350–500. G500+

ST-ALBAN-DE-MONTBEL (see previous page)   St-Alban-Plage

Simple hotel (no restaurant)
Quiet/Gardens/Lake swimming/Parking

A hatful of reasons for seeking out this delectable base: ease of access
from the A43; the tranquil setting alongside Lac d'Aiguebelette; the
invigorating views of lake (the warmest in France) & mountains; the
hotel (two buildings) between the road & water (with its own beach);
and, finally, the delectable English-speaking owner, Jeanine Duport.
Rooms (16) DEF. Cards MC, V. (NE of village; W bank of lake.)
Closed Nov-Easter.
Post 73610 St-Alban-de-Montbel, Savoie. Region Savoie.
Tel 04 79 36 02 05. Fax 04 79 44 10 37. Mich 117/E3. Map 6.

ST-AMAND-MONTROND   Boeuf Couronné

Simple restaurant/Cooking 1-2   FW
Parking

Three dining rooms in this small restaurant at a busy junction NW of the
town. A Grand Canyon wide choice of dishes is a most welcome feature.
Menu B has 6 starters, 4 main courses & 11 desserts. Typical classical &
Bourgeoise bounty could include nuggets like *saumon fumé* (home-
made), filling *faux filet grillé sauce Béarnaise* & *crème caramel*.
Menus AB. Cards MC, V. (Rooms: Le Noirlac, 2km to NW; beside N144.)
Closed 2-23 Jan. Tues evg. Wed. Region Berry-Bourbonnais.
Post 86 r. Juranville, 18200 St-Amand-Montrond, Cher.
Tel 02 48 96 42 72. Fax 02 48 96 33 80. Mich 84/C4. Map 2.

ST-ANTHEME   Pont de Raffiny

Simple hotel/Cooking 2   FW
Parking

Alain Beaudoux has to try so much harder at this remote *logis* 5½km S of
St-Anthème. Modernised bedrooms & an unusual dining room with
fountain & small pool; ask, too, to see the unusual *salon*. Classical fare:
civet de sanglier sauce Grand Marnier, pavé de boeuf au poivre & *rable
de lièvre aux pâtes fraîches* will stop your tummy rumbling for days.
Menus aBC. Rooms (12) CD. Cards MC, V.
Closed Jan-mid Feb. Sun evg & Mon (Sept-mid June).
Post Raffiny, 63360 St-Romain, Puy-de-Dôme. Region MC (Auvergne).
Tel 04 73 95 49 10. Fax 04 73 95 80 21. Mich 114/C3. Map 5.

A100frs & under. B100-150. C150-200. D200-250. E250-350. F350-500. G500+

ST-AVOLD

Europe

Comfortable hotel/Cooking 2-3
Terrace/Lift/Garage/Parking

FW

Easily found: S from A4 exit 39; L after Novotel; R at T; under N3; hotel on right, opp. supermarket. Pity about the view. Charlotte & Eugène Zirn provide bags of compensation at their modern hotel. He drives modern/regional/traditional routes: *jarret de porc sur choucroute nouvelle* & *escalope de saumon à la crème de ciboulette* are typical.
Menus BCDE. Rooms (34) E. Cards AE, MC, V.
Closed Rest: Sat midday. Sun.
Post 7 r. Altmayer, 57500 St-Avold, Moselle. Region Alsace.
Tel 03 87 92 00 33. Fax 03 87 92 01 23. Mich 41/F1. Map 3.

ST-BENOIT

Chalet de Venise

Very comfortable restaurant with rooms/Cooking 2-3
Quiet/Terrace/Gardens/Parking

FW

Do not be misled by the somewhat scruffy exterior & the touch over-the-top interior. A cool garden, shaded by 100-year-old trees, terrace & metre-wide River Miosson are the outside eye-catchers. Inside, Margaret & chef Serge Mautret beguile with appealing modern & regional cooking: witness an unusual *lapin risolle et son jus de vieux Pineau* (a smasher).
Menus b(lun)CDE. Rooms (12) EF. Cards All. (S Poitiers bypass; W D741.)
Closed Rest: 16 Feb-4 Mar. 25 Aug-2 Se. Sun evg. Mon. (D88 from bypass.)
Post r. Square, 86280 St-Benoît, Vienne. Region Poitou-Charentes.
Tel 05 49 88 45 07. Fax 05 49 52 95 44. Mich 95/E1. Map 5.

ST-BENOIT-SUR-LOIRE

Labrador

Simple hotel (no restaurant)
Quiet/Gardens/Parking

Like Le Thouarsais in Bourgueil, bedroom prices at this simple hotel are not outrageous. From the front door you have a superb view of the belfry porch at the great basilica. Be certain to enjoy the Romanesque abbey – & especially the famed Gregorian chants. Don't miss the small church at Germigny-des-Prés (NW); the tiny mosaic roof is a jewel.
Rooms (45) CDE. Disabled. Cards AE, MC, V.
Closed Jan-mid Feb.
Post 45730 St-Benoît-sur-Loire, Loiret. Region Loire.
Tel 02 38 35 74 38. Fax 02 38 35 72 99. Mich 70/A2. Map 2.

A100frs & under. B100–150. C150–200. D200–250. E250–350. F350–500. G500+

ST-BONNET-LE-FROID
Auberge des Cimes

Very comfortable restaurant with rooms/Cooking 4
Secluded (annexe)/Gardens/Parking/Air-cond. (rest)

No chef & no kitchen brigade work harder anywhere in France. Exuberant, modern cooking, highly creative & full of involved detail. Chef Régis Marcon, an English speaker, is a happy, contented family man (now 40); his idiosyncratic, imaginative style makes clever use of his *terroir*. Super new 12-room annexe (Clos des Cimes) with glorious views. Go!
Menus bDEF. Rooms (18) F(Auberge)G(Clos des Cimes). Cards MC, V.
Closed Mid Nov-Easter. Sun evg & Mon (not July/Aug).
Post 43290 St-Bonnet-le-Froid, Haute-Loire. Region MC (Ardèche).
Tel 04 71 59 93 72. Fax 04 71 59 93 40. Mich 129/E2. Map 6.

ST-CAST-LE-GUILDO
Le Biniou

Comfortable restaurant/Cooking 2 FW
Parking

Panoramic view of the sea from the smart modern Breton "bagpipe". Yvette & Jean-Claude Menard are the pipers at "Le Biniou". They squeeze the best from the Armor's piscatorial harvests – which dominate the menus: oysters, mussels, *soupe de poissons aux étrilles, filet de lieu, terrine de poissons, maquereaux, saumon et al*. Who needs to eat meat here?
Menus a(lunch)BCD. Cards MC, V. (Rooms: Dunes & Bon Abri.)
Closed 12 Nov-14 Feb. Tues (mid Sept-mid June but not sch. hols.)
Post à Pen-Guen, 22380 St-Cast-le-Guildo, Côtes d'Armor. (S of St-Cast.)
Tel 02 96 41 94 53. Mich 29/E2. Map 1. Region Brittany.

ST-CERE
France

Comfortable hotel/Cooking 2 FW
Terrace/Gardens/Swimming pool/Closed parking

A modern *logis*, away from St-Céré's busy centre, with spacious lounges, dining room & shady terrace/garden. English-speaking Isabelle Lherm is an attractive young hostess; husband Patrick an assured, able chef. Classical & regional offerings: invigorating *soupe paysanne en croûte, saumon fumé Parmentier* & a diet-killing *pièce de boeuf grillée*.
Menus bCD. Rooms (18) EF. Cards MC, V. (Some rooms have kitchens.)
Closed 7 Nov-19 Mar. Rest: Fri & Sat midday (Sept-June).
Post av. F. de Maynard, 46400 St-Céré, Lot. Region Dordogne.
Tel 05 65 38 02 16. Fax 05 65 38 02 98. Mich 125/D3. Map 5.

A100frs & under. B100–150. C150–200. D200–250. E250–350. F350–500. G500+

ST-CEZAIRE-SUR-SIAGNE

Auberge Puits d'Amon

Simple restaurant with rooms/Cooking 2-3
Air-conditioning (restaurant) `FW`

An ivy-covered ground floor gives some relief to the dour exterior. Nowt dour inside: young Stella & Christian Veysset (trained by Alain Chapel) are having a real go. A classical repertoire shows up well in several tasty, hearty dishes: *terrine de foie de volaille, pièce de boeuf moutarde à l'ancienne & daube façon Grande-Mère.* (Parking no problem.)
Menus bCD. Rooms (5) D. Cards MC, V. Closed 25 Jan-15 Feb. 5-12 June. 3-10 Oct. Wed evg. Thurs (not evgs July/Aug).
Post 06780 St-Cézaire-sur-Saigne, Alpes-Maritimes. Region Côte d'Azur.
Tel 04 93 60 28 50. Mich 163/E2. Map 6.

ST-CHELY-D'AUBRAC

Voyageurs-Vayrou

Simple hotel & very simple annexe/Cooking 1-2 `FW`

Christiane Vayrou & her son-in-law, Patrick Amilhat (his wife, Brigitte, is the sister of Régine Caralp at Le Méjane, Espalion), are the cooks at the long-established family hotel. Classical & regional *cuisine soignée* (see the dining room photographs): *tripoux, terrine de canard, assiette de charcuterie, cou farci et magret fumé & aligot du chef* – all the very essence of Aubrac. Try *fouace au beurre* at the Auguy bakery 50m away.
Menus aBC. Rooms (14) E. Cards MC, V.
Closed Oct-5 Apl. Rest: Sat midday (not July/Aug).
Post 12470 St-Chély-d'Aubrac, Aveyron. Region MC (Auvergne).
Tel 05 65 44 27 05. Mich 141/D1. Map 5.

ST-CIRQ-LAPOPIE (also see next page)

Auberge du Sombral
"Aux Bonnes Choses"

Comfortable restaurant with rooms/Cooking 1-2 `FW`
Quiet/Terrace

The medieval village, high above the Lot, is a photographer's dream; so, too, is Gilles Hardeveld's *auberge* & the evocative place de la Mairie. Unabashed, unrelenting regional nosh: *salade de cabécous rôtis, cuisse de canarde confite, poulet aux champignons, truite au vieux Cahors & gigot d'agneau* are typical. Tricky parking (can be a bit of a walk).
Menus B(bottom-end)CDE. Rooms (8) EF. Cards MC, V.
Closed Mid Nov-Mar. Tues evg & Wed (not July-Sept).
Post 46330 St-Cirq-Lapopie, Lot. Region Dordogne.
Tel 05 65 31 26 08. Fax 05 65 30 26 37. Mich 138/C2. Map 5.

A100frs & under. B100–150. C150–200. D200–250. E250–350. F350–500. G500+

ST-CIRQ-LAPOPIE (also see previous page)   **La Pélissaria**

Simple hotel/Cooking 1-2
Secluded/Gardens

The 13thC house is just off the eastern approach to the photographer's dream village, perched above the Lot. Breathtaking views. Some rooms are smallish, some have a terrace. Marie-Françoise Matuchet is an able chef: classical & regional delights – home-made pasta & sweets are especially praised. Her husband François is *le patron*. English spoken. Dinner only.
Menus D(bottom-end). Rooms (10) FG. Cards MC, V. (Cheaper rooms: below.)
Closed Mid Nov-Mar. Rest: Thurs. Fri. Midday. (Les Gabarres, 2km E.)
Post 46330 St-Cirq-Lapopie, Lot. Region Dordogne.
Tel 05 65 31 25 14. Fax 05 65 30 25 52. Mich 138/C2. Map 5.

ST-CLAUDE   **Au Retour de la Chasse**

Comfortable hotel/Cooking 1
Quiet/Tennis/Parking

Annie & Gérard Vuillermoz are the hosts at the chalet-style hotel 5km S of St-Claude. Attractive environs; smartish hotel exterior; banal interior. Some rooms have kitchens. One plus: an entertaining 3-hole pitch-&-putt course at the rear. Cooking? *Bourgeoise*, classical, grills & the odd dish with Jura wine (*truite meunière* & *poularde de Bresse*).
Menus aBDE. Rooms (16) EF. Cards All. (Use D290 from St-Claude – to S.)
Closed 20-30 Dec. Sun evg & Mon (out of season).
Post Villard-St-Sauveur, 39200 St-Claude, Jura. Region Jura.
Tel 03 84 45 44 44. Fax 03 84 45 13 95. Mich 104/A2. Map 6.

ST-DIZIER   **La Gentilhommière**

Comfortable restaurant/Cooking 1-2   FW

Owners, Florémond (*le chef*) & Corinne Descharmes (*chef de salle*), worked in numerous swish French & Swiss hotels since they won their hotel school diplomas a decade ago. Flowers & shutters dominate the façade (are the handsome figures still on the balcony?). Elegant interior. Neo-classical offerings: *rouelles de dos de lapin à la sauge et ses graines de moutarde* is a typical assured creation.
Menus a(lun)BC. Cards MC, V. (Rooms: Ibis N of town; Picardy 600m walk.)
Closed 15-25 Aug. Sun evg. Mon. Region Champagne-Ardenne.
Post 29 r. J. Jaurès, 52100 St-Dizier, Haute-Marne. (D384 Troyes road.)
Tel 03 25 56 32 97. Fax 03 25 06 32 66. Mich 57/F1. Map 3.

A 100frs & under. B 100–150. C 150–200. D 200–250. E 250–350. F 350–500. G 500+

ST-DONAT-SUR-L'HERBASSE

Chartron

Very comfortable restaurant with rooms/Cooking 3 FW
Terrace/Garage/Parking/Air-conditioning (restaurant)

Like the redoubtable Michael Caines (Gidleigh Park) chef Bruno
Chartron lost his right arm some years ago (serving in the army). Both he
& his wife are an indomitable duo: she's a pleasing *patronne*; he's a
skilled classicist with many light touches. Two lunch lip-smackers: *soupe
glacée à la tomate*; & *daurade grillée beurre citronée fleur de courgette*.
Menus bCDEF. Rooms (7) E. Cards All. (N from centre; quiet backwater.)
Closed Tues. Rest: Mon evg (Sept-June).
Post 26260 St-Donat-sur l'Herbasse, Drôme. Region MC (Ardèche).
Tel 04 75 45 11 82. Fax 04 75 45 01 36. Mich 130/B2. Map 6.

ST-ETIENNE-DE-BAIGORRY

Arcé

Comfortable hotel/Cooking 1-2 FW
Secluded/Terrace/Gardens/Swimming pool/Tennis/Parking

The riverside setting is heaven on earth. A shady terrace, *au bord de
l'eau*, & the pool across the footbridge are enticing pluses. So is the
family Arcé. Emile now leaves the cooking to his son Pascal (the 5th
generation). Some moans about his regional/classical fare: "Anything
with *vinaigrette* was flavoured with curry!" is typical. English spoken.
Menus BCDE. Rooms (24) FG. Cards MC, V. Closed Mid Nov-mid Mar.
Rest: Mon midday (out of season but not sch. hols & pub. hols).
Post 64430 St-Etienne-de-Baïgorry, Pyrénées-Atlantiques. Mich 166/C2.
Tel 05 59 37 40 14. Fax 05 59 37 40 27. Region Southwest. Map 4.

ST-ETIENNE-DU-FURSAC

Nougier

Comfortable hotel/Cooking 1-2 FW
Gardens/Garage/Closed parking

A smart-looking place (called the "Moderne" when I first knew it) opp.
the church & close to the River Gartempe. Artificial "rustic" interior.
Jean-Pierre Nougier walks the classical road: you'll have no unfilled
holes in your stomach with *plats* like *coeur de filet au jus de truffe,
croustillant de pied de cochon forestière* & *confit de canard aux cèpes*.
Menus a(lunch)BCD. Rooms (12) EF. Cards MC, V. (S of La Souterraine.)
Closed Dec-Feb. Sun evg & Mon (Sept-June; not pub. hols). Mon *midi*
(July/Aug). Post 23290 St-Etienne-de-Fursac, Creuse. Region Poit-Char.
Tel 05 55 63 60 56. Fax 05 55 63 65 47. Mich 97/E4. Map 5.

A100frs & under. B100–150. C150–200. D200–250. E250–350. F350–500. G500+

ST-FELIX-LAURAGAIS

Auberge du Poids Public

Comfortable hotel/Cooking 2-3 FW
Terrace/Gardens/Garage/Parking

Panoramic views from the large beamed dining room appeal – perhaps as much as the cooking of acclaimed chef, Claude Taffarello. Both modern & regional dishes. Menu B could be a block of *rillettes de canard, confiture d'oignons*; *thon poêlé, beurre de tomate*; *noisettes* (rissoles) *de pied de porc au jus*; & *pain perdu à l'ancienne* (French toast).
Menus BCDE. Rooms (13) E. Cards AE, MC, V.
Closed Jan. Sun evg (Oct-Apl). Region Languedoc-Roussillon.
Post 31540 St-Félix-Lauragais, Haute-Garonne.
Tel 05 61 83 00 20. Fax 05 61 83 86 21. Mich 153/E4. Map 5.

ST-FLORENTIN

Grande Chaumière

Very comfortable restaurant with rooms/Cooking 3 FW
Quiet/Terrace/Gardens/Closed parking

A stunning readers' favourite: for the handsome house & eye-catching gardens; for the dining room with its glass walls & flagstone floors; for the warm welcome from Lucette Bonvalot; & the neo-classical cooking of her English-speaking husband Jean-Pierre. His sauces are intense & faultless: *suprême de sandre au porto blanc* is one lip-licking example.
Menus B(lunch)DEF. Rooms (11) FG. Cards All.
Closed 26 Aug-1 Sept. Wed & Thurs midday (Sept-May).
Post 3 r. Capucins, 89600 St-Florentin, Yonne. Region Burgundy.
Tel 03 86 35 15 12. Fax 03 86 35 33 14. Mich 56/A4. Map 3.

ST-FLORENTIN

Tilleuls

Simple hotel/Cooking 2 FW
Quiet/Terrace/Gardens/Parking

New owners, Bruno & Nicole Hubert, in their 30s, do a competent job at this tucked-away *logis*: attractively decorated bedrooms; meticulously tended small lawn & flower beds (rare in France); nothing too much trouble for *la patronne*; & her hubby is a talented classicist – proved conclusively with a humdinger *pintadeau au miel, citron et poivre vert*.
Menus a(lunch)BCD. Rooms (9) DE. Cards AE, MC, V.
Closed 29 Dec-4 Jan. 11 Feb-4 Mar. Sun evg (Sept-May). Rest: Mon.
Post 3 r. Decourtive, 89600 St-Florentin, Yonne. Region Burgundy.
Tel 03 86 35 09 09. Fax 03 86 35 36 90. Mich 56/A4. Map 3.

A100frs & under. B100–150. C150–200. D200–250. E250–350. F350–500. G500+

ST-FLOUR   Grand Hôtel Voyageurs

Comfortable hotel/Cooking 2
Lift/Garage

In the *haute ville* with the most delectable of secret sun-trap terraces
(alas, not used for meals). Diego Quinonero mixes creative neo-classical
with regional. The latter, in menu B, included a *cochonnaille des Monts
d'Auvergne (charcuterie);* a pungent *volaille fermière Brayaude aux
morilles, lentilles; fromages;* & a yummy *milliard aux griottes.*
Menus aBCD. Rooms (33) CDEF. Cards DC, MC, V.
Closed Nov-Easter.
Post 25 r. Collège, 15100 St-Flour, Cantal. Region MC (Auvergne).
Tel 04 71 60 34 44. Fax 04 71 60 00 21. Mich 127/D2. Map 5.

ST-FLOUR   Les Messageries/Rest. Nautilus

Comfortable hotel/Cooking 2   FW
Terrace/Swimming pool/Garage/Parking

N of the busy N9/D990, in the low town & near the station. Chef Bruno
Giral (son of the high town Europe's owners) & his wife, Catherine, do a
sound job. Mix of regional, neo-classical & modern creations: on one
hand a light *sandre grillé aux mousserons* & at a more basic, gutsy level
both *tripoux* & *noisette de porc au curry.* Bedrooms much appreciated.
Menus ABCDEF. Rooms (17) DEF. Cards MC, V.
Closed 20 Jan-16 Feb. Fri & Sat midday (Oct-Easter; but not sch. hols).
Post 23 av. Ch. de Gaulle, 15100 St-Flour, Cantal. Region MC (Auvergne).
Tel 04 71 60 11 36. Fax 04 71 60 46 79. Mich 127/D2. Map 5.

ST-GENIEZ-D'OLT   France

Comfortable hotel/Cooking 1-2   FW
Lift/Swimming pool & Tennis (see text)

St-Geniez, beside the River Lot (Olt is local *patois*) is a busy place. Clients
of Madeleine & Michel Crouzet can use the facilities (see above) at their
Club Marmotel, 1km away. What about the cooking? Rating of 1-2 by a
whisker: classical/regional grub. Commendable *Menu Aveyronnais* (A):
charcuterie, terrine de tripoux, aligot & *cabécou grillé.*
Menus ABC. Rooms (48) DE. Cards MC, V.
Closed Nov-19 Mar.
Post 12130 St-Geniez-d'Olt, Aveyron. Regions MC (Auvergne/Cévennes).
Tel 05 65 70 42 20. Fax 05 65 47 41 38. Mich 141/D2. Map 5.

A 100frs & under. B 100–150. C 150–200. D 200–250. E 250–350. F 350–500. G 500+

ST-GERVAIS-D'AUVERGNE

Castel Hôtel 1904

Comfortable hotel/Cooking 2-3 (see text)
Quiet/Gardens/Parking

FW

Over 2000ft above sea-level, & at the heart of the *bourg*; the *logis*, in reality a 17thC château, was opened as an hotel in 1904; the same family Chassagnette/Mouty have owned it ever since. Step back to 1904: for old-time service, furniture, fittings & generous classical dishes – like *poularde poitrine de veau* & *tournedos* from Jean-Luc Mouty. Also bistro.
Menus A(bistro; see below; rating 1-2)bCE. Rooms (17) E. Cards MC, V.
Closed 12 Nov-30 Mar. (Note: bistro is called Comptoir à Moustaches.)
Post 63390 St-Gervais-d'Auvergne, Puy-de-Dôme. Region MC (Auvergne).
Tel 04 73 85 70 42. Fax 04 73 85 84 39. Mich 99/E4. Map 5.

ST-GIRONS

Eychenne

Very comfortable hotel/Cooking 2-3
Quiet/Terrace/Gardens/Swim pool/Parking/Air-cond. (rest.)

FW

A consummate hotel-keeping family: English-speaking Michel Bordeau is the 6th generation at this step-back-in-time hotel; his wife, Sylvette, has now been joined by their delightful daughter Florence (her English is fluent). Copious classical cooking from chef Jean-Marc Granger. Wide-choice menus with fish alternatives for each of the first two courses.
Menus BDE. Rooms (42) EFG(low-end). Cards DC, MC, V.
Closed 22 Dec-end Jan. Sun evg & Mon (Nov-Mar but not pub. hols).
Post 8 av. P. Laffont, 09200 St-Girons, Ariège. Region Southwest.
Tel 05 61 66 20 55. Fax 05 61 96 07 20. Mich 170/B3. Map 5.

ST-GUIRAUD

Mimosa

Comfortable restaurant with rooms (see text)/Cooking 3-4
Terrace/Air-conditioning

Go! Enjoyment factor 10/10: for Bridget Pugh's eclectic cooking – full of natural, harmonious flavours & the epitome of culinary common sense & good taste; for husband David's wine know-how (rare dividend: the chance to order, by the glass, from 20 of the area's best wines). Great news: B&D have bought an hotel in St-Saturnin (2km to N); transport laid on.
Menus c(lunch: low-end; must book ahead)E. Rooms (8) EF. Cards MC, V.
Closed Nov-Feb. Sun evg (not July/Aug). Mon (not midday pub. hols.)
Post 34725 St-Guiraud, Hérault. Region Languedoc-Roussillon.
Tel 04 67 96 67 96. Fax 04 67 96 61 15. Mich 156/A2. Map 5.

A100frs & under. B100–150. C150–200. D200–250. E250–350. F350–500. G500+

ST-HILAIRE-LE-CHATEAU

du Thaurion

Very comfortable restaurant with rooms/Cooking 2-3
Terrace/Gardens/Parking

FW

5 menus welcome you at the completely refurbished home of Gérard (he
was born in the building) & English-speaking Marie-Christine Fanton. His
repertoire covers regional/neo-classical/modern fare: a soup of local *cèpes*
was as delicate as silk & *turbotin beurre blanc* had elegant depth of
flavour. A lowered rating (some moans); but I commend the duo to you.
Menus ACDEF. Rooms (10) EFG. Cards All.
Closed 2 Jan-Feb. 19-28 Dec. Wed & Thurs midday (not July/Aug).
Post 23250 St-Hilaire-le-Château, Creuse. Region Poitou-Charentes.
Tel 05 55 64 50 12. Fax 05 55 64 90 92. Mich 111/D1. Map 5.

ST-JEAN-CAP-FERRAT

Brise Marine

Comfortable hotel (no restaurant)
Quiet/Gardens

I've known my Côte d'Azur base hotel (*sans rest.*) recommendations for a
decade or two – some longer. One certain fact of life has emerged: their
bedroom prices have outstripped inflation by a wide margin. That's true
here. Gardens are a delight; views E over the Med to the mountains above
Monte-Carlo are sensational; & a helpful owner in Yves Maîtrehenry.
Rooms (16) G(mid-range). Cards AE, MC, V.
Closed Mid Nov-Jan. Region Côte d'Azur.
Post av. J. Mermoz, 06230 St-Jean-Cap-Ferrat, Alpes-Maritimes.
Tel 04 93 76 04 36. Fax 04 93 76 11 49. Mich 165/E3. Map 6.

ST-JEAN-CAP-FERRAT

Clair Logis

Simple hotel (no restaurant)
Quiet/Gardens/Parking

At the heart of some of the world's most expensive real estate, the
exclusive Cap Ferrat, a millionaire's paradise. No sea views here but the
largish park, with firs, palm & fig trees, more than compensates. The
green-shuttered, ochre-shaded villa was built 100 years ago. Also an
annexe in the grounds; readers say its bedrooms are a touch cramped.
Rooms (18) EFG. Cards All.
Closed Mid Jan-Feb. 10 Nov-15 Dec. Region Côte d'Azur.
Post av. Centrale, 06230 St-Jean-Cap-Ferrat, Alpes-Maritimes.
Tel 04 93 76 04 57. Fax 04 93 76 11 85. Mich 165/E3. Map 6.

A100frs & under. B100–150. C150–200. D200–250. E250–350. F350–500. G500+

ST-JEAN-DE-COLE

Auberge du Coq Rouge

Very simple restaurant/Cooking 1-2
Terrace

FW

At the heart of Périgord's most evocative village – with *place*, 11thC *église*, cloisters, old covered market, modest château & Gothic bridge. Jean-Francis Parisis' *auberge* is no more than a tiny beamed dining room & terrace in the *place*. Regional/classical/*Bourgeoise*: *soupe*, *omelette aux noix* & *truite de fontaine en persillade* is authentic *terroir* grub.
Menus ABCD. Cards DC, MC, V. (Rooms: France & Russie, Thiviers.)
Closed Jan. Wed. (Above *sans rest.* hotel; easy 7km drive to E.)
Post pl. de l'Eglise, 24800 St-Jean-de-Côle, Dordogne. Region Dordogne.
Tel 05 53 62 32 71. Mich 109/E4. Map 5.

ST-JEAN-DU-BRUEL

Midi-Papillon

Simple hotel/Cooking 2
Quiet/Gardens/Swimming pool/Parking

FW

Surrounded by some of Nature's most seductive corners this spruced-up *logis* appeals to all: a riverside setting; involved 4th-generation owners, Maryse & Jean-Michel Papillon; & the latter's cooking, of all styles, makes clever use of his own-grown vegetables, home-reared poultry & home-made *charcuterie, foies gras et confits.*
Menus aBCD. Rooms (19) BC. Cards MC, V.
Closed 12 Nov-28 Mar.
Post 12230 St-Jean-du-Bruel, Aveyron. Region Massif Central (Cévennes).
Tel 05 65 62 26 04. Fax 05 65 62 12 97. Mich 141/F4. Map 5.

ST-JEAN-PIED-DE-PORT

Plaza Berri

Very simple hotel (no restaurant)
Fairly quiet

As I have said frequently in this guide, hotels don't come more modest than this one. With only 8 bedrooms the "hotel" is no more than a small house tucked away in the SE corner of the walled town & is adjacent to a *pelota* court & car park. The biggest pluses are the reasonable prices & the chance to try many of the close-at-hand restaurant recommendations.
Rooms (8) DE. Cards not accepted. (Public parking adjacent to hotel.)
Closed Mid Nov-mid Dec. Region Southwest.
Post av. Fronton, 64220 St-Jean-Pied-de-Port, Pyrénées-Atlantiques.
Tel 05 59 37 12 79. Mich 166/C2. Map 4.

A100frs & under. B100–150. C150–200. D200–250. E250–350. F350–500. G500+

302

ST-JEAN-PIED-DE-PORT

Very comfortable hotel/Cooking 3-4
Terrace/Swimming pool/Lift/Garage/Air-conditioning (rest.)

Firmin Arrambide has progressed remarkably since I first enthused, in the early 80s, about his innovative modern & regional cooking. So has the hotel (he's the 3rd-generation chef); now with all mod-cons (the lighting, in corridors/bedrooms, needs improving). *Plats*? Punchy *garbue aux choux*; & classic *boeuf grillée à la Béarnaise*. Mingy with coffee.
Menus DEFG. Rooms (20) G. Cards AE, MC, V. Region Southwest.
Closed 5-28 Jan. 20 Nov-22 Dec. Mon evg (Nov-Mar). Tues (20 Sept-June).
Post pl. Ch de Gaulle, 64220 St-Jean-Pied-de-Port, Pyrénées-Atlantiques.
Tel 05 59 37 01 01. Fax 05 59 37 18 97. Mich 166/C2. Map 4.

ST-JEAN-PIED-DE-PORT (Aincillé)

Pecoïtz

Simple restaurant with basic rooms/Cooking 1-2 |FW|
Quiet/Gardens/Parking

A humdinger! Head 7km SE from St-Jean to a hidden village & the down-to-earth home of Jean-Paul & Michèle Pecoïtz. She's a pleasure; the views W are a tonic; & J-P's regional/classical/*Bourgeoise* cooking pleases all. How about good-choice menu B? *Potage, picquillos (piments doux) à la morue, caneton rôti pommes frites*, cheese & sweet.
Menus ABC. Rooms (16) CD. Cards MC, V.
Closed Jan. Feb. Fri (Oct-May).
Post 64220 Aincillé, Pyrénées-Atlantiques. Region Southwest.
Tel 05 59 37 11 88. Mich 166/C2. Map 4.

ST-JEAN-PIED-DE-PORT (also see next page)   Artzaïn-Etchea
(Estérençuby)
Simple hotel/Cooking 1
Quiet/Parking

A *logis*, 11km S of St-Jean & 3 km S of Estérençuby (hotel shown on Mich. maps). In French the Basque name for the hotel is "*La Maison du Berger*" (shepherd). Great terrain to the S. Monsieur Arriaga provides basic regional, classical & *Bourgeoise* dishes: of the *piquillos (piments doux) farcis à la morue, piperade* & *gâteau Basque* variety.
Menus ABC. Rooms (17) CDE. Disabled. Cards not accepted.
Closed 15-30 Mar. 15 Nov-20 Dec. Wed (not high season).
Post 64220 Estérençuby, Pyrénées-Atlantiques. Region Southwest.
Tel 05 59 37 11 55. Fax 05 59 37 20 16. Mich 166/C2-C3. Map 4.

A100frs & under. B100–150. C150–200. D200–250. E250–350. F350–500. G500+

ST-JEAN-PIED-DE-PORT (see previous page) Sources de la Nive
(Estérençuby)
Simple hotel/Cooking 1
Secluded/Parking

There's a touch of Cumbria about the hills & valleys surrounding the
Thistas' remote country *logis*, 13km S of St-Jean & 5km S of Estérençuby.
The old carved & polished furniture pleases the eye; so does the view of
the Nive from the conservatory-like dining room. Grub? Basic classical &
Bourgeoise – like *hors d'oeuvre variés, truite meunière* & *caneton rôti*.
Menus ABC. Rooms (26) D. Cards MC, V.
Closed Jan. Tues (not high season).
Post 64220 Estérençuby, Pyrénées-Atlantiques. Region Southwest.
Tel 05 59 37 10 57. Mich 166/C2-C3. Map 4.

ST-JOSSE-SUR-MER   Le Relais de St-Josse

Simple restaurant/Cooking 2   FW

A four-star *village fleuri* where a young couple are working wonders.
Fabienne Delmer is a self-effacing, English-speaking *patronne*; husband
Etienne a classical cavalier chef. Stylish, assured specialities: of the
marbre de queue de boeuf, pot-au-feu de lotte & *tarte Tatin servi tiède*
type. Mainly praise from readers but one letter was full of doom & gloom
("disgusting fish"). Barn-like *salle*. (Rooms: hotels in Le Touquet.)
Menus ABCE. Cards MC, V. (Rooms: see entry for Ibis at Le Touquet.)
Closed Mid Jan-mid Feb. Sun evg & Mon (Not July/Aug). (Above 9km NW.)
Post 62170 St-Josse-sur-Mer, Pas-de-Calais. Region North.
Tel 03 21 94 61 75. Mich 2/A4. Map 2.

ST-JULIEN-CHAPTEUIL   Vidal

Very comfortable restaurant/Cooking 2-3   FW

I can vouch for chef Jean-Pierre Vidal's references: he was trained by
Forges at Riorges, Troisgros at Roanne & Rostang at Antibes – all in my
earlier guides. Neo-classical virtuosity, exemplified by an aromatic *cannette
rôtie aux épices et pommes gaufrettes*. Chantal Vidal is a bespectacled,
smiling *patronne/sommelière*. First-rate *cave*. (Rooms: Moulin de Barette,
Pont de Sumène – N88, 13km to WNW; also see below.)
Menus b(bottom-end)CDE. Cards AE, MC, V. (Rooms: Barriol in village.)
Closed Mid Jan-Feb. Mon evg. Tues (not July/Aug).
Post 43260 St-Julien-Chapteuil, Haute-Loire. Region MC (Ardèche).
Tel 04 71 08 70 50. Fax 04 71 08 40 14. Mich 129/D2. Map 5.

A100frs & under. B100–150. C150–200. D200–250. E250–350. F350–500. G500+

ST-JULIEN-EN-CHAMPSAUR

Les Chenets

Simple hotel/Cooking 1-2
Quiet/Garage

The Guerins' chalet-style *logis* has an elevated position with views SW over the Drac Valley. Classical cooking with many Italian touches – cooked *"avec passion"*. Plenty of choice on menu B with the likes of *tortelloni aux légumes sauce basilic*; *carpaccio de canard*; an especially liked *fricassée de lapin*; &, alas, a passionless *crème caramel*.
Menus aBC. Rooms (18) CDE. Cards MC, V.
Closed 8-26 Apl. 31 Oct-22 Dec. Sun evg & Wed (not high season).
Post 05500 St-Julien-en-Champsaur, Hautes-Alpes. Region Hautes-Alpes.
Tel 04 92 50 03 15. Fax 04 92 50 73 06. Mich 132/B4. Map 6.

ST-JULIEN-EN-GENEVOIS   Diligence et Taverne du Postillon

Comfortable restaurant/Cooking 2-3 (see text)
Air-conditioning

FW

You can save francs by using the brasserie (low-end B; rating 1-2). I suggest you go down to the Taverne where Christophe Favre continues the classical traditions of his father Robert – with welcome neo-classical additions. Enjoy the likes of *turbot aux algues dans sa carpace de gros sel*, the sea brought to the Alps. (Beside N201; near church/parking.)
Menus Brasserie: B(low-end). Taverne: b(lunch: ceiling)DEF. Cards All.
Closed 2-6 Jan. 28 July-3 Aug (brasserie only). 4-25 Aug. Sun evg. Mon.
Post av. Genève, 74160 St-Julien-en-Genevois, Hte-Savoie. Region Savoie.
Tel 04 50 49 07 55. Fax 04 50 49 52 31. Mich 104/B3. Map 6.

ST-JULIEN-EN-GENEVOIS (also see next page)   Le Soli

Simple hotel (no restaurant)
Fairly quiet/Lift/Closed parking

Aptly-named owners, Gilbert & Marie-Laure Sublet. To the W of the main N201 through St-Julien & just 100m from the Diligence et Taverne restaurant (see above). Geneva is 13km to the N (the Swiss border is only 2km away) &, compared with Swiss hotel prices, the Sublet charges are charitable. Autoroutes & main roads take you in all directions.
Rooms (27) DE. Cards All. Region Savoie.
Closed 23 Dec-3 Jan. (Hotel reception closed on Sunday: 11-18 hours.)
Post r. Mgr Paget, 74160 St-Julien-en-Genevois, Haute-Savoie.
Tel 04 50 49 11 31. Fax 04 50 35 14 64. Mich 104/B3. Map 6.

A100frs & under. B100–150. C150–200. D200–250. E250–350. F350–500. G500+

ST-JULIEN-EN-GENEVOIS
Rey/Rest. Clef des Champs

(see previous page) **(Col du Mont Sion)**
Comfortable hotel/Cooking 1-2
Terrace/Gardens/Swimming pool/Tennis/Lift/Parking

| FW |

At the summit of the Col du Mont Sion, beside the N201 Annecy road & S of St-Julien. Gilbert Rey & his wife have made many friends over the years – readers liking their warm, friendly personalities. The restaurant, Clef des Champs, is in an adjacent building. Chef Gilbert walks neo-classical paths; his fish dishes are especially welcome.

Menus bCDE. Rooms (30) EF. Cards MC, V. Closed 5-25 Jan. 24 Oct-7 Nov.
Rest: 17-23 Oct also. Thurs (not 1st 3 wks Aug). Fri midday.
Post Col du Mont Sion, 74350 Cruseilles, Haute-Savoie. Region Savoie.
Tel 04 50 44 13 29. Fax 04 50 44 05 48. Mich 104/B3-B4. Map 6.

ST-LAURENT-DE-LA-SALANQUE
Commerce

Comfortable restaurant with rooms/Cooking 2
Garage/Air-conditioning (restaurant)

| FW |

Raymonde Siré is the hostess; husband Jean-Louis is the chef. Enjoy classical cuisine, with the odd dip in the *Catalane* pool, in a light yellow-washed *salle*. Noteworthy specialities on menu B include an exemplary *bouillabaisse de lotte à la Catalane*, a sea-scented *méli-mélo* (mixture) *de palourdes & moules bouchots* & an ubiquitous *crème Catalane*.

Menus aBC(ceiling). Rooms (14) CDE. Cards MC, V. Closed 4-19 Mar.
28 Oct-19 Nov. Sun evg (Sept-June). Mon (not evgs July/Aug).
Post 2 bd Révolution, 66250 St-Laurent-de-la-Salanque, Pyr.-Or.
Tel 04 68 28 02 21. Mich 173/D4. Map 5. Region Languedoc-Roussillon.

ST-LAURENT-EN-GRANDVAUX
Moulin des Truites Bleues

Very comfortable restaurant with rooms/Cooking 2-3
Gardens/Parking

| FW |

Pluses? River, cascade (the Lemme falls 15m), woods & an historical site (remains of Roman watchtower). The mill dates back to the Middle Ages; the wheels stopped turning in the 19thC. The label "Rococo" describes the décor (extravagant & fussy); thankfully the heavy classical cooking of the past has been lightened up no end by chef Thierry Volatier. Owners Robert Levavasseur & Denise Pérenet are proud of their *moulin*.

Menus BEF. Rooms (20) FG. Cards All. (Use N5 from village; 6km N.)
Post 39150 St-Laurent-en-Grandvaux, Jura. Region Jura.
Tel 03 84 60 83 03. Fax 03 84 60 87 23. Mich 104/B1. Map 6.

A100frs & under. B100–150. C150–200. D200–250. E250–350. F350–500. G500+

306

ST-LEONARD-DES-BOIS

Touring Hôtel

Very comfortable hotel/Cooking 2
Quiet/Gardens/Swimming pool (indoor)/Lift/Parking

FW

No architectural gem but a host of terrific other benefits more than compensate: a River Sarthe-side site at the heart of the invigorating Alpes Mancelles; an indoor pool & gym; the most caring of owners, Georges & Monique Thommeret; walks galore; & above average neo-classical cooking from chef Christian Baudry. "Go once; return often."
Menus BCD. Rooms (35) EF. Disabled. Cards All.
Closed Mid Nov-mid Feb. Rest: Fri evg & Sat (mid Oct-mid Mar).
Post 72590 St-Léonard-des-Bois, Sarthe. Region Normandy.
Tel 02 43 97 28 03. Fax 02 43 97 07 72. Mich 50/C2. Map 2.

ST-LYPHARD

Les Chaumières du Lac et Aub. Les Typhas

Comfortable hotel/Cooking 1-2
Gardens/Parking

FW

A new complex of thatched buildings, on the W side of the D47 bypass of St-Lyphard. *Le lac* is to the E of the road, as is the Parc Régional de Brière. Stylish, good-taste bedrooms & handsome furniture & furnishings throughout. Wide-choice classical menus: much enjoyed courses were *salade de queue de boeuf aux fèves* & *trio de poissons rôtis croq'sel.*
Menus aCDE. Rooms (20) EF. Disabled. Cards MC, V. Closed Hotel: mid Nov-mid Mar. Rest: Feb. 15-25 Nov. Mon *midi* (summer). Mon evg (Oct-Apl). Tues (not evgs Jul/Aug). Post 44410 St-Lyphard, Loire-Atl. Reg Brittany.
Tel 02 40 91 32 32. Fax 02 40 91 30 33. Mich 63/E3. Map 1.

ST-LYPHARD (Bréca) (also see next page)

Auberge de Bréca

Comfortable restaurant/Cooking 2
Terrace/Gardens

FW

An exceptional setting on the W edge of the marshy La Grande Brière (take punt rides from Bréca). Authentic old thatched *maison briéronne* (all buildings are thatched hereabouts). Gorgeous garden. Classical & *terroir* cooking from Pascal Marinot: *terrine, anguilles ou grenouilles en persillade* & a memorable *saumon cru à la fleur de sel de Guérande.*
Menus BCD. Cards AE, MC, V. (Rooms: Eurocéan; E bypass of Guérande.)
Closed 3 Nov-Mar. Sun evg & Thur (not Jul/Aug). (Bréca S of St-Lyphard.)
Post Bréca, 44410 St-Lyphard, Loire-Atlantique. Region Brittany.
Tel 02 40 91 41 42. Fax 02 40 91 37 41. Mich 63/E3-E4. Map 1.

A100frs & under. B100–150. C150–200. D200–250. E250–350. F350–500. G500+

ST-LYPHARD (Kerbourg) (see previous page) Auberge de Kerbourg

Comfortable restaurant/Cooking 2-3
Terrace/Parking

`FW`

Kerbourg has some fine thatched houses. The exterior of this authentic *maison briéronne* is a touch decrepit but the stone & beamed dining room is heart-warmingly stylish. Canadian Bernard Jeanson is an innovative modern *cuisinier*: superlative *brandade de lieu glacée, jus de poivrons*; & *joues de cochons de 6 heures, petits légumes de cuisson au gingembre.*
Menus BC. Cards MC, V. (Rooms: Eurocéan, E bypass of Guérande.)
Closed Jan-mid Feb. Nov & Dec (not week-ends). Sun evg. Mon. Tues *midi.*
Post Kerbourg, 44410 St-Lyphard, Loire-Atl. Reg Brittany. Mich 63/E3-E4.
Tel 02 40 61 95 15. Fax 02 40 61 98 64. Map 1. (Kerbourg SW St-Lyphard.)

ST-MAIXENT-L'ECOLE   Logis St-Martin

Comfortable hotel/Cooking 1-2
Secluded/Terrace/Gardens/Parking

`FW`

A gorgeous 17thC stone building, with handsome circular tower, in an attractive tree-studded garden above the 10m-wide Sèvre Niortaise (plus 1m-high weir). Cooking, alas, doesn't quite match the seductive 3-star setting. Run-of-the-mill classical & *Bourgeoise* cooking, typified by the likes of *mousseline de foie gras* & *côte de veau romarin.*
Menus a(lunch)BC. Rooms (10) F. Cards All. (SW of town; S of N11.)
Closed 2-28 Jan. Rest: Sun evg & Mon (mid Oct-mid May).
Post ch. Pissot, 79400 St-Maixent-l'Ecole, Deux-Sèvres. Reg Poitou-Char.
Tel 05 49 05 58 68. Fax 05 49 76 19 93. Mich 94/C2. Map 4.

ST-MALO   Le Chalut

Comfortable restaurant/Cooking 3
Air-conditioning

`FW`

All the main French guides have, at last, woken up to the talents of chef Jean-Philippe Foucat. The words I used in *French Leave Encore* are still valid: "go once & you'll return often." Interior a seapool-hued bistro. Classical fish/shellfish extravaganza: *coquillages, saumon, sole, raie, langoustines, St-Pierre, homard et al.* Not for carnivores.
Menus ACE. Cards AE, MC, V. (Rooms: refer to entries which follow.)
Closed Sun evg (not July/Aug). Mon. Region Brittany.
Post 8 r. Corne de Cerf, 35400 St-Malo, Ille-et-Vilaine.
Tel 02 99 56 71 58. Mich 30/A4. Map 1. (In NE corner of walled town.)

A100frs & under. B100–150. C150–200. D200–250. E250–350. F350–500. G500+

ST-MALO (Paramé)   Alba

Comfortable hotel (no restaurant)
Quiet/Parking

Two km to the E of the atmospheric old town of St-Malo (sitting solidly
& contentedly behind its walls & ramparts). The Alba snoozes peacefully
behind the beach & *digue* – the latter wall between the sea & the hotel;
thankfully no traffic uses the promenade. Helpful, friendly owners. The
lounge & more expensive front bedrooms have extensive sea views.
Rooms (20) FG. Cards AE, MC, V.
Closed 3 Jan-10 Feb. 15 Nov-20 Dec. Region Brittany.
Post 17 r. Dunes, 35400 St-Malo (Paramé), Ille-et-Vilaine.
Tel 02 99 40 37 18. Fax 02 99 40 96 40. Mich 30/A4. Map 1.

ST-MALO (Paramé)   Brocéliande

Simple hotel (no restaurant)
Fairly quiet/Parking

300m or so closer to St-Malo than the Alba (see the entry above). The
Brocéliande shares the same pleasing setting: immediately in front of the
beach-side rear of the colourful, small hotel is the traffic-free *digue* (sea-
wall promenade). You can't get much closer to the sea – & the breakers
at high tide when a wind is blowing. Extensive views.
Rooms (9) FG. Cards All.
Closed Mid Nov-mid Dec. Region Brittany.
Post 43 chaussée Sillon, 35400 St-Malo (Paramé), Ille-et-Vilaine.
Tel 02 99 20 62 62. Fax 02 99 40 42 47. Mich 30/A4. Map 1.

ST-MALO (Rothéneuf) (also see next page)   Centre et du Canada

Very simple hotel with basic rooms/Cooking 0-1

There's nowt simpler in this edition of *French Leave* – but no other entry
can boast such big-hearted owners as Alain & Martine Filliette, for
whom nothing is too much trouble. Why do other guides cold shoulder
them? Tuck into copious *cuisine traditionelle*: *darne de merlu sauce
crème, moules sauce poulette, cassolette de crabe gratinée, sole aux
amandes, saumon grillée beurre maître-d', gâteau aux fraises* & more.
Menus A. Rooms (23) BCD. Cards AE, MC, V. (6km NE of St-Malo.)
Closed 21 Dec-Jan. Sun evg & Mon (not high season). Region Brittany.
Post 7 pl. du Canada, Rothéneuf, 35400 St-Malo, Ille-et-Vilaine.
Tel 02 99 56 96 16. Fax 02 99 40 18 28. Mich 30/A4. Map 1.

A100frs & under. B100–150. C150–200. D200–250. E250–350. F350–500. G500+

ST-MALO (Rothéneuf) (also see previous page)   Terminus

Simple hotel (no restaurant)
Quiet/Parking

As unpretentious as any of my base hotel recommendations come: but the
pluses here are a quiet site, N of the busy D201, & a 200m walk to the
village's much appreciated sandy beach. M et Mme Weisser offer clients
inexpensive accommodation & easy access to a handful of enterprising
restaurants on the Cancale peninsula, including many FW enterprises.
Rooms (30) CDE. Cards MC, V. (6km NE of St-Malo.)
Closed Mid Nov-mid Feb. Region Brittany.
Post 16 r. Goélands, Rothéneuf, 35400 St-Malo, Ille-et-Vilaine.
Tel 02 99 56 97 72. Fax 02 99 40 58 17. Mich 30/A4. Map 1.

ST-MALO (St-Servan-sur-Mer)   La Korrigane

Very comfortable hotel (no restaurant)
Quiet/Gardens/Limited closed parking

A 19thC *belle époque* town house which, arguably, would be one of the
contenders for the accolade of France's most stylishly-furnished &
decorated small hotel. Elegance personified. The façade is impressive; at
the rear a small garden provides the perfect spot for breakfast. To the S
of St-Malo in a relatively quiet corner of St-Servan-sur-Mer.
Rooms (10) G. Cards All.
Closed 3-31 Jan. Region Brittany.
Post 39 r. Le Pomellec, 35400 St-Malo (St-Servan), Ille-et-Vilaine.
Tel 02 99 81 65 85. Fax 02 99 82 23 89. Mich 30/A4. Map 1.

ST-MALO (St-Servan-sur-Mer)   Le Valmarin

Very comfortable hotel (no restaurant)
Quiet/Gardens/Closed parking

In St-Malo a château is called a *"Malouinière"*. The Valmarin, a stern-
looking 18thC version, is yet another of St-Malo's treasure-chest of base
hotels; the interior is handsomely & solidly furnished; the park
("gardens" doesn't do it justice) is a treat. Short walk to a beach, park,
the Tour Solidor (fine views S) & Fort de la Cité (views N).
Rooms (12) G. Cards AE, MC, V.
Closed 7 Jan-15 Feb. 15 Nov-23 Dec. Region Brittany.
Post 7 r. Jean XXIII, 35400 St-Malo (St-Servan), Ille-et-Vilaine.
Tel 02 99 81 94 76. Fax 02 99 81 30 03. Mich 30/A4. Map 1.

A100frs & under. B100–150. C150–200. D200–250. E250–350. F350–500. G500+

310

ST-MARCELLIN

Savoyet-Serve

Simple hotel (comfortable annexe)/Cooking 1-2
Lift/Parking/Air-conditioning (restaurant)

The multi-floored S-S is soulless modern – but with all mod-cons. St-Marcellin is famed for its cow's milk cheese; the Serve family's rest. is acclaimed locally for their classical & regional *RQP* menus. Do try *ravioles de Royans* – from down the road. (For something more stylish try *La Tivollière*, a nearby château rest., also run by the family.)
Menus aBCD. (La Tivollière BCDE.) Rooms (51) CDEF. Cards AE, MC, V.
Closed Sun evg. (La Tivollière: Sun evg & Mon.)
Post 16 bd Gambetta, 38160 St-Marcellin, Isère. Regions Htes-Alp/Savoie.
Tel 04 76 38 24 31. Fax 04 76 64 02 99. Mich 130/C2. Map 6.

ST-MARS-LA-JAILLE

Relais de St-Mars

Very comfortable restaurant/Cooking 1-2

FW

A small town with a serious restaurant trying hard to impress. Laurence Cuasante cooks, primarily classical with some regional touches; Pierre welcomes you & demonstrates his nose for & his knowledge of Loire wines. Choice of 4 dishes on each of the menu C courses: the likes of *pièce de boeuf à la moelle à l'Anjou rouge* (highly enjoyable), filling *gâteau chocolat maison* or lip-smacking *crémet d'Anjou* (fresh cream cheese). Menus BCDE. Cards AE, MC, V. (Rooms: Relais Plaisance, Candé.)
Closed 1-15 Aug. Sun evg & Wed evg (Nov-May). (Above 14km E; *sans rest.*)
Post 1 r. Industrie, 44540 St-Mars-la-Jaille, Loire-Atl. Region Loire.
Tel 02 40 97 00 13. Mich 65/D3. Map 1. (Park in *place* opposite rest.)

ST-MARTIN-D'ARMAGNAC

Auberge du Bergerayre

Comfortable restaurant with rooms/Cooking 2-3
Secluded/Terrace/Gardens/Swimming pool/Parking

FW

Pierrette Sarran is *la cuisinière* at this delectable old farm – W of the village & surrounded by vineyards & fields – seemingly infused with the spirit of Armagnac. Rustic dining rooms. Madame's classical/regional fare epitomises Gers: witness *salade paysanne aux gesiers* & *pintadeau rôti, jus court à l'ail* as evidence. Menus inc' wine: guess where from!
Menus ABCD(bottom-end). Rooms (14) EF. Disabled. Cards MC, V.
Closed Rest: Wed.
Post 32110 St-Martin-d'AImagnac, Gers. Region Southwest.
Tel 05 62 09 08 72. Fax 05 62 09 09 74. Mich 150/B2. Map 4.

A100frs & under. B100–150. C150–200. D200–250. E250–350. F350–500. G500+

ST-MARTIN-DE-LONDRES

Les Muscardins

Very comfortable restaurant/Cooking 3

Multi prize-winning *cuisinier* Georges Rousset, a longtime *FL* favourite, leaves much of the modern & neo-classical cooking these days to his talented 32-year-old son, Thierry. Dad acts as *sommelier*. No FW rating alas – nevertheless menu c(lunch: low-end) is great *RQP*. Past highlights have included a lipsmackingly good *cabillaud demi-sel en croûte* & a well conceived *agneau en trilogie (noisettes, poitrine farci et navarin)*.
Menus c(lunch)EDF. Cards All. (Rooms: Host. St-Benoit, Aniane.)
Closed 5-25 Feb. 28 Oct-10 Nov. Mon & Tues (not evgs summer). (26km SW.)
Post 19 rte Cévennes, 34380 St-Martin-de-Londres, Hérault. Reg Lang-Rou.
Tel 04 67 55 75 90. Fax 04 67 55 70 28. Mich 156/B2. Map 5.

ST-MARTIN-DE-LONDRES (Argelliers)

Auberge de Saugras

Simple restaurant with rooms/Cooking 1-2
Secluded/Terrace/Swimming pool/Parking

FW

Hard to find: the stone farmhouse (*mas*; its origins 12thC) is between Viols-le-Fort & Vailhauguès (D127/D127E), both S of St-Martin. *Cuisine autrefois*: nostalgic classical, some slow-cooked dishes (*daube de sanglier*) & cream & *foie gras* used with great gusto – the latter in salads, terrines & *frais de canard poêlé*. The Aurelles need encouraging.
Menus aBCE. Rooms (4) D(bottom-end). Cards AE, MC, V. (E of Argelliers.)
Closed 4-29 Nov. 16-27 June. Tues evg & Wed (not July/Aug).
Post 34380 Argelliers, Hérault. Region Languedoc-Roussillon.
Tel 04 67 55 08 71. Fax 04 67 55 04 65. Mich 156/B2. Map 5.

ST-MARTIN-DU-VAR

Jean-François Issautier

Luxury restaurant/Cooking 4
Parking/Air-conditioning

We've admired J-F & Nicole Issautier for two decades; their present-day, flower-filled home is one of our most loved favourites. Enjoy his super classical skills – "real" French cooking using disparate local produce: *terrine de canard à la ferme* is authentic brilliance; & royal *agnolotti (ravioles) aux herbes dans un bouillon de sauge* is Provence on a plate.
Menus d(lunch: low-end)EFG. Cards All. (Rooms: Servotel; 1km to S.)
Closed Mar. 14-23 Oct. Sun (not *midi* 7 Sept-June). Mon. Region Côte d'A.
Post 06670 St-Martin-du-Var. Alpes-Maritimes. (E side N202; 19km N A8.)
Tel 04 93 08 10 65. Fax 04 93 29 19 73. Mich 165/D3. Map 6.

A100frs & under. B100–150. C150–200. D200–250. E250–350. F350–500. G500+

ST-MARTIN-EN-BRESSE

Au Puits Enchanté

Simple hotel/Cooking 2
Parking

FW

Well-named & a worthwhile detour E from the A6. Chef Jacky Chateau & his wife, Nadine, are *RQP* winners. Elegant but simple applies to both furnishings & cooking: start with a sumptuous *terrine de pintade aux foies de canards en gelée blonde*; then a lighter *rosettes de saumon à la fondue les jeunes poireaux*, cheese & sweet (typical menu B).
Menus ABCD. Rooms (14) CDE. Cards MC, V. Closed 15-31 Jan. Feb school hols. 1st wk Sept. Sun evg (not July/Aug). Mon (Nov-Feb). Tues.
Post 71620 St-Martin-en-Bresse, Saône-et-Loire. Regions Burg/Lyon.
Tel 03 85 47 71 96. Fax 03 85 47 74 58. Mich 88/B3. Map 3.

ST-MEDARD

Le Gindreau

Very comfortable restaurant/Cooking 3-4
Terrace

Old school house (now very chic) with green views over the Vert Valley & cool chestnut-shaded terrace. Elegant Martine & Alexis Pélissou (the chef), both a delight, beguile with flavour-personified neo-classical & regional fare: superb fresh & crisp *tronçon de turbot grillée, beurre blanc*. Fine *cave* (50 halves). 1st-class *sommelier*. Gorgeous flowers.
Menus CEF. Cards AE, MC, V. (Rooms: Campanile & France, Cahors.)
Closed 11 Nov-8 Dec. Sun evg (Sept-June). Mon (not midday pub. hols).
Post 46150 St-Médard, Lot. Region Dordogne.
Tel 05 65 36 22 27. Fax 05 65 36 24 54. Mich 138/B1. Map 5.

ST-MELOIR-DES-ONDES (also see next page)   Le Coquillage

Simple restaurant/Cooking 2
Secluded/Gardens/Parking

FW

Olivier Roellinger is a chef superstar; his shrine, La Maison de Bricourt, is at Cancale. Le Coquillage is his bistro, housed in an annexe, the deluxe but stark H. de Bricourt-Richeux. Enterprising *RQP*. Modern dishes making great use of Brittany's rich harvests (from sea & land) – with clever use of spices & aromatics (both OR trademarks). Superb views to E.
Menus BC. Cards All. (Rooms: Nuit & Jour, Cancale.) Region Brittany.
Closed Mon. Tues *midi*. (Rooms: also see St-Malo (Rothéneuf); Terminus.)
Post 35350 St-Méloir-des-Ondes, Ille-et-Vilaine. (Off D155 to E.) Map 1.
Tel 02 99 89 25 25 & 02 99 89 64 76. Fax 02 99 89 88 47. Mich 30/A4.

A 100frs & under. B 100–150. C 150–200. D 200–250. E 250–350. F 350–500. G 500+

ST-MELOIR-DES-ONDES

Hôtel Tirel-Guérin

(also see previous page) **(La Gouesnière)**
Very comfortable hotel/Cooking 3
Terr/Gardens/Swim pool (indoor)/Tennis/Parking/Air-cond. (rest.)

FW

Family closed shop: Roger Tirel (owners' son) married Annie Guérin;
her brother, Jean-Luc, hitched-up with Roger's sister, Marie-Christiane.
Modern & neo-classical treats (fish predominating) on super menus from
chefs R & J-L. One superb memory: *chausson* of *coquilles & foie gras*.
Ladies are *les patronnes*. Many ½-bottles. Fabulous indoor pool & gym.
Menus bCD. Rooms (60) EF. Disabled. Cards All. (S of St-Méloir.)
Closed Mid Dec-mid Jan. Rest: Sun evg (Oct-Easter) but not sch. hols.
Post la gare, La Gouesnière, 35350 St-Méloir-des-Ondes, Ille-et-Vilaine.
Tel 02 99 89 10 46. Fax 02 99 89 12 62. Mich 30/A4. Map 1. Reg Brittany.

ST-OMER

Bretagne

Comfortable hotel/Cooking 1-2 (see text)
Lift/Closed parking

FW

Jekyll & Hyde hotel. Cooking excellence is no more (Sylvia Beauvalot
won a star in the 80s); now run as an out-&-out big "business" for Brits.
Some readers are "well satisfied"; others say the "food is oily, tired &
tasteless" & the "welcome lacks warmth". Cooking? Rest: big helpings of
classical grub. Maëva: cheap & cheerful grills (rating 0-1; menus A).
Menus aBC. Rooms (75) EF. Cards All. Closed Rest: 2-14 Jan. 11-24 Aug.
Sat *midi*. Sun evg. Evgs pub. hols. Maëva: 23 Dec-2 Jan. Sat *midi*. Mon.
Post 2 pl. Vainquai, 62500 St-Omer, Pas-de-Calais. Region North.
Tel 03 21 38 25 78. Fax 03 21 93 51 22. Mich 2/C2-C3. Map 2.

ST-OMER

Château Tilques

Very comfortable hotel/Cooking 2-3
Secluded/Gardens/Tennis/Parking

FW

English owners, European Country Hotels, & manager Christopher Higgins,
have done a great job in improving all aspects of the hotel. Classical &
neo-classical cooking specialities from chef Patrick Hittos are also much
appreciated by readers: *boudin de ris de veau crème de champignons* &
filet d'agneau cuit en pâté à sel are typical of his repertoire. Small
details count: for example, original appetisers & *petits fours*.
Menus b(lunch: low-end)CDE. Rooms (53) FG. Cards All. (5km NW St-Omer.)
Post Tilques, 62500 St-Omer, Pas-de-Calais. Reg North. (Cheaper rooms:)
Tel 03 21 93 28 99. Fax 03 21 38 34 23. Mich 2/C2. Map 2. (Ibis/St-Omer)

A 100frs & under. B 100–150. C 150–200. D 200–250. E 250–350. F 350–500. G 500+

ST-PARDOUX-LA-CROISILLE

Beau Site

Comfortable hotel/Cooking 2-3
Quiet/Gardens/Swimming pool/Tennis/Parking

The Bidault trio – Madame; her son Dominique; his wife Catherine – have won praise for their attention to detail. So has Jean-Claude, *le père*, for an enterprising mix of neo-classical/regional dishes. Fish *plats* are appreciated in out-of-the-way Corrèze & his *pâtisserie* work, desserts & breakfast *viennoiserie* are highly-rated by all. 1st-class picnic lunches.
Menus bCD. Rooms (32) DE. Cards MC, V.
Closed Oct-Apl.
Post 19320 St-Pardoux-le-Croisille, Corrèze. Region Dordogne.
Tel 05 55 27 79 44. Fax 05 55 27 69 52. Mich 125/E1. Map 5.

ST-PAUL

La Brouette (Chez les Danois)

Simple restaurant/Cooking 1-2
Terrace/Swimming pool/Parking (steep descent)/Air-cond.

Something different – though not liked by all Brits! English-speaking Danish family Bornemann – Olé, Brigitte & son Michel – mix Scandinavian & French at their idiosyncratic, extrovert home. "Salty & smoky" goodies galore: *flétan fumé (ou saumon mariné), harengs marinées ou saumon fumé* (both Danois), *truite fumé*; &, for carnivores, several meat dishes. *Olé!*
Menus a(lunch)B(ceiling). Cards MC, V. (Rooms: see next entry.)
Closed Feb. Mon evg (not July/Aug). (D36 Cagnes-Vence road, E St-Paul.)
Post 830 rte de Cagnes, 06570 St-Paul, Alpes-Mar. Region Côte d'Azur.
Tel 04 93 58 67 16. Mich 165/D3. Map 6.

ST-PAUL

Le Hameau

Comfortable hotel (no restaurant)
Quiet/Gardens/Swimming pool/Parking/Air-conditioning

No wonder readers have fallen in love, over the last 16 years, with this delectable base – just as I did two decades ago. Once a farm (built more than 200 years ago), the hotel is a series of small buildings. A green oasis with fragrant gardens, full of orange, tangerine & apricot trees. Peacock pigeons too. Attentive, English-speaking owner, Xavier Huvelin.
Rooms (14) FG. Cards MC, V. (D7, W of St-Paul.)
Closed 6 Jan-15 Feb. 15 Nov-22 Dec. Region Côte d'Azur.
Post rte de La Colle-sur-Loup, 06570 St-Paul, Alpes-Maritimes.
Tel 04 93 32 80 24. Fax 04 93 32 55 75. Mich 165/D3. Map 6.

A100frs & under. B100–150. C150–200. D200–250. E250–350. F350–500. G500+

ST-PEE-SUR-NIVELLE (Ibarron) Fronton

Comfortable restaurant with rooms/Cooking 2-3 FW
Terrace

Jean-Baptiste & Maritxu (Maritchu) Daguerre are passionate about their
métier. It shows in their unpretentious, flower-dominated Basque home.
Menu B is primarily neo-classical: dishes like *filet de truite saumonée
au beurre blanc, civet de canard aux petits oignons* & *île flottante*.
There's also a super menu of reworked old Basque recipes (D).
Menus BD. Rooms (8) DE. Cards All. (Other rooms: Aub. Basque; 3km NW.)
Closed Mar. Tues evg. Wed evg. Region Southwest. (Ibarron W of Fronton.)
Post Ibarron, 64310 St-Pée-sur-Nivelle, Pyrénées-Atlantiques.
Tel 05 59 54 10 12. Fax 05 59 54 18 09. Mich 148/B4. Map 4.

ST-PERAY (Cornas) Ollier

Simple restaurant/Cooking 1-2 FW
Air-conditioning

Cornas is just N of St-Péray. The ruby-red Cornas wines feature in much
of Jean-Pierre Ollier's rich & hearty classical repertoire. His so, so
helpful wife, Gisèle, will tempt you, in the oh-so-welcome air-cond.
salle, with *terrine du chef, salmis de pintade au Cornas* & *moules
farcies et gratinée* (so good that clients eat 8 kilos every Sunday).
Menus aBC. Cards MC, V. (Rooms: Pôle 2000, St-Péray.)
Closed Feb sch. hols. 6-26 Aug. Mon evg (Oct-Apl). Tues evg. Wed.
Post N86, Cornas, 07130 St-Péray, Ardèche. Region MC (Ardèche).
Tel 04 75 40 32 17. Mich 130/A3. Map 6.

ST-PERAY (Soyons) Domaine de la Musardière

Very comfortable hotel (comfortable annexe)/Cooking 2-3 FW
Terr/Gards/Swim pool/Tenn/Lift/Closed parking/Air-cond. (rooms)

Small estate on W side N86, N of Charmes & S of Soyons (7km S St-Péray).
Everything is swish, with "cheaper" rooms (FG) in La Châtaigneraie, an
annexe. First-class *RQP* in Anne-Marie & Philippe Michelot's dining room:
classical/neo-classical *plats* – witness *estouffe de boeuf au mas de fanny*
(sic) & *papillote de cabillaud aux légumes à l'huile d'olive*. The annexe
has its own pool/tennis/gardens. (Cheaper rooms: Pôle 2000; St-Péray.)
Menus BCE. Rooms (12) G,G2: annexe (18) FG. Cards All.
Post Soyons, 07130 St-Péray, Ardèche. Region Massif Central (Ardèche).
Tel 04 75 60 83 55. Fax 04 75 60 85 21. Mich 130/A3. Map 6.

A100frs & under. B100–150. C150–200. D200–250. E250–350. F350–500. G500+

ST-PERE-SOUS-VEZELAY L'Espérance

Very comfortable hotel/Cooking 4-5
Quiet/Gardens/Swimming pool/Parking/Air-conditioning (rest.)

The only French 3-star in *FLF* & the only one I would spend hard-earned cash to visit. Why? For the eye-pleasing setting; for Marc Meneau, such a gifted chef; for Françoise, his self-effacing wife; for Dominique & Philippe Martin who run the reception & light, airy *salle* with superb precision & friendliness; & for exhilarating, innovative modern cooking.
Menus f(lunch: low-end)G(top-end). Rooms (34) G,G2,G3. Cards All.
Closed Rest: Feb. Tues (not pub. hols). Wed midday. (Cheaper rooms: see)
Post 89450 St-Père-sous-Vézelay, Yonne. Reg Burgundy. (Avallon bases.)
Tel 03 86 33 39 10. Fax 03 86 33 26 15. Mich 72/B4. Map 3.

ST-PERE-SOUS-VEZELAY Le Pré des Marguerites

Comfortable restaurant/Cooking 2 FW
Terrace/Gardens/Parking/Air-conditioning

Marc Meneau's bistro – opp. his rest. *La cuisine/la salle* are staffed by employees who have worked in L'Espérance. How's this for a low-end menu C with a choice for each course: a bravura *galantine de canard* or unfussy *saucisson chaud pommes*; a feisty, ear-to-the-ground *oreilles de porc aux lentilles*; & a discreetly flavoured *sable aux pommes crème anglaise* or a robust *tarte aux raisins de vendange*. Fine service.
Menus aCD. Cards All. (Rooms: La Renommée, 100m E; *sans rest*. Also see)
Post 89450 St-Père-sous-Vézelay, Yonne. Reg Burg. (Avallon base hotels.)
Tel 03 86 33 33 33. Fax 03 86 33 34 73. Mich 72/B4. Map 3.

ST-PIERRE-DE-CHARTREUSE Chalet Hôtel du Cucheron

Simple restaurant with basic rooms/Cooking 1-2 FW
Secluded/Terrace/Parking

Here are more good reasons for driving up into the secretive Chartreuse. At an altitude of over 3500ft, the air is bracing & the views of wooded mountains exhilarating. Better still are the owners, André & Colette Mahaut, much loved by readers. So is Gina, a Great Dane with a glowing blue coat. Cooking? Classical/*Bourgeoise*; expect no miracles. Perhaps 1?
Menus ABC. Rooms (7) BCD. Cards All. (At Col du Cucheron, N St-Pierre.)
Closed 20-26 Jan. 14 Oct-25 Dec. Mon (not sch. hols).
Post Col du Cucheron, 38380 St-Pierre-de-Chartreuse, Isère.
Tel 04 76 88 62 06. Fax 04 76 88 65 43. Mich 117/E4-F4. Map 6.

A100frs & under. B100–150. C150–200. D200–250. E250–350. F350–500. G500+

ST-PIERRE-DES-NIDS

Dauphin

Comfortable restaurant with rooms/Cooking 2
Parking

Don't be put off by the exterior. Hidden behind the dull façade is the remarkable Jean Etienne, an English-speaking *chef/patron* (once with the *French Line*) & dynamic promoter of his *terroir*. *French Line* classical cooking: *escalope de saumon d'Ecosse sur lit vert* & a *cuisse de canard confite à la Pôôtéenne* (the local *pays*) are show stoppers.
Menus ABCDE. Rooms (9) BCDE. Cards AE, MC, V.
Closed Feb sch. hols. 24 Aug-4 Sept. Wed (Sept-Easter).
Post rte Alençon, 53370 St-Pierre-des-Nids, Mayenne. Region Normandy.
Tel 02 43 03 52 12. Fax 02 43 03 55 49. Mich 50/C2. Map 2.

ST-PIERRE-DU-VAUVRAY

Hostellerie St-Pierre

Very comfortable hotel/Cooking 2-3
Quiet/Gardens/Lift/Parking

The triangular-shaped, mock-Norman (half-timbered) hotel is a bit of an eyesore. Readers continue to praise the Seine-side site (L bank) & the new owners, the Potier family. Jeanine & Jean are out front & Alain is in *la cuisine*; harmonious & tasty neo-classical & classical dishes – of the *effeuillée de langue et tête de veau sauce ravigote* variety.
Menus b(lunch)CE. Rooms (14) G. Cards All.
Closed Mid Nov-mid Mar.
Post 27430 St-Pierre-du-Vauvray, Eure. Regions Ile de France/Norm.
Tel 02 32 59 93 29. Fax 02 32 59 41 93. Mich 34/B1. Map 2.

ST-PIERRE-LANGERS

Le Jardin de l'Abbaye

Comfortable restaurant/Cooking 2-3
Parking

Two rustic dining rooms, both with chimneys, at the happy home of Alain & Catherine Duval. The couple love their *métier*; she's a friendly hostess; he walks the classical cloisters. Relish the *Menu Abbaye* (three choices for each of three courses: *nage de daurade au basilic* & *faux-filet au poivre de Guinéc* are both top of the pops treats.
Menus ABCDE. Cards MC, V. (Rms: Michelet, Granville; 11km NW.)
Closed 6-28 Feb. 24 Sept-10 Oct. Sun evg (not July/Aug). Mon.
Post Croix Barrée, 50530 St-Pierre-Langers, Manche. Region Normandy.
Tel 02 33 48 49 08. Fax 02 33 48 18 50. Mich 30/C3. Map 1.

A100frs & under. B100–150. C150–200. D200–250. E250–350. F350–500. G500+

ST-PONS-DE-THOMIERES

Auberge du Cabaretou

Comfortable restaurant with rooms/Cooking 1-2
Secluded/Terrace/Gardens/Parking

FW

Liliane Dubost has gone & a new *patronne*, Marie Brichot, welcomes you to her isolated *auberge* atop the Col du Cabaretou (spectacular views S; refreshing wooded terrain to N). Her early days were disastrous; service especially. Problems now sorted & few grumbles. Modern/neo-classical creations from young chef Hervé Leroy – using *terroir* produce. Menus aBCDE. Rooms (11) E. Cards All. Region Languedoc-Roussillon. Closed Mid Jan-mid Feb. Sun evg & Mon (Oct-Apl).
Post Col du Cabaretou, 34220 St-Pons-de-Thomières, Hérault. (10km to N.)
Tel 04 67 97 02 31. Fax 04 67 97 32 74. Mich 155/D3-D4. Map 5.

ST-POURCAIN-SUR-SIOULE

Chêne Vert

Comfortable hotel/Cooking 2-3
Terrace/Closed parking

FW

The old cobwebs (but not some dusty wall ledges!) have been blown away by the new owners, Jean-Guy & Martine Siret, a normally vigilant *patronne*. The tag spick & span describes the beefed-up hotel fabric & J-G's neo-classical fare. Dig into *saumon cru mariné au gros sel, terrine de faisan en gelée, omble chevalier poêlé* & *civet de chevreuil*. Menus aBC. Rooms (31) DEF. Cards All. Region Berry-Bourbonnais. Closed 5-28 Jan. Sun evg & Mon (mid Sept-mid June).
Post bd Ledru-Rollin, 03500 St-Pourçain-sur-Sioule, Allier.
Tel 04 70 45 40 65. Fax 04 70 45 68 50. Mich 100/A3. Map 5.

ST-QUENTIN (Neuville-St-Amand)

Le Château

Comfortable hotel/Cooking 2-3
Quiet/Gardens/Closed parking

FW

The Meiresonne "château" is more akin to a hunting lodge, hidden behind a wall of trees in a 7-acre park. Claude Meiresonne welcomes guests & chef Jean-François M is a dedicated classicist with many a lighter touch in his well-executed repertoire: from *tournedos poêlé à la crème de morilles* to *marinade de saumon*. (SE of St-Quentin; NE A26 exit 11.)
Menus bCDE. Rooms (15) EF. Cards All.
Closed 28 July-17 Aug. 24-31 Dec. Sat midday. Sun evg.
Post Neuville-St-Amand, 02100 St-Quentin, Aisne. Region North.
Tel 03 23 68 41 82. Fax 03 23 68 46 02. Mich 19/D1. Map 2.

A100frs & under. B100–150. C150–200. D200–250. E250–350. F350–500. G500+

ST-RAPHAEL   Pastorel

Comfortable restaurant/Cooking 2-3
Terrace

At the heart of old St-Raphaël, N of the railway line. There's nothing
flippant about the restaurant or the cooking; chef Charles Floccia has both
Provençal & classical nous. An almost faultless meal of a tasty *amuse-
bouche*, nine oysters with rye bread, an as-it-should-be *blanquette
d'agneau à l'ancienne, salade de Roquefort aux noix* & a dessert.
Menus C. Cards All. (Rooms: see entry for L'Oasis at Fréjus.)
Closed Midday in Aug. Sun evg. Mon.
Post 54 r. Liberté, 83700 St-Raphaël, Var. Region Côte d'Azur.
Tel 04 94 95 02 36. Fax 04 94 95 64 07. Mich 163/E3. Map 6.

ST-REMY-DE-PROVENCE   Canto Cigalo

Comfortable hotel (no restaurant)
Secluded/Gardens/Closed parking

Well-named & to the E of the evocative town. A string of complimentary
letters over the years in praise of the very helpful owners Dominique &
Claude Flogeac. A haven of peace; the attractive gardens are especially
appreciated by readers. What's more bedrooms prices are modest. Of the
two St-Rémy bases my vote would now go to the singing cicada.
Rooms (20) E. Cards MC, V.
Closed Mid Nov-Feb. Region Provence.
Post ch. Canto Cigalo, 13210 St-Rémy-de-Provence, Bouches-du-Rhône.
Tel 04 90 92 14 28. Fax 04 90 92 24 48. Mich 158/B2. Map 6.

ST-REMY-DE-PROVENCE   La Maison Jaune

Comfortable restaurant/Cooking 2-3   FW
Terrace

A three-storey town house with sizeable terrace in centre of St-Rémy.
François Pérraud, the chef (previously at La Regalido; Fontvieille), & his
English-speaking wife, Catherine, opened their new home at the end of
1993. Stylish & clever taste combinations like *minestrone, toasts aux
olives noires* & *blanc de volaille à l'aïoli et au safran*.
Menus b(lunch: bottom-end)CDE. Cards MC, V. (Rooms: see base hotels.)
Closed 22 Jan-8 Mar. Sun evg (winter). Mon. Tues midday (July-Sept).
Post 15 r. Carnot, 13210 St-Rémy-de-Provence, Bouches-du-Rhône.
Tel 04 90 92 56 14. Mich 158/B2. Map 6. Region Provence.

ST-REMY-DE-PROVENCE

Soleil

Comfortable hotel (no restaurant)
Quiet/Swimming pool/Closed parking

An oasis of calm, consistently liked by readers since 1980 – though perhaps not so much these days since Joseph Denante's daughter, Françoise, & her husband, Guy Monset, took over the reins. Nevertheless, the Soleil is close to the town centre (S of St-Rémy), well back from the road & has the added plus of invaluable "closed parking". Rooms (21) DE(bottom-end). Cards All.
Closed Mid Nov-mid Mar. Region Provence.
Post 35 av. Pasteur, 13210 St-Rémy-de-Provence, Bouches-du-Rhône.
Tel 04 90 92 00 63. Fax 04 90 92 61 07. Mich 158/B2. Map 6.

ST-SERNIN-SUR-RANCE

Carayon

Comfortable hotel/Cooking 1-2 `FW`
Quiet/Terrace/Gardens/Lift/Swim pool/Tennis/Garage/Parking

Back after the *FLE* chop. English-speaking Pierre Carayon, 4th-generation chef, & wife Claudette, are energetic *patrons*. The extended, modernised hotel is now a big "business"; coach parties galore. Pierre won an *Ordre national du Mérite* this year for his "enterprise". Classical/regional full-tum fare – ranging from thumbs-down to super. Flies can be a pest.
Menus ABCE. Rooms (55) CDEF. Disabled. Cards All.
Closed Nov. Sun evg & Mon (Dec-Apl).
Post 12380 St-Sernin-sur-Rance, Aveyron. Region Languedoc-Roussillon.
Tel 05 65 99 60 26. Fax 05 65 99 69 26. Mich 154/C1. Map 5.

ST-SULPICE-LE-VERDON

Lionel Guilbaud

Very comfortable restaurant/Cooking 3-4 `FW`

Lionel (born in La Roche-s-Yon in 1950) & Josiane Guilbaud's new home, at La Chabotterie (which evokes part of Vendée history), SE St-Sulpice (see Mich maps: just W of D763 exit). The new setting has more style & atmosphere but Lionel's cooking remains the same – some inventive modern creations & a startling number of personal interpretations of regional specialities (his *pays*). (Rooms: Voyageurs, Montaigu; open every day.)
Menus bC(bottom-end)EF. Cards All. (Above easy 10km drive NE.)
Closed Tues (not high season). (Above: Tel 02 51 94 00 71.)
Post Logis de la Chabotterie, 85260 St-Sulpice-le-Verdon, Vendée.
Tel 02 51 42 47 47. Fax 02 51 42 81 29. Mich 79/E3. Map 1. Reg Poit-Char.

A100frs & under. B100–150. C150–200. D200–250. E250–350. F350–500. G500+

ST-THEGONNEC

Auberge St-Thégonnec

Comfortable hotel/Cooking 2
Terrace/Gardens/Parking

Modern, stone-built *logis* over the road from superb *enclos paroissiaux*. English-speaking Alain Le Coz (he gives a lot of help to Leicester Catering College students) favours flavour in his classical repertoire: *emincé de boeuf Strogonoff et compôte d'oignons au miel* is typical. *Croustillant de fraises de Plougastel* (down-the-road) is super sweet.
Menus ABCD. Rooms (19) EFG(bottom-end). Cards All. Closed 20 Dec-Jan. Sun evg & Mon (15 Sept-15 June). Mon *midi* (15 Jun-15 Sept).
Post 29410 St-Thégonnec, Finistère. Region Brittany.
Tel 02 98 79 61 18. Fax 02 98 62 71 10. Mich 27/D2. Map 1.

ST-VAAST-LA-HOUGUE

France et Fuchsias

Comfortable hotel/Cooking 2
Terrace/Gardens

Famed for exceptional gardens. The owners, the Brix family, make good use of produce grown on their farm. Plenty of fish dishes, too: *crabe mayonnaise* & *filet de cabillaud* are champion; so, too, are *tarte framboise* & *nougat glace*. Cooking rating raised for this edition: readers have had nothing but praise – so I've deleted past criticism.
Menus aBCDE. Rooms (34) CDEF. Cards All.
Closed 5 Jan-25 Feb. Mon (mid Sept-mid May). Tues midday (Nov-Mar).
Post 50550 St-Vaast-la-Hougue, Manche. Region Normandy.
Tel 02 33 54 42 26. Fax 02 33 43 46 79. Mich 12/C2. Map 1.

ST-VALLIER

Albert Lecomte et Hôtel Terminus

Very comfortable restaurant with rooms/Cooking 2-3
Garage/Air-conditioning

Don't be put off by the exterior & the site – by *la gare* & beside the N7. Double-glazed bedrooms, a modern dining room & two first-class neo-classical & classical chefs more than compensate. Albert (helped by son Alexandre) hails from St-Jean-en-Royans (Vercors); the area's famed *ravioles* appear in a *salade* with *magret fumé* & with a *filet de sandre*.
Menus b(lunch)CDEF. Rooms (10) EF. Cards All.
Closed Feb sch. hols. 11-22 Aug. Sun evg. Mon.
Post 116 av. J. Jaurès, 26240 St-Vallier, Drôme. Region MC (Ardèche).
Tel 04 75 23 01 12. Fax 04 75 23 38 82. Mich 130/A1. Map 6.

A100frs & under. B100-150. C150-200. D200-250. E250-350. F350-500. G500+

ST-VALLIER

Comfortable restaurant with basic rooms/Cooking 1-2   FW
Terrace/Air-conditioning

At the heart of St-Vallier, but away from the N7. Chef Jean Brouchard is a well-liked *patron* (even giving some readers seeds for their garden). Uninspiring classical repertoire – *filet de boeuf Béarnaise* is typical. Grills too – *entrecôte* & *porc* as examples. Food is often overcooked. Grumbles about bedrooms; use modern Ibis (N on N7) as alternative.
Menus aBCD(bottom-end). Rooms (9) C. Cards All.
Closed 12 Nov-5 Dec. Sun evg.
Post 2 av. J. Jaurès, 26240 St-Vallier, Drôme. Region MC (Ardèche).
Tel 04 75 23 04 42. Fax 04 75 23 46 99. Mich 130/A1. Map 6.

ST-VIANCE
Auberge des Prés de la Vézère

Simple hotel/Cooking 1-2   FW
Terrace/Parking

Another edition to the Albert Parveaux stable (see Varetz) – though this one is much, much cheaper than the others. Chefs change, but they are all Parveaux trained. Classical & regional dishes on a handful of menus – including welcome fish-based treats like *omble farci aux champignons beurre blanc* & *darne de daurade poêlée au civet au vin rouge*.
Menus ABCD. Rooms (11) E(ceiling). Cards All.
Closed Mid Oct-Apl. (2 min walk to River Vézère.)
Post 19240 St-Viance, Corrèze. Region Dordogne.
Tel 05 55 85 00 50. Fax 05 55 84 25 36. Mich 124/C1. Map 5.

ST-VINCENT-DE-TYROSSE (see next page)
Côte d'Argent

Simple hotel (no restaurant)
Quiet/Gardens/Lift/Parking

A smart, colourful three-storey building with a lounge &, not always the case in France, an attractive, well-tended garden. W of the N10 in a tranquil site & ideally situated for the beaches 12km to the W; the vast pine forests & many *étangs* of the Landes to the N; & providing easy access to fine restaurants at Dax, Magescq, Peyrehorade & St-Vincent (next entry) itself. Note too: open all year; ideal for winter breaks.
Rooms (22) E (low-end). Cards All. Region Southwest.
Post rte Hossegor, 40230 St-Vincent-de-Tyrosse, Landes.
Tel 05 58 77 02 16. Fax 05 58 77 23 96. Mich 148/C2. Map 4.

A100frs & under. B100–150. C150–200. D200–250. E250–350. F350–500. G500+

ST-VINCENT-DE-TYROSSE (see previous page)   Le Hittau

Very comfortable restaurant/Cooking 2-3
Terrace/Gardens/Parking

Le Hittau is described as an 18thC *bergerie* (manger) but, in reality, is a handsome wooden-built *maison* in a tree-filled garden. Max Dando is a classical & regional cooking disciple, capitalising on the rich treasure chest of his *terroir: foie gras, pigeon de pays à l'ail doux confit* & *St-Pierre au vin rouge* are typical. Brother Philippe is a polished MD.
Menus C(bottom-end)DEF. Cards All. (Rooms: see previous entry.)
Closed Feb Sun evg (Sept-June). Mon (not evgs July/Aug).
Post 40230 St-Vincent-de-Tyrosse, Landes. Region Southwest.
Tel 05 58 77 11 85. Mich 148/C2. Map 4. (200m S N10; E of town centre.)

ST-VRAIN   Hostellerie de St-Caprais

Comfortable restaurant with rooms/Cooking 1-2   `FW`
Terrace/Gardens

For those of you who have *FLE* I refer you to p400/401 – & the story of Arlette Malgras & her passion for her courtyard/garden, just sizzling with colour; flowers everywhere, inside & out! Her chef husband's classical/*Bourgeoise* cooking doesn't sizzle with the same panache - just competent stuff like *sole grillée meunière* & the ubiquitous *tarte Tatin*.
Menus B(ceiling)C. Rooms (4) E. Cards MC, V.
Closed 15 July-10 Aug. Sun evg. Mon.
Post 30 r. St-Caprais, 91770 St-Vrain, Essonne. Region Ile de France.
Tel 01 64 56 15 45. Fax 01 64 56 85 22. Mich 54/A1. Map 2.

STE-ANNE-D'AURAY   L'Auberge

Very comfortable restaurant with rooms/Cooking 2   `FW`
Parking

Don't be misled by the unappetising exterior of the *logis* on the D19 Vannes road. The interior more than compensates, as do the appetising offerings from Jean-Luc Larvoir & the welcome from Françoise. Mainly neo-classical with some oddities: *filet de St-Pierre dans sa soup d'ail, tarte de carrelet à la tomate* & *curry de pintade fermière aux moules*.
Menus abCDE. Rooms (6) DE. Cards AE, MC, V.
Closed 7-21 Jan. 24 Feb-3 Mar. 6-20 Oct. Tues evg (not July/Aug). Wed.
Post 56400 Ste-Anne-d'Auray, Morbihan. Region Brittany.
Tel 02 97 57 61 55. Fax 02 97 57 69 10. Mich 46/C4. Map 1.

A100frs & under. B100-150. C150-200. D200-250. E250-350. F350-500. G500+

STE-ANNE-D'AURAY

Le Myriam

Comfortable hotel (no restaurant)
Quiet/Lift/Parking

This base rates no special benefits (other than the lift, essential for a three-storey modern, faceless building); but the hotel has a quiet site, modestly-priced bedrooms & is well placed for the arc of restaurants to the S (&, of course, L'Auberge in Ste-Anne). Just off the D17 Auray road; turn W opposite the village's post office.
Rooms (30) E (low-end). Cards MC, V.
Closed Oct-Apl. Mon evg & Tues (not July/Aug).
Post 56400 Ste-Anne-d'Auray, Morbihan. Region Brittany.
Tel 02 97 57 70 44. Fax 02 97 57 50 61. Mich 46/C4. Map 1.

STE-ANNE-LA-PALUD

Plage

Very comfortable hotel/Cooking 3
Secluded/Gardens/Swim pool/Tennis/Lift/Parking/Air-cond. (rest.)

An idyllic hideaway on the secluded sands of the Baie de Douarnenez & protected by a high headland. A panoramic dining room provides views of sands, sea & sky (sunsets can be spectacular). English-speaking Jean-Milliau & Anne Le Coz are ideal hosts. Modern & classical styles from Jean-Pierre Gloanec, the chef here for 20 years. Numerous half-bottles.
Menus DEF. Rooms (26) G,G2. Cards All.
Closed Nov-Mar. Region Brittany.
Post Ste-Anne-de-Palud, 29127 Plonevez-Porzay, Finistère.
Tel 02 98 92 50 12. Fax 02 98 92 56 54. Mich 44/C1. Map 1.

STE-MENEHOULD

Cheval Rouge

Simple hotel/Cooking 1-2   FW

Catherine & François Fourreau are the hosts at the vine-covered *logis*; Jean-Robert Lafois is the busy chef. He juggles classical, *Bourgeois* & varying regional culinary trotters. Relish *choucroute d'empereur* or an *onglet de veau à la Niçoise*; or tuck into local treats like the famed *pied de cochon à la Ste-Menehould* & *délice d'Argonne*. Some rooms noisy: Le Jabloire (*sans rest.*) at Florent-en-Argonne much quieter.
Menus ABCD. (Brasserie A). Rooms (18) DE. Cards All. (Above 8km to NE.)
Closed 18 Nov-9 Dec. Mon (Sept-Easter).
Post 1 r. Chanzy, 51800 Ste-Menehould, Marne. Region Champ-Ard.
Tel 03 26 60 81 04. Fax 03 26 60 93 11. Mich 39/E2. Map 3.

A100frs & under. B100–150. C150–200. D200–250. E250–350. F350–500. G500+

STE-PREUVE
Château de Barive

Very comfortable hotel/Cooking 2-3 | FW
Secluded/Gardens/Swimming pool (indoor)/Tennis/Parking

An impressive 17thC château, its stone façade shining proudly behind the formal garden, gates & high wall. Readers speak highly of the German-owned hotel: the facilities, welcome, luxury – at not-too-dear prices – & Jos Bergman's neo-classical cuisine. One menu B stunner: *persillade de loup de mer en salade d'hiver*. Excellent Franco-German breakfasts.
Menus BCEF. Rooms (14) FG. Cards All. (Some bedrooms have *cuisinettes*.)
Closed Mid Jan-mid Feb. (App. from D977; SE at Chivres-en-Laonnois.)
Post Ste-Preuve, 02350 Liesse, Aisne. Regions Champ-Ard/North.
Tel 03 23 22 15 15. Fax 03 23 22 08 39. Mich 20/B2. Map 3.

SAINTES
Relais du Bois St-Georges

Very comfortable hotel/Cooking 2-3
Quiet/Terrace/Gardens/Swimming pool (indoor)/Garage/Parking

A fabulous *relais* by any measure. W of Saintes; 1km SE A10 exit 25. The 37-acre park & *étang* add extra sparkle to the man-made comforts. Two pavilions house the bedrooms. Jerômé Emery, the owner, is rightly proud. Chef Philippe Gault weaves modern tapestries making clever use of his Charentes *terroir*: oysters from Marennes, fish & shellfish from the port at La Cotinière (Ile d'Oléron) & both Pineau & Cognac – *bien sûr*.
Menus CDF. Rooms (27) F,G,G2. Cards MC, V. Region Poitou-Charentes.
Post r. Royan (D137), 17100 Saintes, Charente-Maritime.
Tel 05 46 93 50 99. Fax 05 46 93 34 93. Mich 107/D2. Map 4.

STES-MARIES-DE-LA-MER
Hostellerie du Pont de Gau

Comfortable restaurant with rooms/Cooking 2-3 | FW
Parking

Arguably one of the great readers' favourites. Jean & Monique Audry's *logis*, at the heart of the Camargue, is next door to the famed Parc Ornithologique. Vivid regional/classical *plats* from chef Jean, including a gutsy *Menu Carmarguais*. Tuck into the likes of *bouille de congre à la rouille* & a beefy *marinade de toros à la provençale*.
Menus ABCD. Rooms (9) D(ceiling). Cards AE, MC, V. (5km N; D570.)
Closed 4 Jan-20 Feb. Wed (mid Oct-Easter; not sch. hols).
Post 13460 Stes-Maries-de-la-Mer, Bouches-du-Rhône. Region Provence.
Tel 04 90 97 81 53. Fax 04 90 97 98 54. Mich 157/E3-E4. Map 6.

SALERS
Le Bailliage

Comfortable hotel/Cookinq 1-2
Quiet/Terrace/Gardens/Swimming pool/Garage/Parking

FW

Come on Charles Bancarel! You have so many man-made & natural pluses on your side: village, hotel facilities & *terroir*. But you retain an entry by a whisker (after 14 years in my guides). Please provide consistency in your regional/*Bourgeoise*/classical *plats*: among the former *potée*, *tripoux*, *truffade* (served tepid), *pounti* & prime Salers beef & cheese.
Menus ABC. Rooms (30) EF. Cards AE, MC, V.
Closed 20 Dec-1 Feb.
Post 15410 Salers, Cantal. Region Massif Central (Auvergne).
Tel 04 71 40 71 95. Fax 04 71 40 74 90. Mich 126/B2. Map 5.

SALIGNAC-EYVIGUES
La Meynardie

Comfortable restaurant/Cooking 2-3
Terrace/Gardens/Parking

FW

Follow signs N to a dead-end, exquisite setting (woods & pastures) & an old farm with stone walls & deep casement windows. Little touches abound. Hearty regional – *assiette gourmand du Périgord (foie, magret, gésiers, d'oie, crudités)* – & lighter dishes like a spirited *saumon à la feuille de chou, sauce gingembre*. Bravo Gérard Lasserre.
Menus ABCD. Cards MC, V. (Rooms: La Terrasse in village.)
Closed Wed (Oct-mid June).
Post 24590 Salignac-Eyvigues, Dordogne. Region Dordogne.
Tel 05 53 28 85 98. Fax 05 53 28 82 79. Mich 124/B3. Map 5.

SALLES-CURAN
Hostellerie du Lévézou

Comfortable hotel/Cooking 2-3
Quiet/Terrace/Gardens/Parking

FW

A 14thC château with an imposing tower & fine views of the local Welsh-like terrain. The Lac de Pareloup is a couple of km to the N. *Chef/patron* David Bouviala is also the local mayor. Classical/neo-classical/*Rouergate* fare: typical creations of the three styles could inc' *rumsteak aux deux poivres, rouget* & St-Jacques au basilic, & *choux farci*.
Menus a(lunch)BCE. Rooms (20) CDE. Cards All.
Closed Nov-Easter. Sun evg & Mon (not July/Aug).
Post 12410 Salles-Curan, Aveyron. Region Massif Central (Cévennes).
Tel 05 65 46 34 16. Fax 05 65 46 01 19. Mich 140/C3. Map 5.

A100frs & under. B100–150. C150–200. D200–250. E250–350. F350–500. G500+

SALON-DE-PROVENCE

Abbaye de Sainte-Croix

Very comfortable hotel/Cooking 3
Secluded/Terr/Gardens/Swim pool/Closed parking/Air-cond. (rooms)

Parts of the restored abbey date back 800 years. There's a strong sense of peace & tranquillity in the cool interior; the exterior is more dramatic with sensational views S. Fastidious classical & creative neo-classical fare, with little to fault or excite. Nothing dull about *la cave*: plenty of half-bottles & the best local *châteaux/domaines*.
Menus c(lunch: ceiling)EG. Rooms (19) G,G2. Cards All. Region Provence.
Closed Nov-mid Mar. Rest: Mon *midi*. Mon evg & Tues *midi* (15 Mar-5 Apl).
Post 13300 Salon-de-Provence, Bouches-du-Rhône. (5km E; D17 & D16.)
Tel 04 90 56 24 55. Fax 04 90 56 31 12. Mich 158/C2-C3. Map 6.

SALON-DE-PROVENCE

Le Mas du Soleil

Very comfortable restaurant with rooms/Cooking 3
Secluded/Terrace/Gardens/Swim pool/Closed parking/Air-cond.

The modest, unassuming couple – Francis & gentle Christiane Robin – have settled well into their all brightness-&-light modern refurbishment of a 19thC house. Glass & marble floors in *la salle*; what a difference from their old, cramped rest. Spectrum-wide repertoire from Francis: modern/regional/classical/neo-classical. Gérard Paul cheeses & brilliant sweets.
Menus CDEF. Rooms (10) G. Disabled. Cards All. (Off D17, E of Salon.)
Closed Rest: Sun evg. Mon. Region Provence.
Post 38 ch. St-Côme, 13300 Salon-de-Provence, Bouches-du-Rhône.
Tel 04 90 56 06 53. Fax 04 90 56 21 52. Mich 158/C2-C3. Map 6.

SALON-DE-PROVENCE

La Salle à Manger

Very comfortable restaurant/Cooking 2-3   FW
Terrace

Delightful: the self-effacing façade of a *hôtel particulier*; the ornate interior; the courtyard terrace; & the Miège family, led by Francis & wife Elyane in *la cuisine*. Huge choice of classical/Provençals dishes: *foie gras de canard, carpaccio de thon en croûte, daurade de rôti & croustillant d'agneau à la tapenade* were a memorable quartet.
Menus A *la carte* B(ceiling)C. Cards MC, V. (Rooms: Vendôme next door.)
Closed 6-22 Aug. 18 Dec-3 Jan. Sun evg. Mon. (Parking 150m to NE.)
Post 6 r. Mar. Joffe, 13300 Salon-de-Provence, Bouches-du-Rhône.
Tel 04 90 56 28 01. Mich 158/C2-C3. Map 6. Region Provence.

A100frs & under. B100–150. C150–200. D200–250. E250–350. F350–500. G500+

SANCERRE

La Tour

Very comfortable restaurant/Cooking 2 | FW |
Air-conditioning

Sancerre casts a satisfied eye over the famed vineyards surrounding its high dome of a hill. Enter from the N (Porte César), park, & walk a few yards to Daniel & Pascale Fournier's tower: a 14thC *salon* &, on the first floor, a modern room with panoramic views. Daniel is a classical technician. Evidence? A tasty *filet de sandre poché à la Sancerroise. Chariot de fromages* with local/regional cheeses. Super *vins de pays.*
Menus aBCD. Cards AE, MC, V. (Rooms: nearby Panoramic; 300m walk.)
Post Nouvelle Place, 18300 Sancerre, Cher. Regions Berry-Bourb/Loire.
Tel 02 48 54 00 81. Fax 02 48 78 01 54. Mich 85/E1. Map 2.

SANCERRE (Chavignol)

La Côte des Monts Damnés

Comfortable restaurant/Cooking 2 | FW |

Chavignol, 4km NW of Sancerre, is famed for both its wines & goats' milk cheeses. There's now a third good reason for nosing out the small village: the original modern/neo-classical creations from Jean-Marc Bourgeois. Wide choice on his anything but *Bourgeois* menus: tease your tastebuds with alternatives such as *salade de crottin (Chavignol) & pieds de porc*; & spiky *filet de carrelet au beurre de hareng et paprika.*
Menus ABCD. Cards MC, V. (Rooms: Panoramic in Sancerre.)
Closed 3 Feb-4 Mar. Sun evg. Mon.
Post Chavignol, 18300 Sancerre, Cher. Regions Berry-Bourbonnais/Loire.
Tel 02 48 54 01 72. Fax 02 48 54 14 24. Mich 70/C4. Map 2.

SANCOINS

Parc

Comfortable hotel (no restaurant)
Quiet/Gardens/Garage/Parking

Inexpensive bedrooms in a "time-warp" old house; the site, in a quiet, side street, is dominated by fir trees. Madame, alas, is looking much frailer these days. Ideal overnight alternative for the restaurants at Bannegon (to the W) & Magny-Cours (to the NE); see the two entries. Readers report that the nearby L'Ancienne Poste serves good-value fare.
Rooms (11) DE. Cards not accepted.
Closed 1-15 Jan.
Post r. M. Audoux, 18600 Sancoins, Cher. Region Berry-Bourbonnais.
Tel 02 48 74 56 60. Fax 02 48 74 61 30. Mich 85/E3. Map 2.

A100frs & under. B100–150. C150–200. D200–250. E250–350. F350–500. G500+

Le SAPPEY-EN-CHARTREUSE

Le Pudding

Comfortable restaurant/Cooking 2
Terrace

FW

A village setting – on the southern slopes of the Chartreuse, 13km N of Grenoble. Dull exterior but compensated by two generations of the Borrel family. Michel & son Gérard cook; wives Béatrice & Muriel are *les patronnes*. Classical/neo-classical/regional *plats* such as *terrine de gibiers confiture d'oignon* & *filets de perche à la crème de champignons*.
Menus bCE. Cards MC, V. (Rooms: Beau Site, St-Pierre-de-C; 14km N.)
Closed 8-29 Sept. Sun evg. Mon.
Post 38700 Le Sappey-en-Chartreuse, Isère. Region Savoie.
Tel 04 76 88 80 26. Fax 04 76 88 84 66. Mich 131/E1. Map 6.

Le SAPPEY-EN-CHARTREUSE

Skieurs

Simple hotel/Cooking 2
Quiet/Terrace/Gardens/Swimming pool/Parking

FW

Chalet-style hotel with sun-trap terrace (N of village). Christophe (the chef) & Raphaële Jail are an energetic duo. Classical/regional cooking: enjoy *plats* like *terrine de foie de volaille* & *papillote de saumon et sa julienne de légumes*. Ask to see the superb Jail cars: from vintage Ford to modern Ferrari. Christophe & Andrée, his dad, are rallying nutters.
Menus bCDE. Rooms (18) E. Cards MC, V.
Closed Apl. Nov. Dec. Sun evg & Mon (not summer).
Post 38700 Le Sappey-en-Chartreuse, Isère. Region Savoie.
Tel 04 76 88 80 15. Fax 04 76 88 85 76. Mich 131/E1. Map 6.

SARLAT-LA-CANEDA

La Hoirie

Comfortable hotel/Cooking 1-2
Secluded/Terrace/Gardens/Swimming pool/Parking

FW

A re-appearance for this prettily-sited hotel, to the S of Sarlat. Parts of La Hoirie date back to the 13thC. The present-day owners, Robert & Arlette Sainneville-de-Vienne are highly capable *patrons*. She cooks, mixing out-&-out regional with classical – all rich, earthy, filling fare: *magret* (duck breast), *cassoulet périgoudin* & similar grub.
Menus BCE. Rooms (13) FG. Cards All.
Closed Mid Nov-mid Mar. (S of D704, towards La Canéda.)
Post 24200 Sarlat-la-Canéda, Dordogne. Region Dordogne.
Tel 05 53 59 05 62. Fax 05 53 31 13 90. Mich 124/A3-B3. Map 5.

A100frs & under. B100–150. C150–200. D200–250. E250–350. F350–500. G500+

SARLAT-LA-CANEDA — La Madeleine

Comfortable hotel/Cooking 1-2
Terrace/Lift/Garage/Air-conditioning (bedrooms) | FW |

We paid a return call to the town's most famous hotel – 35 years after our first! Over 100 years old, the interior is akin to stepping back to another time. Philippe Melot, wisely, has fashioned a sensible lighter regional & classical repertoire (many fish courses). Both a *flan de mer sauce crustacés* & *filets de sole au beurre blanc* were tonic *plats*.
Menus ABCE. Rooms (22) EF. Cards All. (Town-centre site; parking E&W.)
Closed Hotel: 12 Nov-14 Mar. Rest: 12 Nov-29 Mar. Mon *midi* (not Aug).
Post 1 pl. Petite Rigaudie, 24200 Sarlat-la-Canéda, Dordogne.
Tel 05 53 59 10 41. Fax 05 53 31 03 62. Mich 124/A3. Map 5. Reg Dord.

SARLAT-LA-CANEDA — Mas de Castel

Simple hotel (no restaurant)
Secluded/Gardens/Swimming pool/Parking

I have mixed feelings about Sarlat these days: most of the ancient houses have been restored & their golden stone exteriors cleaned up. But commercialism is rampant. Progress is not necessarily always in a forward gear! Here Jean-Luc Castalian's base has the priceless plus of a tranquil site – 2km S of Sarlat, *la gare* & the D704, towards La Canéda.
Rooms (13) DE. Cards MC, V.
Closed 12 Nov-Easter.
Post Sudalissant, 24200 Sarlat-la-Canéda, Dordogne. Region Dordogne.
Tel 05 53 59 02 59. Fax 05 53 28 25 62. Mich 124/A3-B3. Map 5.

SARLAT-LA-CANEDA — St-Albert et Montaigne

Comfortable hotel (very comfortable annexe)/Cooking 1-2 | FW |
Lift/Air-conditioning (restaurant)

English-speaking Michel Garrigou is a proud ambassador: for his hotel (a modern annexe, the Montaigne, is across the square); his own *pays*; & for the restaurant's copious classical/*Périgord* fare. "Commercial" Sarlat is sardine-packed these days; the hotel, too, is very busy. Dishes? Many – some based on duck: *magret, foie confit, jambon, aiguillette et al*.
Menus ABC. Rooms (61) E. Cards All. (Parking in *place*; if you're lucky.)
Closed Sun evg (17 Nov-Mar). Rest: Mon. (Town-centre hotel.)
Post pl. Pasteur, 24200 Sarlat-la-Canéda, Dordogne. Region Dordogne.
Tel 05 53 31 55 55. Fax 05 53 59 19 99. Mich 124/A3-B3. Map 5.

A100frs & under. B100–150. C150–200. D200–250. E250–350. F350–500. G500+

SARPOIL

La Bergerie

Comfortable restaurant/Cooking 3-4
Parking

FW

Menu B at Laurent & Isabelle Jury's remote home is superb *RQP*. Clever use of regional produce in Laurent's creative culinary rainbow: terrine of lentils, trout & smoked salmon; *pansettes* (faggots) of lamb stuffed with wild thyme & herbs; 12 Auvergne cheeses; *oeufs à la neige*. (Rooms: exquisite Ch. de Pasredon, 2km NW; *chambres d'hôtes*; Tel 04 73 71 00 67.)
Menus BCDE. Cards All. (Château address: 63500 St-Rémy-de-Chargnat.)
Closed Jan. 8-14 Sept. Sun evg. Mon. (Ch. prices low-end F, inc' bkft.)
Post Sarpoil, 63490 St-Jean-en-Val, Puy-de-Dôme. Region MC (Auvergne).
Tel 04 73 71 02 54. Mich 113/E3. Map 5. (La Bergerie 10km SE Issoire.)

SARS-POTERIES

Auberge Fleurie

Very comfortable restaurant/Cooking 3
Parking

FW

Alain & Josette Lequy are the 2nd-generation hosts at their 300-year-old farmhouse. On our first visit, over 30 years ago, his mum was the cook. He has kept her classical clogs on, with no stinting on cream & butter. Numerous inspirational fish specialities. Come pudding time a gallon bowl of cream is left at the table: not for the cholesterol "scweamish".
Menus bE. Cards All. (Rooms: see below.) (His sister is chef at Vervins.)
Closed 15-31 Jan. 15-31 Aug. Sun evg & Mon (not pub. hols). (S D962.)
Post 59216 Sars-Poteries, Nord. Regions Champagne-Ardenne/North.
Tel 03 27 61 62 48. Fax 03 27 59 32 16. Mich 10/A2. Map 3.

SARS-POTERIES

Hôtel Fleuri

Simple hotel (no restaurant)
Quiet/Gardens/Tennis/Parking

A longtime favourite of ours, one which we first visited in the early 60s. The hotel, well back from the D962 & behind the Auberge Fleurie (see above; run as a separate business) was once a farm, built about 100 years ago. Simple rooms with old furniture & run by the self-effacing, gentle sisters, Claudine & Thérèse Carrié-Guinot.
Rooms (11) DE. Cards MC, V.
Closed 22 Dec-5 Jan.
Post 59216 Sars-Poteries, Nord. Regions Champagne-Ardenne/North.
Tel 03 27 61 62 72. Mich 10/A2. Map 3.

A100frs & under. B100–150. C150–200. D200–250. E250–350. F350–500. G500+

SARZEAU

Comfortable restaurant/Cooking 2
Parking

A modern façade gives no inkling of the art museum interior with stone, beams & panelling; almost every square inch of wall is covered with pictures. Unabashed classical cooking: *soupe de poisson, blanc de poulet bourguignonne* & *île flottante* on menu A. More expensive menus feature both fish & meat specialities & a fair choice of above-average sweets.
Menus ACDF. Cards All. (Rooms: Mur du Roy; Penvins; 1km N.)
Closed Jan. Sun evg & Mon (Oct-Mar). Region Brittany.
Post La Grée-Penvins, 56370 Sarzeau, Morbihan. (SE of Sarzeau.)
Tel 02 97 67 34 26. Fax 02 97 67 38 43. Mich 62/C3. Map 1.

SARZEAU

La Tournepierre

Simple restaurant/Cooking 2

FW

A tiny, beamed dining room in a small stone cottage opposite the village church of St-Colombier (NE of Sarzeau). Rich, gutsy classical offerings from chef Alain Jouan: a high-octane opulent *fricassée de ris d'agneau et ses copeaux de foie gras de canard; noisettes d'agneau poêlés aux cocos blancs et son beurre de noix; chèvre chaud;* & a dessert of *pommes rôti au miel* is one typical appetite-satisfying menu B permutation.
Menus a(lunch)BCE(ceiling). Cards AE, MC, V. (Rooms: see above entry.)
Closed 17-30 Nov. Sun evg & Mon (not July/Aug).
Post St-Colombier, 56370 Sarzeau, Morbihan. Region Brittany.
Tel 02 97 26 42 19. Mich 62/C2-C3. Map 1.

SATILLIEU

Gentilhommière

Comfortable hotel/Cooking 1
Quiet/Terrace/Gardens/Swim pools (see text)/Tennis/Lift/Parking

Dynamic is the continuing word for both English-speaking *patron* Jean Astic, & his ever-growing hotel complex. Bedrooms are in a collection of buildings around the site. He also has appartments for rent. The most appreciated feature is the heated indoor pool (also an outdoor one); there's also a gym & sauna. Cooking? Basic classical/*Bourgeoise* fare.
Menus BCD. Rooms (51) EFG. Disabled. Cards MC, V.
Closed Rest: Nov-Mar. Sun evg. Fri evg.
Post 07290 Satillieu, Ardèche. Region Massif Central (Ardèche).
Tel 04 75 69 23 23. Fax 04 75 34 91 92. Mich 129/F2. Map 5.

A100frs & under. B100–150. C150–200. D200–250. E250–350. F350–500. G500+

SAULGES

Ermitage

Comfortable hotel/Cooking 2
Quiet/Gardens/Swimming pool/Closed parking

FW

During lunch black clouds opened their flood gates. We were still able to appreciate the *village fleuri* & the extensive views from the spick-&-span hotel's terrace/garden. Annette Janvier is the pleasant *patronne*; husband Daniel & son Thierry cook neo-classical dishes. Sunny menu C: *terrine de lotte et saumon, pièce de boeuf au Chinon & fraises Melba*.
Menus B(bottom-end)CDE. Rooms (36) F. Disabled. Cards All. (Gym.)
Closed Feb. Sun evg & Mon (Oct-mid Apl).
Post 53340 Saulges, Mayenne. Region Normandy.
Tel 02 43 90 52 28. Fax 02 43 90 56 61. Mich 50/B4. Map 2.

SAUVETERRE-DE-ROUERGUE

Le Sénéchal

Comfortable hotel/Cooking 3-4
Terrace/Swimming pool (indoor)/Lift/Air-conditioning

FW

La Place aux Arcades at the heart of the *bastide* is exhilarating; so is, in different ways, the ultra-modern hotel (with unusual pool). The hotel may not appeal to all but Chantal Truchon's welcome will; the same is true of her chef/husband's inventive modern cuisine. No-choice menu B is great *RQP: terrine de queue de boeuf en gelée à l'orange* a stunner.
Menus BDEF. Room8 (11) G(bottom-end). Disabled. Cards All.
Closed Jan. Feb. Mon & Tues midday (not July/Aug; not pub. hols).
Post 12800 Sauveterre-de-Rouergue, Aveyron. Regs Dord/MC (Cévennes).
Tel 05 65 71 29 00. Fax 05 65 71 29 09. Mich 140/A3. Map 5.

SAUXILLANGES

Chalut

Very simple restaurant with basic rooms/Cooking 2
Garage/Air-conditioning (restaurant)

FW

Have you a sweet tooth? Then head here for a 5-pudding dessert menu (C). Most of you will be content with François Chalut's neo-classical & regional concoctions: a *salade de lapereau tiède et sa ballotine, filet de canard aux poires épicées*, Auvergne cheeses & *crème brûlé aux mures* all appear on an aptly-named, multi-choice *Menu Plaisir* (C).
Menus aBCE. Rooms (6) BC. Cards AE, MC, V.
Closed 20 Jan-15 Feb. 2-19 Sept. Sun evg. Mon.
Post 63490 Sauxillanges, Puy-de-Dôme. Region Massif Central (Auvergne).
Tel 04 73 96 80 71. Fax 04 73 96 87 25. Mich 113/E3. Map 5.

A100frs & under. B100–150. C150–200. D200–250. E250–350. F350–500. G500+

SELESTAT

Jean-Frédéric Edel

Very comfortable restaurant/Cooking 3
Terrace

The *chef/patron* greets you, sends you on your way at the end of the meal – hopefully satiated – &, somehow, finds time to conjure up a mix of classical/modern/Alsace specialities. He reminds some of a benign Nico Ladenis. Highlights? A stunning duck *foie gras*, a signature *sandre au Riesling* & a gossamer-thin topped *crème brûlée au sucre cassonade*.
Menus B(ceiling)DEF. Cards All. (Rooms: Aub. des Alliés; 200m walk.)
Closed 21 July-12 Aug. 23 Dec-3 Jan. Sun evg. Tues evg. Wed.
Post 7 r. Serruriers, 67600 Sélestat, Bas-Rhin. Region Alsace.
Tel 03 88 92 86 55. Fax 03 88 92 87 26. Mich 61/D2. Map 3.

SEMBLANCAY

Mère Hamard

Simple hotel/Cooking 2
Gardens/Parking

FW

An elegant dining room & friendly owners – English-speaking Patrick & Monique Pégué. The gardens & rear aspect are more eye-pleasing than the modest façade. Nothing modest about the grub though: a satisfying menu B of *terrine de canard au foie gras*, rich *rognons de veau au Bourgueil et à l'échalote, salade au Ste-Maure chaude* & a chocolate sweet.
Menus aBCD. Rooms (9) DE. Cards MC, V.
Closed Sch. hols Feb & Nov. Sun evg & Mon (not hotel mid Apl-mid Oct).
Post pl. Eglise, 37360 Semblançay, Indre-et-Loire. Region Loire.
Tel 02 47 56 62 04. Fax 02 47 56 53 61. Mich 67/E3. Map 2.

SEMUR-EN-AUXOIS (also see next page)

Côte d'Or

Simple hotel/Cooking 1
Garage/Parking

An endearing trio: the town; the Côte d'Or; & *les patrons*. A typical unheralded hotel – a 17thC charmer with an old-style *salle* & with owners for whom nothing is too much trouble. Host Christian Chêne employs chefs who walk classical/regional paths: *jambon persillé* & *turbot sauce hollandaise* are the norm. Excellent breakfasts with unlimited coffee.
Menus aBC. Rooms (14) DEF. Cards All.
Closed 18 Dec-6 Feb. Rest: Wed (June-Oct). Region Burgundy.
Post 3 pl. Gaveau, 21140 Semur-en-Auxois, Côte-d'Or.
Tel 03 80 97 03 13. Fax 03 80 97 29 83. Mich 73/D3. Map 3.

A100frs & under. B100–150. C150–200. D200–250. E250–350. F350–500. G500+

SEMUR-EN-AUXOIS (also see previous page) Lac

Simple hotel/Cooking 1
Quiet/Terrace/Parking

The label "quiet" applies only during the week at Michel & Denise Laurençons' *logis* – alongside a lake & near a camping site (youngsters create a racket at weekends). Burgundian/*Bourgeoise* basics: tucker such as *jambon persillé, tête de veau sauce ravigote* & *andouillette grillée*. The Lac is 3km S of town; 6km N of A6 Bierre-lès-Semur exit.
Menus aBCD. Rooms (22) DE. Cards DC, MC, V.
Closed 6 Jan-1 Feb. Sun evg & Mon (mid Oct-mid Apl).
Post Lac de Pont, 21140 Semur-en-Auxois, Côte-d'Or. Region Burgundy.
Tel 03 80 97 11 11. Fax 03 80 97 29 25. Mich 73/D3. Map 3.

SENLISSE Auberge du Gros Marronnier

Simple restaurant with rooms/Cooking 1-2 FW
Quiet/Terrace/Gardens

The Trochon family's *auberge*, a *logis*, is a restored presbytery, adjacent to a church (parts of which are 12thC) & with a pretty *jardin de curé*. The encircling Parc Naturel Régional de la Haute Vallée de Chevreuse is a scenic wonderland. Grills, classical & *Bourgeois plats: civet de lièvre, terrine de biche, tarte Tatin* & similar.
Menus bCE. Rooms (16) F (low-end). Cards AE, MC, V.
Closed 22-27 Dec. Region Ile de France. (Parking no problem.)
Post 3 pl. de l'Eglise, 78720 Senlisse, Yvelines.
Tel 01 30 52 51 69. Fax 01 30 52 55 91. Mich 35/E4. Map 2.

SEPT-SAULX Cheval Blanc

Comfortable hotel/Cooking 2-3
Quiet/Terrace/Gardens/Tennis/Parking

Dropped from *FLE* the attractive hotel now gets another chance. Chef Bernard Robert & his daughter, English-speaking Armelle, a real charmer, are the 5th/6th-generation owners. Armelle's huband, Fabien Abdalalim, works alongside Bernard. Classical/neo-classical dishes with treats such as *poulet de Bresse sauté au thym et au citron* & *bar en croûte de sel*.
Menus b(lunch: ceiling)CEF. Rooms (18) F. Cards All.
Closed 28 Jan-19 Feb.
Post 51400 Sept-Saulx, Marne. Region Champagne-Ardenne.
Tel 03 26 03 90 27. Fax 03 26 03 97 09. Mich 38/B1. Map 3.

A100frs & under. B100–150. C150–200. D200–250. E250–350. F350–500. G500+

SEREILHAC

La Meule

Very comfortable restaurant with rooms/Cooking 3 **FW**
Parking

Readers continue to praise *patronne* Nicole Jouhaud: for doing everything she can to please clients; & for her neo-classical & rich, gutsy *terroir* (Périgord) specialities. She's an extremely capable *cuisinière*. Here's just one example of her seductive style: *sauté de cèpes et girolles aux langoustines*. At last the N21 has at least one redeeming feature.
Menus b(lunch)DF. Rooms (10) EF. Cards All.
Closed 7-20 Jan. Sun evg & Tues (winter).
Post 87620 Séreilhac, Haute-Vienne. Region Poitou-Charentes.
Tel 05 55 39 10 08. Fax 05 55 39 19 66. Mich 110/A2. Map 5.

SERIGNAN-DU-COMTAT

Hostellerie du Vieux Château

Comfortable restaurant with rooms/Cooking 2 **FW**
Terrace/Gardens/Swimming pool/Parking

Well back from D976, behind plane trees. Once a mill site; ask for the history notes (English). Anne-Marie Truchot speaks excellent English; husband Jean-Pierre cooks excellent classical/neo-classical French: *bavarois de tomates coulis au basilic* & *gigolette de volaille Curnonsky* were a tasty duo. Beautifully furnished bedrooms & luxury bathrooms.
Menus BCF. Rooms (7) FG. Cards AE, MC, V. (Cheaper rooms: see Orange.)
Closed 6-20 Jan. 12-22 Nov. 23-30 Dec. Sun evg & Mon (Oct-Easter).
Post 84830 Sérignan-du-Comtat, Vaucluse. Region Provence.
Tel 04 90 70 05 58. Fax 04 90 70 05 62. Mich 144/B3. Map 6.

SERRIERES

Schaeffer

Comfortable restaurant with rooms/Cooking 3 **FW**
Terrace/Garage/Air-conditioning

Bernard & Joëlle Mathe do a great job at their long-established family hotel (busy site; beside N86 & overlooking Rhône); see the old photos. Chef Bernard is a modern, neo-classicist master; colour plays a big part in his *métier:* witness the appetisers & sumptuous desserts. Come autumn BM's *carte de chasseur* (a variety of game dishes) is a hearty highlight.
Menus bCDE. Rooms (12) E. Cards AE, MC, V.
Closed 1-20 Jan. Nov sch. hols. Sun evg & Mon (not July/Aug).
Post 07340 Serrières, Ardèche. Region Massif Central (Ardèche).
Tel 04 75 34 00 07. Fax 04 75 34 08 79. Mich 130/A1. Map 6.

A100frs & under. B100–150. C150–200. D200–250. E250–350. F350–500. G500+

SETE

La Palangrotte

Comfortable restaurant/Cooking 2-3 [FW]
Air-conditioning

An historic port, in parts smart, elsewhere quite grotty. There's nowt grotty about Alain Gémignani's light, airy restaurant – with tinted glass & fitted out in Italian style; nor is his modern/neo-classical cuisine – based on a range of fish dishes. Treats could include a tasty *clafoutis de moules de Bouzigues* (to NW) *à la fondue de tomates*.
Menus b(lunch)C(low-end)E. Cards AE, MC, V. (Rooms: Sables d'Or.)
Closed Sun evg & Mon (not July/Aug). (Above 2km SW, La Corniche.)
Post rampe P. Valéry, quai Marine, 34200 Sète, Hérault. Reg Lang-Rouss.
Tel 04 67 74 80 35. Fax 04 67 74 97 20. Mich 156/B4. Map 5.

SETE

Les Terrasses du Lido

Comfortable restaurant with rooms/Cooking 2 [FW]
Terrace/Swimming pool/Lift/Garage/Parking/Air-conditioning

West of Sète, on La Corniche (on D2, not the N112)) & with views of the distant Med & famed Bassin de Thau. Cool elegance prevails: in *la salle* & on the flower-bedecked terrace beside the first-floor swimming pool. Colette Guironnet is *la cuisinière*. A welcome emphasis on fish dishes (mainly classical) & *coquillages* from the nearby *bassin* (to W).
Menus BDE. Rooms (9) EF. Cards All.
Closed 5-27 Feb. Rest: Sun evg & Mon (mid Sept-mid June).
Post rond-point Europe, 34200 Sète, Hérault. Reg Languedoc-Roussillon.
Tel 04 67 51 39 60. Fax 04 67 51 28 90. Mich 156/B4. Map 5.

SOUILLAC

Le Quercy

Comfortable hotel (no restaurant)
Gardens/Swimming pool/Garage

Though I have not given the hotel a "quiet" tag nevertheless Le Quercy can best be described as having a fairly quiet site, well to the W of the busy N20, N of the D703 & on the R bank of the Borrèze. The *Logis de France* is a modern building; bedrooms have all mod cons: 20 of them have small balconies. One other advantage: reasonable bedroom prices.
Rooms (25) E. Cards MC, V.
Closed Dec-mid Mar.
Post 1 r. Récège, 46200 Souillac, Lot. Region Dordogne.
Tel 05 65 37 83 56. Fax 05 65 37 07 22. Mich 124/C3. Map 5.

A100frs & under. B100–150. C150–200. D200–250. E250–350. F350–500. G500+

SOUILLAC
Le Redouillé

Comfortable restaurant/Cooking 2   FW
Terrace/Gardens/Parking/Air-conditioning

Souillac's best – to S, E side of N20. A shaded terrace; be sure, too, to
see the unusual fountain. Marika Balech welcomes you to her swish
*salle*s; chef/husband Jean-Pierre tantalises with a predominately modern
repertoire. Menu B (no choice) had one welcome surprise: *dos de morue
rôti au jeunes légumes, pommes provençales au beurre de basilic.*
Menus ABCE. Cards All. (Rooms: see previous entry.)
Closed Tues (mid Sept-mid June).
Post 28 av. Toulouse, 46200 Souillac, Lot. Region Dordogne.
Tel 05 65 37 87 25. Fax 05 65 37 09 09. Mich 124/C3. Map 5.

SOUSCEYRAC
Au Déjeuner de Sousceyrac

Comfortable restaurant with basic rooms/Cooking 2-3   FW

Fluent English-speaking Laurence Piganiol & her brilliant young chef
husband Richard, do an outstanding job in an unprepossessing village. A
panelled dining room is a handsome backdrop. Starters – *terrine de
boeuf froide en gelée* & a *brandade de morue et crispie de poitrine
fumée* – were star quality; alas, meat dishes were undercooked to the
point of being almost inedible; & desserts were flamboyantly top notch.
Menus bCD. Rooms (8) C (top-end). Cards MC, V.
Closed Feb. Sun evg & Mon (not July/Aug).
Post 46190 Sousceyrac, Lot. Region Dordogne.
Tel 05 65 33 00 56. Fax 05 65 33 04 37. Mich 125/E3. Map 5.

SOUVIGNY-EN-SOLOGNE
Perdrix Rouge

Comfortable restaurant/Cooking 2   FW
Gardens

A super village with pretty "green" & unusual church with *caquetoir*. The
English-speaking *patronne*, Dominique Beurienne, & the small, beamed
dining room are also eye-pleasers. Husband, Jean-Noël, treads water in
all cooking pools: witness *filet de sandre au beurre blanc, émincé de
boeuf au poivre vert* & *tarte tiède aux pommes façon Sologne.*
Menus aBCE. Cards AE, MC, V. (Rooms: Nouan-le-F. entry.) Closed 22 Feb-
14 Mar. 27 June-4 July. 28 Aug- 5 Sept. Mon (not midday May-Oct). Tues.
Post 41600 Souvigny-en-Sologne, Loir-et-Cher. Region Loire.
Tel 02 54 88 41 05. Fax 02 54 88 05 56. Mich 69/F3. Map 2.

A100frs & under. B100–150. C150–200. D200–250. E250–350. F350–500. G 500+

STAINVILLE

La Petite Auberge

Comfortable restaurant/Cooking 2-3

FW

Elizabeth Abalti, an attractive, elegant *patronne*, with chef Philippe Perée, continues to uphold the reputation of the tiny restaurant made famous by her parents in the 70s. Classical cooking not quite matching the star Michelin first awarded decades ago. Both *poulet à la crème (avec pleurottes et trompettes)* & *carré d'agneau rôti* were run-of-the-mill; desserts, *dame blanche* & *nougat glacé*, were absolutely terrific.
Menus a(lunch)BCE. Cards All. (Rooms: Ibis; N of St-Dizier; 18km W.)
Closed 23 Dec-1 Jan. 21 July-13 Aug. Fri evg. Sat midday. Sun evg.
Post 55500 Stainville, Meuse. Region Champagne-Ardenne.
Tel 03 29 78 60 10. Mich 39/F4. Map 3. (Easy N4 drive to St-Dizier.)

TALLOIRES

Hermitage

Very comfortable hotel/Cooking 2
Secluded/Terrace/Gardens/Swimming pool/Tennis/Lift/Parking

FW

A rejuvenating site, high above Talloires with views W over the lake, Duingt castle & Semnoz mountain. Jean-Jacques & Jacques Chappaz paint classical cooking canvases with the odd *Savoyarde* speciality adding a splash of colour. Typical *plats* include *chaudrée de moules, saladine aux croustillants de Reblochon* & *quenelle de brochet sauce Nantua*. Gym.
Menus B(ceiling)CE. Rooms (37) FG. Cards All.
Closed Nov-20 Dec. (Cheaper rooms: see Annecy; Motel le Flamboyant.)
Post 74290 Talloires, Haute-Savoie. Region Savoie.
Tel 04 50 60 71 17. Fax 04 50 60 77 85. Mich 118/B1. Map 6.

TALLOIRES

Les Prés du Lac

Very comfortable hotel (no restaurant)
Secluded/Gardens/Lake swimming/Parking

A magical marriage of seductive charms. The setting is as captivating as any in France – 100m from Lac d'Annecy with just a *prés* (meadow) between the lake & hotel. Next, light & airy bedrooms decorated with style & flair. Best of all, *la patronne*, English-speaking Marie-Paul Conan (a Joyce Grenfell reincarnation): for one reader – "a special friend".
Rooms (16) G,G2(bottom-end). Cards All.
Closed Nov-Feb.
Post 74290 Talloires, Haute-Savoie. Region Savoie.
Tel 04 50 60 76 11. Fax 04 50 60 73 42. Mich 118/B1. Map 6.

A100frs & under. B100–150. C150–200. D200–250. E250–350. F350–500. G500+

TALLOIRES (Col de Bluffy)   Dents de Lanfon

Simple restaurant with rooms/Cooking 2   FW
Terrace/Parking

Beside the D909, 4km N of Talloires – below the jawbone molars of the
Dents de Lanfon. Danièle Durey speaks English. Husband Jean-Marc does
his classical/regional culinary talking in the kitchen, very effectively too:
evidenced by menu B of *soupe veloutée aux moules, suprême de volaille
aux Reblochon, gratin Savoyard, fromage* & *gâteau aux 3 chocs.*
Menus ABC. Rooms (7) DE. Cards MC, V. Closed 2-31 Jan. 2-10 June. Rooms:
Mon (not July/Aug). Rest: Sun evg (not July/Aug). Mon (not pub hols).
Post Col de Bluffy, 74290 Veyrier-du-Lac, Haute-Savoie. Region Savoie.
Tel 04 50 02 82 51. Fax 04 50 02 85 19. Mich 118/B1. Map 6.

TAMNIES   Laborderie

Comfortable hotel/Cooking 1-2   FW
Secluded/Terrace/Gardens/Swim pool/Parking/Air-cond. (rest.)

A modernised, extended *logis* "business" on a hilltop with fine views
over the Beune Valley. A *Périgourdin* menu C includes feisty, filling
dishes such as *foie gras d'oie mi-cuit, cuisse de canarde confite avec
cèpes et pommes forestière, cabécou chaud* with an aromatic walnut-oil
salad & an inevitable *soufflé glacé aux noix.* Otherwise classical.
Menus ABCD . Rooms (36) DEF . Cards MC, V .
Closed Nov-Mar.
Post 24620 Tamniès, Dordogne. Region Dordogne.
Tel 05 53 29 68 59. Fax 05 53 29 65 31. Mich 124/A3. Map 5.

TARDETS-SORHOLUS   Pont d'Abense

Comfortable restaurant with rooms/Cooking 2   FW
Quiet/Terrace/Gardens/Parking

A great favourite. For Joseph & Agna Ibar, unassuming, gentle owners;
for the shady terrace (ideal for lunches/dinners); the *jardin fleuri*
(lovingly cared for by Joseph); & now for yet another reason – the
couple's English-speaking daughter Isabelle – back from catering college
& bringing a light & improved touch to super regional/classical fare.
Menus aBC(top-end). Rooms (10) CD. Cards MC, V. (Rooms improved.)
Closed Jan. 1-8 Dec. Thurs (not July/Aug). (SW of Tardets/River Saison.)
Post Abense-de-Haut, 64470 Tardets-Sorholus, Pyrénées-Atlantiques.
Tel 05 59 28 54 60. Mich 167/E2. Map 4. Region Southwest.

A100frs & under. B100–150. C150–200. D200–250. E250–350. F350–500. G500+

TARNAC   Voyageurs

Simple hotel/Cooking 2   FW
Quiet/Air-conditioning (restaurant)

Readers continue to praise this modest *logis*, tucked away in adorable
Corrèze. The same adjective could be tied to both Ghislaine & Jean
Deschamps – & to his classical & real *cuisine terroir*. Sauces with beef
dishes are considered "wonderful" & *escargots* "the best ever". Autumn
bonuses of *cèpes, pleurottes et girolles*. I can't wait to go back.
Menus aBC. Rooms (15) D. Cards MC, V.
Closed Mid Dec-mid Mar. Sun evg & Mon (Oct-May; not pub. hols).
Post 19170 Tarnac, Corrèze. Region Poitou-Charentes.
Tel 05 55 95 53 12. Fax 05 55 95 40 07. Mich 111/E2. Map 5.

TAVEL   Hostellerie du Seigneur

Simple restaurant with basic rooms/Cooking 1-2   FW
Terrace

Ange & Juliette Bodo have been great readers' favourites for 13 years.
They'll do anything to help clients. Classical/regional/*Bourgeoise*
cooking, using *terroir* produce: *cuisse de canard au Tavel* is one
example. Relish the couple (from Nice), their art gallery dining room, the
15thC house & the smallest *place* in France (with terrace & carpark).
Menus aB. Rooms (7) CD. Cards MC, V. Region Provence.
Closed Mid Dec-mid Jan. Thurs. (Dinner? Vital to book ahead.)
Post pl. Seigneur, 30126 Tavel, Gard. (Note; near A9 exit 22.)
Tel 04 66 50 04 26. Mich 144/A4. Map 6.

TENCE   Grand Hôtel Placide

Comfortable hotel/Cooking 3   FW
Gardens/Closed parking

A string of compliments from readers for the young, 4th-generation *chef/
patron*, Pierre-Marie Placide (trained by Chabran at Pont-de-l'Isère), &
his bubbling, English-speaking wife Véronique. Modern & regional
masterpieces: dither over cracking choices like lightly-smoked *cochon
aux lentilles de Puy* & *terrine chaude de cèpes, sauce au brebis frais*.
Menus aCDEF. Rooms (17) EF. Cards AE, MC, V.
Closed Dec-Feb. Sun evg & Mon (not high season).
Post av. Gare, 43190 Tence, Haute-Loire. Region MC (Ardèche).
Tel 04 71 59 82 76. Fax 04 71 65 44 46. Mich 129/E2. Map 6.

A100frs & under. B100–150. C150–200. D200–250. E250–350. F350–500. G500+

THANNENKIRCH
Auberge la Meunière

Simple hotel/Cooking 2
Terrace/Parking

Timber predominates at this bright *logis* – both inside & out – & in the vast Vosges forest views (can you spot Haut-Koenigsbourg?). More pluses: a gym, jacuzzi, sauna & billiards. Francesca Dumoulin greets you; hubby Jean-Luc tempts your tastebuds. Classical & regional fare: *canapés de Munster chaud au cumin* & *parfait aux griottes de Thannenkirch* typical.
Menus a(lunch)B(bottom-end)C. Rooms (15) EF. Cards AE, MC, V.
Closed 16 Nov-24 Mar.
Post 68590 Thannenkirch, Haut-Rhin. Region Alsace.
Tel 03 89 73 10 47. Fax 03 89 73 12 31. Mich 61/D2. Map 3.

THIEZAC
Casteltinet

Comfortable hotel/Cooking 2-3
Terrace/Lift/Parking

Built a decade ago with extensive views & now less noise from the main road (bypass to E). Nelly Macua is a helpful hostess; husband Faust is a modern/neo-classical chef. One dish alone – a bursting with flavour *escalopes de sandre de poireaux et fricassée de trompettes aux lardons* – made the trip worthwhile. Another bonus: super Auvergne cheeses.
Menus aBCE. Rooms (23) EF(low-end). Cards MC, V.
Closed 15 Mar-5 Apl. 12 Oct-22 Dec. Rest: Sun evg & Mon (not sch. hols).
Post 15800 Thiézac, Cantal. Region Massif Central (Auvergne).
Tel 04 71 47 00 60. Fax 04 71 47 04 08. Mich 126/C2. Map 5.

THIEZAC
Elancèze et Belle Vallée (annexe)

Simple hotels/Cooking 1-2
Lift (Elancèze)/Parking

A modern *logis* at the heart of the village (rooms with balconies). The annexe, an older, simpler building, is nearby. (Note: village bypass to E.) Michel Lauzet's modest repertoire includes both regional & classical specialities: *coq au vin, truite meunière, tripoux, potée Auvergnate, pounti* & many others. Is the cooking rating of 1-2 too generous?
Menus ABC. Rooms (41) DE. Cards MC, V.
Closed 6 Nov-20 Dec.
Tel 15800 Thiézac, Cantal. Region Massif Central (Auvergne).
Tel 04 71 47 00 22. Fax 04 71 47 02 08. Mich 126/C2. Map 5.

A100frs & under. B100–150. C150–200. D200–250. E250–350. F350–500. G500+

THOMERY   Le Vieux Logis

Very comfortable restaurant with rooms/Cooking 3   `FW`
Terrace/Swimming pool/Parking

Punt upstream on the Seine & Loing & you are in Impressionist *pays*.
Monique-Antonia Plouvier's *hostellerie* is equally eye-pleasing. Jean-Luc
Daligault continues the theme with vibrant modern cooking canvases:
menu B could include *saumon croustillé en peau, polenta et jus de
viande* & a luscious *crème brûlée à la cassonade et vanille Bourbon*.
Another plus: a dozen sensibly-priced, first-class half-bottles of wine.
Menus B(top-end)D. Rooms (14) F. Cards AE, MC, V. Region Ile de France.
Post 5 r. Sadi Carnot, 77810 Thomery, Seine-et-Marne-.
Tel 01 60 96 44 77. Fax 01 60 70 01 42. Mich 54/C2. Map 2.

THONES   Nouvel Hôtel du Commerce

Comfortable hotel/Cooking 2   `FW`
Lift/Parking

Don't be put off by the name or the façade. The 3rd-generation owners
of the 82-year-old *logis* are a cracking duo. Attractive Christiane
Bastard-Rosset is the welcoming hostess; husband Robert is an assertive
chef. Classical/*Savoyards* menus: the former could include a *mousse de
brochet soufflé*; the latter a filling *farcement* (see regional specs.).
Menus aBCDE. Rooms (25) DEF. Cards MC, V.
Closed 28 Oct-28 Nov. Rest: Sun evg & Mon (out of season).
Post r. Clefs, 74230 Thônes, Haute-Savoie. Region Savoie.
Tel 04 50 02 13 66. Fax 04 50 32 16 24. Mich 118/C1. Map 6.

THONES (Manigod)   Chalet Hôtel Croix-Fry

Comfortable hotel/Cooking 1-2   `FW`
Quiet/Terrace/Gardens/Swimming pool/Tennis/Parking

SE of Thônes, between Manigod & Col de la Croix-Fry. The 4000ft-high
site guarantees rejuvenating mountain & valley views. A complex of large
chalet-hotel & smaller ones for rent. *La patronne* is Marie-Ange Guelpa-
Veyrat – sister of Marc Veyrat, the local 3-star wonder chef. Cooking is
classical/regional. Tuck into filling *tartiflette* (see regional specs.).
Menus B(top-end)CDF. Rooms (12) G2,G3. Cards AE, MC, V. (Cheaper rooms:)
Closed Mid Apl-mid June. Mid Sept-mid Dec. (Rosières; col summit; 7km.)
Post 74230 Manigod, Haute-Savoie. Region Savoie.
Tel 04 50 44 90 16. Fax 04 50 44 94 87. Mich 113/C1. Map 6.

A100frs & under. B100–150. C150–200. D200–250. E250–350. F350–500. G500+

THOURS

Château

Comfortable hotel/Cooking 1-2
Terrace/Gardens/Parking

The modern white *logis* is on the E side of the D938 S entrance to
Thouars – with an exceptional panorama of the hill-top town. At lunch
there were no less than 30 French-owned vehicles in the carpark. Gilbert
Ramard's classical fare is popular! *Ballotine de canard aux pistaches,
canette rôtie au poivre vert, pêche Melba, poire belle Hélène* & similar.
Menus ABC. Rooms (20) D. Cards MC, V.
Closed Sun evg.
Post rte Parthenay, 79100 Thouars, Deux-Sèvres. Region Loire.
Tel 05 49 96 12 60. Fax 05 49 96 34 02. Mich 81/D2-D3. Map 2.

THOURS

Clos St-Médard

Very comfortable restaurant with rooms/Cooking 3
Terrace

A captivating 13thC stone, brick & timber house, restored with panache by
Yanelle & Pierre Aracil; the Clos almost touches the W end of the
Romanesque Eglise St-Médard. Madame is an equally captivating *patronne/
sommelière;* her husband is a neo-classical/modern master. Typical delight:
an exuberant *craquant de truite de mer à la fondue d'oignons.*
Menus c(low-end)E. Rooms (4) DE. Cards AE, MC, V.
Closed Feb sch. hols. Sun evg. Mon.
Post 14 pl. St-Médard, 79100 Thouars, Deux-Sèvres. Region Loire.
Tel 05 49 66 66 00. Fax 05 49 96 15 01. Mich 81/D2-D3. Map 2.

THURY-HARCOURT

Relais de la Poste

Comfortable restaurant with rooms/Cooking 1-2 FW
Terrace/Garage/Parking

Readers have consistently praised the owners, the Fermond family; alas,
they also reckon cooking standards are far too inconsistent. The vine-
covered *relais* is an eye-catching plus. Jean-François is a classical fan &
has a fondness for *homard et langouste: à l'américaine, grillé au beurre
d'estragon* & *flambé au cognac.* Other pluses: sauna & solarium.
Menus BDF. Rooms (12) EF. Cards AE, MC, V.
Closed Mid Jan-mid Feb. Sun evg & Mon (mid Nov-mid Apl).
Post 14220 Thury-Harcourt, Calvados. Region Normandy.
Tel 02 31 79 72 12. Fax 02 31 39 53 55. Mich 32/A2. Map 2.

A100frs & under. B100–150. C150–200. D200–250. E250–350. F350–500. G500+

TORCY

Vieux Saule

Very comfortable restaurant/Cooking 2-3
Terrace/Parking

FW

S of Le Creusot. Marie-Madeleine Hervé is a helpful *patronne*; & her husband Christain is a down-to-earth *cuisinier*. His *Menu du Terroir* (C) is a four-course, appetite-quenching blockbuster with two especially hearty *plats* – a *chausson d'escargots au beurre d'orties* & *estouffade de joues de boeuf à la charolaise*. Excellent desserts.
Menus BCDF. Cards MC, V. (Rooms: Novotel, Montchanin.)
Closed Sun evg. Mon. (Above simple 4km drive to SE; use N80.)
Post 71210 Torcy, Saône-et-Loire. Region Burgundy.
Tel 03 85 55 09 53. Fax 03 85 80 39 99. Mich 87/F4. Map 3.

TOUL

Le Dauphin

Very comfortable restaurant/Cooking 3-4
Terrace/Gardens/Parking

Unappetising site in an industrial zone; the interior, cooking & *les patrons* are all very appetising. Véronique Vohmann is an efficient hostess; her chef/husband, English-speaking Christophe, a brilliant modern master. Huge choice: relish delights like a *tartelette d'oignons confits à la moëlle de boeuf* & *rognons de veau au chutney de rhubarbe*.
Menus c(lunch)EF. Cards All. (Rooms: simple Europe, Toul centre.)
Closed 28 July-11 Aug. Sun evg. Mon. (Or Novotel Nancy Ouest; 16km E.)
Post rte Villey-St-Etienne, 54200 Toul, Meurthe-et-Moselle. (D191 – NE.)
Tel 03 83 43 13 46. Fax 03 83 64 37 01. Mich 40/C4. Map 3. Reg Alsace.

Le TOUQUET

Café des Arts

Comfortable restaurant/Cooking 1-2

FW

Two inspection visits: one good, one not so. Well-named: on two floors with contemporary, bizarre décor, 1920s furniture & numerous paintings. Annie Rousseau is the harassed *patronne*, Jérôme Panni *le cuisinier*. Modern & neo-classical cooking scenes, to match the surroundings: *feuilletée de haddock aux pommes de terre, ballotine de lapin farcie* & *gâteau au chocolat orange* is typical menu B. Stick to fish dishes.
Menus BE. Cards All. (Rooms: several hotels nearby; see next entries.)
Closed 10-31 Jan. 15-25 Dec. Mon. Tues (not sch. hols). (Park Aqualud.)
Post 80 r. Paris, 62520 Le Touquet, Pas-de-Calais. Region North.
Tel 03 21 05 21 55. Mich 2/A4. Map 2. (200m E of Aqualud & parking.)

A100frs & under. B100–150. C150–200. D200–250. E250–350. F350–500. G500+

Le TOUQUET   Ibis

Comfortable hotel/Cooking 0-1
Quiet/Terrace/Swimming pool (indoor)/Lift/Parking

I have given space to few group hotels in *FLF* & this entry is justified for
many reasons: the site, on the resort's famed beach; the adjoining indoor
heated sea-water pool (closed Jan); & the latter's thalassotherapy centre.
Cooking? Cheap & cheerful basics. Why not try other nearby restaurants
(without bedrooms), using the Ibis as a base.
Menus AB. Rooms (90) EFG (seasonal rates). Disabled. Cards MC, V.
Post sur la plage, 62520 Le Touquet, Pas-de-Calais. Region North.
Tel 03 21 09 87 00. Fax 03 21 09 87 10. Mich 2/A4. Map 2.
(Bookings: UK 0171 724 1000; US toll free 800 221 4542.)

Le TOUQUET   Novotel-Thalassa

Very comfortable hotel/Cooking 1
Quiet/Swimming pool (indoor)/Lift/Garage/Parking/Air-cond. (rest.)

No prizes for looks; more like a concrete bunker. Like its adjoining
small brother (Ibis) the Novotel is *sur la plage*. The indoor heated sea-
water pool & thalassotherapy centre sit between the two Accor group
hotels. Cooking ? Higher standard than the Ibis & most other Novotels:
classical/regional. Try, instead, Serge Pérard's super fish restaurant.
Menus C(*àlc*). Rooms (149) G,G2. Disabled. Cards All. (Above ½mile walk.)
Closed 4-21 Jan. Post 62520 Le Touquet, Pas-de-Calais. Region North.
Tel 03 21 09 85 00. Fax 03 21 09 85 10. Mich 2/A4. Map 2.
(Bookings : UK 0171 724 1000; US toll free 800 221 4542.)

TOURNUS (also see next page)   Hôtel de Greuze

Very comfortable hotel (no restaurant)
Quiet/Lift/Parking/Air-conditioning

An exceptional hotel in a splendid old building, adjacent to the famed
abbey. Refurbished throughout with elegant furnishings & with ultra-
modern bathrooms. The public rooms are especially handsome. The
hotel is next door to the Restaurant Greuze but is run as a separate
business by the Cachots. Expensive but a terrific luxury base hotel for the
many nearby recommended restaurants.
Rooms (21) G,G2. Disabled. Cards All. Region Lyonnais.
Post 5 pl. de l'Abbaye, 71700 Tournus, Saône-et-Loire.
Tel 03 85 51 77 77. Fax 03 85 51 77 23. Mich 102/C1. Map 6.

A100frs & under. B100–150. C150–200. D200–250. E250–350. F350–500. G500+

TOURNUS (also see previous page)   Restaurant Greuze

Very comfortable restaurant/Cooking 3-4
Air-conditioning

Cooking from an *autrefois*. *Pâté en croûte Alexandre Dumaine, quenelle de brochet, poulet de Bresse sauté nature* (succulence personified), *millefeuille pâtissière* (nowt better) & more. Go while Jean Ducloux still weaves his *haute cuisine* tapestries. An apprentice cook in 1933, he worked for Dumaine in the late 30s & opened here in 1947. Two masters assist: English-speaking MD, Claude Bouillet; & *pâtissier* Jean Léopold.
Menus EF. Cards AE, MC, V. (Rooms: see previous entry.)
Post 1 r. A. Thibaudet, 71700 Tournus, Saône-et-Loire-. Region Lyonnais.
Tel 03 85 51 13 52. Fax 03 85 51 75 42. Mich 102/C1. Map 6.

TOURNUS   Terminus

Comfortable restaurant with rooms/Cooking 1-2
Parking/Air-conditioning (restaurant)

Alongside both the N6 & station. A bright exterior, lined with boxes of geraniums; the interior hides the exciting surprise of a 1900 Gasparini mechanical organ – in the dining room! Michel Rigaud pulls out all the stops in his classical/regional tunes. How about a prize-winning *gâteau de foie blond* & an evocative *quenelle de brochet soufflé*?
Menus aBCDE. Rooms (13) DE. Cards MC, V.
Closed 2-17 Jan. 22 Nov-6 Dec. Tues evg & Wed (not July/Aug).
Post 21 av. Gambetta, 71700 Tournus, Saône-et-Loire. Region Lyonnais.
Tel 03 85 51 05 54. Fax 03 85 32 55 15. Mich 102/C1. Map 6.

TOURNUS   Terrasses

Comfortable restaurant with rooms/Cooking 2   FW
Garage/Parking/Air-conditioning

Competition is fierce in this "intriguing" town (see *Mapaholics' France*; map sheet 102). Like the entry above, the vine-covered, busy-lizzied *logis* is also alongside the N6. Michel Carrette is a friendly host & competent chef. Menu B is bravura classical: we recall, with pleasure, a pungent *cuisse de lapin en civet au Mâcon rouge*.
Menus aBCD. Rooms (18) E. Cards MC, V.
Closed 4 Jan-4 Feb. Sun evg. Mon.
Post 18 av. 23-Janvier, 71700 Tournus, Saône-et-Loire. Region Lyonnais.
Tel 03 85 51 01 74. Fax 03 85 51 09 99. Mich 102/C1. Map 6.

A100frs & under. B100–150. C150–200. D200–250. E250–350. F350–500. G500+

TOURNUS (Brancion)   Montagne de Brancion

Comfortable hotel/Cooking 2
Secluded/Gardens/Swimming pool/Parking

An important change at this longtime readers' favourite – in the hills 14km
SW of Tournus & with extensive views E over the Saône Valley: the
English-speaking owners, Jacques & Nathalie Million have opened a
restaurant. Their chef, Michel Bonthonnou (he has a fine c.v.), treads
modern culinary paths. One worrying new debit: all prices getting dearish.
Menus D(bottom-end)EF. Rooms (20) F(top-end)G. Cards DC, MC, V.
Closed Nov-mid Mar.
Post Brancion, 71700 Tournus, Saône-et-Loire. Region Lyonnais.
Tel 03 85 51 12 40. Fax 03 85 51 18 64. Mich 102/B1. Map 6.

TOURRETTES-SUR-LOUP   Petit Manoir

Comfortable restaurant/Cooking 2   FW

A perched *cité*. The *manoir* is *petit*, accessible only on foot (for the sure-
footed only), 150m from the D2210. Françoise & Dominique Taburet
make you welcome at their old stone house. Chef Dominique is a
classical addict: savour carefully sauced & prepared *croustade
d'escargots, beurre Provençal;* filling *aiguillettes de boeuf braisée aux
carottes*, cheese & a choice of appetising desserts. English spoken.
Menus aBCD(ceiling). Cards AE, MC, V. (Rooms: Floréal, W side Vence.)
Closed 15 Nov-10 Dec. Sun evg (not July/Aug). Wed.
Post 21 Grande Rue, 06140 Tourrettes-sur-Loup, Alpes-Maritimes.
Tel 04 93 24 19 19. Mich 163/F2. Map 6. Region Côte d'Azur.

TOURS (Joué-lès-Tours) (also see next page)   Chantepie

Simple hotel (no restaurant)
Fairly quiet/Closed parking

There's nothing special about this modern hotel, built in 1976. Well clear
of Tours' centre, Chantepie lies N of the D751 (Chinon road), W of the
A10 (exit 14) & just before the new western *rocade* (bypass) with its
junction with the currently being built A85. No grumbles about *le
patron* Gérard Goubault or the modest base hotel. Note: closed parking.
Rooms (28) E. Cards MC, V. (SW of Tours.)
Closed 23 Dec-4 Jan.
Post r. Chantepie, 37300 Joué-lès-Tours, Indre-et-Loire. Region Loire.
Tel 02 47 53 06 09. Fax 02 47 67 89 25. Mich 67/F4. Map 2.

A100frs & under. B100–150. C150–200. D200–250. E250–350. F350–500. G500+

TOURS (Rochecorbon) (also see previous page)   L'Oubliette

Comfortable restaurant/Cooking 2-3   FW
Terrace/Parking

Young Thierry & Anne-Marie Duhamel have won over numerous readers
during their tenure of this most unusual restaurant *taillé dans le roc*;
they've even added a second troglodyte dining room. Modern/neo-classical
plats: on one hand *turbot au curry et riz basmati aux fruits sec* – a touch
odd-ball; &, on the other, a well-sauced *canard du Marais au Chinon*.
Menus aCE. Cards MC, V. (Rooms: Ibis, N10, NE Tours; N152/D29 to N10.)
Closed 2-9 Jan.14-21 Apl. 25 Aug-8 Sept. Sun evg. Mon.
Post rte Parcey-Meslay, 37210 Rochecorbon, Indre-et-Loire. Region Loire.
Tel 02 47 52 50 49. Fax 02 47 52 50 49. Mich 67/E4-F4. Map 2. (E Tours.)

TOURS (St-Symphorien)   Jean Bardet

Luxury hotel/Cooking 4-5
Secluded/Gardens/Swimming pool/Parking/Air-conditioning

English-speaking Jean Bardet is a larger-than-life, hugely likeable &
sizeable chef, the epitome of a modern *cuisinier*; his wife Sophie fits the
same bill. All is set for star 3: 7½-acre park (see *le potager*); luxury lounges
& *salle*; romantic bedrooms; & top-draw staff. Cooking? Opulent
modern. Big-bucks business. (N of Loire; E junction N138/N10.)
Menus eFG. Rooms (16) G,G2. Cards All.
Closed Rest: Sun evg & Mon (Nov-Mar). Mon midday (Apl-Oct).
Post 57 r. Groison, 37100 Tours, Indre-et-Loire. Region Loire.
Tel 02 47 41 41 11. Fax 02 47 51 68 72. Mich 67/F4. Map 2.

TOURS (Savonnières)   Cèdres

Comfortable hotel (no restaurant)
Fairly quiet/Gardens/Swiming pool/Lift/Parking

Of the 8 base hotels recommended in the Loire Valley this is the only one
with a swimming pool. Les Cèdres is a flower-bedecked, modern, whitewashed building, 11km W of Tours & 6km E of Villandry – on the S side
of the D7. Not surprisingly the hotel has been popular with readers – the
site is ideal for exploring many of the *châteaux* E & W of Tours. (There's
also a restaurant, run as a separate business, in the grounds.)
Rooms (37) EFG. Cards AE, MC, V. Region Loire.
Post rte de Savonnières, 37510 Joué-lès-Tours, Indre-et-Loire.
Tel 02 47 53 00 28. Fax 02 47 80 03 84. Mich 67/E4. Map 2.

A100frs & under. B100–150. C150–200. D200–250. E250–350. F350–500. G500+

TOURTOUR
Les Chênes Verts

Very comfortable restaurant with rooms/Cooking 4
Quiet/Terrace/Gardens/Parking

Paul Bajade is a superb modern *cuisinier*: confidence, experience & good taste influence every aspect of his dazzling repertoire. Two signature dishes are masterpieces: *agneau de Sisteron rôti à la sarriette, petits légumes au jus* (the tenderest lamb ever); the other a supreme *risotto aux petites cèpes "bouchons" et rapée de truffe de pays*. Super rooms.
Menus DEF. Rooms (3) G. Cards AE, MC, V. (Cheaper rooms: next line.)
Closed Jan-8 Feb. Tues evg. Wed. (Use nearby Le Mas de Collines.)
Post rte Villecroze (D51), 83690 Tourtour, Var. Reg Côte d'A. (2km W.)
Tel 04 94 70 55 06. Fax 04 94 70 59 35. Mich 162/C3. Map 6.

TREBEURDEN
Ti al-Lannec

Very comfortable hotel/Cooking 3   `FW`
Secluded/Terrace/Gardens/Lift/Parking

A little peace of heaven on earth. Nature has been kind: a secluded, wooded site with extensive views. Just as appreciated (more so?) are the English-speaking owners, Danielle & Gérard Jouanny, masterful hoteliers. Dominique Lanos (their chef for 10 years) has a modern, light & fresh touch. Helpful, top-notch staff. Plus sauna, solarium, jacuzzi & gym.
Menus b(lunch)CEF. Rooms (29)FG,G2. Disabled. Cards All.
Closed 12 Nov-15 Mar.
Post 22560 Trébeurden, Côtes d'Armor. Region Brittany.
Tel 02 96 23 57 26. Fax 02 96 23 62 14. Mich 27/F1. Map 1.

TRELLY
Verte Campagne

Comfortable restaurant wih rooms/Cooking 3   `FW`
Secluded/Gardens/Parking

Climbing roses & rhododendrons are the first visual greetings at the old farmhouse, lost in the *bocage* SE of Trelly (maps show hotel location). Young owners, English-speaking Caroline & Pascal Bernou, are keen as mustard. Chef Pascal is a modern *maître*, full of innovative touches. Even menu B offers good choice. Only one debit: bedrooms are smallish.
Menus BCDF. Rooms (7) EF. Cards MC, V.
Closed 9 Jan-4 Feb. 2-9 Feb. Sun evg (out of season). Mon.
Post 50660 Trelly, Manche. Region Normandy.
Tel 02 33 47 65 33. Fax 02 33 47 38 03. Mich 30/C2. Map 1.

A100frs & under. B100–150. C150–200. D200–250. E250–350. F350–500. G500+

TREMBLAY

Roc-Land

Comfortable hotel/Cooking 2
Quiet/Terrace/Gardens/Tennis/Parking

In 10 acres of wooded grounds NW of the village. *Chef/patron* Jean-Pierre Helleu makes good use of both local & relatively distant produce in his classical repertoire. Menu C provides the chance to have a lightish lunch with two fish courses: *escalope de sandre de Loire* (or a *croustillant de fruits de mer*) & *saumon frais grillée* – both excellent.
Menus ABC. Rooms (2) DE. Cards MC, V.
Closed 2 wks Feb. 2 wks Oct. Sun evg. Mon.
Post 35460 Tremblay, Ille-et-Vilaine. Regions Brittany/Normandy.
Tel 02 99 98 20 46. Fax 02 99 98 29 00. Mich 48/C2. Map 1.

TREMOLAT

Vieux Logis

Very comfortable hotel/Cooking 3-4
Secluded/Terrace/Gardens/Swimming pool/Parking

In the same family's hands for over 400 years (Giraudel-Destord), the evocative hotel is a magical mix of stone, timber, plants & trees. The River Dordogne provides the ideal backdrop. Pierre-Jean Duribreux weaves modern, neo-classical & regional tapestries: *poulet fermier simplement rôti et son jus* is just one example of culinary good taste & a sure touch.
Menus CDF. Rooms (19) G,G2. Disabled. Cards All.
Closed 15 Jan-28 Feb. Tues midday & Wed midday (not mid July-mid Sept).
Post 24510 Trémolat, Dordogne. Region Dordogne.
Tel 05 53 22 80 06. Fax 05 53 22 84 89. Mich 123/E3. Map 5.

La TRINITE-SUR-MER

L'Azimut

Very comfortable restaurant/Cooking 3
Terrace

Blue & white umbrellas & awnings brighten-up the stone-built house overlooking the port. Marie-Hélène & Hervé Le Calvez, the chef, have an impressive c.v. (in France & Switzerland). His repertoire makes clever use of land & sea. Typical fish menu could include *saumon, bar et haddock fumés;* sardines stuffed with an artichoke cream; *saumon sauvage laqué en peau au miel*; & yummy *tarte chibouste tiède à la rhubarbe.* Menus aBCD. Cards MC, V. (Rooms: La Licorne, Carnac; *sans rest.*)
Post 56470 La Trinité-sur-Mer, Morbihan. Region Brittany. (Above 5km W.)
Tel 02 97 55 71 88. Fax 02 97 55 80 15. Mich 62/B2. Map 1.

A100frs & under. B100–150. C150–200. D200–250. E250–350. F350–500. G500+

Les TROIS-EPIS

Croix d'Or

Simple hotel/Cooking 1-2
Terrace/Parking

FW

Views are the highlight at this small hotel (with a new orange livery), 2000ft high – yet only 14km from Colmar. Catherine Bruley & Marianne Gebel stick in a regional/classical groove – a culinary turntable which includes *canard de Barbarie à l'orange, choucroute garnie* & the buffet-style *hors d'oeuvre*, tagged *la table "Hans in Schnokeloch"* (w/end only).
Menus aBC. Rooms (12) CDE. Cards MC, V.
Closed 20 Nov-20 Dec. Tues.
Post 68410 Les Trois-Epis, Haut-Rhin. Region Alsace.
Tel 03 89 49 83 55. Fax 03 89 49 87 14. Mich 61/D3. Map 3.

TRONCAIS

Le Tronçais

Comfortable hotel/Cooking 1-2
Secluded/Gardens/Tennis/Parking

FW

Handsome *logis* in extensive gardens/parkland, the latter bordering, on E edge, a large *étang* – the sum of the parts at the heart of the majestic oak forest of Tronçais. Ghislaine Bajard is a keen, informed hostess; husband Joël a classical chef. In their cosy dining rooms dig into *boeuf à la crème* (Charolais) or an enticing *terrine d'anguille aux mûres*.
Menus AB. Rooms (12) DE. Cards MC, V.
Closed 15 Dec-15 Mar. Sun evg & Mon (not high season).
Post 03360 St-Bonnet-Tronçais, Allier. Region Berry-Bourbonnais.
Tel 04 70 06 11 95. Fax 04 70 06 16 15. Mich 99/E1. Map 2.

TROYES (Bréviandes) (also see next page)

Pan de Bois

Simple hotel/Cooking 0-1
Quiet/Terrace/Parking

"Convenience" is the hotel's redeeming benefit for motorists using the A26. At its junc. with A5 head W for 3km to exit 21; N for 5km on N71 to Bréviandes; then R on N71 to hotel. The latter, in a separate, quieter building, is behind Claude Vadrot's *rôtisserie* rest. Grills (beef/lamb/ duck) *feu de bois* &, *bien sûr*, famed Troyes *andouillettes/boudins*.
Menus ABC. Rooms (31) DE. Disabled. Cards MC, V.
Closed Sun evg. Rest: Mon. Region Champagne-Ardenne.
Post 35 av. Gén.-Leclerc, 10450 Bréviandes, Aube.
Tel 03 25 75 02 31. Fax 03 25 49 67 84. Mich 56/C3. Map 3.

A100frs & under. B100–150. C150–200. D200–250. E250–350. F350–500. G500+

TROYES (Ste-Maure) (also see previous page)   **Aub. de Ste-Maure**

Very comfortable restaurant/Cooking 3   FW
Terrace/Parking

N of Troyes & easily accessed from A26 & N bypass. A delicious spot –
modern glassed-in *salle* in verdant setting beside the River Melda – &
delicious English-speaking *patronne*, Martine Martin. Chef Thierry
Grandclaude weaves modern/neo-classical spells. Two spellbinders:
gâteau de boudin noir aux pommes & *crème croustillant à la passion.*
Menus bC. Cards AE, MC, V. (Rooms: see next entry; & Novotel 6km SW.)
Closed Sun evg. Mon. (Novotel easily reached by Troyes N bypass.)
Post 10150 Ste-Maure, Aube. Region Champagne-Ardenne.
Tel 03 25 76 90 41. Fax 03 25 80 01 55. Mich 56/B2-B3. Map 3.

TROYES (Ste-Savine)   **Chantereigne**

Comfortable hotel (no restaurant)
Quiet/Parking

One of the most unusual hotel structures I know: a horse-shoe shaped,
modern hotel to the W of Troyes (beside N60 but well back from the
road). Easily found: use A5 exit 20, then E towards Troyes; or use N & W
bypass from A26 Troyes-Nord exit (hotel is just W of the bypass/N60
junction). Ideal base for the lovely restaurant above; easy drive.
Rooms (30) E. Disabled. Cards MC, V.
Closed 26 Dec-2 Jan. Region Champagne-Ardenne.
Post 128 av. Gén. Leclerc, 10300 Ste-Savine, Aube.
Tel 03 25 74 89 35. Fax 03 25 74 47 78. Mich 56/B3. Map 3.

TURENNE   **Maison des Chanoines**

Simple restaurant with comfortable rooms/Cooking 2   FW
Quiet/Terrace

A tiny, 16thC stone-built house at the heart of the *bourg* – with a shady
terrace across the alley. Plenty of choice. A typical regional meal could
incorporate an inventive *terrine chaude aux noix, Roquefort et poires*;
a filling *médaillon de veau du Limousin sauce Quercynoise*; & a
refreshing *glace aux noix maison*. Satisfying regional/classical fare.
Menus BC. Rooms (3) EF(low-end). Cards MC, V. Note: book ahead.
Closed Mid Nov-Feb. Tues evg & Wed (not July/Aug).
Post 19500 Turenne, Corrèze. Region Dordogne.
Tel 05 55 85 93 43. Mich 124/C2. Map 5.

USTARITZ

La Patoula

Comfortable restaurant with rooms/Cooking 2 | FW |
Quiet/Terrace/Gardens/Parking

Superlatives flow fast at the exquisitely-sited Patoula. First, in the shape of the friendly hosts, Pierre & Anne-Marie Guilhem; next, the handsome bedrooms & wonderful covered terrace beside the Nive; &, finally, François Rodolphe's modern, neo-classical & regional cuisine with eclectic touches. One vivid menu B memory: *tarte aux anchois*.
Menus BCD(ceiling). Rooms (9) F. Disabled. Cards MC, V.
Closed 5 Jan-9 Feb. Rest: Sun evg (out of season). Mon (not evg summer).
Post 64480 Ustaritz, Pyrénées-Atlantiques. Region Southwest.
Tel 05 59 93 00 56. Fax 05 59 93 16 54. Mich 148/B4. Map 4.

UZERCHE

Teyssier

Simple hotel/Cooking 2 | FW |
Parking

By the time *FLF* is published the A20 bypass will be open – a real bonus for readers who seek out Jean-Michel & Annie Teyssier at their hotel beside the Vézère (the N20 was noisy). J-M sticks to regional/classical styles, his work much influenced by Escoffier: *filets d'oie et de dinde fumés maison, lotte à l'armoricaine* are typical. Good buffet breakfast.
Menus bCE. Rooms (17) CDEF. Cards All.
Closed Dec. Jan. Wed (not evgs mid July-mid Sept).
Post r. Pont Turgot, 19140 Uzerche, Corrèze. Regions Dordogne/Poit-Char.
Tel 05 55 73 10 05. Fax 05 55 98 43 31. Mich 110/C4. Map 5.

VAILLY-SUR-SAULDRE

Auberge du Lièvre Gourmand

Comfortable restaurant/Cooking 2-3 | FW |

"Australian spoken" is one of the welcoming signs on the touch run-down exterior, in a village on the Sologne's E edge. Michèle & William Page are *les patrons*; he's the Aussie. Good to see super down-under wines. Enjoyable neo-classical menu B: *marbré de lapereau à la sauge, confiture d'oignons; joues de lotte cuites à la vapeur, sauce aux palourdes*; & *soufflé à la rhurbarbe*. Bravo, too, for the *Poisson Menu* (C).
Menus ABC. Cards MC, V. (Rooms: La Fontaine, Aubigny-sur-Nère.)
Closed Mid Jan-mid Feb. Mon. (Above easy 17km drive to W.)
Post 18260 Vailly-sur-Sauldre, Cher. Regions Berry-Bourbonnais/Loire.
Tel 02 48 73 80 23. Fax 02 48 73 86 13. Mich 70/B4-C4. Map 2.

A100frs & under. B100–150. C150–200. D200–250. E250–350. F350–500. G500+

VAISON-LA-ROMAINE   Le Beffroi

Comfortable hotel/Cooking 1-2   `FW`
Terrace/Gardens/Parking

I'll put an old snag to bed: church bells don't ring at night. Lots of
pluses: Yann & Catherine Christiansen's 16th/17thC hotel is enchanting;
furnishings are elegant; the setting exquisite; views N exhilarating; the
humming birds are exciting. Cooking? Classical & Provençale. One snag
remains: tricky access/parking (11 places). Lunch only Sat/Sun.
Menus A(Sat/Sun lunch)BC. Rooms (22) EFG. Cards All. (SW Pont Romain.)
Closed 15 Feb-15 Mar. 15 Nov-15 Dec. Rest: 12 Nov-26 Mar. Lunch Mon-Fri.
Post Haute Ville, 84110 Vaison-la-Romaine, Vaucluse. Region Provence.
Tel 04 90 36 04 71. Fax 04 90 36 24 78. Mich 144/C3. Map 6.

VAISON-LA-ROMAINE   La Fête en Provence

Comfortable restaurant/Cooking 1-2   `FW`
Terrace

In the Haute Ville, just off an evocative tiny *place* with fountain & plane
trees (150m W of Le Beffroi). The "terrace" is in a gorgeous courtyard.
Neils (half-brother of Yann at Le Beffroi) & Laurence Christiansen
please with his neo-classical/Provençals & odd eclectic *plats* – like
daube d'agneau & *mignon de porc au curry, riz basmati.*
Menus BC(both bottom-end). Cards All. (Rooms: Beffroi or Logis de Ch.)
Closed Nov-mid Dec. Sun lunch. Mon. Wed. Thurs (out of season).
Post pl. du Vieux-Marché, 84110 Vaison-la-Romaine, Vaucluse. Reg Prov.
Tel 04 90 36 36 43. Fax 04 90 36 21 49. Mich 144/C3. Map 6.

VAISON-LA-ROMAINE (Séguret)   La Table du Comtat

Very comfortable restaurant with rooms/Cooking 2-3
Secluded/Swimming pool/Parking/Air-conditioning (rest.)

The stunning views W (& sunsets) outshine the cooking: La Table, once
an *ancien hospice* (parts date back to 15thC), clings to a rockface.
Franck (the chef) & Josiane Gomez are regularly praised. Cooking, a lot
less precarious but often over-complicated, clings to classical holds: one
simpler, heavenly winning bet – herb-scented lamb (*gigot/côte d'agneau*).
Menus c(lunch: low-end)EF. Rooms (8) FG. Cards All.
Closed Feb. 26 Nov-8 Dec. Tues evg (Oct-May). Wed (mid Sept-June).
Post 84110 Séguret, Vaucluse. Region Provence. (Séguret 10km SW Vaison.)
Tel 04 90 46 91 49. Fax 04 90 46 94 27. Mich 144/C3. Map 6.

A100frs & under. B100–150. C150–200. D200–250. E250–350. F350–500. G500+

VALBONNE

Auberge Fleurie

Comfortable restaurant/Cooking 2-3
Terrace/Parking

Supreme *RQP* & *France Travelauréat* winner. Jean-Pierre Battaglia's
métier is polished classical. Good-choice menus. Gems galore: *pâté de
canard et ses aubergines confites, filet de rascasse au vin rouge* & *pavé
de chocolat crème anglaise* just one trio. Top marks to Colette who runs
the busy show so efficiently. J-P has given us 20 years of great pleasure.
Menus BC. Cards MC, V. (Rooms: Castel' Aras; 2km S on D3.)
Closed Mid Dec-Jan. Wed. (Or Arc Hôtel, D3 towards Mougins.)
Post 06560 Valbonne, Alpes-Maritimes. Region Côte d'A. (On D3, to S.)
Tel 04 93 12 02 80. Fax 04 93 12 22 27. Mich 163/F2. Map 6.

VALBONNE

Bistro de Valbonne

Comfortable restaurant/Cooking 2
Terrace/Air-conditioning

The home of Raymond Purgato for 15 years since he returned from Paris
to his *pays natal*. The tiny stylish *salle* is lost in the criss-cross of lanes
at Valbonne's heart. Classical fare: *pâté Périgourdin au foie gras* &
boeuf Strogonoff a typical duo. Many readers rate his cooking highly.
Another RP venture: the nearby Royal Pub, a wine bar with a difference.
Menus BC. Cards All. (Rooms: expensive Armoiries & cheaper La Cigale.)
Closed 1-15 Mar. 15 Nov-5 Dec. Sun. Mon. Region Côte d'Azur.
Post 11 r. Fontaine, 06560 Valbonne, Alpes-Maritimes.
Tel 04 93 12 05 59. Mich 163/F2. Map 6.

VALDAHON

Relais de Franche Comté

Comfortable hotel/Cooking 1-2
Quiet/Terrace/Gardens/Parking

No prizes for looks at the unattractive modern, but functional, hotel – E
of town & 200m S of D461. *Chef/patron* Daniel Frelin compensates with
a cascade of 6 classical/regional menus. One of 2 menus B (bottom-end)
makes clever use of his *terroir* including *fumé du Haut-Doubs – jambon
cuit, cru, brési & Jésus de Morteau séché* (see regional specialities).
Menus ABCD. Rooms (20) DE. Cards All.
Closed 20 Dec-15 Jan. Fri evg & Sat midday (not July/Aug).
Post 25800 Valdahon, Doubs. Region Jura.
Tel 03 81 56 23 18. Fax 03 81 56 44 38. Mich 90/B1. Map 3.

A100frs & under. B100–150. C150–200. D200–250. E250–350. F350–500. G500+

VALENCE

Bistrot des Clercs

Simple restaurant/Cooking 1-2
Terrace/Air-conditioning

FW

Michel Chabran's "bistro" (see Pont-de-l'Isère). Clever pricing formula: 3
menus (all A) based on a daily-changing *plat du jour* (salmon with
Béarnaise sauce is typical). You can also choose from a wide-choice multi-
regional & classical *carte* (3 courses in price bands BCD). Newly-opened &
already a huge success. Park in Champ de Mars, 200m to S.
Menus A(*àlc* BCD). Cards AE, MC, V. (Bistrot 200m N of Champ de Mars.)
Closed Sun. (Rooms: Alpes-Cévennes, on W side Rhône; easy 2-min drive.)
Post 48 Gde rue, 26000 Valence, Drôme. Region Massif Central (Ardèche).
Tel 04 75 55 55 15. Fax 04 75 43 64 85. Mich 130/B3. Map 6.

VALENCE-d'AGEN

La Campagnette

Very comfortable restaurant/Cooking 3
Terrace/Gardens/Parking

FW

Easily missed: route Cahors (D953), on R, just SW of bypass. Nice shady
garden. Marie-Laure Lerchundi speaks English & is a likeable *patronne*.
Chef/husband Gérard is a consummate modern master. Two delectable
fish dishes remain laser-sharp memories: *filets de rouget à la crème de
romarin* & *alose de Garonne sauce verte et ses oeufs en papillote*.
Menus aCDE. Cards MC, V. (Rooms: simple Tout va Bien, in town centre.)
Closed 1-8 Sept. Sun evg. Mon. (Above: see my *En Route* guide p165.)
Post rte Cahors, 82400 Valence-d'Agen, Tarn-et-Garonne.
Tel 05 63 39 65 97. Mich 137/E4. Map 5. Region Southwest.

VALGORGE

La Tanargue

Comfortable hotel/Cooking 1-2
Secluded/Gardens/Lift/Parking

FW

The anonymous *logis* is 100m N of the D24; the large gardens, tranquil
site & southern outlook more than compensate (in spring a valley of
broom, cherry blossom & chestnut trees). Denise Coste is *la patronne*;
her husband Amedée's cooking is a mix of rich classical & regional – fare
such as *filet de boeuf sauce Périgourdine* & *caille cévenole*.
Menus ABC. Rooms (25) EF. Cards MC, V.
Closed Jan-mid Mar.
Post 07110 Valgorge, Ardèche. Regions MC (Ardèche/Cévennes).
Tel 04 75 88 98 98. Fax 04 75 88 96 09. Mich 143/D1. Map 6.

A100frs & under. B100–150. C150–200. D200–250. E250–350. F350–500. G500+

358

VALLOIRE

La Sétaz/Rest. Le Gastilleur

Comfortable hotel/Cooking 2-3
Gardens/Swimming pool/Parking

FW

The large modern *logis* has two attractive amenities (see above). But, for me, the first-floor dining room & the happy-in-his-work chef, whom I was fortunate to meet, are better bonuses. Jacques Villard is a clever classicist: a superlative *suprême de poulet avec morilles et champignons des bois* & a lip-smacking dessert trolley remain vivid happy memories.
Menus BC. Rooms (22) EF. Cards AE, MC, V.
Closed Mid Apl-May. 22 Sept-19 Dec.
Post 73450 Valloire, Savoie. Regions Hautes-Alpes/Savoie.
Tel 04 79 59 01 03. Fax 04 79 59 00 63. Mich 132/C1. Map 6.

VALS-LES-BAINS

Chez Mireille

Simple restaurant/Cooking 1-2
Air-conditioning

FW

The sainted duo, Albert & Renée Mazet, now run the Europe as *sans rest*. This alternative does very nicely thank you. A warm welcome from Colette Martin & classical temptations from husband Daniel. How about this perm? A salad of fresh & smoked salmon; *petits rôtis de pintade à la crème de laurier*; cheese; &, to finish, *parfait aux marrons* (a *terroir plat*).
Menus ABC. Cards MC, V. (Rooms: see next entry; in same street.)
Closed 3 wks Sept. Wed.
Post 3 r. J. Jaurès, 07600 Vals-les-Bains, Ardèche. Region MC (Ardèche).
Tel 04 75 37 49 06. Mich 129/E4. Map 6.

VALS-LES-BAINS (also see next page)

Europe

Comfortable hotel (no restaurant)
Lift

First the bad news: after 52 years as a chef, Albert Mazet has *quitté ses fourneaux*. The good news is that he and his wife Renée now run the hotel *sans restaurant*. A delightful, amiable couple, full of character &, like their hotel, the very essence of *la vrai France* as she used to be. I understand their daughter & son-in-law now help to run the hotel.
Rooms (32) DEF. Cards All. (Public parking across the road.)
Closed Oct-Apl.
Post 86 r. J. Jaurès. 07600 Vals-les-Bains, Ardèche. Reg MC (Ardèche).
Tel 04 75 37 43 94. Fax 04 75 94 66 62. Mich 129/E4. Map 6.

A100frs & under. B100–150. C150–200. D200–250. E250–350. F350–500. G500+

VALS-LES-BAINS (also see previous page)   **Vivarais**

Comfortable hotel/Cooking 2-3   FW
Terrace/Swimming pool/Closed parking

A fifth-generation chef, Christiane Guiliani-Brioude, is making a name
for herself at the multi-floored, 30s-style spa hotel – with attractive
gardens & a site beside the river & close to the casino. Neo-classical
delights mixed with reworked, old regional recipes: a typical meal could
be a mysterious *salade picodonne; parmentier d'agneau en crépinettes*
with a wild mushroom sauce; & a seductive sweet (choose from 14).
Menus B(ceiling)DE. Rooms (47) EFG(top-end). Cards All.
Post av. C. Expilly, 07600 Vals-les-Bains, Ardèche. Region MC (Ardèche).
Tel 04 75 94 65 85. Fax 04 75 37 65 47. Mich 129/E4. Map 6.

VAL-SUZON   Host. Val-Suzon/Chalet de la Fontaine aux Geais

Comfortable hotel/Cooking 2   FW
Quiet/Secluded (Chalet)/Terrace/Gardens/Closed parking

Attractive, wooded valley setting for the *hostellerie* in grounds of 2½
acres. Yves & Chantal Perreau have won both praise & criticism for their
welcome, the ambience & his neo-classical cuisine (*volaille fermière aux
morilles et foie gras de canard* is one example). Pastry work is a touch
heavy-handed alas. A chalet annexe (in need of repairs) has 9 bedrooms.
Menus b(lunch)D(bottom-end)EF. Rooms (16) FG. Cards All.
Closed Wed & Thurs midday (Oct-Ap!).
Post 21121 Val-Suzon, Côte-d'Or. Region Burgundy.
Tel 03 80 35 60 15. Fax 03 80 35 61 36. Mich 74/A4. Map 3.

Le VALTIN   **Auberge Val Joli**

Comfortable restaurant with rooms/Cooking 1-2   FW
Quiet/Terrace/Gardens/Parking

A delight: for the setting; for the two *salle*s – one ancient (panelled
ceiling), one modern (keeping the stone exterior of the other intact); &
for the Laruelle family – Marie-Thérèse out front & husband Jacques &
their son Philippe in *la cuisine*. Classical, *Bourgeoise* & regional fare:
one tasty memory – *blanc de Sautret au Riesling (poulet Vosgien)*.
Menus aBD. Rooms (16) CDE. Cards MC, V.
Closed 15 Nov-15 Dec. Sun evg & Mon (not sch. hols).
Post 88230 Le Valtin, Vosges. Region Alsace.
Tel 03 29 60 91 37. Fax 03 29 60 81 73. Mich 60/C3. Map 3.

A 100frs & under. B 100–150. C 150–200. D 200–250. E 250–350. F 350–500. G 500+

Le VALTIN
Le Vétiné

Simple hotel (no restaurant)
Secluded/Parking

S of the village & at a higher altitude – over 3000ft above sea-level. The only sound is rushing water in the infant River Meurthe across the valley to the E. Beech woods to the S & pines to the N. This is prime walking terrain – at its best in the spring (wild flowers) & autumn (fungi & fruit). Simple is the word. 14 studios with *cuisinettes*.
Rooms (27) CD. Cards AE, MC, V.
Closed 15-31 Mar. 15 Nov-15 Dec. Sun evg & Mon (not sch. hols).
Post 88230 Le Valtin, Vosges. Region Alsace.
Tel 03 29 60 99 44. Fax 03 29 60 80 95. Mich 60/C3. Map 3.

VANNES
La Morgate

Simple restaurant/Cooking 2 `FW`

Vannes is a busy, bustling town – though less so in the evenings. This small beamed restaurant, between cathedral & *gare*, is worth a detour. Very helpful patrons, Vincenza & David Le Blay. Daniel stirs classical pots: dip into the likes of 10 oysters, an invigorating *dos de bar rôti en peau, fleur de sel de Guérande*, cheese & one of three fine sweets. Rooms: use next entry or La Marébaudière (500m walk SE; with parking).
Menus a(lunch)BC. Cards MC, V. (Parking to NW, W & SW; 500m walk.)
Closed 4-18 Nov. Sun evg. Mon.
Post 21 r. La Fontaine, 56000 Vannes, Morbihan. Region Brittany.
Tel 02 97 42 42 39. Fax 02 97 47 25 27. Mich 47/D4. Map 1.

VANNES (also see next page)
Moulin de Lesnuhé

Simple hotel (no restaurant)
Quiet/Gardens/Parking

The 15thC mill is in a super setting: two buildings straddle a fairly deserted lane; there's a mill race; a refreshing wooded valley; & noisy Vannes is only 5km away. Simple, modern bedrooms. Take D126 NE from Vannes; 2km beyond St-Avé, turn E towards St-Nolff. (I've again given the *moulin* a "quiet" label: is the nearby railway line a noise problem?)
Rooms (12) E(bottom-end). Cards AE, MC, V.
Closed Mid Dec-mid Jan.
Post 56890 St-Avé, Morbihan. Region Brittany.
Tel 02 97 60 77 77. Mich 47/D4. Map 1.

A100frs & under. B100–150. C150–200. D200–250. E250–350. F350–500. G500+

VANNES (also see previous page) — Régis Mahé

Very comfortable restaurant/Cooking 3

Our *FLE* meal was a hit; our *FLF* visit a mixed bag. A handsome beamed *salle* has oak panelling & stained glass windows; when empty – we were the only clients – it's like a chapel of rest. Cooking? 90s modern: *meunière de sole & palourdes beurre noisette* & *persil plat* & a Catalan-influenced (colour & content) *rouget poêlé et poivrons marinés* were great. Thumbs-down for cold soup, cocked-up cheese course & so-so sweet.
Menus c(lunch: low-end)EF. Cards AE, MC, V. (Rooms: see previous entry.)
Closed Feb sch. hols. 18 Nov-2 Dec. Sun evg & Mon. (Above simple drive.)
Post pl. Gare, 56000 Vannes, Morbihan. Region Brittany.
Tel 02 97 42 61 41. Mich 47/D4. Map 1. (Restaurant opposite station.)

VARCES — Relais L'Escale

Very comfortable restaurant with rooms/Cooking 2-3 FW
Quiet/Terr/Gardens/Swim pool/Parking/Air-cond. (bedrooms)

The new owners of this famed *relais*, Frédéric & Géraldine Buntinx, have worked hard to polish up its tarnished reputation. 7 individual chalets (note the air-cond.) are the unusual means of overnight accommodation. FB is a classical fan: witness a tasty *chausson de turbot et St-Jacques au cerfeuil*; & a robust *petite pièce de boeuf aux morilles farcies*.
Menus BCDE. Rooms (7) F. Cards AE, MC, V. (Cheaper rooms: Primevère.)
Closed Jan. Sun evg & Mon (15 Sep-May). Tues (June-15 Sep). (At Claix.)
Post 38760 Varces, Isère. Regs Htes-Alpes/Savoie. (13km S of Grenoble.)
Tel 04 76 72 80 19. Fax 04 76 72 92 58. Mich 131/E2. Map 6.

VARENNES-SUR-ALLIER — Auberge de l'Orisse

Comfortable hotel/Cooking 2-3 FW
Terrace/Gardens/Swimming pool/Tennis/Parking

The *logis*, in large grounds, is well back from the N7/N209 junction, SE of the town. Patrick Paget strives hard to provide clients with culinary reasons for staying awhile. Little choice on menus AB but a good mix of modern/neo-classical offerings: *brandade de morue* & *terrine de poissons de mer et de rivière au coulis crémeux d'Americaine* two top-notch *plats*.
Menus ABC. Rooms (23) E. Cards All.
Closed Fri evg, Sat midday & Sun evg (not hotel Easter-Sept).
Post 03150 Varennes-sur-Allier, Allier. Region Berry-Bourbonnais.
Tel 04 70 45 05 60. Fax 04 70 45 18 55. Mich 100/B3. Map 5.

A100frs & under. B100–150. C150–200. D200–250. E250–350. F350–500. G500+

VARETZ Domaine de Castel Novel

Luxury hotel/Cooking 3
Secluded/Terrace/Gardens/Swimming pool/Tennis/Lift/Parking

The turreted, red sandstone CN – on a hilltop 100-acre site, hidden by woods & overlooking the Vézère Valley – was the home of Colette from 1911-23; she wrote *Chéri* here in 1920. The hotel is one of many owned by Albert Parveaux. Cuisine is a flamboyant mix of contemporary, Périgord & neo-classical – the normal *Relais & Châteaux* formula. Good-value lunch.
Menus D(lunch: bottom-end)EF. Rooms (35) G,G2. Cards All.
Closed Mid Oct-Apl. Rest: Wed midday (not pub. hols). Region Dordogne.
Post 19240 Varetz, Corrèze. (NW of Brive-la-Gaillarde & A20 exit 50).
Tel 05 55 85 00 01. Fax 05 55 85 09 03. Mich 124/C1. Map 5.

VAUX La Petite Auberge

Comfortable restaurant/Cooking 2 FW
Terrace/Parking

New owners, Jean-Marie & Marilyn Carlo (a fluent English-speaker), at the tiller here, a Yonne-side *auberge*, 6km upstream from Auxerre. J-M, after working as an executive chef for an international group, has returned to his *pays*. Accomplished & stylish classical/neo-classical *plats* with eclectic touches. Marilyn is a delightful *patronne*.
Menus aBC. Cards MC, V. (Rooms: Ibis, A6 Auxerre-Sud exit; easy drive.)
Closed Sun evg. Mon. (Also many hotels in Auxerre: see Le Maxime entry.)
Post 89290 Vaux, Yonne. Region Burgundy. (6km S of Auxerre.)
Tel 03 86 53 80 08. Fax 03 86 53 65 62. Mich 72/A2. Map 2.

VAUX-SOUS-AUBIGNY Auberge des Trois Provinces

Simple restaurant with basic rooms/Cooking 1-2 FW

A small, vine-covered, stone building with an equally simple stone & beamed dining room. Young André Jacoulet works hard to survive out in the sticks: inexpensive classical menus with a two-way choice for each course on both menus. Starters could be appetising *moules à la crème ou fricassée de gésiers*; main courses a filling *navarin d'agneau*; cheese; & a sweet (*crème brûlée* is typical). One bonus: 200m or so W of N74.
Menus AB. Rooms (2) D(bottom-end). Cards MC, V.
Closed 27 Jan-15 Feb. Sun evg. Mon. Regions Burgundy/Champ-Ard.
Post 52190 Vaux-sous-Aubigny, Haute-Marne.
Tel 03 25 88 31 98. Mich 74/C2. Map 3.

A100frs & under. B100–150. C150–200. D200–250. E250–350. F350–500. G500+

VELARS-SUR-OUCHE

Auberge Gourmande

Very comfortable restaurant/Cooking 2
Terrace/Parking

FW

The stone-built, flower-bedecked restaurant – rustic, yet refined – is W of Dijon & S of an A38 exit (toll-free). Chef André Barbier & his wife, Louise, play a Burgundy fiddle (with some classical strings): *escargots, oeufs pochés en meurette, coq au vin* & *jambon persillé dijonnais* are all on the menus. You'll not complain about lack of choice here.
Menus aCD. Cards AE, MC, V. (Rooms: La Bonbonnière, Talant.)
Closed 2 weeks Nov. Sun evg. Mon. (Above 6km to NE, quiet & *sans rest.*)
Post 21370 Velars-sur-Ouche, Côte d'Or. Region Burgundy.
Tel 03 80 33 62 51. Fax 03 80 33 65 83. Mich 74/A4. Map 3.

VERCHAIX

Rouge Gorge

Very simple restaurant/Cooking 1-2

FW

Simplicity personified in a fabulous valley (be sure to head E to the dead-end *cirque* before or after your meal). *"Derrière la poste"* & between the village & D907 (6km W of Samoëns). Françoise Thirvaudey tends the tiny *salle*; Roland, her chef husband, paints a classical palette: a *feuilleté de Chavignol sur salade verte, darne de saumon sauce tartare, plateau de fromages* & a *tarte* is a typical tempting menu.
Menus a(lunch)BC. Cards MC, V. (Rooms: Le Sauvageon; nearby Morillon.)
Closed 15-30 June. 15-30 Nov. Sun evg. Mon. (More hotels at Samoëns.)
Post 74440 Verchaix, Haute-Savoie. Region Savoie.
Tel 04 50 90 16 77. Mich 105/E3. Map 6.

VERNET-LES-BAINS

Le Mas Fleuri

Comfortable hotel (no restaurant)
Quiet/Gardens/Swimming pool/Parking

Vernet-les-Bains is a colourful, flower-filled spa with, high above the small resort, a 12thC *église* & restored castle looking serenely over the old town's streets. Le Mas Fleuri is well-named: the *parc ombragé* of the hotel (a much modernised *mas* – farmhouse) is the highlight. Geneviève Bazan's base, surrounded by captivating terrain, is much liked.
Rooms (29) EFG(bottom-end). Cards All.
Closed Oct-May. Region Languedoc-Roussillon.
Post bd Clémenceau, 66820 Vernet-les-Bains, Pyrénées-Orientales.
Tel 04 68 05 51 94. Fax 04 68 05 50 77. Mich 176/C3. Map 5.

A100frs & under. B100–150. C150–200. D200–250. E250–350. F350–500. G500+

VERNON

Les Fleurs

Comfortable restaurant/Cooking 1-2   FW

Just W of the main Seine bridge, the small restaurant is a humdinger – &
well-named with the world-renowned gardens at Giverny upstream on the
other bank. Annie & Michel Graux have a winning formula. Huge choice of
classical tempters (8 entrées; 9 sweets) – the menu price (BCD) depends on
the main course chosen: dig into the likes of *blanquette de veau* (B), *filet
mignon de porc à la moutarde ancienne ou rumsteack au poivre* (C).
Menus BCD. Cards MC, V. (Rooms: Arianotel & Haut Marais – 1km NW.)
Closed 3-17 Aug. Sun evg. Mon. (Parking at bridge/riverside; upstream.)
Post 71 r. Carnot, 27200 Vernon, Eure. Region Normandy.
Tel 02 32 51 16 80. Fax 02 32 21 30 51. Mich 34/C2. Map 3.

VERSAILLES

Home St-Louis

Simple hotel (no restaurant)
Fairly quiet

No hotel comes simpler in Versailles but, equally, I've received no
grumbles about this base during the 15 years I've been recommending it.
Benefits are numerous: in a maze of quiet, one-way streets, 1km SE of
the château; even closer to two R.E.R. stations which allow you to use
the excellent rail network into Paris (rapid is the word) – many readers
have appreciated this aspect; helpful owners; & modest prices.
Rooms (25) DE. Cards AE, MC, V. (Public parking 200m away.)
Post 28 r. St-Louis, 78000 Versailles, Yvelines. Region Ile de France.
Tel 01 39 50 23 55. Fax 01 30 21 62 45. Mich 35/E3-E4. Map 2.

VERSAILLES (St-Cyr-l'Ecole)

Aérotel

Simple hotel (no restaurant)
Quiet/Closed parking

For many years now the base hotel, for long a *Relais du Silence*
member, has been much appreciated by readers. The reasons are many:
for the English-speaking owner (alas Fabienne Seillé, *la directrice*, has
left); for the quiet site, set back from the D7 (on E side) & opposite a
small aerodrome; for the parking area, closed at night; & for the modest
cost of an hotel close to the W edge of the Versaille palace park.
Rooms (26) E. Cards All. (4km W of Versailles.) Region Ile de France.
Post 88 r. Dr Vaillant, 78210 St-Cyr-l'Ecole, Yvelines.
Tel 01 30 45 07 44. Fax 01 34 60 35 96. Mich 35/E3-E4. Map 2.

A100frs & under. B100–150. C150–200. D200–250. E250–350. F350–500. G500+

VERTUS (Bergères-les-Vertus) Mont-Aimé

Comfortable hotel/Cooking 1-2 (bistro 1) `FW`
Quiet/Terrace/Gardens/Swimming pool/Parking

A *logis* at the heart of the village – in Champagne country. Colourful &
idiosyncratic apply to some of Annie Sciancalepore's furnishings &
decorations; her chef/husband, Jean, keeps his end a bit more basic –
both regional & classical. A northern heartwarmer, *waterzoi de pétoncles*
& a hearty *entrecôte grillée md'* both pleased. Bistro across road.
Menus B(bottom-end)CDE. (Bistro B). Rooms (30) EF. Disabled. Cards All.
Closed Sun evg. Region Champagne-Ardenne.
Post Bergères-les-Vertus, 51130 Vertus, Marne.
Tel 03 26 52 21 31. Fax 03 26 52 21 39. Mich 38/B3. Map 3.

VERVINS Tour du Roy

Comfortable hotel/Cooking 2-3
Terrace/Gardens/Parking

An extrovert hotel (ask to see the two tower bedrooms), atop the old
town's ramparts, is run by an equally extrovert owner, English-speaking
Claude Desvignes. His wife, Annie, the chef, is Alain Lequy's sister (see
Sars-Poteries). Cooking? Classical/cream!/hearty regional/Thiérache
produce. Quality furnishings. Regular moans about abysmal service.
Menus CEF. Rooms (15) F(bottom-end)G. Cards All.
Closed Rest: 15 Jan-1 Feb. Sun evg & Mon midday (out of season).
Post 02140 Vervins, Aisne. Regions Champagne-Ardenne/North.
Tel 03 23 98 00 11. Fax 03 23 98 00 72. Mich 20/B1. Map 3.

VEULES-LES-ROSES Les Galets

Very comfortable restaurant/Cooking 3 `FW`

Readers appreciate the warm welcome from Nelly Plaisance at the family
restaurant overlooking the beach. Husband Gilbert & son Jean conjure
up authentic classical fare; their repertoire, not surprisingly, is very
strong in fish/shellfish dishes. Some regional specialities. Gilbert is also
happy to put his fingers in more distant regional pots: *coq au vin de
Bourgogne* & *bouillabaisse* are two contrasting examples.
Menus bCDF. Cards All. (Rooms: Relais Mercure, nearby St-Valéry – to W.)
Closed 5 Jan-3 Feb. Tues evg & Wed (not July/Aug).
Post 76980 Veules-les-Roses, Seine-Maritime. Region Normandy.
Tel 02 35 97 61 33. Fax 02 35 57 06 23. Mich 15/F1. Map 2.

A100frs & under. B100–150. C150–200. D200–250. E250–350. F350–500. G500+

VEZAC
Relais des Cinq Châteaux

Comfortable restaurant with rooms/Cooking 2
Terrace/Swimming pool/Parking/Air-conditioning (restaurant)

Jacky Vasseur (once chef at Domme's Esplanade) is moving up in the world. He's left his tiny home at Vitrac & installed himself in a swanking new *relais*. Modern amenities are welcome but not half as much as his neo-classical cooking; he's especially strong with fish. *Filet de carpe en matelote* & *dos de daurade au fenouil* were both sterling *plats*.
Menus aBCE. Rooms (10) E. Cards MC, V. (D49, 2km SE of Beynac.)
Closed 5-28 Feb. Wed (Nov-Mar).
Post 24220 Vézac, Dordogne. Region Dordogne.
Tel 05 53 30 30 72. Fax 05 53 31 19 39. Mich 124/A3. Map 5.

VIALAS
Chantoiseau

Very comfortable restaurant v ith rooms/Cooking 3-4   **FW**
Quiet/Swimming pool

Readers will fall in love with the wooded terrain, the S-facing setting of the 17thC *relais* &, above all, the remarkable Patrick & Christiane Pagès. He's invigoratingly intelligent, a poet, a consummate wine expert (1000+ different wines) & creative *cuisinier par excellence* ("involved" modern style). Enjoy Christiane's everything-you-need-at-hand bedrooms.
Menus a(lun)BEFG. Rooms (15) F. Cards All. (Cheaper rms: Mt Lozère.)
Closed Mid Oct-Mar. Tues evg. Wed. (Above at Génolhac, 10km to E.)
Post 48220 Vialas, Lozère. Regions Massif Central (Cévennes)/Provence.
Tel 04 66 41 00 02. Fax 04 66 41 04 34. Mich 142/C2. Map 5.

VIC-LE-COMTE (Longues)
Le Comté

Comfortable restaurant/Cooking 2-3   **FW**
Parking

An unprepossessing building N of Longues (4km NW of Vic-le-Comte). Don't be put off by the stained-glass entrance; enjoy the inventive modern & neo-classical repertoire of Gérard Faure. Two crystal-clear memories: *trilogie d'agneau au jus de volaille au thym frais (langue/cervelle/ côte)* & *tartes fine pommes et frangipane sur coulis de mures*.
Menus aBCDE. Cards MC, V. (Rooms: Mon Auberge; Parent-Gare, 9km S.)
Closed Feb sch. hols. Sun evg. Mon.
Post Longues, 63270 Vic-le-Comte, Puy-de-Dôme. Region MC (Auvergne).
Tel 04 73 39 90 31. Fax 04 73 39 24 58. Mich 113/E3. Map 5.

A100frs & under. B100–150. C150–200. D200–250. E250–350. F350–500. G500+

VIEILLE-TOULOUSE

La Flânerie

Comfortable hotel (no restaurant)
Secluded/Gardens/Swimming pool/Garage/Parking

On the R bank of the Garonne with a fine setting (& exceptional views) above the river. Yet just 9km S from horrendously busy, noisy Toulouse (use D4). For once the owner's claim – *une maison de caractère* – is spot on; Jean Grosbois has every reason to be proud of his captivating base. Old furniture, largish bedrooms, cosy lounge & terrace are all bonuses.
Rooms (12) EFG. Cards All.
Closed 23 Dec-10 Jan. Region Languedoc-Roussillon.
Post rte Lacroix-Falgarde, 31320 Vieille-Toulouse, Haute-Garonne.
Tel 05 61 73 39 12. Fax 05 61 73 18 56. Mich 152/C3. Map 5.

VIENNE

La Pyramide

Luxury hotel/Cooking 4
Terrace/Gardens/Lift/Garage/Closed parking/Air-conditioning

My first Patrick Henriroux meal (Mougins 1989) was enough to tell me that this brilliantly talented modern chef would become one of the greats. He now is, before he's 40! Contemporary creations, Point classics (FP's old home), Med touches, superb vegetables & *tour de force* "piano" sweet. Bravo too for Pascale, his lovely wife. 3-star *cave* & *sommelier*.
Menus e(lunch)FG. Rooms (20) G. Disabled. Cards All. (Cheaper rooms:)
Closed Rest: Wed & Thurs midday (mid Sept-mid June). (see next entry.)
Post 14 bd F. Point, 38200 Vienne, Isère. Map 6. (W N7, S of town.)
Tel 04 74 53 01 96. Fax 04 74 85 69 73. Mich 116/A3. Region Lyonnais.

VIENNE (Pont-Evêque)

Midi

Comfortable hotel (no restaurant; see text)
Quiet/Terrace/Gardens/Parking

Some of you will pick me up & say the Midi does have a restaurant these days. So it has – for "snacks" (A) in the evening only. I'll continue to recommend the hotel as a base – ideal for La Pyramide in Vienne, where the bedrooms are dear (& other restaurants to the S). Midi is an easy, short 4km drive to the E of Vienne, at Pont-Evêque (use D502).
Rooms (17) EF. Cards All. Region Lyonnais.
Closed 23 Dec-6 Jan. (No "snacks" served on Sun evg.)
Post pl. Eglise, 38780 Pont-Evêque, Isère.
Tel 04 74 85 90 11. Fax 04 74 57 24 99. Mich 116/B3. Map 6.

A100frs & under. B100–150. C150–200. D200–250. E250–350. F350–500. G500+

VIEUX-MAREUIL   Château de Vieux Mareuil

Comfortable hotel/Cooking 3
Secluded/Gardens/Swimming pool/Parking

FW

15thC château, in elevated site, with 40 acres of woodland & meadows; two experienced owners in English-speaking Jean-Pierre & Annie Lefranc; & menus which offer a range of prices. Good-choice *Menu Régional* is a *RQP* bonus. Chefs change but the Lefranc formula (classical/neo-classical & regional) remains unchanged. Top-class *cave* & bkfts. Bikes for hire.
Menus bDE. Rooms (14)G(top-end). Disabled. Cards AE, MC, V.
Closed Nov-Mar.
Post 24340 Vieux-Mareuil, Dordogne. Region Dordogne.
Tel 05 53 60 77 15. Fax 05 53 56 49 33. Mich 109/D4. Map 5.

VIGNOUX-SUR-BARANGEON   Le Prieuré

Very comfortable restaurant with rooms/Cooking 2-3
Quiet/Terrace/Gardens/Swimming pool/Closed parking

FW

The 19thC priory, with its severe exterior, is in the eastern shadow of the church (D30 to E). The *église* windows of the priory illuminate the culinary church of talented brothers, Jean-Pierre & Didier Besson. Neo-classical tunes, played with flair: *homard et son flan aux girolles* & *saumon rôti lardé au magret de canard* were menu C (low-end) hymndingers.
Menus b(lunch)C(low-end)D. Rooms (7) EF. Cards AE, MC, V.
Closed Feb sch. hols. 24 Aug-3 Sept. Tues evg & Wed (not July/Aug).
Post 18500 Vignoux-sur-Barangeon, Cher. Region Berry-Bourbonnais.
Tel 02 48 51 58 80. Fax 02 48 51 56 01. Mich 84/B1. Map 2.

VILLARS-LES-DOMBES   Ribotel/Rest. Jean-Claude Bouvier

Comfortable hotel & restaurant/Cooking 2-3
Terrace/Lift/Parking

Just N of the terrific Parc Ornithologique. Down-to-earth, friendly duo, Jean-Claude & Christiane, run the *rest.* side – as good an example as any to demonstrate why La Dombes/Bresse/Lyonnais is such a supreme culinary corner. Classical/regional delights: *grenouilles et crêpes Parmentier; volaille de Bresse*; & *faux filet au poivre vert* – just 3 of many.
Menus bCDEF. Rooms (47) DE. Disabled. Cards All.
Closed Rest: 26-31 Dec. Sun evg & Mon.
Post rte Lyon, 01330 Villars-les-Dombes, Ain. Region Lyonnais.
Tel 04 74 98 08 03. Fax 04 74 98 29 55. Mich 102/C4. Map 6.

A100frs & under. B100–150. C150–200. D200–250. E250–350. F350–500. G500+

VILLEDIEU-LES-POELES

St-Pierre et St-Michel

Comfortable hotel/Cooking 1-2
Garage

FW

At the very heart of the small town – famed for copper & surrounded by both *charcuterie* & leather terrain. Jacqueline Duret is *la patronne*; her husband speaks English well. Vast choice menu C: uninspiring classical & Normandy alternatives such as *andouillette sourdine grillée, sole meunière, escalope de veau à la Normande* & ubiquitous *crème brûlée*.
Menus a(lunch)BCD. Rooms (24) E. Cards MC, V.
Closed 2-29 Jan. Fri (Nov-Mar). (Parking in *place* opposite hotel.)
Post pl. République, 50800 Villedieu-lès-Poêles, Manche. Reg Normandy.
Tel 02 33 61 00 11. Fax 02 33 61 06 52. Mich 31/D3. Map 1.

VILLEFORT

Balme

Simple hotel/Cooking 2-3
Terrace/Garage

FW

A small, handsome corner of old-world France. Michel Gomy, an English-speaking Parisian (& tennis nut), & his wife, Micheline, work hard to promote their adopted *pays* (Lozère) in the Far East every year. Touches of the Orient surface in Michel's work – together with modern creations & Cévenols treats. Mont-Lozère-sized choice in menu C.
Menus BCE. Rooms (20) CDE. Cards All.
Closed 13-18 Oct. Mid Nov-Jan. Sun evg & Mon (out of season).
Post 48800 Villefort, Lozère. Region Massif Central (Cévennes).
Tel 04 66 46 80 14. Fax 04 66 46 85 26. Mich 142/C2. Map 5.

VILLEFRANCHE-DE-ROUERGUE

Relais de Farrou

Very comfortable hotel/Cooking 2
Terrace/Gardens/Swim pool/Tennis/Parking/Air-cond. (rooms)

FW

1-star site: N of town at busy D1/D922 junc. Bernard & English-speaking Christine Bouilland have done wonders with the man-made facilities; there's a gym & jacuzzi too. Classical/regional fare: the Menu *Terroir* (B) could include a *buffet hors d'oeuvre et charcuterie du pays; truite de Laguiole ou tripoux*; & *oeufs à la neige et la fouace* (super bread).
Menus a(lunch)BCDF. Rooms (25) EF. Disabled. Cards MC, V.
Closed 25 Feb-11 Mar. 20 Oct-4 Nov. Rest: Sun evg & Mon (out of season).
Post Farrou, 12200 Villefranche-de-Rouergue, Aveyron. Regs Dord/MC(Cév).
Tel 05 65 45 18 11. Fax 05 65 45 32 59. Mich 139/E2. Map 5.

A100frs & under. B100–150. C150–200. D200–250. E250–350. F350–500. G500+

VILLEMUR-SUR-TARN

La Ferme de Bernadou

Very comfortable restaurant/Cooking 3
Terrace/Gardens/Parking

FW

Only one discordant note: little choice on *Menu Marguerite* (B). Rest is pleasure plus: elegant Elisabeth, *la patronne*; the cool terrace & *salle*; the gardens & *étang*; & the neo-classical *plats* from Jean-Claude Voison. Two memorable highlights: *soufflé glacé à la rhubarbe* & *millefeuille aux abricots*. D14 SW town. (Secluded hotel below is easy 9km drive S.)
Menus BCDE. Cards AE, MC, V. (Rooms: Villa des Pins, Vacquiers.)
Closed 1-6 Jan. Feb sch. hols. Sun evg & Mon.
Post 31340 Villemur-sur-Tarn, Haute-Garonne. Regs Lang-Rouss/SW.
Tel 05 61 09 02 38. Fax 05 61 35 94 87. Mich 152/C1 & 153/A1. Map 5.

VILLENEUVE-DE-MARSAN

Europe

Comfortable hotel/Cooking 2
Quiet/Terrace/Gardens/Swimming pool/Parking

FW

Up & down like a roller-coaster & in-&-out of my guides. I should drop the chopper; but, after Robert Garrapit's accident & health problems, I'll not do so. Debits? Maïté Garrapit's wayward addition arithmetic; sniffy *maître d'*; orchestrated dome removal; & rooms need tidying up. Credits? New chef Jean-Jacques Benet's classical/neo-classical fare has done much to overcome the waywardness of his young predecessor.
Menus BDE. Rooms (12) EF. Cards All.
Post 40190 Villeneuve-de-Marsan, Landes. Region Southwest.
Tel 05 58 45 20 08. Fax 05 58 45 34 14. Mich 150/A1. Map 4.

VILLENEUVE-LES-AVIGNON (also see next page) Les Cèdres

Simple hotel/Cooking 1
Terrace/Gardens/Swimming pool/Closed parking/Air-cond.

Between Villeneuve & Les Angles. No prizes for cooking here but Paul Grimonet's *logis* still appeals: for the old house, the cedar trees, the "folly", the modern bungalows, closed parking, the pool & quietish site. Use it as a base. If you eat in then expect classical & Provençale cooking: of the *filet de lapin à la Provençale* & *pêche Melba* variety.
Menus ABC(dinner only). Rooms (21) EF. Cards MC, V. (W of Avignon.)
Closed 15 Nov-15 Mar. Rest; every midday.Region Provence.
Post 39 bd Pasteur, 30400 Villeneuve-les-Avignon, Gard.
Tel 04 90 25 43 92. Fax 04 90 25 14 66. Mich 158/B1. Map 6.

A100frs & under. B100–150. C150–200. D200–250. E250–350. F350–500. G500+

VILLENEUVE-LES-AVIGNON (also see previous page) **Fabrice**

Simple restaurant/Cooking 1-2 | FW |
Terrace/Parking

Between Villeneuve & Les Angles, a short walk from Les Cèdres. Fabrice Guisset has a clever formula for his classical & Provençals *plats* (menu B): 8 starters, 8 main courses, 6 sweets & *apéritifs* included. Typical perm: *gaspachio de moules* (ideal on a hot day), *brochette d'agneau grillé* & 1-star *feuillantine de choco noir au coulis de framboises*.
Menus a(lunch)B. Cards MC, V. (Rooms: Les Cèdres; short walk to SW.)
Closed Feb sch. hols. 3 wks end Aug/Sept. Sun evg. Mon. Region Provence.
Post 3 bd Pasteur, 30400 Villeneuve-lès-Avignon, Gard.
Tel 04 90 25 52 79. Mich 158/B1. Map 6.

VILLENEUVE-LES-AVIGNON **Le Prieuré**

Luxury hotel/Cooking 3
Quietish/Terr/Gards/Swim pool/Tenn/Lift/Closed parking/Air-cond.

There's much to admire: the welcome from Marie-France Mille & François, her son; the rose-scented, herb-perfumed, tree-shaded gardens; & the softly-lit shady terrace for evg dining. Serge Chenet is a modern chef magician, brilliant with herbs. One twist: at breakfast you have the chance to polish off previous evg's left-over puds. Some distant train noise.
Menus C(bottom-end)EF. Rooms (26) G,G2. Cards All.
Closed 3 Nov-7 Mar. Rest: Wed midday & Thurs midday (Mar).
Post 7 pl. Chapître, 30400 Villeneuve-lès-Avignon, Gard. Reg Provence.
Tel 04 90 25 18 20. Fax 04 90 25 45 39. Mich 158/B1. Map 6. (W Avignon.)

VILLENEUVE-SUR-YONNE **La Lucarne aux Chouettes**

Comfortable restaurant with rooms/Cooking 2-3 | FW |
Quiet/Terrace

"The owl's nest", restored with faithful skill & great flair by Leslie Caron, *la patronne*, is four 17thC cottages beside the Yonne; beamed high ceilings, bricks, stone, period furniture & hand-painted bathroom tiles. Chef Marc Daniel paddles classical/neo-classical streams: *darne de colin au beurre blanc* & *coeur de rumsteack poêlé Bearnaise* are typical *plats*.
Menus a(lunch)C(low-end). Rooms (4)G. Cards AE, MC, V.
Closed 15 Feb-15 Mar. Sun evg & Mon (Oct-Apl). (N of bridge; E bank.)
Post quai Bretoche, 89500 Villeneuve-sur-Yonne, Yonne.
Tel 03 86 87 18 26. Fax 03 86 87 22 63. Mich 55/E4. Map 2.

A 100frs & under. B 100–150. C 150–200. D 200–250. E 250–350. F 350–500. G 500+

372

VILLERS-BOCAGE

Trois Rois

Very comfortable restaurant with rooms/Cooking 2 | **FW**
Gardens/Parking

The modern *logis*, alongside the N175 (to SW), is quieter these days; the new southern bypass has at last been completed. Chef Henri Martinotti is a classical king – but for far more than three reasons: for his renowned *tripes à la mode de Caen*; for numerous fish dishes & an appetite-busting *tournedos sauté*; & for an artful, heady *nougat glace au Cointreau*.
Menus BCE. Rooms (14) DEF. Cards All.
Closed Jan. 23-30 June. Sun evg & Mon (not pub. hols).
Post 14310 Villers-Bocage, Calvados. Region Normandy.
Tel 02 31 77 00 32. Fax 02 31 77 93 25. Mich 31/F2. Map 1.

VINCELOTTES

Auberge Les Tilleuls

Comfortable restaurant with rooms/Cooking 2 | **FW**
Terrace

A small, evocative *logis* with pavilion-tented terrace across the road, beside the Yonne & some lime trees. The chef, fluent English-speaking Alain Renaud, & his wife Annette, are an energetic, friendly couple. Classical/regional/*terroir* crackers. Two old-fashioned mouthwatering *plats* on menu B: *coq au vin à l'ancienne* & *tête de veau sauce gribiche*.
Menus bCE. Rooms (5) EF. Cards MC, V. (Parking no problem.)
Closed 18 Dec-Feb. Wed evg & Thurs (out of season).
Post 89290 Vincelottes, Yonne. Region Burgundy.
Tel 03 86 42 22 13. Fax 03 86 42 23 51. Mich 72/A2. Map 2.

VITRAC (Cantal) (also see next page)

Auberge de la Tomette

Simple hotel/Cooking 1-2 | **FW**
Quiet/Terrace/Gardens/Swimming pool

A warm welcome from kindly Odette Chausi at her stone-built *logis* in chestnut-tree terrain. There's nothing prissy about husband Daniel's regional fare. From a trio of choices for each course on regional menu B dig into heart-warmers like *jambon de pays*, *bouriol à la crème fraîche*, *poulet farci aux pruneaux*, Auvergne cheeses & *tarte*. Also garden annexe.
Menus ABC. Rooms (19) DE. Cards AE, MC, V.
Closed Mid Dec-Mar.
Post 15220 Vitrac, Cantal. Region Massif Central (Auvergne).
Tel 04 71 64 70 94. Fax 04 71 64 77 11. Mich 126/A4. Map 5.

A100frs & under. B100–150. C150–200. D200–250. E250–350. F350–500. G500+

VITRAC (**Dordogne**) (also see previous page) **La Ferme**

Simple restaurant/Cooking 1-2 **FW**
Parking/Air-conditioning

Isolated old farm, 200m from the River Dordogne, at Caudon, 3km E of Vitrac. *Périgourdine* fare at Dominique & Arlette Lacour-Escalier's long-established business. Gutsy grub: *soupe de campagne au pain de seigle; rillettes Sarladaises; faux-filet grillé* & *côtes d'agneau* are some of the anything but cissy stomach fillers. Air-conditioned *salle*.
Menus ABC. Cards MC, V. (Rooms: see entry for Mas de Castel, Sarlat.)
Closed Oct. 20 Dec-20 Jan. Sun evg (winter). Mon. (Above 2km S Sarlat.)
Post Caudon-de-Vitrac, 24200 Sarlat-la-Canéda, Dordogne.
Tel 05 53 28 33 35. Mich 124/A3-B3. Map 5. Region Dordogne.

VITRAC (**Dordogne**) **La Sanglière**

Comfortable restaurant/Cooking 2 **FW**
Quiet/Gardens/Swimming pool/Parking/Air-conditioning

A pleasant drive W & N from Vitrac leads you to an isolated & elevated modern restaurant "home" in extensive gardens. Unrelenting regional dishes dominate menus: "light-heavyweight" *salade de magret ou gésier* & *cuisse de canard garnie*; & a "heavyweight" *civet de gésier* are typical. A "lightweight" option could be *flétan à l'oseille*. Top-notch desserts.
Menus ABCE. Cards MC, V. (Rooms: see entry for Mas de Castel, Sarlat.)
Closed Oct-Mar. Sun evg & Mon (not July/Aug). (Above 2km S of Sarlat.)
Post 24200 Vitrac, Dordogne. Region Dordogne.
Tel 05 53 28 33 51. Fax 05 53 28 52 31. Mich 124/A3-B3. Map 5.

VITRE **Hôtel Petit Billot/Rest. Petit Billot**

Simple hotel and restaurant/Cooking 1-2 **FW**

I first visited this simple, beamed restaurant when researching *En Route* (my autouroute guide, p109). Marie-Thérèse Lancelot welcomes you; hubby Bernard works *Bourgeoise*s/classical/regional chopping blocks (*billot* – block): *fromage de tête, rillettes de pays, terrine de maison et son chutney, escalope de veau Viennoise, crème caramel* & *île flottante* are typical. Hotel run as separate business by Paul Fournel. Parking 200m.
Menus ABC. Rooms (17) CDE. Cards MC, V. Region Normandy.
Closed Rest: Sat (out of season). Sun evg. Map 1.
Post 5 pl. Gén. Leclerc, 35500 Vitré, Ille-et-Vilaine. Mich 49/D3.
Tel (H) 02 99 75 02 10. (R) 02 99 74 68 88. Fax (H) 02 99 74 72 96.

A100frs & under. B100–150. C150–200. D200–250. E250–350. F350–500. G500+

VIVONNE

La Treille

Simple restaurant with very basic rooms/Cooking 2

A couple I love dearly will please all readers, especially those with few francs to spare. Geneviève Monteil is a bubbly angel; husband, chef Jacquelin, is an ardent supporter of regional/classical fare. *Mouclade, farci Poitevin, bouilliture d'anguilles*, etc: refer to the regional lists. Valbonne these days is bypassed by N10 & is 10min-drive from A10 exit 20. (Better rooms: Le St-Georges (near church); Rooms (28) DE.)
Menus aBCD. Rooms (4) ABC. Cards MC, V.
Closed Feb sch. hols. Wed (Nov-Apl).
Post av. Bordeaux, 86370 Vivonne, Vienne. Region Poitou-Charentes.
Tel 05 49 43 41 13. Fax 05 49 89 00 72. Mich 95/D2-E2. Map 5.

VOIRON

Serratrice

Comfortable restaurant/Cooking 2

Across the road from the station & an athletics track lap from the famed Caves de la Chartreuse (distillery). *Restaurant de Mer* is the label that Philippe Serratrice gives his edge-of-the-Chartreuse *salle*: absolutely right as his menus confirm. Classical treatment for a range of old-time delights: *soupe de poissons, assiette de fruits de mer, saumon d'Ecosse crème d'algues* & *sole de Boulogne meunière* – all enjoyable *plats*.
Menus BCEDF. Cards All. (Rooms: Relais Bleus; 300m SW.)
Closed 19 June-9 Sept. Sun evg. Mon.
Post 3 av. Tardy, 38500 Voiron, Isère. Region Savoie.
Tel 04 76 05 29 88. Fax 04 76 05 45 62. Mich 117/D4-E4. Map 6.

VOISINS-LE-BRETONNEUX

Port Royal

Simple hotel (no restaurant)
Quiet/Gardens/Closed parking

I have been recommending this modern base hotel, anonymous & unassuming, for a dozen years & I have had no complaints from readers during that time. The most important "benefits", from my point of view, are: the simple-as-pie 5 minute drive E to Alain Rayé's Châteaufort restaurant (see entry); &, if you are a golf fanatic, you'll be happy that there are so many golf courses in the area (including the national course).
Rooms (36) E(low-end). Cards MC, V. Region Ile de France.
Post 20 r. H. Boucher, 78960 Voisins-le-Bretonneux, Yvelines.
Tel 01 30 44 16 27. Fax 01 30 57 52 11. Mich 35/E4. Map 2.

A100frs & under. B100–150. C150–200. D200–250. E250–350. F350–500. G500+

VOLVIC

La Rose des Vents

Simple hotel/Cooking 1-2 `FW`
Secluded/Terr/Gardens/Swim pool/Tenn/Lift/Garage/Parking

All mod cons at hand in this super situated hotel, 2500-ft high & at the heart of the Parc Naturel Régional des Volcans. Head 3km SW from Volvic, then follow signs for Volvic *gare/hôtel*. *Chef/patron* Jean-Pierre Rabanet follows classical flows (*contre-filet forestière* is typical); wife Annie & her English-speaking daughter, Bénédicte, are *les patronnes*.
Menus BCD. Rooms (26) DE. Cards All.
Closed 1-2 Jan. Public hols.
Post Luzet, 63530 Volvic, Puy-de-Dôme. Region Massif Central (Auvergne).
Tel 04 73 33 50 77. Fax 04 73 33 57 11. Mich 113/D1. Map 5.

VONNAS

La Résidence des Saules/Rest. L'Ancienne Auberge

Comfortable hotel & simple restaurant/Cooking 2-3 `FW`
Quiet (hotel)/Terrace

3-star chef Georges Blanc's bistro. Watch supplements on menu C (with 8 dessert options). Two finger-licking hits: a *pâté chaud feuilleté sauce porto* & *crème de champignons aux petites quenelles de volaille*. One miss – overcooked, mushy *filet de lieu jaune à l'échalote*. Great service. Vonnas? No, "Blancville" ("*le business*" at every turn).
Menus b(lunch)CD. Rooms (6) G (low-end). Cards All. (Cheaper rooms?)
Closed 2 Jan-8 Feb. (Use Beaujolais; E bank Saône; Mâcon; *sans rest*.)
Post pl. Marché, 01540 Vonnas, Ain. Region Lyonnais. Mich 102/C3.
Tel (H) 04 74 50 90 51. (R) 04 74 50 90 50. Fax 04 74 50 08 80. Map 6.

VOUGY

Capucin Gourmand

Very comfortable restaurant/Cooking 2-3
Terrace/Parking

Guy & Christine Barbin's chalet-style home has two *salles*; one blue, one white. Hostess Christine is a friendly lass & has improved her English no end. Chef Guy is an assured neo-classicist. Typical of his light, restrained touch are succulent treats like *pigeon des Dombes rôti à l'estragon* & *filet de féra braisé à l'Ayse* (the local white wine).
Menus DE. Cards All. (Rooms: Bellevue & Aub. du Coteau, Ayse.)
Closed 2-10 Jan. 17 Aug-9 Sept. Sun evg. Mon. (Ayse 3km E Bonneville.)
Post rte Bonneville, 74130 Vougy, Haute-Savoie. (Vougy to E Bonneville.)
Tel 04 50 34 03 50. Fax 04 50 34 57 57. Mich 105/D4. Map 6.

A100frs & under. B100–150. C150–200. D200–250. E250–350. F350–500. G500+

WANGENBOURG
Parc

Comfortable hotel/Cooking 2 | FW |
Quiet/Terrace/Gardens/Swim pool (indoor)/Tennis/Lift/Parking

A super site, 1650-ft high, in wooded hills nicknamed the Swiss Vosges. Owned by the same family for 150 years; the 6th generation, Elisabeth & Daniel Gihr, are go-ahead owners. A gym & sauna help you to sweat off the inches after tucking into classical/regional *plats* like *truite au Riesling* & *civet de chevreuil* (infused with *essence de genièvre*).
Menus BCDE. Rooms (34) EF. Cards MC, V.
Closed 3 Jan-22 Mar. 3 Nov-22 Dec.
Post 67710 Wangenbourg, Bas-Rhin. Region Alsace.
Tel 03 88 87 31 72. Fax 03 88 87 38 00. Mich 42/C4. Map 3.

WESTHALTEN
Auberge Cheval Blanc

Very comfortable restaurant with rooms/Cooking 3
Quiet/Lift/Parking/Air-conditioning (restaurant)

There's a handsome, warm interior in the Koehler *logis* at the heart of the wine village. Classical/regional fare. On a cold, wet autumn day a delicate *consommé aux quenelles de moelle*, heart-warming *boeuf en pot au feu, légumes et crudités* & luscious *petits flans à la crème sur coulis de fruits* were just what the doctor ordered. Bravo chef Gilbert!
Menus C(bottom-end)EF. Rooms (12) EF. Disabled. Cards MC, V.
Closed 4-27 Feb. 24 June-3 July. Rest: Sun evg & Mon.
Post 68250 Westhalten, Haut-Rhin. Region Alsace.
Tel 03 89 47 01 16. Fax 03 89 47 64 40. Mich 61/D4. Map 3.

WIMEREUX (also see next page)
La Liégeoise et Atlantic Hôtel

Very comfortable restaurant with rooms/Cooking 3 | FW |
Lift/Parking

The clue is in the new name: Alain & Béatrice Delpierre (she speaks fluent English & wears a bright smile) have left their Liégeoise home in Boulogne & moved N. An uninviting exterior. Don't turn back: enjoy Béatrice & Alain's impressive efforts in the first-floor *salle* beside the sea. He tacks modern/classical courses. Fish *plats* are magnificent: *pavé de bar* with green Puy lentils a sensationally happy marriage.
Menus B(bottom-end)CD. Rooms (10) FG. Cards All.
Post digue de mer, 62930 Wimereux, Pas-de-Calais. Region North.
Tel 03 21 32 41 01. Fax 03 21 87 46 17. Mich 2/A2. Map 2.

A100frs & under. B100–150. C150–200. D200–250. E250–350. F350–500. G 500+

WIMEREUX (also see previous page)

Epicure

Comfortable restaurant/Cooking 2-3

FW

A small, whitewashed restaurant on the corner of the D940 & rue de la Gare. Claudette Carrée is *la patronne*, husband Philippe is the *cuisine moderne* magician. How welcome a mixture of eclectic flavours are: *cabillaud au cerfeuil et poivre de Sichuan* (a Chinese-cracker trick); *navarin de langoustines aux lentilles* (contemporary sleight of hand); & *tarte croustillant de banane et noix de coco* (Indies deception).
Menus BCD. Cards AE, MC, V. (Rooms: Centre, Wimereux.)
Closed Christmas. Sun evg. Wed. (Readers speak well of food at Centre.)
Post 1 r. Gare, 62930 Wimereux, Pas-de-Calais. Region North.
Tel 03 21 83 21 83. Mich 2/A2. Map 2.

WIMEREUX (Wimille)

Relais de la Brocante

Very comfortable restaurant/Cooking 3

FW

Readers' letters urged me to include this intimate, full-of-character *relais* (old presbytery) beneath Wimille's *église*. How right they were. Claude Jansen is a welcoming *MD/sommelier*; & Jean-François Laurent a highly-capable, neo-classical/modern chef. Desserts are a special highlight: *"l'abeille"* – *croustillant de poires beurrées au miel, glace aux éclats de noisettes caramélisées* – a typical "mouthful" marvel.
Menus b(top-end)CE. Cards AE, MC, V. (Rooms: Ibis-Plage & Métropole at)
Closed Sun evg & Mon. (Boulogne – 5km to S; see entry for Métropole.)
Post 62126 Wimille, Pas-de-Calais. Region North. (2km E of Wimereux.)
Tel 03 21 83 19 31. Fax 03 21 87 29 71. Mich 2/A2. Map 2.

YVOIRE

Pré de la Cure

Comfortable hotel/Cooking 2
Terrace/Gardens/Lift/Garage/Parking

FW

A modern, 3-story chalet (bedrooms with balconies) on the edge of the stunning medieval lakeside village (honeypot hive). Both the terrace & the panoramic dining room have lake views. Nicole Magnin is *la patronne*, husband Michel the kitchen boss. Classical/neo-classical fare, typified by a succulent *filet de féra* (from the lake) & *pintade flambé au cognac*.
Menus b(bottom-end)CE. Rooms (25) E. Cards MC, V.
Closed Nov-mid Mar. Rest: Wed (Mar, Apl, Oct).
Post 74140 Yvoire, Haute-Savoie, Region Savoie.
Tel 04 50 72 83 58. Fax 04 50 72 91 15. Mich 104/C2. Map 6. Whew!

A100frs & under. B100–150. C150–200. D200–250. E250–350. F350–500. G500+

Glossary of Menu Terms

A point medium rare

Abatis (Abattis) poultry giblets

Abats offal

Ablette freshwater fish

Abricot apricot

Acajou cashew nut

Acarne sea-bream

Achatine snail (from Far East)

Ache celery

Acidulé(e) acid

Affiné(e) improve; ripen, mature (common term with cheeses)

Africaine (à l') African style: with aubergines, tomatoes, *cèpes*

Agneau lamb

Agneau de pré-salé lamb fed on salt marshes

Agnelet young lamb

Agnès Sorel thin strips of mushroom, chicken and tongue

Agrumes citrus fruits

Aïado lamb with herbs and garlic

Aiglefin haddock

Aigre-doux sweet-sour

Aigrelette sharp sauce

Aiguillette thin slice

Ail garlic

Aile (Aileron) wing (winglet)

Aillade garlic sauce

Aïoli mayonnaise, garlic, olive oil

Airelles cranberries

Albert white cream sauce, mustard, vinegar

Albuféra *béchamel* sauce, sweet peppers

Alénois watercress-flavoured

Algues seaweed

Aligot purée of potatoes, cream, garlic, butter and fresh Tomme de Cantal (or Laguiole) cheese

Allemande a *velouté* sauce with egg yolks

Allemande (à l') German style: with sauerkraut and sausages

Allumette puff pastry strip

Alose shad (river fish)

Alouette lark

Alouette de mer sandpiper

Aloyau sirloin of beef

Alsacienne (à l') Alsace style: with sauerkraut, sausage and sometimes *foie gras*

Amande almond

Amande de mer small clam-like shellfish with nutty flavour

Amandine almond-flavoured

Amer bitter

Américaine (à l') Armoricaine (à l') sauce with dry white wine, cognac, tomatoes, shallots

Amourettes ox or calf marrow

Amuse-bouche appetiser

Amuse-gueule appetiser

Amusette appetiser

Ananas pineapple

Anchoïade anchovy crust

Anchois anchovy

Ancienne (à l') in the old style

Andalouse (à l') Andalusian style: tomatoes, sweet red peppers, rice

Andouille smoked tripe sausage

Andouillette small chitterling (tripe) sausage

Aneth dill

Ange angel

Ange à cheval oyster, wrapped in bacon and grilled

Angevine (à l') Anjou style: with dry white wine, cream, mushrooms, onions

Anglaise (à l') plain boiled

Anguille eel

Anis aniseed

Anis étoile star anise (a star-shaped fruit)

Ansé basted with liquid

Arachide peanut

Araignée de mer spider crab

Arc en ciel rainbow trout

Ardennaise (à l') Ardenne style: with juniper berries

Arête fish bone

Argenteuil asparagus flavoured (usually soup)

Arlésienne stuffed tomatoes *à la provençale*, eggplant, rice

Armoricaine see *Américaine*

Aromates aromatic; either spicy or fragrant

Arômes à la gêne Lyonnais cow's or goat's cheese soaked in *marc*

Artichaut artichoke

Asperges asparagus

Assaisonné flavoured or seasoned with; to dress a salad

Assiette (de) plate (of)

Aubergine aubergine, eggplant

Aulx (plural of *ail*) garlic

Aumônière pancake drawn up into shape of beggar's purse

Aurore (à l') pink sauce, tomato flavoured

Auvergnate (à l') Auvergne style: with cabbage, sausage and bacon

Aveline hazelnut

Avocat avocado pear

Avoine oat(s)

Azyme unleavened (bread)

Baba au rhum sponge dessert with rum syrup

Baguette long bread loaf

Baie berry

Baigné bathed or lying in

Ballotine boned and stuffed poultry or meat in a roll

Banane banana

Bar sea-bass

Barbarie Barbary duck

Barbeau barbel

Barbeau de mer red mullet

Barbue brill

Barigoule (à la) brown sauce with artichokes and mushrooms

Baron de lapereau baron of young rabbit

Barquette boat-shaped pastry

Basilic basil

Basquaise (à la) Basque style: Bayonne ham, rice and peppers

Bâtarde butter sauce, egg yolks

Bâtarde pain crusty white loaf

Batavia salad lettuce

Bâton stick-shaped bread loaf

Baudroie monkfish, anglerfish

Bavaroise bavarois mould, usually of custard, flavoured with fruit or chocolate. Can describe other dishes, particularly shellfish

Bavette skirt of beef

Baveuse runny

Béarnaise thick sauce with egg yolks, shallots, butter, white wine and tarragon vinegar

Béatilles (Malin de) sweetbreads, livers, kidneys, cockscombs

Beaugency *Béarnaise* sauce with artichokes, tomatoes, marrow

Bécasse woodcock

Bécassine snipe

Béchamel creamy white sauce

Beignet fritter

Beignet de fleur de courgette courgette flower in batter

Belle Hélène poached pear with ice cream and chocolate sauce

Belon oyster (see *Huîtres*)

Berawecka Christmas fruit bread stuffed with dried fruit, spices and laced with *kirsch*

Bercy sauce with white wine and shallots

Bergamot variety of pear or orange

Bergamote orange-flavoured sweet

Berlingot mint-flavoured sweet

Berrichone *Bordelaise* sauce

Bêtisse hard mint

Betterave beetroot

Beuchelle à la Tourangelle kidneys, sweetbreads, morels, cream and truffles

Beurre (Echiré) butter. (Finest butter from Poitou-Charentes)

Beurre blanc sauce with butter, shallots, wine vinegar and sometimes dry white wine

Beurre noir sauce with browned butter, vinegar, parsley

Biche female deer

Bière à la pression beer on tap

Bière en bouteille bottled beer

Bifteck steak

Bigarade (à la) orange sauce

Bigarreau type of cherry

Bigorneau winkle

Billy By mussel soup

Biscuit à la cuiller sponge finger

Bisque shellfish soup

Blanc (de volaille) white breast (of chicken): can describe white fish fillet or white vegetables

Blanchaille whitebait

Blanquette white stew

Blé corn or wheat

Blé noir buckwheat

Blettes Swiss chard

Blinis small, thick pancakes

Boeuf à la mode beef braised in red wine

Boeuf Stroganoff beef, sour cream, onions, mushrooms

Boletus type of edible fungi

Bombe ice cream

Bon-chrétien variety of pear

Bonne femme (à la) white wine sauce, shallots, mushrooms

Bonne femme (à la) potato, leek and carrot soup

Bordelais(e) (à la) Bordeaux style: brown sauce with shallots, red wine, beef bone marrow

Bouchée mouthful size (either a tart or *vol-au-vent*)

Boudin sausage-shaped mixture

Boudin blanc white coloured; pork and sometimes chicken

Boudin noir black pudding

Bouillabaisse Mediterranean fish stew and soup

Bouilliture eel stew (see *matelote d'anguilles*)

Bouillon broth, light consommé

Boulangère sauce of onions and potatoes

Boulette small ball of fish or meat

Bouquet prawn

Bouquet garni bunch of herbs used for flavouring

Bourdaloue hot poached fruit

Bourdelot whole apple pastry

Bourgeoise (à la) sauce of carrots, onions and diced bacon

Bourguignonne (à la) Burgundy style: red wine, onions, bacon and mushrooms

Bouribot duck stewed in red wine

Bourrache borage, a herb used in drinks and salads

Bourride creamy fish soup with *aïoli*

Bourriole sweet or savoury pancake

Boutargue grey mullet roe paste

Braisé braised

Brandade de morue salt cod

Brassado (Brassadeau) doughnut

Bréjaude cabbage and bacon soup

Brème bream

Brési thin slices dried beef

Bretonne sauce with celery, leeks, beans and mushrooms

Brioche sweet yeast bread

Broche (à la) spit roasted

Brochet pike

Brochette (de) meat or fish on a skewer

Brouet broth

Brouillade stewed in oil

Brouillés scrambled

Broutard young goat

Brugnon nectarine

Brûlé(e) toasted

Brunoise diced vegetables

Bruxelloise sauce with asparagus, butter and eggs

Bucarde cockle

Buccin whelk

Bugne sweet pastry fritter

Cabillaud cod
Cabri kid (young goat)
Cacahouète roasted peanut
Cacao cocoa
Caen (à la mode de) cooked in Calvados and white wine
Café coffee
Cagouille snail
Caille quail
Caillé milk curds
Caillette pork and vegetable faggot
Cajasse sweet pastry (sometimes made with black cherries)
Cajou cashew nut
Calissons almond and crystallised fruit sweetmeats
Calmar (Calamar) inkfish, squid
Campagne country style
Canapé a base, usually bread
Canard duck
Canard à la presse (Rouennaise) duck breast cooked in blood of carcass, red wine and brandy
Canard au sang see above
Canard sauvage wild duck
Caneton (canette) duckling
Cannelle cinnamon
Capilotade small bits or pieces
Capoum scorpion fish
Caprice whim (a dessert)
Capucine nasturtium
Carbonnade braised beef in beer, onions and bacon
Cardinal *béchamel* sauce, lobster, cream, red peppers
Cardon cardoon, a large celery-like vegetable
Cari curry powder
Caroline chicken consommé
Carpaccio slice raw beef (term often now used for other produce)
Carré d'agneau lamb chops from best end of neck
Carré de porc pork cutlets from best end of neck

Carré de veau veal chops from best end of neck
Carrelet flounder, plaice
Carvi caraway seed
Casse-croûte snack
Cassis blackcurrant
Cassolette small pan
Cassonade soft brown sugar
Cassoulet casserole of beans, sausage and/or pork, goose, duck
Caviar d'aubergine aubergine (eggplant) purée
Cebiche raw fish marinated in lime or lemon juice
Cedrat confit a crystallised citrus fruit
Céleri celery
Céleri-rave celeriac
Cendres (sous les) cooked (buried) in hot ashes
Cèpe fine, delicate mushroom
Cerfeuil chervil
Cerise (noire) cherry (black)
Cerneau walnut
Cervelas pork garlic sausage
Cervelle brains
Cévenole (à la) garnished with mushrooms or chestnuts
Champignons (des bois) mushrooms (from the woods)
Chanterelle apricot-coloured mushroom
Chantilly whipped cream, sugar
Chapon capon
Chapon de mer *rascasse* or scorpion fish
Charbon de bois (au) grilled on charcoal
Charcuterie cold meat cuts
Charcutière sauce with onions, white wine, gherkins
Charlotte sponge fingers, cream
Charolais (Charollais) beef
Chartreuse a mould shape
Chasse hunting (season)

Chasseur sauce with white wine, mushrooms, shallots

Châtaigne sweet chestnut

Chateaubriand thick fillet steak

Châtelaine garnish with artichoke hearts, tomatoes, potatoes

Chaud(e) hot

Chaudrée fish stew

Chausson pastry turnover

Chemise (en) pastry covering

Cheveux d'ange vermicelli

Chevreau kid (young goat)

Chevreuil roe-deer

Chevrier green haricot bean

Chichi doughnut-like fritter

Chicon chicory

Chicorée curly endive

Chiffonnade thinly-cut

Chinoise (à la) Chinese style: with bean sprouts and soy sauce

Chipirones see *calmars*

Choisy braised lettuce, sautéed potatoes

Choix (au) a choice of

Choron *Béarnaise* sauce with the addition of tomatoes

Chou (vert) cabbage

Choucroute (souring of vegetables) usually white cabbage (sauerkraut), peppercorns, boiled ham, potatoes and Strasbourg sausages

Chou-fleur cauliflower

Chou-frisé kale

Chou-pommé white-heart cabbage

Chou-rave kohlrabi

Chou-rouge red cabbage

Choux (au fromage) puffs (made of cheese)

Choux de Bruxelles Brussels sprouts

Choux (pâte à) pastry

Ciboule spring onion

Ciboulette chive

Cidre cider

Citron (vert) lemon (lime)

Citronelle lemon grass

Citrouille pumpkin

Civet stew

Civet de lièvre jugged hare

Clafoutis cherries in pancake batter

Claires oysters (see *Huîtres*)

Clamart with petits pois

Clou de girofle clove (spice)

Clouté (de) studded with

Clovisse small clam

Cocherelle type of mushroom

Cochon pig

Cochonailles pork products

Coco coconut; also small white bean

Cocotte (en) cooking pot

Coeur (de) heart (of)

Coeur de palmier palm heart

Coffret (en) in a small box

Coing quince

Colbert (à la) fish, dipped in milk, egg and breadcrumbs

Colin hake

Colvert wild duck

Compote stewed fruit

Concassé(e) coarsely chopped

Concombre cucumber

Condé creamed rice and fruit

Confiserie confectionery

Confit(e) preserved or candied

Confiture jam

Confiture d'oranges marmalade

Congre conger eel

Consommé clear soup

Contrefilet sirloin, usually tied for roasting

Copeaux literally shavings

Coq (au vin) chicken in red wine sauce (or name of wine)

Coque cockle

Coque (à la) soft-boiled or served in shell

Coquelet young cockerel

Coquillages shellfish

Coquille St-Jacques scallop

Corail (de) coral (of)
Coriandre coriander
Cornichon gherkin
Côte d'agneau lamb chop
Côte de boeuf side of beef
Côte de veau veal chop
Côtelette chop
Cotriade Brittany fish soup
Cou (d'oie) neck (of goose)
Coulemelle mushroom
Coulibiac hot salmon *tourte*
Coulis (de) thick sauce (of)
Coupe ice cream dessert
Courge pumpkin
Courgette baby marrow
Couronne circle or ring
Court-bouillon aromatic poaching liquid
Couscous crushed semolina
Crabe crab
Crambe sea kale
Cramique raisin or currant loaf
Crapaudine (à la) grilled game bird with backbone removed
Crapinaude bacon pancake
Craquelot herring
Crécy with carrots and rice
Crème cream
Crème (à la) served with cream or cooked in cream sauce
Crème à l'anglaise light custard sauce
Crème brûlée same, less sugar and cream, with praline (see *brûlée*)
Crème pâtissière custard filling
Crème plombières custard filling: egg whites, fresh fruit flavouring
Crémets fresh cream cheese, eaten with sugar and cream
Crêpe thin pancake
Crêpe dentelle thin pancake
Crêpe Parmentier potato pancake
Crêpe Suzette sweet pancake with orange liqueur sauce
Crépinette (de) wrapping (of)
Cresson watercress

Cressonière purée of potatoes and watercress
Crête cockscomb
Creuse long, thick-shelled oyster
Crevette grise shrimp
Crevette rose prawn
Cromesquis croquette
Croque Monsieur toasted cheese or ham sandwich
Croquette see *boulette*
Crosne artichoke
Croustade small pastry mould with various fillings
Croustillant crisp, crusty
Croûte (en) pastry crust (in a)
Croûtons bread (toast or fried)
Cru raw
Crudité raw vegetable
Crustacés shellfish
Cuillère soft (cut with spoon)
Cuisse (de) leg (of)
Cuissot (de) haunch (of)
Cuit cooked
Cul haunch or rear
Culotte rump (usually steak)
Cultivateur soup or chopped vegetables
Dariole basket-shaped pastry
Darne slice or steak
Dartois savoury or sweet filled puff-pastry rectangles
Datte date
Daube stew (various types)
Daurade sea-bream
Décaféiné decaffeinated coffee
Dégustation tasting
Délice delight
Demi-glace basic brown sauce
Désossé boned
Demi-sel lightly salted
Diable seasoned with mustard
Diane (à la) peppered cream sauce
Dieppoise (à la) Dieppe style: white wine, cream, mussels, shrimps
Dijonnaise (à la) mustard sauce

Dijonnaise (à la belle) sauce made from blackcurrants
Dinde young hen turkey
Dindon turkey
Dindonneau young turkey
Diot pork and vegetable sausage
Dodine (de canard) cold stuffed duck
Dorade sea-bream
Doré cooked until golden
Doria with cucumbers
Douceurs desserts
Douillon pear wrapped in pastry
Doux (douce) sweet
Dragée sugared almond
Du Barry cauliflower soup
Duxelles chopped mushrooms, shallots and cream
Echalote shallot
Echine loin (of pork)
Echiquier in checkered fashion
Eclade (de moules) (mussels) cooked over pine needles
Ecrasé crushed (as with fruit)
Ecrevisses freshwater crayfish
Ecuelle bowl or basin
Effiloché(e) frayed, thinly sliced
Emincé thinly sliced
Encornet cuttlefish, squid
Encre squid ink, used in sauces
Endive chicory
Entrecôte entrecôte, rib steak
Entremets sweets
Epaule shoulder
Eperlan smelt (small fish)
Epice spice
Epinard spinach
Epis de maïs sweetcorn
Escabèche fish (or poultry) marinated in *court-bouillon*; served cold
Escalope thinly cut (meat or fish)
Escargot snail
Espadon swordfish
Estouffade stew with onions, herbs, mushrooms, red or white wine (perhaps garlic)
Estragon tarragon flavoured
Esturgeon sturgeon
Etrille crab
Etuvé(e) cooked in little water or in ingredient's own juices
Exocet flying fish
Façon cooked in a described way
Faisan(e) pheasant
Fane green top of root vegetable
Far Brittany prune flan
Farci(e) stuffed
Farine flour
Faux-filet sirloin steak
Favorite a garnish of *foie gras* and truffles
Favouille spider crab
Fécule starch
Fenouil fennel
Fenouil marin samphire
Féra lake fish, like salmon.
Ferme (fermier) farm (farmer)
Fermière mixture of onions, carrots, turnips, celery, etc.
Feuille de vigne vine leaf
Feuilleté light flaky pastry
Fève broad bean
Ficelle (à la) tied in a string
Ficelles thin loaves of bread
Figue fig
Filet fillet
Financière (à la) Madeira sauce with truffles
Fine de claire oyster (see *Huîtres*)
Fines herbes mixture of parsley, chives, tarragon, etc.
Flageolet kidney bean
Flamande (à la) Flemish style: bacon, carrots, cabbage, potatoes and turnips
Flambé flamed
Flamiche puff pastry tart
Flan tart
Flétan halibut
Fleur (de courgette) flower

(courgette flower, usually stuffed)
Fleurons puff pastry crescents
Flie small clam
Florentine with spinach
Flûte long thin loaf of bread
Foie liver
Foie de veau calves liver
Foie gras goose liver
Foies blonds de volaille chicken liver mousse
Foin (dans le) cooked in hay
Fond (base) basic stock
Fondant see *boulette*: a bon-bon
Fond d'artichaut artichoke heart
Fondu(e) (de fromage) melted (cheese with wine)
Forestière bacon and mushrooms
Fouace dough cakes
Four (au) baked in oven
Fourré stuffed
Frais (Fraîche) fresh or cool
Fraise strawberry
Fraise des bois wild strawberry
Framboise raspberry
Française (à la) mashed potato filled with mixed vegetables
Frangipane almond custard filling
Frappé frozen or ice cold
Friandises sweets (*petits fours*)
Fricadelle minced meat ball
Fricandeau slice topside veal
Fricassée braised in sauce of butter, egg yolks and cream
Frisé(e) curly
Frit fried
Frite chip
Fritot fritter
Frittons see *grattons*
Friture small fried fish
Frivolle fritter
Froid cold
Fromage cheese
Fromage de tête brawn
Fruit de la passion passion fruit
Fruits confits crystallised fruit
Fruits de mer seafood

Fumé smoked
Fumet fish stock
Galantine cooked meat, fish or vegetables in jelly, served cold
Galette pastry, pancake or cake
Galimafrée (de) stew (of)
Gamba large prawn
Ganache chocolate and *crème fraîche* mixture used to fill cakes
Garbure (Garbue) vegetable soup
Gardiane beef stew with red wine, black olives, onions and garlic
Gardon small roach
Gargouillau pear tart or cake
Garni(e) with vegetables
Garniture garnish
Gasconnade leg of lamb roasted with anchovies and garlic
Gâteau cake
Gâtinaise (à la) with honey
Gaufre waffle
Gayette faggot
Gelée aspic jelly
Géline chicken
Gendarme smoked or salted herring: flat, dry sausage
Genièvre juniper
Génoise rich sponge cake
Gentiane liqueur made from gentian flowers
Germiny sorrel and cream soup
Germon long-fin tuna
Gésier gizzard
Gibelotte see *fricassée*
Gibier game
Gigot (de) leg of lamb. Can describe other meat and fish
Gigot brayaude leg of lamb in white wine with red beans and cabbage
Gigue (de) shank (of)
Gingembre ginger
Girofle clove
Girolle apricot-coloured fungus
Givré frosted

Glacé iced. Crystallised. Glazed
Glace ice cream
Gnocchi dumplings of semolina, potato or *choux* paste
Godard see *financière (à la)*
Gougère round-shaped, egg and cheese *choux* pastry
Goujon gudgeon
Goujonnettes (de) small fried pieces (of)
Gourmandises sweetmeats; can describe *fruits de mer*
Gousse (de) pod or husk (of)
Graine (de capucine) seed (nasturtium)
Graisse fat
Graisserons duck or goose fat scratchings
Grand Veneur sauce with vegetables, wine vinegar, redcurrant jelly and cream
Granité water ice
Gratin browned
Gratin Dauphinois potato dish with cream, cheese and garlic
Gratin Savoyard potato dish with cheese and butter
Gratiné(e) sauced dish browned with butter, cheese, breadcrumbs, etc.
Gratinée Lyonnaise clear soup with port, beaten egg and cheese (grilled brown)
Grattons pork fat scratchings
Gravette oyster (see *Huîtres*)
Grecque (à la) cooked vegetables served cold
Grelette cold sauce, based on whipped cream, for fish
Grenade pomegranate
Grenadin thick veal escalope
Grenouille (cuisses de grenouilles) frog (frogs' legs)
Gribiche mayonnaise sauce with gherkins, capers, hardboiled egg yolks and herbs

Grillade grilled meat
Grillé(e) grilled
Grilot small bulb onion
Griotte (Griottine) bitter red cherry
Griset mushroom
Grisotte parasol mushroom
Grive thrush
Grondin gurnard, red gurnet
Gros sel coarse rock or sea salt
Groseille à maquereau gooseberry
Groseille noire blackcurrant
Groseille rouge redcurrant
Gruyère hard, mild cheese
Gyromitre fungus
Habit vert dressed in green
Hachis minced or chopped-up
Hareng herring
    à l'huile cured in oil
    fumé kippered
    salé bloater
    saur smoked
Haricot bean
Haricot blanc dried white bean
Haricot rouge red kidney bean
Haricot vert green/French bean
Hochepot thick stew
Hollandaise sauce with butter, egg yolk and lemon juice
Homard lobster
Hongroise (à la) Hungarian style: sauce with tomato and paprika
Hors d'oeuvre appetisers
Huile oil
Huîtres oysters
    Les claires: the oyster-fattening beds in Marennes terrain (part of the Charente Estuary, between Royan and Rochefort, in Poitou-Charentes).
    Flat-shelled oysters:
    Belons (from the River Belon in Brittany);
    Gravettes (from Arcachon in the Southwest);
    both the above are cultivated in

387

their home oyster beds.
Marennes are those transferred from Brittany and Arcachon to *les claires,* where they finish their growth.

Dished oysters (sometimes called *portugaises*):
these breed mainly in the Gironde and Charente estuaries; they mature at Marennes.
Fines de claires and *spéciales* are the largest; *huîtres de parc* are standard sized.
All this lavish care covers a time span of two to four years.

Hure (de) head (of). Brawn. Jellied
Ile flottante unmoulded soufflé of beaten egg white and sugar
Imam bayeldi aubergine with rice, onions and sautéed tomatoes
Impératrice (à la) desserts with candied fruits soaked in kirsch
Indienne (à l') Indian style: with curry powder
Infusion herb tea
Italienne (à l') Italian style: artichokes, mushrooms, pasta
Jalousie latticed fruit or jam tart
Jambon ham
Jambonneau knuckle of pork
Jambonnette (de) boned and stuffed (knuckle of ham or poultry)
Jardinière diced fresh vegetables
Jarret de veau stew of shin of veal
Jarreton cooked pork knuckle
Jerez sherry
Jésus de Morteau smoked Jura pork sausage
Joinville *velouté* sauce with cream, crayfish tails and truffles
Joue (de) cheek (of)
Judru cured pork sausage
Julienne thinly-cut vegetables: also ling (cod family, see *lingue*)

Jus juice
Kaki persimmon fruit
Lait milk
Laitance soft roe
Laitue lettuce
Lamproie eel-like fish
Langouste spiny lobster or crawfish
Langoustine Dublin Bay prawn
Langue tongue
Languedocienne (à la) mushrooms, tomatoes, parsley garnish
Lapereau young rabbit
Lapin rabbit
Lapin de garenne wild rabbit
Lard bacon
Lard de poitrine fat belly of pork
Lardons strips of bacon
Laurier bay-laurel, sweet bay leaf
Lavaret lake fish, like salmon trout
Lèche thin slice
Léger (Légère) light
Légume vegetable
Lieu cod-like fish
Lièvre hare
Limaçon snail
Limande lemon sole
Limon lime
Lingue ling (cod family)
Lit bed
Livèche lovage (like celery)
Longe loin
Lotte de mer monkfish, anglerfish
Lotte de rivière (de lac) burbot, a river (or lake) fish; liver a great delicacy
Lou magret see *magret*
Loup de mer sea-bass
Louvine (loubine) grey mullet, like a sea-bass (Basque name)
Lyonnaise (à la) Lyonnais style: sauce with wine, onions, vinegar
Macédoine diced fruit or veg
Mâche lamb's lettuce; small, dark, green leaf
Macis mace (spice)

Madeleine tiny sponge cake
Madère sauce *demi-glace* and Madeira wine
Madrilène Madrid style: with chopped tomatoes
Magret (de canard) breast (of duck); now used for other poultry
Maigre fish, like sea-bass
Maigre non-fatty, lean
Maillot carrots, turnips, onions, peas and beans
Maïs maize flour
Maison (de) of the restaurant
Maître d'hôtel sauce with butter, parsley and lemon
Maltaise an orange flavoured *hollandaise* sauce
Manchons see *goujonnettes*
Mandarine tangerine
Mangetout edible peas and pods
Mangue mango
Manière (de) style (of)
Maquereau mackerel
Maraîchère (à la) market-gardener style: *velouté* sauce with vegetables
Marais marsh or market-garden
Marbré(e) marbled
Marc pure spirit
Marcassin young wild boar
Marché market
Marchand de vin sauce with red wine, chopped shallots
Marée fresh seafood
Marengo tomatoes, mushrooms, olive oil, white wine, garlic, herbs
Marennes (blanche) flat-shelled oyster (see *Huîtres*)
Marennes (verte) green shell
Mareyeur fishmonger
Marinade, Mariné(e) pickled
Marinière see *moules*
Marjolaine marjoram
Marjolaine almond and hazelnut

sponge cake with chocolate cream and praline
Marmite stewpot
Marquise (de) water ice (of)
Marrons chestnuts
Marrons glacés crystallised sweet chestnuts
Massepains marzipan cakes
Matelote (d'anguilles) freshwater red wine fish stew (of eels)
Matignon mixed vegetables, cooked in butter
Mauviette lark
Médaillion (de) round piece (of)
Mélange mixture or blend
Melba (à la) poached peach, with vanilla ice cream, raspberry sauce
Méli-Mélo medley
Mélisse lemon-balm (herb)
Ménagère (à la) housewife style: onions, potatoes, peas, turnips and carrots
Mendiant (fruits de) mixture of figs, almonds and raisins
Menthe mint
Mer sea
Merguez spicy grilled sausage
Merlan whiting (Provence: hake)
Merle blackbird
Merlu hake
Merluche dried cod
Mérou grouper (sea fish)
Merveilles hot, sugared fritters
Mesclum mixture of salad leaves
Meunière (à la) sauce with butter, parsley, lemon (sometimes oil)
Meurette red wine sauce
Miel honey
Mignardises *petits fours*
Mignon (de) small round piece
Mignonnette coarsley ground white pepper
Mijoté(e) cooked slowly in water
Milanaise (à la) Milan style: dipped in breadcrumbs, egg, cheese

Millassou sweet maize flour flan
Mille-feuille puff pastry with numerous thin layers
Mimosa chopped hardboiled egg
Mique stew of dumplings
Mirabeau anchovies, olives
Mirabelles golden plums
Mirepoix cubes carrot, onion, ham
Miroir smooth
Miroton (de) slices (of)
Mitonée (de) soup (of)
Mode (à la) in the manner of
Moelle beef marrow
Mojettes pulse beans in butter
Moka coffee
Montagne (de) from mountains
Montmorency with cherries
Morilles edible, dark brown, honeycombed fungi
Mornay cheese sauce
Morue cod
Morvandelle (jambon à la) ham with a piquant cream sauce, wine and wine vinegar (from Burgundy)
Morvandelle rapée baked eggs, cream and cheese, mixed with grated potato (from Burgundy's Morvan)
Mostèle (Gâteau de) cod mousse
Mouclade mussel stew
Moule mussel
Moules marinière mussels cooked in white wine and shallots
Mourone Basque red bell pepper
Mourtayrol stew with beef, chicken, ham, vegetables and bread (from the Auvergne)
Mousse cold, light, finely-minced ingredients with cream and egg whites
Mousseline *hollandaise* sauce with whipped cream
Mousseron edible fungus
Moutarde mustard
Mouton mutton

Mulet grey mullet
Mûre mulberry
Mûre sauvage (de ronce) blackberry
Muscade nutmeg
Museau de porc (de boeuf) sliced muzzle of pork (beef) with shallots and parsley in *vinaigrette*
Myrtille bilberry (blueberry)
Mystère a meringue desert with ice cream and chocolate; also cone-shaped ice cream
Nage (à la) *court-bouillon*: aromatic poaching liquid
Nantua sauce for fish with crayfish, white wine, tomatoes
Nappé sauce covered
Nature plain
Navarin stew, usually lamb
Navets turnips
Nègre dark (e.g. chocolate)
Newburg sauce with lobster, brandy, cream and Madeira
Nid nest
Nivernaise (à la) Nevers style: carrots and onions
Noilly sauce based on vermouth
Noisette hazelnut
Noisette sauce of lightly browned butter
Noisette (de) round piece (of)
Noix nuts
Noix (de veau) topside of leg (veal)
Normande (à la) Normandy style: fish sauce with mussels, shrimps, mushrooms, eggs and cream
Nouille noodle
Nouveau (nouvelle) new or young
Noyau sweet liqueur from crushed stones (usually cherries)
Oeufs à la coque soft-boiled eggs
Oeufs à la neige see *île flottante*
Oeufs à la poêlé fried eggs
Oeufs brouillés scrambled eggs
Oeufs durs hard-boiled eggs

Oeufs moulés poached eggs
Oie goose
Oignon onion
Oison rôti roast gosling
Omble chevalier freshwater char; looks like large salmon trout
Ombre grayling
Ombrine fish, like sea-bass
Omelette brayaude omelette with bacon, cream, potatoes and cheese
Onglet flank of beef
Oreille (de porc) ear (pig's)
Oreillette sweet fritter, flavoured with orange flower water
Orge (perlé) barley (pearl)
Origan oregano (herb)
Orléannaise (à l') Orléans style: chicory and potatoes
Orly dipped in butter, fried and served with tomato sauce
Ortie nettle
Ortolan wheatear (thrush family)
Os bone
Oseille sorrel
Osso bucco à la Niçoise veal braised with orange zest, tomatoes, onions and garlic
Ouillat Pyrénées soup; onions, tomatoes, goose fat, garlic
Oursins sea-urchins
Pageot sea-bream
Paillarde (de veau) grilled veal escalope
Paille fried potato stick
Pailleté (de) spangled (with)
Paillettes pastry straws
Pain bread
   bis brown bread
   de campagne round white loaf
   d'épice spiced honey cake
   de mie square white loaf
   de seigle rye bread
   doré bread soaked in milk and eggs and fried
   entier/complet wholemeal

   grillé toast
   perdu French toast
Paleron shoulder
Palmier palm-shaped sweet puff pastry
Palmier (coeur de) palm (heart)
Palombe wood pigeon
Palomête fish, like sea-bass
Palourde clam
Pamplemousse grapefruit
Pan bagna long split bread roll, brushed with olive oil and filled with olives, peppers, anchovies, onions, lettuce
Panaché mixed
Panade flour or bread paste
Panais parsnip
Pané(e) breadcrumbed
Panier basket
Panisse fried chickpea or maize fritter
Pannequets like *crêpes*, smaller and thicker
Pantin pork filled small pastry
Paon peacock
Papeton aubergines, fried or puréed, arranged in ring mould
Papillon small oyster (butterfly) from the Atlantic coast
Papillote (en) cooked in oiled paper (or foil)
Paquets (en) parcels
Parfait (de) a mousse (of)
Paris-Brest cake of *choux* pastry, filled with butter cream, almonds
Parisienne (à la) leeks, potatoes
Parmentier potatoes
Pascade sweet or savoury pancake
Pascaline (de) see *quenelle* (of)
Passe Crassane variety of pear
Passe-pierres seaweed
Pastèque watermelon
Pastis (sauce au) aniseed based
Pâté minced meats (of various types) baked. Usually served cold

Pâte pastry, dough or batter
Pâte à choux cream puff pastry
Pâte brisée short crust pastry
Pâte d'amande almond paste
Pâté en croûte baked in pastry crust
Pâtes (fraîches) fresh pasta
Pâtés (petits) à la Provençale anchovy and ham turnovers
Pâtisserie pastry
Pâtisson custard marrow
Patte claw, foot, leg
Pauchouse see *pochouse*
Paupiettes thin slices of meat of fish, used to wrap fillings
Pavé (de) thick slice (of)
Pavot (graines de) poppy seeds
Paysan(ne) (à la) country style
Peau (de) skin (of)
Pêche peach
Pêcheur fisherman
Pèlerine scallop
Perce-pierre samphire (edible sea fennel)
Perche perch
Perdreau young partridge
Perdrix partridge
Périgourdine (à la) goose liver and sauce *Périgueux*
Périgueux sauce with truffles and Madeira
Persil parsley
Persillade mixture of chopped parsley and garlic
Petit-beurre biscuit made with butter
Petit gris small snail
Petite marmite strong consommé with toast and cheese
Petits fours miniature cakes, biscuits, sweets
Petits pois tiny peas
Pétoncle small scallop
Pets de nonne small soufflé fritters
Picanchâgne (piquenchânge) a pear tart with walnut topping

Picholine large green table olives
Pied de cheval large oyster
Pied de mouton blanc creamcoloured mushroom
Pied de porc pig's trotter
Pigeonneau young pigeon
Pignon pine nut
Pilau rice dish
Pilon drumstick
Piment (doux) pepper (sweet)
Pimpernelle burnet (salad green)
Pintade (pintadeau) guinea-fowl (young guinea-fowl)
Piperade omelette or scrambled eggs with tomatoes, peppers, onions and, sometimes, ham
Piquante (sauce) sharp-tasting sauce with shallots, capers, wine
Piqué larded
Pissenlit dandelion leaf
Pistache green pistachio nut
Pistil de safran saffron (*pistil* from autumn-flowering crocus)
Pistou vegetable soup bound with *pommade*
Plateau (de) plate (of)
Pleurote mushroom
Plie franche plaice
Plombières sweet with vanilla ice cream, *kirsch,* candied fruit and *crème chantilly*
Pluche sprig
Pluvier plover
Poché(e) Pochade poached
Pochouse freshwater fish stew with white wine
Poêlé fried
Pogne sweet brioche flavoured with orange flower water
Poire pear
Poireau leek
Pois peas
Poisson fish
Poitrine breast
Poitrine fumée smoked bacon
Poitrine salée unsmoked bacon

Poivrade a peppery sauce with wine vinegar, cooked vegetables
Poivre noir black pepper
Poivre rose red pepper
Poivre vert green pepper
Poivron (doux) pepper (sweet)
Pojarsky minced meat or fish, cutlet shaped and fried
Polenta boiled maize flour
Polonaise Polish style: with buttered breadcrumbs, parsley, hard-boiled eggs
Pommade thick, smooth paste
Pomme apple
Pommes de terre potatoes
  à l'anglaise boiled
  allumettes thin and fried
  boulangère sliced with onions
  brayaude baked
  château roast
  dauphine croquettes
  duchesse mashed with egg yolk
  en l'air hollow potato puffs
  frites fried chips
  gratinées browned with cheese
  Lyonnaise sautéed with onions
  vapeur boiled
Pomponette savoury pastry
Porc (carré de) loin of pork
Porc (côte de) pork chop
Porcelet suckling pig
Porchetta whole roasted young pig, stuffed with offal, herbs, garlic
Porto (au) port
Portugaise (à la) Portuguese style: fried onions and tomatoes
Portugaises oysters with long, deep shells (see *Huîtres*)
Potage thick soup
Pot-au-crème dessert, usually chocolate or coffee
Pot-au-feu clear meat broth served with the meat
Potée heavy soup of cabbage, beans, etc.

Potimarron pumpkin
Potjevleisch northern terrine of mixed meats (rabbit, pork, veal)
Pouchouse see *pochouse*
Poularde large hen
Poulet chicken
Poulet à la broche spit-roasted chicken
Poulet Basquaise chicken with tomatoes and peppers
Poulet de Bresse corn-fed, white flesh chicken
Poulet de grain grain-fed chicken
Poulette young chicken
Poulpe octopus
Pounti small, egg-based, savoury soufflé with bacon or prunes
Pourpier purslane (salad green, also flavours dishes); a weed
Pousse-pierre edible seaweed
Poussin small baby chicken
Poutargue grey mullet roe paste
Praire small clam
Praline caramelised almonds
Praslin caramelised
Pré-salé (agneau de) lamb raised on salt marshes
Primeur young vegetable
Princesse *velouté* sauce, asparagus tips and truffles
Printanièr(e) (à la) garnish of diced vegetables
Produit (de) product (of)
Profiterole *choux* pastry, custard filled puff
Provençale (à la) Provençal style: tomatoes, garlic, olive oil, etc.
Prune plum
Pruneau prune
Purée mashed
Quasi (de veau) thick part of loin of veal (chump)
Quatre-épices four blended ground spices (ginger, cloves, nutmeg and white pepper)
Quatre-quarts cake made with

equal weights of eggs, butter, sugar and flour (four-quarters)

Quenelle light dumpling of fish or poultry

Quetsche small, purple plum

Queue tail

Queue de boeuf oxtail

Quiche (Lorraine) open flan of cheese, ham or bacon

Râble de lièvre (lapin) saddle of hare (rabbit)

Raclette scrapings from specially made and heated cheese

Radis radish

Ragoût stew, usually meat, but can describe other ingredients

Raie (bouclée) skate (type of)

Raifort horseradish

Raisin grape

Raïto sauce served over grilled fish (red wine, onions, tomatoes, herbs, olives, capers and garlic)

Ramequin see *cocotte (en)*

Ramier wood pigeon

Rapé(e) grated or shredded

Rascasse scorpion fish

Ratafia brandy and unfermented Champagne. Almond biscuit

Ratatouille aubergines, onions, courgettes, garlic, red peppers and tomatoes in olive oil

Ratte de Grenoble white potato

Raves (root) turnips, radishes,etc.

Ravigote sauce with onions, herbs, mushrooms, wine vinegar

Ravioles ravioli

Ravioles à la Niçoise pasta filled with meat or Swiss chard and baked with cheese

Ravioles du Royans small ravioli pasta with goat cheese filling (from the terrain under the western edges of the Vercors)

Régence sauce with wine, truffles, mushrooms

Réglisse liquorice

Reine chicken and cream

Reine-Claude greengage

Reinette type of apple

Réjane garnish of potatoes, bone-marrow, spinach and artichokes

Rémoulade sauce of mayonnaise, mustard, capers, herbs, anchovy

Rillettes (d'oie) potted pork (goose)

Rillons small cubes of fat pork

Ris d'agneau lamb sweetbreads

Ris de veau veal sweetbreads

Rissettes small sweetbreads

Rivière river

Riz rice

Riz à l'impératrice cold rice pudding

Riz complet brown rice

Riz sauvage wild rice

Robe de chambre jacket potato

Robert sauce *demi-glace,* white wine, onions, vinegar, mustard

Rocambole wild garlic

Rognon kidney

Rognonnade veal and kidneys

Romanoff fruit marinated in liqueur; mostly strawberries

Romarin rosemary

Roquette salad green

Rosé meat cooked to pink stage

Rosette large pork sausage

Rossini see *tournedos*

Rôti roast

Rouelle (de) round piece or slice

Rouget red mullet

Rouget barbet red mullet

Rouget grondin red gurnard (larger than red mullet)

Rouille orange-coloured sauce with peppers, garlic and saffron

Roulade (de) roll (of)

Roulé(e) rolled (usually *crêpe*)

Rousette rock salmon; dog fish

Roux flour, butter base for sauces

Royan fresh sardine

Rutabaga swede

Sabayon sauce of egg yolks, wine
Sablé shortbread
Sabodet Lyonnais sausage of pig's head, pork, beef; served hot
Safran saffron (see *pistil de*)
Sagou sago
Saignant(e) underdone, rare
Saindoux lard
St-Germain with peas
St-Hubert sauce *poivrade*, bacon and cooked chestnuts
St-Jacques (coquille) scallop
St-Pierre John Dory
Saisons (suivant) depending on the season of the year
Salade Niçoise tomatoes, beans, potatoes, black olives, anchovy, lettuce, olive oil, perhaps tuna
Salade panachée mixed salad
Salade verte green salad
Salé salted
Salicornes marsh samphire (edible sea-fennel)
Salmigondis meat stew
Salmis red wine sauce
Salpicon meat or fish and diced vegetables in a sauce
Salsifis salsify (vegetable)
Sanciau thick sweet or savoury pancake
Sandre freshwater fish, like perch
Sang blood
Sanglier wild boar
Sanguine blood orange
Sanguines mountain mushrooms
Santé potato and sorrel soup
Sarcelle teal
Sarrasin buckwheat
Sarriette savory, bitter herb
Saucisse freshly-made sausage
Saucisson large, dry sausage
Saucisson cervelas saveloy
Sauge sage
Saumon salmon
Saumon blanc hake
Saumon fumé smoked salmon

Sauté browned in butter, oil or fat
Sauvage wild
Savarin see *baba au rhum*
Savoyarde with Gruyère cheese
Scarole *endive* (chicory)
Scipion cuttlefish
Séché dried
Seiche squid or cuttlefish
Sel salt
Selle saddle
Selon grosseur (S.G.) according to size
Serpolet wild thyme
Sévigné garnished with mushrooms, roast potatoes, lettuce
Smitane sauce with sour cream, onions, white wine
Socca chickpea flour fritter
Soissons with white beans
Soja (pousse de) soy bean (soy bean sprout)
Sole à la Dieppoise sole fillets, mussels, shrimps, wine, cream
Sole Cardinale poached fillets of sole in lobster sauce
Sole Dugléré sole with tomatoes, onions, shallots, butter
Sole Marguéry sole with mussels and prawns in rich egg sauce
Sole Walewska *mornay* sauce, truffles and prawns
Sorbet water ice
Soubise onion sauce
Soufflé(e) beaten egg whites, baked (with sweet or savoury ingredients)
Soupière soup tureen
Sourdon cockle
Souvaroff a game bird with *foie gras* and truffles
Spaghettis (de) thin strips (of)
Spoom frothy water ice
Strasbourgeoise (à la) Strasbourg style: *foie gras, choucroute,* bacon
Sucre sugar

Suppion small cuttlefish

Suprême sweet white sauce

Suprême boneless breast of poultry; also describes a fish fillet

Sureau (fleurs de) elder tree (flowers of); delicious liqueur

Tacaud type of cod

Talleyrand truffles, cheese, *foie gras*

Talmousse triangular cheese pastry

Tanche tench

Tapé(e) dried

Tartare raw minced beef

Tartare (sauce) sauce with mayonnaise, onions, capers, herbs

Tarte open flan

Tarte Tatin upside down tart of caramelised apples and pastry

Telline small clam

Tergoule Normandy rice pudding with cinnamon

Terrine container in which mixed meats/fish are baked; served cold

Tête de veau vinaigrette calf's head *vinaigrette*

Thé tea

Thermidor grilled lobster with browned *béchamel* sauce

Thon tunny fish

Thym thyme

Tiède mild or lukewarm

Tilleul lime tree

Timbale mould in which contents are steamed

Tomate tomatoe

Topinambour Jerusalem artichoke

Torte sweet-filled flan

Tortue turtle

Tortue sauce with various herbs, tomatoes, Madeira

Toulousaine (à la) Toulouse style: truffles, *foie gras*, sweetbreads, kidneys

Tournedos fillet steak (small end)

Tournedos chasseur with shallots, mushrooms, tomatoes

Tournedos Dauphinoise with creamed mushrooms, *croûtons*

Tournedos Rossini with goose liver, truffles, port, *croûtons*

Touron a cake, pastry or loaf made from almond paste and filled with candied fruits and nuts; also see *ouillat*, a Pyrénées soup

Tourte (Tourtière) covered savoury tart

Tourteau large crab

Tourteau fromager goat's cheese *gâteau*

Tranche slice

Tranche de boeuf steak

Traver de porc spare rib of pork

Tripes à la mode de Caen beef tripe stew

Tripettes small sheep tripe

Tripoux stuffed mutton tripe

Trompettes de la mort fungi

Tronçon a cut of fish or meat

Trou water ice

Truffade a huge sautéed pancake, or *galette*, with bacon, garlic and Cantal cheese

Truffe truffle; black, exotic, tuber

Truffée with truffles

Truite trout

Truite (au bleu) trout poached in water and vinegar; turns blue

Truite saumonée salmon trout

Tuiles tiles (thin almond slices)

Turbot (turbotin) turbot

Vacherin ice cream, meringue, cream

Valenciennes (à la) rice, onions, red peppers, tomatoes, white wine

Vallée d'Auge veal or chicken; sautéed, flamed in Calvados and served with cream and apples

Vapeur (à la) steamed

Varech seaweed

Veau veal

Veau à la Viennoise (escalope de) slice of veal coated with egg and breadcrumbs, fried

Veau Milanaise (escalope de) with macaroni, tomatoes, ham, mushrooms

Veau pané (escalope de) thin slice in flour, eggs and breadcrumbs

Velouté white sauce with *bouillon* and white *roux*

Velouté de volaille thick chicken soup

Venaison venison

Ventre belly or breast

Verdurette *vinaigrette* dressing with herbs

Vernis clam

Véronique grapes, wine, cream

Verte green mayonnaise with chervil, spinach, tarragon

Vert-pré thinly-sliced chips, *maître d'hôtel* butter, watercress

Verveine verbena

Vessie (en) cooked in a pig's bladder; usually chicken

Viande meat

Vichy glazed carrots

Vichyssoise creamy potato and leek soup, served cold

Viennoise coated with egg and breadcrumbs, fried (usually veal)

Vierge (sauce) olive oil sauce

Vierge literally virgin (best olive oil, the first pressing)

Vigneron vine-grower (wine-maker)

Vinaigre (de) wine vinegar or vinegar of named fruit

Vinaigre de Jerez sherry vinegar

Vinaigrette (à la) French dressing with wine vinegar, oil, etc.

Viroflay spinach as a garnish

Volaille poultry

Vol au vent puff pastry case

Xérès (vinaigre de) sherry (vinegar)

Yaourt yogurt

Zeste (d'orange) rubbing from (orange skin)

Regional Cuisine

In the notes which follow I examine first the French regions with Atlantic seaboards, starting in the north and finishing at the Spanish frontier; then the regions bordering Belgium, Germany, Switzerland, Italy and the Mediterranean; and, finally, the regions of inland France.

North Fish takes pride of place, freshly landed at the ports of Boulogne, Calais, and smaller ones like Le Crotoy. *Sole, turbot, maqueraux, barbue, lotte de mer, flétan, harengs, merlan, moules, crévettes*; all appear on menus. So do soups and stews, many with root vegetables: *waterzooï* – fish or chicken stew; *hochepot* – meat and vegetable *pot-au-feu*; *carbonnade* – beef stew with beer. Leeks are super; enjoy *flamiche aux poireaux* (*quiche*-like pastry). Seek out the *hortillonages* (water-gardens) of Amiens and their fine vegetables. Try *gaufres* (yeast waffles) and *ficelles* (variously stuffed pancakes). Beer, too, is good.

Normandy Land of cream, apples and the pig. Vallée d'Auge gives its name to many dishes, including chicken, veal and fish; the term means cream, apples or cider, or apple brandy (Calvados) have been added. Cider is first class. Pork products are everywhere: *andouilles* – smoked tripe sausages, eaten cold; *andouillettes* – small grilled tripe sausages. Fish are superb: *sole à la Normande, à la Dieppoise, à la Fécampoise, à la Havraise* (the last three are ports); *plats de fruits de mer*; shrimps; oysters; *bulots* (whelks); mussels. Enjoy tripe; *ficelles* – pancakes; cow's milk cheeses; rich cream; butters, both salty and sweet; salad produce and potatoes from Caux; exquisite apple tarts; *canard à la Rouennaise*; and fish stews.

Brittany Fish and shellfish are commonplace: lobsters, *huîtres, langoustes*, crabs, of varying sorts, *moules*, prawns, shrimps, *coquilles St-Jacques*; to name just a few. Enjoy *cotriade* – a Breton fish stew with potatoes and onions; *galettes* – buckwheat flour pancakes with savoury fillings; *crêpes de froment* – wheat flour pancakes with sweet fillings; *far Breton* – a batter mixture with raisins; *gâteau Breton* – a mouthwatering concoction; *agneau de pré-salé* – from the salt marshes near Mont-St-Michel (fine omelettes are also made there); and *poulet blanc Breton*. Brittany is one of France's market-gardens: enjoy artichokes, cauliflowers, cabbages, onions and strawberries.

Charentes/Vendée western half of Poitou-Charentes. La Rochelle is a famed fishing port; consequently fish predominates. Oysters are glorious (see *Huîtres* in Glossary). The port of La Cotinière, on the island of Oléron, is renowned for its shrimps. Challans, in the Vendée, is reputed for its quality ducks. Charentes is second to none for butter, goat's milk cheeses, Charentais melons, Cognac, cabbages, mussels, *mojette* (white beans) and salt-marsh lamb from the Marais Poitevin.

Southwest One of the great larders of France; can be divided into several distinct areas. From the countryside that lies in a semicircle to the north-west, west, south and south-east of Bordeaux comes: lamb from Pauillac; oysters (*gravettes*) from Arcachon; eels (*pibales*); beef (*entrecôte Bordelaise* is the bestknown); onions and shallots; *cèpes*; *alose* (shad); and *lamproie* – lamprey (eel-like fish). The Garonne Valley is one vast orchard: try prunes from Agen; peaches; pears and dessert grapes.

South of the Garonne is **Gascony**: famed for *foie gras* (duck and goose); *confit* (preserved meat from both birds); jams and fruits; and Armagnac. Try a *floc* (Armagnac and grape juice).

To the south and west of Gascony are **Béarn** and the **Landes**. From the latter came *palombes* and *ortolans*, ducks and chickens. Among traditional Béarn specialities are *garbue* – the most famous of vegetable soups; *poule au pot* – the chicken dish given its name by Henri IV; *tourin, ouliat* and *cousinette (cousinat)*. See the Southwest for further details.

West of Béarn is **Basque** country: tuna, anchovies, sardines and salmon (from Béarn also) are great; Bayonne ham, *piments* (peppers), *piperade, ttoro* (fish stew) and *gâteau Basque*.

Champagne-Ardenne & Ile de France Many of the specialities listed earlier in the North appear in the former, renowned for its potatoes and turkeys. In the Ardenne you'll enjoy smoked hams, sold in nets; *sanglier*; *marcassin*; and red and white cabbages. West of Verdun, at Ste-Menehould, try *pieds de cochon* (pig's trotters); *petits gris* (snails); and the many differing sweets and sugared almonds (Verdun is famous for them). Troyes is renowned for pork and *andouillettes*.

Regional specialities and produce are all but non-existent in the Ile de France. Look out for cherries from Poissy, beans from Arpajon and tomatoes from Montlhéry. Enjoy *pâtés* and *terrines* and tempting *pâtisseries* and *galettes*.

Alsace There is a strong German influence in much of the cooking; pork, game, goose and beer are common. *Foie gras* (fattened goose liver) is superb. So, too, is a range of tarts; *flammekuchen* – flamed open tart; and some with fruit (*linzertorte* – raspberry or bilberry open tart); jams, fruit liqueurs and *eaux-de-vie* (see Alsace wines). Stomach-filling *choucroute* and local sausages are on most menus; as are *kougelhopf*, *beckenoffe* and *lewerknepfle* (see Alsace specialities). Enjoy *tourte Alsacienne* – pork pie. Use *winstubs* (wine bars).

Lorraine on the north-west borders is known for its *madeleines* (tiny sponge cakes), *macarons*, mouthwatering *quiche Lorraine*, fruit tarts, omelettes and *potée*.

Jura This is dairy country; witness the numerous excellent cheeses encountered in the region. Try *Jésus de Morteau* – a fat pork sausage smoked over pine and juniper; *brési* – wafer-thin slices of dried beef; and many local hams. *Morilles* and other fungi are common; so are freshly-caught trout and other freshwater fish.

Savoie & Hautes-Alpes *Plat gratiné* applies to a wide variety of dishes; in the Alps this means cooked in breadcrumbs; *gratins* of all sorts show how well milk, cream and cheese can be combined together. Relish *fondue* and *gougère*. Freshwater lake fish are magnificent (see the regional specialities for Savoie). Walnuts, chestnuts, all sorts of fruits and marvellous wild mushrooms are other delights.

Côte d'Azur & Provence A head-spinning kaleidoscope of colours and textures fills the eyes: aubergines, peppers, beans, tomatoes, cauliflowers, asparagus, olives, garlic, artichokes, courgettes; the list is endless. Fruit, too, is just as appealing: melons from Cavaillon; strawberries from Monteux; cherries from Remoulins; glacé fruit from Apt; truffles from

Valréas and Aups. Fish from the Med are an extra bonus: *bar* and *loup de mer, daurade, St-Pierre*, monkfish and mullet; these are the best. Lamb from the foothills of the Alps near Sisteron; herbs of every type from the *département* of Var; nuts from Valensole; honey and olive oil; *ratatouille*; sardines; *saucisson d'Arles*; *bouillabaisse* and *bourride*; *soupe de poissons* and *soupe au pistou*; what memories are stirred as I write.

Languedoc-Roussillon & Cévennes The same products and dishes listed under Provence are available here. Also oysters and mussels (*les coquillages*) from the lagoons (particularly the Bassin de Thau; visit Mèze and Bouzigues). Excellent shellfish; cherries from Céret; anchovies; apricots and pumpkins. Enjoy *brandade de morue* (salt cod), *confit d'oie* (and *canard*), *cassoulet* and *saucisses de Toulouse*.

Loire The river and its many tributaries provide *alose, sandre, anguille*, carp, perch, pike, salmon and *friture*. A tasty *beurre blanc* is the usual sauce with fish. *Charcuterie* is marvellous: *rillettes, rillons, andouillettes, saucissons, jarretons* and other delights. Cultivated mushrooms come from the limestone caves near Saumur.

The **Sologne** is famous for asparagus, frogs, game, fungi, lake and river fish and wildfowl. You'll be offered, too, many a *pâté*, fruit tarts (it's the home of *tarte Tatin*) and pies.

Burgundy Refer to the often seen regional specialities. Many dishes are wine based: *coq au Chambertin* and *poulet au Meursault* are examples. Enjoy hams, freshwater fish, vegetables, *escargots*, mustard and gingerbread from Dijon and blackcurrants (used for *cassis*, the term for both the fruit and the liqueur made from them).

Lyonnais The culinary heart and stomach of France. There is a variety of top-class produce on hand: Bresse poultry (*chapons* – capons – are unforgettable treats); *grenouilles* and game from Les Dombes; Charolais cattle from the hills west of Beaujolais; fish from the rivers and pools (pike *quenelles* appear everywhere); *charcuterie* from Lyon, particularly sausages called *sabodet, rosette, saucisson en brioche* and *cervelas*; and chocolates and *pâtisseries* from Lyon.

Auvergne & Ardèche Both areas which keep alive old specialities. Refer to the regional lists but here are some of the best: *potée Auvergnate* – a stew of cabbage, vegetables, pork and sausage; *friand Sanflorin* – pork meat and herbs in pastry; *aligot* – a purée of potatoes, cheese, garlic and butter; *pounti* – a small egg-based savoury souffle with bacon or prunes; and delectable *charcuterie*, hams, *saucisson, saucisses sèches* (dried sausages), *pâtés* and so on. The quality and variety of cheeses are second to none. Cabbages, potatoes, bacon and cheese feature on menus. The area around Le Puy is famed for its lentils and Verveine du Velay –

yellow and green liqueurs made from over 30 mountain plants. The Ardèche is renowned for its sweet chestnuts (relish *marrons glacés*).

Berry-Bourbonnais & Poitou – eastern half of Poitou-Charentes. The flat terrain of Berry-Bourbonnais is dull country, the granary of France. The area is renowned for beef, deer, wild boar, rabbits, hares, pheasants and partridge.

Much of Poitou lies in the deserted, wooded hills of Limousin (as do the western edges of Auvergne). Apart from the specialities listed look out for *mique* – a stew of dumplings; *farcidure* – a dumpling, either poached or sauteed; and *clafoutis* – pancake batter, poured over fruit (usually black cherries) and baked. Limousin is reputed for its *cèpes* – fine, delicate, flap mushrooms; and also for its reddish-coloured cattle.

Dordogne A land of truffles, geese, ducks, walnuts, *cèpes*, chestnuts, sunflowers and fruit. *Foie gras* (goose and duck) is obligatory on menus; as are *confits* of both birds (preserved in their own fat) and *magrets* (boned duck breasts which have become so popular in the last decade throughout France). *Pâtés* incorporating either poultry or game, and truffles, are common place. If you see *miques* (yeast dumplings) or *merveilles* (hot, sugar-covered pastry fritters) on menus, order them. In the south, in the Lot Valley and towards the Garonne, it's a land of orchards: plums, prunes, figs, peaches, pears and cherries.

Regional Specialities

ALSACE

Beckenoffe (Baeckeoffe) (Baeckaoffa) "baker's oven"; a stew, or hotpot, of potatoes, lamb, beef, pork and onions, cooked in a local wine
Choucroute garnie sauerkraut with peppercorns, boiled ham, pork, Strasbourg sausages and boiled potatoes. Try it with a beer (*bière*)
Chou farci stuffed cabbage
Flammekueche (Tarte flambée) bacon, onion and cream tart
Foie gras goose liver
Kougelhopf a round brioche with raisins and almonds
Krapfen fritters stuffed with jam
Lewerknepfle (Leber Knödel) liver dumpling (pork liver dumpling)
Matelote Alsacienne in Alsace made with stewed eels (in the past from the River Ill) – sometimes with freshwater fish
Pflutters Alsacienne potato puffs
Potage Lorraine potato, leek and onion soup
Schifela shoulder of pork with turnips
Tarte (aux mirabelles) golden plum tart. Also with other fruits
Tarte à l'oignon Alsacienne onion and cream tart

BERRY-BOURBONNAIS

Bignons small fritters
Bouquettes aux pommes de terre grated potato, mixed with flour, egg white and fried in small, thick pieces
Brayaude (gigot) lamb cooked in white wine, onions and herbs
Chargouère (Chergouère) pastry turnover of plums or prunes
Cousinat (Cousina) chestnut soup (*salée* – salted) with cream, butter and prunes; served with bread
Gargouillau a *clafoutis* of pears
Gouèron a cake of goat cheese and eggs
Gouerre (Gouère) a cake of potato purée, flour, eggs and *fromage blanc* (fresh cream cheese), cooked in an oven as a *tourtière*
Lièvre à la Duchambais hare cooked slowly in a sauce of cream, chopped-up shallots, vinegar and pepper
Milliard (Millat) (Milla) a *clafoutis* of cherries (see Poitou-Charentes); pancake batter, poured over fruit (usually black cherries)
Pâté de pommes de terre a tart of sliced potatoes, butter, bacon and chopped-up onions, baked in an oven. Cream added to hot centre
Poirat pear tart
Pompe aux grattons a cake, in the shape of a crown, made up of a mixture of small pieces of pork, flour, eggs and butter
Sanciau thick sweet or savoury pancake; made from buckwheat flour
Truffiat grated potato, mixed with flour, eggs and butter and baked

BRITTANY

Agneau de pré-salé leg of lamb, from animals pastured in the salt marshes and meadows of Brittany
Bardatte cabbage stuffed with hare, cooked in white wine and served with chestnuts and roast quail
Beurre blanc sauce for fish dishes; made from the reduction of shallots, wine vinegar and the finest butter (sometimes with dry white wine)
Cotriade fish soup with potatoes, onions, garlic and butter
Crêpes Bretonnes the thinnest of pancakes with a variety of sweet fillings; often called **Crêpes de froment** (wheat flour)
Far Breton batter mixture; vanilla-flavoured sugar, rum, dried prunes
Galette takes various forms: can be a biscuit, a cake or a pancake; the latter is usually stuffed with fillings like mushrooms, ham, cheese or seafood and is called a **Galette de blé noir** (buckwheat flour)
Gâteau Breton rich cake with butter, flour, egg yolks and sugar
Gigot de pré-salé same as *agneau de pré-salé*
Kouign-amann crisp, flaky pastries of butter, sugar and yeast
Palourdes farcies clams in the shell, with a *gratiné* filling
Poulet blanc Breton free-range, fine quality white Breton chicken

BURGUNDY

Boeuf Bourguignon braised beef simmered in red wine-based sauce
Charolais (Pièce de) steak from the excellent Charolais cattle
Garbure heavy soup; mixture of pork, cabbage, beans and sausages
Gougère cheese pastry, based on Gruyère cheese
Jambon persillé parsley-flavoured ham, served cold in its jelly
Jambon en saupiquet, **Jambon à la crème**, **Jambon à la Morvandelle** ham with a piquant cream sauce, wine and wine vinegar
Matelote freshwater fish soup, usually based on a red wine sauce
Meurette red wine-based sauce with small onions. Accompanies fish or poached egg dishes
Pain d'épice spiced honeycake from Dijon
Pochouse (Pouchouse) stew of freshwater fish and garlic, usually white wine based. Rarely seen on restaurant menus
Potée see *Garbure*

CHAMPAGNE-ARDENNE

Flamiche aux Maroilles see *Tarte aux Maroilles*
Flamiche aux poireaux puff-pastry tart with cream and leeks
Goyère see *Tarte aux Maroilles*
Rabotte (Rabote) whole apple wrapped in pastry and baked
Tarte aux Maroilles a hot creamy tart based on the local cheese

COTE D'AZUR

Aïgo Bouido garlic and sage soup – with bread (or eggs and cheese)
Aïgo saou fish soup (no *rascasse* – scorpion fish) with *rouille*
Aïoli (ailloli) a mayonnaise sauce with garlic and olive oil
Anchoïade anchovy crust
Berlingueto chopped spinach and hard-boiled eggs
Bouillabaisse a dish of Mediterranean fish (including *rascasse*, *St-Pierre*, *baudroie*, *congre*, *chapon de mer*, *langoustes*, *langoustines*, *tourteaux*, *favouilles*, *merlan* and, believe it or not, many others) and a soup, served separately with *rouille*, *safran* and *aïoli*
Bourride a creamy fish soup (usually made with big white fish), thickened with *aïoli* and flavoured with crawfish
Brandade (de morue) à l'huile d'olive a mousse of salt cod with cream, olive oil and garlic
Capoum a large pink *rascasse* (scorpion fish)
Pain Bagna bread roll with olive oil, anchovies, olives, onions, etc.
Pieds et paquets small parcels of mutton tripe, cooked with sheep trotters and white wine
Pissaladière Provençal bread dough with onions, anchovies, olives, etc.
Pistou (Soupe au) vegetable soup bound with *pommade*

Pollo pépitora Provençal chicken *fricassée* thickened with lemon-flavoured mayonnaise

Pommade a thick paste of garlic, basil, cheese and olive oil

Ratatouille aubergines, courgettes, onion, garlic, red peppers and tomatoes in olive oil

Rouille orange-coloured sauce with hot peppers, garlic and saffron

Salade Niçoise tomatoes, beans, potatoes, black olives, anchovy, lettuce and olive oil. Sometimes tuna fish

Tapénade a purée of stoned black olives, anchovy fillets, capers, tuna fish and olive oil

Tarte (Tourte) aux blettes open-crust pastry with filling of Swiss chard (not unlike Chinese cabbage) and pine nuts

Tian Provençal earthenware dish

DORDOGNE

Bourrioles d'Aurillac sweet pancakes, made from buckwheat flour

Cèpes fine, delicate mushrooms. Sometimes dried

Chou farci stuffed cabbage. Sometimes *aux marrons* – with chestnuts

Confit de canard (d'oie) preserved duck (goose)

Cou d'oie neck of goose

Foie de canard (gras) duck liver

Friands de Bergerac small potato cakes

Merveilles hot, sugar-covered pastry fritters

Mique stew or soup with dumplings

Pommes à la Sarladaise potatoes, truffles, ham or *foie gras*

Rilletes d'oie soft, potted goose

Sobronade soup with pork, ham, beans and vegetables

Tourin Bordelais (Ouillat) onion soup

Tourin Périgourdine vegetable soup

Truffes truffles; black and exotic tubers or fungi, as large as walnuts, which grow on the roots of certain oak and hazelnut trees

Truffes sous les cendres truffles, wrapped in paper (or bacon) and cooked in ashes

Walnut oil As you explore the region you'll soon realise that walnut trees thrive. Be sure to buy some *huile de noix*

HAUTES-ALPES

See those listed in the Savoie region

ILE DE FRANCE

Refer to these five regions: Normandy to the west; the North; Champagne-Ardenne to the east; and Burgundy and the Loire on the southern borders of the Ile de France.

JURA

Brési wafer-thin slices of dried beef
Gougère hot cheese pastry – based on Comté cheese
Jésus de Morteau fat pork sausage smoked over pine and juniper
Poulet au vin jaune chicken, cream and *morilles*, cooked in *vin jaune* (a rare wine, deep yellow and very dry)

LANGUEDOC-ROUSSILLON

Aïgo Bouido garlic soup. A marvellous, aromatic dish; the garlic is boiled, so its impact is lessened. Served with bread
Boles de picoulat small balls of chopped-up beef and pork, garlic and eggs – served with tomatoes and parsley
Bouillinade a type of *bouillabaisse*; with potatoes, oil, garlic and onions
Boutifare a sausage-shaped pudding of bacon and herbs
Cargolade snails, stewed in wine
Millas cornmeal porridge
Ouillade heavy soup of bacon, *boutifare*, leeks, carrots and potatoes
Touron a pastry of almonds, pistachio nuts and fruit

LOIRE

Alose à l'oseille grilled shad with a sorrel sauce
Bardette stuffed cabbage
Beuchelle à la Tourangelle kidneys, sweetbreads, morels, truffles, cream
Bourdaines apples stuffed with jam and baked
Rillauds chauds strips of hot bacon
Rillettes potted pork
Sandre freshwater fish, like perch
Tarte à la citrouille pumpkin tart
Tarte Tatin *upside-down* tart of caramelised apples and pastry
Truffiat potato cake

LYONNAIS

Bresse (Poulet, Poularde, Volaille de) the best French poultry. Fed on corn and, when killed, bathed in milk. Flesh is white and delicate
Gras-double ox tripe, served with onions
Poulet demi-deuil *half-mourning*; called this because of the thin slices of truffle placed under the chicken breast; cooked in a *court-bouillon*
Poulet au vinaigre chicken, shallots, tomatoes, white wine, wine vinegar and a cream sauce
Rosette a large pork sausage;
Sabodet see *Glossary of Menu Terms*
Tablier de Sapeur *gras-double* coated with flour, egg-yolk, breadcrumbs

MASSIF CENTRAL (Auvergne, Ardèche and Cévennes)

Aligot purée of potatoes with Tomme de Cantal cheese, cream, garlic and butter

Bougnette a stuffing of pork, bread and eggs – wrapped in *crépine* (caul)

Bourriols d'Aurillac sweet pancakes, made from buckwheat flour

Brayaude (gigot) lamb cooked in white wine, onions and herbs

Cadet Mathieu pastry turnover filled with slices of apple

Clafoutis baked pancake batter, poured over fruit, usually cherries

Confidou Rouergat ragout of beef, red wine, tomatoes, garlic and onions

Cousinat (Cousina) chestnut soup (*salée* – salted) with cream, butter and prunes and served with bread

Criques grated potato, mixed with eggs and fried – in the form of pancakes. Related to the *truffiat* of Berry

Farçon large *galette* of sausage, sorrel, onions, eggs and white wine

Farinette buckwheat flour pancakes – meat and vegetable filling

Friand Sanflorin pork meat and herbs in pastry

Jambon d'Auvergne a tasty mountain ham

Manouls see *Trénels*

Milliard (Millat) (Milla) a *clafoutis* of cherries (see Poitou-Charentes)

Mourtayol a stew with beef, chicken, ham, vegetables and bread

Omelette Brayaude eggs, pork, cheese and potatoes

Perdrix à l'Auvergnate partridge stewed in white wine

Potée Auvergnate stew of vegetables, cabbage, pork and sausage

Pountari a mince of pork fat in cabbage leaves

Pounti small, egg-based savoury soufflé with bacon or prunes

Rouergat(e) Rouergue; the name of the area to the west of Millau

Salmis de colvert Cévenole wild duck, sautéed in red wine, onions, ham and mushrooms

Soupe aux choux soup with cabbage, ham, pork, bacon and turnips

Trénels mutton tripe, white wine and tomatoes

Tripoux stuffed mutton tripe

Truffade a huge *galette* of sautéed potatoes

NORMANDY

Andouillette de Vire small chitterling (tripe) sausage

Barbue au cidre brill cooked in cider and Calvados

Cauchoise (à la) with cream, Calvados and apple

Douillons de pommes à la Normande baked apples in pastry

Escalope (Vallée d'Auge) veal sautéed, flamed in Calvados and served with cream and apples

Ficelle Normande pancake with ham, mushrooms and cheese

Marmite Dieppoise a fish soup with some, or all of the following: sole, turbot, *rouget*, *moules*, *crevettes*, onions, white wine, butter and cream

Poulet (Vallée d'Auge) chicken cooked in the same way as *Escalope*

Vallee d'Auge
Tripes à la mode de Caen stewed beef tripe with onions, carrots, leeks, garlic, cider and Calvados
Trou Normand Calvados – a "dram", drunk in one gulp, between courses; claimed to restore the appetite

NORTH

Carbonnade de Boeuf à la Flamande braised beef with beer, onions and bacon; if only more chefs would prepare this great dish
Caudière (Chaudière, Caudrée) versions of fish and potato soup
Ficelles Picardes ham pancakes with mushroom sauce
Flamiche aux Maroilles see *Tarte aux Maroilles*
Flamiche aux poireaux puff-pastry tart with cream and leeks
Gaufres yeast waffles
Goyère see *Tarte aux Maroilles*
Hochepot a *pot-au-feu* of the North (see *Pepperpot*)
Pepperpot stew of mutton, pork, beer and vegetables
Sanguette black pudding, made with rabbit's blood
Soupe courquignoise soup with white wine, fish, *moules*, leeks and Gruyère cheese
Tarte aux Maroilles a hot creamy tart based on Maroilles cheese
Waterzooï a cross between soup and stew, usually of fish or chicken (Don't bypass Serge Pérard's exhilarating fish restaurant at 67 rue de Metz in Le Touquet; his *soupe de poissons* is fabulous.

POITOU-CHARENTES

Bouilliture (Bouilleture) a freshwater eel stew with shallots and prunes in Sauvignon white wine
Boulaigou thick sweet or savoury pancake
Bréjaude cabbage, leek and bacon soup
Cagouilles (also called **Lumas**) snails from the Charentes
Casserons en matelote squid in red wine sauce with garlic and shallots
Cèpes fine, delicate, flap mushrooms; please do try them
Chaudrée a ragout of fish cooked in white wine, shallots and butter
Chevrettes local name for *crevettes* (shrimps)
Clafoutis pancake batter, poured over fruit (usually black cherries), and then baked; another treat you must not miss
Embeurrée de chou white-heart cabbage, cooked in salted water, crushed and served with butter
Farcidure a dumpling – either poached or sautéed
Farci Poitevin a *pâté* of cabbage, spinach and sorrel, encased by cabbage leaves and cooked in a *bouillon*
Migourée a sort of *chaudrée*
Mique a stew of dumplings

Mogette (Mojette) small pulse beans in butter and cream

Mouclade mussels cooked in wine, egg yolks and cream; can be served with some Pineau des Charentes

Oysters for an explanation of *les claires, belons, gravettes, marennes* and other terms see the *Glossary of Menu Terms* (under *Huîtres*)

Soupe aux fèves des Marais soup of crushed broad beans with bread, sorrel, chervil and butter

Soupe de moules à la Rochelaise soup of various fish, mussels, saffron, garlic, tomatoes, onions and red wine

Sourdons cockles from the Charentes

Tartisseaux fritters

Tourtou thick buckwheat flour pancake

PROVENCE

Please see the specialities listed in the Côte d'Azur

SAVOIE

Farcement (Farçon Savoyard) potatoes baked with cream, eggs, bacon, dried pears and prunes; a hearty stomach filler

Féra a freshwater lake fish

Fondue hot melted cheese and white wine

Gratin Dauphinois a classic potato dish with cream, cheese and garlic

Gratin Savoyard another classic potato dish with cheese and butter

Lavaret a freshwater lake fish, like salmon

Longeole a country sausage

Lotte a burbot, not unlike an eel

Omble chevalier a char, it looks like a large salmon trout

Tartiflette potato, bacon, onions and Reblochon cheese

SOUTHWEST

Besugo *daurade* – sea-bream

Chorizos spicy sausages

Confit de canard (d'oie) preserved duck meat (goose)

Cousinette (Cousinat) vegetable soup

Echassier a wading bird of the Landes

Garbure (Garbue) vegetable soup with cabbage and ham bone

Gâteau Basque a shallow, custard pastry – often with fruit fillings

Grattons (Graisserons) a *mélange* of small pieces of rendered down duck, goose and pork fat; served as an appetiser – very filling

Hachua beef stew

Jambon de Bayonne raw ham, cured in salt. Served as paper-thin slices

Lamproie eel-like fish; with leeks, onions and red Bordeaux wine sauce

Lou-kenkas small, spicy sausages

Loubine (Louvine) grey mullet (like a sea-bass)
Ortolan a small bird (wheatear) from the Landes
Ouillat (Ouliat) Pyrénées soup; onions, tomatoes, goose fat, garlic
Palombes (Salmis de) wild doves and wood pigeons from the Landes and Béarn, sautéed in red wine, ham and mushrooms
Pastiza see *Gâteau Basque*
Ramereaux ring doves
Salda a thick cabbage and bean soup
Tourin (Tourain) see *Ouillat*. (*Touron*: see Languedoc-Roussillon)
Tourtière Landaise a sweet of Agen prunes, apples and Armagnac
Ttoro (Ttorro) a Basque fish stew

Regional Cheeses (**Vache** cow; **Chèvre** goat; **Brebis** ewe)

ALSACE

Cow's milk
Carré-de-l'Est soft, edible white rind, made in a small square; milder than Camembert. Bland taste. Available all year
Gérardmer same cheese as Gérômé, alternative name
Gérômé soft, gold-coloured cheese, a little more solid than Munster, often covered with fennel or caraway. Made as a thick disk. Spicy taste and at its best in summer and autumn. Good with full-bodied red wines
Munster soft, gold-coloured, stronger taste than Gérômé, made as a small disk. Munster *laitier* (made by commercial dairies) available all year; *fermier* (made by farms) at its best in summer and autumn. Try them with Traminer wines. Munster *au cumin* (with caraway seeds)

BERRY-BOURBONNAIS

Cow's milk
Chambérat fruity-tasting; made as a flat, pressed disk
Goat's milk
Chevrotin du Bourbonnais a truncated cone and creamy tasting. Best in summer and autumn. Also know as **Conne**
Crézancy-Sancerre small ball, similar taste to Chavignol (see Loire cheeses). **Santranges** is a related, similar cheese
Graçay nutty, soft cheese; made as a dark, blue-coloured cone

BRITTANY

Cow's milk
Campénéac a pressed, uncooked cheese. Strong smell and made in thick disks. Good all the year
Meilleraye de Bretagne at its best in summer. Light smell, ochre-yellow rind, made in large squares
Nantais dit Curé (Fromage du Curé) (Nantais) strong smell, supple, small square of cheese. Good all the year

Port-Salut is a semi-hard, mild cheese, good all the year. Port-du-Salut was the monastery where the cheese was originally made – at **Entrammes** (Mayenne); the name was sold to a dairy company, though a variety of the type is still produced there. St-Paulin is a related cheese

St-Gildas-des-Bois a triple-cream cheese with a mushroom smell; cylinder shape and available throughout the year

St-Paulin semi-hard, yellow, mild, smooth-textured with a washed, bright orange rind. Made commercially throughout northern France

BURGUNDY

Cow's milk

L'Ami du Chambertin salty, washed in Marc de Bourgogne

Aisy-Cendré cured in Marc and stored in wood ashes. Firm, strong-smelling, fruity taste; good with full-bodied red wines

Boulette de La Pierre-Qui-Vire amusingly named; made at the abbey of the same name near St-Léger-Vauban. Small, firm herb-flavoured ball

Cîteaux thick disk, very rare and made by the monks at Cîteaux Monastery - once a rival of Cluny

Ducs made near Tonnere; a soft cylinder ideal with St-Bris whites

Epoisses soft, orange-dusted, made as a flat cylinder. At its best in the summer, autumn and winter; goes well with full-bodied red wines

Langres small, cone-shaped and strong. Related to Epoisses

Rouy related to Epoisses. Strong smell, soft and made as a square

St-Florentin related to Epoisses. Smooth, red-brown appearance with spicy taste. Season summer to winter

Soumaintrain strong tasting, russet crust, brine washed

Goat's milk

Dornecy just west of Vézelay. Small, firm, upright cylinder

Lormes south of Avallon, related to both Dornecy and Vézelay

Montrachet soft, mild and creamy; made as a tall cylinder

Pourly slight nutty flavour, soft and made as a small cylinder

Vézelay a farm-produced cheese, at its best in summer and autumn. Soft, and in the form of a cone, with a bluish rind

CHAMPAGNE-ARDENNE

Cow's milk

Barberey from the area between Chaource and Les Riceys. A soft, musty-smelling, small cylinder. Best in summer and autumn

Boulette d'Avesnes soft, pear-shaped and pungent bouquet. Sharp and strong

Caprice des Dieux soft and mild, packed in oval-shaped boxes

Cendré d'Argonne from north of Châlons-s-Marne; soft, ash coated

Cendré de Champagne (Cendré des Riceys) mainly from Châlons-s-Marne and Vitry-le-François area. Flat disk and coated with ashes

Chaource at its best in summer and autumn; a creamy cheese, made in

cylinders and with a mushroom smell. From the borders of Burgundy
Chaumont related to Epoisses and Langres cheeses (see Burgundy); cone-shaped, soft cheese with strong smell
Dauphin from the Avesnes area. Soft, seasoned, crescent-shaped, heart or loaf. Is related to Boulette d'Avesnes
Evry-le-Châtel truncated cone; firm with a mushroom smell
Igny made by monks at the Igny monastery; a pressed flat disk
Maroilles soft, slightly salty and gold. Appears in many regional dishes
Les Riceys from the area south of Troyes, home also of the good Rosé des Riceys wine. Best seasons, summer and autumn. Flat disk, no strong smell and fruity taste. Try the local wine with the cheese
Saint Rémy a spicy-tasting, strong-smelling, reddish-coloured square

COTE D'AZUR

Goat's milk
Banon a soft cheese made in a small disk, usually wrapped in chestnut leaves; sometimes *au poivre* (covered with black pepper)
Poivre-d'Ane flavoured with rosemary or the herb savory (*sarriette*). Aromatic taste and perfume
Ewe's milk
Brousse de la Vésubie from the Vésubie Valley, north of Nice; a very creamy, mild-flavoured cheese

DORDOGNE

Cow's milk
Bleu du Quercy a blue cheese with parsley-like veins
Echourgnac pressed, uncooked, small disk – made by monks
Goat's milk
Cabécou de Rocamadour gets its name from the patois for little goat. Very small size with nutty taste. At its best in summer and autumn

HAUTES-ALPES

Goat's milk
Annot (Tomme d'Annot) a nutty-flavoured, pressed disk; made from ewe's or goat's milk
Picodon is a goat cheese; soft, mellow taste and doughnut size

ILE DE FRANCE

Cow's milk
Brie soft, white rind, the size of a long-playing record. It will frequently be described with the addition of the name of the area in which it is made: **Brie de Coulommiers**; **Brie de Meaux**; **Brie de Melun**; and **Brie de Montereau** are the best known. Faint mushroom smell
Chevru similar in size and taste to Brie de Meaux

Coulommiers like Brie, but a smaller, 45 rpm disc. At its best in summer, autumn and winter. Both cheeses are ideal with Côte de Beaune reds

Délice de Saint Cyr a soft, triple-cream cheese – nutty-tasting and made in small disks

Explorateur a mild, triple-cream cheese – made in small cylinders

Feuille de Dreux fruity-flavoured, soft disk. Ideal with fruity red wines

Fontainebleau a fresh cream cheese with whipped cream; add a dusting of sugar and it really is great

JURA

Cow's milk

Cancoillotte very fruity flavour, prepared from **Metton** (an unmoulded, recooked cheese) and looks like a cheese spread. It is available all through the year and is eaten warm in sandwiches or on slices of toast

Comté a hard, cooked cheese, made in great disks. Has holes the size of hazelnuts. Best seasons are summer, autumn and winter

Emmental Français – the French version; another hard, cooked cheese, also made in huge disks but with holes the size of walnuts

Gex (Bleu de) a *fromage persillé*, with blue veins, like the pattern of parsley. Made in large disks; at its best in summer and autumn

Morbier strong-flavoured thick disk with ash stripe through middle

Septmoncel (Bleu de) made in thick disks; blue veins, slightly bitter

Vacherin Mont-d'Or soft, mild and creamy; made in cylinders

Goat's milk

Chevret faint goat smell; small flat disk or square-shaped cheese

LANGUEDOC-ROUSSILLON

Cow's milk

Chester Français French Cheshire cheese from Castres and Gaillac

Montségur bland, pressed and uncooked disk

Les Orrys strong-flavoured, big disk; drink with fruity Corbières

Goat's milk

Pélardon a *generic* name; small disks, nutty-tasting and soft. A similar, related cheese is **Rogeret des Cévennes**

LOIRE

Cow's milk

Olivet Bleu small disk, often wrapped in leaves. A fruity taste and a light scent of blue mould. Try it with a red Bourgueil

Olivet Cendré savory taste. Cured in wood ashes. Same size as Olivet Bleu. **Gien** is a related cheese

Frinault a soft, small disk; ideal with light Loire wines

Pithiviers au Foin also known as **Bondaroy au Foin**. A soft cheese, made in thin disks and protected by a covering of bits of hay

Saint-Benoît a fruity, soft, small disk
Saint-Paulin semi-hard, yellow, mild, smooth-textured with a washed, bright orange rind. Made commercially throughout northern France
Vendôme Bleu (Vendôme Cendré) related to the Olivet cheeses
Make sure you try some of the delicious fresh cream cheeses called **Crémets**, eaten with sugar and fresh cream

Goat's milk

Crottin de Chavignol from the area just west of Sancerre, which, with Chavignol, makes the ideal wine to accompany it. Takes the form of a small, flattened ball
Levroux identical to Valençay. Nutty flavour
Ste-Maure summer and autumn season. Soft cylinders, full goat flavour cheese. **Ligueil** is a similar related cheese
Selles-sur-Cher from the Sologne; also known as **Romorantin**. Dark blue skin, pure white interior with mild, nutty flavour. Both **Montoire** and **Troo** are similar related cheeses
Valençay pyramid shaped; usual best seasons for all goat's milk cheeses – summer and autumn. Mild, soft and nutty taste. Often called **Pyramide**

LYONNAIS

Cow's milk

Bresse (Bleu de) available all the year. A mild, soft, blue cheese, made in small cylinders. One of the poorest French blue cheeses
Mont-d'Or from just north of Lyon; small disks, delicate, savory taste

Goat's milk

Bressan a small, truncated cone – also known as **Petit Bressan**
Charolais (Charolles) soft, nutty-flavoured, small cylinder
Chevreton de Mâcon if made of pure goat's milk it is at its best in summer and autumn. A light blue rind and slightly nutty taste
Without fail try **fromage blanc**; a fresh cream cheese, eaten with sugar and fresh cream. If you've never tried some, you've missed a treat

MASSIF CENTRAL (Auvergne, Ardèche and Cévennes)

Cow's milk

Auvergne (Bleu d') when made on farms at its best in summer and autumn. Strong smell, soft, made in the same way as Roquefort. **Bleu de Laqueuille** is a related cheese
Cantal from the Auvergne. The best comes from **Salers**. The cheese is made from milk of Salers cows. Praised by Pliny
Causses (Bleu des) a blue cheese with parsley-like veins, hence the term *persillé*. At its best in summer and autumn
Fourme-d'Ambert has a summer and autumn season. A blue cheese from the Auvergne and in the shape of a tall cylinder
Fourme de Montbrison a bitter blue – as is **Fourme de Pierre-s-Haute**
Gapron (Gaperon) a garlic-flavoured, flattened ball

Laguiole related to Cantal. Big cylinders, penetrating bouquet
Loudes (Bleu de) blue-veined and from the Velay hills, near Le Puy
Murol a semi-hard, mild cheese, like St-Nectaire. Made in small disks
St-Félicien a salty-tasting cheese from the hills west of Tournon
St-Nectaire has a purply-brown skin, made in larger disks than Murol. A semi-hard, mild cheese. **Savaron** and **Vachard** are related
Thièzac (Bleu de) related to Bleu d'Auvergne
Tomme de Cantal a fresh, softish, cream-coloured, unfermented cheese
   Goat's milk
Brique du Forez also known as **Chevreton d'Ambert**. A small loaf with a nutty flavour. **Galette de la Chaise-Dieu** – a flat cake – is similar
Rigotte de Condrieu soft, small cylinders with no special flavour; available all the year. **Rigotte de Pelussin** is a related cheese
   Ewe's milk
Roquefort the best blue cheese of all. Sharp and salty. Roquefort, the "King of cheeses", is ripened in the village's unique caves, said to be the best natural "refrigerators" in the world. The caves are a unique geological site where a mountain top collapsed creating numerous rock faults, fissures and caverns (*fleurines*). The fresh air that blows through them provides the ideal atmosphere for the "penicillium Roqueforti", a microscopic mushroom, to mature within the heart of the creamy rounds. Salt is added to the surface of the cheese to slow down the growth of mould on the outside, while the inside matures

NORMANDY

   Cow's milk
Bondon (also called **Neufchâtel**) from Pays de Bray (north-east of Rouen). Small cylinder, soft and smooth. **Bondard** is related
La Bouille red-speckled, white rind; strong smell, fruity-tasting small disk
Bricquebec made by monks at the abbey of the same name. A mild-tasting, flat pressed disk. Available all the year
Brillat-Savarin mild, creamy disk – a triple-cream cheese. **Magnum** is the same cheese but much older
Camembert soft, milky flavour with a white rind, made as a small, flat disk. Available all the year
Carré de Bray small, square-shaped, mushroom-smelling cheese
Coeur de Bray fruity-tasting, heart-shaped cheese. Best in summer
Demi-sel mild, fresh and salted – made as a small square
Excelsior best in summer and autumn. Small cylinder, mild and soft
Gournay a one inch thick disk; slightly salty, soft and smooth
Livarot best in autumn and winter. Semi-hard, strong and gold. Spicy flavour; try it with a Riesling. **Mignot** is similar
Monsieur soft, fruity cylinder – strong smell
Pavé d'Auge (Pavé de Moyaux) spicy-flavoured, soft cheese, made in a yellow square. Try it with full-bodied reds

Petit-Suisse available all the year; a small, round, fresh cream cheese
Pont-l'Evêque rectangular or square shape, strong, soft and gold; at its best in summer, autumn and winter. First made in 13th-century

NORTH

Cow's milk
Boulette de Cambrai a small, ball-shaped, soft, fresh cheese – flavoured with herbs. Available all the year
Edam Français a red ball without holes or with tiny ones
Gouda Français mild, yellow-coloured, small wheel
Gris de Lille a really salty square of cheese with a strong smell
Maroilles soft, slightly salty and gold. Appears in many regional dishes
Mimolette Française orange-coloured, ball-shaped cheese
Rollot spicy-tasting, soft, small yellow disk; sometimes heart-shaped

POITOU-CHARENTES

Cow's milk
Jonchée from Saintonge area. Fresh cream cheese – served with sugar and cream. **Caillebote** is a similar cheese
Pigouille small, creamy-flavoured disk – served on straw. Can also be made from goat's or ewe's milk

Goat's milk
Chabichou Poitou area cheese: *laitier* (dairy made) and *fermier* (farm made); small, truncated, upright cylinders; soft and sharp-tasting
Couhé-Vérac soft, nutty cheese made in small squares
Jonchée from Niort area. Mild, soft, creamy – best in summer and autumn. A cheese called **Lusignan**, made as a disk, is similar
La Mothe-St-Héray best in summer and autumn. A small disk, one inch thick. Try it with the reds of Haut-Poitou. **Bougon** is a related cheese
Pouligny-St-Pierre pyramid-shaped; strong smell, soft cheese. A cheese called **Tournon-St-Pierre** is related
Pyramide pyramid-shaped, soft cheese
Ruffec fruity taste, made in a small disk
Taupinière packed and served in chestnut leaves

Ewe's milk
Oléron best in spring; mild, creamy, fresh cheese. Made on Ile d'Oléron; known also as **Jonchée d'Oléron** or **Brebis d'Oléron**

PROVENCE

Goat's milk
Picodon de Valréas soft, nutty-tasting, small disk

Ewe's milk
Brousse du Rove creamy and mild-flavoured cheese; best in the winter
Cachat also known as **Tomme du Mont Ventoux**. A summer season; very

soft, sweet and creamy flavour

SAVOIE
Cow's milk
Abondance from the hills and valleys encircling the town of the same name. Best in summer and autumn. Small, firm wheel

Beaufort at its best in winter, spring and summer. A hard, cooked cheese, equivalent to Gruyère, but with no holes

Beaumont mild, creamy, hard disk. Related to Tamié

Chambarand made by monks near Roybon. A mild, creamy-tasting, small disk. Ideal with the light wines of Savoie

Colombière from the Aravis area; mild-flavoured, flat disk

Fondu aux Raisins (Fondu au Marc) big disk of processed cheese and covered in grape pips

Reblochon best in summer and autumn. Semi-hard, gold colour with a mild and creamy flavour. Made in flat, small disks

St-Marcellin available all the year. Small, mild-flavoured disks

Ste-Foy (Bleu de) a blue-veined cheese, made in a flat cylinder. Best in summer and autumn. **Bleu de Tignes** is a related cheese

Sassenage a summer and autumn season. A soft, spicy-flavoured, blue-veined cheese, related to Bleu de Gex (see Jura region)

Tamié (Trappiste de Tamié) made by monks at the monastery of the same name, south of Lake Annecy; light rind, pressed, uncooked disk

Tomme de Savoie a semi-hard, flat cylinder with a slight nutty smell. A summer and autumn season. Has many relations – all called **Tomme**

Vacherin d'Abondance mild, soft and the size of a thick pancake. At its best in winter. Ideal with Crépy or a Chautagne wine

Goat's milk
Chevrotin des Aravis a small, flat cylinder with a summer and autumn season. Mild, no particular smell. From Aravis area

Persillé des Aravis blue-veined, sharp-tasting, tall cylinder. Also known as **Persillé de Thônes** and **Persillé du Grand-Bornand** (nearby towns)

SOUTHWEST
Cow's milk
Belle des Champs from Jurançon; white, mild and an aerated texture

Bethmale a hard cylinder from the valleys south of St-Gaudens

Fromage des Pyrénées a mild, semi-hard, large disk with a hard rind

Passe-l'An a strong, hard cheese; made as a huge wheel

Goat's milk
Cabécous small, flat cheese. Mild, nutty flavour. At its best in winter

Ewe's milk
Esbareich in the form of a big, flat loaf. A summer and autumn season; ideal with Madiran. Related cheeses: **Laruns**, **Amou** and **Ardi-Gasna**

Iraty a strong-flavoured, pressed loaf. Contains some cow's milk